THE DIVINE VERDICT

STUDIES

IN THE HISTORY OF RELIGIONS

(SUPPLEMENTS TO *NUMEN*)

EDITED BY

M. HEERMA VAN VOSS • H.G. KIPPENBERG • R.J.Z. WERBLOWSKY

VOLUME LII

THE DIVINE VERDICT

A STUDY OF DIVINE JUDGEMENT
IN THE ANCIENT RELIGIONS

BY

J. GWYN GRIFFITHS

E.J. BRILL
LEIDEN • NEW YORK • KØBENHAVN • KÖLN
1991

Library of Congress Cataloging-in-Publication Data

Griffiths, John Gwyn.
   The divine verdict: a study of divine judgement in the ancient religions/by J. Gwyn Griffiths.
     p.   cm.—(Studies in the history of religions. ISSN 0169-8834; v. 52)
   Includes bibliographical references and index.
   ISBN 90-04-09231-5
   1. Judgment of God—Comparative studies. 2. Future life-Comparative studies. 3. Ethics, Ancient. I. Title. II. Series: Studies in the history of religions: 52.
BL475.8.G75   1990
291.2'11—dc20   90-48119
                                                                          CIP

ISSN 0169-8834
ISBN 90 04 09231 5

© *Copyright 1991 by E.J. Brill, Leiden, The Netherlands*

All rights reserved. No part of this book may be reproduced or translated in any form, by print, photoprint, microfilm, microfiche or any other means without written permission from the publisher

PRINTED IN THE NETHERLANDS

To
MATTHEW HEERMA VAN VOSS
with
Admiration
and
Gratitude

CONTENTS

Preface	xi
Abbreviations	xvii

PART I
JUDGEMENT IN HISTORY AND IN THIS LIFE

I. Israel and Some of Her Neighbours	3
1. Amos, a Prophet of Judgement	4
2. The Divine Control of History	11
3. Deuteronomy and the Deuteronomic History	23
4. Some Hittite Parallels	25
5. The Babylonian Theodicy	35
6. The Concept of Justice in Ancient Iranian Religion	40
II. The Greek Concept of a Moral Law with Divine Sanction	47
1. Aeschylus: The Individual and the Nation	48
2. The Erinyes: Activity in Two Worlds	53
3. Divine Intervention as Atê in Early Greek Poetry	58
4. Herodotus: Theology and History	65
5. Plato, Plutarch, and Others	72
6. A Sociological Question	89
7. The Human Verdict on Murder in Greece	93
III. Roman Applications	95
1. Divination and Dependence	96
2. Livy on Rome's Success	98
3. Vergil: Commissioned but Inspired	102
4. Rome's Atonement for Sin	106
IV. Aspects of Christian Doctrine	110
1. Second Advent and Judgement	110
2. Rewards and Punishments	112
3. The Exegesis of Current Events	114
4. The Judgement on Jerusalem	118
5. Judging within the Community	122
6. Judgement and the Sacraments	124
7. Human and Divine Vengeance	126
V. Some Indian Doctrines	132
1. Varuna in the Rigveda	132
2. Heaven, Hell, and Rebirth	135

CONTENTS

3. Compensation and Retribution in Karma	137
VI. Confucianism, Mohism, and Taoism	146
1. Confucius and the Intervention of Heaven	146
2. Mohism and Taoism	148
3. Chuang-tzu	154
4. The Transference of Merits	156
5. Avenging Ghosts	157
VII. Egypt: Pharaoh and People	160
A) The Gods and the God-King	160
1. Theological Status	160
2. A Dogma Doubted	161
3. God-given Qualities	164
4. Criticism of a King	167
5. Some Changed Emphases	173
6. A Revealing Test-case	176
VIII. Egypt: Pharaoh and People	184
B) Divine Impact on Human Affairs	184
1. Divine Impact on this Life	184
2. Sinuhe's God-given Success	186
3. Later Biography	187
4. Sin and Suffering in the Confessional Literature	189
5. Behind the Changed Outlook	195

PART II
JUDGEMENT AFTER DEATH

IX. A) Egypt and Judaeo-Christian Thought	201
1. Present and Future Judgement	202
2. Posthumous Litigation	203
3. Diverging Divine Roles	204
4. The Combination of Test and Ordeal	210
5. Magic and Morality	213
6. The Priestly Connection and the Basic Situation	218
7. Some Changed Emphases and their Influence	224
(1) The Weighing of the Heart	224
(2) The Blissful Right and the Baleful Left	225
(3) Shaï, Meskhenet, and Renenet	226
(4) A Triad of Assistant Arbiters	227
(5) Heaven, Hell, and a Pointer to Purgatory	230
(6) Transference to the Living	234
8. Facets of Impact on Judaeo-Christian Thought	237
(1) The Second Death	237

	(2) The Crown of Righteousness	238
	(3) Weighing and Recording	239
	B) Iran, Judaism, and the Christian Consummation	242
	1. The Impact of Iranian Eschatology	243
	2. Judaism's Distinctive Contribution	258
	(1) The Messianic Figure	259
	(2) The Judgement of the Nations	262
	3. The Other Ancient Cultures	266
	4. The Christian Consummation	268
	(1) Revelation	268
	(2) Paul	271
	(3) The Synoptic Gospels	275
X.	From Egypt to Greece via Crete	280
	1. Types of Influence	282
	2. Symbolic Scales	287
	3. The Evidence of Linear B	291
	4. The Minoan Judges of the Dead	294
XI.	Posthumous Judgement in Israel	298
	1. The Lack of a Posthumous Application	300
	2. The Book of Job	304
XII.	Divine Judgement in the Mystery Religions	313
	1. The Isiac Mysteries	313
	(1) Confession	315
	(2) Judgement	317
	(3) Forgiveness	322
	2. Anticipated Eschatology	323
	(1) The Change of Perspective	324
	3. The Eleusinian Experience	327
	4. Mithraism: Judgement as Ordeal	332
	5. The Dionysiac Mysteries	337
	(1) From the Villa dei Misteri	337
	(2) Textual Evidence	340

Epilogue	344
Bibliography	358
Index	390

PREFACE

The theme of divine judgement in the ancient religions, and indeed with a more general scope, is often treated with a concentration on one of its two main aspects: either that which is deemed to affect man's present life or that which is believed to occur only after death. It seems to me that it would be more satisfying to combine the two aspects in a single investigation. The material studied, not surprisingly, does not regularly segregate the two; sometimes the same composition refers to both, although one cannot always be sure which area is intended. For practical purposes, at the same time, it is useful to draw a line of demarcation as I have done in the two parts of the work.

To cover the whole spectrum of the ancient religions may seem a bold venture. The aim issues partly from my personal scholarly interests. After graduating in Latin and Greek in the University of Wales at Cardiff, I studied Egyptian and Hebrew at the Universities of Liverpool and Oxford. In all my work since then I have tried to maintain these interests. My Hebrew studies have been stimulated by contact with my friend of student days, Professor W.D. Davies, lately of Duke University, Durham, North Carolina, and then of Texas Christian University, Fort Worth. My study of Plutarch's *De Iside et Osiride* (1970) introduced me to the Avestan literature, and during my tenure of a Visiting Fellowship at All Souls College, Oxford, in 1976–77 I was fortunate in gaining help on Avestan linguistic matters from Dr. M.E. Tucker at the Oriental Institute. Similarly, for the literature of India, Professor B.K. Matilal, also of the Oriental Institute and of All Souls College, gave me helpful advice; likewise Professor Paul Thieme during my stay at the University of Tübingen in the summer semester of 1977. On the religions of Mesopotamia I have received occasional aid from Professors O.R. Gurney and W.G. Lambert. I have naturally relied much on the translations of accepted authorities.

Quite apart from these personal experiences and contacts it does appear to me that the wider approach has now won general approval. This is due in part to the higher status achieved by the studies of Comparative Religion and Comparative Literature as well as by projects in which interdisciplinary co-operation has played a role. Beyond the new expansionism in the formal academic sense there is a decided change in temper. This has been hardest to achieve, perhaps, in the area of classical studies. Within this area itself there has been a successful struggle to remove the constraints of a too rigid definition of the epochs regarded as exclusively important. Thus the Hellenistic age is now regarded as one of vital significance. Again, the whole relation of the classical world to its wider environment in the Eastern Mediterranean is now more keenly appreciated. Witness, for example, the fact that Professor Hilary Armstrong has been able to give to a volume edited by him in the series *World Spirituality* (published by Crossroad of New York) the title *Classical Mediterranean Spirituality: Egyptian, Greek, Roman.* (1986) (There is, of course, a major omission—the religion of the Jews—but this is treated in two other volumes.) The broader viewpoint is well represented in the work of recent exponents of Greek religion such as Walter Burkert, Martin West, and Reinhold Merkelbach. Nor is their breadth of view related only to an interest in neighbouring cultures; it relates to the whole range of studies covered by religious phenomenology, including especially anthropology, ethnology, sociology, and psychology.

False hopes, I fear, may be raised by such remarks. My own study is devoted to one circumscribed theme. In Part II I have given prominence to the Egyptian material because I believe that its influence on the other cultures was of basic significance in respect of belief in posthumous judgement. The idea of divine judgement in this life, on the other hand, was much more thoroughly espoused by the Jews and the Greeks, and Egypt became, at least eventually, a debtor nation in this intellectual activity. After the opening discussion in Part II, where I have drawn on my first treatment of the theme in my *Conflict of Horus and Seth* (1960), pp. 54–84, I have ventured to deploy, albeit with much revision and pruning, a number of studies which have been previously published in scattered locations. 'From Egypt to Greece via Crete' (Chapter 10) is only partly based on my inaugural lecture at University College, Swansea in 1974 (*The Divine Tribunal*); a section on 'The Evidence of Linear B' broaches a theme which I then ignored. 'Posthumous Judgement in Israel' (Chapter 11) follows the main lines of a lecture to the Old Testament Society in 1974 which later appeared in an expanded form in *Fontes atque Pontes* (Festgabe für Hellmut Brunner): *Ägypten und Altes Testament*, 5 (Wiesbaden, 1983), 186–204. I have been indebted to Professors Hellmut Brunner and Emma Brunner-Traut for constant comments and criticisms; my closest contact with them was when my wife and I spent a semester at Tübingen University in 1977, when Brunner was head of the Egyptological Department and Institute; before and after that our converse has been mainly by correspondence save for their visit to the Wellcome Museum at University College, Swansea, of which my wife is Hon. Curator. Previously, in 1969, I had spent a semester at the University of Bonn, and profited from a similar relation with Professor Elmar Edel.

'Divine Judgement in the Mystery Religions' (Chapter 12) includes some material from a paper delivered to an international colloquium on the soteriology of the oriental cults in the Roman imperial era; it was held at Rome in September 1979 and the Acta were published in the volume edited by Ugo Bianchi and Maarten J. Vermaseren, *La Soteriologia dei culti orientali nell' Impero Romano* (Leiden, 1982), pp. 192–222. On several points I now offer revised opinions. I should add that the paper embodies interpretations which I presented in the Forwood Lectures in the Philosophy and History of Religion at the University of Liverpool in March 1980 on 'The Achievement of Salvation in the Mystery Religions'. Professor A.F. Shore presided on those occasions and my private discussions with him afterwards proved most helpful. More frequent discussions have naturally occurred with my wife, Dr Kate Bosse-Griffiths, who fully shares my interest in these themes, and also with my brother, the Rev. D.R. Griffiths, formerly Lecturer in New Testament Studies at University College, Cardiff. Dr David Hawkes, of All Souls College, formerly Professor of Chinese in the University of Oxford, has kindly helped me on some points of exegesis in that field. The usual *caveat* applies with special force to all these scholars. I am alone responsible for any remaining errors and infelicities.

I have devoted special attention to Israel, Greece, and Egypt. Israel's neighbours are also considered, and there are discussions of Judaism, Christianity, and Zoroastrianism. The early traditions of India and China provide a contrast in religious belief: in the developed doctrine of *karma* we find a distinctively dogmatic approach, but the whole theme lacks prominence in the Chinese schools of thought. In several areas, notably in Egypt and Israel, it is shown that punishment in this life is sometimes presented as a fate that man brings upon himself rather than as one imposed by God, though always against a moral background derived from religion. More often, however, God himself is regarded as the intervening judge, who may also apportion rewards.

In my second part I have discussed judgement after death, the first part having been allotted to the idea of God's judgement in history and in this life. Posthumous judgement is here regarded in general as complementing the first theme, although it has usually been treated hitherto on a separate basis. Attention is focussed on the question of the origins of the Judaeo-Christian tradition. Zoroastrian influence has often been regarded as dominant. The present analysis reveals a complex ideology in which three strands are recognized: first, a general judgement which coincides with the end of the world; secondly, a judgement of the individual after death; and thirdly, a judgement of the nations. The first idea is here derived from Zoroastrianism, while the second, especially in its symbolic detail of weighing and recording, is ascribed to Egyptian influence. A judgement of the nations is seen as a distinctively Judaic element. In the Mystery Religions, on the other hand, a doctrine of 'anticipated eschatology' is sometimes, though not consistently, found to operate, since the initiate is reborn to new life after his 'voluntary death' with its experience of confession, judgement, and forgiveness.

It will be seen that one of my aims is to discuss the way in which the ancient religions, within this defined field, have influenced one another. An overriding aim, at the same time, is to analyse the content and purpose of each religion, so far as the extant evidence allows this, in its attitude to divine judgement. To some extent the evidence is iconographical; inscriptions also have their role; but the main sources are literary, and the result is that the treatment is basically an essay in Comparative Literature. Comments on form and style may thus emerge, especially on form in the sense of genre. In my view, however, a more important aspect is the consideration of literature as a mirror of society and its beliefs. From time to time I have tried to pose such questions as, How far are the authors quoted representative of the societies and times in which they lived? and What other evidence can point to current beliefs? The clearest answer to the second question may well be found in a national legal system and I have not neglected this source of information. Obviously ideas of divine judgement may be closely related to judicial processes which operate on the purely human level and to the ethical standards embodied in them. The link between authors and their societies is often more difficult to define; it is certainly a complex and varied relationship. In several ancient cultures the authors are anonymous and very little is known of their life and times. Nor does it follow that they are therefore fully representative. Another restrictive fact which applies generally to the ancient world is that only a small minority in any society were fully literate.

I am indebted to the Committee of Egypt Exploration Society for allowing me to reproduce in a revised form my contribution to *Pyramid Studies and Other Essays presented to I.E.S. Edwards* (London,

1988), 92–102: see my Chapter 8 here. A debt of a more personal nature relates to scholars I have already mentioned; and there are others to whom I am most grateful. My colleague in Swansea, Professor Alan B. Lloyd, has always favoured me with willing and enlightened aid. At the Griffith Institute, Oxford Dr Jaromir Málek and his team of bibliographers have been a valued stand-by. In Swansea, again, my wife and I have enjoyed the constant support of Professor Christopher Collard, a Hellenist who has merited the rare good fortune to preside, even in these adverse times, over a flourishing Department of Classics and Ancient History.

Finally, my profound thanks go to the Editors of the *Numen* Supplements, Professors M. Heerma van Voss, R.J.Z. Werblowsky, and H.G. Kippenberg, for accepting this book into the series. The other two will forgive me, I am sure, if I pay special thanks to Professor Matthew Heerma van Voss, and not only in connection with this book. I have enjoyed the privilege of his friendship over many years, meeting mostly in Amsterdam and in international conferences. This has also meant a regular exchange of *opuscula* and frequent discussions. As an Egyptologist he has established himself as an authority on aspects of religious literature, especially on that of the Twenty-first Dynasty, including those which are highly relevant to the present work, as will be clear from my references to his studies. His professional career has also embraced wider academic interests. He has recently retired from his post as Professor Ordinarius in the History of the Ancient Religions in the University of Amsterdam; he first occupied this chair in 1969 and he has consistently invested it with much distinction. Nor is his outlook limited to the ancient world. He has always impressed me with his lively appreciation of the pluralism inherent in modern European culture as an orbit where languages such as Dutch and Welsh will continue to flourish. My book is dedicated to this fine scholar.

University of Wales
University College
Swansea

JOHN GWYN GRIFFITHS

June 1989

ABBREVIATIONS

See also *Annual Egyptological Bibliography* (Leiden); *Lexikon der Ägyptologie* (Wiesbaden); O. Eissfeldt (tr. P.R. Ackroyd), *The Old Testament* (Oxford, 1965, repr. 1974); *Oxford Classical Dictionary* (2nd Ed., 1970); *Cambridge History of Judaism*, I (1984); M. Boyce, *History of Zoroastrianism*, I and II (1975; 1982); J. Gonda, *Die Religionen Indiens* (Stuttgart, 1960).

Abh.	Abhandlungen
ANET[3]	*Ancient Near Eastern Texts relating to the Old Testament*, ed. James B. Pritchard. 3rd Ed., Princeton, 1969.
Arch. Rel.	*Archiv für Religionswissenschaft*
ASAE	*Annales du Service des Antiquités de l'Égypte*
BD	*Book of the Dead*
BDB	Brown, Driver, and Briggs, *Hebrew and English Lexicon of the Old Testament*
BdE	Bibliothèque d'Étude, IFAO
BSFE	*Bulletin de la Société française d'Égyptologie*, Paris
Bull. Ryl.	*Bulletin of the Journal of the John Rylands University Library*
CHJ	*Cambridge History of Judaism*
EPRO	Études Préliminaires aux Religions Orientales dans l'Empire Romain, ed. M.J. Vermaseren
FGrH	*Fragmente der griechischen Historiker*, ed. F. Jacoby
FS.	Festschrift
Harv. Theol. Rev.	*Harvard Theological Review*
ICC	International Critical Commentary, Edinburgh
IFAO	L'Institut Français d'Archéologie Orientale, Cairo.
JAOS	*Journal of the American Oriental Society*
JDAI	*Jahrbuch des Deutschen archäologischen Instituts*
JEA	*Journal of Egyptian Archaeology*
JHS	*Journal of Hellenic Studies*
JNES	*Journal of Near Eastern Studies*
JSSEA	*Journal of the Society for the Study of Egyptian Antiquities*, Toronto
JTS	*Journal of Theological Studies*
LÄ	*Lexikon der Ägyptologie*, ed. Wolfgang Helck, Eberhard Otto, Wolfhart Westendorf. 6 Vols. Wiesbaden, 1975–1986.
Lichtheim, *Lit.*	Miriam Lichtheim, *Ancient Egyptian Literature*. 3 Vols. Berkeley, 1973–1980.
Liverpool Annals	*Annals of Archaeology and Anthropology*, Liverpool
LSJ	Liddell and Scott, *Greek-English Lexicon*. 9th Ed., rev. H. Stuart Jones, Oxford, 1925–1940.
MÄS	Münchner Ägyptologische Studien
MDAIK	*Mitteilungen des Deutschen Archäologischen Instituts, Abteilung Kairo* (A = Athen, R = Rom).
NEB	New English Bible
Nilsson, *Gr. Rel.*	M.P. Nilsson, *Geschichte der griechischen Religion*
NTS	*New Testament Studies*
OBO	Orbis Biblicus et Orientalis
PW	Pauly, Wissowa, Kroll, and Mittelhaus, *Real-Encyclopädie der klassischen Altertumswissenschaft*, Stuttgart, 1893–
Pyr.	*Pyramid Texts*, ed. K. Sethe
RAC	*Reallexikon für Antike und Christentum*, Stuttgart, 1950–
RdE	*Revue d'Égyptologie*
Rev. Arch.	*Revue archéologique*

Rev. Hist. Rel.	Revue de l'Histoire des Religions
Rhein. Mus.	Rheinisches Museum für Philologie
RSV	Revised Standard Version
RVV	Religionsgeschichtliche Versuche und Vorarbeiten
Schürer, Hist. Jewish People	rev. Vermes-Millar-Black, *History of the Jewish People in the Age of Jesus Christ*, I–III, 1973–1987, Edinburgh
Seeber, Untersuchungen.	Christine Seeber, *Untersuchungen zur Darstellung des Totengerichts im Alten Ägypten*, Munich, 1976
SPAW	Sitzungsberichte der Preussischen Akademie der Wissenschaften
TAPA	*Transactions of the American Philological Association*
TDNT	*Theological Dictionary of the New Testament*, ed. G. Kittel, tr. and ed. G.W. Bromiley, Vols. I–X.
TWNT	*Theologisches Wörterbuch zum Neuen Testament*, ed. G. Kittel and G. Friedrich.
VT	*Vetus Testamentum*
VTS	Vetus Testamentum, Supplements
Wb.	*Wörterbuch*. In Egyptian contexts = Erman-Grapow, *Wörterbuch der ägyptischen Sprache*
ZÄS	*Zeitschrift für Aegyptische Sprache und Altertumskunde*
ZAW	*Zeitschrift für die altestamentliche Wissenschaft*
ZDMG	*Zeitschrift der deutschen morgenländischen Gesellschaft*
ZPE	*Zeitschrift für Papyrologie und Epigraphie*

PART I

JUDGEMENT IN HISTORY AND IN THIS LIFE

CHAPTER ONE

ISRAEL AND SOME OF HER NEIGHBOURS

In the story *Michael Kohlhaas* by Heinrich von Kleist a vivid portrayal is presented of a man obsessed by the passion for justice and fair dealing in human affairs. The story is to a large extent historical and tells how a horse-dealer from near Brandenburg in the mid-sixteenth century loses two fine black horses because they have been illegally detained and maltreated by a nobleman. He tries to recover them by legal means, but fails owing to corrupt intervention by a relative of the nobleman. Kohlhaas is bitterly disillusioned and decides to resort to illegal means. He gathers a band of armed supporters who burn down the nobleman's castle and also a part of Wittenberg. A civil war threatens to ensue, but Martin Luther persuades Kohlhaas to disband his forces and to seek legal redress once more. A court at Dresden orders such redress; the two black horses are returned in good condition; and the nobleman is sentenced to two years' imprisonment; but at the same time the court condemns Kohlhaas to death for his acts of rebellion. He is beheaded, but faces death calmly in the assurance that his long and terrible struggle has been in some way vindicated: an act of injustice has been reversed.

In his long struggle Kohlhaas is mainly concerned with righting the wrong which a corrupt system of justice has condoned. It is true that he resorts to the aid of religion, particularly in the person of Martin Luther; he also assumes himself, at one stage, an apocalyptic role claiming to represent the Archangel Michael. But the achievement of justice on the human plane is his great purpose, even though this, after the death of his wife, becomes to some degree an affair of revenge, *das Geschäft der Rache*.[1] Yet it begins with a confidence that integrity and justice will be honoured and with a sense of divine protection rather in the spirit of Friedrich von Logau's faith, which Longfellow memorably rendered:

> Though the mills of God grind slowly, yet they grind exceeding small;
> Though with patience He stands waiting, with exactness grinds He all.

---

[1] Cf. Walter Silz, *Heinrich von Kleist* (Philadelphia, 1961), 183; and Nietzsche's idea that *ich bin gerecht* (I am just) really means *ich bin gerächt* (I am avenged).

The saying has a Greek origin: see below, Chapter 2, Section 5. A concern with justice, both human and divine, is a feature of many ancient religions, and the religion of the Hebrews displays it with special clarity. It is conspicuous in the work of the earliest literary figure among the prophets, the eighth-century prophet Amos.

1. *Amos, a Prophet of Judgement*

He is forthright about corruption in the law-courts of Israel:

> You that turn justice upside down[2]
> and bring righteousness to the ground . . .
> you that hate a man who brings the wrongdoer to court
> and loathe him who speaks the whole truth.
> (Amos 5:7 and 10. *NEB*.[3])

The word for 'justice' here is *mishpât* (מִשְׁפָּט), often used of a judicial sentence. Amos calls for justice too in the rather wider sense of *tsedaqâh* (צְדָקָה), and he combines the two when he represents Yahweh as demanding that both be honoured:

> Let justice roll on like a river
> and righteousness like an ever-flowing stream.
> (Amos 5:24.)

The second term often implies the demands of a social relationship in a less lofty sense, in particular the demands of the covenant laid down between Yahweh and Israel; and these demands denote, from the human standpoint, the fulfilment of needs relating to cult and ritual.[4] It is true that Amos rebukes the merely formal satisfaction of such needs, invoking the luxury and oppression practised by those who may be zealous in ritual. At the same time he announces an impending judgement of nations, first of nations who are neighbours of Israel, and then of Israel herself. The judgements will involve the disaster and destruction of cities, ills which will result from the direct intervention of Yahweh as a punishment of sin (3:6). A series of oracles announced by the prophet indicates that palaces will be burnt and populations exterminated as a punishment for cruelties inflicted by these nations; and each punishment is introduced by the formula which figures in the first utterance:

---

[2] From an emended reading; the text has 'turn justice to wormwood'.
[3] Unless otherwise stated (as with RV, Revised Version, and RSV, Revised Standard Version), this translation is followed.
[4] Cf. Gerhard von Rad, *Gesammelte Studien zum Alten Testament* (München, 1958), 230 f.

> For crime after crime of Damascus
> I will grant them no reprieve.
>
> (Amos 1:3.)

They are therefore presented as penalties fixed by Yahweh as judge; and in each case the punishment may be said to fit the crime; retribution is enacted along the lines of a *lex talionis*. It is surprising, after strictures on the Syrians, Philistines, Phoenicians, Edomites, Ammonites, and Moabites, to find Judah added to the list; Yahweh threatens that fire will consume the palaces of Jerusalem because false gods have been followed. This may well be a later addition, but the attack which then ensues on corruption in Israel (2:6 ff.) is fully consonant with an emphasis found in many parts of the work. If the prophecies add up to a gloomy prospect in which death and destruction are dealt out as penalties to various peoples by Yahweh, yet there is a distinct lack of favouritism about the verdicts, and this balances the refreshing universalism which is present in the declaration that Yahweh has not only brought out Israel from Egypt but also arranged the movement of Philistines from Caphtor and the Aramaeans from Kir (9:7). That declaration is also refreshing in another way: it stands out, in contrast to the chastisements to be inflicted, as an assurance that Yahweh has intervened positively and considerately in the destiny of nations. He is responsible for rewards as well as punishments.

A note of comfort is likewise struck at the end of the work with regard to Israel's future. Amid the desolation a remnant of her people shall witness renewed prosperity:

> I will restore the fortunes of my people Israel;
> they shall rebuild deserted cities and live in them.
>
> (Amos 9:14.)

This has been widely regarded as a post-exilic addition to the original; if it is regarded as authentic, it will apply mainly to the restoration of the fallen house of David, implying thus a vindication of the southern against the northern kingdom, a wider interpretation on messianic lines being later possible.[5] The prophet's own oracles raise another question: does their portrayal of doom for many nations partake of the nature of apocalyptic or is it a more precise prophecy relating to events in the eighth century? At first one is invited to reject an element of apocalyptic vision, for Amos is

---

[5] It is defended as early by H. Graf Reventlow, *Das Amt des Propheten bei Amos* (1962), 91 ff., as cited by G.H. Jones in *Efrydiau Beiblaidd Bangor* (FS. B.J. Roberts, Swansea, 1973), 73 n. 1; see also J. Alberto Soggin, *Introduction to the Old Testament* (Rev. Ed., London, 1980), 244.

scornful of those who long for the *Day of Yahweh* (5:18 ff.) since they are likely to be bitterly disappointed; normally the *Day of Yahweh* is the vehicle of apocalyptic prophecy, careering to judgement and salvation. Yet Amos does not reveal clear signs of linking his oracles to contemporary events. If he was writing in 760 B.C.,[6] as is generally believed, the expansion of the Assyrian Empire was to be a conspicuous feature of the century. Certainly the desolation and destruction described in the oracles might easily mark the ruthless power-struggle of Assyria. But it was not till 722 that Israel fell to Sargon II of Assyria,[7] and in the reign of Jeroboam II (782-743 B.C.) Israel had conducted a successful war of liberation against Syria, retrieving territory that Syria had seized. During the same period, however, Assyria had been attacking Syria under Shalmaneser IV,[8] and many were probably able to divine the shape of things to come from Assyria's growing intrusions. In spite of the lack of detail it is on the whole preferable to relate the prophecies of Amos to the context of eighth-century events.

The divine judgement pronounced against various nations and cities raises a significant question about literary form. It is a pattern followed by prophets after Amos, notably by Isaiah (19:1-25, against Egypt and 23:1-18, against Tyre and Sidon), by Jeremiah (chs. 46-51, against Egypt, Tyre and Sidon, Moab, the Ammonites, Edom, Damascus, Babylon, and others), by Ezekiel (chs. 25-32, mainly against Tyre and Egypt), and by Joel (3:4-8, against Tyre and Sidon). These vary in elaboration, and the details of doom pronounced by Amos are brief in comparison with the elaborate and expansive style adopted by Jeremiah and Ezekiel. They all share, however, the view that the doom predicted is the result of the sin of the peoples named; the instruments of the penalties inflicted may be earthly powers which are themselves tainted by sin, but divine justice uses them in the manner of a whip or rod:

The Assyrian! He is the rod that I wield in my anger.

(Isa. 10:5.)

Reverting to the question of form—a list of towns or peoples with prophecies of doom against them—we note that a parallel has been seen in the Egyptian 'Execration Texts' which appear on parts of

---

[6] John Marsh, *Amos and Micah* (London, 1959), 36; James L. Mays, *Amos* (London, 1969), 20.

[7] Cf. D.J. Wiseman, in D. Winton Thomas (ed.), *Documents from Old Testament Times* (London, 1958), 58 f.

[8] Ibid. 51; and cf. 2 Kings 14:25-28.

bowls and figurines belonging to the Twelfth and Thirteenth Dynasties (19th–18th centuries B.C.)[9] These too contain the names of foreign towns and princes which the writer wishes to consign to destruction. Thus Ashkelon and Jerusalem are named on pottery fragments now in Berlin:

> the Ruler of Asqanu, *Khalu-kim*, and all the *retainers*
> who are with him; . . .
> the Ruler of Jerusalem,[10] Yaqar-'Ammu and all the
> *retainers* who are with him; . . .
> (J.A. Wilson, in *ANET*,³ 329.)

No words of doom or threat accompany this and similar elements of the list, for the attitude is forcefully expressed in a ritual act—the breaking of the pot or figurine. A magical means of destruction is clearly implied. It is of interest too that imprecation applies to evil things also, such as plans and dreams, and eventually turns from foreigners to Egyptians—either those categorized generally as rebels or regarded in a personal sense as threatening the royal family—just as Amos ends with his own people. The Danish scholar, A. Bentzen, in adducing the Egyptian execration texts, has established a pointed parallel as far as *genre* is concerned, and the arguments against the parallel, in so far as they rest on chronology—more than a thousand years separates Amos from these Egyptian texts[11]—are scarcely cogent when the Egyptian literary sequels[12] are considered. Thus the famous 'Israel Stela' of Merenptah (c. 1230 B.C.) purports to be a 'Hymn of Victory' over various foreign peoples and ends with a list of defeated nations and towns, the first of which comprises the traditional 'Nine Bows'. The last two of the named nations, now said to be laid low, are described thus:

---

[9] For earlier examples see Georges Posener, in *Lex. der Ägyptologie*, I (1975), 67 ff. ('Ächtungstexte').

[10] *r ( ) w=u-šl-m-m*. The equation has been questioned by Jirku, but is cogently defended by W. Helck, *Die Beziehungen Ägyptens zu Vorderasien im 3. und 2. Jahrtausend v. Chr.* (2nd Ed., Wiesbaden, 1971), 48; cf. J. Ebach, in *Lex. der Ägyptologie*, III (1980), 267 f. on this the earliest mention in an Egyptian text. For the text see Sethe, *Die Achtung feindlicher Fürsten, Völker und Dinge*. APAW 1926.

[11] See J.A. Soggin, *Introd.* 243 ff. with refs. both to Bentzen's study and to those of his critics.

[12] In *OTS* 8 (1950), 92 ff. A. Bentzen makes the point that the Israelite New Year Festival as the pre-exilic forerunner of the Day of Atonement contained 'a definite element of judgment'. James L. Mays, *Amos* (1969), 27 believes that in the case of the early prophets and of Amos there was no 'cultic setting' to the statements against the sinning nations.

>   Israel is laid waste, his seed is not:
>   Hurru is become a widow for Egypt.
>   (J.A. Wilson, in *ANET*³ 378.)

An element of 'poetic eulogy'¹³ is doubtless present here, although a firm historical allusion has been seen by some.¹⁴ Ralph Giveon¹⁵ wisely remarks that 'the mention of Israel on the Israel-Stela ... does not prove that Merenptah made war against them. It shows, however, that such a group was known to exist in Palestine at the time.' That the execration texts were ideologically akin to the lists of toponyms is also made clear by Giveon, who connects them with the idea of prophylactic magic: they served at once as a triumphal declaration and as a warning to potential enemies. In some Egyptian texts a distinction is made between towns which are in jubilation and those where terror reigns. Thus in the *Book of the Victory over Seth*, which emanates from the Thirtieth Dynasty (iv B.C.) and the Ptolemaic Era, a ritual attack on an image of the god Seth made of red wax is described (the attack ends in the burning of the image and spitting on it); then the victory of Horus is related; and a signal feature of this outcome is that whereas jubilation prevails in the cities of Horus, misery afflicts the cities of Seth:

>   Sesu is in lamentation, Wenes is in sorrow ...
>   Ḥenu (Hypselis) is a desolate¹⁶ place, Ombos has been overthrown.
>   (Schott, *Urk*. VI, 16 f.)

These places are all in Egypt, but several allusions refer to the banishment of Seth to foreign countries. A similar situation is portrayed in the Ptolemaic *Legend of the Winged Disk* and in *The Triumph of Horus*.¹⁷ The Ptolemaic texts are of course much later than Amos, but they preserve an earlier tradition. It would be unwise to ignore the clear affinities between the Hebrew oracles and the Egyptian declarations of doom; and it is likely that the cultic prophets who preceded Amos pointed a contrast, in the Egyptian manner, between the joys of Judah and Israel as opposed to the desolation of foreign countries. That Judah and Israel are

---

¹³ Wilson in *ANET*³ 376.

¹⁴ Wilson, ibid. 378 n. 18 on the people of Israel then (c. 1230 B.C.) in or near Palestine, though not yet a settled people. Cf. K.A. Kitchen *Ancient Orient and Old Testament* (London, 1966), 59 f.

¹⁵ 'Remarks on the Transmission of Egyptian Lists of Asiatic Toponyms', in *Fragen an die altägyptische Literatur* (FS. E. Otto, Wiesbaden, 1977), 171–183, this on pp. 172 f.

¹⁶ An amended form: see Schott *Urk*. VI, 1, 17 (Leipzig, 1939).

¹⁷ For translations see Fairman, in *JEA* 21 (1935), 26–36 and in *The Triumph of Horus* (London, 1974).

also now condemned is the mark of a heightened moral sensibility, although Amos doubtless betrays a firm 'Standort in Juda'.[18]

After brushing aside Bentzen's thesis rather too brusquely, Shalom M. Paul[19] makes the valuable point that the oracles of Amos 'are concluded by a verdict in which the deity speaks in the first person and condemns each nation to punishment by fire.' That a divine judicial verdict is implied becomes clear, as we have seen above, by the introductory formula which refers to the crimes which have produced the verdict. Similarly the visions of chapter 7 culminate in that of Yahweh standing in his sanctuary, ready to proclaim his judgements. The ritualist of the Egyptian 'Execration Texts' is also proclaiming judgement, but not from an explicitly judicial background; nor are the related texts thus couched; their setting is rather the priestly utterance in time of war and victory.[20] Outside the oracles on the nations Amos uses a certain variety of literary forms. Thus the funeral dirge is the vehicle of lament on Israel as a fallen virgin:

> She has fallen to rise no more,
> the virgin Israel,
> prostrate on her own soil, with no one to lift her up.
>
> (Amos 5:2.)

Before this the prophet himself calls it *the dirge* (qinah) *of the house of Israel*. The following lines show that the nation's doom through the ravages of war is seen as the judgement: the virgin is violated by the foe and lies dead.

Yet another form used by Amos is the prophetic vision, a form afterwards found in several other prophetic books. The visions are presented (7:1 ff.) as revelations which Yahweh has conveyed and which, when interpreted, express his judgements. In the case of the first two visions—the locust-swarm and the rain of fire—the threat is mercifully revoked through the prophet's intercession. But the vision of the plumb-line is followed by no such intercession or withdrawal; and after the intervening account of the prophet's disturbing visit to Bethel comes the vision of the basket of ripe summer fruit. Again it is Yahweh's interpretation that adds the prophecy of doom:

---

[18] Cf. Klaus Koch et al. *Amos* (Alter Orient und Altes Testament, Bd. 30, 2, Neukirchen-Vluyn 1976), 121, referring esp. to the phrase 'children of Israel' in Amos 3:1.

[19] In *JBL* 90 (1971), 397–403 ('Amos 1:2–2:3: A concatenous literary pattern'); this remark on p. 401, adducing verses 4, 7, and 12 in ch. 1; and 2:2.

[20] Cf. Max Löhr, *Untersuchungen zum Buch Amos* (Giessen, 1901), 1; Hans Walter Wolff, *Amos* (Neukirchen-Vluyn, 1967), 135 f.; 254 ff.

> Then the Lord said to me, 'The time is ripe for my people Israel.'
> (Amos 8:2.)

A natural symbol is implied: the ripe fruit is ready to fall, and that is Israel's sad moral state. But the Hebrew reinforces this with the paronomasia between *qaits* (קָיִץ), 'summer', and *qets* (קֵץ), 'end'. Amos employs hymnic elements too, especially when lauding the power of Yahweh in nature (4:13; 5:8 f.; 9:5 f.), but in these compositions the note of judgement as applied to human affairs is rare:

> that bringeth sudden destruction upon the strong,
> so that destruction cometh upon the fortress.
> (Amos 5:9. RV.)

It remains true, in spite of the variety of forms used by Amos to express condemnation, that the direct medium of declaration by the divine judge is most often chosen. Before the pronouncement of the verdict the grounds for it are usually elucidated, and sins of corruption and idolatry are listed against Israel in several parts of the book. In one case the very privilege of election by Yahweh is made a means of reproach, for the high promise entailed by the privilege has not, it is suggested, been carried out by Israel:[21]

> For you alone have I cared
> among all nations of the world;
> therefore will I punish you for all your iniquities.
> (Amos 3:2.)

In several sayings there is an exhortation to listen, and it is addressed in this context (3:1) to the children of Israel, who seem to be referred to as the persons accused in the court:

> Listen, Israelites, to these words that the Lord addresses to you,
> to the whole nation which he brought up from Egypt.
> (Amos 3:1.)

Yahweh on occasion seems to be calling on witnesses:

> Listen and testify against the family of Jacob:
> This is the very word of the Lord God, the God of Hosts.
> (Amos 3:13.)

But another passage

---

[21] Cf. H.W. Wolff, *Amos*, 212: 'Erwählung als Grund des Gerichts'.

> Stand upon the palaces in Ashdod
> and upon the palaces of Egypt,
> and proclaim aloud.
>
> (Amos 3:9.)

appears to envisage the sending of heralds to proclaim a royal message.[22] In prophetical writings after Amos the setting of a court-procedure becomes more pronounced. The address to witnesses is a clear formal element, as in the prelude which Isaiah assigns to the accusations made by Yahweh:

> Hark you heavens, and earth give ear,
> for the Lord has spoken:
>
> (Isa. 1:2.)

The whole creation is thus summoned to listen,[23] in a sense that poetically transcends the idea of any ordinary earthly tribunal.[24] J. Bright[25] well remarks that here 'Yahweh himself appears both as accuser of his people and as the judge who brings indictment against them.' Yet the prophet quickly moves from the court setting to a consideration of sin as an act which disturbs the *pietas* expected of children towards their father.[26] Nor does the juridical-moralistic assessment of sin affect the whole of the treatment even when such imagery is present.

2. *The Divine Control of History*

We have seen that Amos only occasionally refers to the positive side of Yahweh's intervention in historical events in order to help Israel. His book is replete with judgements that are imminent. An allusion to past judgements includes a reference to Sodom and Gomorrah, although Israel is mentioned as the object of the Lord's saving grace:

---

[22] Ibid. 229. In 4:1 ('Listen to this, you cows of Bashan'), the accused are addressed; in 5:1 the same formula introduces a hymn of lament.

[23] Cf. Ed. J. Kissane, *The Book of Isaiah* (Dublin, 1941), 8; he points out on p. xii that the prophet is equally expansive on the subjects of Yahweh's judgement, since the terms 'man', 'earth', and 'world' are used in connection with the 'Day of Yahweh'.

[24] For the use of this terminology in the prophets see S. Amsler, 'Le thème du procès chez les prophètes d'Israel', in *Revue de Théologie et de Philosophie* 111 (1974), 116–31, a ref. I owe to J.A. Soggin, *Introd.* xxxi.

[25] In Peake's Comm. (New Ed., London, 1962), 490.

[26] Cf. Walther Eichrodt (tr. J.A. Baker), *Theology of the Old Testament*, I (Philadelphia, 1961), 375.

> I brought destruction amongst you
> as God destroyed Sodom and Gomorrah;
> you were like a brand snatched from the fire.
>
> (Amos 4:11.)

Sodom and Gomorrah, two of the 'Cities of the Plain', are often named, before and after this, as examples of the divine wrath which brings a direct punishment of sin in the course of history.

Our survey of the theme of judgement in the book of Amos has shown how basic it is in his whole thought, however varied the literary expression may be. If we attempt a broader (and inevitably sketchier) view of Old Testament literature in search of this theme, we find that it occupies a dominating place throughout. That God controls history with a moral motive is implied from the very beginning in the interpretation of the creation stories and their sequel; in particular he is said to exact penalties firmly and consistently for sins committed. There are positive and negative aspects of the divine activity, as we have noted, and German scholars, especially Gerhard von Rad,[27] have given great prominence of late to the quality of Old Testament history as *Heilsgeschichte*, 'salvation-history'. This view lays stress on the 'deeds of God in history', the chief of which are seen to be the call of the Patriarchs, the deliverance of the children of Israel from the bondage of Egypt, the bestowal upon them of the land of Canaan, the election of David and Zion. A feature of this interpretation is that it concentrates on the bright interventions at the expense of the dark records of punishments for disobedience. Von Rad[28] indeed admits that later hymnic synopses, such as in some of the Psalms, provided contrasts with the divine acts of deliverance—'the infidelity and disobedience of Israel now increasingly became objects of importance in the presentation.' Von Rad's emphasis throughout is on the historical sense of the community of the faithful; to him it is the kerygmatic purpose in addressing this Hebrew community that gives meaning to 'the deeds of God in history'. It has been complained that the process really undermines the objective historical value of much of the Old Testament, and that von Rad has done for the Old Testament what Bultmann has done for the New.[29] The various traditions need to be critically assessed. Thus there are clear accretions present in the traditions concerning Moses; but the

---

[27] See Gerhard von Rad (tr. D.M.G. Stalker), *Old Testament Theology* (Edinburgh, 1961), I, 121 ff., emphasizing the 'Credo' of Deut. 26:5–9. Mr Stalker renders the term as 'saving history'; 'salvation-history' is preferable.
[28] Ibid. I, 123.
[29] Cf. W. Eichrodt, op. cit. I, 514.

belief that Yahweh brought Israel out of Egypt through him can be firmly linked to a historical foundation.[30]

The creation stories are in a different category, but the interpretation on the lines of sin and punishment is already vigorously at work. Adam and Eve are driven from the Garden because of their sin, and the trouble arises because the fruit of the Tree of Knowledge of Good and Evil is forbidden to them—a really baffling element. Doctrinally, of course, the influence of the several episodes in chapters 2–11 of Genesis which elaborate on human offences and divine penalties has been of immense significance. Its impact has extended not only to later developments in the Old Testament but also to Rabbinical Judaism as expressed in the Talmud and Midrash and then, later still, to the Jewish mysticism enshrined in the literature of the Kabbalists.[31] The impact on Christianity was likewise powerful, particularly in the doctrine of Adam's Fall and the emergence of the new Adam. On Islâm too the influence was strong to the extent that Old Testament traditions were accepted by the Prophet;[32] a firm teaching about sin and punishment is not invalidated by occasional emphases on predestination.[33]

If we ask by what rationale the divine penalties are inflicted in the Old Testament, a variety of behaviour emerges. The first penalties are imposed on the Serpent, Eve, and Adam, and they spring from the ban placed on the fruit of the Tree of Knowledge. Instant death was threatened (Gen. 2:17) as the result of breaking the ban, but none of the penalties includes this although ultimate death is threatened to Adam (Gen. 3:19)—one of the many inconsistencies of presentation in this mythic material. Punishment can obviously not be simultaneous with the offence, and the treatment of Cain is a simple example of how the process works. With the sending of the Flood the bond of cause and effect is again apparent, for the wickedness of mankind provokes it. In this episode the emphasis has shifted to the whole community of men, although some of the individuals previously dealt with, especially Adam, are representative in a wider sense. The episode of the Flood invites examination with the comparative material, particularly that

---

[30] See the painstaking assessment by Siegfried Herrmann in *Israel in Egypt* (Studies in Biblical Theology, 27, London, 1973), 65 f.

[31] See Gershom Scholem, 'On Sin and Punishment: Some Remarks concerning Biblical and Rabbinical Ethics' in *Myths and Symbols* (FS. M. Eliade), ed. J.M. Kitagawa and C.H. Long (Chicago, 1969), 163–177.

[32] Cf. Arthur N. Wollaston, *Muhammad: His Life and Doctrines* (London, 1904), 102 ff.

[33] Claus Schedl, *Muhammad und Jesus* (Vienna, 1978), 97 ('Gott und Hölle').

which centres on Utnapishtim, the Babylonian Noah; the Egyptian myth of 'The Deliverance of Mankind' is also comparable. Is the element of moral chastisement equally prominent in these stories? Like Noah, Utnapishtim is honoured and excepted from disaster because of his piety, but the cause of the Flood in the Babylonian context is the offending noise made by men, a noise which proves disturbing to the gods, especially to Enlil, the ruling deity.[34] Admittedly an attempt has been recently made to introduce a moral nuance into the relevant words, and with some cogency.[35] The words *ḫubūrum* and *rigmum*, it is argued, are shown by the contexts in which they occur rather than by their derivation, to imply respectively 'mutinous uproar' and 'cry of woe' (or 'rebellious cry'); so that the causal background suggested is that of men in rebellion against the gods. An imputation of moral evil is not directly made, but the general sense supports the idea. Pettinato alludes to the strong moral emphasis of the Bible episode and also of the classical myth of the Flood which Deucalion and Pyrrha survived. He does not refer to the Egyptian tale, which tells of the planned slaughter, but not by drowning, of mankind, and which gives prominence to the anger of the sun-god Rê. Here the mutinous attitude of men is recorded as the cause of the divine anger;[36] it is said that 'mankind plotted something in the (very) presence of Rê' and the sun-god says of them, 'They have plotted things against me.' No ethical offence is spelled out. Perhaps the Babylonian and Egyptian tales are here akin. From the religious point of view, of course, disobedience and rebellion against the gods are sinful attitudes.

It remains true that the hostile judgements elaborated in the Old Testament amount to a devastating total, and Klaus Koch[37] has quoted, in the Introduction to a volume devoted to this and related themes, a statement by Schleiermacher which holds that the lasting impression left by the ancient Jewish religion is one of a deity who is forever exacting retribution, in sharp contrast to the Christian emphasis on forgiveness. Koch goes further, maintaining that most contemporary men of culture consider it to be self-evident that the *lex talionis—eye for eye, tooth for tooth, hand for hand, foot for foot* (Ex.

---

[34] W.G. Lambert and A.R. Millard, *Atra-Ḥasīs. The Babylonian Story of the Flood*. (Oxford, 1969), 5 and 66 f.

[35] G. Pettinato, 'Die Bestrafung des Menschengeschlechts durch die Sintflut', in *Orientalia* 37 (1968), 165–200.

[36] John A. Wilson, in *ANET*³ 10, in a synopsis of the tale, speaks of 'the sin of mankind'. The quotations are from his translation on p. 11.

[37] (Ed.) *Um das Prinzip der Vergeltung in Religion und Recht des alten Testaments* (Wege der Forschung, 125; Darmstadt, 1972), vii ff.

21:24)—constitutes the centre-point of Old Testament practice in law and religion. A misleading aspect of this belief is that it extends a post-exilic emphasis to the whole range of Israel's experience. The developed doctrine is eminently clear in the eighteenth chapter of Ezekiel which begins with the repudiation of the proverb

> 'The fathers have eaten sour grapes, and the children's teeth are set on edge.'
> (Ezek. 18:2.)

Yahweh responds thus: *Every living soul belongs to me; father and son alike are mine. The soul that sins shall die.* Examples are then presented of the principle that *the righteous man shall reap the fruit of his own righteousness, and the wicked man the fruit of this own wickedness.* The chapter ends with a call to repentance, and a reaffirmation of the basic law:

> Therefore, Israelites, says the Lord God, I will judge every man of you on his deeds. Turn, turn from your offences, or your iniquity will be your downfall.
> (Ezek. 18:30.)

In spite of the apostrophe to Israelites, it is evident that the doctrine here enunciated is applied primarily to individuals, and that it is based on a system of reward or punishment for good or bad behaviour.

It is axiomatic, one might think, that any concept of Yahweh as a judge who assesses conduct and acts accordingly to allot praise or blame must bear some relation to actual judicial practice. In a study of Israel's sacral law Wolfgang Preiser[38] comes to the conclusion that retaliation did not have a central place in that system, although the idea is sometimes present. He does not give much attention to parallels in the ancient world; it is fairly clear that the idea of restitution or retribution was widespread. Yet it is noteworthy, as von Rad[39] remarks, that 'law in ancient Israel diverges from the Codex Hammurabi in giving a considerably greater place to private vengeance, especially to the blood-feud;' the Hammurabi Code, he adds, reflects a system in which the state operates more widely in the administration of justice and the punishment of crime, while in Israel there was no state provision to act on behalf of an injured individual. The *Go'el* (גֹּאֵל), 'Avenger', was the next of kin in the blood-feud and retribution devolved on him. At the same

---
[38] In Koch (ed.), op. cit. 236–277 ('Vergeltung und Sühne im altisraelitischen Strafrecht').
[39] *Old Testament Theology*, I, 31.

time a careful distinction was maintained between accidental and intentional homicide, as indeed was the practice in other areas of the ancient world.[40] The blood-feud itself was by no means a peculiarly Hebraic concept; it is still potent in Egypt and the Sudan as I know from experience. Furthermore, the collection of laws found in the 'Book of the Covenant' (Ex. 21:1–22:19) has been shown to relate mainly to 'the interests of village and town-dwelling peasants',[41] and it is a reasonable inference that the collection represents 'the law of Canaanite municipalities taken over by Israel'.[42] Before this the Israelites had been semi-nomadic, and they now adopted a settled agricultural life. It follows that several elements in their early laws were not of strictly Hebraic origin.

A system of tribal judges is ascribed to Moses (Ex. 18:13 ff.) on the advice of Jethro, and under the monarchy a similar system prevailed, tribal and local and in no way dependent on the priesthood. The description in Exodus, where the trustworthy men to be appointed as judges are placed in charge of thousands and hundreds, fifties and tens, suggests the organization of a military levy rather than a tribal division. Moses is himself to deal with matters of higher import. The delegation of his authority is practical good sense, but a separation of sacral and civic justice is also suggested.[43] Under the monarchy the King was naturally the final court of appeal, while the priests dealt with purely sacral matters. After the Exile the importance of the elders in the local courts persisted, an open space near the town gate being used as the venue; the number on the bench of community magistrates varied from seven to twenty-three, and it was the Sanhedrin in Jerusalem that decided appeals in major matters. An accusation could not be proceeded with unless it was supported by at least two witnesses, who had to be adult males and free citizens.

It would evidently be wrong to expect the judgements of Yahweh, whether through his prophets or in his direct control of events, to be conveyed in terms of the juridical background thus outlined. Accusers or witnesses and details of charges are indeed sometimes mentioned, but not of course in a factual sense, for Yahweh's is the supreme court and he is the supreme Judge who judges alone and

---

[40] David Daube, *Roman Law* (Edinburgh, 1969), 165, including refs. to Biblical and Greek ideas.
[41] Max Weber (tr. H.H. Gerth and D. Martindale), *Ancient Judaism* (Glencoe, Ill., 1952), 62.
[42] G. von Rad, op. cit. I, 31.
[43] Martin Noth, *Exodus* (London, 1962), 150.

not as one of a panel of judges. His interventions in the course of events are regarded as judgements which reflect his righteousness. Examples of judgements of this kind are the destruction of Sodom or the sending of the Flood or the rebuke of the Tower of Babel, and they are examples that bear out the title of *Judge of all the earth* (Gen. 18:25, a context where the *outcry* against Sodom is a technical legal term and where Abraham intercedes with Yahweh as a pleader in court appeals to the judge; the modern parallel would be an adjournment of the court to discuss legal issues arising).[44] Yet in the early history of Israel it is in the context of war that Yahweh intervenes to vindicate his righteousness, and he does this by ensuring victories for his people Israel. The idea occurs in the Song of Deborah (Judg. 5:11); and Jephthah appeals to Yahweh's judicial decision in the struggle between Israelites and Ammonites:

> The Lord who is judge will judge this day between the Israelites and the Ammonites.
> (Judg. 11:27.)

Walter Eichrodt,[45] who correctly describes this phenomenon, adds that 'it is obvious that a connection is frequently understood between Yahweh's activity as Judge and the defeat of external enemies;' he might have added too that the idea is all too common in the ancient world, although not exclusively in the judicial sense, and that it has often survived, unhappily, into later centuries. Its origin lies ultimately, perhaps, in a social form akin to that ascribed to totemism, a form which identifies the clan or tribe with its god and sacred animal.[46] A feature of the aid thus proffered is that on occasions of stress and crisis the divine presence is said to be experienced, and there are parallels to this idea in the ancient literature of Mesopotamia, where 'The Exaltation of Inanna' sometimes implies intervention in historical events and the simultaneous exaltation of a human leader. The Exodus narrative includes several well-known instances.[47]

---

[44] Gerhard von Rad (tr. J.H. Marks), *Genesis* (London, 1956), 205 ff.
[45] *Theology of the Old Testament*, I, 242.
[46] Cf. J. Gwyn Griffiths, *The Conflict of Horus and Seth* (Liverpool, 1960), 145 f. That totemism as described by anthropologists is not a self-consistent or unified system or even that the very idea of totemism is illusory has been strongly urged by Claude Lévi-Strauss: see his *Totemism* (tr. R. Needham, London, 1964), 45. But the identification of clan-leader and sacred animal is clearly exemplified by the relation between the Pharaoh and the Horus-falcon.
[47] Cf. Charles D. Isbell, in *JNES* 40 (1981), 143, reviewing *Divine Presence and Guidance in Israelite Traditions: The Typology of Exaltation*, by Thomas W. Mann (Baltimore, 1977).

Perhaps the most direct expression of how divine judgement shapes human destiny is found in the First Psalm in the contrast drawn between the fate of the godly and the ungodly:

> in all that he does he prospers.
> Wicked man are not like this;
> they are like chaff driven by the wind.
>
> (Ps. 1:3–4.)

It is a simple equation that is here presented: godliness brings prosperity, wickedness misfortune. The psalm is late and post-exilic,[48] and probably represents the conventional orthodoxy of its day. It might seem to be addressed to the individual; but two parties within the Jewish congregation might be implied (the piously obedient and the ungodly apostates); or indeed a national antithesis of Jewish worshippers of Yahweh as opposed to gentiles who do not know him.[49] In any case its expression of eudaemonism is akin to utilitarianism in that it stresses what produces worthy and pleasant results, for happiness is seen as the product of good behaviour. Yet it is well known that the Psalms sometimes rise above such a view and face the fact that prosperity may be achieved by the unworthy and that suffering may be the lot of the godly. One reply to the problem is the idea that the prosperity of the wicked is short-lived (Psalm 37), for though he may spread himself like a green bay-tree, he soon vanishes:

> I passed by one day, and he was gone.
>
> (Ps. 37:36.)

Another reply is the affirmation that the righteous are received by God at death, whereas the ungodly survive only in Sheol (Psalm 49); or it is suggested that final retribution is not always possible in this life, and the account will be balanced only after death (Psalm 73).[50]

It is the immortal classic of the Book of Job that provides the most searching exposition of the problem posed by the suffering of the righteous. Job himself is a righteous and sensitive soul, but his great merits do not save him from falling into deep trouble. Eliphaz the Temanite presents him with the traditional view of virtue's claims:

---

[48] 'About the middle of the third century B.C.': W.O.E. Oesterley, *The Psalms* (London, 1939, repr. 1962), 119.
[49] Cf. S. Mowinckel (tr. D.R. Ap-Thomas), *The Psalms in Israel's Worship* (Oxford, 1962, repr. 1967), I, 207 ff. Cf. below 303.
[50] Oesterley, op. cit. 86 ff.

> For consider, what innocent man has ever perished?
> Where have you seen the upright destroyed?
> This I know, that those who plough mischief and sow trouble
> reap as they have sown.
>
> (Job 4:7–8.)

It was the opinion of S.R. Driver that the book's chief aim was to controvert this doctrine which implied that suffering was a result of divine displeasure. Whereas Job certainly denies the doctrine in one sense, for he asserts his innocence, yet to him the important thing is that in all his sorrow he is not cut off from God; indeed he maintains that his sorrow has resulted in giving him a deeper experience of God.[51] At the same time the book goes some way to provide a vindication of God's justice in its relation to the world of men; elements of this theodicy are concerned, however, as we shall see in a later chapter, with the possibility of divine retribution after death. Within the context of this life Job's arguments, as opposed to those of his counselling friends, constitute a 'great counter thrust against these ideas about a straight and direct relationship between sin and punishment.'[52] If the disputations of the friends are unconvincing, the response assigned to God himself is not exactly relevant, for it is not a response that concerns itself with the question posed, namely the suffering of the innocent and righteous. As Scholem[53] remarks, 'Instead, God answers him with—to be precise—the entirely meaningless question of whether Job had been present at the Creation.' The challenge is overwhelming:

> Where were you when I laid the earth's foundations?
> Tell me, if you know and understand.
>
> (Job 38:4.)

and it is followed by a magnificent description of the mysterious glories of earth and heaven. Job's reaction is to submit in humility:

> What reply can I give thee, I who carry no weight?
>
> (Job 40:4.)

Then, in a further challenge, the question of justice is admittedly raised:

> Dare you deny that I am just
> or put me in the wrong that you may be right?
>
> (Job 40:8.)

---

[51] H.H. Rowley, *Job* (Century Bible, New Series, 1970), 18–21; cf. Norman G. Habel, *The Book of Job* (Cambridge Bible Comm., 1975), 6 f.
[52] Scholem, in *Myths and Symbols* (FS. M. Eliade, 1969), 170.
[53] Ibid.

but a return is afterwards made to the wonders of the creation, and Job repeats his submissive rejoinder: *I repent in dust and ashes.* (42:6.) The divine appeal is to majesty, for the grandeur of the universe points to Job's insignificance and also in a general sense to man's insignificance since the panorama of the animal world is presented with keen sympathy and admiration. There is an emphasis too on the careful ordering of the universe and its elaborate design,[54] and this would be relevant to the book's main theme if it included the idea that the cosmic plan is based on justice. Questions like *Do you hunt her prey for the lioness?* (38:39) and *Who provides the raven with its quarry?* (38:41) show that the divine approach takes for granted the predatory nature of animal subsistence.

Job himself emerges as a nobly Stoic figure rather like the Oedipus of Sophocles. He maintains his faith in God even when smitten by adversity:

> The Lord gives and the Lord takes away;
> blessed be the name of the Lord.
>
> (Job 1:21.)

It is said of him, *Throughout all this Job did not sin; he did not charge God with unreason.* (1:22.) When a further stage is reached in the onset of bodily affliction, the emphasis remains: *Throughout all this, Job did not utter one sinful word.* (2:10.) On the other hand, the scrutiny of divine providence in relation to the righteous and unrighteous man, although it is pursued in the lengthy disputations of the counselling friends, reaches no effective conclusion. It is transferred in some passages (to be discussed in a later chapter) to a court which belongs to the life after death. In the context of the present life it faces the problem of reconciling God's omnipotence with the existence of evil and injustice—'the most classic of all the classic dilemmas of theology: omnipotence and evil.'[55]

A feature of the book is its concentration on Job as an individual; this may be an indication, among others, of the post-exilic origin of the body of the work. Admittedly, the individualism is not limned in historically convincing detail. Job lives *in the land of Uz* (1:1), where the reference is uncertain (perhaps in or near Edom); and a spaciously vague aura comes from the statement *Thus Job was the greatest man in all the East.* (1:3.) The plunderers of his property are

---

[54] Cf. the Comm. by Victor E. Reichert (Soncino Books of the Bible, Hindhead, 1946), 196.

[55] Leszek Kolakowski, *Religion* (Fontana Masterguides, 1982), 30. His first chapter ('God of Failures: theodicy') is devoted to this theme.

the Sabaeans of South Arabia; and then, surprisingly, the Chaldaeans (1:17)—a throw-back, perhaps, to the beginning of the first millennium B.C. Such allusions confirm the affinities of the book with the Wisdom Literature of the Near East, including that of Israel itself. Yet a searing *Einsamkeit* finds expression from time to time:

> The wolf is now my brother,
> the owls of the desert have become my companions.
> (Job 30:29.)

V.E. Reichert (1946) renders: *I am become a brother to jackals, / And a companion to ostriches*, quoting Ibn Ezra's comment, 'They are wild animals which have a cry of desolation.'

In the early religion of Israel it is usually through the Covenant (*berith*) with his people that Yahweh is represented as establishing his role in history. The individual is subsumed in this relationship, which is presented, as in Exodus 24, as being initiated by Yahweh; if Moses plays the part of spiritual intermediary, his prominence does not indicate a covenant which is primarily sought from the human side. The first move is on the part of the divine, as Moses makes clear to the Israelites: *This is the blood of the Covenant which the Lord has made with you on the terms of this book.* (Ex. 24:8.) If the Hebrew word *berith* denotes 'bond of communion' or the like—'a circle enclosing both partners, not so much a "limitation" (Buber) as a being brought together into an intimate relationship'[56]—yet its primary mundane contexts concern an alliance between peoples, as between Abraham and the Amorites, or a pact between a monarch and his subjects, as between David and the elders of Israel at Hebron (2 Sam. 5:3). A more intimate ambience refers to the bond of friendship, as between David and Jonathan (1 Sam. 18:3), or the pact of marriage (Mal. 2:14).[57] The latter idea is applied by Hosea (2:22 ff.) to the Covenant that binds Yahweh and Israel, but the basic thought is the relationship between sovereign and people, so that it is not a pact between equal partners. It is true that Israel is a people specially elected by God according to the relationship envisaged, but she becomes a servant people (*'ebed*)[58] whose role is to obey him. (Isa. 42:1 ff.) If Israel fails to carry out her obligations as laid down in the Covenant, God punishes her through historic

---

[56] T.C. Vriezen, *Outline of Old Testament Theology* (Oxford, 1960), 141, who avers, however, before this, that 'Yahweh and Israel are not coequal partners.'
[57] See Koehler and Baumgartner (1967), 150 ff.; Brown-Driver-Briggs, 136.
[58] For the application of the term, in other allusions, to individuals see C.R. North, *Isaiah 40–55* (Torch Comm., London, 1952 repr. 1959), 60.

interventions. Yet the Covenant stands. Varied emphases occur in the types of pledges made—to Abraham (Gen. 17), to Moses (Ex. 24), and to Noah (Gen. 9:9 ff.), the last of these being a pledge which involves mankind and the creation in general. According to Deutero-Isaiah a part of the function of the Servant of Yahweh is to bring forth judgement to the Gentiles:

> Here is my servant whom I uphold,
> my chosen one in whom I delight;
> I have bestowed my spirit upon him,
> and he will make justice shine on the nations.
>
> (Isa. 42:1.)

Here 'justice' (*mishpât*) may have a wider sense than the particular judgement affecting a special situation.[59] But in what follows the Lord is portrayed as an active warrior triumphing over his foes (42:13) who are idolaters. If Israel is in a sad condition, that is Yahweh's rebuke for her infidelity. Even so he will redeem her, and when the nations are gathered together, the truth will be upheld in a scene which is plainly presented as a court of law:

> Let them produce witnesses to prove their case,
> or let them listen and say, 'That is the truth.'
> My witnesses, says the Lord, are you, my servants,
> you whom I have chosen.
>
> (Isa. 43:9–10.)

Nor is this vindication of the truth merely a religious matter. It will have political and military results:

> For your sakes I have sent to Babylon;
> I will lay the Chaldaeans prostrate as they flee,
> and their cry of triumph will turn to groaning.
>
> (Isa. 43:14.)

The Hebrew is, however, obscure and probably corrupt. C.R. North (p. 74) renders literally: *For your sake I (will) send to Babylon, and will bring down (as) fugitives all of them, and the Chaldaeans in the ships of their ringing cry.* The reference is of course to the Neo-Babylonian empire, and its fall is apparently prophesied, an event which occurred in 539 B.C., through the invasion by Cyrus the Great, thus enabling the Jewish exiles to return to Jerusalem.

---

[59] North, op. cit. 61: 'It is almost equivalent to "the true religion".'

3. *Deuteronomy and the Deuteronomic History*

We have referred to the significance of the Covenant in relation to the activity of God in history. It is the Book of Deuteronomy that sets out most clearly the basis of the Covenant: God's election of Israel has established it, and his love has prompted both the election itself and his act of deliverance in her favour. After a command to put to death all opposing nations, including Amorites and Canaanites, comes an assurance of divine election and love with an allusion to the deliverance from Egypt:

> It was not because you were more numerous than any other nation that the Lord cared for you and chose you, for you were the smallest of all nations; it was because the Lord loved you and stood by his oath to your forefathers, that he brought you with his strong hand and redeemed you from the land of slavery, from the power of Pharaoh, king of Egypt.
>
> (Deut. 7:7–8.)

If the Lord will be faithful to those who love him, those who defy him will face destruction:

> Know then that the Lord your God is God, the faithful God; with those who love him and keep his commandments he keeps covenant and faith for a thousand generations, but those who defy him and show their hatred for him he repays with destruction: he will not be slow to requite any who so hate him.
>
> (Deut. 7:9–10.)

Although the nucleus of the book probably derives from the reign of Josiah in 621 B.C., it purports to be in the main a series of addresses delivered by Moses to the nation before the entry into the promised land. These addresses expound the essence of their faith, as in the words just quoted, where rewards and punishments seem evenly balanced. In Chapter 28, on the other hand, curses much outnumber the blessings, doubtless reflecting a similar imbalance in the sanctions featured in ancient Near Eastern treaties. From time to time there are retrospective allusions to the deliverance from Egypt and the trials overcome in the wilderness. The initial divine impetus is seen in the promise made to the forefathers. Penalties inflicted on Egypt are regarded as a rebuke of the sheer force of oppression, but also as a means of furthering Israel's deliverance. The conquest of Canaan completes the latter process and redeems the initial promise; at the same time it is a punishment of the peoples of Canaan for their sins: *it is because of the wickedness of these nations that the Lord your God is driving them out before you* (Deut. 9:5).

Virtuous obedience to God results in security and prosperity, while sinful disobedience produces failure and suffering: this is the view of history put forward in Deuteronomy and it is equally present in the books from Joshua to the Second Book of Kings, books thus properly called the 'Deuteronomic History'.[60] No single authorship is thereby implied nor indeed a single source. Discrepancies appear in the narratives, notably as between Joshua and Judges: Joshua 1–12 depicts Canaan being conquered by a unified Israel led by one military leader, while Judges 1, especially in its second part, gives an account of a fragmented campaign with several failures or partial successes. Moreover, within Joshua itself there are two varying accounts of the fall of Jericho. Yet a unity binds these books together, and its essence is theological. Divine judgement, whether on people or king, is what brings disaster, and it is caused by disobedience to divine commands; faithful obedience, on the other hand, brings the reward of success.

This does not mean that every single event falls within the grid of a God-controlled system. The course of the campaign in Canaan certainly does, for Yahweh expressly sanctions and even commands it. Whereas the term 'Yahweh War' (cf. 1 Sam. 17:47 and 18:17) is preferable to 'Holy War' to describe the concept, its historical reality as a religious phenomenon is beyond question. (See G.H. Jones, *VT* 25 (1975), 642–58 and T. Veijola in *Studies in the Historical Books of the Old Testament*, ed. J.A. Emerton, Leiden, 1979, 238.) Minor incidents in the campaign include the subterfuge practised by the prostitute Rahab in the fall of Jericho and the condign punishment of Achan for his illicit partaking of the spoil; Achan confesses (Josh. 7:20), *I have sinned against the Lord the God of Israel*. In the narrative of Judges (19–21) the account of later phases of the settlement in Canaan features the savage vengeance taken on the tribe of Benjamin, where the near-extermination of the tribe involves an 'utter disproportion between the crime and the punishment' (Soggin, *Introd.* 281). An inter-tribal assembly delivers judgement, but with divine sanction.

The books dealing with the rise of the monarchy and its development reveal, in their separate assessment of each reign, a quite remarkable narrowing of outlook. The phase is preceded, it is true,

---

[60] Martin Noth, *The Deuteronomistic History* (tr. Sheffield, 1981; German original, 1943, rev. 1957); Moshe Weinfeld, *Deuteronomy and the Deuteronomic School* (Oxford, 1972, repr. 1983); A.D.H. Mayes, *The Story of Israel between Settlement and Exile* (London, 1983); G.H. Jones, *1 and 2 Kings* (2 Vols.; New Century Bible, London, 1984).

by an episode which illustrates divine judgement in relation to a wider question of morality: when David destroys Uriah and his family in order to possess his wife Bathsheba, his own family is to suffer a similar fate, as the prophet Nathan tells him in God's name (2 Sam. 12:7-12). It is in the Books of Kings that the more restricted approach becomes evident. The Deuteronomistic redactors present assessments that are governed almost solely by theological considerations, with little weight given to political and economic matters. Josiah's reforms, in their opposition to syncretism with Canaanite cults, were admittedly maintaining the stance of the Covenant; but the demeaning of Omri and Ahab meant concentrating entirely on their fondness for those cults. Elijah's contest on Carmel scarcely implies a 'divine judgement', as Soggin (p. 203) puts it; rather does it point to a struggle between two sanctuaries, the one Israelite and the other Canaanite (or Phoenician, with Sidonian Melqart as the Baal) on an ancient site. An ironical feature of the struggle is that Yahweh wins by excelling as a lightning-producer—an attribute that might suit Melqart or Hadad or the Hittite god Teshub.

In subsequent reigns the Deuteronomists condemned the kings who refused to follow the centralization of the cult in Jerusalem, in accordance with Josiah's reforms, preferring instead to support the 'high places' of the local sanctuaries. It is thus a framework that contains 'an evaluation of the rulers of Israel and Judah which is based on the criterion of cultic purity found in the book of Deuteronomy' (G.H. Jones, *1 and 2 Kings*, 1984, I, 29). This reflects a narrowly dogmatic approach. On the other hand, the interpretation of the disasters which assailed Israel in 722 and Judah in 597 and 587 was in line with the much wider doctrine which saw in these and similar events the operation of divine judgement. It was an interpretation which was fully in agreement, as we have seen, with the views of the principal prophets, and it was one which strongly persisted, albeit with interesting variations. Habakkuk is concerned about contradictions in the workings of divine justice; Nahum revels in the fall of Nineveh as an act of vengeance which the Lord of Hosts inflicts with every good reason; and Jonah, although his narrative lacks historicity, presents the divine compassion as embracing even Nineveh.

4. *Some Hittite Parallels*

The idea of divine judgement is so strongly presented in the Old Testament that one might be tempted to think that it was an idea peculiar to Hebraic thought. J.A. Soggin[61] warns us that this may be far from being so. Discussing revelation in history—and judgement and revelation are evidently related ideas—he states that 'to assert that in the Old Testament revelation takes place *in* rather than *through* history is clearly not to assert that other people did not have similar experiences;' and he proceeds to maintain that 'all people of the ancient world, both East and West, saw in war, pestilence or earthquake, the hand of the God who judged human sin.' What distinguishes Biblical history, according to him, is its 'organic character' and its 'coherent attempt to eliminate myth'. At first sight the assertion appears to be rather boldly comprehensive and to invite modification. The causality of natural phenomena, such as pestilence or earthquake, is ascribed in many ancient religions to the deities within whose domain these occurrences fall. Beyond this simple ascription lies the question of their possible link with rebuke or punishment. War, on the other hand, is a humanly activated occurrence. The gods naturally give victory to their adherents. But how far is defeat interpreted as a penalty for infidelity or sin?

Soggin refers to a very relevant study by A. Malamat[62] who is able to call attention to a Hittite text attributed to King Mursili II (c. 1320 B.C.), the so-called 'Plague Prayer', in which a sequence is discovered relating to 'conclusion of treaty, violation of treaty and consequent national catastrophe'.[63] A deadly disease which lasted for twenty years is described, and its ultimate cause is put down to the fact that, when the Egyptians and the Hattians were bound by oath to the Hattian Storm-god, *the Hattians promptly broke their word.* The text adds the question, *Has this perhaps become the cause of the anger of the Hattian Storm-god, my Lord?*[64] Malamat aptly compares 2 Sam. 21:1–3, which concerns the famine in the time of King David, another narrative where a national disaster is explained as the result of the violation of a treaty. In Hittite sources there is also a threat of famine and disease for ignoring an oath.[65]

Other Hittite texts reveal the belief that victory comes from the gods and that they should be suitably honoured for this. Thus a cuneiform text of about 1600 B.C. tells of how the Great King Hattushili I, after conquering a city beyond the River Puran, took

---

[61] *Introd.* 45.
[62] 'Doctrines of causality in Hittite and Biblical historiography: a parallel', *VT* 5 (1955), 1–12.
[63] Op. cit. 12.
[64] A. Goetze, *ANET*³, 395, § 5.
[65] Ibid. 353 ff.

its many riches to his own capital city of Hattusha (near the modern Turkish village of Boğăzköy). There he delivered part of the rich booty *to the Sun Goddess of Arinna* and part *to the temple of the goddess Mezulla*.[66] It may be assumed that these splendid gifts, mostly of silver and gold, were offered to the deities 'as votive gifts, evidently as a token of thanks for their support during the battles'.[67] In defeat, on the other hand, there was sometimes a ritual of purification which included animal and human sacrifice:

> If the troops have been beaten by the enemy they perform a ritual, 'behind' the river as follows: they 'cut through' a man, a goat, a puppy, and a little pig; . . . and the troops walk right through, and when they come to the river they sprinkle water over them.
> (O.R. Gurney, *The Hittites*,² 1954, 151.)

Gurney[68] compares the covenant in Genesis 15:9–18, where Abraham is ordered to make animal sacrifices. But the context is not there one of military defeat. In the text quoted it is evident that the soldiers have to be purified because they are deemed to have offended by the act of failure; and the sacrifices are to deities who must be expiated because they have been compromised by the same act. The fault is carefully assigned to the human element.

A prominent theme in Hittite mythology is the anger of the gods, although its causes, whether in the narrative sense or in the moral connotation, are not always clear. In the Old Testament, on the contrary, the causes of Yahweh's anger are usually explained as when the destruction of the Cities of the Plain is put down to the breaking of the Covenant. It is said that the nations will ask, *Why has the Lord so afflicted this land? Why has there been this great outburst of wrath?* The answer is thus given:

> Because they forsook the covenant of the Lord the God of their fathers which he made with them when he brought them out of Egypt. They began to worship other gods and to bow down to them . . .
> (Deut. 29:25 f.)

No ethical condemnations are uttered here; it is sheer infidelity that has offended. In the Hittite myth of the disappearance of Telipinu, a Hattian weather-god, the divine anger produces conditions of drought and barrenness which affect the whole of nature as well as men and gods. Themselves afflicted by hunger, the gods institute a search for the vanished Telipinu. An eagle is sent out, but returns

---

[66] Kurt Bittel, *Hattusha* (New York, 1970), 5–6.
[67] Ibid. 6.
[68] Gurney, loc. cit.

without success. Then the mother goddess Hannahanna sends out a bee, which finds the god, but makes him angrier by stinging him. In his heightened anger Telipinu produces a dangerous flood, and now the gods, especially the goddess of health, resort to magical rites, such as the burning of various objects; when the fire is put out, an incantation urges the cessation of the god's wrath:

> As this fire is put out, so too shall [Telipinu's] anger, wrath and fury be put out. Telipinu, let go your anger, let go your wrath, let go your fury![69]
> (Cord Kühne, 'Hittite Texts' in *Near Eastern Religious Texts relating to the Old Testament*, ed. W. Beyerlin London, 1978, 163.)

This and other rites are effective and Telipinu, now that his wrath is removed, resumes his beneficent energies, thus restoring order and fertility to the natural world. Other versions show that the rites were used too in relation to other gods and often enacted in times of disaster. According to Cord Kühne[70] 'the aim of the myth is to demonstrate the efficacy of the ritual against divine anger embedded in the action.'

But what has caused Telipinu's anger? Twelve lines are lost from the beginning of the Hittite text quoted by Kühne, and they may have denoted the cause. Another version, where the vanished god is called 'the Storm-god' (without the name Telipinu) is provided by Hans G. Güterbock,[71] and this version shows considerable concern about the allocation of the sin which caused the Storm-god's anger:

> The Storm-god's Father went to his (i.e. the Storm-god's)
>   Grandfather and said to him:
> 'Who sinned (so that) the seed perished and everything
>   dried up?'
> The Grandfather said:
> 'No one sinned, but you alone sinned!'
> The Storm-god's Father replied:
> 'In no way did I sin!'
> (Hans G. Güterbock, op. cit. 145 f.)

Yet what seems a family quarrel is placated by the kindly intervention of the mother goddess Hannahanna:

---

[69] Sympathetic magic is obviously implied. Cf. Albrecht Goetze, 'The Telepinus Myth', in *ANET³*, 126–28, this section on p. 128.
[70] Op. cit. 160.
[71] 'Hittite Mythology', in S.N. Kramer (ed.), *Mythologies of the Ancient World* (New York, 1961), 141–79, esp. 143 ff. On possible affinities between Telepinu and the 'black Demeter' of Phigalia in Arcadia, see Walter Burkert, *Structure and History in Greek Mythology and Ritual* (Berkeley, 1979, repr. 1982), 125–29.

> Now my father says to me:
> 'It is your fault!
> I shall investigate the matter and kill you!'
> Now, how shall I proceed? What has happened?
>   Hannahanna replied:
> 'Fear not!
> If it is your fault I shall put it straight,
> and if it is not your fault I shall (also) put it straight.'
>
> (Ibid. 146.)

Any system of thought which connects sin and misfortune is bound to argue sometimes from the misfortune to the sin. The allocation of sin becomes, therefore, an important task. *Rabbi, who sinned, this man or his parents? Why was he born blind?* (John 9:2.) Directly from this arises the concern with the possible transmission of the punishment for sin from one generation to another, the sins of the fathers being visited on the children. In the Hittite text the Storm-god's Father and Grandfather are both suspected of causing by their sin the instigation of the divine anger. The mother goddess Hannahanna nobly reaches out of this rigidly causal schema. Her promise of help is generously constructive and forgiving:

> 'If it is your fault I shall put it straight,
> and if it is not your fault I shall (also) put it straight.'

Hans Güterbock, whose translation has here been used, does not offer an interpretation on these lines, but it seems to follow the import of his version.

It is doubtful, none the less, whether such thoughts are typical of the Hittite approach. That the gods are responsible for both boon and bane is an assumption underlying many prayers, like those of Mursili II (c. 1320 B.C.) in which the request is made that freedom from plague be granted, and also help against external enemies.[72] In the 'Plague Prayers of Mursilis'[73] the breaking of an oath made to the Hattian Storm-god is given as the reason for a disaster, as we have noted above with reference to Malamat's interpretation. These prayers are addressed to the Hattian Storm-god and to other Hattian gods and the King Mursili II states that the *anger of the gods* has been disturbing him. The offence of the broken oath is admitted, but it is significantly located in the reign of his father (Suppiluliumas):

---

[72] Hans G. Güterbock, 'Religion und Kultus der Hethiter', in *Neuere Hethiterforschung* ed. G. Walser (Historia Einzelschriften, 7, Wiesbaden, 1964), 54–73, this on p. 58, citing Gurney in *Liverpool Annals* 27 (1940), 24 ff.
[73] See the translation by Albrecht Goetze in *ANET*³, 394 ff.

> See now! I have admitted my guilt before the Storm-god (and said): 'It is so. We have done it.' I know for certain that the offence was not committed in my days, that it was committed in the days of my father ... But, since the Hattian Storm-god is angry/ for that reason and people are dying in the Hatti land, I am (nevertheless) making the offerings to the Hattian Storm-god, my lord, on that account.
>
> (A. Goetze, in *ANET*³, 395.)[74]

Here the passage begins with a suggestion that Mursili II should be excused of the offence since it was committed in his father's reign; but then comes an acceptance of the idea that a *continuum* of responsibility extends from generation to generation. Later this is propounded with bitter clarity:

> It is only too true that man is sinful. My father sinned and transgressed against the word of the Hattian Storm-god, my lord. But I have not sinned in any respect. It is only too true, however, that the father's sin falls upon the son. So, my father's sin has fallen upon me. Now, I have confessed before the Hattian Storm-god, my lord, and before the gods, my lords (admitting): 'It is true, we have done it.' And because I have confessed my father's sin, let the soul of the Hattian Storm-god, my lord and (those) of the gods, my lords, be again pacified! Take pity on me and drive the plague out of the Hatti land!
>
> (Ibid.)

Whereas this is the exact opposite of the doctrine enunciated in the Book of Ezekiel, 18 (see above, p. 15), it is significant that the very same problem was causing concern to these ancient writers.[75] Further, the Old Testament itself sometimes gives answers which are closer to this Hittite attitude, as in the warning contained in the Decalogue: *I punish the children for the sins of the fathers to the third and fourth generation of those who hate me.* (Ex. 20:5.) Yahweh may be *a god compassionate and gracious*, but he is also *one who punishes sons and grandsons to the third and fourth generation for the iniquity of their fathers.* (Ex. 34:7; cf. Num. 14:18.) It was a view that persisted into the sixth century:

> Our fathers sinned and are no more,
> and we bear the burden of their guilt.
>
> (Lam. 5:7.)

---

[74] Cf. Cord Kühne, in *Near Eastern Religious Texts etc.* O.R. Gurney, *Some Aspects of Hittite Religion* (Schweich Lectures, 1976; Oxford, 1977), 1–2; see also his 'Hittite Prayers of Mursili II', in *Liverpool Annals*, 27 (1940), 3–163.

[75] Cf. the comparison made between the Apology of Hattusili III and the royal propaganda of David and Solomon by Harry A. Hoffner Jr. in *Unity and Diversity: Essays in the History, Literature, and Religion of the Ancient Near East* ed. H. Goedicke and J.J.M. Roberts (Baltimore, 1975), 50.

Yet the prophet Jeremiah, like Ezekiel after him, firmly rejected the doctrine: *for a man shall die for his own wrongdoing.* (Jer. 31:30.)[76]

A related Hittite prayer voices a complaint about the apparent inequity of the operation of divine judgement:

> Rested are the rebellious countries but the Hatti land is a weary land.
> (A. Goetze, in *ANET*³, 396.)

An appeal ensues for discrimination in favour of the good:

> Whatever rage (or) anger the gods may feel, and whosoever may not have been reverent toward the gods—let not the good perish with the wicked! If it is one town, or one [house], or one man, O gods, let that one perish alone!
> (Ibid.)

It is fairly clear, at the same time, that the term 'good' here should be applied only in the ritually religious sense of those who carry out their formal obligations to the gods. In a Middle Hittite hymnic prayer to Istanu, the sun-god, the judgements of the god are stressed: he is addressed as *upright Lord of the Tribunal, King of heaven and earth*; he is said to be both just and merciful, but his reactions to the good and the evil are differentiated thus:

> The righteous man is dear to thee, and thou exaltest him . . .
> On wicked and evil men dost thou deliver judgement.
> (Güterbock in *Altorientalische Literaturen*, 226–7.)

His tenderness to the downtrodden is praised in a memorable phrase reminiscent of the Great Aten-Hymn of Akhenaten:

> Istanu, thou art Father and Mother for the oppressed and
> lonely men,

a phrase which occurs earlier too: *Thou art the Father and Mother of all lands*. Gurney points out (in *Liverpool Annals*, 27, 1940, 80) that a phrase *ama-a-a*, 'mother-father' occurs in Sumerian, and *abi ummi*, 'father-mother', in Akkadian; but that the Hittite here (*attaš annaš*) should be understood as an asyndeton—'the father (and) the mother'—and that this order is frequent in Hittite. He also cites the Egyptian parallel in which 'mother' precedes 'father'. A curious feature of the same composition is that the sun-god is seen as the judge of litigious strife among animals.

---

[76] Cf. Cord Kühne, op. cit. 173.

> Thou art judge in the legal strife of dog and pig,
> and thou dost decide even the legal strife of the animals
> who do not speak with the mouth.

The versions are those of Hans G. Güterbock[77] (translated from his German), who points out that the Babylonian elements in this work are easily recognizable, especially the sun-god's role as judge, following that function of the Babylonian Shamash.

Some Hittite prayers exhibit the concept of a personal god to whom the main deities addressed are asked to convey the message. This concept also reverts to Akkadian and Sumerian prototypes.[78] W.G. Lambert translates the openings of some examples as follows:

> He shall recite, 'Ea, Šamaš and Marduk, what are
>   my iniquities?'
> He shall stand facing the ritual paraphernalia of a man's
>   god and goddess and
> He shall recite, 'My god, I did not know', and
>   'My god, my lord.'

In such prayers the basic idea is that disease is the result of the god's anger because of sins committed by the worshipper. It was customary in actual courts of law for the person who confessed his offences to be treated more leniently; hence the emphasis on confession in these prayers. The god is now being addressed instead of the King. In the Hittite prayers, indeed, the King is the petitioner before the god, and so the prayers become 'pleas of confession and self-defence (Hittite *arkuwar*) before the tribunal of the god.'[79]

Whether king or commoner, the Hittite worshipper before his god has the status of subject or servant before a sovereign power who is also the supreme judge. Religious duties therefore imply obedient service to the god; and disobedience results in punishment and humiliation in which the servant's whole family suffers together with all his descendants according to the concept of 'penal co-responsibility' which is also prominent, as we have seen, in areas of Hebraic thought. The essence of sin is disobedience: the servant breaks his master's commands; but confession removes or mitigates the penalty.[80] In a study of divine judgement in the religious

---

[77] 'Hethitische Literatur' in *Altorientalische Literaturen* ed. W. Röllig (Wiesbaden, 1978), 211–53, this work on pp. 226–27. For an earlier translation by Güterbock see his study, 'The Composition of Hittite Prayers to the Sun', in *JAOS* 78 (1958), 237–45.

[78] See W.G. Lambert, in *JNES* 33 (1974), 267–322 and the Appendix by Hans G. Güterbock on Hittite parallels, pp. 323–27.

[79] Gurney, *Some Aspects of Hittite Religion*, 2.

[80] See Giuseppe Furlani, 'The Basic Aspect of Hittite Religion', in *Harv. Theol. Rev.* 31 (1938), 251–62.

doctrine of the Hittites, G. Furlani[81] shows that the sun-god, as in several religions of the ancient Near East, is given the function of supreme judge. He is the deity who sees everything and perceives the thoughts of men. Certainly Rê in Egypt and Shamash in Babylon are given this function, though not exclusively. Analysing the Apology (or Autobiography, as he terms it) of Hattusili(s) III, Furlani shows that underlying its thought is the idea that the outcome of war is really a judgement of the god, the two opponents being regarded as contending litigants in a court of law. In this way every war is viewed as an ordeal through which the god declares his verdict as to which side is in the right. Furlani adds that the concept expressed by Friedrich Schiller in the saying *Die Weltgeschichte ist das Weltgericht* could well be applied to Hittite thought; and that a logical consequence was the belief that the victor is always in the right—at least according to the victor. The divine decision is stressed by the goddess through a communication in a dream:[82]

> On your own ye are weak, but I, Ishtar, have turned all the Hittite lands to the side of Ḫattusili.

In another document (written in Akkadian) the Storm-god decides a matter of politico-dynastic controversy between the Hurri and the Mitanni. In this case it is not war but a treaty under divine auspices that decides the issue: the Hittite King Suppiluliuma is compelled, as it were, by the god to favour the restoration of Mattiwaza (Kurtiwaza) on the throne of the Mitanni.[83] However, the treaty was preceded by a successful military campaign, conducted by Pyassilis.[84]

A Hittite approach which has recently been illuminated by Gurney[85] is the idea that the punishment of the gods may be deflected to another direction by means of a medium similar to that

---

[81] 'Il giudizio del dio nella dottrina religiosa degli Hittiti', in *Rev. Hittite et Asianique* III, 18 (1934), 30–44. See also his book *La Religione degli Hittiti* (Bologna 1936), esp. Ch. 20 ('Il peccato'). Here he notes (p. 355) that the offended deity could allow a considerable interval of time to pass between the sin and its punishment.

[82] Harry A. Hoffner, Jr., op. cit. (n. 75), 54 and in *JNES* 28 (1969), 228 (correcting previous translations).

[83] Ernst F. Weidner, *Politische Dokumente aus Kleinasien* (Boghazköi Studien, 8; Leipzig, 1923), 16–18; cf. Furlani in *Rev. Hittite et Asianique* III, 18, 40–41; K.A. Kitchen, *Suppiluliuma and the Amarna Pharaohs* (Liverpool, 1962), 4.

[84] Kitchen, loc. cit.; cf. H.G. Güterbock, in *Journal of Cuneiform Studies* 10 (1956), 48. Furlani, op. cit. 41–42, refers to two instances in the Annals of Mursili II which mention judgements conveyed in the context of war.

[85] *Some Aspects of Hittite Religion*, 47–58.

of the Hebrew scapegoat which is to bear upon him all the iniquities of the people and to be sent into the wilderness (Lev. 16:22). One might compare the sending of the evil spirits into the Gadarene swine (Mt. 8:32); or the hope of Horace that pestilence will be averted from Rome and despatched to the distant Persians or Britons (*Carm.* I. 21). In origin this rite, as Gurney shows (p. 47), is 'a purely magical procedure', and what is diverted elsewhere is 'evil', especially disease or pain. There are some differences in the Hittite parallels presented. In one instance,[86] portraying a situation after a battle which has brought pestilence from an enemy country, a bull and an ewe from that country are sent back to it with the avowal that the pestilence goes back with it, and also with the hope that the god or goddess who caused the pestilence will now be appeased. It appears, then, that magical and religious elements co-exist here; and the second element reverts to the familiar idea that pestilence is caused by the gods.

Perhaps it would be wrong to suggest that Hittite theology included a system of divine judgement consistently and thoroughly applied to human affairs. According to Gurney[87] 'a Hittite king might acknowledge the incorrigible sinfulness of Man; but there was always a chance that misfortune might befall a man or the nation not as a result of punishment for sin but merely through divine negligence;' and he quotes the rather titivating riposte made to the gods in the 'Plague Prayer' of King Mursili II:[88]

> What is this, O gods, that you have done? You have let in a plague and the land of Hatti, all of it, is dying, so no one prepares the offerings of food and drink. And you come to us, O gods, and for this matter you hold us guilty . . .

The gods will themselves suffer, it is suggested, if they do not stop the plague. A similar bargaining attitude of *do ut des* is present in a prayer of King Muwatallis; the gods are praised for their deed on his behalf, especially in making him king; and yet a touching faith is expressed; *No sooner will the gods have heard my words, than they will put right (and) remove the evil that is in my soul.*[89]

---

[86] Ibid. 48; cf. the translation in H.M. Kümmel, *Ersatzrituale für den hethitischen König* (Wiesbaden, 1967), 113 ff. A very similar text, on which a ram figures, is given by Gurney, loc. cit., and by Goetze in *ANET*^{3}, 347.
[87] *The Hittites* (repr. London, 1975), 157.
[88] Cf. A. Goetze, in *ANET*^{3}, 396 (b, init.).
[89] Ibid. 398.

5. *The Babylonian Theodicy*

To some extent Hittite literature is said to have depended on Mesopotamian prototypes, and these provide plentiful examples of the idea that human affairs are much influenced by divine decisions. It was an idea applied, it seems, exclusively to this life. According to S.H. Hooke,[90] 'the Babylonian conception of divine retribution for sin and reward for righteousness was entirely confined to this life.'

Professor W.G. Lambert has fortunately provided a detailed presentation, with translation and commentary, of the texts which are most relevant to our purpose, and his introductory survey of thought and literature in ancient Mesopotamia is also a very welcome guide.[91] He describes man's relation to the gods as being that of the servant and lord, and shows how the idea of sin or transgression merged the ritual and ethical categories—'the offence might be transgressing a ritual taboo or oppressing the widow and orphan.'[92] The gods as bestowers of victories in war become implicated, as far as Sumerian is concerned, in a situation which mirrors the political pluralism of the country. Each city-state had its own deity, and he was regarded as taking part in the military struggles of the state. The defeat of one city-state meant that the local deity shared the grief, and this is evident in the Sumerian lamentations over cities[93]—a theme which we have observed in Biblical literature. When a city has been defeated and destroyed, its protecting deity is regarded as having abandoned it; and a poetic Sumerian song lists the cities and temples of Sumer and names the deities who have abandoned them, beginning with *Enlil has abandoned Nippur*.[94] A similar idea was applied to the individual, who was deemed to have his own protective god and goddess; and 'if man became impure or sinned, his guardian deities abandoned him.'[95] Their return could be induced by magic or prayer.

As for the gods of the defeated cities, they are presented as being angry with the King or his subjects for their wickedness. This attitude was adopted by the Assyrians, who were often ruthless in conquest. Yet they sometimes gave a theological justification to

---

[90] *Babylonian and Assyrian Religion* (London, 1953), 100.
[91] W.G. Lambert, *Babylonian Wisdom Literature* (Oxford, 1960).
[92] Ibid. 4.
[93] Lambert, loc. cit., quotes from Samuel N. Kramer, *Lamentation over the Destruction of Ur* (Assyriological Studies, 12; Chicago, 1940), 23, lines 46–47.
[94] Kramer, op. cit. 2.
[95] B. Landsberger, *Three Essays on the Sumerians* (Los Angeles, 1974), 16.

their devastation. When Sennacherib destroyed Babylon, his successor Esarhaddon stated that the citizens of Babylon had oppressed the weak and had pursued bribery and plunder, selling temple property to Elam; thus they incurred the anger of Marduk, the god of the city, and he instigated its destruction.[96]

With the rise of Old Babylonian literature (from *c.* 1700 B.C.) Lambert sees the emergence of a more sophisticated, and also more questioning, attitude to the role of the gods in human affairs. If the belief in a universe controlled by the gods was persistent, it posed problems about the obvious injustices seen in the life of the individual. There are several Babylonian texts which present the tension between a challenging scepticism and the viewpoint which represented, one supposes, a kind of orthodoxy. In view of their subject-matter they have invited comparison with the Book of Job.

The *Ludlul Bêl Nēmeqi* (*I will praise the Lord of Wisdom*) is a long and impressive monologue described by Lambert[97] as 'The Poem of the Righteous Sufferer' in which 'a certain noble relates how he met with every conceivable calamity, and was eventually restored to health and prosperity by Marduk.' The *Lord of Wisdom* is Marduk, though he is strangely left unnamed in the section describing the nobleman's suffering. This includes social degradation (I, 78, Lambert p. 35: *Though a dignitary, I have become a slave*) and much physical pain portrayed in miniscule detail. Marduk is often named in the section which exults in the restoration to health and honour, and here the power that caused the misery is left nameless:

> Marduk, he restored me.
> He smote the hand of my smiter,
> It was Marduk who made his weapon fall.
>
> (Tablet IV, 10–12, Lambert, p. 59.)

If we examine the criticism levelled at the gods, we find that it expresses disillusion and disappointment. Here is a man who has served his gods faithfully, but feels that they have not kept their part of the contract. Instead of rewarding him[98] they have humiliated him. When he prays to his personal god and goddess, they seem to take no notice. Nor can the diviner or the dream priest

---

[96] Lambert, op. cit. 5, citing R. Borger, *Die Inschriften Asarhaddons* (Graz, 1956), 12–13.

[97] Op. cit. 21 ff. See also Robert H. Pfeiffer, in *ANET*³, 434–7; Hartmut Schmökel, in W. Beyerlin, *Near Eastern Religious Texts etc.* (1975, tr. 1978), 137–40; Erica Reiner, in *Altorientalische Literaturen* (1978), 195–99.

[98] Cf. Lambert, op. cit. 289 n. 26: 'The Babylonians had no hesitation in demanding a practical return from their religious observances . . .; a personal name declares, "There is profit in righteousness" . . .'

explain the trouble. Some *divine wrath* is operating against him. He is treated as though he has omitted all religious obligations

> Who in his negligence has despised the god's rites,
> Has not taught his people reverence and worship,
> But has eaten food without invoking his god[99]
> (Tablet II, 17–19, Lambert, p. 39.)

whereas in fact he has honoured all such duties:

> For myself I gave attention to supplication and prayer:
> To me prayer was discretion, sacrifice my rule.
> The day for reverencing the god was a joy to my heart.
> (Ibid. 23–25.)

The divine order is open to the gravest criticism simply because it is inscrutable:

> Who knows the will of the gods in heaven?
> Who understands the plans of the underworld gods?
> Where have mortals learnt the way of a god?
> (Ibid. 36–38.)

From the humiliation caused by it comes the *Schadenfreude* of the community:

> All my country said, 'How he is crushed!'
> The face of him who gloats lit up when he heard.
> (Ibid. 116–17.)

The work does not, however, expatiate on the causation of suffering; and the criticism of the divine order does little probing. Lambert[100] therefore suggests that 'The Babylonian *Pilgrim's Progress*' would be a better comparison than 'The Babylonian Job'. Its underlying doctrine, albeit challenged, is that religion brings its due recompense.

The work is dated to the late Cassite period (1500–1100 B.C.); and of slightly later[101] origin is the *Babylonian Theodicy*, which is also referred to sometimes as 'An Akkadian dialogue on the unrighteousness of the world', 'The Acrostic Dialogue', and 'The Babylonian Koheleth'.[102] In form it presents a dialogue between a sufferer and a friend, and this is more clearly reminiscent of the

---

[99] In a cultic meal, perhaps, rather than an ordinary meal. Cf. Lambert, 289 n. 13.
[100] Op. cit. 27. Cf. H. Schmökel, in op. cit. (n. 97), 137: 'the problem of theodicy is dealt with in a restrained fashion . . .; the author probably regarded it as insoluble.'
[101] 'Probably written about 1000 B.C.': Lambert, op. cit. 63.
[102] Cf. H. Schmökel, op. cit. 133.

Book of Job.[103] Thematically it is also close to that work, since it questions the divine ordering of human affairs in view of the manifest fact that the righteous are sometimes seen to suffer whereas the wicked flourish. The more orthodox friend argues against this that the fate of the wicked is often otherwise: they eventually encounter catastrophe which may be explained as the divine rebuke of their conduct. Prosperity, on the other hand, is seen by him as the regular result of piety. Among the injustices which the sufferer condemns is the advantage bestowed on the first-born in a family; he describes himself as one born late to his parents and left by them in the condition of an orphan. A localized predicament seems to be reflected, although primogeniture has carried precedence in many societies. What is significant is the nature of the friend's reply: Aruru (the goddess who created man) ordained that in animals and man the first offspring is weak, but the later offspring bigger and stronger. The friend harps too on the familiar note of the remoteness and inscrutability of the divine mind:

> In your anguish you blaspheme the god.
> The divine mind, like the centre of the heavens, is remote;
> Knowledge of it is difficult; the masses do not know it.
> (*Theodicy*, XXIV, 255–7; Lambert, p. 87.)

Unlike the *Ludlul Bêl Nēmeqi*, this work does not end with a restoration to happiness and affluence. The sufferer instead pleads with his friend to help him, maintaining the while a sweet humility of spirit and appealing anew to his personal gods to resume their aid. He lauds the sun-god also:

> May the god who has thrown me off give help,
> May the goddess who has [abandoned me] show mercy,
> For the shepherd Šamaš guides the peoples like a god.
> (*Theodicy* XXVII, 295–7; Lambert p. 89.)

But this quiet end is not achieved without a measure of success for the sufferer in the debate. He points to the oppression inherent in society; the rich and powerful dominate the poor and weak, and are able even to interfere with the course of justice in the courts. To this the friend acquiesces:

> Solemnly they speak in favour of a rich man,
> 'He is a king', they say, 'riches go at his side.'
> But they harm a poor man like a thief.
> (*Theodicy* XXVI, 281–3; Lambert, ibid.)

---

[103] Cf. James Barr, in *Bull. Ryl.* 54 (1971), 36 f.

He asserts before this, rather surprisingly, the belief that the creator-gods have assigned to man a nature which tends to falsehood rather than truth:

> Narru, king of the gods, who created mankind,
> And majestic Zulummar, who dug out their clay,
> And mistress Mami, the queen who fashioned them,
> Gave perverse speech to the human race.
> With lies, and not truth, they endowed them for ever.
> (*Theodicy*, XXVI, 276–80; Lambert, ibid.)

This sounds like a doctrine of Original Sin, but in fact goes further since it makes the inherent tendency to evil a primary state, and not one which followed a Fall from a state of original purity.

A text which also uses the dialogue form is entitled *The Dialogue of Pessimism* by Lambert.[104] The speakers are a master and his slave. The former makes a series of decisions about doing this and that—visiting the palace, dining, hunting, making love—but in each case, after the slave has praised the idea, the master quickly abandons it, whereupon the slave also attacks it. In the end, exhausting his ideas, he asks the slave what is worth doing. The slave is now prepared to make a suggestion of his own: death is the only thing worth doing.

Akkadian documents from the site of the ancient Mari on the Middle Euphrates throw light on a direct relationship with the divine which explicitly rested on reciprocal service. In a letter of the eighteenth century B.C. addressed to Zimri-Lim, King of Mari, by a member of his court, a report is given of a man who heard the god Dagan speak to him in a dream with words in which he complained of the King Zimri-Lim:

> Why are the messengers of Zimri-Lim not in constant attendance upon me, and why does he not lay his full report before me? Had this been done, I would long ago have delivered the kings of the Yaminites into the power of Zimri-Lim.
> (Tr. William L. Moran in *ANET*^{3}, 623.)

There follows a promise of triumphant action if the King will show respect and consult the god. In these writings prophecies of success in war or politics are frequent. A handmaid who fell into ecstasy gives the King a divine assurance: *Zimri-Lim, although you neglect me, (for my part) I will continue to love you. I will give your enemies into your hand.* (H. Schmökel in *Near Eastern Religious Texts etc.* ed. W. Beyerlin,

---

[104] Op. cit. 139 ff. He suggests *The (Humorous) Dialogue of Pessimism* if the work is interpreted as a satirical skit; cf. R.H. Pfeiffer, in *ANET*^{3}, 437–8.

London, 1978, 125.) But the woes and warnings of the Hebrew prophets are rarely paralleled, and discussions of the Mari writings often focus more on the medium than the message, especially the use of dream-visions and transports of ecstasy. See the literature mentioned by William L. Moran and Hartmut Schmökel in the works cited above.

6. The Concept of Justice in Ancient Iranian Religion

A tremendous thrust in the direction of eschatology: that is one of the major impressions made by the religious traditions[105] of ancient Iran. The central doctrine of Zoroaster concerned the unceasing struggle of Ahura Mazda and Ahriman (Angra Mainyu). It was 'wholly a struggle between the right, *aša*, and the false, *drug*.'[106] But it is to enter its final phase only after a trebled period of three thousand years, when the decisive triumph of the right will be achieved.[107] If ultimate triumph is thus guaranteed, the question naturally arises as to the operation of the beneficent divine will in the interim. Does it have any controlling power over the lives of men? A similar question arises in relation to divine judgement, which is envisaged as happening to the individual after death or in a collective sense in the phase of the final victory over Ahriman.[108] Does such a belief allow any moral judgement or rebuke within this life?

A Dualistic System

To some extent the problem is solved by the dualism of the system. Since the 'Destructive Spirit', Ahriman, is responsible for all evil and has beings called *daēvas* to serve his purpose, Ahura Mazda is not regarded as in any way implicated in the resulting moral confusion. The Greeks, not surprisingly, identified Ahura Mazda with Zeus and Ahriman with Hades.[109]

Like the Egyptian in its use of the concept of *mâat*, Avestan had a word which was used both of a principle and a divinity: 'for

---

[105] For the plural cf. Geo Widengren, *Die Religionen Irans* (Die Religionen der Menschheit, 14; Stuttgart, 1965).
[106] Mary Boyce, *A History of Zoroastrianism* (Hdb. der Orientalistik, I. 8; Leiden, 1975), 198. (Hereafter Boyce, *Hist.*)
[107] Ibid. 287 ff.
[108] Ibid. 236–246.
[109] M.L. West, *Early Greek Philosophy and the Orient* (Oxford, 1971), 189. Cf. Plutarch, *De Is. et Os.* 46, 369 E and my Comm. (1970), ad loc. p. 473.

Zoroaster there existed both the principle *aša* and Asha who was a divinity, one of the seven Bounteous Immortals of his own great vision.'[110] There is a further similarity in that *aša* originally implies cosmic and social order as well as moral order or truth.[111] *Drug*, the opposing principle, is likewise related to Ahriman. Within the life of the individual it follows that obedience to Ahura Mazda and in particular to his chosen spirit of truth, Asha, was regarded as the path to upright conduct. Thus in the *Gāthās* Zoroaster prays to Ahura Mazda to show him Asha and is bidden to go to Asha to receive guidance.[112] There is no dichotomy of significance between Ahura Mazda and Asha, for the latter is a creation of the supreme god.[113] As in the experience of Zoroaster himself, a crucial moral choice is imposed on man: either he must fight on the side of Asha or he must follow Drug. In either case he incurs the hostility of the opposing powers; but he also enlists the sympathy and actual support of the powers which he has chosen to follow. Since the choice is completely free, a thoroughly moral basis is possible for life and outlook. Indeed it has been said that 'Zoroastrianism is predominantly an ethical religion.'[114] It is true that a belief in the power of fate sometimes impinged on the concept of moral freedom. In a text which is much later than Zoroaster the problem is encountered by a text stating that *the material is according to fate, the spiritual according to action*,[115] and interpreted as denoting that 'we depend on fate only for the material things whereas in the spiritual order our action is autonomous.' Spiritually, however, the devoted follower is not immune from the attacks of the evil *daēvas*, who can even lure the followers to worship them.[116] It would doubtless be wrong to externalize this conflict entirely as though it is being fought only between divine powers and not within the soul of man.

Yet man's life is subject to divine judgement, and Ahura Mazda, acting through Asha, is regarded as the arbiter of rewards and punishments:

> That satisfaction which thou hast created for both factions (the truthful and the deceitful) together with Thy spirit and hast promised

---

[110] Boyce, *Hist.* 199.
[111] Ibid. 27.
[112] S. Insler, *The Gāthās of Zarathustra* (Acta Iranica, 8; Leiden, 1975), Yasna, 43.10–12, pp. 62–65; cf. Boyce, *Hist.* 199.
[113] Yasna, 31.7; Insler, *The Gāthās*, 38–39.
[114] R.C. Zaehner, *The Teachings of the Magi* (London, 1956), 97.
[115] *Videvdat* as quoted by J. Duchesne-Guillemin, *Symbols and Values in Zoroastrianism* (Religious Perspectives, 15; New York, 1966), 153.
[116] Boyce, *Hist.* 201.

> (to them) through fire and truth, that commandment which is for thy adherents—speak, Wise One, with the tongue of Thine own mouth, in order for us to know (all) that, by means of which I might convert all the living.[117]
>
> (Yasna, 31.3.)

A slightly different version is quoted by Martin West:[118]

> The reward which thou shalt give by the spirit and the fire
> And which thou shalt divide, as Righteousness, among the
>   two parties . . .
> Do thou tell us, that we may know. . . .
>
> (Yasna, 31.3.)

'Reward' or 'recompense', where Insler has 'satisfaction', makes little difference, for the latter explains (p. 182) that he means 'satisfaction' in the legalistic sense. The differing tenses may appear a more serious divergence. According to Insler (ibid.) the promise was made in the past, but pertains to 'the final judgement'; so that basically his interpretation is the same as that of West (p. 178):[119] 'And at the end he will judge them in the name of Aša.'

Moral Reckoning

The idea of moral reckoning is certainly present in the *Gāthās* and is well exemplified in one which Duchesne-Guillemin[120] has called 'the *gatha* of Conversations' and in which Zoroaster and his Lord conduct a dialogue. He translates one strophe thus:

> I recognized thy beneficence, O Wise Lord,
> When I saw, at the birth of existence, in the beginning,
> that you assigned a recompense for deed and words:
> Evil retribution for evil, good for good,
> Through thy power, at the last turning of creation.
>
> (Yasna, 43.12.)

The various versions of this strophe exemplify also, incidentally, the difficulties attending these texts. Maria W. Smith (1929), 104, thus renders it:

---

[117] Translated by Insler, p. 37.

[118] *Early Greek Philosophy and the Orient*, 178. The translator is J. Duchesne-Guillemin, *The Hymns of Zarathustra* (London, 1952), 109; cf. the same author's *Zoroastre* (Paris, 1948), 246.

[119] Cf. Maria Wilkins Smith, *Studies in the Syntax of the Gathas of Zarathushtra* (Philadelphia, 1929), 74–75. Helmut Humbach, *Die Gathas des Zarathustra* (Heidelberg, 1959), I, 88, uses present tenses.

[120] In *Religions of the Ancient East* (Faith and Fact Books, 141; London, 1959), 128. His version in *The Hymns of Zarathustra* (1952, repr. 1979), 137, is rather different.

And when thou didst tell me; Go to teach justice—(Z:) then didst thou prescribe for me (things which were) not disobeyed. (Ah:) Hasten before there comes for me obedience, accompanied by great-gifted destiny, which shall apportion the rewards of the two-parties, salvation-and-Damnation.

Gone is the crystal clarity of the first version quoted, but two other more recent versions share the greater abstruseness. Thus Helmut Humbach (1959) I, 114:

Und wenn du zu mir sagst: 'Zur Wahrhaftigkeit gelangst du in
    Umsicht',
so sagst du mir das, nicht ohne mich erhört zu haben.
Aufstehen will ich, noch bevor die Erhörung zu mir gelangt
im Verein mit der Reichtum verleihenden Anteilsspendung,
die die Anteile verteilen wird, um die Beine zu kräftigen.

A startling divergence emerges in the last clause ('to strengthen the legs'), and it rests on a preferred variant reading (cf. Humbach in II, 51). Insler's version (1975, p. 65) differs on that point, but otherwise approximates to Humbach's:

However, that Thou didst say to me: '*Thou hast come to the truth in thy discernment; moreover, thou hast never contradicted Me in disobedience*', it was for me to arise before obedience was to come to me accompanied by a wealth-granting reward, (for it is obedience) according to which one should distribute the rewards to both factions at the time of (our) salvation.

Insler italicizes the words of Ahura Mazda, and he is at one with other commentators in applying the last phrase, about 'the time of salvation', to the final judgement which awaits man in the future. A previous phrase, however, mentions 'a wealth-granting reward', and the question clearly arises as to the temporal application of such a reward. Does it not apply to the reward available to the righteous here and now? That is not the opinion of Insler, for he avers (p. 238) that 'Zarathustra is saying that he was to become obedient to AhM before the reward for such good behavior was to come to him;' and he adds that 'the next line qualifies that such rewards (both good and bad) are to be dispensed at the final judgment', comparing 51, 15c, *These prizes have been promised to you by good thinking and truth during the times of salvation!* In the much later Dēnkart (ninth century A.D.) there is a stress on the disinterested pursuit of virtue. Among the sayings of Aturpat, son of Mahraspand, who lived in the fourth century A.D., occurs this one: *Do good simply because it is good.*[121]

---

[121] Zaehner, *The Teachings of the Magi*, 113; cf. Duchesne-Guillemin, *Symbols and Values in Zoroastrianism*, 153.

It may be, none the less, that a problem remains. Of what use will a 'wealth-granting reward' be in the final judgement? In the present life such a reward can be a distinct advantage; and one tends to question whether the phrase itself rules out an allusion to a distant future. Here the economic background of Zoroastrianism is of course relevant. A pastoral and cattle-breeding people were often endangered by the attacks of nomadic tribes. The prophet naturally equates the aggressors with the followers of the Lie and he questions his God about the possibility of retribution:

> This do I ask thee, Lord: what retribution will there be for him who would secure the kingdom (political power) for the follower of the Lie, for the evil-doer who cannot earn a livelihood except by doing violence to the husbandman's herds and men, though they have not provoked him?
>
> (Yasna, 31.15.)[122]

Translations of *maēniš* ('retribution' above) have not surprisingly varied in colour. Bartholomae's *Altiranisches Wb.* (Strassburg, 1904), 1107 gives for g. (gaθisch-awestisch) *maēnay-f-*, 'Strafe, Bestrafung'; cf. Maria W. Smith, p. 79 ('I ask (about) this, the punishment'); Duchesne-Guillemin (1948), 'peine'; Humbach, 'Vergeltung'; Insler, 'payments'. If the last-quoted version seems colourless in comparison, especially with Zaehner's 'retribution', it does raise the question of whether tangible payments, perhaps in kind, could be demanded in such unhappy events. Yet the main significance must be wider. The helpless condition of the ox when violence is threatened is portrayed in the *Gāthā* which contains its appeal to Ahura Mazda:

> Violence, fury, cruelty, frightfulness, and might hem me in. No other husbandman have I but you; so assign me good grazing lands.
>
> (Yasna, 29.1.)[123]

The God eventually names Zoroaster as the ideal pastor, albeit himself without much strength until he becomes assured of King Vishtaspa's help.

The appeal of the ox for a divine pastor and for good grazing lands suggests the possibility of succour and security here and now. For man too obedience to the Wise Lord is not without its condolences in this life, even if hope for the next life is more often

---

[122] Tr. by Zaehner in *The Dawn and Twilight of Zoroastrianism* (London, 1961), 34; cf. Insler, 40–41, who ends with 'the cattle and men of the undeceiving pastor', as does Humbach, I, 92.

[123] Zaehner, ibid. 34. Insler, p. 29, ends with, 'I have no pastor other than you. Therefore appear to me with good pasturage.'

displayed. The beginning of Yasna 51 points to good fortune and the best of everything as results of devotion to the good rule:

> That good rule must be chosen which best brings good fortune to the man serving it with milk. In alliance with truth, it shall encompass the best (for us) through its actions, Wise One. This very rule shall I now bring to realization for us.
> (Yasna, 51.1; tr. Insler, p. 103.)

'To serve with milk' implies offering in general and also 'the metaphoric sense of strength'.[124] The 'good rule' (*khshathra*) relates to earthly power.[125] Further, Ahura Mazda is credited with the creation of both material and spiritual entities:

> You, O Mazdā, created for us in the beginning by your thought material objects and consciences.
> (Yasna, 31.11.)[126]

Other allusions describe him as 'the creator of everything' (Yasna, 44.7) and as one who has 'fashioned the cow as well as the waters and the plants by reason of Thy most virtuous spirit' (Yasna, 51.7).[127] A question that clearly arises, at the same time, is that of the control of Ahura Mazda over the world which he created. If he has fashioned everything, is he also regarded as the shaper of destiny? If so, his judgements may be expected to influence the life of man on a moral basis.

'For Zoroaster', according to Duchesne-Guillemin,[128] 'Righteousness led to bliss.' He adds, however, that 'he does sometimes ask the Lord, rather pathetically, for reassurance on this point, but on the whole he is certain of the final beatitude of the righteous, and is, therefore, willing to suffer among men.' In his own life, it is maintained, Zoroaster enjoyed a measure of prosperity; if at an early stage he was compelled to flee, King Vishtaspa afterwards ensured his success. The prophet does complain of a vexatious interlude—being denied hospitality in the wintry season by the favourite of a prince. The latter is assured that his punishment will come at the *Bridge of the Separator*, that is, on the final day of judgement; and in this poem the prophet draws a parallel between the *Bridge of the winter* and the *Bridge of the Separator*, where the last

---

[124] Insler, ibid. 103.
[125] Humbach, *Gathas*, II, 86.
[126] Tr. Mary Boyce, *Hist.* I, 195. Cf. Insler, p. 39; Humbach, I, 90–91.
[127] Insler's translations. Cf. Mary Boyce, *Hist. II. Under the Achaemenians* (Leiden, 1982), 192, where the influence on the Old Testament is discussed, including creation through the Spirit.
[128] *The Hymns of Zarathustra*, 7.

noun refers to the segregation of the good and the wicked:[129]

> The minion of the prince, at the Bridge of the winter,
> Offended Zarathustra Spitama by refusing him shelter...
> His soul, stripped bare, shall fear at the Bridge of the Separator.

No penalty in this life is therefore envisaged here.

---

[129] Ibid. 8.

CHAPTER TWO

THE GREEK CONCEPT OF A MORAL LAW WITH
DIVINE SANCTION

As we move from the countries of the ancient Near East to consider the ideas of the Greeks and Romans, we face a contrast, for the most part, in the evidence concerning authorship. We know the names of the major Hebrew prophets and also, to some extent, the nature of their *Sitz im Leben*—a phrase which includes their political and religious situation. The Deuteronomists, it is true, are a faceless group, but even they are firmly linked historically to the reforms of Josiah at the end of the seventh century. Anonymity is what we mostly encounter (apart from some named Hittite kings) in the relevant literature of the Hittites, Babylonians, and Iranians. By comparison the literature of Greece and Rome is highly personal. Names of authors are known and often something of their life and times. Homer, of course, poses a special problem. If the *Iliad* and the *Odyssey* were eventually written in a final form by a single poet of that name, it is abundantly clear that a long tradition of orally transmitted verse lay behind him.

The bond which links the writer and his people is often hard to define. Among the classical writers here discussed are the tragedians Aeschylus, Sophocles, and Euripides. While a strongly individualist element marks each of them, Athenian drama always relied on close *rapport* with its large audiences. This does not mean that the ideas or sentiments expressed reflected a majority view of the audience, but it does imply that they were likely to evoke a response. The historian Herodotus, although not an Athenian, probably gave lectures in Athens and thus enjoyed intellectual contacts there as in many other places. To ascertain how representative of contemporary thought any author may be is an impossible task. It is axiomatic that no author has ever lived in a vacuum and to some degree his work must be related to the society in which he lives. In the following discussions we have chosen authors and works which give prominence to our theme, sometimes opting an aspect of the theme (as with the Erinyes and Atê) as a subtitle. At the same time we have examined some other evidence which is not linked to any particular author, especially that which illustrates ideas embodied in the judicial system.

1. *Aeschylus: the Individual and the Nation*

The author who gives the clearest and most impassioned impression of the Greek view of the moral law which is seen to operate in human affairs is Aeschylus, the earliest of the great writers of tragedy in Athens. In his *Agamemnon* and *Persae* he presents the theme as it affects both the individual and the nation, although these two aspects are of course open to interpenetration. Some earlier interpreters were doubtless too eager to establish a systematic theology in the works of Aeschylus, while some more recent observers relate themselves too rigidly to sociological categories such as 'Shame-Culture' and 'Guilt-Culture'. All these elements, theological, sociological and several others, are certainly present, and it is well to remember that Aeschylus is writing, at the same time, as an individual artist with his own vision.[1] Writing, of course, for a particular society with its manifest preconceptions about human life in relation to the gods, and yet writing with an aspiration to universal validity.

When Agamemnon, King of Argos, the victorious Greek leader in the Trojan War, is depicted arriving home from Troy, there are two events in his recent past that cloud his triumphant return. One is the sacrifice of his own daughter, Iphigeneia, slain at Aulis as an offering to Artemis in order to secure a safe passage for the Greek fleet. The second misfortune, especially from the point of view of Clytemnestra his wife, is that he brings with him the prophetess Cassandra, daughter of Priam King of Troy, who is now Agamemnon's unwilling paramour. She is the 'flower, gift of the army, chosen especially from much wealth' (954–955)—a captive, then, a spoil of war, doubtless with the usual sexual connotation. Eduard Fraenkel[2] rightly says that 'not with a single word does Aeschylus indicate whether the king has any other feeling towards his captive beyond that of pity for her fate.' The bestowal of female captives on victorious chiefs was, however, common practice.[3] Yet Peter Walcot in a perceptive study[4] views the situation as that of 'the wife who sees her husband bring home a mistress' and as 'the most

---

[1] With his own realization, too, of what was possible through the theatre as his medium and also an awareness of the contemporary political and social climate; cf. Peter Walcot, *Greek Drama in its Theatrical and Social Context* (Cardiff, 1976), 95 and passim.

[2] *Aeschylus, Agamemnon*, II (Oxford, 1950, repr. 1962), 433.

[3] Cf. H. Lloyd-Jones, *Agamemnon*, Translation with Comm. (Prentice-Hall, 1970), 68.

[4] *Envy and the Greeks* (Warminster, 1978), 23.

obvious illustration of sexual jealousy'. This interpretation is in fact borne out by the words of Clytemnestra after the slaying of her husband and Cassandra (lines 1431–1447). Here she 'stresses the charge that Cassandra is both prophetess and concubine;' (thus Denniston and Page ad loc. (1957), 203); and in a plural reference to Chryseïs she alludes to other amours in which Agamemnon had indulged. She does, however, accept Cassandra as a new slave of the house (1035 ff.)

It is the sacrifice of her daughter Iphigeneia that counts most with her. Cassandra's dire prophecies of doom also contribute to the explanation of the disasters which ensue. Clytemnestra and her lover Aegisthus are the perpetrators of the deeds which encompass the deaths of both Agamemnon and Cassandra. Clytemnestra's words indicate a motive of avenging the slaying of Iphigeneia; and others refer to the ancestral curse of the blood-feud that lies on the family of Agamemnon.

That curse is of divine origin, and there are several ways in which the gods are said to intervene in the sad human story of war, of lost love, and of revenge. On the plane of the gods, too, there is a theme of revenge and retribution, and sometimes the two planes converge. If Orestes is to be the avenger of his father's death within the orbit of the family, he is also the instrument of divine retribution. In general terms the Chorus (750 ff.) proclaim a doctrine that has been sanctioned of old: misery can result from prosperity and good fortune; yet the poet, speaking through the Chorus, maintains that it is the deed of iniquity that produces more iniquity, while the righteous house enjoys a blessed state. Most dangerous in evil men is arrogance (*hubris*) and unholy recklessness (*thrasos*). Righteousness (*dikê*) shines in humble homes and shuns the power of wealth. If misery can result from prosperity, as the popular notion has it, the underlying reason is that prosperity causes envy (*phthonos*), especially the envy of the gods. Although Aeschylus does not accept the positing of prosperity as the cause of misery, preferring to see iniquity as the cause, yet he gives some prominence to the force of envy. When Clytemnestra spreads sumptuous cloths for Agamemnon to walk on, he expresses concern and fear, for it is a path that may arouse envy (line 921). Not the envy simply of mortals, since gods alone deserve such honours. When the king eventually consents to tread the purple cloths, he hopes that no envious eye of the gods will strike him from afar (lines 946–7).

After Orestes has exacted retribution by killing Clytemnestra and Aegisthus, the span of the *Oresteia* covers 'an almost systematic series: a father killing his daughter, a wife killing her husband, a son killing his mother'.⁵ It is Apollo who commands Orestes to return from exile to encompass the matricide, but in the *Eumenides* of Aeschylus the whole issue is discussed by a human court, that of the Areopagus, which has to face the problem of how to save Orestes from the unrelenting pursuit of the Furies, the Erinyes, who have given him no peace from the moment when he killed his own mother. If the Areopagus is a human court, in this case divine powers are given an important role. The Erinyes here defend the cause of Clytemnestra, and like her, they disdain the ties of marriage.⁶ But the goddess Athena is the president of the court of Athenian citizens, and Apollo appears as the advocate of Orestes—not surprisingly, since Orestes has acted at his behest (though ultimately that of Zeus). The verdict of the court is indecisive, the votes being equally divided; but Athena gives her casting vote in favour of Orestes. At the same time Athena succeeds in mollifying the Erinyes. They are given a cult-centre in Athens, at the foot of the Acropolis, and blessed with a new name, the Eumenides, 'the Kindly Ones'. Outside Aeschylus the matter is not allowed to end there, for Orestes is said to have expiated his sin in various ways.⁷ If the Aeschylean dénouement seems arbitrary in its decisive simplicity, the moral issues presented by him are complex; so is the sociological background of the final decision.⁸ The end of the *Eumenides* portrays the serenity which comes from the reconciliation of rival claims, and in this trilogy as elsewhere Aeschylus proclaims his faith in the justice and wisdom of a ruling providence which he finds embodied above all in the figure of Zeus.

In the *Persae* the doctrine of divine retribution is applied by him to the fate of nations in a way that is altogether more direct and telling. The key word of the tragedy is undoubtedly *hubris*. It is used of the Persian King Xerxes in particular, but also of the Persian imperial designs in general. At the end of the play Xerxes appears in rags before the palace of Susa. His mother Atossa is deeply concerned about his tattered robes, and some scholars have argued

---

⁵ Walter Burkert, *Structure and History in Greek Mythology and Ritual* (Berkeley, 1979), 19; cf. A.F. Garvie *Aeschylus, Choephori* (Oxford, 1986), 74.

⁶ On the contrasted and inverted role of the sexes in this context see Jean-Pierre Vernant, *Myth and Thought among the Greeks* (London, 1983), 137, Clytemnestra and Electra being seen as equally manly.

⁷ H.J. Rose, *A Handbook of Greek Mythology* (6th Ed., London, 1958), 87; Robert Parker, *Miasma* (Oxford, 1983), 386–8.

⁸ George Thomson, *Aeschylus and Athens* (London, 1941; 3rd Ed., 1966), 288 sees in it the passage from a matrilineal society to male dominance. The matriarchy posited reverts, however, to a distant past, and its existence even then is hypothetical. On p. 52 he describes the Erinyes as 'ancestral spirits of a matrilineal society'.

that the aim of the dramatist was to raise a laugh among the Athenians by ridiculing the Persian disaster and extolling the Athenian victories. The play certainly coincided with the celebration of those victories; but the text is throughout infused with a deeply religious conviction that the fall of Persia was due to the overweening arrogance which aroused the jealousy (*phthonos*) of the gods.[9] When Darius appears before his tomb, he explicitly points the same moral. It is noteworthy that Aeschylus refrains from dwelling on the considerations of strategy, tactics, and politics that might well be regarded as the vital instruments of the Greek triumph. He does not even name a single Greek. Instead he insistently points to the blasphemous arrogance which incurred the divine envy and wrath[10] and so led inevitably to the retributive punishment by which the events themselves are explained. In this religious ambience Athens has no cause for proud self-congratulation; she is merely the instrument of the divine will, rather in the way that Babylon's conquest of Israel was explained by Hebrew prophets as a manifestation of Yahweh's wrath.

Psychologically there was doubtless room for these beliefs in popular attitudes. Envy of the prosperous is a widespread phenomenon, and a stage further is reached when prosperity, or at least self-glorification through it, is regarded as an invitation to disaster, if only in the sense that 'pride comes before a fall'. The causal link between *hubris* and *nemesis* was connected in the popular mind with the idea of *baskania*, 'witchery', in the sense of the danger which results from excessive praise.[11] In political life the ideas of *eunomia*, 'good order', and *dikê*, 'justice', were regarded as belonging together, and defiance of them brought an inevitable penalty. Heraclitus expressed this with a significant allusion to the Erinyes: *The Sun will not overstep his bounds, otherwise the Erinyes, the ministers of Dikê, will find him out.*[12] Here the Erinyes are clearly seen as beings who avenge every violation of natural laws.[13]

There are some problems attaching to *nemesis*, 'righteousness', 'retribution'. As a goddess, Nemesis is occasionally implicated in a

---

[9] See esp. verse 362. Cf. H.D. Broadhead, *The Persae of Aeschylus* (Cambridge, 1960), xv ff.

[10] For the attitudes of Hesiod and Herodotus see Walcot, *Envy and the Greeks*, 8–14. He discusses the 'envy of the gods' in his Chs. 3 and 4, with remarks on the *Persae* on pp. 32–34.

[11] Cf. Martin P. Nilsson, *Greek Folk Religion* (1940, repr. New York, 1961), 109.

[12] Diels-Kranz, *Die Fragmente der Vorsokratiker*, I, 22, 94. Cf. B.C. Dietrich, *A Sense of Guilt* (Cardiff, 1980), 13.

[13] Cf. M. Marcovich, *Heraclitus* (Merida, Venezuela, 1967), 277, quoting Jaeger.

surprising mythology which includes her being chased by an infatuated Zeus. But by and large she stands for the abstract idea of divine punishment. Herodotus is content with the abstraction, and he liberally applies the doctrine, as in his account of the retributive rebuke administered to Croesus. Pindar (*Pyth.* 10.44), on the other hand, refers to Nemesis as ὑπέρδικος, 'more than just, severely just', and his notion is amply confirmed by the role usually ascribed both to the goddess and to the principle.

Problematic also is the Aeschylean emphasis on the envy of the gods, *phthonos theôn*, not so much in itself as in the slant given to it by some modern interpreters. In lines 750–62 of the *Agamemnon*, to which we have referred above, the chorus seek to deny the old belief that a man's prosperity and good fortune produce misery for a family; rather it is impiety that causes misery; a life of integrity is not afflicted. Although *phthonos* is not specifically mentioned here, it is clearly regarded as the motivating force of the old belief. Albin Lesky[14] is therefore able to speak of 'the attack the poet makes on the contemporary belief that the gods destroy man's all too good fortune through malicious envy.' Lesky, by the way, very properly remarks that the *Oresteia* is not just a moral tractate about sin and retribution. What is undeniable is that lines 750–762 of the *Agamemnon* reject a doctrine which is given overwhelming prominence in the *Persians* fourteen years earlier. So much was pointedly recognized by Wilamowitz, but denied by Eduard Fraenkel,[15] who maintained that Aeschylus never accepted 'the cruder conceptions of φθόνος θεῶν.' He would ascribe to both Aeschylus and Pindar 'the purified idea of φθόνος θεῶν', but this idea is not clearly explained by him. The 'fundamental truth' which he finds (p. 349) to be espoused by Aeschylus is that 'the gods (or Zeus) see to it that sooner or later the impious man is punished while the righteous will be spared.' Applying the idea to Xerxes, he says that he has overstepped the limits fixed by God. This certainly explains *hubris*, but it is not clear how *phthonos* comes into it. Nor is it clear that here, 'as in Herodotus and Pindar, the primitive concept of divine envy has undergone refinement', as Hugh Lloyd-Jones[16] states.

One must agree with Walcot that Aeschylus was not above being influenced by the popular Greek idea of envy in both human and divine contexts. When he proceeds to brush aside the possibility of

---

[14] *Greek Tragedy* (2nd Ed., London, 1967), 77. Cf. Walcot's discussion in *Envy and the Greeks*, 47 ff. Lesky's remarks in his 3rd Ed., *Die tragische Dichtung der Hellenen* (Göttingen, 1972), 113, are more briefly presented.
[15] *Aeschylus, Agamemnon*, II, 349–50. See also Walcot, loc. cit.
[16] *The Justice of Zeus*, 69.

a development of thought as between the *Persians* and the *Oresteia*, he may be going too far. 'In other words', he says (p. 51), 'Aeschylus was a typical Greek, and as a typical Greek he was not likely to have been excessively bothered at the gods displaying feelings of envy.' This seems to demean his stature as a literary and dramatic artist. Just before this (p. 48) Walcot favours the view that 'the chorus says what is dramatically necessary and effective in each particular context.' A different religious sentiment might be equally effective dramatically; indeed, if he was thinking in terms of what was acceptable to his audience, why does the poet go out of his way to correct a traditional view? What the messenger says in the *Persae* about the envy of the gods is, on the other hand, admirably suited to the Athenian mood after Salamis, and the poet is basically transferring to the gods a feeling which the Athenians were then fervidly experiencing. Not for the first time in human history, and certainly not the last, the conflict inherent in war was able to deploy the sanction of religion. Among the Greeks the commemoration of victories was linked to various deities (and not only Nikê), but the divinization of triumphant warriors was also on the cards.[17]

2. *The Erinyes: Activity in Two Worlds*

Of special relevance to our theme are the Erinyes or Furies, for they are the agents of divine retribution in two worlds, this world and the next.[18] They are conspicuous in avenging wrongs done to kinsfolk; in particular it is the murder of a kinsman or kinswoman that arouses them. Originally, then, an Erinys may well have been the spirit of a murdered person crying out for vengeance.[19] This function is seen in the *Oresteia* of Aeschylus, as we have just noted, and the theme is represented also in art.[20] At the end of the *Eumenides*, Orestes is freed from the pursuit of the Erinyes, and so the family vendetta comes to an end. At the same time the Erinyes are given an honoured place in Athenian cult, although a reconciliation of conflicting claims has been achieved. The significance of this serene ending has been variously interpreted. According to

---

[17] Raoul Lonis, *Guerre et religion en Grèce à l'époque classique* (Paris, 1979), 265–319.
[18] H.J. Rose, *Handbook of Greek Mythology*, 86.
[19] Nilsson, *Geschichte der griechischen Religion*, I (3rd Ed., Munich, 1967), 100, following Rohde and pointing to the Genitive of the slain person which often comes after the noun.
[20] Jane Henley, *Greek Myths: A Vase Painter's Notebook* (Bloomington, 1973), 157–60 with Figs. 14–15 on pp. 22–23.

Hugh Lloyd-Jones[21] 'Aeschylus insists strongly on the value of the punitive element in the government of both the universe in general and of the Athenian state.' The Erinyes, he argues, are given an allotted place in the Athenian law of the fifth century in relation to the blood-feud. That may well be so, but the crucial element in the dénouement of the *Eumenides* is the verdict that the Erinyes shall no longer be allowed to pursue Orestes; that is certainly the implication of Athena's acquittal of Orestes in verse 752, which is scarcely 'punitive'; here she declares him to have escaped the charge of murder (αἵματος δίκην) after accepting before this that the son is more closely related to the father than to the mother, thus endorsing the principle of the Attic law of inheritance, which was essentially patriarchal.[22] The Erinyes (778–792) naturally protest against this reversal of their ancient claims, and it is when Athena appeases them with her decision of an honoured place for them in Athens, that she ordains (930–937) that perjurers will still have to fear them. In words which seek to mollify the Erinyes, Athena lauds their power over all human affairs (930–931), a power which brings bliss to some and bane to others (954–955). In this last passage Erinys is mentioned in the singular as 'mistress (*potnia*) Erinys', who has great power 'over the immortals (the gods) and over those below the earth'. Power over the gods is a surprising attribute, but it is confirmed in Hesiod, *Theogony*, 220, where the Kêres of 217 are perhaps to be equated with the Erinyes: see M.L. West ad loc. (p. 229); cf. too verse 472 with an allusion to retribution meted out to Cronus. The reference to the underworld clearly alludes to their power over humanity after death. In verses 267–268 they threaten to drive Orestes living to the world below; in verses 338–340 they threaten to pursue the murderer of kinsfolk until he goes down below, and even then he shall not be 'too free'.

Their activity in this respect is portrayed in vase-paintings,[23] and in literature too it is vigorously, if distressingly, conveyed in descriptions assigned to the 'Hell of Eleusinian and Orphic tradition'.[24] Here the Erinyes are tormenting punishers, but the crimes over which they exercise powers of execution are by no means confined to homicide and the connected blood-feud. The Homeric tradition already assigns them the right to exact retribution for perjury, filial impiety, and the flouting of the rights of hospitality,

---

[21] *The Justice of Zeus*, 94.
[22] Cf. George Thomson, *The Oresteia of Aeschylus*, I (2nd Ed., Amsterdam, 1966), 55.
[23] Cf. below, pp. 329 ff.
[24] George Thomson, op. cit. II, 201–202.

and these contexts would seem to obstruct the theory that the Erinys was in origin the ghost of a murdered person claiming redress. Another theory which finds in the Erinys simply the outraged conscience of a sinner, can derive support from the way in which Euripides in his *Orestes* (396) does precisely that to the Erinyes that torment Orestes. When Menelaos asks him what is causing his suffering and what disease is destroying him, Orestes replies, 'It is conscience, my realization that I have done terrible deeds.' This may be described as a process of 'internalization',[25] and evidently takes us away from the original significance in a rationalizing manner often found in Euripides.

It is not easy to understand the exact role of the Erinyes in the underworld. As portrayed in the *Oresteia* their task is to seek out a murderer (Orestes) who has fled, and to bring him to justice. In the theory here presented the establishment of the Court of the Areopagus will in future expedite the trial of cases of homicide; but the psychological and moral pressure of the Erinyes will still be necessary. In this particular instance the person charged is acquitted by the court. In other cases, if the defendant is found guilty, the court imposes its penalty—in the classical era death for intentional homicide and exile if it was unintentional, but with the proviso that a defendant might choose to go into exile, if he so wished, at the end of his first speech.[26] A convicted murderer (or criminal of other categories) was regarded as a target for the Erinyes even after death, when he would be tormented by them in Hades. Torment and punishment, that is now their only role, it seems. This gruesome idea has elaborate parallels in Egypt.

It is noteworthy that the Erinyes were sometimes the object of a cult, though not frequently. Occasionally they shared a cult with the Moirae.[27] The epithet Erinys *Tilphossaia* which occurs in Callimachus (fr. 652 Pfeiffer) relates to a myth about a miraculous horse, Areion, being born to Poseidon and a goddess in Boeotia; and a similar myth concerns Poseidon and Demeter Erinys in Arcadia. But in Boeotia there is no evidence of a cult of either Erinys Tilphossaia or of Demeter Erinys,[28] the latter of the names being mentioned by Lycophron, *Alexandra*, 153, (ed. Carl von Dolzinger, 1895, 98). In Arcadian Phigalia, on the other hand, as

---

[25] Robert Parker, *Miasma*, 310.
[26] Douglas M. MacDowell, *The Law in Classical Athens* (London, 1978), 119–20.
[27] B.C. Dietrich, *Death, Fate and the Gods* (London, 1965), 92–93. On p. 96 he remarks that an independent cult of the Erinyes is attested 'in only a very few instances'.
[28] Albert Schachter, *The Cults of Boeotia*, I (London, 1981), 164.

well as in Arcadian Thelpusa, the cult of Demeter Erinys is firmly attested.[29] There is evidence, if the wider conspectus be taken, for seeing in the original concept of the goddess Erinys 'a deity connected with the underworld and with nature in general'.[30] In the function with which we are concerned—the Erinyes as agents of divine retribution—the significant conceptual elements are the sense of justice, the desire for vengeance, and the fear of the pollution associated with death. Although the Erinyes are sometimes regarded as being capable of punishing the gods themselves, in general they are presented simply as their agents, and the question of divine envy does not therefore enter into their approach. The picture of them in Aeschylus is certainly gruesome in the extreme, but it does not include what Wilamowitz-Moellendorff[31] called 'the meanest element in human nature... envy'. An Orphic text on a papyrus roll discovered in 1962 at Derveni, a little north-west of Thessaloniki, was accompanied by a prose composition of perhaps the early fourth century B.C. in which an exegesis of Orphic verses is provided. A discussion of the Erinyes or Eumenides takes up more than half of this prose text, and it is said to proffer allegorical interpretations which regard these beings as souls and expatiate on their role as punishers of perjurers.[32]

There are various figures parallel to the Erinyes. The names Eumenides, Semnae, and Potniae are used of them; an affinity characterizes too the Moirae, the Praxidicae, Aulis, and Maniae.[33] Dietrich[34] has diligently studied these and other similar figures. It is significant, however, that whereas chthonic features are often present in these goddesses, the Erinyes alone have the role of pursuing and punishing offenders. The Moirae can be seen as 'gloomy divinities that represented death',[35] and the Maniae (Madnesses) are equated by Pausanias (8.34.2) with the Eumenides.[36]

---

[29] Dietrich, *Death, Fate, and the Gods*, 121–3, in an admirable chapter (pp. 91–156) devoted to the Erinyes. Cf. Burkert, *Structure and History in Greek Mythology and Ritual*, 127.

[30] Dietrich, op. cit. 101; cf. p. 117, 'chthonic deities... primarily concerned with vegetation', which explains the link with Demeter.

[31] *Griechische Tragoedien übersetzt*, II (8th Ed., Berlin, 1919), 22 ('das gemeinste der Menschennatur,... Neid'). Cf. the remarks of the Danish sociologist Sven Ranulf, *The Jealousy of the Gods and Criminal Law at Athens*. I. (London & Copenhagen, 1933), 117.

[32] See M.L. West, *The Orphic Poems* (Oxford, 1983), 77–82.

[33] Also used as titles of Demeter and Korê. Cf. the Demeter-cult at Potniae in Boeotia, on which see Nilsson, *Geschichte Griech. Rel.* I³, 151.

[34] *Death, Fate, and the Gods*, 91–125.

[35] Ibid. 86.

[36] Ibid. 107–8, with doubt expressed about the connection.

An association with Demeter often emerges, but here the pointer is to vegetation. A Demeter Erinys as a horse may indicate an original horse-shape for Erinys,[37] although the snake is also a candidate in view of the descriptions in Aeschylus and the portrayal in art of wild females with snakes in their hair.[38] It is the pursuing and punishing aspect that is missing in the parallel figures. A more convincing correlate from this point of view might be what Dietrich (p. 141) terms 'The figure of the winged Snatcher: Potnia, Gorgo, Siren, Harpy etc.'; and here the winged Sphinx is relevant, as well as the 'Etruscan Erinys'.[39] All appear to be agents of death rather than of vengeance or retribution; and this may be true of the original function of the Erinyes too.

Another similar divine being, often called a daemon, is Alastor, a 'spirit of destruction, spirit of vengeance, evil spirit'.[40] Its root meaning is in doubt,[41] though none of the suggestions made relates to vengeance. Yet vengeance is the idea implied by several occurrences in tragedy. Clytemnestra (in *Ag.* 1501) says that 'the ancient fierce Alastor' is working through her in the sense of taking vengeance for the misdeed of Atreus; not that a sudden impulse has seized her, rather is she 'working out the rule of divine vengeance, of which she is the minister.'[42] Elsewhere it is the thought of avenging the death of Iphigeneia that moves her. In the *Eumenides* (236) Orestes describes himself as an *alastor*; doubt as to the basic meaning is reflected in translations: 'graciously receive a wanderer' (Verrall, accepting Wecklein's derivation from ἀλάομαι, 'wander', cf. LSJ—'the obligatory wandering of one who has shed blood'); 'graciously receive a wretched man' (H. Lloyd-Jones); 'receive this outcast graciously' (R.C. Trevelyan). In later usage, especially in Euripides and Demosthenes, the figure of a daemon yields to that of a human agent, although the idea of vengeance is often present. But the thought of the impact of ancestral guilt, as in Aeschylus, *Agamemnon* (1501 and 1508), does not persist so strongly.

---

[37] Ibid. 138.

[38] A punitive role in the Egyptian traditions is often attached to menacing females aided by snakes and brandishing knives. See Erik Hornung, *Tal der Könige* (Zürich, 1982), 153; 161; 164; id. *Ägyptische Unterweltsbücher*² (Zürich, 1984), 314 f.; 405.

[39] Cf. Franz de Ruyt, *Charun, Démon Étrusque de la Mort* (Brussels, 1934), 101 with Fig. 45 ('Charun ailé').

[40] Fraenkel, *Aeschylus, Agamemnon*, III, 711.

[41] H. Frisk, *Griechisches Etym. Wb.* I (Heidelberg, 1954), 64.

[42] See Denniston and Page ad loc. (Oxford, 1957), 208.

3. *Divine Intervention as Atê in Early Greek Poetry*

It is not surprising that ideas found in the tragedies of Aeschylus are present also in the works of earlier Greek poets, especially in those of Hesiod, Theognis, Solon, and Pindar. The still earlier Homeric poems provide ample evidence of the idea of divine intervention in human affairs. This is true in a general sense. While the protagonists are human beings, yet their actions are influenced by the role both of the gods and of the agencies of Fate (Moira). Moreover, the gods can decide the course of great issues, such as, in the *Iliad*, the result of the Trojan War, and the more personal issues, such as, in the *Odyssey*, the return of Odysseus to Ithaca and the punishment of the suitors of Penelope.[43]

We are here concerned, however, with intervention in a narrower field, in the working of the moral order which impinges on the conduct of individuals. If a man transgresses the accepted code of conduct, he is likely to face punishment in this life; if he honours the accepted code, he is likely to gather the welcome fruits of his just endeavours, and these may be glittering prizes if he excels in *aretê*, 'valour, skill'.[44] But both rewards and punishments, in the Homeric view, are to be expected in this life. There is another life in Hades, a shadowy existence which barely merits being called life. Not there in a vague future, but here and now is the operation of moral recompense to be observed. The implied system is a just one, although it is still a matter of debate how far the concept of justice is associated with Zeus in the *Iliad*.

What is embarrassing to the justice of the system is the role played by *atê*, 'infatuation caused by the gods'. A well-known instance in the *Iliad* (19.86 ff.) is the defence put forward by Agamemnon concerning his action in taking from Achilles his mistress Briseis. *It is not I who am responsible*, says Agamemnon, *but Zeus and Moira*,[45] *and air-wandering Erinys, who in the assembly infused wild* atê *into my mind on the day when I myself took the prize of Achilles from him*. (19.86–89). He continues his defence thus: *But what could I do? God achieves his end in everything. The eldest daughter of Zeus is Atê, who infatuates all and is the cause of ruin* (90–92). We are then told that Atê brought infatuation even to Zeus, who angrily threw her from Olympus to earth, where she henceforth causes misfortune. Taken

---

[43] Cf. Dietrich, *Death, Fate, and the Gods*, 335–7.

[44] For the meaning 'reputation' see Peter Walcot, *Greek Peasants, Ancient and Modern* (Manchester, 1970), 6–7.

[45] Dodds, *The Greeks and the Irrational*, 3, prefers to translate 'and my portion', but admits on p. 7 that Agamemnon is treating his 'portion' as an agent.

by itself, the significant episode relating to Agamemnon would seem to diminish considerably any serious claim that the *Iliad* offers an ethical structure in which the justice of Zeus is paramount. After an extremely culpable deed—and the seizure of Briseis was deemed to be such by the other Achaeans, including Achilles, as Nestor pointedly tells Agamemnon in *Iliad* 9.108—the guilty person disclaims responsibility, laying the blame on Zeus, Moira, and Erinys because they infused 'wild *atê*' into his understanding. Even to admit such a possibility is to undermine the whole concept of free choice on the part of an individual. Admittedly in his reply to Nestor Agamemnon seems ready to concede his own responsibility: *I was infatuated and gave way to my sorry passion* (*Il.* 9.119). The two statements cannot easily be reconciled, and a facile way out is to reiterate that Homeric events are displayed on two planes, the human and the divine, and that such a presentation is bound to involve occasional contradictions. Yet the role of Atê[46] is more extensive than this one episode might suggest.[47] Sometimes the treatment suggests the personification of an abstraction, as in *Iliad* 9.505, following a passage where Prayers (*Litai*) are similarly treated, being called daughters of Zeus. This might lead to a general interpretation which attenuates the theology to the point of being a form of expression intended to portray what is really a human predicament. Whereas E.R. Dodds rejects such an approach, his own explanation is basically on the same lines: 'we may class all instances of nonalcoholic *ate* in Homer under the head of what I propose to call "psychic intervention".'[48] At the same time, he explains actions performed by men 'in a state of *ate*' as those which can be traced indifferently 'either to their *moira* or to the will of a god'; in each case the actions are beyond the field of personal choice, and are 'overdetermined' (p. 7).

Theologically the concept of *atê* is one of disturbing moral connotation. Ranulf[49] goes too far, perhaps, when he designates it as 'the idea that the gods force men to commit crimes' and adds that it meant, among other things, 'the blindness that leads to crime, the crime itself, and the punishment for it, all indissolubly interwoven in one conception'. A more sophisticated analysis of the Homeric concept of personality in relation to supernatural forces

---

[46] For a comprehensive analysis see Josef Stallmach, *Ate. Zur Frage des Selbst- und Weltverständisses des frühgriechischen Menschen.* (Beitr. zur klassischen Philologie, 18; Meisenheim am Glan, 1968).
[47] See Dodds, op. cit. 2-13.
[48] Ibid. 5.
[49] *The Jealousy of the Gods etc.* I, 33.

was provided by Bruno Snell. He succeeded in showing that the individual in Homer's world is equipped with various powers, for which the words σθένος, βίη, κῖκος, ἴς, κεάτος, ἀλκή, and δύναμις are used, but that no holistic notion of the soul is developed. 'Spirit' (θυμός) and 'mind' (νόος) are used to describe the source of emotional and mental states, but the idea of an organic whole is missing. Having this interpretation of their inner selves, Homer's men regard themselves as an 'arena for arbitrary and sinister powers'.[50] Against this, the *Iliad* may be regarded as 'a profoundly moral story' which shows that 'to the Greek mind sin was sooner or later followed by punishment;' the scheme of sin and punishment is 'transformed into poetry by the pathos with which he (the poet) invests its victims.'[51]

A 'profoundly moral story' would seem, however, to merit closer attention to the ethical considerations which are constantly implicit. Such attention has certainly been forthcoming from Hugh Lloyd-Jones,[52] who maintains (p. 10) that 'when a human action, whether right or wrong, is put down to the action of a god, that does not mean that the human actor is not held to be responsible for his decision.' The claim is evidently self-contradictory. We have seen that in one place (*Il.* 9.119) Agamemnon does aver his own responsibility, but that in another (*Il.* 19.86) he denies that. Well may it be admitted[53] that 'this double motivation and double responsibility, human and divine, has always been difficult to grasp;' and it is highly questionable whether 'we must acknowledge that Homer's gods are effective and his religion real, but that his human characters are free to decide and are responsible for their decisions.' The same problem arises with Achilles. Speaking before a sacrifice (*Il.* 19.270 f.), Achilles seeks to defend his action in causing the death of Patroclus: '*Father Zeus, you give to men great* atai;' and he maintains that Agamemnon would never have aroused *thumos* in his breast nor would he have taken the girl (Briseis) against the will of Achilles, had not Zeus wished that many of the Achaeans should die. Here again, a slightly different account is given (in *Il.* 9.628–42). But the passage itself lacks consistency. Achilles has of his own will infused a wild *thumos* into his breast

---

[50] Bruno Snell, *Die Entdeckung des Geistes* (3rd Ed., Hamburg, 1955), 40–42, the quoted phrase on p. 42. The translation by T.G. Rosenmeyer, *The Discovery of the Mind* (Oxford, 1953), is of the 2nd Ed. For a critical assessment see H. Lloyd-Jones, *The Justice of Zeus*, 9–10.
[51] C.M. Bowra, *Tradition and Design in the Iliad* (Oxford, 1930), 25–26.
[52] *The Justice of Zeus*, 8–27.
[53] Ibid. 10.

(verse 628); the gods, however, have done this to him (verse 637), and this time it is an evil *thumos*. (The words are those of Ajax.) Perhaps the situation is rightly summarized thus: 'like Agamemnon, Achilles blames Zeus, but he does not deny his own responsibility.'[54] But there is a good deal more of blaming Zeus than there is (one line) of accepting responsibility.

This is not the place to consider in detail the wider question of the Homeric conception (or lack of conception) of the soul. Tensions certainly arise through the function ascribed to Atê. Psychologically the attitude expressed by *Not I, but the God* shows concern with the question of ultimate responsibility together with a desire to shift the blame from the actual doer, especially when the results of a sinful action seem to go beyond what might be reasonably expected and to call for a divine explanation.[55] But the Homeric problems seem to be smoothed out when we turn to Hesiod, Solon, and Pindar. In their works Atê denotes mischief or harm brought about by the gods. The process is now, however, thoroughly moralized, for the harm is seen as a punishment for human guilt. According to Hesiod (*Op*. 230-31) neither famine (*Limos*) nor Atê[56] follows those who honour justice, and the righteous man need not fear to meet the Atai, envisaged as 'ruffians encountered on the road'.[57] If Atê is the punishment for crooked living, *Kerdos*, 'Gain', is the reward of straight living; and *hubris* is the specific sin for which Atê is the punishment (*Op*. 213-16). Hesiod (*Theog*. 230) names Atê among the melancholy children of Eris, 'Strife', thus flouting the Homeric tradition which makes her the eldest daughter of Zeus (*Il*. 19.91). This indicates the tenuous status of Atê as a goddess, and it is not surprising that no cult is attested for her. Yet Hesiod himself must have believed in the existence of all the divinities named by him. The whole of the *Theogony* would make no sense at all otherwise, and its power derives from the way in which the writer is giving religious meaning to the world of men and to the nature of the cosmos as he knows it.[58] Both in the *Theogony* and in the *Works and*

---

[54] Ibid. 23.
[55] Cf. Stallmach, *Ate*, 97.
[56] M.L. West, ad loc., p. 214, thinks that here it is 'a vague word, perhaps referring here to spoilage of crops . . .' But in verse 216 he explains the plural form as 'afflictions, calamities'.
[57] West, op. cit. 210.
[58] Bruno Snell, 'Die Welt der Götter bei Hesiod', in *Hesiod* ed. E. Heitsch (Wege der Forschung, 44. Darmstadt, 1966), 714; also in *Die Entdeckung des Geistes*³ (1955), 70–71. The verb νομίζω does not occur in Hesiod. See Wilhelm Fahr, *Theous Nomizein* (Spudasmata, 26; Hildesheim, 1969), 10. He shows that the expression treated by him appeared first in the questioning milieu of the fifth-century sophistic movement.

Days Hesiod eschews the sanguine and at times frivolous picture of the gods displayed in Homer. He is clearly anxious to include the darker side as well as the felicitous aspect, as with the Muses. The place he gives to Atê accords with the earnestness of his approach, and consonant with this is his readiness, in the *Theogony*, to embrace elements borrowed from Near Eastern sources.[59]

Like Hesiod, Theognis places Atê and Kerdos in antithesis, but he reverts to the Homeric emphasis in making the gods arbiters of causation and consequence:

> No one, Cyrnus, is himself responsible for disaster or success, but the gods are the givers of both. Nor does any man perform an action with sure knowledge of whether it will result in a good or bad end.
> (Theognis, *Eleg.* 1. 133–6, ed. Douglas Young, 1961, 9.)

He adds in verse 142 that *the gods bring all things to fulfilment according to their mind*. This outlook makes man helplessly dependent on the divine will and purpose, and it is futile for him to pursue his own purposes, however good they may be. There is much in Homer to support the doctrine, but Dodds[60] finds here a 'new accent of despair' which places Theognis 'nearer to the world of the *Oedipus Rex* than to the world of the *Iliad*'. Elsewhere, however, the same poet—if it be the same one—has a very different gospel to preach:[61]

> Nor is any one of the immortal, blessed gods, Cyrnus, open to be accused by us. It is the violence of men and their shameful greed and their arrogance that has hurled us from opulence into misery.
> (Theognis, *Eleg.* 1. 833–6, ed. Young, 51.)

The reference to violence and arrogance appears to echo the *Odyssey*,[62] while the variation of emphasis, as we have seen, is paralleled in the *Iliad*.

To Solon it is *hubris* that is bound to invoke the punishment of Atê, and the vital sanction in the struggle against *hubris* is the realization that it inevitably leads to failure. Upright living, on the other hand, brings prosperity.[63] It is Zeus who ensures the penalty (*tisis*), which is likened to the wind in spring driving away the clouds and helping the sun to break through. The course of man's

---

[59] See Peter Walcot, *Hesiod and the Near East* (Cardiff, 1966); cf. M.L. West, Hesiod, *Theogony* (Oxford, 1966), 18–31 and 106–7.
[60] *The Greeks and the Irrational*, 30.
[61] Cf. T. Hudson-Williams, *The Elegies of Theognis* (London, 1910), 183: 'cf. 833–6, which give quite a different point of view; both elegies are undoubtedly genuine.'
[62] Antonio Garzya, in his Comm. (Florence, 1955), 250, points out that the phrase ὕβρις τε βίη occurs in *Od.* 15. 329; cf. Douglas Young ad loc.
[63] Solon, *Eleg.* 1. 9–15, ed. Diehl, 17–18. Cf. Stallmach, *Ate*, 60–61.

life, according to these principles, might seem predictable, but Moira is said to bring to mortals an evil or noble element, and these elements are inescapable gifts of the gods (verses 63–66), so that no one knows how actions begun in a certain way will turn out. Here, then, Solon is thinking of an activity of Atê which cannot be averted by man. A kind of fatalism is present which is due, perhaps, to 'a residue of disbelief in the universal justice of heaven' and implies that 'Moira, Fate, makes all human effort fundamentally insecure, however earnest and logical it may seem to be.'[64]

No such ambivalence seems to cloud Pindar's treatment of the theme. In his descriptions of the punishment of Tantalus (*Ol.* 1.54 ff.) and of Ixion (*Pyth.* 2.25 ff.) he holds firmly to the sequence of guilt and punishment. In the case of Tantalus the punishment has to be everlasting because he has been granted immortality, but the guilt is incurred in the manner of a mortal who was not able to bear his great good fortune (*olbos*), a word which implies massive wealth. Certainly the myth made Tantalus a paragon of Lydian wealth, his father being Zeus and his mother Plutô (a minor goddess related to Ploutos, 'Wealth'). His crime does not seem particularly heinous: granted the boon of enjoying the food of the gods, nectar and ambrosia, he dared to share it with human guests. The punishment of the hanging stone does not locate Tantalus in Hades; he is allowed to come to the table of the gods.[65] An idea introduced by Pindar to accompany that of Atê is *Koros*, 'surfeit, satiety' (*Ol.* 1. 56–57): *through his surfeit of wealth he (Tantalus) brought on himself an overpowering Atê*. In another passage (*Ol.* 13.10) he describes Hubris as *the bold-tongued mother of Surfeit (Koros)*. Hubris and Koros had been previously connected by Solon (fr. 5.9–10), though with a differing relationship: *for Koros gives birth to Hubris.*[66] In other ways Pindar shows a fondness for the personified abstract deities such as Angelia, Euphrosyna, Eunomia, Hêsychia and Chronos.[67] He is also keen, it appears, on genealogy for its own sake. Either sequence provides a logical course: the amassing of wealth can lead to a surfeit of it, thus engendering a sense of arrogance; or an initial sense of arrogance can cause the pursuit of wealth to a point of surfeit.

---

[64] Werner Jaeger, tr. Gilbert Highet, *Paideia*, I (Oxford, 1939), 143. It is doubtful, however, whether one is justified, as Jaeger does, in seeing here a second meaning of Atê. The sense of injury inflicted on men without their guilt or causation being involved is present in Homer. Cf. Stallmach, op. cit. 61–62.

[65] Cf. Gilbert Norwood, *Pindar* (Sather Classical Lectures, 19; Berkeley, 1945), 216 n. 49; C.M. Bowra, *Pindar* (Oxford, 1964), 79.

[66] For the variation of relationship in Tragedy see H. Lloyd-Jones, *The Justice of Zeus*, 110 and 193 n. 23.

[67] Cf. Nilsson, *Geschichte Griech. Rel.* I³, 748.

Hubris is conspicuous for Pindar in the guilt and punishment of Ixion also (*Pyth.* 2.25 ff.) which are treated as one. We are told that he was not able to withstand the 'long good fortune' (*makron... olbon*) which he received from the gods, the boon, namely, of a life of delight among the gracious gods themselves; instead his *hubris* was such that in a frenzied state of mind he dared to desire sexual union with Hera, the wife of Zeus, but was made to embrace Nephelê (a cloud) instead, the montrous Centaurus being the result of the union. Another crime ascribed to him (verse 32) was that he was the first to shed the blood of a kinsman. Here Pindar calls him (verse 31) a 'hero', but later (verse 37) refers to him as an 'ignorant man'. He does not mention the tradition to which Aeschylus (*Eum.* 441 and 718) alludes, that Ixion made due purification for the killing of his father-in-law and was consequently received by Zeus on Olympus—a notable instance of the divine pardon being extended to a sinner who was ritually cleansed. Ixion's second offence became therefore more serious since it also implied ingratitude, and his punishment is correspondingly condign: he is bound to a wheel which is winged and cannot escape from its ceaseless turning. Yet in another context Pindar (*Pyth.* 4.291) refers to the pardon extended by Zeus to the Titans whom the Olympian gods had hurled into Tartarus and imprisoned there: *Immortal Zeus set the Titans free*. It is not clear, however, that he envisages the punishment of Ixion as taking place in Tartarus, and he gives no hint, as we have seen, of any subsequent purification and pardon. Such a hint 'might have diverted attention from the uninterrupted cycle of ὄλβος, κόρος, ὕβρις and ἄτη.'[68]

According to Stallmach[69] Pindar tries to give ethical depth to the story of Coronis, the daughter of a Thessalian king who was wooed by Apollo but then yielded to the passion of Ischys; her penalty was to be slain by the arrow of Artemis. It may be doubted whether Pindar has succeeded in his ethical striving, for this girl's crime was to flout the erotic privilege of a god.[70] Further, she had union with a stranger from Arcadia. If one queries whether to a Thessalian girl Apollo himself was not a stranger (at least if his origin is placed in Lycia, though here he is linked to Delphi), the answer is that as a god he transcends geographical affinities; a god, moreover, who

---

[68] R.W.B. Burton, *Pindar's Pythian Odes* (Oxford, 1962), 116.
[69] *Ate*, 63.
[70] Hesiod uses the word 'marry' of the action of Ischys: Ἴσχυς γῆμε Κόρωνιν. See R. Merkelbach and M.L. West, *Fragmenta* (Oxford, 1983), 60. 3. Cf. Pindar's use of γάμος in *Pyth.* 3.13.

had already made her pregnant with the future Asclepius,[71] who is snatched from her womb on the funeral pyre. 'So great infatuation' had occupied the heart of Coronis, and the poet sees no breath of injustice in the god's conduct although in other ways he is a purist in rejecting scandalous tales about the gods. The rigid demarcation of the divine and human spheres is what especially concerns him, and at the end of the poem the principle is again illustrated by the way in which Asclepius is punished for daring to accept a commission, for great gain, to raise a man from the dead. What is regarded as inviolable is the line between divine and human activities, death being regarded as irrecoverably beyond the human area. Yet in the case of Coronis it is the god Apollo who, according to the legend, is the first to cross the line through his becoming enamoured of a mortal girl.

4. *Herodotus: Theology and History*

In his general approach to countries and their peoples, and especially in his descriptions of their manners and customs, Herodotus is imbued with the kind of rationalism which was prevalent among Ionian writers.[72] His own programmatic statement (I.1 init.) is naturally not concerned with method and outlook, although the mention of an exposition of what he has learnt by investigation is a pointer to an objective aim. The preservation of the memory of the past is not a very revealing purpose; but the bestowal of renown on 'the great and marvellous achievements of both Greeks and foreigners' is an aim which indicates the wide sweep of his plan and also the positive and laudatory nature of the central motive. At the same time the stress on the 'marvellous' (*thômasta*) does not ostensibly fit in with a rationalist outlook, and it is a stress which figures not only in the programme but consistently in its execution. It is none the less a concern which is sometimes consonant with a rationalist urge. Herodotus is always ready to be puzzled and amazed, but his involvement goes beyond a superficial sense of curiosity. Above all, he wants to know and to understand.[73]

Even his comparisons of religious phenomena could be related to such an attitude, his achievement in this field having led to his

---

[71] Cf. Burton, op. cit. 83: 'Coronis' sin was that she lay with a mortal while pregnant by a god.'
[72] Cf. A.B. Lloyd, *Herodotus II*, i (Leiden, 1975), 156 ff. He speaks (p. 163) of H.'s 'thoroughgoing empiricism'.
[73] Max Pohlenz, *Herodot* (Leipzig, 1937, repr. Stuttgart, 1961), 45.

being greeted as the founder of Comparative Religion.[74] Yet a very different attitude confronts us when we consider his interpretations of major historical themes. His proemium ends on a note of concern with causation, in particular with the causes of war between Greeks and foreigners; it is the war of Greeks and Persians that is his main theme. What eventually emerges with great force is that his basic interpretations are moral and theological.[75] He is not content with a factual narrative. He aims rather at an over-all view of history in which divine providence dominates human affairs. Such a view is admittedly not obtruded at every point, but it is not an incidental addition to the narrative; nor is it the pouring of a moralistic sauce over a meal of meaty events.[76]

The encounter of Greeks and Persians as presented by him shows his thinking most clearly and, insofar as it is interpreted theologically, invites comparison with the earlier views of Aeschylus. One similarity is the prominence given to characterization. In drama that is a requirement of the literary form; in historical writing the thematic choice was more open, but attention to biography was becoming apparent in the fifth century, and Herodotus tells us something of the life of Greek leaders such as Themistocles, Leonidas, and the Spartan king Cleomenes, whose importance he probably underestimated.[77] More detail is provided about Croesus, and about the Persian kings Cyrus the Great, Cambyses, Darius the Great, and Xerxes. Monarchy and tyranny were political forms that furthered the emphasis; and in the case of the Greek protagonists Herodotus presents Leonidas and Themistocles as leaders of the Spartans and Athenians rather than as overpowering individuals.[78] Herodotus does not indulge in long passages of character delineation in the manner later adopted by Sallust, Tacitus, and Plutarch. He prefers to present scattered comments which are linked to particular events, but when added together, such comments form, in some cases, a fairly detailed study. On the birth and upbringing of Cyrus the Great he is fervently expansive (1.107 ff.) and the whole portrait of Cyrus is favourable; equally the society which produced him is admiringly sketched. The simplicity and toughness are lauded: *soft lands breed soft men.* (9.122)[79] Their respect

---

[74] A.B. Lloyd, op. cit. I, 169, citing Jacob Burckhardt.
[75] Cf. J. Wells in How and Wells, *Comm. on Herodotus*, I (Oxford, 1912), 43: 'with H. the philosophy of history is wholly theological.'
[76] Cf. Pohlenz, *Herodot*, 91.
[77] A. Momigliano, *The Development of Greek Biography* (Harvard, 1971), 34.
[78] Ibid. 40.
[79] Cf. A.R. Burn, *Persia and the Greeks* (London, 1962), 61.

for truth is reflected in the saying about the three essentials of Persian education: learning to ride, to shoot with the bow, and to tell the truth. (1.136) Herodotus mentions also their readiness to adopt foreign customs: they borrowed items of dress and armour from the Medes and Egyptians, and paederasty from the Greeks. (1.135) A hint of decline appears here, and it is deepened by the theme of austere simplicity giving way to sophistication and luxury, while the sheer expansion of empire leads to a state of wealth and power which provokes the traditional divine reaction. But as far as the kings themselves are concerned it is not a Hesiodic regression. Cyrus is succeeded by Cambyses, whose character, in spite of further conquests, represents a steep decline. Afterwards, however, Darius the Great largely restores the royal image in Herodotus; one may compare the remarks of an Athenian speaker in Plato's *Laws* (694 C), maintaining that the Persians were ruined under Cambyses but almost restored under Darius.[80] When Herodotus analyses (7.10) the eventual disastrous failure of Xerxes, a warning to the king by his uncle Artabanus points to the divine habit of prostrating any person or thing that is inordinately large; also to the fact that a large army may be defeated by a lesser one, since God in his envy may strike fear or a thunderbolt into the midst of the larger force. Needless to say, this was no part of Iranian doctrine about kingship. Their kings were regarded in Zoroastrian belief as deriving their right to rule from Ahura Mazda himself.[81] In their inscriptions they devoutly acknowledge this, but the concept of divine envy is far removed from their religion except in the sense that it belongs, like all other moral and physical evils, to the orbit of Ahriman (Angra Mainyu) and his *daēvas*.[82] What was especially abhorrent to Zoroaster was *Drug*, 'Deceit',[83] and it is in rather striking contrast that deceit is sometimes an attribute of Atê in Greek thought.

The theological element in the final assessment provided by Herodotus concerning the conclusion of the encounter of Greeks and Persians is of basic import. It is not the only element, admittedly. Indeed Momigliano[84] goes so far as to say that he 'explained

---

[80] Cf. Walcot, *Envy and the Greeks*, 68.
[81] Mary Boyce, *Zoroastrians* (London, 1979), 55. At the same time she points out (p. 52) that the Achaemenid kings were embalmed in burial, contrary to the Zoroastrian rite of exposing the body.
[82] Mary Boyce, *Hist.* I, 201.
[83] Ibid. 200. Cf. above 41.
[84] *Essays in Ancient and Modern Historiography* (Oxford, 1977), 29. He also tends to ignore the theology of Herodotus in the paean of praise which he offers to him in *Studies in Historiography* (London, 1966), 127–42.

the victory of the Greeks as due to the superiority of their way of life, and more especially to the democracy of Athens'. Reviewing the main purpose of Xerxes, which is defined as the subjugation of the whole of Greece, Herodotus (7.139) assigns the highest praise for the Greek victories to the Athenians: it was the Athenians, he says, after God (μετά γε θεούς), who repelled the Persian king. To Herodotus, then, the victory of the Greeks, as the brief but pointed phrase makes clear, is 'primarily a work of special intervention from above'.[85] The speech of Themistocles after Salamis emphasizes the same idea with greater force and with particular reference to the way in which Xerxes had challenged divine providence:

> It was not we who achieved this, but our God and our divine protectors, who enviously resented the idea that one man should rule both Asia and Europe, and he a blasphemous and arrogant character, one who merges the sacred and the profane, who burns and overthrows the statues of the gods, and who even whipped the sea and put down chains into it.
> (Herodotus, 8.109.)

Similar charges are made by Aeschylus, *Persae* (809 ff.), not against Xerxes in particular, but against the Persians in general. Broadhead (ad loc., p. 201) reminds us that in 1.131 Herodotus avers that the Persians had no statues or temples or altars. The words in the *Persae* are spoken by the ghost of Darius, and the enormities of Xerxes are doubtless intended; indeed in a previous passage (718 ff.) Darius and Atossa refer to Xerxes by name when condemning him, although they are his parents.[86] The similarity in the moral approach of Aeschylus and Herodotus has often been noted, and a partial dependence of the latter on the former has naturally been suggested.[87] There is a marked difference, however, in the more detailed treatment of the character of Xerxes supplied by Herodotus. In contrast to the fatal flaws eventually stigmatized there are mentions of his liberality, mercy, appreciation of honest advice, and readiness to acknowledge error. His faults include a lack of sustained courage, a fear of the supernatural, and indulgence in

---

[85] R.W. Macan (1908), I, 186.

[86] Cf. Ann N. Michelini, *Tradition and Dramatic Form in the Persians of Aeschylus* (Leiden, 1982), 117–21, with a suggestion (p. 121) that the theme of sacrilege is associated with *hubris*, which is 'the extension on the moral plane of the theme of superabundance or πλῆθος.' Cf. pp. 95–96.

[87] Michelini, ibid. 95, compares the dialogue between Artabanus and Xerxes (Herodotus, 7.49) on the dangers of an army's size with the emphasis on πλῆθος in *Persae*, 429–32.

human sacrifice; and of course the much stressed defiance of the divine.[88]

Sometimes Herodotus conveys the principle of retribution through the word *tisis*. When Cyrus (in 1.86) is causing Croesus to be burnt alive, he repents of the idea of killing a man who had once been as fortunate as himself. 'Moreover,' we are told, 'he feared the retribution (*tisin*),' and reflected that there was no stability in human affairs. It is unlikely that the retribution here envisaged implies a vendetta pursued by the descendants of Croesus against Cyrus; the latter's position was too powerful to allow that possibility. A more general law of retribution is suggested, a law which perhaps would mean that Cyrus would have to pay for his cruelty later in life. It is also possible that the idea intended is that a just recompense would be exacted from him in a life to come. In the case of Hermotimus, on the other hand, who inflicts castration on his castrator Panionius and on his sons (8. 106), the retaliation is in this life and tallies closely with the original crime. It is the just law (*nomos dikaios*) of the gods that encompasses this; and we are told that Panionius was overtaken by retribution (*tisis*) and by Hermotimus himself. In this instance, therefore, private vengeance coexists with the divine law.

Herodotus does not, of course, devote himself entirely to this rather negative approach to human actions. He praises the virtuous, as when he introduces Aristeides (8.79) as 'the best and most just man in Athens'.[89] But moral repayment is often mentioned, and occasionally in an extreme form. When Gyges kills Candaules in obedience to the latter's wife's order, following his arrangement to allow her to be seen naked by another man, it is said (1.13) that the Pythian priestess announced that the Heraclidae, to whom Candaules belonged, should take vengeance (*tisis*) on the progeny of Gyges up to the fifth generation; and the utterance, we are told, was fulfilled. In line with all this is the extreme interest shown in portents, dreams, and oracles, an interest which can be fairly dubbed to be naive.[90] Kurt von Fritz seems rightly to infer, after a highly favourable assessment of the contribution made by Herodotus to the chronological ordering of history, that his scientific approach was constantly threatened by his religiosity.[91] The

---

[88] For details see Joseph Wells in How and Wells, *Comm.* I (1912), 47–48; and a still more elaborate analysis in Kenneth H. Waters, *Herodotos on Tyrants and Despots* (Wiesbaden, 1971), 65–85.
[89] Other examples are given by Pohlenz, *Herodot*, 92.
[90] Kurt von Fritz, *Die Griechische Geschichtsschreibung*, I (Berlin, 1967), 465.
[91] Ibid. 462–65, with a question left open on the validity of the general theology of history.

primacy of divine determinism is well illustrated at the end of the Croesus-Cyrus encounter (1.87). When the fire which was planned to kill Croesus cannot be quenched even after the decision of Cyrus to stop it, Croesus is said to have prayed to Apollo, who at once causes a merciful downpour. Cyrus then realizes that Croesus is 'beloved by the gods[92] and a good man'. Cyrus then asks him what man persuaded him to invade his country; Croesus replies that he himself had done it, but adds that 'the god of the Greeks was the cause of these events since he urged me to take the field'. Human good sense, he explains, would not choose war rather than peace, 'but somehow the gods willed that this should happen.' Here we see the element of fatalism which complicates the theology.

It is one thing to believe that there is a divine force operating in history which eventually achieves the reward of the virtuous and the castigation of the wicked; quite different is the belief that the divine will is sometimes inscrutable and even capricious, operating with no apparent rationale in a moral sense. It is an outlook which cannot evade the charge of obscurantism, for it defies explanation or consistency. Everything sometimes appears to be predetermined; yet the major gods can interfere with the course of things, at least up to a point. Apollo tries to get the Moirae to change things to rescue his favourite Croesus, but he achieves only a postponement.[93]

In one respect Herodotus offends against the idea of a coherent and consistent theology still more stridently. It is when he imputes to the divine will a deceitful technique which preys on man's ignorance and gullibility. The technique includes false dreams 'sent to deceive.'[94] Of this the clearest example is the dream-vision sent to Xerxes and Artabanus (7.12–19). When Artabanus has been trying to persuade the Great King to desist from his invasion of Greece, Xerxes is twice visited by a dream-figure who urges him to carry on with his plan. Then Artabanus himself, dressed in the royal robes, experiences a similar visitation who gives the same advice, whereupon Artabanus withdraws his resistance to the plan, and a third vision seen by Xerxes is interpreted by the Magians as signifying his sovereign rule of the whole earth, although it ends with the sudden disappearance of the triumphant crown. The Magian interpretation is to be regarded, one assumes, as wrong, so

---

[92] The adjective θεοφιλής sometimes has an active sense, 'loving the gods', but in later authors such as Philo: see LSJ.
[93] Cf. Kurt von Fritz, op. cit. I, 242.
[94] Oswyn Murray, *Early Greece* (Glasgow, 1980), 31. He would locate the tendency in 'a moralizing tradition of story-telling' found mainly in Ionia.

that the third vision is not really deceitful. It is otherwise with the first two, for a divine figure in them is giving Xerxes very misleading advice.[95] Artabanus in this context (7.16) provides a rationalist comment on the significance of dreams:

> The wandering dreams that come to men are of a kind that I shall explain to you, and I am many years older than you. These dream-visions that wander among us usually come from the thoughts which absorb us during the day; and over the last days we have been much concerned with the expedition.
> (Herodotus, 7.16.)

It is tempting to accept such a comment as being really that of Herodotus himself, just as the general warning given to Xerxes by Artabanus against the dangers of greed and arrogance is certainly the view of Herodotus.[96] On the other hand, his attitude to portents and oracles is in no way consistent. Three times (1.66; 1.75; 5.91) he uses the adjective *kibdêlos*, 'evasive', of oracular responses, and in the instance last cited it is clear that they were 'not quibbling or evasive but downright frauds and shams',[97] procured as they were by corrupt means. Yet in other cases he obviously believed that oracles, especially those of Delphi, might be divinely inspired. He was undoubtedly aware, at the same time, of the old tradition that deliberate deceit was a legitimate arm of divine procedure. It is conspicuous in the *Iliad*. Occasionally the idea is used of purely human relations, as when Dolon complains (*Il.* 10.391) that Hector has confounded his judgement 'with many infatuate feelings', but usually it conveys blinding deceptions of divine origin. Indeed we are roundly told (*Il.* 19.97) that Hera deceived (ἠπάτησεν) Zeus through her guile; just before that it is Atê that infatuated him. In Tragedy 'deceitful Atê' is the medium by which human knowledge is obstructed, either through injury inflicted on the mind or through a process by which the understanding is deceived.[98] The emphasis on divine deceit is scarcely ennobled, however, by the Homeric antecedent. If Herodotus describes Xerxes being swayed

---

[95] Cf. T.R. Glover, *Herodotus* (Berkeley, 1924), 268, where, however, the deceitful nature of the advice is not remarked on.

[96] Cf. Heinrich Bischoff, 'Der Warner bei Herodot', in Walter Marg (ed.), *Herodot* (Wege der Forschung; München, 1962), 312–14 ('Die Warnergedanken gehören Herodot selbst.') See also Seth Benardete, *Herodotean Inquiries* (The Hague, 1969), 186–90.

[97] T.R. Glover, op. cit. 269. Drachmann, *Atheism in Pagan Antiquity* (1922), 28, argues that the apologetics of both Herodotus and Sophocles point to the rising scepticism about divination.

[98] Stallmach, *Ate*, 43, citing Aeschylus, *Ag.* 1523; Sophocles, *Trach.* 850–51; Euripides, *Troad.* 530.

by a dream-vision which is completely false, there may well be an 'obvious exemplar' in 'the deceptive dream sent by Zeus to Agamemnon in the second book of the *Iliad*'.[99] The falsity here concerns not only the content of the dream but also its medium in the likeness of Nestor. In the last analysis it is the gods who decide to punish Xerxes and they do this in a way that is offensive to human susceptibility.[100] Herodotus in his presentation of the issues is close to the *Iliad* and to Aeschylus, but his theology is flawed in its ethical inconsistency. His record of rewards and punishments in this life embraces great extremes of generosity and mercy,[101] often ascribed to Persians. His writing shows of course several other concerns, and Kurt von Fritz sees him as basically more of a geographer and ethnographer than a historian. Further, his style and technique are often ironic and tragic in tone, with much attention to the development of character, as in the instances of Pausanias and Themistocles.[102] Initially these qualities were directed to an audience of hearers, and many who heard him doubtless shared his views about the workings of divine intervention in history.

5. *Plato, Plutarch and Others*

For differing reasons neither the Stoics nor the Epicureans had much room in their systems for the idea that human behaviour produces punishments or rewards in this life. In the case of the Stoics the strong element of determinism in their thought tended to militate against the very idea of free choice in a man's life. The element of determinism extended even to the definition of character, which they regarded as the product of an inherited nature and of a particular environment; yet they could argue that, in spite of this, a person was responsible for his actions.[103] Punishments, according to the Old Stoics, served as retribution and as a warning

---

[99] H. Lloyd-Jones, *The Justice of Zeus*, 61. K.H. Waters, *Herodotus the Historian* (London, 1985), 109, regards the final dream of Xerxes as 'an invention of a moralising kind'.
[100] Cf. the figure of Apatê (Deceit) misleading Asia in the Apulian vase depicting the Persians: see Pohlenz, *Herodot*, 125 with refs.
[101] Hans Drexler, *Herodot-Studien* (Hildesheim, 1972), 174–8.
[102] Cf. Charles W. Fornara, *Herodotus. An Interpretative Essay.* (Oxford, 1971), 65. But whether his antithesis in the dictum, 'Herodotus' method is artistic, not historical', can be justified is doubtful. Certainly a number of great historians have been fine literary artists.
[103] Charlotte Stough in J.M. Rist (ed.), *The Stoics* (Berkeley, 1978), 226.

to others.[104] The reconciliation of Providence (*Pronoia*) and Destiny (*Heimarmenê*) is based on the belief that everything that happens is related to a chain of causes which enables a responsible choice to be possible. On this freedom of choice depends the validity of all praise and blame, reward and punishment; yet the choice which an individual makes can be causally explained.[105]

As for the rival Epicurean movement, here was a school of thought which did not indeed deny the existence of the gods, but steadfastly rejected any idea of their influence on human affairs. The theology of Epicurus is eloquently presented by Lucretius, and it is worthy of note that he not only decries, with considerable contempt, the popular beliefs about the penalties that await men in the afterworld; he also praises the calm and unruffled life of the gods, and maintains that they cannot conceive anger against man nor seek to do him any harm in this life either.[106] Before this the rise of agnosticism and also of atheism had weakened in many Greek minds the hold of the traditional belief in divine intervention. It is significant that in the history of Thucydides this whole approach is conspicuously missing.[107] Lloyd-Jones has been able to show, none the less, that Thucydides, even without any invocation of the divine apparatus or of the operation of Hubris and Atê, achieves an interpretation that comes rather close to these ideas in its psychology. In his account of the Melian massacre he exposes the 'brutal imperialist policy' which the Athenians had pursued; and that massacre was followed by their fateful decision to invade Sicily.[108]

In Tragedy a comparable change may be observed in the passage from Aeschylus to Euripides. The passionate moral simplicities of Aeschylus are also absent from the outlook of Sophocles. He sometimes uses phrases which seem to anticipate the psychological emphasis found in Euripides, as when the Chorus in the *Antigone* (603) declares that among the misfortunes that have brought ruin to the house of Oedipus is the 'Erinys in the mind' (φρενῶν ἐρινύς), with an allusion, it seems, to a kind of mental Fury that afflicted Antigone. In general, however, Sophocles retains the old

---

[104] J.M. Rist, *Stoic Philosophy* (Cambridge, 1969), 83, in a chapter entitled 'All Sins are Equal' (a Stoic belief).

[105] Max Pohlenz, *Die Stoa* (2nd Ed., Göttingen, 1959), 104, with reference to Zeus and Chrysippus.

[106] Benjamin Farrington, *The Faith of Epicurus* (London, 1967), 117, with a quotation in translation from the *De Rerum Natura*, 6.68 ff.

[107] 'In the history of Thucydides the gods are conspicuous by their absence; the divine motivation which Herodotus took over from the epic has been totally abandoned.' Thus H. Lloyd-Jones, *The Justice of Zeus*, 137.

[108] Ibid. 143.

theology, while achieving a presentation of it which gives priority to its emotional impact on the human level. He 'expressed the full tragic significance of the old religious themes in their unsoftened, unmoralized forms—the overwhelming sense of human helplessness in face of the divine mystery, and of the *ate* that waits on all human achievement . . .'[109] While he usually avoids the word *hubris*, its significance is fully exploited as in the case of Ajax. Athena praises the temperate (*Ajax*, 132) and castigates pride in power or wealth. Later the word *hubris* is pointedly used of the arrogance of Ajax (1061), which a god has rebuked by directing it on to his flocks and herds.[110] In psychological terms the fury of Ajax may be said to turn to madness, and his eventual suicide is an attempt to retrieve his injured honour.[111] To some extent, at the same time, Athena is the medium of divine displeasure,[112] and the traditional theological framework is maintained.

Perhaps the most problematic of the plays of Sophocles from this point of view is the *Philoctetes*. Up to the intervention of Heracles at the very end Philoctetes has been refusing to return to Troy; throughout he displays his anger with the Greeks who are fighting there because they have left him in Lemnos in great physical pain; and he succeeds, after long discussions, in persuading Neoptolemus to agree with the idea that he should take him home instead. But when Heracles suddenly appears at the end, he commands Philoctetes to go to Troy after all; there, he is told, his wound will be healed and he will lead the Greeks to victory, because no success is possible without the bow and arrows which Philoctetes holds and which had formerly belonged to Heracles himself. In a brief speech of three lines Philoctetes obeys at once in spite of his previous obstinate opposition to the whole idea. He says now that he had longed to hear the god's voice and that he will not disobey his command.

This unexpected change is made possible only by the *deus ex machina*. As Joe Park Poe remarks in his book *Heroism and Divine Justice in Sophocles' Philoctetes* (Leiden, 1974), 7, 'Happy ending, nice and tidy'. A wide variety of exegesis has emerged. Some take the line described by Poe as 'pietistic', and these include Bowra:

---

[109] Dodds, *The Greeks and the Irrational*, 49. By 'the divine mystery' he presumably means that the events decreed by the gods are often beyond human scrutiny.
[110] 1060 f. Cf. Nilsson, *Geschichte Griech. Rel.* I³, 757.
[111] Cf. J.C. Kamerbeek, *The Ajax* (Leiden, 1953), 6–8.
[112] Gilbert Norwood is quoted ibid. 8 as saying that 'Athena is simply divine punishment personified', to which Kamerbeek wisely reacts, 'Not incorrect, but too simple.'

Philoctetes in yielding to the god is giving a fine example of man's will co-operating with God's will. Others like Kitto and Linforth see the *deus ex machina* here as a purely external intervention which contravenes the psychological trend of the drama. Poe himself sees the end as an exposition of man's helplessness in the face of a divine providence which is thoroughly unjust. This last interpretation has some cogency; its weakness is the brevity and lack of clarity in the dramatic exposition itself. Philoctetes in the course of the play has certainly attacked divine dispensations; he even finds the gods to be evil (v. 452 τοὺς θεοὺς εὕρω κακούς).

A change of atmosphere can quickly be sensed in Euripides. In general his portrayal of religion shows both negative and positive aspects. A sceptical reaction to divination appears and there are occasional allusions to the vanity of offerings. If one cannot easily envisage Euripides as an Eleusinian initiate, yet in his *Ion* there are beautiful lines in praise of Iacchus and in his *Bacchae* he gives a vibrantly sympathetic view of Dionysiac ecstasy.[113] King Pentheus of Thebes, who opposes the ecstatic god, suffers a cruel fate at the hands of the frenzied Maenads, and at the end of the play Cadmus expresses horror and revulsion. A kind of orthodoxy is therefore built into the pattern of events: no challenge to the divine can succeed; yet the pitiless quality of the punishment finds no approbation. The character of Pentheus, while not a stereotype of villainy, is unfavourably portrayed in its hysterical and brutal traits, and the play 'contrasts transcending, "religious" experience with a too human, frightened, and disastrous attempt to deny it.'[114] But whether the play recognizes or condemns the god Dionysus is a question purposely left open by the playwright.

The theme of revenge appears too in the *Medea*, *Hecuba*, and *Electra*, with a similar ebb and flow of feeling; 'the spectator's sympathy is first enlisted for the avenger and then made to extend to the avenger's victims.'[115] In some of these cases it is revenge on the human plane that matters most, though in no case is the divine plane ignored. It may be asked whether the human factors are subordinated to 'a kind of justice, natural or absolute, or one superintended by the traditional Olympians.'[116] In the *Hippolytus* and the *Medea*, an *alastor* and a daemon are said to have instigated

---

[113] Otto Kern, *Die Religion der Griechen*, II (Berlin, 1935), 292–3.
[114] Christopher Collard, *Euripides* (New Surveys in the Classics, 14, Greece and Rome; Oxford, 1981), 33.
[115] E.R. Dodds, *Euripides, Bacchae* (2nd Ed., Oxford, 1960), xlvi.
[116] Collard, op. cit. 33.

the troubles, and in the *Hippolytus* the word *atê* is used of the source of the madness (v. 241, 'I was mad, I fell through the *atê* of a daemon'). In origin the notion is of course that of 'supernatural interference as the cause of mental disorder',[117] but it may be doubted whether the traditional notion has not now become merely symbolic—an idea repugnant to Lloyd-Jones,[118] who in these matters is very much of a Fundamentalist. He rightly stresses the role of contemporary thought in later interpretations, pointing to the importance of Ibsen's *Hedda Gabler* in relation to the exposition by Wilamowitz of Phaedra in the *Hippolytus* of Euripides.[119] There is certainly a strong feminist element in the plays of Euripides, as anyone who heard Kathleen Freeman expounding his *Medea* could forcefully realize. Modern feminism, it could be argued, is worlds apart, and the interpreter's first duty is to consider the writer's own intention within the ambience of his age. A part of the Euripidean ambience was undoubtedly the sophistic Enlightenment of fifth-century Athens. If it is true that 'he did not quite escape the charge of atheism even in his own day',[120] the palpable prejudice of Aristophanes is the main source. On the other hand, he can scarcely be held up as a defender of the traditional faith on the divine dispensation of human life. In the *Medea*, the *Hecuba*, the *Trojan Women*, the *Andromache*, and the *Bacchae* the justice of Zeus is certainly apparent, but often it is shown as something harsh and terrible. The *Heracles Furens* includes a strong protest against divine injustice although in the end Heracles is prevailed upon to give up his plan of suicide.[121]

Justice (*dikaiosunê*) is the basic theme of Plato's *Republic*, and it is treated as something related to the private individual, his community, and his *polis*.[122] In the Myth of Er, as well as in the Myth of the *Phaedo*, Plato dwells on the theme of rewards and punishments

---

[117] W.S. Barrett, ad loc. (Oxford, 1964), 206.

[118] *The Justice of Zeus*, 149.

[119] Ibid. 145–6. Comparable is the treatment of Antigone by Hölderlin, Cocteau, Anouilh and Brecht: see George Steiner, *After Babel* (London, 1975), 414.

[120] Drachmann, *Atheism in Pagan Antiquity*, 51. Statements denying or doubting the existence of the gods are shown to be those of individual characters in the plays—a constant trap in the study of drama.

[121] Lloyd-Jones, op. cit. 152–5 is at his least convincing in his attempt to find the traditional beliefs in these plays.

[122] Cf. Gregory Vlastos, 'The Theory of Social Justice in the *Polis* in Plato's *Republic*', in Helen F. North (ed.), *Interpretations of Plato* (Suppl. Mnemosyne, 50; Leiden, 1977), 1–40. He argues that 'justice' is the meaning followed by Plato, and that the other sense, 'righteousness', is not considered by him. He also argues, against Karl Popper, that economic equality is an important element in Plato's scheme.

in the afterworld, and it would be misleading to make a sharp dichotomy between his myths and his doctrine as presented otherwise.[123] Thus the *Phaedo* provides arguments for the immortality of the soul and the myth in that work gives a picture of what awaits the good and bad soul in the life after death. Nor are historical elements lacking in some of the mythical accounts, as in 'the myth of ancient Athens and the fabled city of Atlantis', which is found in the *Timaeus* and the *Critias*.[124] At the end of the unfinished *Critias* moral causes are adduced to explain the fall of Atlantis: unjust ambition and power had replaced earlier ideals. Atlantis was eventually submerged in ocean, and it was Zeus himself who decided to punish its people, the sequence of *hubris* and *nemesis* being clear.[125]

In general, however, Plato does not pay much attention to any system of rewards and punishments which may be observable in this life. The idea of divine providence (θεοῦ πρόνοια) is basic to his thought, but it is not treated at length in relation to the problem of evil here and now. Discussing the theology of Plato's *Laws*, Paul Elmer More[126] described it as 'the first serious theodicy of the western world'. Book X of the *Laws* is concerned, initially, with belief in the existence of the gods; then with the belief that the gods pay regard to human affairs; and the conviction (903 B) that 'all things have been ordered by Him who cares for the whole world, with a view to the salvation and excellence of the whole.' Each part, according to its ability, enacts and suffers what is proper to it.

It was left, none the less, to Plutarch, a follower of Plato in a later age, to examine an aspect of this doctrine in some detail. Writing at the beginning of the second century A.D., Plutarch ventured to discuss the objection which was often raised against the belief in an active and compensating providence: why was divine vengeance often so slow in dealing with crime and sin in the lives of men and women in this world? Hence his work *On the Delays of the Divine Vengeance*, Περὶ τῶν ὑπὸ τοῦ θείου βραδέως τιμωρουμένων, a title

---

[123] John F. Callahan, 'Dialectic, Myth and History in the Philosophy of Plato', in Helen F. North (ed.), op. cit. 64–85, esp. 69, modifying J.A. Stewart.

[124] Ibid. For possible historical elements in the story of Atlantis see J. Gwyn Griffiths, 'Atlantis and Egypt', in *Historia* 34 (1985), 3–28. Cf. Callahan. op. cit. 74.

[125] The earthquake which destroyed the town of Helice in Achaea in 373 B.C. may possibly have influenced Plato, or at least the pious and popular reaction to it. Cf. my remarks ibid. 28 n. 109, citing Hans Herter.

[126] *The Religion of Plato* (2nd Ed., Princeton, 1928), 145. For the excerpt which follows cf. Trevor J. Saunders, *Plato, the Laws* (Penguin Classics, 1970, repr. 1972), 437.

Latinized as *De Sera Numinis Vindicta*.[127] His general attitude was that of 'a declared and consistent Platonist',[128] and he was respected as such by contemporary Athenian Platonists. To him the supreme object of man's life, the *telos* at which he should aim, was likeness to God—not the Stoic aim of Conformity with Nature.[129] In the work *On the Delays of the Divine Vengeance*, 5, 550 D, Timon, Plutarch's brother, quotes Plato on the principle of *Imitatio Dei*:[130]

> Consider first that God, as Plato says, offers himself to all as a pattern of every excellence, thus rendering human virtue, which is in some sort an assimilation to himself, accessible to all who can 'follow God'.

The maxim 'follow God' appears in Plato's Laws (716 B): *Every man should be intent on belonging to those who follow in the company of God*; and it is echoed too in the *Phaedrus* (248 A). But it may well derive ultimately from Pythagoras.[131]

In this dialogue of Plutarch's, which is located at Delphi, there are four speakers: Plutarch himself, his brother Timon, his son-in-law Patrocleas, and his friend Olympichus. We are told in the opening paragraph that Epicurus had been speaking, but had suddenly left the company without waiting for comments on his speech. This was not, of course, Epicurus the philosopher, but a person named after him (hence the emendation Epicureios, by Fabricius); or perhaps the suggestion is that someone had been reading aloud a book by Epicurus; still more likely is that it means simply 'an Epicurean'.[132] The ensuing discussion deals with remarks made from the Epicurean standpoint, which included an attack on the idea of providence. When they denied divine intervention in human affairs, the Epicureans often pointed to the prosperity of the wicked and the misery of the good; and Patrocleas opens the responding discussion by admitting that their most telling argument is the delay and postponement of the divine punishment of the wicked. It is a delay, he argues, that encourages the wicked and disheartens the good. Epicureanism in its attack on

---

[127] An admirable modern edition and translation are by Phillip H. De Lacy and Benedict Einarson in Vol. VII of the Loeb Library's *Plutarch's Moralia* (London, 1959). Also valuable are the edition, translation and commentary by Yvonne Vernière (Budé, Paris, 1974).

[128] D.A. Russell, *Plutarch* (London, 1972), 63. For a detailed exposé of his philosophy see John Dillon, *The Middle Platonists* (London, 1977), 184–230.

[129] John Dillon, op. cit. 192.

[130] The translation is by De Lacy and Einarson. Cf. John Dillon, ibid.

[131] De Lacy and Einarson, op. cit. 194 n.c.

[132] Ibid. 175 n.a. Yvonne Vernière in the Budé edition, 130 n. 1, accepts, like Wyttenbach and Pohlenz, the emendation by Fabricius, regarding the person as representative of Epicureanism.

divine providence is thus the main target. To the Stoics, on the other hand, providence had a certain measure of validity; and although Plutarch[133] rejects their view of 'one reason and one providence, dominating and ruling everything', arguing that this cannot explain the existence of evil, yet his Platonism shows a considerable Stoic impact.[134]

The delay in divine punishment, according to Olympichus, leads people to reject any idea of providence; it also prevents the wrongdoer from benefitting from the rebuke since it is far removed in time from the evil action. Timon's objection is that the delay may often mean that the wrongdoer's descendant is punished—an obviously unjust procedure. Bion is quoted (the philosopher of the third century B.C., not the later pastoral poet) for the saying that God was more ludicrous in punishing a descendant for the crimes of an ancestor than a physician who treats a descendant for an ancestor's disease. It is Plutarch himself who deals with these points, and he begins on a note of humility, disavowing any absolute dogmatism. He urges that God's delay in punishing is salutary for his human imitators, who may often punish in error; it also allows the offender time to recover if he is amenable to being reformed. The deferment of punishment means, moreover, that the most suitable manner and time can be chosen, as when Callippus was murdered with the very dagger with which, though ostensibly a friend, he murdered Dion. There is one type of punishment, it is added, which is not deferred at all: this is the anguish of the guilty soul. On the question of the punishment of descendants for the offences of their ancestors, one reply is that the rewarding of descendants for the services made by their ancestors is readily approved of. Why not apply the same logic to punishments? An analogy is claimed, in this context, between the city and the family and the individual; they have the same kind of continuity, and the misdeeds of the past call for penalties. On Bion's objection about the treating of a descendant for an ancestor's disease, Plutarch replies that punishment may be preventive and save a descendant from yielding to an inherited tendency to evil.

After these discussions comes the myth which concludes the work. This concerns punishments in the afterworld, and is thus irrelevant to our present topic, though there are some links with the

---

[133] *De Iside et Osiride*, 45, 369 A. See my *Plutarch's De Iside et Osiride* (Cardiff, 1970), 44–45 and 469.

[134] Cf. John Dillon, *The Middle Platonists*, 228, on the absorption of Stoic logical concepts.

preceding *logos*. For instance, mention is made of the punishment of ancestors whose descendants have also been punished in the life on earth. Thus no sin is left unpunished. A feature of the *logos* itself is the provision of numerous historical or mythical instances in which the principle discussed is seen to be operating. At one point indeed (557 E–F) Plutarch objects that many of the instances are fictitious. Reference is made by Olympichus (549 D–E) to the proverb which talks of 'the slow grinding of the mills of the gods', which was much later followed by Friedrich von Logau and Longfellow[135] but which, according to the speaker, makes the fact of punishment obscure and extinguishes the fear of wickedness. Whereas the Myth is clearly indebted to the Myths of Plato in the *Republic* and the *Phaedo*, the preceding discussion shows the sensitive and tolerant spirit of Plutarch at its best, so that the work has not surprisingly been described as 'perhaps the most admired of Plutarch's philosophical writings'.[136] In both the Myth and the *logos* there is a constant emphasis on the coherence and responsibility of the individual, an emphasis which pertains to this world and the next; and Plato is doubtless here the principal guide.[137]

Yet in spite of the many instances which the *De Sera* adduces of the operation of divine retribution in human lives, it can hardly be maintained that the strength of the work lies in this direction. The concession made by Plutarch himself to the doubtful nature of some of the instances is one disabling factor, as we have noted.[138] That is why a recent study of religious themes in the *Moralia* and the *Lives* has perceptively devoted one chapter to 'Divine Retribution in the *Lives*'.[139] Here at any rate we see Plutarch the historian at work, and it is revealing to note how his theory of divine intervention works out in the exposition of particular lives. Brenk begins by referring (p. 256) to 'the undeniable fact that Plutarch's *Lives* are case histories in crime and punishment'; he then qualifies this by saying that 'his thought is somewhat complex and oscillates considerably

---

[135] See above pp. 3–4 and von Leutsch, *C. Paroem. Gr.* II, 199, 85, ὀψὲ θεῶν ἀλέουσι μύλοι, ἀλέουσι δὲ λεπτά.

[136] De Lacy and Einarson, op. cit. 170. Cf. John Oakesmith, *The Religion of Plutarch* (London, 1902), 107, referring to his 'eloquent sermon on the text, "God moves in a mysterious way"'.

[137] Cf. Yvonne Vernière, *Symboles et mythes dans la pensée de Plutarque* (Paris, 1977), 154.

[138] Cf. De Lacy and Einarson, op. cit. 176.

[139] Frederick E. Brenk, *In Mist Apparelled* (Mnemosyne Suppl. 48; Leiden, 1977), 256–75. A less felicitous title is given to the chapter: 'Clinging like Bees or Bats'. For a general assessment of the book see my review in *JHS* 100 (1980), 227–8.

between the two poles of vice bringing its own punishment, and vice punished through supernatural intercession.'

The *Lives* are shown to contain frequent reference to the theme of retribution, and probably the concentration, in each case, on one central individual invited a treatment reminiscent in some way of Tragedy. Brenk refers (p. 261) to 'the frequency of retribution endings'. These, however, do not always concern the central character himself. Thus in the *Life of Timoleon* the death of his mercenaries, who had been guilty of sacking Delphi, is presented as an event of retribution; and so is the death of Pausanias in the *Life of Cimon*, after he mistakenly kills a girl whom he has compelled to visit him at night. In the *De Sera* (555 C) the word *hubris* is used of his action, and a vision of the dead girl plays a part in the sequence of events. Other factors which seem to conflict at times with the process of retribution are *tuchê*, 'fortune' or *eutuchia*, 'good fortune', both attached to the main character, and *to daimonion*, 'the divine'. Callippus, the assassin of Dion, is himself killed by the sword which he used to kill Dion (*Dion*, 58); and Cassius similarly falls (*Caesar*, 69) to the sword with which he killed Caesar. Brenk (p. 260) is rightly suspicious of these particular details in the case for retribution, and he shows that in the instance of the punishment of Callippus it is *tuchê* and the gods who are credited with the deed. As far as the gods are concerned, there is nothing basically unexpected in the notion that they bring about retribution. Indeed that is the traditional Greek doctrine and Zeus himself is the prime instigator. What intrigues Brenk is that in the *De Sera* the sequence of retaliatory justice, although ascribed to divine action, is often seen as an inherent and inevitable moral process:[140]

> The title suggests the direct intervention of the divine, but in fact vice is usually seen to bring its own punishment; and if retribution comes at all, it is not by a supernatural action on God's part, but through the use of human instruments.

There is also inconsistency in the treatment of Tuchê. If the events of history are directed by a blind Fortune, that directly contradicts the idea of a just and beneficent Providence. In several of the *Lives*, and especially in the *De Fortuna Romanorum*, an early philosophical work, Plutarch is ready to elevate *tuchê* to a position of key importance, as when he assigns the successes of the Romans to their *tuchê*. But in the majority of the philosophical essays he reduces its role to a minimum; and in the matter of divine retribution

---

[140] Ibid. 259.

it would of course have been impossible to link that to a Fortune that was wayward and fickle. The two different standpoints are irreconcilable.[141] A dichotomy must therefore be accepted. Yet the role of *tuchê* is not usually conveyed in absolute terms. Sometimes prominence is given in the *Lives* to personal valour and virtue, *aretê*, or to a combination of this with *tuchê*, as when the victory of Pelopidas is assigned to both factors (*Life of Pelopidas*, 25). In general the *Lives* are teeming with instances of retribution. In the *Life of Caesar* he is killed in the portico of Pompey's theatre— suitable retaliation for his virtual killing of Pompey. Caesar's killers are likewise dealt with. Brutus commits suicide after seeing visions of his own evil genius, his *daimon* (here a kind of Erinys),[142] and the suicide of Cassius is carried out with the very sword that killed Caesar. The vision which appears to Brutus the second time is described as *to daimonion*, and probably represents Caesar himself appearing after his death. It has, then, the precise role of the Erinys.[143]

Although the *De Sera* is also replete with incidents which exploit similar themes, it has a distinctly higher level of spirituality. A number of passages extol the value of inner anguish as opposed to external punishment. It is urged (555 E–F) that neither man nor God need impose penalties on evildoers when the workings of conscience and remorse are such that in time men realize the folly of their misdeeds, and the emptiness, shame and confusion which they have caused. The delay in divine punishment enables the evildoer to return in repentance (*metanoia*, 551 D) to a more upright life. Moreover, the rewards or punishments which may occur in a life to come should not, it is urged, affect our life here and now (560 F–561 A); the sanctions of this life are more important. In several of his other works Plutarch shows great interest in the furtherance of an ideal of personal virtue and assiduously tenders practical advice to those who aim at this ideal. Problems of moral psychology and mental therapy are discussed in several of his philosophical essays, especially in those on the control of anger, on talkativeness, on curiosity, on harmful shyness, and on self-praise without

---

[141] Cf. Brenk, ibid. 163: 'The conclusion one must arrive at is that Plutarch is a schizophrenic when it comes to *tyche*.'

[142] A detail omitted in the *Life of Brutus*.

[143] Guy Soury, *La démonologie de Plutarque* (Paris, 1942), 143–4. Brenk, op. cit. 263 is unclear on the matter: 'the great *daimon* of Caesar seems to avenge him', but Brutus sees the vision 'of his evil *daimon*'. See also D.A. Russell, *Plutarch*, 77–78, who doubts whether 'any firm system' of demonology can be found in Plutarch.

offence.[144] Plutarch's warm humanity is reflected in his over-all attachment to *philanthropia*, a favourite word of his,[145] denoting the benevolence and good will which is the ideal of the man who has imbibed Greek culture and civilization. Nor was it an ideal which excluded women from its orbit. One of the finest of Plutarch's writings is the Letter of Consolation addressed by him to his wife on the loss of their infant daughter. This work praises the daughter's 'natural goodness'.[146] Plutarch draws a contrast between *philanthropia* and *philautia*, 'love of self' (in an unfavourable sense). At the same time his moral essays show a lively consciousness of the evils which assail man's ethical aspirations. Self-control and self-discipline (*askêsis*) are firmly inculcated[147] and it is significant that Apollo, the god of moderation who is also a god of healing, is conspicuous in his thinking on such matters, including his therapeutic aims.[148] Another of his essays, *Progress in Virtue*, offers a programme by which analysis and correction of self are deemed to show the way to mental and moral health.[149]

All this does not mean that the *De Sera* is primarily devoted to spiritual exhortation. The hand of a retaliatory providence is given pride of space and emphasis; and there is a resulting lack of cohesion and consistency, as often in Plutarch's work. A quite different view assigns an overriding importance to the spiritual emphasis:[150]

> Furthermore, Plutarch, in his interpretation, finds it necessary to abandon the concept of divine punishment altogether, and to replace it with what he understands to be a process of therapy for the soul. What popular religion calls 'punishments' must, according to Plutarch, be reinterpreted sociologically as corrective and preventive measures deriving from the divine therapy for the soul. The confirmation of this truth cannot be achieved by the λόγος, but only by the μῦθος, since it is in this 'myth' that we learn about the destiny of the soul in the afterlife.

---

[144] See Heinz G. Ingenkamp, *Plutarchs Schriften über die Heilung der Seele* (Hypomnemata, 34; Göttingen, 1971), who makes a study of these five essays.

[145] Cf. the chapter devoted to the concept by Rudolph Hirzel, *Plutarch* (Das Erbe der Alten, 4; Leipzig, 1912), 23–32.

[146] Cf. Moses Hadas, *On Love, the Family, and the Good Life*. Selected Essays of Plutarch. (New York, 1957), 93: 'Near as Plutarch comes to Christian Ethics, he is characteristically pagan in his belief in man's natural goodness. Little Timoxena was naturally good . . .'

[147] Ingenkamp, op. cit. 101.

[148] Ibid. 140.

[149] D.A. Russell, *Plutarch*, 87–90.

[150] Hans Dieter Betz, Peter A. Dirkse, and Edgar W. Smith, Jr. in *Plutarch's Theological Writings and Early Christian Literature* ed. Hans Dieter Betz (Studia ad Corpus Hellenisticum Novi Testamenti, 3; Leiden, 1975), 182.

The same scholars find a contrast between Plutarch and Early Christian Literature, maintaining that 'in Plutarch we are presented with a consistent philosophical argument, while in ECL all of the various ideas coexist with one another without being harmonized into a theological system.'[151] In one way the contrast is unfair because Early Christian Literature comprises many varied works, whereas Plutarch's one work on this theme is being considered. Even so, that work is a dialogue divided between different speakers. Plutarch himself is given the lion's share,[152] and priority should perhaps be assigned to his arguments. It is he who conveys the whole of the argument about the force of inner suffering (553 F–555F); he urges that the happiness of evil-doers is illusory, since the punishment in the soul's agony begins at once with the perpetration of the deed, the external punishment being merely the completion of this, and may be a long process proving more painful than a swift death imposed by God, which would really mean a soft treatment. It is a process of meditation in which the soul realizes the folly of its crimes in the pursuit of pleasure, power, and wealth, repeating to itself and arguing with itself how it may escape the memory of sinful deeds and throw out the witness of conscience in the hope that it may be purified and begin an entirely new life (556 A). In such a meditation the sinful soul is not aided by its many foibles and fears, but it is brought to a state of bitter self-knowledge and self-hatred (556 B).

It is not clear that Plutarch views the anguish of the sinner's soul as an experience that can replace the traditional punishments inflicted by the divine. There is indeed one sentence which could be thus explained:

> For my part I do not think, if it is right to say so, that the doers of wickedness need the attention of either God or man as punishing judge, but that their life itself suffices, since it is entirely destroyed and brought into confusion by evil.
>
> (*De Sera*, 11, 556 D.)

This statement can scarcely be reconciled with Plutarch's thoroughgoing defence (in words assigned to him in the dialogue) of divine chastisement in the events of men's lives, while the Myth defends the same process in the afterlife, where men who have often been punished already in a previous life receive renewed and heightened penalties. When Timon raises the problem of how

---

[151] Ibid. 184.
[152] Five-sixths according to Yvonne Vernière (Budé), 99.

unjust it is to visit the sins of parents upon their children (556 E),[153] Plutarch in his reply is prepared to defend even this. He argues, as we have already noted, that if rewards are acceptable in their transmission from one generation to another, the same approval should extend to punishments (557 F). Collective responsibility is urged as another defence: a city and a family have the same kind of continued moral obligation as an individual, and evil deeds enacted in the past must be penalized (558 F–559 F). After a championing of the survival of the soul, Plutarch returns to argue that the punishment of descendants has a deterrent effect on others (561 A).

On the whole, then, he emerges in this essay as an apologist for traditional beliefs. His discussion of the inner anguish experienced by the guilty does run counter to them in some degree, and one challenging statement goes to the extent of suggesting the priority of the spiritual, as opposed to the external, intervention by the divine. Yet much the greater part of Plutarch's contribution to the dialogue supports the working of a patient, though relentless, providence in human lives. It is a wide-ranging essay, including as it does a treatment of the soul's survival and, in the Myth, its experience after death. It also gives prominence to the idea that God's example should be followed. In several ways, therefore, its content goes beyond the limits suggested by its traditional title, which deals only with the delays in divine retaliation. It is really concerned with 'the whole problem of theodicy'.[154] Nor is it surprising that there are many parallels in Early Christian Literature as well as several dissimilarities.[155]

In the historical writings of the post-classical era such themes are not much to the fore. Writing mostly in the third century B.C., Timaeus of Tauromenium in Sicily dealt especially with the history of Sicily, although he lived in Athens for fifty years. His work survives only in fragments,[156] many of them in Polybius and Diodorus Siculus, by whom he was virulently attacked for inaccuracy and partisanship—a controversial approach that has naturally affected the choice and quality of the surviving fragments.[157]

---

[153] A belief in this type of punishment was common among ancient cultures. Cf. Betz et al. op. cit. 209.
[154] Ibid. 181, following Ziegler.
[155] Ibid. 183–4.
[156] See Felix Jacoby, *Fragmente der Griechischen Historiker*, III B (Leiden, 1950), 566, pp. 581–658, with his Kommentar in III b (Leiden, 1955), 526–594 and the volume of Noten (Leiden, 1955), 311–347.
[157] Cf. Truesdell S. Brown, *Timaeus of Tauromenium* (Univ. of California Publications in History, 55; Berkeley, 1958), 23. That Timaeus himself may have

Timaeus was often concerned with the rise and fall of important Sicilian cities, and he viewed as a primary cause of decline the moral failure which he saw as the result of lush prosperity with its attendant softness and decadent sophistication. This attitude is of course familiar in the approach of earlier Greek historians to the encounter of Greece and Persia. The clash of two Greek cities, Sybaris and Croton, in the South of Italy in 510 B.C. became a favourite illustration of the dangers of luxurious living; and Timaeus gloats on the obliteration of Sybaris for this reason. He gives still more detail about the fall of Acragas to Carthage in 406, and his manner has been described as 'flamboyant'.[158] A key word in the vocabulary of condemnation is now *truphê*, 'softness' (as in F 9),[159] which in the Hellenistic era seems to replace words like *koros*, 'satiety', save that the sense of 'effeminacy' is now added.[160] Later it was especially applied to the Ptolemies of Egypt, particularly to Ptolemy VIII Euergetes II, whose reception of an embassy from Rome in 140 B.C. led to rhetorical descriptions of Roman austerity as contrasted with Ptolemaic laxity. The Dionysiac ideal of the Ptolemaic dynasty has undoubtedly influenced the contrast.[161]

As for the fall of Acragas to Corinth, luxury and prosperity are equally conspicuous as causative factors.[162] Divine punishment in a more specific way is sometimes portrayed by Timaeus. When the Carthaginians after a victory killed and burned captives as offerings, fire is said to have broken out in their camp, so that many of them perished in the flames; their blasphemous conduct therefore brought upon them, he adds, the very same fate as they had inflicted on others.[163] There is a Herodotean touch about his account of how retribution came to Agathocles after his murder of Ophellas, for on the very same day Agathocles lost his sons and his army.[164]

Although Polybius made scathing attacks on Timaeus—the lat-

---

provoked criticism is admitted by Brown on p. 106: 'He (Polybius) is probably right, also, in finding Timaeus waspish in his comments on other writers, though here he and his critic stand on the same level.'

[158] A.G. Woodhead, *The Greeks in the West* (London, 1962), 88.

[159] Jacoby, Komm. 549–50 shows that there is here a filling out of the brief account in Herodotus, 5.44. *Truphê* does not figure in the earlier account.

[160] See Hans Herter, 'Effeminatus', in *RAC* 4 (1959), 620–50, where many other expressions are also noted.

[161] Heinz Heinen, 'Die Tryphè des Ptolemaios VIII, Euergetes II', in *Althistorische Studien* (Fs. H. Bengston, Historia Einzelschr. 40; Wiesbaden, 1982), 116–128.

[162] T.S. Brown, *Timaeus of Tauromenium*, 69–70.

[163] Apud Diodorus Sic. 20. 65; cf. Nilsson, *Geschichte Griech. Rel.* II, 188.

[164] Diodorus Sic. 20.70 and Nilsson, ibid.

ter's continuing popularity apparently irked him[165]—and approached the problems of historical causation in a rationalistic manner, yet he occasionally reveals signs of the traditional belief in divine retribution. Thus in his account (11.24.8) of a Roman encounter with the Carthaginians in which Scipio was facing Hasdrubal, the completion of a Roman victory is prevented only by a sudden downpour of rain. The event is presented as the interception of a deity, θεός . . . τις, and in this case on the side of the Carthaginians. It has been argued that this is no more than a 'manner of speaking',[166] or that it corresponds merely to what we would call 'an act of God'[167]—a phrase with a minimum of theological content. This attenuation can hardly be read into the account given by Polybius (in 18.54) of how Dicaearchus, the admiral of Philip V of Macedon, set up, during his voyages in the Aegean Sea, two altars, one to Asebeia (Blasphemy) and one to Anomia (Lawlessness), making offerings to them and honouring them as gods. Polybius says that after living by unnatural principles (παρὰ φύσιν) he met his destined death (τῆς εἱμαρμένης ἔτυχε) in a punishment he deserved from both gods and men. (He was put to death after torture.) The behaviour ascribed to Dicaearchus was not without precedent.[168] In his account of the revolt of the mercenaries against Carthage Polybius (1.84) tells of how Hamilcar reduced his enemy to such straits that they were driven through famine to eat each other; and he adds that God (*to daimonion*)[169] had thus brought upon them fitting retribution for their impious and lawless treatment of their neighbours. Commenting on this passage, Walbank[170] states that *to daimonion* 'is virtually equivalent to τύχη . . . which is a bringer of retribution' in several other episodes. But he adds that 'elsewhere the action of *Tyche* shades off into caprice.' *Asebeia* is a basically religious concept, while *paranomia* belongs to the political sphere; they therefore imply 'outrage to the laws of God and man'.[171] *Tuchê*, 'Fortune', is,

---

[165] 'Polybius has set out deliberately to smash his reputation'—T.S. Brown, op. cit. 105.
[166] Nilsson, op. cit. 189: 'nicht mehr als eine Redewendung'.
[167] F.W. Walbank, *A Historical Commentary on Polybius*, I (Oxford, 1957), 17; also ad loc. in II (1967), 304.
[168] Walbank ad loc., II, 626, refers to altars erected at Athens to Hubris and Anaideia, the motive being protection against these powers. Dicaearchus, he thinks, was 'seeking appropriate protection', that is, for actions which were impious and lawless.
[169] W.R. Paton (Loeb, 1922), 229, renders it as 'Providence', but this is misleading.
[170] Ad loc. I, 147.
[171] Ibid.

however, a far more important concept in the work of Polybius, and Walbank has wisely devoted a long section to his discussion of it (pp. 16–26).[172] His conclusion is an ambiguous one: 'Consequently, to the question whether he believed in an objective power directing human affairs, the answer cannot be an unqualified "No"; but in so far as it is a qualified "Yes", his belief was neither sufficiently strong nor sufficiently clear for him to recognize any inconsistency with his normal, rational formulation of the character of *Tyche*' (p. 26).

In part the ambiguity is inherent in the concept of *Tuchê*. As an abstract idea it denotes the domination of chance in human affairs and as such is opposed to any belief in divine control; yet *Tuchê* is also worshipped as a goddess and in this sense is herself a religious phenomenon. Polybius discusses in one place (36.17) when *Tuchê* should be used to explain events: it is when the causes are difficult to grasp; then they may be referred *to God . . . and to Tuchê*—a significant collocation. But the second of these is sometimes portrayed by him as an inconstant, irrational, and even capricious force which tends to bring a reversal to men in a state of prosperity; clearly an earlier doctrine is echoed here; and the same is true of the several instances where *Tuchê* is a power that castigates evil deeds,[173] for she seems now to act as an agent of divine justice. At other times her role is like that of Fate or Providence, in the manner of Heimarmenê or Pronoia on Stoic lines. There are occasions, however, where he maintains with much emphasis that rational explanations are preferable, and his attitude to religion is basically that of a sceptic. This view is confirmed by the occasional qualifications made by him when divine retribution is mentioned. The death of Antiochus Epiphanes is represented as an act of swift divine retaliation after sacrilegious excess, but the words *as some people say* are added.[174]

In general there can be no question that the emphasis on *Tuchê* and Fortuna was a challenge to the belief in divine intervention.[175] Philosophical and religious trends sought to answer the challenge by asserting man's independence of the caprices of fate (a figure blind and irresponsible) or the superiority of divine control. A profane fatalism was doubtless distasteful to many; hence the

---

[172] See also Nilsson on 'Tyche und Daimon' in *Geschichte Griech. Rel.* II, 190–207.
[173] See Walbank, I, 20–21.
[174] Ibid. I, 25.
[175] '... Tyche drives the gods into the background'—Drachmann, *Atheism in Pagan Antiquity*, 92. He finds indications of this as early as Thucydides.

increasing popularity in the Hellenistic and Roman eras of the religiously sanctioned figure of Fortuna.[176]

6. *A Sociological Question*

Modern discussions of religion are often a far cry from the definition by A.N. Whitehead[177] which was once popular: 'Religion is what the individual does with his own solitariness.' Before saying that, he noted that 'this doctrine (that religion is the art and theory of the internal life of man) is the direct negation of the theory that religion is primarily a social fact'; while admitting that 'social facts are of great importance to religion, because there is no such thing as absolutely independent existence.' There can be little doubt, whatever one's view of these words, that Whitehead was accurately stating his own feeling and experience, and also—although his position may thereby be challenged—the way of thinking which was characteristic of the society in which he lived. The subsequent half-century has certainly, in its probing of religious experience, tended to very different directions. It is true that phenomenology, with its emphasis on the psychology of religion in a widely diachronic sense, has favoured the analysis of the individual's mental and spiritual states; at the same time group psychology has attracted much attention, with a natural projection from the living contemporary community to communities that have lived in the past. Again, the sociology of religion has exerted potent influence as a special field of study. A good instance of its vitality in the study of Greek religion can be seen in the words of the French scholar Jean-Pierre Vernant in his chapter on 'The Structure of the Human Cosmos' in a work entitled *The Origins of Greek Thought*:[178]

> *Koros, hybris, pleonexia* were the irrational forms assumed by aristocratic arrogance in the Iron Age—that spirit of *eris* [strife] which now bred not high-minded emulation, but only injustice, oppression, *dysnomia* [disorder].
>
> The idea of *sophrosyne* took shape in contrast to the *hybris* of the rich. It consisted of moderation, proportion, fair limits, the golden mean. 'Nothing in excess' was the motto of the new wisdom. This valuing of the moderate, the mean, gave the Greek idea of *arete* almost a 'bourgeois' aspect: it was the middle class that was able to play a moderating role in the city by striking a balance between extremes on both sides.

---

[176] Nilsson, op. cit. II, 197.
[177] *Religion in the Making* (Cambridge, 1927), 6.
[178] (London, 1982), 84; tr. from a book published in Paris in 1962.

The wide sweep of these ethical and sociological equations seems rather facile until we recall that before this Vernant has been quoting Solon and Theognis, and that after this he again refers to Solon as a man of the centre who set out to be 'arbiter, mediator, and reconciler'. With that particular juncture of Attic history in mind, the equations become more convincing.

Embedded in the Greek morality of retaliation is the right of vendetta. An act of homicide, whether deliberate or accidental, against a member of a clan (*genos*) demanded the shedding of blood for blood.[179] Thus Achilles emerges from his tent to avenge Patroclus. Vendetta is a war, just as war is an indefinite series of vendettas;[180] and such acts of vengeance are sanctioned by the gods.[181] On the divine plane, too, it is not the individual that counts, but the family or clan and the city; and the operative principle is collective responsibility; it is this that enables Plutarch, as we have seen, to approve of retaliation as applied to a man's descendants.

It is no easy task to apportion ideology in such matters to various strata of society. Looking at an Isthmian ode of Pindar (I. 41 ff.), Arthur Adkins[182] finds the ideal of the poor modestly stated as 'seek a livelihood, and *arete* when a livelihood is attained.' A man of higher class, however, an *agathos*, does not seek material gain for himself; through victory in war or in the games, he wins glory (*kalon*) for the city. The *agathos* may be troubled by the envy of his fellows, and also by the envy of the gods—an outcome which Adkins sees as equated with any disaster that befalls him. From the logic of his social position it is the *agathos* who tends to become open to both types of envy and concomitantly to incur the charge of *hubris*. It is doubtful, none the less, whether the whole rationale of arrogance and reprisal should therefore be rigidly linked to one class. In the wider sense of general outlook an attribution to a particular class may often be justified, and it may be broadly true that both Plato and Aristotle entertained aristocratic values, that is, the values of the class to which they belonged,[183] although neither of them was content to follow conventionally accepted

---

[179] Gustave Glotz, *La Solidarité de la famille dans le droit criminel en Grèce* (Paris, 1904, repr. New York, 1973), Ch. 3 ('La vengeance de famille à famille').
[180] Ibid. 92.
[181] Ibid. 558 ff.
[182] *Moral Values and Political Behaviour in Ancient Greece* (London, 1972), 76.
[183] Ellen M. Wood and Neal Wood, *Class Ideology and Ancient Political Theory* (Oxford, 1978), 119–257. They have considerable difficulty, however, in establishing aristocratic affiliations for Socrates (pp. 83–94).

ideas. Belief in a Last Judgement was eventually a part of the convictions held by Greeks who had been initiated into the Eleusinian Mysteries, but an estimate of the percentage of the population, let alone their class, who believed thus, cannot be confidently essayed. It has been described as 'a belief of a minority in Greece'.[184] Belief in a divine justice which operates in the control of human affairs in the present life is attested more widely, as our survey has shown. Although our sources for it derive from the upper and literate strata of society, we can be confident that its broad teachings were familiar to the whole community. In a society such as Athens the evolution of the polis meant that certain general principles were subsumed into the legal system. Thus the right of the vendetta, which began as part of a tribal order, was incorporated into a body of criminal law which controlled and delimited its function.

Of an ideology which was distinctive of the oppressed classes there are inevitably few traces. 'The difficulty here is the scantiness of the evidence, even for the humbler *citizens*' (as opposed to the slave population).[185]

Plutarch's *De Sera*, as we have seen, mentions several instances of divine vengeance being exacted from individuals, although he also includes families and cities as legitimate targets; and Callimachus devotes two hymns to the fate of Teiresias and Erysichthon under penalties imposed by the gods. A good example of the Greek idea that an offence against the gods could sometimes implicate not merely the individual offender but the whole community to which he belonged can be seen in the tradition about the Locrian maidens. The offending act is that of Ajax the Lesser, a native of Eastern or Opuntian Locris: he is said to have raped Cassandra in the temple of Athena at Troy, an event which featured in the lost epic *Iliou Persis*. Cassandra had been dragged, it was said, from the image of Athena, the *palladium*, which she had clung to in the hope of protection; and the goddess was clearly thought to be offended more by the sacrilege of her temple and image than by the act of rape. Since Ajax died at sea in a storm during the return of the

---

[184] A.W.H. Adkins, *From the Many to the One* (London, 1970), 66. In his note 2 he points out that 'the belief is certainly rare in extant literature, but we have only the recorded thoughts of a small minority of Greeks, mostly drawn from Athens, and from one special class of Athenians.' Yet he admits that Democritus 'speaks of it as a belief which blights the life of many.'

[185] G.E.M. de Ste. Croix, *The Class Struggle in the Ancient Greek World* (London, 1981), 441. What he then elaborates on is the negative side of the ideology, as in the struggle against imperialism.

Achaean fleet from Troy, that might be regarded as due retribution. But no, the Locrians must pay for the shameful deed, first by suffering a plague in their land and then by having to send two maidens every year to Athena's temple in Troy, where they had to spend the rest of their lives cleaning the temple. They risked death at the hands of the Trojans when approaching the temple; and when they died thus or otherwise, they were denied burial. After a long interval the Locrians stopped sending the maidens, and then a disease afflicted their women in their child-bearing until the practice was resumed in the third century B.C., as an inscription from Naryka in Locris confirms.[186]

Details of this tradition have been questioned, especially by J. Fontenrose. Minor discrepancies in the tradition do not, however, amount to invalidation. He finds firm evidence for a ritual in the third century B.C. but questions the story of a thousand-year tribute and remarks on 'the legendary character of the story'. If this is too sweepingly dismissive, he might seem to have a point (p. 135) when he notes that 'in Physkos, a few miles from Naryka, there was a temple of Athena Ilias;' the rites and the service by the maidens were, he suggests, carried out there rather than in a very distant Ilion, although Ilion continued to be inhabited. There is every likelihood, however, that the custom was connected with Ilion, and that the tradition arose before 700 B.C.[187] Even if early historicity is doubted, many Greeks believed that this was happening, and there is never any breath of criticism.[188] It remains a prime example of

---

[186] Among the sources are Lycophron, *Alexandra*, 1141–73, ably discussed by Stephanie West, *JHS* 104 (1984), 127 ff. See also J. Fontenrose, *The Delphic Oracle* (Berkeley, 1978), 131–7; both these authors refer to the principal previous discussions.

[187] H.W. Parke, *History of the Delphic Oracle* (Oxford, 1939), 331–4; H. J. Rose, *Hdb. of Greek Mythology*, 143: 'no piece of mythology but historical fact'; cf. L. R. Farnell, *Greek Hero Cults* (Oxford, 1921), 263–305.

[188] Not of this particular case, unless the pathos of Lycophron's description be taken as implied criticism. But the doctrine of inherited guilt, which was first formulated by Solon, was certainly challenged, as by Euripides: see Plutarch, *De Sera*, 12, 556 E; cf. Robert Parker, *Miasma*, 199 ff. On pp. 202–3 Parker deals all too briefly with the Locrian maiden-tribute and follows F. Graf in seeing its origin in 'temple service of a familiar kind' which was re-interpreted and perhaps misunderstood 'by outsiders'—this last term being an odd way to describe the many Greek providers of the evidence. The concept of tribute paid by one state to another finds an early parallel in the tradition of the human tribute imposed on Athens by King Minos of Crete in revenge for the death of his son in Attica; seven youths and seven maidens were annually involved in this tribute. A political significance is probably implied, in the sense that Athens in the Late Bronze Age was dominated by Crete; see G.S. Kirk, *The Nature of Greek Myths* (Penguin, 1974), 153–6.

divine vengeance being visited on a man's descendants for centuries, a dogma which even Plutarch defended; and it features also the principle of collective responsibility, notably in the dictum of Polybius that the maidens were taken from the hundred noble families of Locris. There are several pointers, at the same time, to a concentration on the family or clan of Ajax; the third-century inscription mentions the town of Naryka in Eastern Locris and the family of Aianteioi. In this way it typifies the Greek concept of vendetta; it goes far beyond any definition of a *lex talionis*;[189] and it wins the grim accolade, in its studied and enduring sadism, of being the most cruel episode in the ancient annals of divine vengeance.

The force of the guilt that is shared communally and is transmitted over a long space of time may strike us as something beyond reason. According to N.R.E. Fisher (*Social Values in Classical Athens*, 45) Athenian society was 'remarkable for its sense of community', and this is clear in traditions concerning retribution for outrageous acts. Christian ideology is not without similar emphases within wider orbits; witness the idea that the whole of humanity was implicated in Adam's fall or in the crucifixion of Christ (*Were you there when they crucified my Lord?*); and the argument in the twentieth century about shared responsibility for the Holocaust which destroyed more than six million Jews.

7. *The Human Verdict on Murder in Greece*

We have referred from time to time (above pp. 50, 54 f., 91) to the retributive element in the Greek judicial system. If the right to pursuit of a family vendetta in a case of murder was embodied in the Athenian law of the fifth and fourth centuries, as the speeches of Antiphon and Demosthenes make clear, it was a right which was severely controlled by rigid procedures. The victim's family were regarded as responsible for seeking vengeance and purification, and the duty of prosecution was therefore assigned to them. After proclamation in the Agora the charge was presented to the *basileus*,

---

[189] Dr West, op. cit. 149, remarks on the 'gross disproportion between crime and punishment'. Fritz Graf, *SSR* 2 (1978), 61–79, shows that the tribute could scarcely have been annual since this would have led to the presence of 60 or 100 maidens at one time; they were sent, probably, at various intervals to complement the small number when death removed one or two of them. Graf is also attracted to the location of the rite in Physkos rather than Ilion, but his attempt to interpret the rite as one of passage from childhood to adulthood does not convince; it makes too clean a break with the mythic background.

the archon with religious duties, and the trial proceeded before the Areopagus or the *ephetai*. Intentional homicide was punished with death, unintentional with temporary exile.[190] For other Greek states the evidence is less clearly defined. Sparta's *Gerousia* was parallel in function to the Council of the Areopagus in dealing with cases of homicide; and Crete also had a council of elders. An inscription from Teos (CIG 3044) is said to show the legislator relying entirely 'upon the religious sanction in the matter of punishment' and making 'no reference to the secular authority of the state'.[191]

The evident truth is that these human verdicts, couched though they usually are in terms of judicial processes, are firmly based on religious beliefs and sanctions.[192] In Book Ten of the *Laws* Plato maintains that law is the human embodiment of the divine Reason that rules the universe; he also states (716 C) that *God is the measure of all things, not man, as they say*, rebutting Protagoras. In Book Nine he gives an elaborate analysis of types of homicide. Yet in the types concerned with the family vendetta the religious origin is simpler and more firmly embedded in folk consciousness: behind the façade of law stand the clamant figures of the Erinyes.

---

[190] See Douglas M. MacDowell, *The Law in Classical Athens* (London, 1978), 109–120 ('Homicide and the Family'); cf. Kathleen Freeman, *The Murder of Herodes* (New York, 1963), 14–20.

[191] George M. Calhoun, *The Growth of Criminal Law in Ancient Greece* (Berkeley, 1927, repr. Westport, Conn., 1973), 120. He then remarks, 'here unquestionably we have primitive survival, suggesting the conviction noted in Hesiod that the gods will intervene to punish crime.' He is referring to *Works and Days*, 238 ff.

[192] Cf. Burkert, *Greek Religion*, 252, on the basic import of oaths linked to the gods: 'Just as the oath governs the law of states, so it dominates penal law and civil law . . .'

CHAPTER THREE

ROMAN APPLICATIONS

A problem in discussing the Roman attitudes to our theme is that the reflective and philosophical literature of the Romans is almost always heavily indebted to Greek thought, so that a survey of this literature would inevitably lead to a coverage of ground already covered. A largely distinctive feature of Roman experience was the link between religion and military expansionism, first within Italy itself and afterwards to imperial status in the Mediterranean and beyond. It is true that warlike activity and religious belief have been energetically associated in most early societies. The primitive tribe did not go to war save under the sign of the totem,[1] or at least of a sacred symbol.[2] When the Romans went to war, religious sanction was regarded as necessary.

In a wider sense, both communally and privately, they were anxious to know the will of the gods and to secure their favour. An implicit inference is their belief that the gods were a determining factor in the course of human events and experiences. It is relevant, in view of this, to examine their ideas and practices in connection with divination; they are often marked by caution and fear. Then I propose to look at the more positive and often confident conviction that Rome's imperial role was a destiny planned and actively supported by the gods.

The principal exponents of this conviction in the Augustan age were the historian Livy and the poets Vergil and Horace. Proximity to the contemporary ruling regime raises some problems in the study of their writings, and we have to ask whether they were impelled by a simple propagandist urge to establish, in some cases with suitable rewards, the divinely ordained destiny of the regime

---

[1] This does not imply the presence of totemism as a unique institution recurring in a great number of societies. See Claude Lévi-Strauss (tr. R. Needham), *Totemism* (London, 1964), 44. As an elaborate system it was not known to either Italic or Greek societies; cf. F. Altheim (tr. H. Mattingly) *A History of Roman Religion* (London, 1938), 66 with n. 82. In primitive societies the totemic system probably implied an important imaginative element; see Rodney Needham, *Primordial Characters* (Charlottesville, 1978), 51–54.

[2] In historical times the twelve figure-eight shields, the *ancilia*, exemplified this, not in war itself, but in a ceremony connected with Mars and marked by the war-dance of the Salii. Cf. R.M. Ogilvie, *The Romans and their Gods* (London, 1964), 79.

in question. On the whole, none the less, ample signs of heart-searching are also evident; even a sense of sin and a demand for atonement.

1. *Divination and Dependence*

The elaborate system of divination practised by the Romans is good evidence for their consciousness of dependence on the gods. To some extent, they believed, the will of the gods could be ascertained. There were some indications in natural phenomena, and the observation of these could provide simple guides. Thunder and lightning were obviously not a good prelude to any enterprise, and were explained as preventive signs probably in private as well as public affairs. Sound common sense would be enough to show this; but to any believer there was more to it than that, for Jupiter himself was the producer of thunder and lightning, and their occurrence accordingly pointed to intervention by him. The wise reaction was to delay or cancel the action intended, or even to carry out expiatory rites in order to avert the threat. Basically such procedures were fairly passive in nature;[3] and the whole business was entirely devoid of moral considerations. If errors were implied, they were of a purely ritual nature, and amends could be made by rites correctly enacted. Rules applied to the flight of birds and to various startling signs, and portents carried a similar ritual emphasis.

The other main system of divination used by the Romans was a less passive procedure. It involved the inspection of the entrails of animals, with a verdict which explained a healthy condition as a favourable omen, and an adverse verdict on an unhealthy condition. This system was derived from the Etruscans and has parallels in Babylon.[4] By the end of the Republic divination in general was a target of scepticism in the minds of some of the intelligentsia. In his book on the subject Cicero barely conceals his contempt, although he avers that he himself has presided over auspices. Yet there are clear signs of the view that rejection could bring divine reprisal. Julius Caesar is sometimes cited by ancient authors as guilty of arrogant rejection and as a victim, subsequently, of the wrath of the gods.[5] In some cases he is reported as practising adroit re-

---

[3] Cf. Kurt Latte, *Römische Religionsgeschichte* (Munich, 1960), 158.
[4] Ibid. Cf. Ogilvie, op. cit. 65–67.
[5] Georges Dumézil (tr. P. Krapp), *Archaic Roman Religion*, II (Chicago, 1970), 543–6.

interpretation rather than rejection. Before his campaign in Africa against Scipio and Juba he made the due sacrifice, but the animal escaped—a seriously bad omen, which Caesar is said to have ignored, thus rejecting its import.[6] Yet there is evidence that Caesar did delay his departure because the winds were unfavourable.[7] According to Suetonius (59) his landing in Africa was also marred by an ominous mishap: he fell to the ground as he left the ship. By declaring 'I hold thee, Africa' (*Teneo te, Africa*) he made the omen favourable. Nor did he eventually lack success. An ambivalence likewise marked his attitude to Fortuna. He often stressed his faith in his own personal Fortuna, but whether he believed even in that is doubtful.[8]

The appetite, or lack of it, shown by sacred chickens when offered food, became another valid omen, and the test was obligatory before a campaign. We may feel attracted to the impatience shown by Claudius Pulcher, who was consul in 249 B.C., when he threw the chickens into the Tiber (or into the sea)[9] after they had refused to eat, adding scornfully, 'Well, let them drink' (*vel bibant*). Catastrophe followed, with the loss of the Roman fleet. What strikes one is that the derisory attitude to divination is attested so early, and by an officer of the state. In the following century, perhaps under Greek influence, the derision is expressed in literature and affects even a conservative figure like the elder Cato.[10] In spite of all this the system continued to be observed, and persisted well into imperial times.[11]

If divination plainly indicated a sense of dependence on the gods and a desire to know beforehand whether an action was acceptable to them, the question arises whether it sometimes went further and was regarded as influencing or even causing events. 'Do signs forecast or do they actually *cause* events?'[12] Liebeschuetz[13] cites the

---

[6] Suetonius, *Divus Julius*, 59.

[7] Stefan Weinstock, *Divus Julius* (Oxford, 1971), 98, citing *Bellum Africum*, 1.3.44. Portents relating to the Ides of March were not accepted by him on the grounds that the haruspex had wrongly interpreted them; see Weinstock, 345–6.

[8] H. Erkell, 'Caesar und sein Glück' in *Caesar* ed. D. Rasmussen (Wege der Forschung, 43; Darmstadt, 1967), 60. Rather surprisingly Weinstock, op. cit. 115, sees this faith as the one exception to his scepticism.

[9] The later sources state this, connecting the act with the disaster at sea that followed. See Latte, *Römische Religionsgeschichte*, 266 n. 1.

[10] Latte, op. cit. 265.

[11] Cf. the mention of 'chicken-minders' (*pullarii*) in inscriptions: see ibid. 267 n. 1 (end).

[12] J.H.W.G. Liebeschuetz, *Continuity and Change in Roman Religion* (Oxford, 1979), 27.

[13] Ibid.

case of Marcus Crassus setting out in 54 B.C. to campaign against the Parthians although adverse omens had been announced by the tribune Ateius Capito. As Crassus was leaving Rome, Capito austerely cursed him. Later, in 50 B.C. Appius Claudius the censor condemned the tribune for falsifying the omens, a procedure upbraided by Cicero (*Div.* 1.16 (29–30)). There followed the disastrous defeat and death of Crassus near Carrhae. The Roman interpretation of these events leaves room for ambiguity. It seems, on one view, that the disaster was deemed to be caused by the ignoring of bad omens as they were announced. Cicero's view, however, was that the omens merely predicted what would happen unless due precautions were observed. An additional complication is the ceremonial cursing of Crassus by Capito; also the latter's apparent opposition to the campaign. On the whole, it appears that a directly causative element should not be assigned to the Roman view of divination. The Romans certainly believed that the favour of the gods could be secured; but the two accepted methods were prayer and sacrifice.

2. *Livy on Rome's Success*

If 'history to the Romans was the story of divine intervention in the affairs of men',[14] that intervention was usually regarded by them as favourable, especially in the sense that Rome's imperial destiny was seen as a process sanctioned and indeed ordained by the gods. This was a conviction fervently presented in the Augustan age. In prose its chief protagonist was Livy, in poetry Vergil.

Livy's Preface gives his professed aim: it is to commemorate the actions of the foremost people of the world (*principis terrarum populi*). Humble about his own qualities as a historian, he is grandiloquent about Rome's renown. Her glory in war is such that the legend concerning Mars as the father of Romulus and founder of the Roman people may seem acceptable, even if its historicity is in doubt; indeed antiquity may be allowed the license of mingling the divine and the human in order to make the origins of cities more impressive. Yet Livy concedes that in his own day the very power of Rome has engendered evils, chief of which is *avaritia*. To some extent he echoes Sallust's verdict: to the earlier historian the destruction of Carthage in 146 B.C. had brought a period of decline in public morality, leading especially to the vices of *avaritia* and *ambitio*. Livy does not mention *ambitio*, and it has been well sug-

---

[14] Ogilvie, *The Romans and their Gods*, 59. He is there discussing prodigies.

gested that the omission derives from his lack of political experience. Unlike Sallust, he never held public office and was aloof, therefore, from the petty struggles of political rivalries.[15]

Whereas a degree of scepticism is apparent in Livy's treatment of some religious themes, particularly in his discussion of Rome's early legendary traditions, as on the apotheosis of Romulus and the occasional divine epiphanies reported, he is fairly consistent in his advocacy of the view that the gods have championed Rome's cause. The Polybian interpretation of religion as a useful social cement colours Livy's presentation of Numa as the founder of religious rites, but throughout his history religion is generally displayed as a force of basic significance.[16] The brand of Stoicism promulgated by Posidonius probably influenced him; the determinism of an all-powerful Fate is accepted, but human character is seen as a significant element in its contribution to the course of history. It is reasonable to detect the same kind of doctrine in points made by the Stoic Balbus in Cicero's *De Natura Deorum* (2.8 (20–21)), as when he mentions the failures incurred by Roman generals who ignored religious demands of a divinatory nature.[17] It was essentially, in each case, a failure in their regard for religion.

It is to be expected, then, that Livy often uses the term *Fatum*, though his use of it is not rigidly shaped by Stoicism. Much more often does he use the term *Fortuna*.[18] Important also is the expression *Fortuna populi Romani*, not of a capricious force, but one steadfastly guarding the interests of the Roman people; it is significant too that the phrase is often associated with *virtus Romana*.[19] In the Preface the origin and power of Rome are attributed to the fates and to the help of the gods; and the claim is also made that no other state has surpassed Rome in moral qualities, especially in frugality

---

[15] Ogilvie, *A Commentary on Livy, Books I–5* (Oxford, 1965), 24. For a different view of the relation to Sallust see T.J. Luce, *Livy: The Composition of his History* (Princeton, 1977), 250–51. On Sallust's political moralism see D.C. Earl, *The Political Thought of Sallust* (Cambridge, 1961, repr. Amsterdam, 1966), 41–59.

[16] Cf. P.G. Walsh, *Livy: His Historical Aims and Methods* (Cambridge, 1961, repr. 1976), 49: '. . . the importance of *religio* is so frequently emphasized that it is impossible to believe that Livy is an utter sceptic.'

[17] Walsh, op. cit. 50.

[18] Iiro Kajanto, 'Die Götter und das Fatum bei Livius' in *Wege zu Livius* ed. E. Burck (Wege der Forschung, 132; Darmstadt, 1967), 481, records 493 instances of *fortuna* (not counting Fortuna as a goddess) as opposed to 40 of *fatum*. He notes that not always is *fortuna* used of a cause beyond human control.

[19] Ibid. 481–2. Cf. Walsh, op. cit. 53–59. According to Gerhard Stübler, *Die Religiosität des Livius* (Stuttgart, 1941, repr. Amsterdam), 109, Fortuna stands with *virtus* and the gods as the most important factor in the history.

and moderate living. The extreme partiality of such a claim is plain enough. Walsh[20] notes still more blatant examples:

> ... if a Roman like Tarquinius Superbus achieves his ends by guile and deceit, this is a non-Roman trait. (5.28.3; 1.53.4) Most incredible of all are Livy's words after condemning the execution of the Alban leader Mettius, who was tied to waggons which were driven in opposite directions: 'This was the first and last punishment exacted by the Romans which showed insufficient regard for human law; in other cases we can boast that no other race has been more gentle in its punishments.' (1.28.11.)

Walsh adds that 'in every book such undisguised chauvinism can be exemplified;' and Montesquieu remarked on the falsity of the claim to *clementia* in view of very cruel decrees which are present in the Roman civil code of the Twelve Tables.[21]

Yet the concern with moral qualities, particularly those deemed to be productive of greatness, is a saving grace. The qualities most often lauded are *pietas, fides, concordia, disciplina, prudentia, ratio, clementia, pudicitia, virtus, dignitas, gravitas, frugalitas*. After listing and interpreting them, Walsh[22] maintains that 'these abstract qualities, clothed in the accidental garb of the leaders of each generation, are the true and enduring heroes of the *Ab Urbe Condita*.' This does not mean, of course, that unfavourable qualities are ignored. These include pride, rashness, and savagery—*superbia, temeritas, ferocia*—and such demerits are often attached to particular individuals. Flaminius was thus morally responsible for the disaster at Lake Trasimene against Hannibal, just as the heroic Camillus is in contrast invested with every religious acclaim.

At the core of Livy's account of Rome's conquest of Italy is the principle of ethical causation: the gods have sanctioned the whole process because the Romans have so plainly excelled in moral qualities. 'Fair treatment of allies and military discipline' are the two factors described by one scholar[23] as predominant in his account. The second factor is clearly convincing. It is also true that Livy often emphasizes the first, using the words *fides* or *clementia*. He tells us that the Romans were always ready to stand by the treaties and promises which they had solemnly given; he also tells us that

---

[20] Op. cit. 65.
[21] Sheila M. Mason, 'Livy and Montesquieu' in *Livy* ed. T.A. Dorey (London, 1971), 145. Montesquieu was thinking especially, it seems, of the treatment of children and slaves.
[22] Op. cit. 66.
[23] James Lipovsky, *A Historiographical Study of Livy*, Books VI-X (New York, 1981), 170.

they were often ready to treat defeated enemies with generosity. It is admitted that when the Romans themselves are sometimes defeated, the urge for vengeance is paramount. The pattern of expansion in Campania is scantily plotted, and the successes there and against the Samnites point to the moral superiority of the Roman stand. We are asked to believe that this is the basic reason why Rome, and not Samnium, became the sovereign power in Italy. Politically the wise deployment after conquest of a system of alliances, and of an extension of citizenship, was undoubtedly an important element in the success of expansionism.[24]

Whenever war was declared, the Romans enacted an elaborate ceremony in which the priestly heralds, the *fetiales*, took part. It was a ceremony of much interest to Livy,[25] and one which confirmed the constant conviction that they had divine support in the war. Brunt[26] has thus defined their position:

> We must not forget that for the Romans a just war was one in which the gods were on their side. The very formalism of Roman religion made it possible for them to believe that this divine favour could be secured, provided only that all the necessary ceremonies and procedures had been duly followed.

In the phase of achieving world dominion Cicero's argument was that Rome had succeeded in this mainly because she was intent on defending her allies. Livy and Sallust had similar views. Self-defence, according to this doctrine, included the right to repel any disadvantage that might threaten; and this might well imply the mere existence of a powerful neighbour. Divine sanction in such a context was easily and superficially secured. According to Lactantius (*De div. inst.* 6.9.4) Rome took possession of the world by 'inflicting injuries under cover of law and unceasingly coveting and carrying off what belonged to others'. Brunt[27] aptly remarks that 'Roman reactions to the possibility of a threat resembled those of a nervous tiger, disturbed when feeding.'

Although pessimistic about his own age and its moral decline, Livy was ideologically much influenced by the religious revival which Augustus furthered. It is significant that he claims to have kindled the interest of Augustus himself in details of his historical theme (4.20.7), describing him as 'the founder or restorer of all the

---

[24] Cf. Cicero, *Pro Balbo*, 31 and P.A. Brunt, 'Laus imperii' in *Imperialism in the Ancient World* ed. P.D.A. Garnsey and C.R. Whittaker (Cambridge, 1978), 165.
[25] Cf. John Briscoe, *A Commentary on Livy Books XXXI-XXXIII* (Oxford, 1973), 77.
[26] Op. cit. 178.
[27] Ibid. 177.

temples' (*templorum omnium conditorem aut restitutorem*).[28] But he maintained a certain independence of mind.[29] Much closer to Augustus was the poet Vergil, whose *Aeneid* was virtually the result of a commission given to the poet by the Emperor.

3. *Vergil: Commissioned but Inspired*

In the third book of the *Georgics* the poet avows that in a future work he will tackle an exalted theme and that Augustus himself will be the central figure, worshipped in his shrine:

> in medio mihi Caesar erit, templumque tenebit.
> (*Georg.* 3.16.)

It is relevant to note that Vergil read the whole of the *Georgics* aloud to the Emperor over a period of four days at the Campanian town of Atella.[30] These details from Donatus and Servius are overshadowed by the poet's own startling prediction that Octavian will become a god and his plan to place him at the centre of his epic. Clearly the association with Augustus was very close, and it was heightened by the Emperor's constant concern about the progress of the epic. Maecenas was also, of course, an important figure in this literary converse. There was a material side to the intimacy, but it would be wrong to make that a primary motive in the minds of the several poets of the circle. We have been well reminded[31] that 'Maecenas did not just employ Horace as a poet but made him an *amicus*.' The same applies to Vergil, who refers to Maecenas as the patron who ordered the difficult task of writing the *Georgics* (3.41, *tua, Maecenas, haud mollia iussa*).

To Vergil, however, Augustus was the more significant and insistent influence, especially in relation to the *Aeneid*. It is a moot

---

[28] The reading *aut* is preferable to *ac* since no one could be both a founder and a restorer of a temple. Even with *aut* the claim of *omnium* is plainly excessive; cf. Ogilvie, *Commentary I-V*, 565: 'Augustus founded some and restored others;' and Walsh, op. cit. 14–15. For Livy's admiration of the religious reforms under Augustus see G. Stübler, *Die Religiosität des Livius*, 87–89 and 206–7 (Augustus as God and son of God, a *Romulus redivivus*).

[29] Walsh, op. cit. 18, although he quotes (p. 11) Syme's view that Livy's history was 'fostered by the government' and that 'the Emperor and his historian understood each other.' According to Liebeschuetz, *Continuity and Change* etc., 61, 'Livy was much less committed to the *princeps* than Vergil ...'

[30] Schanz-Hosius, *Geschichte der römischen Lit.* I. i⁴ (1935), 49. Cf. W.F. Jackson Knight, *Roman Virgil* (London, 1944), 64. K. Büchner, 'P. Vergilius Maro' (*RE* 1961), 37, rejects doubts which have been raised concerning the tradition.

[31] I.M. Le M. DuQuesnay in *Poetry and Politics in the Age of Augustus* ed. T. Woodman and D. West (Cambridge, 1984), 24.

point, admittedly, whether the ambitious work envisaged in the *Georgics* turned out to be the *Aeneid*. Augustus cannot be said to be exactly *in medio* as far as this poem is concerned, although he belongs very intimately to the central theme of Rome's God-given imperial destiny. The striking tribute of deification accorded to him in the third book of the *Georgics* has suggested the idea that this poem is itself the realized ambition.[32] But the tense is future and a venture into epic is suggested, although the eventual result concerned a different theme.

Loftily poetic and intensely religious, Vergil's *Aeneid* is in some ways the highest expression of a faith which binds Rome's destiny to the will and sanction of the gods. In the view of Simone Weil this high spiritual level sinks to the lowest abyss through the nature of the poet's relation to Augustus. To her the essence of the relation was mercenary:[33]

> Virgil had far too deep a sense of the proprieties to publicly place on record a commercial transaction of this nature. Nevertheless, this was, in fact, the transaction which took place between him and Augustus. His verse is often delightful to read; but in spite of that, for him and others like him, another name should be found than that of poet.

If the disparagement seems 'almost wilful',[34] it is worth considering further the nature of the relation. If Augustus was to Vergil more of an *amicus* than of a *patronus*, we may ask, to start with, what Vergil gained from the friendship. From the literary point of view he probably gained more, in the intellectual sense, from other friendships, particularly from converse with Gallus, Pollio, and Varius. Material gains, however, point to Augustus and Maecenas. When lands in the region of Cremona and Mantua were conferred on veterans of the Civil War in 42 B.C., Vergil lost the family estate in the process, and probably it was his appeal to Octavian that secured its restoration. While Meliboeus still laments his loss in Eclogue I, Tityrus avows (*Ecl.* I. 6) that it 'was a god that gave us this peace' (*deus nobis haec otia fecit*). Perhaps Tityrus stands for Vergil[35] and his newly elevated god is Octavian. Yet in *Georgics* 2.198 Mantua seems still to be lost. If the internal evidence is

---

[32] Friedrich Klingner, *Virgil: Bucolica, Georgica, Aeneis* (Zürich, 1967), 278, rejected afterwards in favour of a future epic poem in the manner of Ennius.
[33] Simone Weil (tr. A.F. Wills), *The Need for Roots* (London, 1952), 223.
[34] T.S. Eliot in his Preface to the same work, p. ix.
[35] Strongly denied by H.J. Rose, *The Eclogues of Vergil* (Berkeley, 1942), 49, but his arguments are mainly geographical. There are admittedly ambiguities in many of the personal allusions; cf. Eleanor W. Leach, *Vergil's Eclogues* (Ithaca, 1974),

therefore debatable, the *Lives* of Vergil put his debt beyond doubt.

Whatever troubles arose at this stage, the poet's economic future was assured, for by the time of the *Georgics* he had become 'a member of Maecenas' circle and practically a court poet'.[36] Each book of the Georgics is in fact dedicated to Maecenas and the whole work is a plea for agricultural revival—quite probably the suggestion of a munificent patron. R.D. Williams[37] tells us, in spite of this, that 'the poem should not be thought of as a commissioned work', while admitting that 'it chimed in well with the political needs of the time, to get the Romans back to the land that had been so neglected . . .' It is hard to deny the claim that 'it springs essentially and personally from Virgil's own intense love for the beauty of nature'. What has happened here, as in the *Aeneid*, is that the commissioned laureate is also an inspired bard. It was not the first or the last time in the history of literature that an external award accompanied a work of genius. That was true of several prize-winners in the dramatic festivals of Athens; it is true occasionally of the bardic victors in the National Eisteddfod of Wales, and more often, perhaps, of the winners of the Nobel Prize for Literature.

After his success with the *Eclogues* Vergil's path was smooth. Octavian's court in Rome was able, through Maecenas, to make liberal offers to the most promising literati, and Vergil was given a villa in the gardens of Maecenas on the Esquiline, probably with the intention of attracting him permanently to Rome;[38] but the poet preferred to stay near Naples, coming but rarely to Rome.[39] Henceforward the link with Augustus remained close, and the considerable fortune left by Vergil was divided among relatives and friends, of whom Augustus himself was bequeathed a quarter.[40] It was Augustus, in particular, who saw to it that the epic was published although Vergil had wished to see it burned.

If Vergil owed a great deal to Augustus, it could be argued that he repaid the debt tenfold by making him, in the *Aeneid*, the main instrument of the divine favour bestowed on Rome. Since the epic tells of the origins of Rome, Aeneas was the chosen hero; and yet he

---

273: 'Tityrus seems unable to identify his *deus*.' Vergil's friends, Pollio, Gallus, and Varus acted as commissioners in this situation, and an appeal to Octavian may credibly have resulted in reinstatement or compensation; see H.H. Huxley, *Virgil, Georgics I and II* (London, 1963, repr. Bristol, 1979), 4.

[36] Cyril Bailey, *Religion in Virgil* (Oxford, 1935, repr. New York, 1969), 192.
[37] In *Virgil: His Poetry throughout the Ages* (with T.S. Pattie; London, 1982) 15.
[38] Tenney Frank, *Vergil: A Biography* (Oxford, 1922), 141.
[39] Karl Büchner, *P. Vergilius Maro* (RE 1961, Sonderdruck), 37.
[40] Büchner, op. cit. 40.

is meant to 'pre-figure Augustus'.[41] In Vergil's Sixth Book a panorama of Rome's history is displayed, culminating in the glorious figure of Augustus, the man of divine origin who will restore the golden ages once enjoyed in Latium under the reign of the god Saturn:

> Augustus Caesar, divi genus, aurea condet
> saecula qui rursus Latio regnata per arva
> Saturno quondam, . . .
>
> (*Aeneid*, 6.792–4.)

It is added, at the same time, that this benign ruler will extend his empire to include the Garamantians (from mid-Africa) and the Indians. Vergil's constant vision combines extended imperial sway with the idea of benevolent rule which aims at the peaceful coexistence of conquerors and conquered. The theme of peace is given special prominence in the celebrated lines on the mission of Rome in the Sixth Book of the *Aeneid*: it will be Rome's task 'to establish the rule of peace, to spare those who have been subdued and wear down in war the arrogant':

> pacisque imponere morem,
> parcere subiectis et debellare superbos.
>
> (*Aeneid*, 6.752–3.)

Brunt[42] has pertinent remarks to offer:

> When Virgil defined Rome's mission as *parcere subiectis et debellare superbos* he was in effect dividing mankind into two categories, those too insolent to accept her god-given dominion, and those who submitted to it. The latter were to be spared; what of the former? Germanicus was to set up a monument boasting that he had 'warred down' the Germans, after exterminating one community with no distinction of age or sex (Tac. *Ann.* 2.21 ff.).

Vergil must have been aware of similarly brutal events, but we have to credit him with the sincere belief that the establishment of peace after the Civil Wars would make Augustus a true founder of a happier world. The ideal was vividly portrayed in the Ara Pacis Augustae, even if we bear in mind that 'the word "pax" can seldom be divorced from notions of conquest, or at least compulsion.'[43] We must assume too that, on a personal level, the poet had been impelled by his friendship with Augustus and by the strain of

---

[41] G. Karl Galinsky, *Aeneas, Sicily, and Rome* (Princeton, 1969), 53, showing how the *pietas* assigned to both is reflected in art.
[42] In *Imperialism in the Ancient World*, ed. Garnsey and Whittaker, 184.
[43] Ronald Syme, *The Roman Revolution* (Oxford, 1939, repr. 1967), 304.

idealism which tinged his very pragmatic outlook.[44] Details of the friendship are not sufficient to explain his appeal to Vergil.

4. *Rome's Atonement for Sin*

Vergil never shows an urge to glorify in the carnage of successful warfare. His narrative of the conquests achieved by Aeneas is shadowed by a constant sense of his being a reluctant conqueror. His successes follow the path ordained by the gods, but even in the final episode of the vanquishing of Turnus it is a very muted victory—until Aeneas is spurred on by recalling the killing of Pallas, so that the death of Turnus becomes an act of retribution. If the poet accepts such acts as a necessity and regards Rome's triumphal career in war as a just gift of providence, yet he is intensely disturbed by the experiences of Civil War. To him this is the type of war that stands condemned, because it is a kind of fratricide. In a preview of these events Aeneas is urged by Anchises to give a lead in throwing away weapons of war (*proice tela manu, sanguis meus! Aen.* 6.835) In the Fourth Eclogue, although it was written some ten years before the Battle of Actium, Vergil voices hopes for an era of general calm and happiness. It is in this poem that he shows concern not only with the advent of peace (for the child that is to be born will rule a world 'made peaceful by his father's virtues'), but also by the end of age-long fears and the removal of all 'traces of our past wickedness' (*sceleris vestigia nostri*).[45] The coming Golden Age will restore primitive innocence.

It is possible that Vergil's ideas about man's early sinfulness point to Jewish-Alexandrian influences via the Sibylline Oracles. In the context, however, of the Augustan revival of religion it is Horace who provides the clearest compendium of contemporary theology. If the Civil Wars which followed Julius Caesar's death were offensive to the gods, a religious explanation of the offence and its punishment was forthcoming. In the sixth of the 'Roman odes' Horace begins with a prophecy that is at once matter-of-fact and openly theological: 'thou shalt continue to expiate, O Roman, the

---

[44] Syme, op. cit. 479, puts it more strongly: 'But was Augustus the ideal Princeps? That might be doubted. The person and habits of Augustus were no less detestable than his rule.' For the more favourable tradition see E. Gabba in *Caesar Augustus: Seven Aspects* ed. F. Millar and E. Segal (Oxford, 1984), 61–85.
[45] *Ecl.* 4.13. Occasionally *scelus* can mean misfortune, but H.J. Rose, *The Eclogues of Vergil*, 163, unwisely remarks on 'the traces still left of wickedness, or ill luck, for *scelus* can mean both . . .' The moral emphasis is borne out by the later phrase *priscae vestigia fraudis* (line 31).

sins of thy fathers, though innocent thyself, until thou dost restore the tottering temples and shrines of the gods and their statues which are foul wih black smoke':

> Delicta maiorum immeritus lues,
> Romane, donec templa refeceris
>   aedisque labentis deorum et
>   foeda nigro simulacra fumo.
>
> (Horace, *Odes*, 3.6.1–4.)

The following line presents the belief that underlies the prophecy: 'it is through conducting thyself as one subservient to the gods that thou rulest':

> dis te minorem quod geris, imperas.

The gods have given a host of evils to sorrowing Hesperia because they have been neglected. Hitherto, then, the emphasis is entirely on the lack of observance of religion's external demands, its call for the upkeep of temples and statues and the implied performance of related rites. Clearly a campaign of restoration and rededication was needed, and this was precisely what Augustus organized. Elsewhere (*Odes*, 1.2.29–30) Horace asks who shall be given the task of atoning for the guilt (*scelus expiandi*) involved in the falling empire: Jupiter, he suggests, will choose Apollo or Venus or Hermes. The same basic assumption again appears: Rome's *imperium* was divinely ordained, but the gods could withdraw it if they were not duly respected.[46]

If the suggestion arises of a bargain which is almost commercial in its superficiality, it should not be forgotten that the ode beginning 'Delicta maiorum' proceeds to lament the decline in morality. The poet's times are said to be 'fertile in sin' (*fecunda culpae saecula*); and examples are found in the luxury and uninhibited adulteries of a young wife, a life-style contrasted with the austere simplicity of the early Sabine mode. Whereas each cameo is a telling one in the quick etching of the Horatian master-hand, the very directness of the moral message is much at variance with the poet's usual manner. Here we are conscious that he is delivering a 'grand message to the nation'[47] and inevitably the question arises as to whether the poet has been able to practise what he preaches. More importantly, from the artistic point of view, is there an ethical consonance in the *Odes* generally with the intensity of this message?

---

[46] Cf. Liebeschuetz, *Continuity and Change etc.*, 56.
[47] F. Solmsen in *AJPh.* 68 (1947), 340. Cf. Ed. Fraenkel, *Horace* (Oxford, 1957), 262.

Solmsen[48] has rightly noted that Horace is a fairly consistent advocate of moderation. Yet the celibate poet, who delights in his affairs with women and boys,[49] engagingly described himself to Tibullus as 'a pig from the sty of Epicurus' (*Epicuri de grege porcum*, *Ep.* 1.4.16); and if the saying is in the manner of a jest, it points to his basic belief, which is one of 'full adherence to the Epicurean creed'[50] and which was only momentarily upset by the 'conversion' of *Odes* 1.34 with its reflection on Jupiter's thunder in a clear sky.[51] In the Fourth Book of the *Odes* Horace returned to the 'grand message' of the Roman Odes, at least in the Carmen Saeculare; but he presents too a number of amatory and playful pieces. As an apostle of the Revival of Religion espoused by Augustus he cannot compare with Vergil.

If the gods who have been offended by the neglect of religion now call for an act of expiation, as Horace termed it, the act itself is attributed to the lead given by Augustus. Temples are rebuilt, ancient priesthoods are resuscitated, and religious observance in general restored to its pristine dignity. Expiation in most ancient religions was expressed in rites such as sacrifice, fasting, and penance. In the Rome of Augustus an attempt was made to link religion and morality through the law concerned with marriage and adultery. At first the programme for moral reform failed to gain acceptance; and even when it was legally enforced, its effectiveness remained doubtful, and the claimed link with religion was only vaguely expressed.[52] Roman religion may be said to have persisted for another three hundred years, but it would be wrong to attribute such an enduring result to the Augustan revival, although it did have a marked effect in a crucial phase of Rome's history.

That Rome's destiny was favoured by her gods was a belief, as we have seen, passionately proclaimed by both Vergil and Horace; and Livy was equally committed to the doctrine. When the time

---

[48] Op. cit. 340–41.

[49] Cf. D.R. Shackleton Bailey, *Profile of Horace* (London, 1982), 67–75, arguing against the view of Gordon Williams that male homosexuality in Rome was merely a 'poetic convention'.

[50] Fraenkel, *Horace*, 255, referring to the 'serious culmination' of *Ep.* 1.18. In *Horace* ed. C.D.N. Costa (London, 1973), 26, Margaret Hubbard writes of 'Horace's sympathy with the great poet (Lucretius) who had made an Epicurean of him', but does not substantiate the claim. When she goes on to aver that Lucretius had also 'made an Epicurean of Vergil', she is wildly misleading.

[51] 'Of course we must not take the recantation seriously', according to Nisbet and Hubbard, *A Commentary on Horace, Odes, Book I* (Oxford, 1970, rev. 1980), 377. It impresses one as serious enough, but reflects only a passing phase.

[52] See the admirable analysis by Liebeschuetz, *Continuity and Change etc.* 90–100, esp. 95.

came for Rome's imperial collapse, the relationship between religion and power was a question which was bound to arise and still arises in the multitude of modern discussions of the 'Decline and Fall'. Rome's official recognition of Christianity was an obvious factor for change.[53] But a plethora of other factors comes into the count. If the 'Fall' is dated to the sacking of Rome by Alaric in A.D. 410, manifest importance must be assigned to military, economic and administrative considerations.[54] The wider social and religious questions lead to easy confusions, such as that of 'morale' and 'morality'. They even raise the doubt as to whether the 'Fall' was not really a good thing. It caused chaos, but eventually liberated many nascent cultures, in which case the invocation of a moral nemesis, whether in pagan or Christian terms, is out of place.[55] At the same time a measure of continuity persisted in some of the new cultures, as was notably the case with the *Romanitas* inherited by the early Welsh Church and society.[56]

---

[53] Cf. A. Momigliano on the rise of Christianity as 'the most important of all social changes' in *The Conflict between Paganism and Christianity in the Fourth Century*, also edited by him (Oxford, 1963), 6. In some cases the Christian view led to a new Roman patriotism, as in the belief of Prudentius that a Christian Rome will be young and strong; cf. Joseph Vogt (tr. J. Sondheimer), *The Decline of Rome* (London, 1965), 191.

[54] The military collapse affected, of course, only the Western Empire.

[55] Cf. M.I. Finley, 'War and Empire', in *Ancient History: Evidence and Models* (London, 1985), 67–87, where economic motivations are stressed.

[56] A.W. Wade Evans, *Welsh Christian Origins* (Oxford, 1934), 23–36. Cf. Santo Mazzarino (tr. G. Holmes), *The End of the Ancient World* (Westport, Conn. 1966), 173–189 ('Decadence and Continuity').

CHAPTER FOUR

ASPECTS OF CHRISTIAN DOCTRINE

The imprint of eschatology is often so strong in the New Testament that it seems sometimes to obliterate the concern with divine judgement in this life. One feature of the eschatological emphasis is belief in the Last Judgement. In the doctrine eventually evolved by the Church this belief embraces several distinctions. The difference between Particular and General Judgement is sometimes stressed. According to an edict of Pope Benedict XII, 'Benedictus Deus' (1336), the approved doctrine was that on death the soul is at once admitted either to the Beatific Vision or to purgatory or to hell—an idea unlike that of early theologians such as Tertullian, who believed that between the day of death and the final resurrection of the body there intervened a state of sleep with partial happiness or suffering. Scriptural support for this idea of Particular Judgement was found in the parable of Dives and Lazarus (Luke 16:19 ff.) and in the words of Christ to the penitent thief; but it is not easy to reconcile it with the teaching about the General or Last Judgement, which concerns mankind in general after the resurrection of the dead, but includes the idea of judging the soul and body of each individual.[1]

1. *Second Advent and Judgement*

These doctrines are still further complicated in the New Testament by the continual claims that the Messiah, after his death, resurrection, and ascension, will return to the world and himself inaugurate the Last Judgement. In this phase the end of the world will supervene. Yet it will be an event not long delayed, as the sayings of both Jesus and Paul make clear:

> Truly, I say to you, this generation will not pass away before all these things take place.
>
> (Mark 13:30.)

---

[1] F.L. Cross and E.A. Livingstone, *Oxford Dictionary of the Christian Church* (2nd Ed., 1974), 564 and 1035. The word *purgatorium* first occurs at the end of the twelfth century: see Jacques Le Goff (tr. A. Goldhammer), *The Birth of Purgatory* (London, 1984), 3–4. He devotes a chapter to ancient antecedents of the idea ('Ancient Imaginings', pp. 17–51).

> For this we declare to you by the word of the Lord, that we who are alive, who are left until the coming of the Lord, shall not precede those who have fallen asleep.
> (1 Thess. 4:15.)

Long past is the day when sayings like that quoted first could be dismissed as interpolations derived from Jewish-Christian apocalyptic of the first century.[2] The apocalyptic which developed in Judaism was clearly a part of the doctrine received and accepted by Jesus, although it may be difficult in particular cases to exclude the possibility that the evangelists may have coloured his words with expressions used in the early Church.[3] The earlier Hebraic tradition is also drawn upon. We have had occasion (pp. 5 ff. above) to discuss the 'Woes' pronounced on cities and nations. The tradition is closely followed in the 'Woes' pronounced by Jesus on the Galilean towns of Chorazin, Bethsaida, and Capernaum. Because they have not repented, their fate will be worse than that of Sodom:

> But I tell you that it shall be more tolerable on the day of judgement for the land of Sodom than for you.
> (Matt. 11:24; cf. Luke 10:13–15.)

Capernaum has been exalted, but will be laid low—an echo, perhaps, of what Isaiah said about Babylon:

> And Babylon, the glory of kingdoms,
>   the splendour and pride of the Chaldeans,
> will be like Sodom and Gomorrah
>   when God overthrew them.
> (Isa. 13:19.)

We must remember that the book of Isaiah was a work which particularly appealed to Jesus. Yet there is a palpable difference in the punishment predicted in these 'Woes': the fall of Babylon will soon be realized historically because the Medes are being stirred by God to oppose the Babylonians (Isa. 13:17); but it is only *on the day of judgement*, that is, of the Last Judgement, that the little towns of Galilee will meet their fate. Not one of the towns named is actually charged in the Gospels with unbelief, unlike Nazareth; and so the possibility does arise again that the saying should not be ascribed to Jesus himself, but rather to the early Church. One might also be tempted to argue that at the end of the same discourse Jesus

---

[2] Cf. Albert Schweitzer, *Geschichte der Leben-Jesu-Forschung*, I (6th Ed., 1950, repr. Munich, 1966), 247.
[3] Cf. T.W. Manson, *The Sayings of Jesus* (London, 1949, repr. 1957), 241–2 on Matt. 24:30. In this chapter I have used the Revised Standard Version.

describes himself as *gentle and lowly in heart*, so that the terror-bringing judge now promises *rest for souls*, thus producing an unlikely contradiction which puts the first picture into question. Yet the contrasting facets appear elsewhere.

2. Rewards and Punishments

If the emphasis on judgement in the latter instance is in any case eschatological, the question arises whether the many dominical sayings concerned with rewards and punishments are not more easily related to a system of payment according to merit and demerit which operates in the present life. A saying which warns about ostentatious alms-giving seems to fit such a framework. The people who do this, we are told, aim at being given the praise of men; and they succeed in their aim: *they have their reward* (ἀπέχουσιν τὸν μισθὸν αὐτῶν, Matt. 6:2); in other words, they do get praised by men. In such contexts the word *misthos* is regularly used. It does not mean a reward in the sense of an unexpectedly bountiful gift, but rather the wage or salary to which one is fully entitled; and if one's action has been unworthy, the same word can indicate the punishment.

If the allusion is plainly to a reward here and now, the subsequent contrast relies on a different idea. The right way to give alms is in secret; *and your Father who sees in secret will reward you* (Matt. 6:4, where the verb means literally 'pay back' or 'recompense'); and in 6:18 the same term is used of God's recompense for prayer in secret. It is therefore hardly true to say that 'Jesus also refrains from any depiction of reward and punishment',[4] although he admittedly gives little detail about the reward. What is clear is that he defers the recompense to a future state. One may compare the consolation to the unjustly persecuted: *Rejoice and be glad, for your reward is great in heaven* (Matt. 5:11). The eschatological blessing of the Kingdom of Heaven may warrant succour for 'the condition of the Church face to face with Judaism', as W.D. Davies[5] argues; the vital thing, for our purpose, is that it is eschatological. Keeping this proviso in mind, we have to admit that the whole idea of reward and punishment has some prominence in the sayings of Jesus. Its operation on

---

[4] W.G. Kümmel (tr. J.E. Steely), *The Theology of the New Testament* (London, 1974), 56. The contrasting emphasis probably belongs to the series of antitheses in which the Pharisees are rebuked; cf. W.D. Davies, *The Setting of the Sermon on the Mount* (Cambridge, 1964), 291–2.

[5] Op. cit. 289.

the usual worldly level is given scant respect, for the servant who merely fulfils his duty deserves no special praise:

> So you also, when you have done all that is commanded you, say, 'We are unworthy servants; we have only done what was our duty.'
> (Luke 17:10.)

In the parable of the vineyard owner (Matt. 20:1–15) the latecomers are given the same wage as the early workers, with a blatant rebuttal of the normal time-counting rate for the job. The procedure seems unjust, but 'undoubtedly behind the employer is concealed God, who declares without any restraint that he has the right to give rewards in the measure corresponding to his goodness.'[6] The parable of the talents ends with the praise given by the master to the slaves who have wisely used the money entrusted to them:

> His master said to him, 'Well done, good and faithful servant; you have been faithful over a little, I will set you over much; enter into the joy of your master.
> (Matt. 25:21 and 23.)

Again, the reference is to God's reward in his heavenly Kingdom. If the underlying relationship envisaged is that between God as lord and man as his servant, yet 'herewith the servant is not paid and dismissed, but is received into the closest and most lasting relationship with the lord.'[7] According to an exhortation in Luke 14:12–14 one should give generous invitations not to the rich in the hope of repayment, but to the poor and the unfortunate; *and you will be blessed, because they cannot repay you. You will be repaid at the resurrection of the just.* Once again, the idea of earthly recompense is dismissed in favour of the divine reward beyond this world; and one has to concede that 'this is not necessarily different from saying that virtue is its own reward.'[8] In this way any contradiction between the teaching of the Gospels and Paul's emphasis on justification by grace alone is removed; so also is the ethical objection that expectation of rewards tends to corrupt the motive for human conduct and that a good act done with a view to the reward is not inherently good, since one should do good for the sake of the good itself, as G.E. Lessing and Immanuel Kant averred. The Christian doctrine

---

[6] Kümmel, op. cit. 57.
[7] Günther Bornkamm (tr. I. and F. McLuskey), *Jesus of Nazareth* (London, 1960), 138–9.
[8] C.F.D. Moule, *Essays in New Testament Interpretation* (Cambridge, 1982), 239, in a study of 'Punishment and Retribution: An Attempt to Delimit Their Scope in New Testament Thought'.

denotes that the divine reward, unlike the common idea of *misthos*, is freely promised and given, but is not merited and earned by man.[9]

There is a sharp renunciation, accordingly, of any belief in earthly reward or punishment, and this implies a break with contemporary Jewish thought.

3. *The Exegesis of Current Events*

Fully consonant with the rejection of any quest of recompense in this world is the incisive refusal to see God's judgement at work in recent or current events. This becomes especially clear in a passage in which Jesus discusses two tragic happenings in Jerusalem:

> There were some present at that very time who told him of the Galileans whose blood Pilate had mingled with their sacrifices.
> And he answered them, 'Do you think that these Galileans were worse sinners than all the other Galileans, because they suffered thus? I tell you, No; but unless you repent you will all likewise perish.
> Or those eighteen upon whom the tower in Siloam fell and killed them, do you think that they were worse offenders than all the others who dwelt in Jerusalem?
> I tell you, No; but unless you repent you will all likewise perish.'
> (Luke 13:1–5.)

The passage is followed by the parable of the fig-tree which the owner of a vineyard wishes to cut down after three unfruitful years, but for which the vinedresser appeals that it be given a year's grace; here the vineyard recalls 'the vineyard of the Lord' mentioned in Isaiah 5:1–7 as a symbol of the house of Israel which brings bitter disillusion and the threat of destruction. But Luke's account suggests that the possibility of repentance is still an alternative.

The fate of Israel is also very much the concern of the passage quoted, especially in the incident first mentioned. While the incident itself is not recorded by Josephus, similar outrages relating to Jewish resistance to Roman dominion are described by him as occurring under Pilate's rule. In his account of the later Jewish War of A.D. 66–70 he relates of the slaughter of worshippers in the courts of the Temple, including the killing of many by Jewish factions who were fighting in the inner court and who thus sprinkled the altar with libations of their own blood.[10] In Luke's

---

[9] Hans Conzelmann (tr. J. Bowden), *An Outline of the Theology of the New Testament* (London, 1969), 122–3.

[10] Josephus, *Bell. Iud.* 5.1.3; cf. G.W.H. Lampe, in Peake's Comm. (Walton-on-Thames, 1962, repr. 1981), ad loc.; G.B. Caird, (Harmondsworth, 1963, repr. 1974), ad loc.

reference one has to envisage a group of Galileans coming to the Temple in Jerusalem and being slain at Pilate's behest while offering sacrifices. The anti-Roman animus of the Galileans is well-known, and the Zealot movement may well have originated in the family of Judas the Galilean, probably to be identified with Judas the son of Ezekias.[11] It may be conceded that 'those pilgrims whose blood Pontius Pilate mingled with their sacrifices must have been Galilean revolutionaries.'[12] Of relevance here is the fact that two sons of Judas the Galilean were crucified for anti-Roman activities,[13] as well as the abundant evidence that Jesus of Nazareth, as a Galilean, was regarded by the Romans in the same light. He very probably realized that even a stance of pacific resistance to Rome would invite the punishment of crucifixion, and when he called his disciples to follow him in carrying the cross, the only possible meaning, if the saying is fully assigned to him, is that they were asked to face the threat of crucifixion similarly and for the same reason:

> If any man would come after me, let him deny himself and take up his cross and follow me.
> (Mark 8:34.)

> And he who does not take his cross and follow me is not worthy of me.
> (Matt. 11:38; cf. 16:24)

> And he said to all, 'If any man would come after me, let him deny himself and take up his cross daily and follow me.'
> (Luke 9:23; cf. 14:27.)

The Synoptic Gospels thus agree in recording the saying and they are given here in the likely chronological order. A part of the saying occurs also in Mark 10:21, but there it is spurious. If these words are not the genuine words of Jesus, they may be explained as a retrospective saying assigned to him by the early Church; in that case the expression 'take up the cross' will be demoted to the level of a metaphor. The one indubitable instance where a later standpoint is conveyed is the adverb which is added in Luke 9:23: *let him . . . take up his cross daily*. If the disciple is to take up his cross

---

[11] Geza Vermes, *Jesus the Jew* (London, 1973, repr. 1976), 46.
[12] Ibid. 47.
[13] Emil Schürer, rev. Vermes, Millar and Black, *The History of the Jewish People in the Age of Jesus Christ*, II (Edinburgh, 1979), 600. Judas the Galilean is mentioned by Gamaliel in Acts 5:37. E. Mary Smallwood, *The Jews under Roman Rule* (Leiden, 1976), 153 n. 40, argues against the identity of Judas the Galilean and Judas the son of Ezekias, partly on chronological grounds. These are not decisive; and the difference of emphasis seen in their claims is not of basic import; cf. H. Paul Kingdom in *NTS* 19 (1973), 80.

daily, then it cannot be the cross which will come once only as the result of national martyrdom. But since this accretion occurs nowhere else, it can be safely regarded as an editorial embellishment, allowing the rest of the saying to derive from the actual words of Jesus, whose outlook is thus attested as that of a Messiah who rejects the Zealot commitment to armed rebellion but who nevertheless champions the release of his people from the Roman yoke.[14]

Crucifixion by the Romans was a common occurrence in Palestine. According to Josephus[15] the Judaean revolt under Herod the Great in 4 B.C. was quelled by Varus, who searched for the instigators and crucified 2000 on this charge. The slaughter of the Galileans in the Temple by Pontius Pilate belongs to the same pattern of events; and it is noteworthy that Jesus, when accosted on this matter, refuses to endorse any suggestion that these Galileans have been thus punished for their sins.

The second event mentioned seems, at first sight, to imply a sheer accident—the fall of the 'tower in Siloam' on eighteen people who were instantly killed. But a similar question arises: were these people punished in this way for their sins? The incident appears to refer, not to a 'tower in Siloam', but to the Pool of Siloam to which water had been conducted to Jerusalem through a tunnel from the Gihon Spring (cf. 2 Kings 20:20 on Hezekiah; and John 9:1–12). It seems that Pilate had been active in a reconstruction of this aqueduct and that in the task he had used money reserved for the Temple (the *qorbân*). National sentiment was inevitably offended by such behaviour, and Josephus (*Bell. Iud.* 2.9.4) refers to a disturbance which gave vent to the resentment felt. In Luke's context the eighteen mentioned as having been killed were possibly workmen engaged in carrying out Pilate's building plan and were buried under falling masonry, the term 'tower in Siloam' being used perhaps of one of the towers in the city wall overlooking the Pool of Siloam. A popular view may well have been that these workmen deserved their fate since they were betraying the Jewish nation in serving Pilate's blasphemous scheme; God had punished them with

---

[14] J. Gwyn Griffiths, 'The Disciple's Cross', in *NTS* 16 (1970), 22–25. See also S.G.F. Brandon, ibid. 17 (1971), 453; and my further remarks, ibid. 19 (1973), 483–5. Cf. T.W. Manson, *The Sayings of Jesus*, 131 ('the voluntary acceptance of martyrdom at the hands of the Roman Empire'); Martin Hengel, *Die Zeloten* (Leiden, 1961), 266 n. 2 ('taking up the cross' as a Zealot formula); Brandon, *Jesus and the Zealots* (Manchester, 1967), 145 (the cross as a symbol of Zealot sacrifice).

[15] *Ant.* 17.10.10 (295) and *Bell. Iud.* 2. 5. 2 (75); cf. Smallwood, *The Jews under Roman Rule*, 113.

death. Another possibility is that those killed were Zealots who had attacked Pilate's aqueduct because its construction meant a sacrilegious use of the Temple fund;[16] and this view is the more likely since it brings the two incidents into line as examples of disaster in the wake of nationalist agitation. But Jesus refuses again to condemn the perpetrators. The suffering and death thus experienced, he urges, should not be explained as a punishment of sin; these people were not more sinful than others; and here one can detect a degree of sympathy with their motives—quite the opposite of Lampe's exegesis that 'there may be an implicit condemnation of nationalist political ambitions.' Still further off the mark is Brandon's[17] view that 'the political aspect of both incidents ... is not evident.' The subsequent parable of the fig-tree, as we have seen, continues the concern with Israel's fate.

Yet the final stress is a call to repentance: *unless you repent you will all likewise perish*. In these words the role of divine punishment in history is reinstated, even if the too easy application of the doctrine is rejected. In general terms Bultmann[18] aptly sums up the principle: 'those who suppose inordinate misfortune to be a punishment for particularly heinous sin are reminded that they themselves are no better than any one else.' The summation, however, should include the application to Israel; it is not merely individual sinners, but all Israel that is called to repentance, otherwise she will perish.[19] The thought of the coming downfall of Jerusalem is present and the call is for national repentance,[20] and an interpretation on the lines of purely personal conversion must be rejected.[21]

In the Gospel of John the possible connection between suffering and sin is acutely raised at the beginning of the account of how Jesus cured the affliction of a man who was born blind:

> As he passed by, he saw a man blind from his birth.
> And his disciples asked him, 'Rabbi, who sinned, this man or his parents, that he was born blind?'

---

[16] See G.W.H. Lampe in Peake's Comm. (1962, repr. 1981), 835. A rather speculative view of the two incidents was given by Robert Eisler, who postulated an occupation of the Temple area by Jesus and his followers and an assessment by him, in Luke 13:1-9, of the failure of the action, in words spoken on the last day before his arrest. Cf. Ernst Bammel in *Jesus and the Politics of His Day* ed. Bammel and Moule (Cambridge, 1984), 32.
[17] *Jesus and the Zealots*, 316 n. 6.
[18] *Primitive Christianity in its Contemporary Setting* (tr. R.H. Fuller, 1956, repr. Edinburgh, 1960), 86.
[19] Cf. Lampe, op. cit. 835.
[20] Cf. D.R. Griffiths, *The New Testament and the Roman State* (Swansea, 1970), 47.
[21] Such is the view of W.G. Kümmel, *The Theology of the New Testament*, 43; cf. the remarks of his as quoted by D.R. Griffiths, loc. cit.

Jesus answered, 'It was not that this man sinned, or his parents, but that the works of God might be made manifest in him.'
(John 9:1–3.)

It may be assumed that the account was taken by John from a collection of miracle-stories[22] about Jesus, and perhaps the question and answer also came from the collection. John himself, on the other hand, seems more interested, in his expansive commentary on the event, in the question of whether Jesus could be rightly regarded as a sinner, rather than in the possible sin of the man or his parents.[23] The question posed seems reminiscent of a type of theological problem, as C.K. Barrett suggests (ad loc.), which might have featured in Rabbinical discussions, and fairly learned ones at that, since the idea of sin in the womb or of sin in a previous existence,[24] is necessary to explain the first strange alternative. The second alternative, that the effects of sin may be transmitted from father to son, was of course well known to Hebraic thought, being first expressed in Exodus 20:5 (the Decalogue), where Yahweh is *a jealous god, visiting the iniquity of the fathers upon the children.* In the case of blindness the transmission is perfectly possible genetically; and in a wider context the healing of congenital ailments has great significance, for 'if a prophet were to inspire genuine hope of a new age in store for mankind, he must offer an assurance that this intolerable constraint on human dignity and freedom would, in God's own time, be removed.'[25]

4. *The Judgement on Jerusalem*

Although Jesus died in 29 A.D., several sayings attributed to him present him as the prophet of the doom of Jerusalem, which was destroyed by the Romans at the end of the Jewish War of 68–70 A.D. In Matthew 23:29–39 he denounces the scribes and Pharisees

---

[22] R.T. Fortna, *The Gospel of Signs* (Cambridge, 1970), 22–25 and 70–74.

[23] Fortna, op. cit. 71. Cf. Rudolf Schackenburg, *The Gospel according to John*, ii (London, 1980, German original 1971), 240. Bultmann (tr. Beasley-Murray, Oxford, 1971) in his Comm., 329, ascribes verses 2–3 to the source. C.H. Dodd, *The Interpretation of the Fourth Gospel* (Cambridge, 1953), 354, sees in Chapter 9 a simple Johannine unit of narrative and discourse. In his *Historical Tradition in the Fourth Gospel* (Cambridge, 1965), 181–8, Dodd draws parallels with the stories of healing in the Synoptic Gospels; and comparing the teaching about judgement in those Gospels, he asserts (pp. 187–8) that 'down to the end of verse 3 . . . there is nothing alien to the tradition as we know it from the Synoptics . . .'

[24] Cf. Wisdom 8:19–20. In Mark 2:3–12 the grant of forgiveness to the paralytic prior to the act of healing does suggest a link between disease and sin.

[25] A.E. Harvey, *Jesus and the Constraints of History* (London, 1982), 117; see also E.P. Sanders, *Jesus and Judaism* (London, 1985), 161.

as *sons of those who murdered the prophets* and tells them that the righteous blood which has been shed will come upon them. This will happen, he says, within a fairly short time, and Jerusalem itself will suffer desolation:

> Truly, I say to you, all this will come upon this generation. O Jerusalem, Jerusalem, killing the prophets and stoning those who are sent to you! How often would I have gathered your children together as a hen gathers her brood under her wings, and you would not! Behold, your house is forsaken and desolate. For I tell you, you will not see me again, until you say, 'Blessed is he who comes in the name of the Lord.'
> (Matt. 23:36–39; cf. Luke 13:34–35.)

Afterwards, when the disciples point out to him the buildings of the Temple, he tells them that *there will not be left here one stone upon another, that will not be thrown down* (Matt. 24:2; cf. Luke 21:6). Temple and city will be brought down, and in the case of the city the reason is made plain: she will suffer through God's judgement for her rejection and murder of the prophets. Mingled with the angry denunciation is a note of ardent solicitude: Jesus would have willed it otherwise, but his own attempts were also rejected. Such attempts, it may be assumed, were not thought of as taking place in Jerusalem itself; several of the parables (e.g. that of the vineyard, Matt. 21:33 ff.) adumbrate the theme of rejection. Indeed a vague allusion to the fall of Jerusalem might be seen in the parable cited, but that seems a hazardous procedure, although Jeremias, *The Parables of Jesus* (1963), 77, is prepared to do so, comparing the parable of the marriage feast and the words, *The king was angry, and he sent his troops and destroyed those murderers and burned their city* (Matt. 22:7).

The Lukan account of the crucifixion includes the address of Jesus to the women of Jerusalem, warning them of disasters to come:

> Daughters of Jerusalem, do not weep for me, but weep for yourselves and for your children. For behold, the days are coming when they will say, 'Blessed are the barren, and the wombs that never bore, and the breasts that never gave suck!' Then they will begin to say to the mountains, 'Fall on us'; and to the hills, 'Cover us.' For if they do this when the wood is green, what will happen when it is dry?'
> (Luke 23: 28–31.)

A major problem of exegesis is to decide whether such predictions are prophecies after the event, ascribed to Jesus through the medium and conviction of the early Church, as Bultmann maintains, or whether they may be genuine prophecies prompted by wise observation of how the tension between Rome and the Jews was tending. When Luke (11:49) assigns to the Wisdom of God the saying that *I will send them prophets and apostles, some of whom they will kill and persecute* . . ., the word *apostles* certainly bears the stamp of the early Church.

In a judicious survey of the evidence in the New Testament and outside it G.W.H. Lampe ('A.D. 70 in Christian reflection', in *Jesus and the Politics of His Day* ed. Bammel and Moule, 1984, 153–71)keeps a fairly open mind on the question. He says (p. 153) that the New Testament passages are 'somewhat enigmatic', adding that 'some are fairly certainly *vaticinia post eventum*, but most, and perhaps even all, could just be interpreted without total implausibility as genuine prophecies of a catastrophe which the troubled history of Judaea in the three or four decades preceding the outbreak of war would make it easy to foresee.' But he assigns to the period after 70 'very probably' (p. 161) some of the Gospel allusions to the fate of Jerusalem, including the predictions about the destruction of the Temple. A strong candidate for this category is undoubtedly the remark in Mark and Matthew concerning the 'abomination of desolation':

> But when you see the desolating sacrilege set up where it ought not to be (let the reader understand), then let those who are in Judea flee to the mountains.
>
> (Mark 13:14.)
>
> So when you see the desolating sacrilege spoken of by the prophet Daniel, standing in the holy place (let the reader understand), then let those who are in Judea flee to the mountains.
>
> (Matt. 24:15–16.)

The allusion in Daniel (11:31) is to the altar (and probably statue) of Zeus set up in the Temple by Antiochus Epiphanes. A parallel profanation might be seen, as Lampe shows, in the attempt made by Caligula in 39–40 to set up a statue of himself in the Temple. Luke (21:20) re-phrases the saying in this way: *But when you see Jerusalem surrounded by armies, then know that its desolation has come near.* All three evangelists may well be referring to an invasion of the Temple by Roman forces and to the act of desecration by Titus when his troops installed their standards there and offered sacrifices to them, as Josephus describes at the beginning of the Sixth Book of his *Jewish Wars*. In view of the several Old Testament echoes, Lampe goes on to suggest that the prophecy may yet be 'only a general warning'; but then he veers round again to say (p. 163) that it is really a prophecy after the event. In my view these Gospel sayings probably contain a nucleus of the Lord's words;

only the more precise allusions to events during the fall of Jerusalem should be regarded as accretions contributed by the faith of the early Church, and one example is plainly present in the act of desecration we have just discussed.

References to the fall of the city are not so numerous in the New Testament (cf. Moule, *The Birth of the New Testament*, 3rd Ed., 1981, 172 ff.), but it is doubtful whether their paucity should affect considerations of dating the literature itself. Our concern, at any rate, is mainly with the concept of divine judgement revealed. In the words of Jesus we find punishment inflicted on Jerusalem for its consistent and cruel rejection of God's prophets. None of the well-known prophets figures in the list (unless the prophet Zechariah is meant in Matt. 23:35), but the grand prophetic style of the early tradition leaves a sure imprint, as from the words of Micah (3:12), *Jerusalem shall become a heap of ruins*, although both priests and prophets are lashed in his condemnation. Contemporary religious leaders are impugned by Jesus, especially the *scribes and Pharisees*. If we compare the judgements pronounced by the prophets of the Assyrian era—Amos, Hosea, Micah, Isaiah and Joel—we find in them a wider spectrum of condemned vices, including infidelity, idolatry, social injustice, judicial bribery and corruption, sexual immorality, and religious obtuseness. Of course Jesus attacks some of these evils in other sayings. The pattern of political tensions is broadly similar in several eras: they come from major military threats, Israel being at the mercy of ruthless imperial powers— Assyria, Babylon, Rome. A feature of the whole tradition is the agonizing soul-searching which often led the prophets to find the main cause of Israel's distress in her own unfaithfulness to God, while ascribing to the oppressing power the role of a divinely ordained scourge. This latter concept is absent from the Gospel sayings. According to the ancient view a time of reckoning awaits the oppressors too: it will come with the 'Day of Yahweh' or with the triumph of the Messiah.

In later Christian thought the dominant idea is that the judgement inherent in the fall of Jerusalem is God's punishment of the Jews for the crucifixion. (See Lampe, op. cit. 166 ff.) Justin, the Gospel of Peter, Tertullian, Origen, Hippolytus, Eusebius, Hilary, Jerome, and Augustine all exemplify this idea. To them Christ's death was avenged not only in the fall of the city, but also in the subsequent sufferings of the Jews.

5. Judging within the Community

The rejection by Jesus (in John 9:1–3) of the interpretation which rests on divine punishment is another mark of his deviation from contemporary Jewish thought. In the teaching of Paul we find an elaborate system of rewards and punishments applied to both this world and the next, with a preference, on the whole, for the operation of divine judgement in this world. Indeed Paul is so minutely explicit on sins and their proper punishment that it surprises one to note that he apparently neglects to dwell on sins transmitted from father to son.[26] It can be inferred, however, from the rebukes administered by him that he would have accepted an explanation imputing sin to the parents. In 1 Cor. 5:1–5 he expresses the view that a man who has committed incest with his mother or step-mother will die in consequence of his sin.[27]

In the Dead Sea Scrolls, particularly in the Manual of Discipline (1QS), which concerns a sect established at Qumrân at the beginning, probably, of the first century A.D., a system of monitoring the purity of adherents is indicated, and the renunciation of the evil ways of the outside world is a basic tenet. There was clearly a dedication to a strict mode of life. Within man, it is taught, there are two spirits, that of truth and that of perversity; the man devoted to the pursuit of truth has implanted in his heart *fear for the judgements of God.*[28] At the same time a series of penalties is outlined, some of which involve temporary or permanent expulsion from the community. A list of vices to be eschewed is comparable to some which occur in the New Testament, particularly those in Mark 7:20–23 and Galatians 5:13–21.[29] The Church discipline practised in the Jerusalem Church is certainly reminiscent of the penalties detailed in the Qumrân Manual. According to Acts 5 Ananias and Sapphira were miraculously smitten dead for *lying to the Holy Spirit* by concealing part of their wealth; a similar falsifying act is marked as punishable in the Manual (6.25),[30] though much more mod-

---

[26] For an analysis of the transgressions condemned by Paul see E.P. Sanders, *Paul, the Law, and the Jewish People* (Philadelphia, 1983), 107–14.

[27] Cf. Sanders, op. cit. 108 and 120 n. 51, noting that Lev. 18:8 is the source of the prohibition.

[28] Theodor H. Gaster, *The Scriptures of the Dead Sea Sect* (London, 1957), 54. Cf. G. Vermes, *The Dead Sea Scrolls in English* (Harmondsworth, 1962), 76.

[29] Cf. W.D. Davies in *The Scrolls and the New Testament* ed. K. Stendahl (New York, 1957, repr. Westport, 1975), 169–71. Marcel Simon has put forward the suggestion that a list of vices noted by Apuleius provides an echo of the Christian catalogue: see my *Apuleius, The Isis-Book*, 359.

[30] Gaster, op. cit. 61; and Sherman E. Johnson in Stendahl (ed.), op. cit. 131–2.

erately. All such procedures, however, are not applications of divine judgement even if they are in accordance with Torah. The overwhelming stress is eschatological:

> He is to be zealous to carry out every ordinance punctiliously, against the Day of Requital.
> (Gaster, op. cit. 69.)

It is the Final Count that will settle all outstanding matters. A similar emphasis appears in the Zadokite or Damascus Document, which begins with a discussion of God's vengeance and providence (Gaster, p. 71); in the reckoning to come the punishment of the wicked will be condign, but those who have been faithful to the Torah will find that God will forgive their iniquities in accordance with the Covenant which he made with the people of Israel (p. 75). This doctrine of forgiveness is one which cuts across the theory of Klaus Koch[31] that the Old Testament does not know a system of retribution. He constantly emphasizes 'the concept of actions with built-in consequences', with a parallel set of constructs—the Sin-Disaster Construct and the Good Action—Blessings Construct; and in the first construct he sees it being depicted often without the active intervention of Yahweh (his p. 70). A judicial record of sins can, however, be dismissed through Yahweh's forgiveness:

> If thou, O Lord, shouldst mark iniquities,
>   Lord, who could stand?
> But there is forgiveness with thee,
>   that thou mayest be feared.
> (Psalms 130:3–4.)

At the end of John's Chapter 9, where the healing of the blind-from-birth is described, a process of present judgement is posited in the words *For judgement I came into this world* (9:39). The phrase *eis krima* can clearly be either active or passive—'to judge' or 'to be judged'; and the context shows that both meanings are intended, for the debate that has followed the healing shows Jesus himself being judged and also judging. Of this judgement it has been rightly said[32] that it is 'no dramatic cosmic event, but takes place in the response of men to the word of Jesus.' It is envisaged, then, as happening at the time and also in future spiritual encounters. It is true that in John 12:48 we find a transposition of the process to the Last Judgement: *the word that I have spoken will be his judge on the last*

---

[31] In *Theodicy in the Old Testament* ed. J.L. Crenshaw, 57–87. Of course he is aware of the doctrine (p. 73), but hardly succeeds in his argument that it leaves intact his theory about in-built consequences.

[32] R. Bultmann, *Theology of the New Testament*, ii, 38.

day; but Bultmann[33] properly marks the concluding phrase as a 'later ecclesiastical redaction'. Whether John really began with the idea of the Last Judgement and then transposed it to that of a judgement enacted in the present life, as Bultmann argues, is a moot point. A 'de-mythologizing of eschatology' would certainly be afoot if that were happening. What is clear is that the words attributed to Jesus in the whole discourse are couched in John's own style and reflect his intellectual approach.

6. *Judgement and the Sacraments*

The words of Jesus himself are far more accessible in the Synoptic Gospels, and some occur in the records both there and in the Pauline epistles which relate to the sacraments; and the theme of judgement is found in accounts of both baptism and eucharist.[34] In the case of baptism it is not immediately evident. Indeed Bultmann[35] is able to discuss baptism without a mention of judgement. He describes it (p. 133) as 'a sacramental bath which washes away the guilt of sin'. Repentance, confession, and forgiveness were the chief spiritual elements of the Baptism of John; also a threat of punishment to those who do not repent, although this is absent in the accounts of Mark and John. According to Moule[36] 'the Christian rite is, in the New Testament, essentially *dying* with Christ, and so rising again with him: even if it is 'the bath of the new birth', it is manifestly *death* first; and death, as clearly, represents, to biblical thinking, the ultimate verdict on sin.' He then adds, 'If Baptism is voluntary death, then it is also a pleading guilty, an acceptance of the sentence.' Here it is significant that in using the phrase 'voluntary death' he is not quoting the New Testament but (unconsciously perhaps) the words *voluntaria mors* used by Apuleius of the first rite of initiation into the Isis Mystery-cult.[37] Rebirth follows in the Mystery-cult and there is a clear parallel in Paul's interpretation of baptism:

> Do you not know that all of us who have been baptized into Christ Jesus were baptized into his death?

---

[33] Ibid. ii, 39.

[34] See esp. C.F.D. Moule, 'The Judgment Theme in the Sacraments' in *The Background of the New Testament and its Eschatology* ed. W.D. Davies and D. Daube (In honour of C.H. Dodd, Cambridge, 1954, repr. 1964), 464–81. See also J. Jeremias (tr. N. Perrin), *The Eucharistic Words of Jesus*, London, 1964.

[35] Op. cit. ii, 133–4.

[36] Op. cit. 465.

[37] Apuleius, *Metam.* 11.21; cf. my Comm. (1975), 94; 280; 296 ff.

> We were buried therefore with him by baptism into death, so that as Christ was raised from the dead by the glory of the Father, we too might walk in newness of life.
>
> (Rom. 6:3–4.)

In the Isiac cult too there is a sequence of confession, forgiveness, death, and rebirth. Judgement is conspicuous there in the priest's response to the sinner's confession; and the Osirian pattern constantly assumes the eventual justification of the believer before the god. Leaving aside the question of whether Paul's formulation is indebted to the Mystery-cults,[38] one observes that Paul, like Apuleius, does not obtrude the issue of final justification into his discussion of baptism. If Matthew (3:15) describes Christ's baptism as an endeavour *to fulfil all righteousness*, the expression hardly suffices to give a prominent role to judgement in the theology of Christian baptism; nor do the other suggestions collected by Moule,[39] leading him to maintain that 'baptism is essentially pleading guilty, accepting the verdict . . . so that by baptism an individual, or indeed the whole Church corporately, is (in a sense) brought past the great assize, past the final judgment of the last day, into the life of the new age . . .' He then quotes John 5:24: *he who hears my word and believes him who sent me, has eternal life; he does not come into judgment, but has passed from death to life*. No specific link with baptism is indicated here. It may readily be admitted that a judgement in the midst of life is implicit in the confession, repentance, and forgiveness which characterize the rite; and that final justification is also adumbrated in the act of faith thus witnessed. Yet these ideas are not explicitly displayed in the sacrament.

Moule is on firmer ground when he discusses the eucharist from the same point of view. He finds here (p. 469) an 'antecedent preparation of self-judgment and fresh acceptance of God's verdict on sin'; and he quotes Paul's warning:

> Whoever, therefore, eats the bread or drinks the cup of the Lord in an unworthy manner will be guilty of profaning the body and the blood of the Lord.

---

[38] Günter Wagner (tr. J.P. Smith), *Pauline Baptism and the Pagan Mysteries* (Edinburgh, 1967), resolutely rejects all claims of outside influences on Paul. For a more reasoned, although unconvincing rejection see W.D. Davies, *Paul and Rabbinic Judaism*, 89–94. A Hellenistic influence is accepted by G. Bornkamm, *Paul* (tr. Stalker, London, 1971), 190, and by H.J. Schoeps (tr. H. Knight), *Paul: the Theology of the Apostle in the light of Jewish Religious History* (London, 1961), 112–13. In *Paul and Paulinism* ed. M.D. Hooker and S.G. Wilson (In honour of C.K. Barrett, London, 1982), 245, John Painter sees an 'influence of the mysteries on Christianity at Corinth' and also a Gnostic element.
[39] Op. cit. 467.

> Let a man examine himself, and so eat of the bread and drink of the cup.
> For any one who eats and drinks without discerning the body eats and drinks judgement upon himself.
>
> (1 Cor. 11:27–29.)

The following verse suggests that this judgement, in the case of some Corinthian Christians, has resulted in death: *that is why many of you are weak and ill, and some have died.* It seems that the unworthy behaviour at the Table of the Lord refers to unseemly greed in approaching the food and drink; but failure to 'discern the body' means something much more profound: it is the participant's failure to realize his unity with Christ and with his fellow Christians, for to Paul the body of Christ symbolizes the unity of redeemed humanity in Christ.[40]

If by such a failure a person *eats and drinks judgement upon himself,* it may be questioned whether the reference is to self-condemnation at the moment or to damnation in the final prospect. There are other allusions[41] to self-judgement, as in Romans 14:22 (*happy is he who has no reason to judge himself for what he approves*), though not in eucharistic contexts.[42] A reference in 1 Corinthians 11:26 gives an eschatological touch to Paul's discourse: *for as often as you eat this bread and drink the cup, you proclaim the Lord's death until he comes*, where the last clause alludes to Christ's second coming, an event which is to inaugurate the Final Judgement. However, the emphasis on self-judgement appears to exclude the eschatological explanation since the final verdict is pre-eminently a divine decision; repentance and forgiveness will ensure a favourable verdict in that context: *there is therefore now no condemnation for those who are in Christ Jesus* (Rom. 8:1). Even so, God's punishment has already smitten by death some Corinthian Christians who have been guilty of misconduct in the Supper.

7. *Human and Divine Vengeance*

In the sense of self-judgement a man may condemn his own spiritual state. In other connections the theme of judgement and

---

[40] W.D. Davies, *Paul and Rabbinic Judaism*, 55–57, where it is argued that behind this symbolic use of *sôma* is the 'traditional Rabbinic doctrine of the unity of mankind in Adam'. Cf. Bornkamm, *Paul*, 192, on the *corpus mysticum ecclesiae*.

[41] For others see Moule, op. cit. 470.

[42] Cf. Moule's conclusions (pp. 480–81). On p. 472 his perspective is unduly narrowed: 'Emphatically, therefore, the Eucharist is an occasion of judgment . . .' As depicted by Paul, 1 Cor. 11:24, the principal purpose of the Eucharist is *remembrance (anamnêsis).*

consequent retribution is pursued by Paul on the wider level of a man's relationship to others; and consideration of the divine role sometimes leads to a sharp contrast. The best known expression of this contrast presents the view that God alone is entitled to take vengeance:

> Beloved, never avenge yourselves, but leave it to the wrath of God; for it is written, 'Vengeance is mine, I will repay, says the Lord.'
> No, 'if your enemy is hungry, feed him; if he is thirsty, give him drink; for by so doing you will heap burning coals upon his head.'
> Do not be overcome by evil, but overcome evil with good.
> (Rom. 12:19–21.)

What strikes one initially here is that a lower ethical standard is assigned to God than is allowed to men. The idea that God alone has the right of vengeance is explicit in the Old Testament: *vengeance is mine, and recompense* (Deut. 32:35); so is the corresponding prohibition of human vengeance (Lev. 19:18), though its application is limited to the sons of your own people.[43] The generous treatment of the enemy is also inculcated in the Old Testament, and the words used here by Paul practically reproduce Proverbs 25:21–22.[44] But it is only in Matthew 5:44–45 that the higher ethic is applied to God: *love your enemies ... so that you may be sons of your Father who is in heaven; for he makes his sun rise on the evil and on the good ...* It is of course possible that Paul had access to a collection of the words of Jesus; and W.D. Davies[45] has provided examples suggestive of this, as in Romans 12:17 (*Repay no one evil for evil*) which is compared with Matthew 5:39 ff. (*Do not resist one who is evil ...*) But Paul here, in a passage that is clearly eclectic in approach,[46] fails to echo Christ's application of the higher ethic of 'no vengeance' to God himself.

There are many allusions in the Pauline letters to the *wrath of God*, and Stephen H. Travis has shown in *Christ and the Judgment of*

---

[43] For the national emphasis cf. Deut. 32:36; Ps. 99:80; Isa. 34:8; 2 Thess. 1:6–8; Heb. 10:30–31.

[44] There, however, after *you will heap live coals on his head* comes *and Yahweh will give you your reward*. The former expression may derive from an Egyptian ritual of penitence: see S. Morenz in *Theol. Literaturzeitung* 78 (1953), 187–92 and W. McKane, *Proverbs: A New Approach* (London, 1970, repr. 1980), 591–2.

[45] *Paul and Rabbinic Judaism*, 138; cf. id. *Jewish and Pauline Studies* (Philadelphia, 1984), 113–14. H.J. Schoeps, *Paul: The Theology etc.*, 56, observes that 'Logia of Jesus are very seldom expressly cited;' cf. his quotation from Kümmel (p. 57): 'Paul does not feel himself to be a disciple of the historical Jesus, but a man commissioned by the risen Lord.' Matt. 5:44–45 does not rule out God's claim to punish those who reject him. Indeed several words of Jesus uphold this claim in relation to the Last Judgement. See below, Chapter 9 B (4) (pp. 275 ff.)

[46] On the eclectic character of the present locus see Bornkamm, *Paul*, 203.

God (Basingstoke, 1986), 31–44, that sometimes the application is to present judgement, but more often to an eschatological phase, as in the reference to *the day of wrath when God's righteous judgment will be revealed* (Rom. 2:5). He rightly rejects the idea that the *wrath of God* should be regarded as an impersonal phenomenon because there are several allusions to *the wrath* simply; obviously a reference to God can always be understood.

To associate wrath with judgement is not a normal human approach. The ideal judge, whether mortal or divine, is righteous, incorruptible, absolutely fair and scrupulous. Such an ideal, one might think, excludes the possibility that the judge can be moved to wrath, save perhaps in the final phase when the case against the accused person has been decisively established and the imposition of the penalty is announced and elaborated. The retributive anger of Yahweh in the Old Testament can be usually classified in the latter category. There are parallels, it seems, in Greece, where the Erinyes, 'Furies', are wrathful beings relentlessly exacting vengeance; in Egypt too the infliction of punishment is carried out by fierce assessors. In each of these cases, however, the angry forces are ancillary only; they implement the verdict of the supreme judge. Yahweh, on the other hand, is himself wrathful, as when he describes Assyria as the rod of his anger (Isa. 10:5; cf. above p. 6). In wider contexts of the Old Testament he is of course extolled for his mercy and for being *slow to anger* (Ps. 104:8); but the rulers of the earth are advised to fear his anger (Ps. 2:11–12), and many examples are given of the way in which his punishments have been inflicted upon sinful nations.[47] Paul's debt to this tradition, as well as to the later stress on eschatological judgement found in Judaism, is constantly clear. His verdicts on moral and religious infringements within the Church, especially at Corinth, are invested by him with divine authority, as when he says of the man guilty of incest, *I have already pronounced judgment in the name of the Lord Jesus on the man who has done such a thing* (1 Cor. 5:3–4); and he has stated previously (v. 2), *Let him who has done this be removed from among you.* Thus too in his treatment of unworthy partaking of the Lord's supper, he says that *when we are judged by the Lord, we are chastened* (1 Cor. 5:32). While Paul claims to be conveying the Lord's judgement, he also emphasizes his own personal role: *for though absent in body I am present in spirit* (1 Cor. 5:3). In this way the early Church, like the Qumrân community, was following ethical guid-

---

[47] See above Chapter 1, Sections 1–2; cf. Stephen H. Travis, *Christ and the Judgment of God* (1986), 6–13.

ance which claimed the highest sanction.[48] Paul's injunction concerning the incestuous man is certainly severe: his flesh is doomed to destruction, *that his spirit may be saved in the day of the Lord Jesus* (1 Cor. 5:5)—a possible hope in the Parousia. Another severe saying of his in another context is *If any one will not work, let him not eat* (2 Thess. 3:10). But Lampe[49] has achieved a measure of mitigation here: the meaning may be 'Let him be excluded from the common meal'. His general conspectus is also a kindly one when he says that 'the discipline of the first-century Church is pastoral rather than penal . . .'[50]

Whether the Pauline strictures merit the rubric of divine judgements seems doubtful. In the Gospels the emphasis on God's retributive wrath is a good deal less prominent. It occurs, as we have noted, in the woes pronounced by Jesus on the unrepentant cities; here the judgement is clearly the Last Judgement, although the comparison with Sodom might suggest a fate which is imminent within history. The many forceful references to Gehenna also point to punishment after death.

An outstanding act of judgement which Jesus carried out during his life and which he probably intended to apply immediately to the religious life of his people was his cleansing of the Temple in Jerusalem. It is reported in Mark 11:15–18; Matthew 21:12–16; Luke 19:45–48; and John 2:13–17. The scene is charged with righteous indignation. According to John 2:17, *His disciples remembered that it was written, 'Zeal for thy house will consume me'*, with an allusion to Psalms 69:9. The culminating action is the expulsion of the traders and money-changers, and it is followed by these words of denunciation:

> And he taught, and said to them, 'Is it not written, "My house shall be called a house of prayer for all the nations"? But you have made it a den of robbers.
>
> (Mark 11:17.)

The words *for all the nations* are omitted by the other evangelists, although they are present in one of the two original sources of the saying:

---

[48] Cf. J.S. Ruef, *Paul's First Letter to Corinth* (Harmondsworth, 1971), 40; Bornkamm, *Paul*, 183.

[49] 'Church Discipline and the Interpretation of the Epistles to the Corinthians', in *Christian History and Interpretation: Studies presented to John Knox*, ed. Farmer, Moule, and Niebuhr (Cambridge, 1967), 337–61, this on p. 342.

[50] Ibid. 341; cf. Travis, op. cit. 81.

> For my house shall be called a house of prayer
> for all peoples.
>
> (Isa. 56:7.)
>
> Has this house, which is called by my name,
> become a den of robbers in your eyes?
>
> (Jer. 7:11.)

Several scholars regard the quotation in Mark 11:17 as an addition which invalidates the authenticity of the whole verse.[51] The quotation is present also in the reports of Matthew and Luke, and it seems quite likely that these evangelists were here following Mark, but left out *for all the nations*, thus failing to preserve an important emphasis.[52] It is preferable to regard the verse as authentic. It renews the early prophetic vision which saw the Gentiles, in a blessed future, joining in the worship at Jerusalem; now the Court of the Gentiles in the Temple was being used only for trade and profit. On this latter point Jesus is delivering, to my mind, a condemnation of the whole system of sacrifices which necessitated the trading and money-changing. '*I desire mercy, not sacrifice*' was a quotation (from Hosea 6:6) used by him in Matthew 9:13 and 12:7.[53]

As the Son of Man Jesus is both Judge and Saviour,[54] the former role being for the most part embedded in eschatology. A rare instance of his being invited to judge in a real-life case is found in the account of the woman caught in adultery (John 8:2–11). The Mosaic law which demanded the death of such a woman was not regularly adhered to, it seems, in the time of Christ, but the Pharisees hoped to elicit a statement which would, in any case, prove embarrassing. This account does not occur in the early manuscripts of John, nor was John its likely author,[55] although he

---

[51] See E.P. Sanders, *Jesus and Judaism*, 66 ff. with notes 40 ff. This is also his own view.

[52] C.H. Dodd, *The Founder of Christianity* (1970), 152 and 187 n. 12. Cf. W.D. Davies, *The Gospel and the Land* (Berkeley, 1974), 350 f.

[53] Cf. E.P. Sanders, op. cit. 67 and Moule, *The Birth of the New Testament* (1981), 24–25. It is true that Matt. 5:23 assumes obedience to the sacrificial system. Sanders argues, unconvincingly, that the action in the Temple was a symbolic act prefiguring the destruction of the Temple, to be followed by a phase of restoration.

[54] Cf. Morna D. Hooker, *Jesus and the Servant* (London, 1959), 162: 'Ultimately, the Son of Man is a greater figure than the Messiah, for he is both Judge of all men, and Saviour of his people.'

[55] Travis, *Christ and the Judgment of God*, 157–63, shows that John often emphasizes judgement in the present time. Cf. above p. 117 f. on the man born blind and Travis, p. 160.

later (8:15) represents Jesus as saying, '*You judge according to the flesh, I judge no one*'—a dictum that agrees with his verdict here (8:11), '*Neither do I condemn you; go, and do not sin again.*' A genuine tradition is probably represented in this account.[56]

---

[56] C.H. Dodd, *The Founder of Christianity*, 57–58 and 180 n. 18; cf. John Marsh, *Saint John* (Harmondsworth, 1968, repr. 1974), 681–8.

CHAPTER FIVE

SOME INDIAN DOCTRINES

If we except the later parts of the Upanishads, some of which are as late as the fifteenth century A.D., the Vedic literature can be definitely assigned to the Ancient World, although none of its earliest manuscripts can claim such a date. A long oral tradition is assumed to precede the first developed forms. Unquestioned priority is ascribed to the 'Rigveda-Samhita', 'The Collection of the Rigveda'. The Hymns of the Rigveda, since they are pre-Buddhistic in content, must antedate 600 B.C. A little prior to that date, probably, occurred the formation of the Samhita text, but the oral creativity and transmission may well have entailed many centuries before that.[1]

1. *Varuna in the Rigveda*

The Hymns of the Rigveda comprise some 10,000 lines of verse, roughly equivalent in size to the Homeric epics. Mythology is the staple content. Much is detailed about the deeds of Indra, the warrior god, Varuna, the guardian of cosmic order and morality, Agni, the fire-god, and Soma, the god associated with a stimulating beverage (perhaps not intoxicating, however) used in sacrificial rites. Of these deities it is clearly Varuna that is most likely to be invoked in a context concerned with the moral control of human life. He is one of 'the chief upholders of the moral law'; if the gods are angry with the evil-doer, 'it is Varuna's wrath which is most closely connected with the conception of guilt and sin.'[2] It is therefore not surprising that to Varuna is addressed a request for forgiveness:

> Forgive us the sins of our fathers, forgive us what we ourselves have done.
>
> (Rigveda, 7.86.5.)[3]

---

[1] Jan Gonda, *Vedic Literature* (Wiesbaden, 1975), 20–22; James A. Santucci, *An Outline of Vedic Literature* (American Academy of Religion, Aids to the Study of Religion Series, 5; Missoula, Montana, 1976), 1 and (on the Upanishads), 49. Naturally it is rarely that evidence appears of the 'processes of creativity' on the part of the Vedic ritualists; see J. Gonda, *Prajāpati's Rise to Higher Rank* (Orientalia Rheno-Traiectina, 29; Leiden, 1986), 195.

[2] A.A. Macdonell, *The Vedic Mythology* (Strassburg, 1897, repr. Delhi, 1971), 18.

[3] Tr. K.F. Geldner, *Der Rig-Veda*, ii (Harvard, 1951), 257 (here tr. from his

If the god is the source of forgiveness, he offers the possibility of appearing sinless before him:

> We wish to appear sinless before Varuna, and may he also forgive the sinner; we follow uprightly the commands of Aditi.
> (Rigveda, 7.87.7.)[4]

At the same time it is implied that Varuna can punish sin, and this idea is clearly expressed in a hymn addressed to the god by an invalid who suffers from dropsy:

> Whatever, O Varuna, we men commit in sin against the divine race, if in unwisdom we have thwarted thy ordinance, for that offence, O God, harm us not.
> (Rigveda, 7.89.5.)[5]

Perhaps the 'harm' envisioned there is the infliction of disease. Certainly he is said to punish sinners severely by binding them in fetters; and yet it has been said that 'there is in fact no hymn to Varuna in which the prayer for forgiveness of guilt does not occur.'[6] There is also a positive side to his intervention in human life, for *he speeds the experienced man to wealth*,[7] a belief that evokes the prayer, *Let us have prosperity in possession, prosperity also in acquisition. Do ye protect us evermore with blessings*.[8] At the same time a hope of bliss in the hereafter can colour the worshipper's thought.[9]

The god Mitra is often associated with Varuna, and their association has tended to merge the distinctive qualities of Mitra into those of Varuna.[10] In the hymns addressed jointly to the two gods it is the character of Varuna that predominates. They are celestial gods whose eye is the sun. The hymns present them as 'barriers against falsehood, which they dispel, hate, and punish' and as deities who 'afflict with disease those who neglect their worship'.[11] It is true that this ethical element in the hymns, as indeed other various elements, is open to sceptical interpretations.[12] We are

---

German). Cf. Edward J. Thomas, *Vedic Hymns* (Wisdom of the East; London, 1923), 59.

[4] Tr. Geldner.
[5] Edward J. Thomas, op. cit. 58.
[6] A.A. Macdonell, *A Vedic Reader* (Oxford, 1917, repr. Madras, 1965), 135.
[7] Ibid. 140, with a tr. of 7.86.7.
[8] Ibid. 141 (= 7.86.8).
[9] Ibid. 135 ('The righteous hope to behold in the next world Varuna and Yama, the two kings who reign in bliss.')
[10] Arthur B. Keith, *The Religion and Philosophy of the Veda and Upanishads*, i (Harvard, 1925, repr. Westport, 1977), 96. On p. 98 he sees Mitra as a friendly god invoked in compacts.
[11] Macdonell, op. cit. 119. Cf. 7.61.5 (p. 122): *Avengers follow the falsehoods of men*.
[12] Cf. Richard Gombrich, *On Being Sanskritic* (Inaugural lecture, Oxford, 1978),

reminded by A.B. Keith[13] that the 'moral element in the Rigveda and the subsequent literature is of comparatively small extent, and the vast majority of the Vedic hymns are not concerned in the remotest degree with questions of morals.' With regard to Hymn 7.89, where the dropsical invalid appears to ascribe his disease to the god's punishment of sin, Keith (p. 246) makes the suggestion that the idea was initially of purely physical origin in that 'the disease of dropsy by its accumulation of fluid suggested the action of this god who is always connected with the waters;' but from this idea, he argues, it was an 'easy step' to evolve the view of the disease as a punishment for sin inflicted by the god. Keith also discusses critically the analysis of sin given in Hymn 7.86.6:[14]

> It was not my own intent, O Varuna, it was seduction; liquor, anger, dice, thoughtlessness; the elder is in the offence of the younger; not even sleep is the warder off of wrong.

Keith remarks (p. 246) that it is possible 'to exaggerate the moral character of this confession of sin'; he sees the poet taking a position 'with a calm which is not expressive of any deep movement of repentance or consciousness of sin'; and he notes the imputation of sin to an ancestor or the idea that it was committed in sleep—easy excuses, one might think. Yet he concedes that 'the attitude is clearly moral; the punishment is admitted to be just, repentance is expressed, and the god is asked to forgive.' In this hymn there is certainly a measure of agitated uncertainty about the nature of sin and the god's likely attitude to it:[15]

> When will I behold his mercy, my mind at rest? I meditate on my sin, O Varuna, desiring to see what it is. I turn to men of discernment, asking them, and the wise all say the same: 'Varuna is angered against thee.'

The awe and *Angst*, it is true, are mitigated by the hope of forgiveness. Yet the sense of sin is the first stage, and if in modern times Vivekānanda, the pupil of Ramakrishna, proclaimed in Europe and America 'the absolute divinity of man and the sinfulness of the

---

25: 'The Veda could remain authoritative because it was so obscure . . . that any doctrine could at least be said to be compatible with it.' Cf. p. 23: 'The Veda was of course the repository of all wisdom; acceptance of this tenet is a defining criterion of Hindu orthodoxy. But it existed to be venerated, not to be understood.'

[13] Op. cit. 249.

[14] Tr. Macdonell, op. cit. 139, who admits that 'the exact sense of three important words is, however, somewhat doubtful.'

[15] Tr. R.C. Zaehner, *Hinduism* (Oxford, 1962, repr. 1975), 32; cf. Edward J. Thomas, *Vedic Hymns*, 58.

Christian preoccupation with sin',[16] it was a far cry from the Vedic roots of Hinduism.

2. *Heaven, Hell, and Rebirth*

The examples we have cited of concern with sin and forgiveness are relevant to experience in this life. If disease, for instance, is regarded as the divine punishment of sin, it is obviously a part of present experience. This does not mean, however, that the concepts of reward and punishment are always restricted in this way. Heaven and hell are amply represented in the Vedas, and the general approach indicates a heaven for the good and a hell for the bad.[17] Yama, the god of the dead, rules in highest heaven in a domain of eternal light; it is also the abode of the Fathers, who are united with the sun, as in Hymn 10.14, addressed to Yama,[18] a god who is given two four-eyed dogs, perhaps with the idea of his investigating power. Yet the abode of the wicked is less clearly referred to, and it is not beyond doubt that it is a place of punishment.[19] It is only in the Atharva-Veda, a work of comparatively modern origin, that an abode of nether darkness is presented, where specific punishments are assigned according to deeds enacted.[20]

The concept of reward, on the other hand, is sometimes associated with that of sacrifice, and it is given an application which relates to the blessings of this life. In Hymn 10.90 of the Rigveda the sacrifice of Primal Man, the gigantic Purusha, is explained as the source of the whole of creation, a quarter of him accounting for living beings on the earth, and three quarters the immortal beings in heaven.[21] A direct beneficence is bestowed by Soma, identified with the stimulating nectar-like juice, for a hymn to Indra and Soma relates how Soma made the warrior-god Indra a victorious smiter of the dragon;[22] probably the hymn accompanied the offering of Soma, who is also greeted, with Indra, as the upholder of truth against falsehood, and one who protects the upright.[23] Offerings and

---

[16] Zaehner, op. cit. 168.
[17] Macdonell, *The Vedic Mythology*, 165–74; Louis Renou, *Vedic India* (London, 1957, repr. Delhi, 1971), 79–81.
[18] See Thomas, *Vedic Hymns*, 112–14.
[19] Macdonell, op. cit. 169.
[20] L. Renou, *Vedic India*, 80.
[21] Rigveda, 10.90.3–4; Zaehner, *Hindu Scriptures* (London, 1966), 9; Jan Gonda, *Die Religionen Indiens*, i (Stuttgart, 1960), 186–7.
[22] Rigveda, 4.28.1, tr. Geldner.
[23] Rigveda, 7. 104, in S. Radhakrishnan and Charles A. Moore, *A Source Book in Indian Philosophy* (Princeton, 1957), 28.

sacrifices in a more general sense connote various ideas, such as the removal of sin and the sharing of a communal meal—shared, that is, by gods and men. Another basic sense which is common to many religions is the hope of reciprocity: the gods in return will grant 'long life, an abundance of offspring, wealth, health, victory, and the other good things of this world'.[24] The Rigveda often records gifts offered to the priests and other holy men by rich donors, and these acts of liberality are praised by the poets in the *danastutis*, 'Praise of liberality'. Such effusions have been castigated by H. Oldenberg and B.K. Ghosh, the former describing them as poetry in the service of a class interest, and the latter as expressions of 'Brahmanical greed in its worst aspect'.[25] Jan Gonda tends to defend these eulogies, pointing to the honour and distinction thus conferred on the donor and explicitly comparing the relation between god and worshipper. This relation he sees as going beyond 'a mere matter of bartering with gods'; both god and worshipper give and receive, sharing in a process which maintains the world-order and perpetuates life; and thus the formula *do ut des* should be replaced by *do ut possis dare*, in the sense that man, in his offerings, adds to the god's power.[26] The carefully sustained argument does not delete, however, the bargain-hunting aspect (as indeed in other religions), and Gonda admits the increased emphasis on this in the post-Vedic period, as in the saying that *the objects given to brahmans become treasures in the next world* (p. 225).

The gifts, of course, are received in this world, and eventually a doctrine of rebirth in this world assumes an important role in the Indian tradition, resulting in the invalidation of the simple eschatology of the Rigveda. The Satapatha Brahmana (The Brahmana of the Hundred Ways; sometimes called 'the Hindu Talmud'), a priestly Vedic commentary, is cited[27] as providing the origins of this idea of rebirth. There a man is said to be born again in the present world as a reward for knowing a certain mystery, thus pointing to a doctrine of retribution and transmigration. If parts of the Rigveda find that the elements of an individual pass into units of the cosmos, such as the wind, the sun, the plants, and the waters, this can hardly be viewed as a comparable doctrine; rather is it one of cosmic dispersal. Admittedly it implies a continued life in other

---

[24] Zaehner, *Hinduism*, 44.
[25] See Jan Gonda, *Change and Continuity in Indian Religion* (Disputationes Rheno-Trajectinae, 9; The Hague, 1965), 211.
[26] Ibid. 214. He cites Rigveda, 10.36.
[27] Macdonell, *The Vedic Mythology*, 168.

forms,[28] but the teaching of the Satapatha Brahmana seems to be more directly relevant, as in passages which threaten that failure to perform certain ceremonies properly can lead to rebirth after death and to a state of being *ever again food for death*. This type of rebirth is therefore a bane and not a blessing, and is developed in classical Hinduism in the concept of the *samsāra* or cycle of existence with a never-ending sequence of rebirths.[29]

3. *Compensation and Retribution in Karma*

Intimately bound up with the idea of rebirth, which is also often termed transmigration, reincarnation, or metempsychosis, is the doctrine of *karma* or *karman*. The word means 'action' and its application in a wide causal sense is made possible by the belief in *rita*, the system of universal order. This system is in turn linked to the fundamentally important principle of *dharma*, which has both a cosmic and a personal relevance, *sanatana dharma* being the term used for the cosmic and eternal law governing the universe, while *dharma* is used, on the personal level, of the source of moral law. Social and family obligations enter prominently into this orbit.

When *karma* is used of a ritual act, the expected result points to the operation of cause and effect; a sacred act properly performed led to the favourable result for which it was intended; an improper performance, on the other hand, could lead to disaster. When *karma*, however, was used of an act in a general sense, the principle of cause and effect now led to a creed of moral retribution. In the social context of the four castes it referred to deeds which it was proper for members of the castes to enact; thus the second caste, that of the warrior, the *kshatriya*, was expected to follow the military virtues. But a wider interpretation ensued: *karma* was used of 'good' and 'bad' actions and of the results inexorably attached to them;[30] and these results determined the type of rebirth which was available to a person. A person whose past deeds have been good will find rebirth from the womb of a Brahman woman, but evil deeds will bring rebirth from the womb of an outcaste woman, or indeed from the womb of an animal. The teaching is expressly presented in the Chāndogya Upanishad (5.10.7):

---

[28] 'A new body in heaven' is at times indicated. See Wendy Doniger O'Flaherty, *The Rig Veda* (Penguin Classics, 1981, repr. 1984), 48.
[29] L. Renou, *Vedic India*, 79 and 89; Zaehner, *Hinduism*, 4.
[30] Zaehner, *Hinduism*, 59.

'Those whose conduct on earth has given pleasure, can hope to enter a pleasant womb, that is, the womb of a Brāhman, or a woman of the princely class, or a woman of the peasant class; but those whose conduct on earth has been foul can expect to enter a foul and stinking womb, that is, the womb of a bitch or a pig or an outcaste.'
(Zaehner, *Hindu Scriptures*, 101.)

Here is a text which derives from one of the earliest of the Upanishads; it dates perhaps from about 500 B.C.[31] Since the doctrine does not occur in the Rigveda, it could possibly be assumed that it was known to the pre-Aryan population of India. Indeed such an assumption has been confidently made by Trevor Ling,[32] following Gilbert Slater's work on *The Dravidian Element in Indian Culture*, where it is suggested that the idea arose from ignorance of the facts of physical reproduction. Ignorance of these facts is cited in relation to certain Australian aborigines even today, the belief being held that reproduction is caused by the entry of a spirit into the body of a young woman. It seems an apposite analogy, but the attribution of the idea to pre-Aryan India is purely speculative. It is true that a suggestion of yogic practices[33] occurs in the archaeological record of Mohenjo-daro, Harappā, and Chanu-daro, especially in the famous 'yogi' statuette from Mohenjo-daro.[34] But were yogic practices an essential feature of the approach to *karma*? This seems very doubtful, although the doctrine of release from the cycle of rebirths called for the attainment of liberation in a transcendental sphere, and this state was typically achieved 'by the practice of austerity and yoga: self-denial and self-discipline . . .'[35]

If its origins must therefore remain uncertain, it is clear that the teaching about *karma* became a rigid system which involved an almost mechanical and automatic determinism. It reminds one of Klaus Koch's theory about retribution in the Old Testament: it is not a vengeful urge ascribed to Yahweh, but a system in which

---

[31] Juan Mascaró, *The Upanishads* (Penguin Classics, 1965, repr. 1975), 7, where the oldest are dated, however, 'between 800 and 400 B.C.'; cf. his p. 45. His selection does not include this passage.

[32] *A History of Religion East and West* (London, 1968), 27–29.

[33] E.J.H. Mackay, *Further Excavations at Mohenjo-daro* (Delhi, 1938), i, 335 and ii, Pl. 87, No. 222 (a seal showing a figure in perhaps a yogi attitude with the heels pressed together).

[34] Sir John Marshall, *Mohenjo-daro and the Indus Civilization* (London, 1931), i, 44 and 356–7 (by Mackay) with iii, Pl. 98. The half-closed eyes concentrated on the tip of the nose suggest a yogi, particularly as they are set straight and are not Mongolian in type. It is probably a priestly figure; cf. L. Schulberg, *Indien: Reiche zwischen Indus und Ganges* (Reinbek, 1971, repr. 1976), 27.

[35] Ninian Smart, *The Religious Experience of Mankind* (New York, 1969, repr. Glasgow, 1971), 99.

every action has its in-built consequences. The dispiriting aspect of the *karma* teaching is clearly given vent in a statement made by the god Krishna to the hero Arjuna in the Bhagavad-Gita (18.60): he tells him that his *karma*, which is born of his own nature, has fettered him in such a way that even if, through delusion, he does not want to do something, he will have to do it in spite of himself:

> Bound art thou by thine own works (*karma*)
> which spring from thine own nature;
> [For] what, deluded, thou wouldst not do,
> That wilt thou do perforce.
> (Zaehner, *Hindu Scriptures*, 324.)

We are reminded of Ovid's words

> video meliora, proboque;
> deteriora sequor.
> (*Metam.* 7.20.)

and of Paul's admission *For I do not do what I want, but I do the very thing I hate* (Rom. 7:15). Paul claimed an escape from this condition through the guidance of the Spirit. An escape is proffered too in the various Indian traditions. In Jainism, where *karma* is a subtle material force and accordingly more difficult to counter, liberation is deemed possible only through knowledge, self-discipline, and asceticism.[36] *Moksha*, 'liberation', in the developed doctrine of Hinduism rests on the belief that the self, *ātman*, can be integrated with the Absolute (*Brahman*); and it is a belief that involves a pantheistic approach. Krishna expatiates on this to Arjuna:

> '[And] thus [all] flaws transcending,
> The man of Yoga, constant in integrating self,
> With ease attains the highest joy,
> Brahman's [saving] touch.
> With self by Yoga integrated, [now] he sees
> The self in all beings standing,
> All beings in the self:
> The same in everything he sees.'
> (Bhagavad-Gita, 6.28–29
> tr. Zaehner.)

If a blissful outcome is therefore envisaged as possible, as it is also in Buddhism, which finds liberation in Nirvana, yet both Jains and Buddhists see the world as a place of terror and pain.[37]

The burden of *karma* constitutes one of the most oppressive systems of moral and social retribution evolved by man. Its intellectual

---

[36] Ibid. 100–109.
[37] Zaehner, *Hinduism*, 67.

attraction arose partly from its ability to explain human inequalities and misfortunes. If a man was seen to suffer misfortune without an obvious cause, it could be attributed to an evil committed by him in a previous existence; similarly, if a man lived evilly without a resulting sequence of suffering, a future existence could be invoked to include the suffering imposed.[38] A search for a theological definition of the theory raises, however, a difficult question: can the operation of *karma* be properly regarded as an instance of divine assessment and control of human life?

There are two religious systems, Jainism and Buddhism, both of which give prominence to *karma*, that invite a firm negative reply since they both deny the existence of a creator-god. According to Jainist belief the cosmos is eternal and uncreated; it is of vast dimensions and includes a number of heavens and purgatories. The heavens are peopled by gods, but these do not include a sovereign creator; and the many purgatories serve as places for the reincarnation of evil men.[39] Yet liberation from the process of rebirth is promised to the believer who withdraws from the world's evil influences and practises self-discipline to the point of rigorous austerity. The retributive system was doubtless inherited from previous beliefs; and the position with Buddhism was exactly the same, although the existence of a creator-god was equally and firmly denied. In the sixth and fifth centuries B.C., when early Buddhism and Jainism were spreading, a belief in *karma* was already in vogue.[40] The Buddha doubtless 'taught the path of *nirvāna*, which could be attained through one's own efforts'; and doubtless too 'he refused to accept the mediation of any gods and of any priesthood;'[41] he did not, it seems, accept a 'primordial Absolute', but regarded *karma* as 'operating with an almost autonomous deterministic finality'.[42] It has been suggested that the initial readiness to assume the deterministic doctrine was due to its popularity at the time, together with the idea of transmigration.[43]

---

[38] Cf. Trevor Ling, *History of Religion East and West*, 28.
[39] Ninian Smart, op. cit. 104–105.
[40] V.P. Varma, in *Philosophy East and West* 13 (1963), 34—a valuable study which does not convince, however, in finding the doctrine in the Rigveda (p. 29: '*tapas* also is a kind of *karman*'). In these texts *karma* means simply 'action': see Wendy D. O'Flaherty in the opening essay of *Karma and Rebirth in Classical Indian Traditions* (1980), noting 40 occurrences of the word there.
[41] Ibid. 39.
[42] Ibid. 38.
[43] Hajune Nakamura, *Indian Buddhism* (Tokyo, 1980), 64: 'Buddhists adopted the notion of transmigration which was prevalent among common people in those days, taking it for granted, without examining it philosophically.'

SOME INDIAN DOCTRINES

While Buddhism was committed to a crucial rejection of the divine in relation to the cosmos and its creation and therefore of its moral ordering, it by no means rejected popular religion at a lower level. A multitude of gods, demons, and spirits peopled its local religious activities. Furthermore, images of the Buddha, the Bodhisattvas, and of the celestial Buddhas became popular; and when Buddhism spread to China, the cult of ancestors was not impugned, nor that of traditional deities. In Mahayana Buddhism the doctrine of *karma* was circumvented by a particularly popular appeal: invoking the name of the Buddha could bring the promise that the next rebirth would be in paradise, where the achievement of nirvana would obviously be a more accessible aim.[44]

In the Vedic tradition, on the other hand, there can be no doubt that the system of *karma* is related to a strong theistic conviction. The Upanishads view the universe as divinely ordered; and if a plurality of gods appears, there are clear indications of a simple personal, or sometimes impersonal, God seen as the final reality behind everything. Certainly the workings of *karma* here have this foundation,[45] but the release from them may also have divine sanction. In another respect the doctrine has an unusual aspect. It looks before and after, being concerned with both previous and future lives. Yet at any given moment it can be construed as delivering judgement in the present life. It denotes 'a continuous process of judgment both before and after death', 'an unceasing judgment operative in the very being of every person';[46] and it is therefore somewhat misleading to include it in the category of 'judgement of the dead'.[47]

A feature of the concept of ages rotating in slow and relentless cycles is that it permits the recurrence many times of mythological events in which the gods themselves are subject to the operation of *karma* and of the changes effected through reincarnation. There is a striking example which concerns the warrior-god Indra. He is addressed in a description of 'The Parade of Ants' and shown to have experienced the process himself:[48]

> I saw the ants, O Indra, filing in long parade. Each was once an Indra. Like you, each by virtue of pious deeds once ascended to the

---
[44] Ninian Smart, *The Religious Experience of Mankind*, 221.
[45] Not that any deity is specifically named in connection with it; cf. Brandon, *The Judgment of the Dead* (London, 1967), 173.
[46] Ibid. 175 and 176.
[47] Brandon admits as much, ibid. 176.
[48] Heinrich Zimmer, ed. Joseph Campbell, *Myths and Symbols in Indian Art and Civilization* (New York, 1946, repr. 1953), 7.

rank of a king of gods. But now, through many rebirths, each has become again an ant. This army is an army of former Indras.

A contrast emerges here when other depictions of Indra are recalled, some of which show him as 'a rowdy amoral deity, fond of feasting and drinking' and as the wielder, like Zeus and Thor, of the thunderbolt which destroyed his enemies.[49] Perhaps the contrast is a salutary one, with its distressing sense of humiliation: the king of the gods is now an ant.

An impression of fatalistic resignation is often conveyed by the doctrine of *karma*, as I have observed earlier. Perhaps a distinction should be made between the intellectual definition of the doctrine and the spiritual effect it has on those who believe in it. On the former point R.F. Gombrich declares that 'the doctrine is logically very far from fatalism; indeed it might be said to go to the other extreme.'[50] He elucidates the doctrine in this way:

> This law (of *karma*) applies to all living beings, always. *Karma* means 'deed' or 'act'. Strictly speaking, your *karma* is what you do, not what is done to you—that is the maturation (*vipāka*) of your *karma*, the result of one of your previous acts in this or one of your former lives. *Karma* is a doctrine of free will. Indeed, will is paramount, the doctrine is that what counts is the intention, not the effect. 'It is intention (*cetanā*) that I call *karma*', said the Buddha.

Gombrich then proceeds to discuss the psychological attitudes of villagers with whom he had converse in Ceylon. According to him, when a villager meets with misfortune, he says, 'It's *karma*', implying that the mishap is the result of his former bad actions; 'it can't be helped' is partly the sense, but that does not mean, emphasizes Gombrich, that it is not his fault or that he is not responsible. 'Determinism', he adds, 'is a heresy.' Yet he goes on to say (pp. 145–6) that 'the response to misfortune 'karumē' does in fact have a fatalistic ring, which suggests that on the affective level the villager may not accept the total responsibility which he admits cognitively.'

This revealing comment takes us, of course, into the sphere of religious experience in contemporary life, and our concern is rather with the ancient classical doctrine and its ethical implications. An eloquent defence of its relation to both freedom and morality was

---

[49] A.L. Basham, *The Wonder that was India* (3rd. Ed., 1967, repr. London, 1988), 234, with a hymn quoted from the Rigveda, 10, 119, 2–9.

[50] Richard F. Gombrich, *Precept and Practice. Traditional Buddhism in the Rural Highlands of Ceylon.* (Oxford, 1971), 145.

offered by Sir Sarvepalli Radhakrishnan. On the former claim he wrote thus:[51]

> The doctrine of Karma is sometimes interpreted as implying a denial of human freedom, which is generally regarded as the basis of ethical values. But when rightly viewed the law does not conflict with the reality of freedom ... The theory of Karma recognizes the rule of law not only in outward nature, but also in the world of mind and morals.

He goes on to say that 'Karma is not a mechanical principle but a spiritual necessity. It is the embodiment of the mind and will of God.' The type of judgement at work is said to show justice as an attribute of God:[52]

> Every act, every thought is weighed in the invisible but universal balance-scales of justice. The day of judgment is not in some remote future, but here and now, and none can escape it. Divine laws cannot be evaded. They are not so much imposed from without as wrought into our natures. Sin is not so much a defiance of God as a denial of soul, not so much a violation of law as a betrayal of self. We carry with us the whole of our past. It is an ineffaceable record which time cannot blur nor death erase.

The scheme also leaves room, he argues, for repentance and forgiveness; and he stresses that 'the past guilt cannot be wiped away by the atoning suffering of an outward substitute. Guilt cannot be transferred. It must be atoned for through the sorrow entailed by self-conquest.' While he admits (p. 55) that a 'philosophy of despair' has sometimes been the outcome of the system, he urges that there is no necessity for this; indeed he claims that 'the law of Karma encourages the sinner that it is never too late to mend.'

What seems to be glossed over in this impassioned apologetic is the importance of rebirth and reincarnation in the system. When we are told that 'we carry with us the whole of our past', it is not made clear that this may include our experience in previous lives, perhaps in lives even as animals or insects.[53] In another study,[54] where a chapter is devoted to Buddhism, Radhakrishnan does pay some attention to this matter. He refers to 'the conception of the world as *saṁsara*, a stream without end, where the law of karma functions' as being common to all Indian systems, Hindu, Jain,

---

[51] S. Radhakrishnan, *The Hindu View of Life* (London, 1927, repr. 1960), 52.
[52] Ibid. 53.
[53] See however p. 89: 'the law of Karma tells us that the individual life is not a term, but a series.'
[54] S. Radhakrishnan, *Religion and Culture* (New Delhi, 1968), 127.

Buddhist and Sikh. Buddhism, he maintains, has no room for fatalism:[55]

> The conduct of the individual in one life cannot determine his everlasting destiny. The Buddha does not accept a fatalistic view. He does not say that man has no control over his future. He can work out his future, become an *arhat* (a worthy one), attain *nirvāna*.

Concerning *nirvāna* a misunderstanding has sometimes arisen, as when R.C. Zaehner[56] associated 'the absolute monism ... of the Indian idealists' with 'moral ambivalence'. We are reminded by B.K. Matilal[57] that 'no Vedāntic or Buddhist philosophers of repute ever suggested that men should abandon the good-evil distinction before they achieved Nirvāna;' the distinction becomes an inessential detail in the ultimate reality only because 'evil has been overcome'.

Karma has a certain moral appeal in view of these arguments. To Western minds it is the theory of reincarnation that flaws it since a continuum of moral consciousness cannot easily be envisaged in a series of very varied forms and lives. Yet the transmigration of souls was a doctrine spread also by the Western philosopher Pythagoras and by Pherecydes of Syros before him. An anecdote about Pythagoras tells of him seeing a puppy being beaten and ordering the man to desist with the words, 'Stop! That's the soul of a friend of mine; I recognize the voice.'[58] According to the Jainist creed transmigration takes place immediately after the death of the previous body. The soul was regarded as a constant and unchangeable element, although the idea of the interdependence of soul and body was also a potent factor; even in the situation of the liberation denoted by *moksha* the Jainists were reluctant to dispense with the corporeal element. Upon the coming of death the soul was thought to move within a single moment into a new embryo.[59] In the early Indian mythology various ideas of rebirth are not surprisingly attested, and it is of interest that a nexus with the animal world

---

[55] Ibid.

[56] *Our Savage God* (London, 1974), 15 and often elsewhere of a timeless state of Being which transcends good and evil.

[57] *The Logical Illumination of Indian Mysticism* (Oxford, 1977, Inaugural Lecture), 25–26.

[58] M.L. West, *The Orphic Poems*, 18–19, citing Xenophanes, fr. 7a. For a study of linguistic claims relating to reincarnated human lives see J. Gwyn Griffiths, 'Some Claims of Xenoglossy in the Ancient Languages', *Numen* 33 (1986), 141–69.

[59] P.S. Jaini, 'Karma and the Problem of Rebirth in Jainism', in *Karma and Rebirth in Classical Indian Traditions* ed. Wendy Doniger O'Flaherty (Berkeley, 1986), 217–38, esp. 219–21.

sometimes appears, as in the theme of rebirth from the Devouring Goddess, so that allowing oneself to be devoured by the goddess is a way of achieving immortality.[60] Eventually the idea of moral causation and of moral rebuke enters into both Brāhmanic and Jainist interpretations of *karma*.

The emphasis on the punitive element found in this connection raises the question of how far the legal system was similarly inclined. Writing in about 300 B.C. on the customs and culture of Northern India between the Indus and the Ganges, the Greek diplomat and historian Megasthenes described the Indians as very law-abiding and rarely addicted to crimes.[61] Other sources offer varied evidence, and the much later Hindu law has been keenly defended with the claim that the *ius talionis* was less conspicuous than elsewhere.[62] The Laws of Manu, it is true, laud the idea of punitive control:[63]

> The whole world is controlled by punishment, for a guiltless man is hard to find . . .

In one way the concept of *karma* dispenses with any sense of accumulated punishment imposed from without, since it is seen as a self-operating law of moral causation. A universal moral order is assumed to exist, and a basic text of the classical theory points to the bond between action and character:

> According as one acts, according as one conducts himself, so does he become. The doer of good becomes good. The doer of evil becomes evil. One becomes virtuous by virtuous action, bad by bad action.
> (Brihad Āranyaka, 4.4.5.)[64]

If this looks like a simple doctrine of behaviourism, the passage does go on to show how action is preceded by desire and resolve.

A complication arises in the concept of *karma* as presented in the 'theistic Upanishads'. In these writings, unlike those of the Buddhist and Jainist traditions, a belief is propounded that 'human fortunes are in the hands of God.'[65] Such a belief is evidently contrary to the doctrine of a self-operating system.

---

[60] Wendy Doniger O'Flaherty, *Sexual Metaphors and Animal Symbolism in Indian Mythology* (Oxford, 1980), 266.
[61] A.L. Basham, *The Wonder that was India*, 115, in a survey of legal literature and administration.
[62] Ramaprasad Das Gupta, *Crime and Punishment in Ancient India* (New Delhi, 1973), 57–60. Cf. Terence P. Day, *The Concept of Punishment in Early Indian Literature* (Waterloo, Ontario, 1982), 71 ff.
[63] Basham, op. cit. 114.
[64] Ainslie T. Embree, *The Hindu Tradition* (New York, 1972), 62; J. Mascaró, *The Upanishads* (1965), 140; Terence P. Day, op. cit. 73.
[65] Terence P. Day, op. cit. 77 ff.

CHAPTER SIX

CONFUCIANISM, MOHISM, AND TAOISM

In the first century A.D. and afterwards Indian Buddhism spread to China and developed there in distinctive ways. Ideologically, however, it is of greater moment to consider what contributions were made to our theme by the two outstanding religious movements of purely Chinese origin.

1. *Confucius and the Intervention of Heaven*

Although he has sometimes been classified as an agnostic, Confucius (K'ung-fu-tzū), who was born in the middle of the sixth century B.C., included a clearly religious element in his teaching. Of the works associated with him, the *Analects* are accepted as the compilation most genuinely credited with his authorship; they were compiled, it seems, not more than some seventy years after his death. A great zeal for education and for offering it to all is apparent; an emphasis on *li*, 'ceremonial', with an attendant sense of reverence and propriety; and a basic aim in presenting the Way (*Tao*), sometimes called the Way of Heaven and thus invested with a religious aura.[1] Virtue (*te*) is also said to be a gift of Heaven: *Heaven is the author of the virtue that is in me* (7.23).[2]

A variety of topics is touched on in the Analects, but a certain reserve is shown in the Master's approach to the gods:

> The topics the Master did not speak of were prodigies, force, disorder, and gods.
> (*Analects*, 7.21; tr. D.C. Lau, 88.)

Arthur Waley[3] translates thus: *The Master never talked of prodigies, feats of strength, disorders or spirits.* A similar reserve appears when Confucius is asked *how the spirits of the dead and the gods should be served*:

> The Master said, 'You are not able even to serve man. How can you serve the spirits?'

---

[1] Ninian Smart, *The Religious Experience of Mankind*, 202. Cf. D.C. Lau, *Confucius, The Analects* (Penguin Classics, 1979, repr. 1986), 11–12, with a mention of other phrases such as 'the ways of the Former Kings' and 'the way of the Master'.
[2] D.C. Lau, op. cit. 89.
[3] *The Analects of Confucius* (London, 1938), 127 (with the numbering 7.20).

> 'May I ask about death?'
> 'You do not understand even life. How can you understand death?'
> (*Analects*, 11.12; tr. Lau, 107.)[4]

One may compare the dictum (6. 22, Lau, 84) about wisdom: *To work for the things the common people have a right to and to keep one's distance from the gods and spirits while showing them reverence can be called wisdom.* To the disciple Tzu-hsia is ascribed a saying which gives big roles to Destiny and Heaven and outlines, at the same time, a doctrine of universal brotherhood:

> Ssu-ma Niu appeared worried, saying, 'All men have brothers. I alone have none.'
> Tzu-hsia said, 'I have heard it said: life and death are a matter of Destiny; wealth and honour depend on Heaven. The gentleman is reverent and does nothing amiss, is respectful towards others and observant of the rites, and all within the Four Seas[5] are his brothers. What need is there for the gentleman to worry about not having any brothers?'
> (*Analects*, 12.5; tr. Lau, 113.)

It appears that wealth and honour, according to this saying, are bestowed by Heaven, presumably as rewards for good moral conduct. Yet in another saying by Confucius himself the concept of reward is firmly rejected. Asked about the exaltation of virtue and the reformation of the depraved, he said: *To put service before the reward you get for it, is that not exaltation of virtue? To attack evil as evil and not as evil of a particular man, is that not the way to reform the depraved?* (12.21; tr. Lau, 116.).[6] Heaven is credited with maintaining a cosmic (and presumably moral) order, although it keeps silent about it. Confucius is himself tempted to maintain silence in view of this:

> The Master said, 'What does Heaven ever say? Yet there are the four seasons going round and there are the hundred things coming into being. What does Heaven ever say?'
> (*Analects*, 17.19; tr. Lau, 146.)

Destiny is mentioned as the powerful arbiter of disease and death:

> Po-niu was ill. The Master visited him and holding his hand through the window, said, 'We are going to lose him. It must be Destiny. Why else should such a man be stricken with such a disease?'
> (*Analects*, 6.10; tr. Lau, 82.)

---

[4] See also the discussion by Waley, op. cit. 31–33.
[5] The Four Seas 'that bound the universe'; Waley, op. cit. 164 n. 1.
[6] The last sentence is quite different in Waley's version (p. 169): 'Attack the evil that is within yourself; do not attack the evil that is in others' (with certain textual revisions).

The disease was probably leprosy.[7] There is no suggestion, however, that this is a punishment for evil conduct. A mention of the Master's own serious illness (7.35; tr. Lau, 91) tells of a disciple offering a prayer to the gods above and below, to which the Master responds, *In that case, I have long been offering my prayers*, suggesting a constant observance of prayer. Yet Waley (p. 31 n. 3) supplies an ethical explanation: 'What justifies me in the eyes of Heaven is the life I have led. There is no need for any rite now.'

If Confucius believed that 'Heaven can and does intervene in human affairs',[8] the *Analects* give little elaboration of the belief. Death and disease are occasionally attributed to Destiny, but with no explicit moral causation. Service without thought of reward is certainly extolled, so that it can be rightly said of Confucius that 'he did not believe in a kind of divine determinism, implying that Heaven necessarily rewards the virtuous and punishes the evil . . .;' nor, on the other hand, did he espouse a naturalistic fatalism,[9] although a patient acceptance of Heaven's decrees is urged. Doctrinally, thus, the *Analects* give a somewhat pallid lead in such matters, the main reason being that the divine role is not expressly defined and that human conduct in the family and in society at large receives the prior attention. It is rather ironic that in later ages Confucius himself became the centre of a religious cult.[10]

2. *Mohism and Taoism*

It was after the death of Confucius that the Mohist and Taoist movements became important, although early traditions regarded Lao Tzu, the founder of Taoism, as an older contemporary of Confucius. Mo Tzu, the founder of Mohism, probably lived in the second half of the fifth century B.C. With his principle of universal love he was the first to challenge the doctrines of Confucius; he aimed at testing traditional rules with the measure of the benefit or harm accruing from them to people generally (and not merely to one class).[11] His doctrine of the Will of Heaven (*T'ien Ming*) gave

---

[7] Cf. Waley, 117 n. 6. But he gives 'Heaven' for 'Destiny'.
[8] Ninian Smart, *The Religious Experience of Mankind*, 204.
[9] Ibid. Cf. David Hawkes, *Chinese: Classical, Modern and Humane* (Inaugural Lecture, Oxford, 1961), 10: 'Confucianism is rather like a secular religion invented by a benevolent agnostic for the harmonious functioning of a human beehive.'
[10] Laurence G. Thompson, *Chinese Religion* (3rd Ed., Belmont, California, 1979), 71; Cyril G. Williams, *Crefyddau'r Dwyrain* (Religions of the East; Cardiff, 1968), 291.
[11] A.C. Graham, *Chuang-Tzu, The Inner Chapters* (London, 1981, repr. 1986), 4.

him sanction for stressing universal love;[12] but it also enabled him to challenge Confucius on the question of divine intervention in human affairs. Reward of virtue and punishment of evil occurs, according to him, in this life; natural calamities indicate Heaven's rebuke. He also defended the popular belief in spirits and minor deities, and in all these opinions, as well as others, he was opposing the teaching of Confucius.[13]

In the tract *The Will of Heaven* Mo Tzu illustrates his doctrine by alluding to four righteous kings. (I quote from the translation by Burton Watson in his *Basic Writings of Mo Tzu, Hsün Tzu, and Han Fei Tzu*, New York, 1967, 81.)

> How did Yü, T'ang, Wen, and Wu win reward? Mo Tzu said: Above they honored Heaven, in the middle realm they served the spirits, and below they loved men. Therefore the will of Heaven announced: 'These men love all those I love and benefit all those I would benefit. They love men widely and benefit them greatly.' Therefore Heaven caused them to be honored with the position of Son of Heaven, and enriched with the possession of the world. They were succeeded by their sons and grandsons for countless generations, and their goodness was praised throughout the world. Even today people praise them, calling them sage kings.
>
> (*The Will of Heaven*, Section 26.)

We are then told that four evil kings of antiquity incurred punishment: *they were the ones who disobeyed the will of Heaven and incurred punishment*:

> Above all they blasphemed against Heaven, in the middle realm they blasphemed against the spirits, and below they did harm to men ... Therefore Heaven caused them to die before their time and to perish in a single generation, and even today people condemn them, calling them evil kings.
>
> (Ibid.)

It is further stated (p. 93) that *obedience to the will of Heaven is the standard of righteousness*. In these statements, as in many others, Mo Tzu comes close to regarding Heaven as a personal God. Certainly, as Rowley remarks (*Prophecy and Religion in Ancient China and Israel*, 131), 'he cannot be said to have thought of Heaven as a pale abstraction.'

The Taoist movement also rejected aspects of the teaching of Confucius. This movement's most celebrated text, *Tao Te Ching* ('Classic of the Way and of Power')[14] originated probably in the

---

[12] Stuart McFarlane, in *Dict. of Religions* ed. J.R. Hinnells (Penguin, 1984), 217.
[13] Ninian Smart, op. cit. 207.
[14] See A.C. Graham, op. cit. 7 and 34 n. 10, correcting Waley's translation of the title, *The Way and its Power* (London, 1934).

latter half of the fourth century B.C., although the date of Lao Tzu, its traditional author, seems very uncertain.[15] There is much that is attractive in the naturalistic quietism urged in the work, as well as in the mystical view of the Tao as the Way which is at one with cosmic creation as *the mother of the myriad creatures* (tr. Lau, I. 2, p. 57). Behind the natural world, then, is this divine principle, and the aim of the wise is to live in harmony with it—'in tune with the Infinite' as Charles Fosdick used to present a Christian emphasis or in line with Nature (*phusis* or *natura*) as the Stoics put it. Our question is whether this system or outlook—it is not a system elaborated coherently—implies divine intervention or control. Individual immortality in an afterworld is not sought, but failure to follow the Tao brings unhappy results. While Tao usually replaces Heaven in this work, the phrase 'Way of Heaven' occurs sometimes in parts that may reflect an earlier tradition. Certainly an intervening Heaven is here portrayed:

> Is not the way of Heaven like the stretching of a bow?
>   The high it presses down,
>   The low it lifts up;
>   The excessive it takes from,
>   The deficient it gives to.
>   (*Tao Te Ching*, 77.184; tr. Lau, p. 139.)[16]

It rightly adds that the *way of man* is quite different:

> The way of man is otherwise. It takes from those who are in want in order to offer this to those who already have more than enough.
>   (Ibid. 77.184 a.)

D.C. Lau (p. 23) points out that this does not agree with the view of the Tao generally taken in the work, where it is 'something non-personal and amoral'. He quotes a forceful instance of the exceptional view:

> It is the way of heaven to show no favouritism.
> It is for ever on the side of the good man.
>   (Ibid. 79.192; tr. Lau, p. 141.)[17]

---

[15] D.C. Lau, *Lao Tzu, Tao Te Ching* (Penguin Classics, 1963, repr. 1976), 11, avers that 'in all probability Lao Tzu was not a historical figure at all', but that seems too bold a break with tradition.

[16] See also his discussion on p. 23.

[17] Gia-fu Feng and Jane English (London, 1973, repr. 1978) render thus: 'The Tao of heaven is impartial. It stays with good men all the time.' In their brief introduction in *Lao Tsu, Tao Te Ching* these writers adhere to the tradition: 'Lao Tsu, an older contemporary of Confucius, was keeper of the imperial archives at Loyang in the province of Honan in the sixth century B.C.' Michael Saso,

Heaven therefore intervenes here and now on behalf of the good man. The general tenor of the work may not support such divine interventionism, but it may be questioned whether the usual approach is 'amoral'. It is true that conventionally accepted tenets of morality are attacked, as in the famous Chapter 19:

> Banish wisdom, discard knowledge,
> And the people will be benefited a hundredfold.
> Banish human kindness, discard morality,
> And the people will be dutiful and compassionate.
> Banish skill, discard profit,
> And thieves and robbers will disappear . . .
> Give them Simplicity to look at, the Uncarved Block to hold,
> Give them selflessness and fewness of desires.
> (*Tao Te Ching*, 19; tr. Arthur Waley.)[18]

Zaehner says of these lines that they 'might be taken as the hippies' charter;' for the Taoists were 'quite literally the drop-outs of their time—anti-intellectual, anti-organization, anti-status-seeking, anti-moralist'. The last adjective is, however, quite misleading, for the lines clearly envisage a state when the removal of authorized wisdom, technology, and profit-making will release the natural goodness in man and make true morality possible: *the people will be dutiful and compassionate; . . . thieves and robbers will disappear*. The Uncarved Block is the symbol of 'that primitive state of unity in which man felt himself to be at one with all Nature and with his fellow-men.'[19]

There are certainly sayings where accepted morality seems to be challenged. The opening of Chapter 2 is thus rendered by Lau (p. 58):

> The whole world recognizes the beautiful as the beautiful, yet this is only the ugly; the whole world recognizes the good as the good, yet this is only the bad.

A quite different version comes from Gia-fu Feng and Jane English:

> Under heaven all can see beauty as beauty only because there is ugliness.
> All can know good as good only because there is evil.

'Chinese Religions', in *A Handbook of Living Religions* ed. J.R. Hinnells (Penguin, 1985), 346, gives a similar date to 'the works of Lao-tzu'; but others date the sage to the fourth or third centuries B.C. Cf. W. Eichhorn, in *Concise Encycl. of Living Faiths* ed. R.C. Zaehner (2nd Ed., London, 1971, repr. 1983), 375, who prefers the idea of a school of writers; A Bertholet, rev. K. Goldammer, *Wb. der Religionen* (Stuttgart, 1976), 337, where two sets of dates are given as alternatives.

[18] Quoted by R.C. Zaehner, *Drugs, Mysticism and Make-Believe* (London, 1972), 130. Lau's version (p. 75) differs in minor details.
[19] Ibid.

The immediately following context points to the complementary function of opposites, as Lau's own version has it:

> Thus Something and Nothing produce each other;
> The difficult and the easy complement each other;
> The long and the short off-set each other.

and Dr David Hawkes, in a detailed analysis, assures me of its correctness. The general sense of the alternative version is thus supported. A degree of moral ambiguity, none the less, appears in Chapter 20:

> Between yea and nay
> How much difference is there?
> Between good and evil
> How great is the distance?
>
> (*Tao Te Ching*; tr. Lau, p. 76.)

Here Gia-fu Feng and Jane English are in broad agreement with Lau, even if they are more incisive: *Is there a difference between good and evil?*

In other parts of the work there is a firm stance on moral issues and indications too of the beneficent results accruing to the virtuous and corresponding disaster to the evil:

> In an ally it is benevolence that matters;
> In speech it is good faith that matters.
>
> (*Tao Te Ching*, 8.21; tr. Lau, p. 64.)

> To be overbearing when one has wealth and position
> Is to bring calamity upon oneself.
>
> (Ibid. 9.23; tr. Lau, p. 65.)

> Are you capable of keeping to the role of the female? . . .
> It benefits them yet claims no possession;
> It benefits them yet exacts no gratitude;
> It is the steward yet exercises no authority.
>
> (Ibid. 10.24–26; tr. Lau, p. 66.)

> In his every movement a man of great virtue
> Follows the way and the way only.
>
> (Ibid. 21.48; tr. Lau, p. 78.)

> That which goes against the way will come to an early end.
>
> (Ibid. 30.70; tr. Lau, p. 88.)

> 'The violent will not come to a natural end.' I shall take this as my precept.
>
> (Ibid. 42.97; tr. Lau, p. 103.)

> Know contentment
> And you will suffer no disgrace;

> Know when to stop
> And you will meet with no danger.
> You can then endure.
> (Ibid. 44.100; tr. Lau, p. 105.)[20]

> There is no disaster greater than not being content;
> There is no misfortune greater than being covetous.
> (Ibid. 46.105; tr. Lau, p. 107.)

> The way of heaven benefits and does not harm.
> (Ibid. 81.196; tr. Lau, p. 143.)

It is made clear that the basis of these moral sentiments is man's natural goodness: *Yet the way is revered and virtue honoured not because this is decreed by any authority but because it is natural for them to be treated so.* (51.114 a; tr. Lau, p. 112.) The quality of the ethical appeal is exemplified by the precept *Do good to him who has done you an injury.* (63.148; tr. Lau, p. 124.) Admittedly its quality has been impugned by Rowley,[21] although he accepts F. Legge's translation *Recompense injury with kindness*: he argues that the context shows 'that the principle does not spring from any root of love for the injurer, but rather from complete indifference to him.' The previous section certainly urges non-action and the avoidance of trouble, and this agrees with a frequent Taoist emphasis. Non-interference or quietism is implied, but 'complete indifference' should be questioned; still more the claim that 'the maxim springs ... from a radical selfishness of spirit, from the view that the superior man must guard his own superiority.'[22] Man's natural intuition, according to this doctrine, unites him with the cosmic Tao and enables him to keep *the role of the female* which *benefits yet expects no gratitude.* (See above.) In Chapter 67 three *treasures* are mentioned; the first is *compassion*, the second *frugality*, and the third *not daring to take the lead in the empire*. The last phrase shows that this chapter is concerned with political reactions; and the subsequent comments confirm this:

> Being compassionate one could afford to be courageous,
> Being frugal one could afford to extend one's territory.
> (Ibid. 67.164; tr. Lau, p. 129.)

In the final comment a similar concern is apparent: *What heaven*

---

[20] Cf. Lau's discussion on p. 28.
[21] H.H. Rowley, *Submission in Suffering* (Cardiff, 1951), 77–82.
[22] In fact Lao Tzu denies superiority. Cf. 49.110; tr. Lau, p. 110: *The sage has no mind of his own. He takes as his own the mind of the people.* There follow the words which even Rowley is loath to impugn: *Those who are good I treat as good. Those who are not good I also treat as good. In so doing I gain in goodness.*

succours it protects with the gift of compassion. (67.165; tr. Lau, p. 129.)

A nexus of conduct and result is often indicated, and the sequence is sometimes ascribed to *heaven*, as in the last quotation. Whether this amounts to a firm belief in divine intervention is rather doubtful. More often it looks like an automatic system of moral give-and-take.[23] Occasionally the term *T'ien, Heaven*, has been translated as *God*,[24] but no belief in a personal God is shown. If we equate Heaven with Providence, then the teaching of the Taoist is seen to include the idea of a divine principle that affects human life.

3. *Chuang-tzu*

Taoist thought found a brilliant representative, probably in the fourth century B.C., in Chuang-tzu, some of whose works have recently become accessible in an authoritative English translation and commentary.[25] We find in him a similar plea for a 'Return to Nature'; he has indeed been dubbed the 'Rousseau of the East';[26] but there is no trace of the influence of *Lao-tzu* on the *Inner Chapters* of Chuang-tzu.[27] The word 'nature' (*hsing*) is not actually used in the *Inner Chapters* although it occurs often in the other parts of the *Book of Chuang-tzu* which are of miscellaneous origin.[28] Intuition and spontaneity are praised; yet they do not lead to a facile surrender to passions and instincts, for *the utmost man uses the heart like a mirror*,[29] suggesting a reflective calm. Chuang-tzu is credited with an attitude of numinous awe towards Heaven; an impersonal power though it remains, as for Confucians and Taoists alike, it is sometimes personified by Chuang-tzu as *the maker of things*.[30] If we ask whether this power, in a personal or impersonal form, assesses the life of man here and now with a verdict that impinges on it, it seems that Heaven's mode of justice differs from man's, since it judges not his deliberate actions, but his Heaven-given essence:

---

[23] Cf. N. Vandier-Nicolas, in *Le Jugement des Morts* (Sources orientales, 4; Paris, 1961), 233.

[24] See Rowley, op. cit. 81.

[25] A.C. Graham, *Chuang-tzu, The Inner Chapters* (London, 1981, repr. 1986); on p. 31 *The Inner Chapters* are said to be 'generally recognized as his work'.

[26] C.G. Williams, *Crefyddau'r Dwyrain*, 317, referring to K.L. Reichelt.

[27] Graham, op. cit. 5. He is clearly referring to detailed literary dependence, rather than to matters of general approach.

[28] Ibid. 16.

[29] Ibid. 98 with the discussion on p. 14.

[30] Ibid. 18. According to C.G. Williams, op. cit. 318–19 he speaks of the Tao in a similar manner.

> When the maker of things recompenses a man, he recompenses not the man but what is from Heaven in the man.
>
> (*Inner Chapters*, related passages; tr. A.C. Graham, p. 108.)

Presumably, then, the judgement is a kindly one since Heaven's endowment to man is beneficent. The context concerns a certain Huan who became a Confucian scholar, but whose bounty *spread only to the clans of his father and mother and wife*, a restriction that caused his brother to become a Mohist in support of the doctrine that love should be equal for all. Later Huan killed himself. Chuang-tzu appears to interpret this as a kind of judgement from Heaven: *Thinking of one's own as the alternative that is It—one who has Power in him wouldn't know how to do that, not to mention one who has the Way. Of old this was called the punishment for retreating from Heaven.*[31]

In general, however, these writings give little attention to our theme. If we turn to the 'Syncretist Writings' deriving from the second and first centuries B.C., we find that elements from the teaching of various schools are blended in the *Chuang-tzu* collection by editors of this era.[32] Ideas about reward and punishment are sometimes applied to the performance of administrative officials, albeit without conspicuous emphasis.[33] A section entitled *The Way of Heaven* presents an ideology then generally accepted:

> Emptiness and stillness, calm and indifference, quiescence, Doing Nothing, are the even level of heaven and earth, the utmost reach of the Way and the Power; therefore emperor, king or sage finds rest in them.
>
> ('Syncretist Writings' in Graham, *Chuang-tzu*, 259.)

The subsequent development of Taoism has been condemned for implying that 'social inaction and lethargy were necessary virtues.'[34] Yet in *The Way of Heaven* occurs an enchanting poem ascribed to Chuang-tzu in which he describes the state of the believer who *knows the joy from Heaven*; for him there is no shadow of divine wrath or human rebuke:

> There is no wrath from Heaven,
> No blame from man,

---

[31] *Chuang-tzu*, Chapter 32; tr. Graham, op. cit. 108. Cf. his discussion on p. 17, with its mention of the reference by Confucius to his being *one of those under sentence from Heaven*.

[32] Graham, op. cit. 258–85.

[33] Graham, op. cit. 258 and esp. 262.

[34] Trevor Ling, *A History of Religion East and West*, 106. He then quotes even more trenchant remarks by C.K. Yang (1961), a Chinese writer who feels that to include Taoism in a Chinese history of religion is 'a great humiliation'. Cf. H.H. Rowley, *Submission in Suffering*, 81.

No being tied by other things,
No retribution from ghosts.

(Ibid.; tr. Graham, p. 260.)

4. *The Transference of Merits*

The way in which Buddhism was able to influence Taoism in China belongs to the second century A.D. and afterwards; it does not pertain strictly, then, to the area of Ancient Religions; still less does the flowering of Buddhism in Japan.[35] It is worth describing briefly, however, a phase in the Chinese experience which illustrates a remarkable reversal of the doctrine of the sins of the fathers being visited on the children, which is prominent in both Israel and Greece, as we have seen.

This phase has its likely origin, to some extent, in the devotional Buddhism of an Indian text which became authoritative to the 'Pure Land sect', also called Amida Buddhism. A basic doctrine here was the idea that merit can be transferred, particularly from a great Buddha to a believer who may himself be unworthy. As a result, and simply by uttering the sacred name in true faith, the believer could be warranted a place in 'The Pure Land of the West'—a process which was a far cry from the original message of the Buddha.[36] When Buddhism spread in China, it proved itself accommodating in many ways, and it skilfully blended with both Taoism (in some respects) and the cult of ancestors. In the latter connection it applied the principle of the transference of merit in a significantly extended manner. Official Buddhist sanction was given to ceremonies in honour of the dead;[37] and some of these rites and prayers were now directed to the purpose of saving the deceased from the torments of hell and securing for him a happier afterworld. Rooms in the Buddhist temples were specially reserved for this type of intercession, and the whole ceremonial rested smoothly on the traditional fabric of the Chinese cult.[38] Taoist communities practised a rite of repentance in order to obtain pardon, the aim being to ensure that their numerous ancestors and relatives, who were either already dead or would die later, should be without sin during many cycles of time.

---

[35] See Trevor Ling, *The Buddha* (London, 1973, repr. Harmondsworth, 1976), 283 ff. referring to the sixth century A.D. and later.
[36] Ninian Smart, *The Religious Experience of Mankind*, 225–6.
[37] Cf. Trevor Ling, *A History of Religion East and West*, 233.
[38] C.G. Williams, *Crefyddau'r Dwyrain*, 136.

Thus were the merits of the living transferred in many instances to the dead; and the impress of Buddhism is apparent in the concept,[39] which bridges this world and the next.

5. *Avenging Ghosts*

A feature of Buddhism in China was its intense elaboration of the idea of hell and of the grading of punishments according to the nature of the sins committed. In her book *Chinese Hells*, subtitled *The Peking Temple of Eighteen Hells and Chinese Conceptions of Hell* (St. Augustin, 1981), Anne S. Goodrich (p. 68) states that the whole idea was 'quite foreign to early Chinese thought', having been brought into China with Buddhism and amalgamated with old Chinese notions.[40] She points out (p. 67) that 'Hell' is not an exact translation of *Ti-yü*, literally 'earth prison'; 'Purgatory',[41] she feels, is a closer concept since the sentences to this prison are not for eternity; further, prisoners are released to live in society again or to go to Paradise. Hill eight, we are told,[42] is the 'superlative hot hell for crimes against the rules of Confucianism, for bandits, and for special types of sex crimes'. Yet Confucianism itself countenanced no such system, and in the early doctrines there were no ideas of judgement and punishment after death.[43]

On the other hand there are interesting early examples, from the third century B.C., of the idea of retribution colouring historical writing. Several have been provided by Alvin P. Cohen,[44] who points to the ancient belief that the 'soul' of a person who had been unjustly killed could return as an avenging ghost and take revenge on the murderer. A general approach with a moral slant is seen in Chinese historiography—an assumption that 'history contained a kind of "moral dynamic" which ultimately required good acts with

---

[39] N. Vandier-Nicolas, in *Le Jugement des Morts* (en Chine), 236, of the second to the fifth centuries A.D.

[40] Cf. Anne S. Goodrich, *The Peking Temple of the Eastern Peak* (Nagoya, Japan, 1964), 205 ff. ('Gods of Death and the Underworld'); and p. 217: 'The Taoists have only ten hells.'

[41] Cf. Wolfram Eberhard, *Guilt and Sin in Traditional China* (Berkeley, 1967), 17 n. 14, with the remark that 'most sinners stay only temporarily', but are not completely 'purged'.

[42] Ibid. 39.

[43] Ibid. 17. In his n. 13 Eberhard mentions an official called the *Sih-ming* (Controller of Fate) who appears in pre-Han texts as an official who 'keeps the lists and controls men and spirits'.

[44] 'Avenging Ghosts and Moral Judgement in Ancient Chinese Historiography: Three examples from Shih-chi', in *Legend, Lore, and Religion in China* (in honor of Wolfram Eberhard; San Francisco, 1979), 97–108.

just rewards and success, and evil acts with punishment and failure' (pp. 97–98). But in pre-Buddhist China the process was believed to take place 'either within the individual's own life or among his or her posterity'. These avenging ghosts, who recall the Greek Erinyes, were clearly distinguished, according to Cohen (p. 99 n.3), from other ghosts, demons, or spirits, in that 'they had received express permission from Heaven to carry out their vengeance as an act of justice'. In the first two episodes described by him there is a long interval between the death of the victims and vengeance effected by the ghosts; and less moralistic historians could have described the retributive deaths as mere accidents, without invoking the action of the ghosts. The episodes, as presented, therefore point to 'a living belief in the just and moral workings of the world' (p. 108).

I suppose there is a slight margin of doubt as to the motives of these early writers in introducing such episodes. The indulgence of a whim for the fantastic or the quest for an additional attraction in the narrative might be plausible possibilities. Tendencies in this direction might well incur, however, the charge of unreliability, as Cohen points out; and it is more likely that the gruesome events did happen and that the intervention of ghosts was supplied, at the time, as an explanation. In the background, very probably, was a genuine belief which corresponded in the affairs of individuals to the invocation of heavenly intervention in the affairs of the nation or community.[45]

A sense of outrage at the unjust actions of new dynastic regimes is occasionally expressed in poetry:[46]

> I grieve that the good, who gave all their devotion,
> Are, for their pains, undone by little men.

The sorrowful protest is not directed, be it noted, at any ruling providence, but at the 'little men'. A similar sentiment finds expression in another poem from this collection (*The Songs of the South*), which existed already by the time of Confucius in the

---

[45] Cohen, op. cit. 107 n. 18 remarks on the intervention of Heaven in the latter sense, that it operated 'as a kind of "deified cosmos" and supreme deity of the state religion and of various philosophies, or as a personified deity that usually appears as the Heavenly Emperor...' On the general didacticism of early Chinese historians see Burton Watson, *Early Chinese Literature* (New York, 1962), 111; and on Mo Tzu's emphasis on the spirits of the ancestors and those of the unjustly killed see Eichhorn, *Die Religionen Chinas* (Stuttgart, 1973), 53.

[46] David Hawkes, *Ch'u Tz'u: The Songs of the South* (Oxford, 1959), 117 (Hsi Shih).

beginning of the fifth century B.C. A part of this poem ('On Encountering Sorrow') is rendered thus by David Hawkes (p. 23):

> The fools enjoy their careless pleasure,
> But their way is dark and leads to danger. . . .
> How well I know that loyalty brings disaster.

CHAPTER SEVEN

EGYPT: PHARAOH AND PEOPLE

A) The Gods and the God-King

Egypt's contribution to our theme is best known for the conspicuous place it gives to judgement after death. Certainly much more attention has been given to this aspect than to the idea of divine impact on the present life and on history. My present chapter, therefore, deals with a comparatively neglected area, and I have realized from the start that the special position of the King (and I capitalize him because of his official divinity) means that the material relating to kingship demands separate treatment.

1. *Theological Status*

The theological status of the Pharaoh is obviously a matter of some import in any explanation of his historical relationship to the gods. His official titulary is the clearest indication of his status since it applies to the contemporary living King. In the third edition of his *Egyptian Grammar* (Oxford, 1957), 71–76 Sir Alan Gardiner expounds the royal titulary and illustrates it by quoting that of Sesostris I of the Twelfth Dynasty, whose reign began about 1971 B.C. He translates it as follows:

> Horus 'Life-of-Births', Two Ladies 'Life-of-Births', Horus of gold 'Life-of-Births', King of Upper and Lower Egypt, 'Kheperkerē' ['the *ka* of Rē' comes into being'], Son of Rē', 'Sesostris' ['man of (the goddess) Wosret'] granted life, stability and wealth like Rē' eternally.

It is at once clear that the names and designations thus listed are replete with theological claims. Two of the names are within cartouches and Sir Alan calls them respectively the *prenomen* and *nomen*. In the *prenomen* is often found a statement about the sun-god Rê, in this case 'the *ka* of Rê comes into being', implying a close relationship between this god and the actual life of the King. The *nomen* is roughly the equivalent of our family name, and in this case, as often, it again links the King to a deity, since Sesostris means 'man of Wosret', a goddess associated with Hathor. Apart from the two personal names, however, there is a whole series of divine equations or connections. Most prominent of all is the identification with Horus. It opens the series and occurs again in 'Horus of gold', which probably meant at first 'Horus over the Ombite' or '... and the Ombite', with an allusion to Seth.[1] A connection with the sun-god Rê is asserted three times. Once in the *prenomen*, as we have seen; then once again in the ancient designation 'Son of Rê'; and finally in the concluding expression which assigns life, stability and wealth to the King, 'like Rê eternally'.

The 'Two Ladies' mentioned in the second designation are the goddesses Wadjet of Buto and Nekhbet of Hierakonpolis who figure as representatives of Lower and Upper Egypt respectively. As such they contribute the uraeus and vulture to the royal crowns. They are not, however, implicated in a direct identification with the King, since the word referring to them is a nisbe-form *Nbty-y*, meaning 'He who belongs to the Two Ladies'.[2] It is Horus who is above all the vehicle of the divine equation. The living King is identified with the god in the official titulary throughout the millennia of Pharaonic rule and beyond that into the Macedonian and Roman eras. Occasionally the identity was also expressed in art, as in the statue of the Pharaoh Khefren which shows the King's head being held between the wings of a falcon, the suggestion being that King and falcon-god are one.[3] Intimately bound up with the concept of the living King as Horus was the belief that the deceased King became Osiris; and the whole religious approach to royal burial was that the King's son as Horus was enacting his duty to his deceased father, thus honouring the Horus-Osiris relationship. Among the King's most frequent designations was 'the good God' (*nṯr nfr*) and 'the great God, (*nṯr ꜥꜣ*).[4]

2. *A Dogma Doubted*

Details of the dogma concerning the Pharaoh's divinity are ably presented in Henri Frankfort's *Kingship and the Gods* (Chicago, 1948), where prominence is given not only to the titulary but also to the rites of coronation, theogamy, and renewal. It was in the New Kingdom that the rites of theogamy became evident; they incorporated the doctrine that the King was of divine origin through the

---

[1] See my *Conflict of Horus and Seth* (Liverpool, 1960), 124 and my remarks in *ASAE* 56 (1960), 64–86.
[2] See Jürgen von Beckerath, *Handbuch der ägyptischen Königsnamen* (MÄS, 20; Munich, 1984), 1; and 14–17. Gardiner's rendering should therefore be revised.
[3] W. Stevenson Smith, *The Art and Architecture of Ancient Egypt* (Harmondsworth, 1958, repr. 1965), Pl. 40; cf. my *Origins of Osiris and his Cult* (Leiden, 1980), 103–4.
[4] See Winfried Barta, 'Königsbezeichnung', in *LÄ* III (1980), 478 with refs.

physical union of his mother with a god. This doctrine has been well expounded by Hellmut Brunner in his *Die Geburt des Gottkönigs* (Wiesbaden, 1964),[5] where it is rightly compared with the Christian doctrine of incarnation. One striking feature of Frankfort's study was the contrast drawn by him between the tradition of Egypt and that of Mesopotamia: in the latter area the King is seen as an associate of the gods whereas in Egypt he is seen to be on a par with them—a true god himself.

A strong reaction to these claims was expressed in a study by Georges Posener, *De la divinité du Pharaon* (Paris, 1960), which has left its impress on several subsequent studies by other scholars. He shows that the concentration on religious literature has obscured the very different approach revealed in other sources, where the Pharaoh's human qualities are dwelt on. Posener admits the frequent use of *nṯr*, 'god', to refer to the King, but doubts whether it was always used with the same full force; in the case of the King, he suggests, a divinity of a distinctly inferior grade is implied. It is striking, however, that Mesopotamian literature does not apply divine terms to the sovereign rulers.[6] Where Posener undoubtedly succeeds is in his demonstration that the official dogma of the Pharaoh's divinity was far from colouring Egyptian attitudes in general. To some limited extent Posener's conclusions were supported by the study published by Hans Goedicke in the same year, *Die Stellung des Königs im Alten Reich* (Wiesbaden, 1960). Confining himself to the non-religious literature of the Old Kingdom, he examines the use of terms applied to the King, and concludes (p. 89) that the term *ḥm* is concerned with the human nature of the King and that its use shows that the Pharaoh in the Old Kingdom was in no way regarded as a god, but in the first place as a man. With the term *nysŵt* or *nsw*, on the other hand, he finds that the concern was with the King's office as sovereign and that this was regarded as the result of the divine will. He is thus led to aver that 'it is not the King that is divine, but the office held by him' (p. 90). The King appears therefore as a mediator between two spheres, the human and the divine; further, he represents justice and order.

A study of kingship in the Middle Kingdom by Elke Blumenthal[7] offers, in its first volume, a collection of source material classified under various headings. Although interpretation is reserved for a

---

[5] Cf. my Review in *JEA* 51 (1965), 218–19.

[6] Cf. C.J. Gadd, *Ideas of Divine Rule in the Ancient East* (Schweich Lectures, 1945; London, 1948), 34 ff.

[7] *Untersuchungen zum ägyptischen Königtum des mittleren Reiches*. I. *Die Phraseologie*. (Abh. Leipzig, 61; Berlin, 1970.)

further volume, the second chapter, on 'The King and the Gods', is especially relevant to our theme. Thus a god is often mentioned (pp. 62 ff.) as the King's father, and this idea includes even physical fatherhood. While the canonical titulary designates the King as the son of Rê, these allusions mention several other gods as his father, probably as cult or place demanded. It is an exalted relationship and yet conveys subordination and dependence (p. 65) vis-à-vis the gods. Education, election, and loving care are also ascribed to the gods in the relationship; and they are the givers of many blessings, among them health, power, and prosperity. The King's divinity is abundantly attested. He is referred to as *nṯr* and sometimes said to act *mi nṯr*, 'like a god'. Several sayings identify him with a particular god, and with pointed emphasis, as in 'He is himself Atum' (*Tm pw ds.f*, Urk. VII, 29, 6, here p. 99). Bastet, Rê, Horus, Khnum, Sia, and Sakhmet are other deities in similar equations.

What is very clear in this material is that the divine attitude to the King is portrayed as wholly beneficent. He is treated consistently to rewards, blessings, and boons, and never to chastisements and punishments. It is in the section devoted to the King and Maat that such possibilities might arise. The King is the upholder of Maat in the double sense of righteous conduct and cosmic order. What is to happen if he fails in his duty? In the Instruction for Merikarê, where a King is speaking to his son, we find the sentence 'Do what is right so that thou mayest endure on earth (*ỉr m3ʿt w3ḥ.k tp t3*), with the clear suggestion that a long life is the reward of upright conduct. Elke Blumenthal's translation (p. 432) is similar to the one I have just given. Unhappily there is some doubt as to the exact force of the second clause, which is a virtual subordinate adverbial clause where the initial meaning has to be supplied. Erman[8] translated 'Do right as long as thou abidest on earth,' giving the clause a purely temporal sense, and J.A. Wilson[9] agreed with this view. From the general ethical standpoint it is true that longevity as a reward of virtue is a doctrine often inculcated for private individuals. Is it now being pointedly applied to the kingship also? Certainly there is much in this Instruction that is specifically meant for kings. According to Posener[10] it is an authentic *Speculum regum*, but has little light to throw on a regal sense of divinity.

---

[8] Tr. Blackman (1927; repr. New York, ed. Simpson, 1966), 77.
[9] *ANET*³ (1969), 415 (*Do justice whilst thou endurest upon earth.*) Gardiner, *JEA* 1 (1914), 26 and Faulkner, in *The Lit. of Ancient Egypt*, ed. Simpson (New Haven, 1972), 183, are in line with the other version.
[10] *LÄ* III (1980), 987.

3. *God-given Qualities*

One must admit that this Instruction lays tremendous stress on the judgement after death, with barely a hint that a moral dispensation is already at work in this life. On the positive side there is indeed an indication that the King is inherently entrenched in his God-given qualities:

> ... the ruler of the Two Banks is a wise man, and a king who possesses an entourage cannot act stupidly. He is wise from birth, and God will distinguish him above millions of men. The kingship is a goodly office.
>
> (*Merikarê*, 115 ff.)[11]

He is protected from folly by his courtly advisers (as Wilson renders it, 'The king and lord of courtiers cannot be a fool'), but the greater stress is on the wisdom which is his from birth and which God has conferred. In other words, the implicit doctrine is that the King can do no wrong. He is specially favoured by the gods, and, if we accept the evidence of other sources, he is himself a god. He is therefore quite outside the orbit of divine assessment in this life.

At this point, nevertheless, we must look at recent attempts to engulf the doctrine of Pharaoh's divinity in a sea of reductionism. Here I refer principally not to Posener's work, which for the most part is concerned to show that the Egyptians did not normally think of the Pharaoh as a god, whatever the official dogma claimed, but to more recent attempts to destabilize the content of the official dogma itself. Admittedly Posener furthered the process, after Moret and Baillet, by questioning the force of some words and expressions. He argued that *ntr*, 'god', and phrases in which it figures can embrace a variety of status positions, some of them being distinctly inferior; even the application of divine names, such as Horus and Rê, could be construed, he suggests, in a metaphorical sense. It is this approach that has been developed by Winfried Barta in his book on the divinity of the reigning King.[12] Like Goedicke, he confines his attention to the Archaic Period and the Old Kingdom, and his main conclusion is that to the Pharaoh was ascribed, not divinity ('Göttlichkeit') but similarity to divinity ('Gottähnlichkeit'). The status was conferred on him, it is urged, by ritual, particularly by the ceremonies attached to birth, corona-

---

[11] Tr. Faulkner, op. cit. 190.
[12] W. Barta, *Untersuchungen zur Göttlichkeit des regierenden Königs* (MÄS 32; Munich, 1975). Cf. the Reviews by A.B. Lloyd in *JEA* 65 (1979), 188–90 and David Lorton in *JAOS* 99 (1979), 460–65.

tion, and renewal, the Sed Festival being the vehicle of renewal. With the idea of similarity to the divine is connected the symbol of the image; words such as *mỉ*, 'like', and *twt*, 'image', are invoked.[13] If we return to the implications of the titulary, we recognize that 'son of Rê' and 'granted life, stability and wealth like Rê eternally', as well as royal names compounded with Rê, are all properly categorized under terms like 'similarity' or 'association'. The glaring exception to all this is Horus. With him the King is expressly identified, and the early evidence on the Horus-cult shows how the identification arose. It was probably based on the identification of the tribal ruler with his god.[14]

In the Old and Middle Kingdoms there is no clear evidence of a belief that the Pharaoh was amenable to the discipline of moral assessment by the gods with the attendant sequence of success or failure in his life. The royal biographies imply consistently that the Pharaoh is efficient and prosperous; his successes stem from his own valour and his exalted status is an in-built guarantee. In any case, since these are funerary effusions, they are naturally devoted to praise. The biographies embedded in the Instructions are more promising material, for they include with some personal details a series of meditations of the King's office and the experiences arising from it. Here a parallel to the Instruction for Merikarê is that of King Ammenemes I for his son Sesostris. The opening passage in this text speaks of the King imparting truth 'to his son the Lord of All.' It continues thus:[15]

> He said: O you who appear as a god, hear what I shall say to you, that you may be king of the land and rule the Banks, and achieve abundance of good fortune.

If the Instruction for Merikarê tends to focus on the King's human qualities, the above words clearly aim at highlighting his divinity, especially in the terms 'Lord of All' and 'god'.[16] There is a hint, at the same time, that the son's hearkening to good advice will lead him to prosperity, a thought that is in line with the conditional eudaemonism expressed in writings relating to private individuals. Other parallels naturally occur in the two categories, for general

---

[13] Cf. Elke Blumenthal, op. cit. 96–99; Erik Hornung (tr. Baines), *Conceptions of God in Ancient Egypt* (London, 1982), 139–42.

[14] See my *Conflict of Horus and Seth* (1960), 40; cf. H. Goedicke, in *Unity and Diversity* ed. Goedicke and Roberts (Baltimore, 1975), 201–17.

[15] Tr. Faulkner in *The Lit. of Ancient Egypt*, ed. Simpson, 194.

[16] W. Helck, *Der Text der 'Lehre Amenemhets I. für seinen Sohn'*. (Kleine Ägyptische Texte, Wiesbaden, 1969), 14.

advice about behaviour is not easily segregated into royal and non-royal compartments.

Succinct expression to a doctrine of divine recompense, which presumably applies to the Pharaoh, is given by a maxim on the pedestal of a post-Saïte statue from Coptos: see Pascal Vernus in *GM* 84 (1985), 71–79. It is there said of the sun-god: *Rê shines, observing and reciprocating (ḏb3) the action of the doer. To him who does good he does good; to him who does evil he does the same*; cf. the saying in P. Vernus, *Athribis* (Cairo, 1978), 206 (1) and (m) and remarks by H. de Meulenaere in FS. W. Westendorf (Göttingen, 1984), I, 555–9, with slightly diverging translations. Such sayings reflect the position of Rê as the judge of human actions; but Osiris also assumes the role, as in the saying from a Ptolemaic stela which Vernus quotes in *Athribis*, 206 (m). The general principle of recompense is seen in several facets of Egyptian law, where civil offences demand compensation to the injured party, while criminal offences are penalized by corporal punishment, imprisonment, and death; see David Lorton, 'The Treatment of Criminals in Ancient Egypt' (1976), 7 and S. Allam, *Everyday Life in Ancient Egypt* (1985), 80. Except in the sense of a general supporting sanction, divine judgement does not explicitly enter into the juridical, as opposed to the experiential, punishment or reward. Even the decree of Antef, the founding Pharaoh of the Seventeenth Dynasty, although it concerns an offence against the temple of Min at Coptos (*an enemy has been taken in*), does not describe the penalty in terms of divine retribution, unless we take the allusion to the offending priest as *a criminal and enemy of his god* as implying that. It seems that the offence had a political complexion, since the enemy harboured in the temple may well have been a Hyksos leader with whom Antef was contending for power in Upper Egypt; see Lorton, ibid. 19 n. 84; he gives a sound exposition, with translation, of the whole text. The word *ḫfty* is twice used in a key phrase; first, it seems, of a political-military opponent, but then with a more religious aura; cf. Lorton, *The Juridical Terminology of International Relations in Egyptian Texts* (Baltimore, 1974) 119 and 165 n. 6.

In the Qadesh Inscriptions of Ramesses II occurs an instance of a complaint made by a Pharaoh to one of the gods—in this case Amûn—concerning an alleged divine failure to reciprocate the King's faithful adherence. The complaint begins thus:

> His majesty spoke, 'What is this, father Amun?
> Is it right for a father to ignore his son?'
>
> (Lichtheim, *Lit.* II, 65.)

If the Hittites have won an initial success, that is a reproach to the god who favours Egypt and its Pharaoh: *What are these Asiatics to you, O Amun, the wretches ignorant of God?* (Ibid.) The Pharaoh then lists his many services to the god, and pleads for a just return for the services rendered: *Do good to him who counts on you, then one will serve you with loving heart.* Amûn hears the plea and duly intervenes on Pharaoh's behalf, and as a result the King, although quite unsupported by his own troops, wins splendid success. The general approach, of course, has many ancient parallels in the idea that divine intervention is demanded on a reciprocal basis. What is distinctive in this text is that the King uses a similar ploy in addressing his unfaithful troops:

Is there none among you whom I helped in my land?

(Ibid. 67.)

After rehearsing his many services to them, he gains their renewed and triumphant support. The double pattern of reciprocity which features the principle of *do ut des* has been ably expounded by Scott Morschauser in *Perspectives on the Battle of Kadesh*, ed. H. Goedicke (Baltimore, 1985), 123–206; and I am grateful to Dr David Lorton for drawing my attention to the study. Dr Miriam Lichtheim (*Lit.* II, 58) rightly regards the text as poetic; for the original Egyptian see Kitchen, *Ramesside Inscriptions*, II, 2–64 and cf. his *Pharaoh Triumphant* (Warminster, 1982), 56 ff.

4. Criticism of a King

Whereas Herodotus paints a picture of Cheops or Khufu, the builder of the Great Pyramid, as a cruel oppressor, it is noteworthy that the Egyptian sources present him as a pious ruler. Suggestions have been made, it is true, that the Middle-Egyptian text called the Westcar Papyrus imputes impiety and cruelty to him, and Dr David Lorton has kindly drawn my attention to some of these discussions. The papyrus tells us that Khufu searched for sacred information about the sacred chambers of the enclosure of Thoth. It was in connection with the building of his tomb that he sought the information; yet B.J. Kemp (in *Ancient Egypt, A Social History*, Cambridge, 1983, 77) describes the search as 'impiety'. He cites Hornung's article (in *ZÄS* 100 (1973), 33–35), but Hornung there compares a reference to 'fields of Thoth' connected with seven shrines of flint on the sarcophagus of Ieqer now in Turin (see *CT* VI, 272d ff.) without the slightest hint of anything but an enlightened funerary purpose. Further, the search is aided in the story by the revered sage Djedi, even though it leads to Heliopolis. At the same time Kemp quite rightly dubs the story as 'The doom of the house of Khufu' since it ends with the foundation of a new dynasty. Here then, if ever, there was a splendid chance to display the theme of retribution; but it is conspicuously absent.

Admittedly a possible flaw in the picture of Khufu is suggested by Hellmut Brunner in the fourth edition of his admirable *Grundzüge einer Geschichte der altägyptischen Literatur* (Darmstadt, 1986). He remarks (p. 36) that Khufu in his first meeting with Djedi addresses him as 'servant' whereas his father King Sneferu had addressed his magician as 'my brother'—a deliberate characterization it is urged, of the two Pharaohs. I cannot locate any 'servant'; perhaps Brunner is thinking of the King's general mode of treating Djedi. In any case, the contrast would be a rather flimsy ground to justify the expansive term 'characterization'.

Later in the story Khufu orders the execution of a prisoner in order to test Djedi's claim that he can rejoin a severed head. Djedi protests that a human being should not be used, and animals are used instead. Some argue that a contrast is intended between the 'personal humane attitude of Djedi' and 'the cruelty of Khufu'; cf. the balanced discussion by David Lorton in 'The Treatment of Criminals in Ancient Egypt' in *Journal of the Economic and Social History of the Orient* 20 (1976), 16, rejecting this particular antithesis while upholding Djedi's protest as representative of a humane Egyptian standard. What should be noted is that Khufu concedes Djedi's point; if he had insisted, in spite of the protest, on killing the prisoner, now that would indeed, as Dr K. Bosse-Griffiths remarks to me, impute cruelty to him.

It is not until the New Kingdom that overt criticism of royal deeds and policies emerges. Up to then the general attitude, based on the doctrine of the King's divinity, is that 'the King can do no wrong'. At the close of the Amarna era, when Tutankhamûn became King, the large stela which he arranged to be erected at Karnak expressed forthright condemnation of the confusion and chaos which was now ascribed to previous reigns:[17]

> When His Majesty arose as king, the temples of the gods and goddesses, beginning from Elephantine down to the marshes of the Delta had fallen into decay, their shrines had fallen into desolation

---

[17] Tr. Sir Alan Gardiner, *Egypt of the Pharaohs* (Oxford, 1961), 236–7. The text is in *Urk.* iv, 2025–32. See also John Bennett, *JEA* 25 (1939), 8–15; J.A. Wilson, *ANET*[3] 251–2.

and become ruins overgrown with weeds, their chapels as though they had never been and their halls serving as footpaths. The land was topsy-turvy and the gods turned their backs on this land.

The condemnation is levelled primarily, one may infer, at the flouting of the traditional religion by Akhenaten when he eventually proclaimed the exclusive monotheism of the Aten with an attendant ban on the worship of other deities; and in the lengthy subsequent part the new King elaborates on the measures taken by him to restore the dignity of all the gods by ensuring that their shrines, statues, and rites are well equipped and honoured, so that the gods now rejoice. Rather ironically the name of Haremheb replaces each occurrence of the name of Tutankhamûn, although the traces of the latter's name are still discernible. By claiming to have restored the temples and their prestige, the young King is implicitly condemning the outright neglect of the previous King, Akhenaten; in fact it had been more than neglect, it was plain proscription. Even if Haremheb, the King's general and vice-regent, is to be regarded as essentially the author of this text,[18] the attack on the work of a previous Pharaoh is forceful. The text begins with a reference to the setting up of justice ($m3't$)—a traditional role of the Pharaoh. Traditional too was the King's duty to the upkeep of temples;[19] and from purely religious matters we are led to a wider comment: 'The land was topsy-turvy and the gods turned their backs on this land,' which is followed by 'If messengers were sent to Djahi (Syria) to extend the boundaries of Egypt, they had no success' and the complaint that gods then did not answer prayers. An accusation of chaotic conditions at home and ineffective policies abroad is again levelled against Akhenaten, both charges being probably much exaggerated. What is significant is that the charges are made at all; and they appear to have no precedent.

Before this in Egypt there had been periods of undoubted anarchy and chaos. After the break-up of the Old Kingdom frequent reference is made to the disturbed condition of Egypt. In these writings it is very rare to find a suggestion that the King's acts are criticized, although the Instruction for Merikarê implies in one section (120 ff.) that an act of spoliation is often followed by a similar counter-blow: 'A blow is repaid by the like of it, and all that

---

[18] Cf. C. Desroches-Noblecourt, *Tutankhamen* (London, 1963), 182.

[19] Cf. the name of Tutankhamûn's temple at Faras in Lower Nubia: *He who sets the gods at rest*. See Hornung (tr. Baines), *Conceptions of God in Ancient Egypt*, 250.

is achieved is a hitting.'[20] To King Akhtoy is ascribed a teaching that vengeance had best be left to God:[21]

> Be inactive about the violent man who destroys altars, for God will attack him who rebels against the temples.
>
> (*Merikarê*, 110 f.)

In *The Admonitions of an Egyptian Sage* the sage Ipuwer is telling an unnamed King of the dire straits to which Egypt had been reduced by revolution and civil wars. The powerful, including noblemen and magistrates, are said to be stripped of authority; foreign barbarians have invaded Egypt. The inversion of the social order is bewailed rather repetitiously, and especial poignancy enters into the portrayal of how the King and his office have been thrown aside:

> Behold, things have been done which have not happened for a long time past; the king has been deposed by the rabble.
> Behold, he who was buried as a falcon < is devoid > of biers, and what the pyramid concealed has become empty.
> Behold, it has befallen that the land has been deprived of the kingship by a few lawless men.
> Behold, men have fallen into rebellion against the Uraeus, the [. . .] of Re, even she who makes the Two Lands content.
>
> (*Admonitions*, 7. 1 ff.)[22]

A little later it is said that 'the secrets of the Kings of Upper and Lower Egypt are divulged'; and also that 'the king's storehouse is the common property of everyone, and the entire palace is without its revenues.' All this is part of the lamented decline. But in one place (10, 6 ff.; Faulkner, p. 224) Ipuwer urges the King to take action: 'Destroy the enemies of the august Residence, splendid of magistrates . . .', an exhortation that is repeated several times, although the text is often disturbed by lacunae. Then the King is urged to carry out all the customary ritual demands.

These exhortations give an immediacy of reference, and allusions to particular threatening foreigners may well imply a date at the end of the Thirteenth Dynasty,[23] when the Delta was dominated by the Hyksos. What is of concern to us, however, is the attitude

---

[20] Faulkner, op. cit. 190. E. Blumenthal, *Untersuchungen zum ägyptischen Königtum des mittleren Reiches*, I, 439, sees in the context an expression of royal self-criticism, as also in 70–71; cf. Wilson, *ANET*³ 417.
[21] Tr. Faulkner, ibid. 189.
[22] Tr. Faulkner, ibid. 219.
[23] John Van Seters, *JEA* 50 (1964), 13–23; cf. id. *The Hyksos* (New Haven, 1966), 103–120. J. Spiegel, in *LÄ* I (1975), 65–66, adheres to a date at the end of the Old Kingdom.

towards the kingship which emerges in the work. It is clear in the earlier sections that, in spite of the dire picture of revolution and chaos, there is no breath of criticism of the King. At no point in these sections is it suggested that the breakdown is due to a fault of his. Even when we come to the exhortation to the particular King who is addressed, that he should destroy the enemies, there is no suggestion that he is responsible for the calamities that have befallen. It is therefore puzzling to read Faulkner's[24] synopsis of Ipuwer's content:

> He describes the chaotic state into which the realm has fallen and blames the king for his failure to keep order; the sage urges the king to 'destroy the enemies of the august Residence' and to attend to his religious duties so as to bring the gods to his aid; the attributes of the monarch should be authority, knowledge, and truth, yet the present incumbent has let the land fall into confusion.

It is hard to see where the prophet 'blames the king for his failure to keep order'; and it is significant that a little later Faulkner offers two alternative explanations of the general message of the work:

> It may have been intended as a lesson in kingship by way of showing the monarch the consequences of misrule. On the other hand, it may have had a political purpose of supporting the reigning dynasty by contrasting its beneficent rule with the chaos which had gone before.

In view of the previous consistent tradition of respect for the King, which in this text is confirmed by the poignant allusions to the violent disrespect shown to royal monuments in a time of chaos, Faulkner's second alternative interpretation is much the more cogent. It may be objected that the lamentation concerning previous anarchy is parallel to the statements in the 'Restoration Stela' of Tutankhamûn. The difference is indeed dependent on our knowledge of the historical sequence: we know that the state of affairs there described is attributed, by clear implication, to Akhenaten. Admittedly, it is only implication, since the offending King is not named. If Ipuwer bewails the absence of God: 'Where is he today? Behold, his power is not seen;'[25] the 'Restoration Stela' also tells of how 'the gods turned their backs on this land.'

The literature of complaint and scepticism might seem a likely source, at first sight, for disloyal ideas levelled at kingship in a theological sense. *The Man who was Tired of Life* observes the

---

[24] Op. cit. 210.
[25] Ibid. 226 (12, 5 f.); cf. 216 (5, 3: *Indeed, the hot-tempered man says, 'If I knew where God is, then would I serve Him.'* It is not Ipuwer who says this, however, as Hornung seems to suggest, *Conceptions of God in Ancient Egypt*, 227.

transitory nature of royal pyramids, but does not suggest that the gods have thereby punished the kings; personal and social ills are lamented without historical or political comment. Still more general are the Lamentations of Khakheperrê-sonbe.[26] On the other hand, the 'Loyalist Instruction from the Sehetep-ibrê Stela' is an exhortation to adore the King, and it is accordingly to be expected that the King himself is here the arbiter of rewards and penalties:[27]

> The one whom the king loves shall be a well-provided spirit: there is no tomb for anyone who rebels against His Majesty.

Yet both dispensations clearly relate to the afterworld. Another work, 'The Prophecy of Nefer-ti', is intimately concerned with kingship; and although it is set in Sneferu's Fourth Dynasty, it is plainly related to the collapse and chaos which preceded the Twelfth Dynasty. These troubles are presaged powerfully, but the main purpose of the work is propagandist and becomes manifest when we reach the prophecy *A king of the South will come, Ameny by name*, a reference to Ammenemes I, the founder of the Twelfth Dynasty.[28] He was in fact a usurper, but the text hails him as the saviour who restores order after chaos. From our point of view the question of religious import is whether the previous kings are expressly blamed for the chaos. In other words, are the calamities and sufferings explained as divine retaliation for moral failure? The absence of the sun-god is remarked on: *Rê separates himself from men*,[29] but this is explained in the sequel on physical lines, in that the sun fails to achieve its full radiance, as a kind of concomitant gloom to add to human misery. It is striking, at the same time, that the human failure behind it all is described in studiously vague terms:[30]

> See, there are great men in the governance of the land, yet what has been done is as though it had never been done. Rê must begin by refounding the land, which is utterly ruined, and nothing remains.

In the first sentence here Helck prefers the negative form supplied by an ostracon reading, 'See, there are no longer officials in the business of the land,' where he also seems to read *srw*, 'officials',

---

[26] See Faulkner, op. cit. 230–33.
[27] Faulkner, op. cit. 200. See also Posener in *LÄ* III (1980, 982–4 ('Lehre, loyalistische') with refs.
[28] Faulkner, op. cit. 239.
[29] W. Helck, *Die Prophezeiung des Nfr.tj* (Wiesbaden, 1970), 43, XI d; cf. Faulkner, 238.
[30] Helck, op. cit. 19, IV b ff.; Faulkner, 236. M. Lichtheim, *Lit.* I, 141, gives *Lo, the great no longer rule the land*.

instead of Faulkner's presumed *wrw*, 'great ones'. Helck's preferred reading (the first one) is grammatically more cogent, and the sense is also acceptable. The reference to officials makes it unlikely that Rê is now asked to restore the whole cosmic order which is envisaged as destroyed; *the land* must rather mean Egypt.[31] Whatever the exact interpretation, it is significant that the author has not dared to blame the King. He concentrates beautifully on the civil servants although he later stipulates what the sun-god must now do. The basic ideology thus re-asserts itself: whatever calamity occurs, you are not allowed to blame the divine Pharaoh.[32]

The prophet Nefer-ti is described as a lector priest who was a native of the Heliopolitan nome. His wisdom is praised, and socially he doubtless represents the propertied class which included the high officers of state.[33] Yet in his eagerness to exonerate the kingship it is precisely these people that are attacked by him,[34] as we have seen. As for the two kings named in the work—Sneferu and Ameny—they are both treated with the utmost veneration, Sneferu being shown as a popular and beloved monarch. In the picture of Ameny some niceties are lacking, as though to cover his non-royal origin.[35] But his saving act of restoration has a quality that invites comparison with Jewish Messianism: he is 'he that cometh' and will bring joy to his people through his restoration of Maat to its rightful sphere.[36] If one has to infer that previous kings, in comparison, were guilty of misrule, yet no specific charge is levelled against any single one of them.

5. *Some Changed Emphases*

Whereas a change of ideology is to be expected in the New Kingdom, neither of the two 'Instructions' deriving from this period are

---

[31] E. Blumenthal in *ZÄS* 109 (1982), 3, favours the cosmic sense. The context is much concerned rather with the disorder in the administration of Egypt, as H. Goedicke argues in *The Protocol of Neferyt (The Prophecy of Neferti)* (Baltimore, 1977), 77 f.

[32] Cf. the allusion in 57 (= Helck, XII, 9) to the birthplace of the Lord God (*ntr nb*) in Heliopolis.

[33] E. Blumenthal, op. cit. 22.

[34] Blumenthal, ibid. appears to overlook this. She cites a study by F. Junge, 'Die Welt der Klagen', in *Fragen an die altägyptische Literatur* (FS. E. Otto, Wiesbaden, 1977), 275–84, where he shows (p. 275) that the corruption of administrators is a common theme in these writings.

[35] Blumenthal, op. cit. 26.

[36] It also recalls the later development of apocalyptic writings. Cf. Jan Bergman, in *Apocalypticism in the Mediterranean World and the Near East* ed. D. Hellholm (Tübingen, 1983), 55, regarding the work as a precursor of this trend.

much concerned with kingship. The author of the 'Instruction of Ani' was himself, probably, a scribe who belonged to the lower middle class, and he preaches 'quietude, personal piety, and ritual activity'.[37] In the 'Instruction of Ani' we find a touching example of the principle of compensation, applied here to the relationship of mother and son:[38]

> Double the food your mother gave you.
> Support her as she supported you;
> She had a heavy load in you,
> But she did not abandon you.

There is an allusion also to judgement:[39]

> It is the god who judges the righteous,
> His fate comes and takes him away.

But it is unclear whether it is envisaged as happening here and now. Vengeance, it is urged, should be left to God:[40]

> Don't rush to attack your attacker,
> Leave him to the god;
> Report him daily to the god,
> Tomorrow being like today,
> And you will see what the god does,
> When he injures him who injured you.

At no point, however, are these principles applied to the King. At the end of the work the son answers the father on the question of the value and method of his teaching. It is a debate that recalls the tenor of Greek philosophical dialogue, and in particular the discussion in Plato, *Protagoras*, 325 D.[41]

The 'Instruction of Amenemope' is of somewhat later date. It derives from the Ramesside era,[42] and the opening lines describe the author's role as 'overseer of fields' who acts as controller of harvest-dues 'in the great name of His Majesty'. Allusions to the Pharaoh are, as ever, full of respect. But the main stress of the work is the primacy of the divine ordering of life:[43]

---

[37] J.A. Wilson, *ANET*³ 420. Cf. the analysis by H. Brunner in *Hdb. der Orientalistik: Ägyptologie, Lit.*² (Leiden, 1970), 130–32, also in *LÄ* III (1980), 975–7.
[38] Tr. by M. Lichtheim, *Lit.* ii, 141.
[39] Ibid.
[40] Ibid. 142.
[41] Brunner, op. cit. 131. Cf. id., *Altägyptische Weisheit* (Zurich, 1988), 468.
[42] Irene Grumach (- Shirun), *Untersuchungen zur Lebenslehre des Amenope* (MÄS 23; Munich, 1972), 3; also in *LÄ* III (1980), 971.
[43] Grumach, op. cit. 124–5; cf. M. Lichtheim, *Lit.* ii, 157; Brunner, op. cit. 133.

> The words which man speaks are one thing,
> That which God enacts is another.
>
> (*Amenemope*, 19. 16–17.)

There is no suggestion, however, that the King is amenable to present judgement.

In many ways the concept of kingship which prevailed in the New Kingdom and the Late Period showed a continuity with the ideas of previous periods.[44] Some changes in the King's power base are observable in the late New Kingdom[45]—a matter of inner-political adjustment rather than of dogmatic ideology. In the Saïte Period (664–525 B.C.) a conscious effort was made to imitate ancient forms of the royal titulary, and variations in iconography can be traced to more distinctive predilections.[46] An instructive variation occurs in a representation of Nectanebo II, the last of the Pharaohs, who is shown with a huge Horus-falcon; Khefren in the Fourth Dynasty is also shown with the falcon in a well-known statue, but here the King is not dwarfed by the falcon with which he is equated. In the example from the Late Period the differing scale seems to suggest 'total dependence on the beneficence of the god'.[47] Already in the late Eighteenth Dynasty some diminution in the theological status of the King is apparent in the fact that a part of the 'Protestations of Innocence' occurs on the sarcophagus of Tuthmosis IV,[48] thereby making the King amenable to a process applied hitherto only to commoners. Less significant are examples of the folk tradition which enjoys tilting at Pharaonic dignity with flippant tales. An old tradition persists in this approach and its psychological motive is probably 'comic relief'.[49] The variegated sources illustrate the difference between the *Idealbild* and the *Realbild* of the Pharaoh, the latter being best seen in the Demotic and Greek texts, provided that we allow for the element of burlesque exaggeration in the popular stories about such kings as Psammetichus I, Apries, and Amasis.[50]

---

[44] Cf. Barry J. Kemp in *Ancient Egypt, A Social History* (Cambridge, 1983), 71–76 ('Divine Kingship'); David O'Connor, ibid. 188–202, although he speaks of 'quasi-divine kingship' (p. 190); and Alan B. Lloyd, ibid. 288–99.
[45] O'Connor, ibid. 229–32.
[46] A.B. Lloyd, ibid. 289–91.
[47] Lloyd, ibid. 291.
[48] L. Kákosy, *Selected Papers* (Budapest, 1981), 264 (this first publ. in 1973).
[49] Lloyd, op. cit. 293. Cf. A. Spalinger in *Orientalia* 47 (1978), 13, in a discussion of the concept of the monarchy during the Saïte Epoch, pp. 12–36.
[50] Cf. 'König Amasis und der Schiffer' in E. Brunner-Traut, *Altägyptische Märchen* (Düsseldorf, 1963), 153–5; and 'Il re Amasi si diverte' in Edda Bresciani, *Letteratura e Poesia dell'antico Egitto* (Turin, 1969), 613–14.

6. *A Revealing Test-Case*

The very culpable follies thus divertingly ascribed to some Pharaohs are, however, at some remove from an assessment of royal policy and behaviour which is based on religious sanction or censure. A Demotic document that derives from the third century B.C. provides exactly the material which illuminates this theme. Traditionally called *The Demotic Chronicle*, it is not really a chronicle, but a series of prophetic and oracular sayings, interlaced with historical comments.[51] The beginning and end of the papyrus have not been preserved, and the original text may have included a narrative framework.[52] At the heart of the apocalyptic message of the work is a promise of deliverance: after a period of rule by foreigners Egypt will be saved by a ruler emanating from Heracleopolis in Middle Egypt. Although mention is made of *foreigners and Ionians*, probably denoting Persians and Greeks, there are stylistic affinities to ancient works like the *Prophecy of Nefer-ti*, a New-Kingdom text which avers, as we have seen, that *a King of the South will come*.[53] It is, however, the element of retrospective divine assessment that concerns us. An indication of this appears in the role of the god Thoth. It is said of him (Col. II, 4) that *what they* (recent Egyptian Pharaohs) *have done has been written down by Thoth when he examined their affairs in Heracleopolis*. Thoth is of course familiar as the Recorder of the gods in the tribunal after death; here his function is to assess recent royal behaviour. It is still a posthumous judgement, but its relation to current events in Egypt gives it a historical flavour.

Vent is given to the condemnation of certain Pharaohs, but the verdict is not always uniformly adverse. A varied balance-sheet is thus presented for King Hakoris:

> The fifth ruler who came after the Medes was Hakoris, Lord of the Crown, whose time of sovereignty was made full since he was beneficent to the temples. He was overthrown because he abandoned the Law, and did not have solicitude for his brothers.
> (*Demotic Chronicle*, Recto Col. IV, 9–10.)

---

[51] See Janet H. Johnson, 'The Demotic Chronicle as a Statement of a Theory of Kingship', in *JSSEA* 13.3 (1983), 61–72; also her studies in *Enchoria* 4 (1974), 1–17 ('The Demotic Chronicle as a Historical Source'); and in *Grammata Demotika* (FS. E. Lüddeckens) ed. Heinz-J. Thissen and Karl-Th. Zauzich (Würzburg, 1984), 107–124 ('Is the Demotic Chronicle an Anti-Greek Tract?'). One eagerly awaits a full Edition, with Translation and Commentary, by Dr Johnson.

[52] Cf. P. Kaplony, 'Demotische Chronik'. in *LÄ* I (1975), 1056–60.

[53] Cf. my remarks in *Apocalypticism etc.* ed. David Hellholm, 279–83; cf. J. Bergman, ibid. 53–55; and J. Assmann, ibid. 357–61.

Favour shown to the temples is a natural, if superficial, cause of divine approval. Lack of concern for 'brothers' is a moral complaint extending, one supposes, only to the royal family, although the reference might be wider. A slight contradiction appears in the allusion to 'making full' the time of sovereignty, for it is then said that *he was overthrown*; so there *was* a cutting short of the reign, but not before a respectable time-span was over. Length of reign is therefore dependent on divine favour; Hebrew parallels abound, but earlier Egyptian sources often present the idea, though not in royal contexts, that longevity is a gift accorded by the gods to the virtuous.

The statement that Hakoris *was overthrown because he abandoned the Law* is by no means an isolated dictum in this text. In fact the upholding of the Law (*ḥp*) becomes a fairly constant criterion in the rationale of moral assessment. In one case, that of Nepherites II, the sin is imputed to the Pharaoh's father:

> The sixth ruler who came after the Medes was Nepherites. 'He has not lived.' That means, the order was not made to allow him to live. It happened that the Law at the time of his father was abandoned . . . Thus the sacrilege was avenged after him on his son.
> (Ibid. Recto, Col. IV, 11–12.)

It seems that the reign of Nepherites II was indeed a short one, lasting four months only. It was not he, nevertheless, who flouted the Law, but his father. Visiting the sins of the fathers on the children is an idea again prominent in the Hebrew tradition. Yet the approach is not always negative. It is said (III, 19) of Amyrtaeus that *the Law was restored in his time*; and the restored Egyptian ruler will be loyal to the Law:

> Rejoice over the ruler that will be, for he will not abandon the Law.
> (Ibid. Recto, Col. III, 16.)

In *JEA* 72 (1986), 152 J.D. Ray assembles some of the negative statements and talks of the 'final lurch into depravity' made by Hakoris; he suggests too that the portrayal of Psammuthis as 'impious' derives merely from the 'short length of his reign' and 'need not be taken seriously'. Certainly the correspondence conveyed seems to be rather mechanical. Ray is more concerned here, however, with matters of chronology. He proposes to locate Psammuthis as a usurper who intruded after the second year of Hakoris, and remarks that 'history in this case was more complex than theology would have liked it to be.'

One of the earliest commentators on the Demotic Chronicle was

Eduard Meyer,[54] and it was his view that these assessments of rulers through theological criteria show the impress of Hebrew thought. Points of language may well support this view. The term *hp*. 'Law', instantly invokes the Hebrew Torah; and the phrase *mi̯ (.t) p3 ntr*, 'the way of God' (IV, 7), was well compared by Spiegelberg,[55] the first editor and translator, with the Hebrew *děrěkh Yăhweh*, 'the way of Yahweh'. In the latter case, however, Egyptian antecedents can be cited.[56] The word *hp*, 'law', 'Justice', is used in Middle Egyptian and afterwards, usually in the plural; in the *Demotic Chronicle* it is consistently and significantly in the singular, usually with the definite article, and it bears the meaning 'law, right, or justice'.[57] In *VA* 2 (1986), 53–62 David Lorton discusses 'The King and the Law', and his careful analysis of the terminology bears out the juxtaposition, in several instances, of the plural *hpw* and the singular *M3't*, the latter only being used, before the Demotic texts, of 'law' in an abstract sense.

Yet it is not on linguistic resemblances that the argument for extraneous influence mainly depends. It is on the striking recurrences of the theological concepts. In her admirable study of the *Demotic Chronicle* and its doctrine of kingship, Janet H. Johnson[58] is very ready to note parallels in non-Egyptian sources, but she finally posits the idea that the theory of kingship here expounded is 'solidly rooted in earlier Egyptian tradition'.[59] That this tradition was susceptible to changes is apparent in some detail from the above discussion and the change so forthrightly enounced in the *Chronicle* demands an explanation from outside the native outlook. As we have seen, Meyer drew attention to the possibility of Hebrew influence, basing his case on contemporary developments in Judah. He refers especially to the Books of Judges and Kings and to the fact that the idea of the 'Law' in a special sense was being developed in Egypt at a time when the Law of Deuteronomy was introduced in Judah. The punishment for disobedience to the Torah is exemplified in the Book of Chronicles too, as in the account of the fate of Rehoboam:

---

[54] 'Ägyptische Dokumente aus der Persenzeit', *SPAW* (Berlin, 1915), 287–311.
[55] *Die sogenannte Demotische Chronik* (Leipzig, 1914), 18 n. 3; cf. Alan B. Lloyd in *Historia* 31 (1982), 43.
[56] Janet H. Johnson in *JSSEA* 13 (1983), 69.
[57] Charles Nims in *JNES* 7 (1948), 243–60. The wider abstract concept is denoted in Egyptian by *M3't*; cf. Lloyd in *Historia* 31 (1982), 43, noting a phrase *hpw nw M3't*, 'the laws of Justice', from the New Kingdom. For some wider senses in Demotic writings, such as 'the laws of nature', see my remarks on observations by E.A.E. Reymond in *Apocalypticism etc.* (1983), 282.
[58] Op. cit.
[59] Ibid. 72.

> When the rule of Rehoboam was established and was strong, he forsook the law of the Lord, and all Israel with him.
> (2 Chron. 12:1; followed by the coming of Shishak against Jerusalem.)
>
> Thus says the Lord, 'You abandoned me, so I have abandoned you to the hand of Shishak.'
> (2 Chron. 12:5.)

Thus too does the end of Jehu come in 2 Kings 10.31 (*Jehu took no heed to walk in the law of the Lord*). Much can now be added to reinforce Meyer's approach when the cultural interchange of later centuries is taken into account. In the third century B.C. (when the *Demotic Chronicle* was written) such interchange was possible in both directions. There were Jewish communities active in Lower Egypt who were patently exposed to the influence of their environment in respect to the Greek culture of the country's rulers and also to the native Egyptian culture of all parts of the *chôra*. That the Hellenistic age was an age of syncretism is long since a cliché. Its detailed validity rests largely on the pursuit of Comparative Literature, and it is fortunate that recent studies have flourished in this field. In some instances, admittedly, lively debate has ensued on the question of the direction in which influence has been exerted, even when the presence of influence is clearly manifest. In the case of the 'Instruction of Amenemope', an earlier text which derives from the eleventh or tenth century B.C., parallels with the Book of Proverbs (mainly 22:17–23:11) are evident, and some scholars, including the Egyptologist Étienne Drioton, have favoured the view that here the Hebrew tradition has influenced that of Egypt. It has now been decisively shown, however, that the passage common to the two works have much earlier antecedents in Egyptian Wisdom and that the Hebrew work makes detailed references to Amenemope, as in the mention of 'thirty chapters' (Prov. 22:20) which alludes to the thirty sections of the Egyptian work.[60]

The 'Instructions of Onkhsheshonqy' appear in a manuscript of Ptolemaic date (it may date from the second century B.C.),[61] and various debates have gathered around its content. It is introduced by a story in which one of the two protagonists is implicated in a plot against the life of the Pharaoh. The other protagonist, who is

---

[60] See Ronald J. Williams, 'The Alleged Semitic Original of *Amenemope*', *JEA* 47 (1961), 100–106; and in *The Legacy of Egypt* (2nd Ed., ed. J.R. Harris, Oxford, 1971), 246–7.

[61] S.R.K. Glanville, *Cat. of Demotic Papyri in the British Museum*, Vol. II (London, 1955), xii; cf. H.S. Smith in *Serapis* 6 (1980; in honor of Charles F. Nims), 155.

the author of the Instructions, suffers imprisonment although innocent, and he complains to the god Prê:[62]

> Oppression and misfortune, my great lord Prê, imprisonment and oppression are what have been inflicted upon me because I did not kill a man. It is your abomination, O my great lord Prê! Is this the way in which Prê vents his anger upon a land?
> (*Onkhsheshonqy*, IV, 19–20.)

Here the complaint is addressed to the god, but it is the Pharaoh who is accused of causing unjust oppression. A little later the anger of Prê is seen as inflicting retaliation for the Pharaoh's offence, and once more the emphasis is on the neglect of the Law:[63]

> [If] Prê is angry with a land, its ruler neglects the law.
> If Prê is angry with a land, he makes the law cease in it.
> If Prê is angry with a land, he makes sanctity cease.
> If Prê is angry with a land, he makes justice cease in it.
> If Prê is angry with a land, he makes value scarce in it.
> (Ibid. V, 2–7.)

On the other hand, retaliation on a personal level should be avoided according to his counsel:[64]

> Do not retaliate, do not let one retaliate against you.
> (Ibid. XII, 16.)

While it is not mainly concerned with the culpability of the Pharaoh, this Book of Instructions shares with the *Demotic Chronicle* a readiness to broach that possibility quite forcibly. It is a book that raises in other ways too the question of religious and cultural contact. Peter Walcot's studies have well illustrated the range of interpenetration which must be considered. In his book *Hesiod and the Near East* (Cardiff, 1966) he was able to show that Hesiod's *Theogony* has clear links with the Hittite Epic of Kumarbi and the Song of Ullikummi.[65] But in another study[66] he suggested that the influence of Hesiod is apparent in the 'Instructions of 'Onkhsheshonqy'. Chronologically there seems to be no difficulty in the suggestion, for Hesiod probably wrote towards the end of the

---

[62] Tr. by H.S. Smith, ibid. 152–3.
[63] Tr. M. Lichtheim, *Late Egyptian Wisdom Literature in the International Context* (Freiburg, Schweiz, 1983), 23.
[64] Ibid. 32, with further examples.
[65] See also M.L. West, *Hesiod, Theogony* (Oxford, 1966), 20–31, ending 'Greek literature is a Near Eastern literature;' see too his account of 'Wisdom Literature' in *Hesiod, Works and Days* (Oxford, 1978), 3–25.
[66] P. Walcot, 'Hesiod and the Instructions of 'Onchsheshonqy', *JNES* 21 (1962), 215–19.

eighth century B.C. whereas the Egyptian work is unlikely to have had its origin earlier than the fourth century B.C. Walcot points to a number of parallel features, especially the peasant audience with which both are concerned; also the doctrine of hard work and the danger of procrastination. A basic question that goes beyond the comparative dating of the works is that concerning the literary antiquity of the concepts presented—a problem faced by Walcot himself. For instance, both the Greek and the Egyptian works stress the need for restraint in speech. Here is a virtue much extolled in the very earliest stratum of the Egyptian Wisdom Literature, more than ten centuries before Hesiod. There are other facets which do not have ancient antecedents, and the concern with agriculture is perhaps the most important parallel point in Walcot's thesis.[67]

It is of course desirable to list all parallels between such works even if the establishment of a literary influence is a difficult procedure. A recent expositor[68] of Onkhsheshonqy preserves a cautious attitude, while inclining to the view that the sayings derive from Egyptian tradition. It is caution that is certainly excessive. A contrast is found in the recent work of Miriam Lichtheim,[69] who prefers to speak of 'international wisdom literatures'. In a book which provides studies, with translations, of Onkhsheshonqy's Instructions, of the Louvre Demotic Papyri 2414 and 2377, and of the Instruction of Papyrus Insinger, she defines one of her considered conclusions thus:

> The detailed study of the genre has led to the conclusion that Demotic Instructions had absorbed many elements of non-Egyptian origin, for their authors had been acquainted with, and influenced by, the currents of international wisdom literatures, Near Eastern and Greek, which flowed through the internationalized cultures of the Hellenistic world.
>
> (M. Lichtheim, op. cit. (1983), p. x.)

The term 'international' might seem somewhat expansive. Perhaps

---

[67] Cf. R.J. Williams, 'The Sages of Ancient Egypt in the Light of Recent Scholarship', *JAOS* 101 (1981), 1–19, esp. p. 5 on Walcot ('the interesting and plausible conjecture'). On the importance of 'The Silent Man' in the Egyptian tradition see Emma Brunner-Traut in *Studien zu altägyptischen Lebenslehren* ed. E. Hornung and O. Keel (Freiburg, Schweiz, 1979), 174–216, where she deals mainly with its survival in Coptic Egypt.

[68] H.J. Thissen, *Die Lehre des Anchscheschonqi* (Bonn, 1984), 6–7.

[69] *Late Egyptian Wisdom Literature in the International Context* (1983). Cf. the saying in Matt. 6:34 (*Take no care for the morrow* . . .) which doubtless derives immediately from Jewish proverbial lore, but which ultimately provides an instance of Egyptian influence on the gnomic literature of the Hebrews. See my 'Wisdom About Tomorrow' in *Harv. Theol. Rev.* 53 (1960), 219–22.

'Near Eastern' would be better, remembering Martin West's dictum that 'Greek literature is a Near Eastern literature'. It is surprising, in view of this, that Dr Lichtheim finds Walcot's thesis 'unconvincing'.[70]

The theory that the *Demotic Chronicle* is indebted to Hebrew tradition for its basic doctrine on the moral condemnation of kingship is fortunately a more restricted theme than the whole sweep of Near Eastern Wisdom Literature. We have seen some evidence for the doctrine in the 'Instructions of Onkhsheshonqy'; and there is certainly testimony to other literary commerce between Hellenistic Egypt and Judaism. A number of sayings in the Demotic Papyrus Insinger can be compared in content and form with sayings in Qoheleth and Ben Sira;[71] prominence is given, at the same time, to the teaching about 'Tyche-Nemesis', where Demotic uses the term *p3 tb3*, 'retaliation', referring in P. Insinger to the 'divine avenger' who in the Tefnut legend takes the form of a griffin.[72] However, retaliation for crimes in general is meant, and it is not applied especially to the conduct of kings.

The impact of Egypt is revealed in some Jewish ritual practices, such as the placing of sacred scrolls in tombs, for which there is evidence in Palestine and in Roman catacombs, as well as in the synagogue of Priene.[73] The religious Jewish community, the Therapeutae, who lived in seclusion near Alexandria, betrayed some Egyptian influences, as Daumas[74] has shown. In religious ideas the doctrines attached to Isis have been rightly linked with Philo's concept of the Logos and of Sophia, and also with the Wisdom of Solomon.[75] Again, Demotic Wisdom had a clear impact on Ben Sira;[76] and the debt of the Hermetic literature to Egyptian religion has been detailed by Erik Iversen in matters of cosmology.[77] Nor is

---

[70] M. Lichtheim, *Ancient Egyptian Literature*, iii (Berkeley, 1980), 160.

[71] M. Lichtheim in *Studien zu altägyptischen Lebenslehren*, ed. Hornung and Keel, 301–3; and in *Late Egyptian Wisdom Literature etc.*, 141–4, where Stoic doctrine is also compared; further, 157–8; 184–7.

[72] M. Lichtheim, ibid. 151–2; Emma Brunner-Traut in *Fragen an die altägyptische Literatur* (Gedenkschr. E. Otto, 1977), 125–42; H. Brunner, 'Petbe', *LÄ* IV (1982), 992–3, who invokes possible Greek influence.

[73] E.R. Goodenough, *Jewish Symbols in the Greco-Roman Period* (New York, 1953–58), iv, 142, who rightly recalls the Egyptian use of the Book of the Dead.

[74] In his edition of Philo, *De vita contemplativa* (Paris, 1963), Introduction.

[75] Wilfred L. Knox, *Some Hellenistic Elements in Primitive Christianity* (London, 1944), 51 and 78 n. 2; cf. A.D. Nock, *Essays on Religion and the Ancient World* (Oxford, 1972), i, 460; ii, 882.

[76] Jack T. Sanders, *Ben Sira and Demotic Wisdom* (Chicago, 1983).

[77] Erik Iversen, *Egyptian and Hermetic Doctrine* (Copenhagen, 1984); cf. my Review in *CR* 36 (1986), 323–4.

it without significance that the earliest Jewish synagogues arose in Egypt.[78] It would be strange, amid such abundant testimonies, if traffic in the other direction, were not attested. A Hymn to Isis from Philae includes an episode in which the King (in this case Ptolemy II Philadelphus) is subjected to scrutiny and humiliation in the manner of the Jewish and Babylonian New Year ceremonies.[79] This is clearly relevant to the condemnation of certain kings in the *Demotic Chronicle*.

It is true that an inner-Egyptian change of emphasis might partly explain the revised outlook. The Egyptians had consistently regarded the ordinary man as being susceptible to divine control and chastisement, and in the Late Period there are signs that the King was being mentally reduced to the same level, especially after the disasters experienced by Egypt after the Persian conquest in 525 B.C.[80] This view does not make any allowance, however, for possible foreign influences, one clear example of which occurs in relation to the idea of retribution. In the Late Period and afterwards the term *petbe*, deriving from an Egyptian expression meaning 'recompense', was used in Demotic and Coptic, and a personification ensued in which the Greek Nemesis clearly played a part in both iconography and ideology.[81]

---

[78] See my 'Egypt and the Rise of the Synagogue', *4th International Congress of Egyptology, Abstracts* (Munich, 1985), 74–76 and more fully in *JTS*, 38 (1987), 1–15.

[79] Louis V. Žabkar, *Hymns to Isis in her Temple at Philae* (Univ. Press of New England, 1988), Hymn VIII, pp. 115 ff., esp. 121–3. He does not himself point the parallel mentioned. See also my remarks on 'Royal Renewal Rites in Ancient Egypt' in *La Commémoration* ed. Ph. Gignoux (Louvain-Paris, 1988), 35–46.

[80] Cf. E. Otto, *Die biographischen Inschriften der ägyptischen Spätzeit* (Leiden, 1954), 116–18; cf. A.B. Lloyd in *Historia* 31 (1982), 43–44 and in *Ancient Egypt, a Social History* (Cambridge, 1983), 299; Janet H. Johnson in *JSSEA* 13 (1983), 69–72. Both Lloyd and Johnson tend to argue for a continued ancient tradition, although Lloyd is prepared to concede a diminution in the Pharaoh's moral status. John D. Ray in *Divination and Oracles*, ed. M. Loewe and C. Blacker, 183, remarks of the Demotic Chronicle that 'in more than one case moral character is equated with length of reign' and points also to the 'nationalistic themes'. In *JEA* 72 (1986), 149–58 ('Psammuthis and Hakoris') he is mainly concerned with dynastic sequence, but discusses the theological emphases (see esp. pp. 151–2), finding (p. 156) that 'history in this case was more complex than theology would have liked it to be.'

[81] H. Brunner, in *LÄ* IV (1982), 992, s. v. 'Petbe'.

CHAPTER EIGHT

EGYPT: PHARAOH AND PEOPLE

B) DIVINE IMPACT ON HUMAN AFFAIRS IN NON-ROYAL BIOGRAPHY

A feature often ascribed to Egyptian religious thought is the belief that the gods are able to intervene in human life. The intervention may be beneficent in the sense that it saves from danger or calamity or confers rewards, in the long view, on the upright and virtuous; or it may be malevolent in the sense that it brings suffering or injury which is interpreted as a punishment inflicted on wrongdoers. This general approach is of course present in several other ancient religions, notably in the theology of the Hebrews and the Greeks, as we have seen. A field of literature which might seem a promising area to test the nature and strength of this belief among the Egyptians is that of biographical writings. Many such writings are concerned with private individuals and are therefore free of the theological complexities which might apply to statements made by, or about, the Pharaohs, particularly the complexity that the King himself was officially described, and to some debatable extent regarded, as a god.

1. *Divine Impact on This Life.*

Egypt was the home of the non-royal autobiography, and the earliest autobiographies, such as that of Weni of the Sixth Dynasty, were funerary texts. This is also true of many other biographical writings both early and late. A conceptual difficulty may sometimes arise from the funerary context. By the New Kingdom the Egyptians had evolved a firm and vividly illustrated system of posthumous judgement. Every deceased person was believed to have to face, after death, a tribunal which decided his fate in the afterworld according to the result of a scrutiny of his life which purported to apply moral criteria. It was not until the New Kingdom that this belief was given the iconographical expression that secured its potent popularity;[1] but the belief itself, including the symbolism of

---

[1] Christine (Beinlich-) Seeber, *Untersuchungen zur Darstellung des Totengerichts im Alten Ägypten* (MÄS 35; Munich, 1976), 2.

'weighing the heart' which was attached to it, is attested earlier in literature;[2] as in the Instruction of Merikarê. Funerary texts, including those of a biographical character, naturally refer to the judgement after death. The question which is bound to arise is whether this judgement affected in some way the idea that a divine assessment is being operated during the course of this life. Does the second judgement cancel out the first? Is success or failure in the life on earth related to expressions of divine sanction or chastisement?

In some ways the Egyptians dealt with the possibility of divine impact, whether favourable or unfavourable, on the level of magical equipment and competence. This is the approach behind the 'Calendar of Lucky and Unlucky Days'.[3] It was important to know, in relation to the triple division of each day (thus in Book III), what parts were favourable (*nfr*) and adverse (*ḥ3*), and for what reasons, mythological or theological. It was also important to know what actions it was proper to pursue or to avoid. The actions detailed are generally of ritual significance, and there is a singular lack of ethical emphasis in the whole business. Predictions abound concerning people born on particular days. Certain texts from Deir el-Medîna are of a more personal nature in that they record the reaction of individuals to the experience of the 'manifestation' (*b3w*) of a god.[4] For the most part these texts describe the effect of the divine encounter on the individuals concerned, but they do not deal in a wider sense with the control exerted by the gods upon the lives of these individuals. (An outstanding exception is the case of a man who may have believed he had suffered blindness as a punishment inflicted by a god, although the interpretation is contested.) I tend to demur, therefore, to the use of the term 'Divine Intervention' in the title of the learned essay by Dr Borghouts, particularly as he makes no attempt to cover the whole field in the way suggested by the title.[5] The type of experience with which he deals is well exemplified by his fourth instance (pp. 5–7).[6] Here the

---

[2] Reinhard Grieshammer, *Das Jenseitsgericht in den Sargtexten* (Wiesbaden, 1970), 46 ff.

[3] A.M. Bakir, *The Cairo Calendar No. 86637* (Cairo, 1966); see esp. his synopsis, pp. 2–5. P. Sallier IV (BM 10184) is partly similar. The Cairo Papyrus sometimes designates a whole day or half of a day with the basic sign.

[4] See J.F. Borghouts, 'Divine Intervention in Ancient Egypt and its Manifestation (*b3w*)' in *Gleanings from Deir el-Medîna* ed. R.J. Demarée and Jac J. Janssen (Leiden, 1982), 1–70.

[5] In other ways he is finicky about terminology, preferring on p. 1 to call the article *p3* in *p3 b3w* 'a singular prepositive determiner'.

[6] = Kitchen, *Ramesside Inscriptions* III (Oxford, 1980), 687, No. 12.

sculptor Qen addresses the sun (*šw* with the sun determinative) and the gods of heaven and earth. He then says that he has made a statement falsely (*m 'd̲3*) to the lady of the house, but that a manifestation of a god (*b3w nt̲r*) afterwards occurred, with the result that he now says to various gods *ḥtp n.ỉ, be merciful to me*. Probably he is asking for forgiveness.[7]

2. *Sinuhe's God-given Success*

Religious ideas and motifs appear often in *Sinuhe*, the favoured classic of Middle Egyptian, and it is not surprising to find that the climax of the story, which concerns the victorious fight of Sinuhe against the champion of the Retenu, the Syrians, gives a clear example of a successful outcome being ascribed to a god who has supported Sinuhe in his wanderings and extended mercy to him after an initial phase of anger. Sinuhe kills the doughty challenger and then seizes his property. He now enjoys a state of renown and wealth. This climactic triumph stresses his debt to divine support. I quote from Dr Lichtheim's translation:[8]

> Thus I became great, wealthy in goods, rich in herds. It was the god who acted, so as to show mercy to one with whom he had been angry, whom he has made stray abroad. For today his heart is appeased.

The god is not named, but just before this, at the moment of victory, Sinuhe says *I gave praise to Mont*, referring to the well-known god of warlike prowess. A deity of wider powers is probably envisaged as the one who ordained the whole course of events. In fact the question is left open in the slightly later plea: *Whichever god decreed this flight, have mercy, bring me home!* (Simpson's *O God, whoever you are . . .* develops the sense of *nb* as 'any',; one wonders whether it does not mean 'lord' here, for *nb*, 'lord', follows *nt̲r* in *Sin*. B 206 and 210; if so, it will be *O Lord God, who decreed . . .*) The traditional translation implies a deliberate withholding of the god's name, and there are parallels, of course, to this tendency—in Egypt itself and in the Athenian *agnostos theos* discussed by Paul.

What is of some interest and relevance is that this passage in

---

[7] *Wb*. III, 186 ff. It is noteworthy that a rendering 'vergeben' is missing; the word is also absent from the German-Egyptian Index, although two other words are supplied under 'verzeihen'.

[8] Miriam Lichtheim, *Ancient Egyptian Literature*, I (Berkeley, 1973), 228; W.K. Simpson, *The Literature of Ancient Egypt* (New Haven, 1972), 65. On the unnamed god see Emma Brunner-Traut in *LÄ* I (1973), 281–91 and H. Brunner in *Der Name Gottes* ed. H. von Stietencron (Düsseldorf, 1975), 42, with a discussion of this passage.

Sinuhe flatly contradicts the generalization propounded by Eberhard Otto[9] in his valuable study of the biographical inscriptions of the Late Period. He there (pp. 22–23) sums up the doctrine of earlier eras as one claiming to be based on the natural order: 'Behave uprightly on earth, then success cannot fail to follow; and indeed in the earlier period the sequence of behaviour and success has the appearance, so to speak, of a naturally decreed order. Now, however (i.e. in the Late Period), God is presented as the causation of behaviour and success.' (Translated) The sequence is now a free decision by God; it cannot be compelled. In this work Otto is naturally not concerned to provide detailed examples from earlier periods apart from a few quotations from the Wisdom Literature.

3. *Later Biography*

Although *Sinuhe* happens to supply a strikingly different approach, it would be unwise to represent it as entirely typical. Certainly Otto offers abundant instances to illustrate his statement about the Late Period; and we are now well placed to study some of these instances in a publication which reproduces the original texts *in extenso* together with a Translation and Commentary.[10] For the more limited period with which he is dealing Jansen-Winkeln has assembled (II, pp. 387–92) statements to illustrate the influence of God on men. One of these (II, p. 387: B22, Takeloth II) is *sb3.n nb.f, whom his lord has instructed*; it seems that Amûn is meant here (cf. I, p. 293), while the following clause refers to the pupil becoming a *strong-armed Horus*.[11] Other benefits mentioned as divine bestowals are the banishment of ignorance, longevity on earth, temporal power, the recognition of able efficiency, election before his kinsmen, exaltation to headship of state and temple, a pleasant and respected old age, the gift of a son and also the establishment of a son in the line of succession. Several of these favours relate to kings (as with Takeloth II above), and a problem arises in that the Pharaoh occupies a distinctively lofty position. Priestly privileges, which are often subsumed by the royal status, are also in a special category.[12] Among a collection of more general sentiments too there

---

[9] *Die biographischen Inschriften der ägyptischen Spätzeit* (Leiden, 1954), 22 f.

[10] Karl Jansen-Winkeln, *Ägyptische Biographien der 22. und 23. Dynastie* (Wiesbaden, 1985). The first volume gives a Translation and Commentary, the second a treatment of the phraseology followed by the texts themselves.

[11] Cf. R.A. Caminos, *The Chronicle of Prince Osorkon* (Rome, 1958), 87, note kk. citing *Wb.* IV, 84, 4–5 and Černy, *Inscrs. of Sinai*, II, 105 n. f (*whom Horus, lord of the palace, taught*).

[12] Jansen-Winkeln, op. cit. II, 392–402.

is a sense of the blessedness which comes from obedience to God:

> How beautiful it is, to walk uprightly on the way of God.
> (II, p. 424, 6.6.)

> If you (the gods) are satisfied with the upright on earth, his God loves him who does not know two ways in his affairs.
> (II p. 424, 6.7.)

> I know that God acts in favour of the upright man.
> (II, p. 425, 6.8.)

> I completed the years in contentment; that is the reward for one who does good.
> (II, p. 426, 6.16.)

While Jansen-Winkeln makes no claim to assess the general significance of these texts, his analytical compendium is most helpful. The last quotation used above makes no mention, be it noted, of God or gods, but as a rule such a mention does occur.

Perhaps it is in the inscriptions of Petosiris (*c.* 320 B.C.) that we find the most striking expressions of the doctrine:[13]

> Thy lord, Thoth, has caused this to happen for thee; for thou wert friendly to everyman.
> (Lefebvre, II, 31, Inscr. 58 d, 40; with I, 90.)

> O loved one of all the gods, thy barns are full because thou hast enabled men (thy subordinates) to live.
> (Ibid. II, 30, Inscr. 58 c, 24; with I, 88.)

> He who keeps his heart on God's way
> maintains his life-span on earth.
> He who has great fear of God in his heart
> has great favour on earth.
> (Ibid. II, 38, Inscr. 62.2; with I, 82.)

Thoth is named in the first of these quotations, and Petosiris was a High Priest of Thoth in Hermopolis. When no god is named, as in the other quotations, it is likely that Thoth is intended; likewise generally, the anonymous god is probably the local god.

---

[13] G. Lefebvre, *Le Tombeau de Petosiris*, 3 Vols. (Cairo, 1903–4); E. Otto, *Die biographischen Inschriften*, 23 with refs. Cf. M. Lichtheim, *Lit.* III, (1980), 45–54; Susanne Nakaten, 'Petosiris' in *LÄ* IV (1982), 995–8; Emma Brunner-Traut, *Lebensweisheit der Alten Ägypter* (Freiburg im Breisgau, 1985), 66–71.

4. Sin and Suffering in the Confessional Literature

If the doctrine portrays the virtuous as being thus consistently rewarded, the treatment of the wicked is assumed to be otherwise, but these biographies, which normally praise the subject, do not refer to an outcome of that kind. An instance occurs, however, in a biographical allusion contained in a well-known hymn to Ptah from Deir el-Medîna.[14] Here Neferabw narrates how he swore a false oath to Ptah, whereupon the god caused him *to see darkness by day*, and he ends with a warning that it is dangerous to offend Ptah in this way. *To see darkness by day* has usually been explained as blindness, perhaps temporary.[15] If the phrase metaphorically implies 'disgrace'[16] or spiritual disfavour, the theological point remains clear: it is a punishment for immoral conduct. Whereas the concept of Maat and its derivatives often appears in these texts, it cannot be said that Maat whether viewed as an abstract principle or a personal entity, is usually regarded as the agent that determines good or bad fortune. That role is normally assigned to a deity. The literary *Gattung* concerned may have something to do with this. It is not a matter of affixing a mere label such as 'Biography' as opposed to 'Wisdom Literature'. What goes on in the biographical writings is inherently more personal in the sense that an individual's career or experience is recorded; and this invites a more personal record of any encounter with the divine. In the Wisdom Literature, on the other hand, aphorism and doctrine are the expected mode and the whole presentation is usually more impersonal, although the tradition of instruction for a son is at-

---

[14] T.G.H. James, *Hieroglyphic Texts in the British Museum*, 9 (1970), 36–37 and Pl. 31.

[15] Thus Borghouts, op. cit. in n. 4 above, 7; cf. M. Lichtheim, *Lit.* II, 109; E. Brunner-Traut, op. cit. 37.

[16] Thus Erik Hornung according to Borghouts, 43 n. 31. H. Brunner, 'Blindheit' in *LÄ* I (1975), 828–33, discusses the metaphorical usages (830–31), but regards this allusion as pointing to physical blindness (828). Jan Assmann, *Ägyptische Hymnen und Gebete* (Zürich, 1975), devotes pp. 347–417 to 'personal piety' with this text as No. 150 B, pp. 355–6 with notes on pp. 598–9, where he compares his No. 147, 29–30 (with n. on p. 596): *Thou dost cause me to see darkness, which thou givest; shine for me, that I may see thee!* In his *Ägypten—Theologie und Frömmigkeit einer frühen Hochkultur* (Stuttgart, 1984), 260–64, Assmann shows that darkness is several times used metaphorically to denote the absence or distance of God. See also H. Brunner, 'Gottesnähe und -ferne', in *LÄ* II (1977), 817–19; but Brunner sees some instances as implying both physical and metaphorical darkness; that is, a blindness inflicted which points also to the distance of God. Yet the allocation of darkness and daylight can be present symbolically, as Assmann shows; thus in P. Bremner-Rhind, 7, 3–4, Isis sings of the absence of Osiris: *Darkness is here for us in my sight even while Rê is in the sky.*

tested early. Even in the Wisdom Literature it is misleading to view the role of Maat as an automatic process. An important study by Hellmut Brunner[17] shows how the gods are often invoked as the true arbiters of human destiny. He quotes the saying in the early wisdom of Ptah-hotep (115 f.): *The plans of men are never realized, but it is what God commands that prevails.* In the Instruction of Ani (8. 15–16) personal retribution, it is urged, should be left to God: *Thou wilt see what God does, when he injures him who injured thee.*[18] Brunner is able to show that in the later Wisdom Literature, such as that of Amenemope, there are clear marks of the influence of the spiritual approach shown in the biographical confessional literature; in particular a loving and forgiving relationship between God and man finds expression. The term 'personal piety' is often used to describe these writings of the Late New Kingdom. It appears that Breasted[19] was the first to use the term, and as a too convenient label[20] it is unfortunate in its suggestion that this age had an exclusive right to be so regarded. 'Personal piety' certainly appeared in other ages. The literature of the Amarna age, although contrasting in its elitism, includes masterpieces which merit the description.

Among the compositions thus labelled are several which show concern with divine judgement in this world and the next; nor is the distinction always clear. A hymn in praise of Amen-Rê[21] extols the god as an impartial and incorruptible judge. He is called *the vizier of the poor*; he does not receive bribes from the guilty. The brief eulogy ends thus:

> Amûn judges the earth with his fingers
> and speaks to the heart.
> He judges the guilty and assigns him to the East (?)
> and the just to the West.
> (Caminos, *LEM*, 9–10; cf. Jan Assmann, *Ägyptische Hymnen–und Gebete* (Zürich, 1975), 379, No. 174.)

Here the first sentence clearly applies to judgement here and now, even if *with his fingers* is a little uncertain in reference. Caminos takes the noun as synonymous with 'hands'; Fecht thinks that the sun's

---

[17] 'Der freie Wille Gottes in der ägyptischen Weisheit' in *Les Sagesses du Proche-Orient Ancien* (Paris, 1963), 103–120.
[18] Brunner, op. cit. 107; cf. M. Lichtheim, *Lit.* II, 142.
[19] *Development of Religion and Thought in Ancient Egypt* (London, 1912), 349; cf. id. *The Dawn of Conscience* (New York, 1946), 313.
[20] Cf. Gerhard Fecht, *Literarische Zeugnisse zur 'Persönlichen Frömmigkeit' in Ägypten* (Heidelberg, 1965), 11 n. 7, referring to it as a 'necessary evil'.
[21] Gardiner, *Late-Egyptian Miscellanies* (Brussels, 1937), 2; R.A. Caminos, *Late-Egyptian Miscellanies* (London, 1954), 9–11; Fecht, op. cit. 39–41.

rays are meant, with an allusion to the judicial function carried out by the sun-god in the solar barque (perhaps with the symbolism borrowed from Amarna); fingers are, however, often mentioned with reference to scribal efficiency in accounting,[22] and Thoth as a recorder of the gods is the paradigm of this expertise.[23] If Amûn *speaks to the heart*, his cogent address to the conscience and knowledge of hearers in an earthly court must be envisaged. But the final sentence confronts us firmly with his judgement after death, with a suggestion in 'East', as Caminos shows, of a burning hell.

The 'Prayer of a defendant to Amûn'[24] has no double aspect; it is concerned solely with the fate of a defendant in an Egyptian court of law. He is a poor defendant, and the court is defrauding him of silver and gold. His prayer is that Amûn may be found[25] to change himself into the presiding vizier in order to ensure the triumph of the helpless pleader. A pathetic wishful fantasy is implied. In a 'Hymn to Thoth'[26] the judicial background is abandoned, and the god is praised for the prosperity and happiness which his worshipper has enjoyed in this life:

> My gateway is happy from the time that Dog has entered it;
> it has thriven and has been furnished
> from the time that my lord has trodden it.
> Be happy, you of my street!
> Rejoice, all my neighbours!
> Behold my lord: it is he who has made me . . .
> (Caminos, *LEM*, 88; cf. Assmann, *Hymnen*, 381–2, No. 178.)

The last sentence probably refers, not to creation, but to the securing of advancement, as Caminos points out; the hymn's main emphasis is that the baboon-god, whose image was installed in the house, is the source of his follower's well-being and material prosperity. An appealing touch in this hymn is that the adorer wants his neighbours to rejoice with him; doubtless he enabled them to do that in a convivial way.

A 'Supplication to Amûn in a year of need'[27] reflects the belief that the god has control over seasonal and climatic conditions and can thus reverse the distress caused in an exceptional year; the god

---

[22] Cf. *Wb.* V, 563, 6. It is suggested, ibid. 8, that the present allusion may mean that Amûn judges the world with a mere beckoning of his fingers.
[23] Cf. M.-T. Derchain-Urtel, *Thot* (Brussels, 1981), 95 ff.; Dieter Kurth in *LÄ* VI (1985), 506–7 on Thoth's import for accountancy.
[24] Gardiner, *LEM*, 17; Caminos, *LEM*, 56–58; Fecht, *Lit. Zeugnisse*, 44–46.
[25] Accepting Fecht's explanation of *gm* as an optative passive $s\underline{d}m.f$.
[26] Gardiner, *LEM*, 25; Caminos, *LEM*, 88–91; Fecht, op. cit. 52–58. Fecht's verse-divisions are followed.
[27] Gardiner, *LEM*, 45; Caminos, *LEM*, 171; Fecht, op. cit. 58–62.

is also urged to permit the worshipper to flourish.[28] A more specific temporal favour is requested in 'A prayer to Amûn to favour the scribe': the worshipper seeks advancement among the magistrates on behalf of the scribe Qay-geb. The prayer ends thus:

> Put the magistrates in the place of the magistrates,
> the great in the place of the great.
> Put the scribe of the treasury, Qay-geb,
> in front of Thoth, your righteous one.
> (Caminos, *LEM*, 174; cf. Assmann, *Hymnen*, 383, No. 180.)

A plea for the scribe to be placed in the protection of Thoth is understandable since Thoth was pre-eminently the divine scribe. But does the plea relate to Qay-geb's activity in this life? The two lines beginning *Put the magistrates in the place of the magistrates* can only make sense if they are related to a place in the necropolis; and this interpretation is fully confirmed by the lines of the opening prayer for Amûn's gracious treatment of Qay-geb:

> you being in favour among the magistrates
> and established in the Place of Truth.
> (Caminos, ibid.; cf. Assmann, ibid.)

Here *the Place of Truth* (*st M3't*) can refer only, as Caminos shows, to a part of the Theban necropolis;[29] so that there is nothing here, after all, which urges divine favour in this present life. What is being sought is a place of honour in the West. In that blessed region the protection of Thoth befits the afterlife of the scribe of the treasury.

In clear contrast is the 'Prayer to Thoth for skill in writing'.[30] The call to Thoth here is unequivocally concerned with the ambitions of a scribe in this life. Efficiency in their profession, material wealth, and social importance have accrued, it is said, to scribes whom Thoth has supported:

---

[28] A meaning of *ḫpr* adduced by Fecht from the Index (574–5) which Caminos supplies. Cf. Assmann, *Hymnen*, 382, No. 179, 11.

[29] Gardiner, in *JEA* 24 (1938), 163, defined it as 'a general name of the Theban necropolis'; Caminos, more cautiously and with many refs., as 'a name of at least a section' thereof which 'certainly included ground near the Ramesseum'. To him the wider definition is 'still open to question'. Another point raised by this prayer is how far burial places were organized and divided according to rank and profession. The Pharaohs, of course, were distinctively treated, but it seems that the higher and lower nobility were not rigidly demarked in line with office or status. 'Tomb' or 'Tomb of Pharaoh' are the two principal meanings ascribed by Černý to 'Place of Truth': see his *Community of Workmen at Thebes in the Ramessid Period* (Cairo, 1973), 29–85.

[30] Gardiner, *LEM*, 60; Caminos, *LEM*, 232–4; Fecht, op. cit. 65–73.

> I have seen many for whom thou didst act,
> and (now) they are among the Thirty (Judges),
> strong and wealthy through what thou hast done.

If advice is forthcoming from the god, then the earnest scribe promises ample gratitude: he will not stint his praise of the god:

> Suffer me to relate thy feats in whatever land I be.
> Then the multitude of men shall say,
> 'How great are the things that Thoth has done!'
> (Caminos, *LEM*, 232; cf. Assmann, *Hymnen*, 383–4, No. 181.)

Since he serves the god in one of his temples (*I am the slave of thy house*), he is well equipped to undertake this task. His promise in return for services rendered is of course a commonplace of religious votive texts in many cultures. A more significant statement in this prayer is *Fate and Fortune are in thy hand* (*š3yt rnnt m-ʿ.k*). Destiny and prosperity are therefore regarded as being within the gift of divine dispensation, in the case of the god Thoth. The divine control of Destiny is particularly noteworthy.[31]

Another 'Prayer to Thoth'[32] contains a rather daunting crux in the way it refers to an apparently judicial procedure. After a plea that he may be placed in Khmûn (Hermopolis), the city of Thoth, the worshipper desiderates the god's support in a court scene:

> Would that I had Thoth
> behind me tomorrow!
> 'Come', they say,
> when I am entered in the presence of the lords ⟨of Justice⟩,
> 'and come out triumphant.'
> (Caminos, *LEM*, 73; Cf. Assmann, *Hymnen*, 384–5, No. 182.)

What is desired, according to Caminos, is 'to enjoy Thoth's good offices at the posthumous ceremony of the weighing of the heart'. The word *m3ʿ-ḫrw*, 'triumphant', supports this interpretation; so does the special role of Thoth in the *Totengericht*. However, the reference of the word *tomorrow* (*dw3w*) brings a disturbing doubt. Daumas[33] argues that this relates to the morning prayer, and the word *tomorrow* does seem too specific to suit posthumous judgement. The end of Ch. 125 of the Book of the Dead includes the words '*Come!' says Thoth*, as Fecht (p. 77) points out, and the theme

---

[31] S. Morenz and D. Müller, *Untersuchungen zur Rolle des Schicksals in der ägyptischen Religion* (Berlin, 1960), 29–34; cf. Jan Quaegebeur, *Le dieu égyptien Shaï* (Leuven, 1975), 108–9.
[32] Gardiner *LEM*, 85 f.; Caminos, *LEM*, 321; Fecht, op. cit. 73–89.
[33] See Fecht, 76–77 with refs.

there is the successful outcome of the tribunal.[34] Yet the following lines in the 'Prayer to Thoth' are not easily connected with the afterworld. Thoth is here addressed as a *dom-palm* fruitful in water-bearing nuts and he is asked to rescue *the silent one*:

> Thou that takest water <from> a place afar off,
> come that thou mayest rescue me, the silent one.
> (Caminos, *LEM*, 321; cf. Assmann, *Hymnen*, 384.)

The god is then called *a pleasant well to a thirsty man <in> a desert*, and Daumas has found the background in the actual locale of the Thoth-temple in the district of Tuna el-Gebel, although he explains the thirst as a 'mystic thirst'. Fecht[35] concedes that the reference has now abandoned the afterworld for present cult realities. The different levels are not incompatible. Apropos of the *tomorrow* in the previous verses, an allusion to a posthumous judgement can be defended in the sense that *tomorrow* and *yesterday* in religious and wisdom texts can have a general application to future and past.[36] This poem indulges, then, in a change of focus in respect of such matters. It would be clearly wrong to argue from a rigid expectation concerning the genre. Whereas the Wisdom Literature, for instance, is not primarily directed to fate in the afterlife, there are occasional allusions to it.[37]

A feature of the confessional compositions from Thebes is the place they give to misfortunes suffered or evil deeds enacted. Herein lies the revolutionary difference that marks them off so sharply from the previous products of the Egyptian biographical tradition over a long period. Mostly funerary in origin, the earlier biographies are exclusively devoted to praiseworthy deeds, and the tradition has persisted, in a funerary context, right up to our own times. The very act of burial is an act of remembrance, and the concomitant literary record aims at achieving a kind of immortality.[38] Shakespeare (in Anthony's *oratio funebris*) took a pessimistic view of man's influence after death:

---

[34] Naville, *Tb.* 125 Schlussrede A.a. 44; cf. Hornung, *Das Totenbuch der Ägypter* (Zürich, 1979), 244, 211.

[35] Op. cit. 83.

[36] Cf. J. Gwyn Griffiths, 'Wisdom about Tomorrow', *Harv. Theol. Rev.* 53 (1960), 219–221. (Wrongly ascribed to F.Ll. Griffith in *Studien zu altägyptischen Lebenslehren* ed. Hornung and Keel (Freiburg, 1979), 371.) Cf. Fecht's remarks p. 81 and see also the parallels quoted by Assmann, *Hymnen*, 610, where allusion to the day of death is seen.

[37] Cf. Erik Hornung, 'Lehren über das Jenseits?' in op. cit. n. 36, 218–224.

[38] Jan Assmann, 'Schrift, Tod und Identität' in *Schrift und Gedächtnis* ed. Assmann and Hardmeier (Munich, 1983), 64–93, esp. 64 on the tomb as a 'sign' (*sema*) of personality.

The evil that men do lives after them;
The good is oft interred with their bones.

To ensure that the good was permanently proclaimed, that seemed to be the aim of the early Egyptian biographers. While the surrounding society is a potent factor, with its collective identity,[39] yet the achievements of an individual form the centrepiece of each record. At the same time the record appeals to passers-by and to posterity, so that survival in their remembrance is the aim.

5. *Behind the Changed Outlook*

The considerable extent of the biographical literature from the Fourth Dynasty to the end of the Eighteenth reveals an attitude which is both elaborately personal and devotedly pious. A mark of the personal interest is the presence of the portrait statue in early tombs. While the amount of detail concerning an individual's career varies a good deal from time to time, it is often sufficient to be of much factual value in the historical sense.[40] On the other hand, elements of an 'ideal biography' are present from the start, giving maxims of a general ethical type which the subject claims to have followed. What is theologically relevant is that such maxims, although they purport to refer to the deceased's conduct in this life, are sometimes directed to act as a defence in the judgement after death.[41] Thus Harkhuf says:

> Never did I speak any evil thing to a powerful one against any man, for I desired that it might be well with me before the Great God.
> (*Urk.* I, 123, 1–2.)

In other words, good conduct can claim its reward, but in the life to come.

The successes of this life, in contrast, are attributed to the King, and a spirit of utter devotion and commitment to him is frequently revealed. Admittedly, the deceased in the Old Kingdom sometimes lays claim to magical and moral powers of his own, as when he says *I am an excellent and well-equipped glorified spirit, a lector-priest who knows his speech.* (*Urk.* I, 122, 13).[42] But his dependence on the King is a

---

[39] Ibid. 65–67.
[40] For a survey of this writing see E. Otto, 'Biographien', in *Hdb. der Orientalistik* ed. B. Spuler, I. i. 2, *Ägyptologie: Literatur* (2nd Ed., Leiden, 1970), 179–88.
[41] Cf. my *Conflict of Horus and Seth* (Liverpool, 1960), 79–80, where other examples are also cited. In the type of sentence quoted the words *before the King* are often added: see E. Edel, in *MDAIK* 13. 1 (1944), 32. Similarly, *that it might be well with me among the people* occurs in some texts: ibid. 34.
[42] See Edel, op. cit. 19 ff. and 88–89.

constant sentiment. The nome-rulers show a sturdier standing, especially in the transition from the Old to the Middle Kingdom. In the New Kingdom more attention is given to details of successful careers, but indebtedness to the King is regularly stressed,[43] and most profoundly of all under Akhenaten. In general a realistic reason for this stress is plain: the careerists of the higher nobility actually did owe their advancement to the Pharaoh or his advisers. It is significant that when this could not happen, as at the break-up of the Old Kingdom, a ruler of This says that he has been elevated *by the might of Onuris*.[44] Another nomarch, Ankhtifi, avers that Horus brought him to Edfu to restore order from anarchy; the allusion here will be to the god and not to the Pharaoh as the living Horus.[45] At the same time loyalty to the reigning King—and in a normal situation there certainly was one available—is a strongly recurrent theme in Egyptian biography.

In the Middle Kingdom it was a devotion that assumed the force of a proselytizing faith.[46] Even Sinuhe, who assigns victory and prosperity, as we have seen, to the impact of divine aid, shows a blind devotion to Sesostris I.[47] Dependence on the King is considerably lessened in the biographies of the Late Period, as in those of the prophets of Amûn in the Twenty-second and Twenty-third Dynasties, when a more free and individual stance is revealed.[48] Correspondingly there is also a fairly constant acknowledgement that the gods have granted temporal blessings here and now. Surveying his life's achievements, Hor, a prophet of Amûn in the Twenty-third Dynasty, pays literary obeisance to the King (Petubastis), but makes it abundantly clear that his successes were due to the god's inspiration, and that part of the divine plan was to ensure Hor's longevity on earth.[49] When we reach Petosiris in the fourth century, it is striking that he makes no mention of any king. God's benefactions, received in this life and warranted for the next, are his major theme. He lived, however, in unsettled times, prob-

---

[43] E. Otto, 'Biographien', 185–7.

[44] Dows Dunham, *Naga-ed-Dêr Stelae of the First Intermediate Period* (Boston, 1937), 92–94, No. 78; cf. W. Schenkel, *Memphis, Herakleopolis, Theben* (Ägyptol. Abh. 12; Wiesbaden, 1965), 183, No. 260; and Lichtheim, *Lit.* I, 84–85.

[45] J. Vandier, *Mo'alla* (Cairo, 1950), 163, Inscr. No. 2, init. and 164 n. a. (Horus the god of Edfu is probably meant; cf. p. 20). H. Kees, in *Orientalia* 21 (1952), 88, thinks that a king, at least in the formal sense, is meant.

[46] Posener, *Littérature et Politique dans l'Égypte de la XIIe Dynastie* (Paris, 1956), 121.

[47] Posener, ibid. 99; cf. id. *De la divinité du Pharaon* (Paris, 1960), 66–67.

[48] E. Otto, 'Biographien', 187–8.

[49] E. Otto, *Die biographischen Inschriften*, 148–9 with refs., but correcting '22. Dyn.' on p. 147 to '23. Dyn.' (See his p. 126, No. 10.) Cf. S. Morenz, *Ägyptische*

ably spending his last years under Alexander the Great, and this may partly account for his passing over of royal names.

With Petosiris, of course, one has to face the probability of influences from outside Egypt on both artistic and religious manifestations.[50] At that time the door was wide open to such influences. It was beginning to open, indeed, in a much earlier period. The Amarna experience was in itself a disturbing and challenging process, and the reaction to it was probably conducive to a more intense spirituality which led away from the King and even from Maat to a greater emphasis on the major gods.[51] At the same time Amarna's outlook had become to a degree consciously cosmopolitan with the ascription of universal concerns to the sun-god; and shortly afterwards this cosmopolitanism is reflected even in the Book of Gates.[52] Nor is it without import that the middle of the second millennium saw the largest influx into Egypt of Syro-Palestinian deities.

The possibility of Near-Eastern influence on the main stream of Egyptian biography in the late New Kingdom should not be excluded, at least as far as religious ideas are concerned. The case is clearer, however, when we consider the biographical cameos embedded in the hymns and prayers of Deir el-Medîna. They have a special quality of penitence based on a firm belief that divine control is responsible for both success and suffering in this life. Within the Egyptian tradition one might be tempted to explain the radical change purely in sociological terms: this is the religion of the unprivileged *plebs*, the unofficial, popular, implicit faith which was hitherto unattested—an approach signalized by Gunn in the early study which he entitled 'The Religion of the Poor' (*JEA* 3, 1916, 81–94; he also uses the term 'folk-faith', p. 93). Sometimes the emphasis is expressly pointed in the texts, but by no means uniformly; one notes, for instance, the status-pride of the man who wants to be buried among the magistrates. These were royal

---

Religion (Stuttgart, 1960), 68–69. In Ann Keep's translation, *Egyptian Religion* (London, 1973), 65, the ideas are quite wrongly assigned to the King himself.

[50] S. Nakaten, in *LÄ* IV (1982), 995.

[51] Cf. Jan Assmann, 'Weisheit, Loyalismus und Frömmigkeit', in Hornung and Keel, ed. op. cit. (1979), 12–72. Although Wisdom is his main interest here, Assmann analyses biography and confessional literature too and ably shows the interaction of the three types. He fortifies his discussion with diagrammatic aids and with a wealth of illustrative quotations.

[52] Erik Hornung, tr. Baines, *Conceptions of God in Ancient Egypt* (London, 1983), 167; id. *Das Buch von den Pforten des Jenseits*, I (Geneva, 1979), 176–81 (Scene 30) and II (1984), 134–7. Here Horus is the tutelary deity of Egyptians and Nubians, and Sakhmet that of Asiatics and Libyans.

workers, and the higher strata were fairly well-off.[53]

The basic explanation of the changed outlook is probably to be sought in a wider Near-Eastern context. There are Hittite prayers, such as that of Kantuzilis[54] about 1380 B.C., which express penitence, petition, and dependence on the divine; and behind such writings, with a patent influence upon them, is a rich source of Mesopotamian hymns and prayers which begin towards the opening of the second millennium. Israel's penitential psalms are a millennium later, but they show the impress of the same tradition.[55] A feature of this tradition in Mesopotamia itself was belief in a personal god assigned to one individual. In short, a spiritual climate had established itself to which Egypt was not immune. One might object that Deir el-Medîna was a small and closed community, not likely to be penetrated by influences from so wide an external orbit. Small it certainly was. But closed? Among the deities worshipped here were Reshep, Qudshu, Anat, and Astarte, none of them of pure Egyptian pedigree, but 'foreign Asiatic divinities'.[56] A version of the story of Isis and Rê on an ostracon includes 'exotic names of deities—Hetebteni and Asembeni.[57] Again, a prophylactic charm against a threatening demon names his mother as Nedjerhesmem and his father as Djewebshet, a variant of the latter name, Tewetw-beshed, being compared by Albright to 'a whole series of Syrian and Anatolian mountain gods'.[58] The magician himself claims the name of '*Trws* who is behind his shrine' and Edwards (p. 160) invokes, hesitantly and yet cogently in view of the context, an obscure Hittite deity named Tarawa or Daraw.

---

[53] Jac J. Janssen, *Commodity Prices from the Ramessid Period* (Leiden, 1975), 536, where three social strata are distinguished; cf. Morris Bierbrier, *The Tomb-Builders of the Pharaohs* (London, 1982), 83: 'their lot was far above that of the average peasant.'

[54] A. Goetze, in *ANET*³ (1969), 400 f.; Cord Kühne, in *Near Eastern Religious Texts relating to the Old Testament* ed. W. Beyerlin (London, 1978), 167 ff. In the latter volume H. Brunner presents the comparable Egyptian material, pp. 30–44. See also H.G. Güterbock, in *Altorientalische Literaturen* ed. W. Röllig (Wiesbaden, 1978), 226–8.

[55] Thorkild Jacobsen, *The Treasures of Darkness* (New Haven, 1976), 147–64. Cf. Kate Bosse-Griffiths, in *Studien zu Sprache und Religion* Ägyptens (FS. W. Westendorf; Göttingen, 1984), II, 746–7. I am indebted to her for calling my attention to Jacobsen's very relevant discussion.

[56] M. Bierbrier, *Tomb-Builders of the Pharaohs*, 90.

[57] Hornung, *Conceptions of God in Ancient Egypt*, 89 with refs.

[58] I.E.S. Edwards, in *JEA* 54 (1968), 155–60, this on pp. 158–9. In his *Hieratic Papyri in the British Museum, Fourth Series: Oracular Amuletic Decrees of the Late New Kingdom* (London, 1960), I, xxi, Edwards shows that magical texts often offer succour aganist actions of gods which may prove harmful to a person; they therefore illustrate the negative aspect of our theme. For this chapter see also my contribution to *Pyramid Studies and Other Essays* (presented to I.E.S. Edwards; London, 1988), 92–102.

PART II

JUDGEMENT AFTER DEATH

CHAPTER NINE

A) EGYPT AND JUDAEO-CHRISTIAN THOUGHT

In the second part of my investigation I turn to ideas about judgement after death. My first concern will be to describe and explain the ideas themselves as they appear in Egypt, Iran, Judaism, and Christianity. I shall try to discern the distinctive qualities of each tradition and how they developed. At the same time an attempt will be made to ascertain the influence exerted by these traditions on one another. The combination of these aims is bound to produce, I fear, a sense of unease, and perhaps even of confusion, in both writer and reader. It is rather like a juggler's attempt to keep three or four balls on the move in the air simultaneously. Such an attempt may result in failure, but happily not in disaster. The origins of religious beliefs which still have vital force are always worth pondering.

Several works have been devoted to the development of the concept within Egypt itself, and there have been two notable attempts to record parallel ideas in other religions. I refer to *Le Jugement des Morts* (Sources Orientales, 4; Paris, 1961) to which Jean Yoyotte contributed the section on Ancient Egypt; and to S.G.F. Brandon, *The Judgment of the Dead* (London, 1967), a book described in its subtitle as 'An Historical and Comparative Study of the Idea of a Post-Mortem Judgment in the Major Religions'. While Brandon's work is clearly indebted in several respects to its French predecessor, the advantage of single authorship enables him, on occasion, to indulge more freely in the process of comparison. Normally he does not, however, discuss questions of influence and is content to note the parallels. An exception is his discussion (pp. 122–3) of *The Testament of Abraham*, a work probably penned by a Jewish Christian in Egypt in the second century A.D. Since the judgement here is viewed as applying to individual souls and not as 'the Great Assize of the nations according to Jewish apocalyptic tradition', and since the supervising archangel Dokiel is called *the just keeper of the balance*, Brandon feels that there is an exact equivalence to the role of Anubis in the Osirian scene of judgement, and that 'an Egyptian derivation of this *psychostasia* appears most probable' (p. 123). Yet he does not attempt an examination of the relative claims of Egypt and Iran as factors of influence on this area of Jewish and Christian eschatology. In his Preface (p. ix) he ventures the opinion that 'the notion of a *post mortem* judgment . . . constitutes the ultimate authentication of the traditional ethic of Western society.' Its presence in Zoroastrianism and Islam, leave alone Egypt, would seem to demand a more expansive adjective than 'Western'.

In what follows I shall be content to sketch, in barest outline, the evolution of the idea of posthumous judgement in Egypt, calling attention to some facets which have received particular comment in recent discussions.

1. *Present and Future Judgement*

In the first part of this study we attempted a survey of the idea of divine judgement as it affects life in this world. Too often, it seems, has a rigid line of demarcation been drawn between the two spheres of divine activity, with the suggestion that posthumous judgement alone gives God's final verdict and that his assessment of life here and now must be something partial and temporary. A consideration of manifold texts ostensibly relating to judgement before death reveals the fact that quite frequently the precise reference is not beyond question. When the Psalmist tells us (1:5) that *the wicked will not stand in the judgement*, we may feel that the subsequent statement, *the way of the wicked will perish*, suggests the finality of a last condemnation. Yet we cannot rule out the possibility that judgement both here and hereafter is envisaged. Many similar instances occur; and sometimes a text combines, in separate loci, allusions to both types of judgement.

Although Egyptian tradition, especially in the non-royal sphere, often shows concern with rewards and punishments in this life, there can be no question that its emphasis on judgement after death became more conspicuous from the New Kingdom onwards. As far as influence is concerned, it is certainly in this area that Egypt made its greatest impact. Ideas of present judgement reflect possible influences from outside, particularly from Israel. But the concept of future judgement was one which revealed Egypt as a potent irradiating influence in the direction of Hebraic, Greek and Christian thought. Two main reasons may be suggested for this phenomenon. First is the fact that Egyptian belief in life after death was much more firmly based. At an early stage the Hebraic and Hellenic belief in immortality seems remarkably pallid and tenuous by comparison. The second reason derives largely from iconography. In the developed pictorialism of the weighing of the heart the Egyptian tradition assumed a paramount appeal; and the accompanying texts reflect a strongly moral ambience even if a magical element was often present.

2. *Posthumous Litigation*

Before the emergence of the belief in a trial that awaited every man and woman after death we find evidence of belief in a variety of judicial procedures that were possible at that stage.[1] In general, following the conviction that life in the hereafter continued the features of this life, the Egyptians believed that litigation was possible after death. Clear indications of such a belief occur in the 'Letters to the Dead' edited by Gardiner and Sethe and dated by them to the Old and Middle Kingdoms. We find the writer of one letter urging his father to take legal action against the writer's brother, although the brother is now dead; in another letter on a papyrus now at Leiden a widower threatens to bring a case against his dead wife:[2]

> I will lay a charge against you in the presence with words of my mouth in the presence of the Divine Ennead of the West, and it shall be decided between you and me.
> (Gardiner and Sethe, *Egyptian Letters to the Dead*, London, 1928, Pl.10, No. 2, with p. 10.)

There are modern contexts, of course, in which a case could occur in a court of law concerning the property left by a deceased person. What is radically different about the above litigation is that the court is firmly placed in the afterworld—*in the presence of the Divine Ennead of the West,* where *the West* relates to the funerary area and in general to the world beyond. A judicial struggle between opposing parties is envisaged in these documents, and it might seem that the idea of a general judgement of the dead is not mentally connected with such a struggle. Some contribution to the wider idea was, however, probably made by the concept of litigation. Thus there is a statement in the Pyramid Texts (386 *a* WPMN): *There is no living one who complains against the King.* A possible accuser or co-litigant is clearly presupposed here. And in the series of denials (*Pyr.* 892 *a* PN ff.) beginning *I have not opposed the King*, we can recognize a close

---

[1] For studies of the development see J. Spiegel, *Die Idee vom Totengericht in der ägyptischen Religion* (Leipziger Ägyptologische Studien, 2; Glückstadt, 1935); J. Yoyotte, 'Le Jugement des Morts dans l'Égypte ancienne' in *Sources Orientales*, 4 (Paris, 1961), 17–80; R. Grieshammer, *Das Jenseitsgericht in den Sargtexten* (Wiesbaden, 1970); Christine Seeber, *Untersuchungen zur Darstellung des Totengerichts im Alten Ägypten* (MÄS 35; Munich, 1976); ed. 'Jenseitsgericht', *LÄ* III (1980), 249–52.

[2] The version of the editors has been revised in minor respects.

affinity to the form of denials made in the *locus classicus* of posthumous judgement in Chapter 125 of the Book of the Dead—the denials usually referred to as 'Negative Confessions' or 'Protestations of Innocence'.[3] Further, the litigation of opposing parties is given an aura of divine association in that in the Pyramid Texts and in later sources the judicial strife of Horus and Seth is a prominent theme often concerned with the struggle of these deities for the sovereignty of Egypt.[4]

3. *Diverging Divine Roles*

The struggle is often presented as one between Osiris and Seth, the former god replacing Horus. It is significant that some allusions portray Seth being accused of the murder of Osiris, the charge being now part of a criminal prosecution, whereas the litigation between Horus and Seth suggests a civil lawsuit concerned with the question of rightful succession to the throne of Egypt. The distinction accurately reflects the equation of Horus with the living King and of Osiris with the dead King, the latter's claim being made to concern sovereignty over the domain of the dead.[5]

A related question of some importance is the identity of the deity under whom the whole procedure is said to be conducted. He is often referred to as *the Great God*, a phrase which has been connected frequently by modern scholars with Rê, although the role of Osiris as sovereign of the domain of the dead would seem to make him a powerful candidate. That the phrase $n\underline{t}r$ *'3* means 'the greatest god' has been suggested by Barbara L. Begelsbacher-Fischer, *Untersuchungen zur Götterwelt des alten Reiches* (OBO 37; Freiburg, Schweiz, 1981), 22 and passim (89; 122; cf. 59, of Hathor); on p. 22 n. 1, she refers to W. Barta, *Aufbau und Bedeutung der altägyptischen Opferformel* (AF 24; Glückstadt, 1968), 8 and 15. Barta's p. 8 does not appear to refer to it; on p. 350 he renders it 'der Grosse Gott', cf. p. 15; and on pp. 291–2 he discusses its possible application to various gods and the King, but without suggesting a superlative meaning. Such a meaning would undoubtedly suit the deity responsible for judging the dead, but it would suit Rê or Osiris equally.

From the conceptual point of view it is clear that in general

---

[3] Cf. my *Conflict of Horus and Seth* (Liverpool, 1960), 79.
[4] Ibid. Chapter 3, pp. 54–84 ('The Trial'). Cf. Grieshammer, op. cit. 11–45 and esp. 43–45.
[5] See my *Origins of Osiris and his Cult* (Leiden, 1980), 178–81.

Egyptian ideas about law and legal systems were heavily influenced by religion; and we must assume, at the same time, that judicial procedures located in the afterworld inevitably reflect practices followed on earth. Thus a distinction between civil and criminal procedures has been seen in the evidence from Deir el-Medîna, although the dividing line is sometimes rather vague.[6] Conceptually of basic importance was the principle and personality of Maat. The idea of cosmic order and equilibrium was often connected with Maat, but in judicial contexts the idea of truth and justice was its dominant meaning. Already in the Old Kingdom frequent reference is made to Maat. Yet it is clear that as a goddess she is not presented in judicial contexts as a presiding deity; rather is she (or the Two Maats) often named as sanctioning the process of justice.[7] A passage in Utterance 260 of the Pyramid Texts describes King Wenis being judged in a trial of some kind, and the Two Maats are said to *hear* and to *judge* the King; but Tefen and Tefenet are named before that as judges, and Shu is named as a witness (*Pyr.* 317 a–b W). A significant point is that the King is said to be justified (*m3ʿ ḥrw.f*) concerning what he has done (*m irt.n.f*; 316 d); that is, the trial is based on an examination of his deeds, and he is said to carry Maat with him (323 e).[8]

Whereas Tefen and Tefenet seem to reflect the same dualism as the Two Truths, referring perhaps to the two litigants originally involved in the case, neither of these groups appears as the presiding college of judges. Rê or Osiris seem to bear that role. Geb also occurs as judge, particularly in the litigation of Horus or Osiris against Seth, but also in the wider sense of a tribunal of the dead. But there is some evidence that Anubis was regarded occasionally in this capacity. In Utterance 610 of the Pyramid Texts, which Sethe describes as a variant of Utterance 437, Anubis is described as *sr ḏ3ḏ3t*, *Magistrate of the Court*, and the deceased King is equated

---

[6] Schafik Allam, *Das Verfahrensrecht in der altägyptischen Arbeitersiedlung von Deir el-Medineh* (Tübingen, 1973), 40.

[7] Cf. S. Allam, 'De la Divinité dans le droit Pharaonique', *BSFE* 68 (1973), 17–30, esp. 19. For a possible association of Maat with a very different ceremony which included ritual slaughter see John D. Ray in *Abstracts of Papers: Fourth International Congress of Egyptology*, ed. Sylvia Schoske (Munich, 1985), 183–4 (to be published in full later).

[8] Allam, op. cit. 19. See also A. Moret, 'La Doctrine de Maât', *RdE* 4 (1940), 1–14, esp. 5. Moret proceeds to argue that Maat's cult influenced neighbouring areas, including Palestine. Cf. the offering of Maat portrayed on an ivory plaque from Samaria: see J.W. and Grace M. Crowfoot, *Early Ivories from Samaria* (London, 1938), Pl. 1.2 with pp. 12–13; cf. their p. 49: 'The influence of Egypt . . . is all-pervasive.' Cf. too R. Giveon, *The Impact of Egypt on Canaan* (OBO 20; Freiburg, Schweiz, 1978), 111.

with him, as also with Thoth (*Pyr.* 1713 *c* MN). The King, it is said, will make himself a glorified spirit *as Thoth and as Anubis, Magistrate of the Court*. It is an utterance, admittedly, which lavishes the King with a lush variety of divine equations: as a glorified spirit he will become Horus, Seth, Osiris (not named, but clearly referred to), Ḥa, Min and Sokar; and now Thoth and Anubis too. The urge to identify the King so freely with other gods was spiritually advantageous to him of course, and it was probably a potent factor in spreading the process of syncretism in other ways.[9] Doubtless the funerary eminence of Anubis aided his occasional choice as a judge, although his role is usually that of the embalmer god. He is referred to sometimes as one who *reckons hearts* (*Pyr.* 157 *c* W; 1287 *a* P) or *claims hearts* (Faulkner) with a context suggesting power over them; so that a judicial function may here be denied.[10] A passage in the Coffin Texts (IV 311 *c*–314 *e*) begs Atum to save the deceased from a destructive deity with the face of a dog, a deity who tears at hearts—a being rather like the Devourer in the later judgement scenes; and the allusion to the canine face suggests Anubis.[11] When Anubis is said to make seats, in the same context, for the spirits who follow *the Lord of the Nomes*, allusion is made to *that day of 'Come from there!'* (*CT* IV 260 a). It has been well suggested that the exhortation may refer in the original text to the order given by Anubis to the seven spirits, but that the added gloss in the later Book of the Dead implies an invitation from Osiris to Rê to come to the judgement scene.[12] Probably the role of Anubis in connection with judgement became more significant as the idea itself took a stronger hold; in the private tombs of the Fourth and Fifth Dynasties his other funerary functions were stressed, albeit in a predominantly beneficent sense, especially as a giver of life.[13] His eventual

---

[9] See my remarks in *Studies in Egyptian Religion* (In honour of Jan Zandee; Leiden, 1982), 43–55.

[10] Grieshammer, *Jenseitsgericht*, 88. He notes that such a function is not ascribed to Anubis elsewhere in the *Coffin Texts* apart from possible allusions in IV 311 *c* ff. and IV 252 *c* ff.

[11] Grieshammer, ibid. 89. He also cites *CT* IV 252 *c*, but this is rather different. Mention is made in 253 *c*–254 *a* of the Lords of Justice, the Court (*ḏ3ḏ3t*) behind Osiris, and in 258 *b* Anubis is said to *have made their seats*, referring to the seven spirits who follow *the Lord of the Nomes*.

[12] M. Heerma van Voss, *De oudste Versie van Dodenboek* 17 a (Leiden, 1963), 77 with n. 309. Ursula Rössler-Köhler, *Kapitel 17 des ägyptischen Totenbuches* (Wiesbaden, 1979), 221, in a note (4) on the text of the archetype, states that late parallels give Rê instead of Anubis as the one who gives orders to the gods protecting Osiris.

[13] Barbara L. Begelsbacher-Fischer, *Untersuchungen zur Götterwelt des alten Reichs* (OBO 37; Freiburg, Schweiz, 1981), 19–31.

role in the tribunal is described in the Book of the Dead (125) and is plain to see in the numerous depictions of that scene: he is the supervisor of the balance in which the heart of the assessed person is weighed. As such he bears the title *He who is in charge of the balance* (*iry mḫ3t*) or simply *Lord of the Balance* (*nb mḫ3t*);[14] and the vignettes show him actively engaged in this activity, although Horus often assists him in the task.

Two other functions enacted by Anubis are the reporting of the result to Thoth as Recorder, and the guiding of the successful candidate to the presence of Osiris as presiding judge; the latter function is likewise performed sometimes by Horus.[15] The sporadic early appearance of Anubis as *Magistrate of the Court* has been illumined by a study of a Leiden papyrus of the Book of the Dead (T 3) which belongs to the Twenty-first Dynasty and bears the name of a lady called Tajoeheriet, a musician of Amun.[16] Here a scene that depicts the exit-door from the hall of judgement in Spell 125 shows a 'tribunal of the gate' which consists of demons (*3ḫw*). While Anubis does not figure in the weighing scene itself (Horus here takes care of the balance),[17] he plays a role in the subsidiary phase of judgement which is a kind of appendix to the main tribunal and is connected with the gate.[18] This judgement is a test concerning the door, as in the Papyrus of Ani, Pl. 30, 18–26 (ed. Budge, Vol. II, London, 1913, p. 571), where Anubis questions Ani on the name of the door and its parts, and on receiving the correct answers pronounces, *Pass on, for thou hast knowledge* (*rḫ*). In the Papyrus of Tajoeheriet occurs a significant section:

> To be spoken by Anubis: 'To me as magistrate (*sr*) spoke the voice of someone who comes from Egypt (*Ta-Meri*)'![19]
> (Heerma van Voss, *Zwischen Grab und Paradies*, Taf. 19, cols. 8–9; cf. id. *Anoebis en de demonen*, 4.)

Here the mention of Egypt clearly implies that the tribunal has a world-relevance or perhaps a heavenly status that overlooks the

---

[14] Seeber, *Untersuchungen*, 154.
[15] Seeber, ibid. 154–63. She points on p. 161 to three instances of an anthropomorphic Master of the Balance, but suggests that Horus may be intended by these figures.
[16] M. Heerma van Voss, *Anoebis en de demonen* (Leiden, 1978). See also *Zwischen Grab und Paradies* (Basel, 1971) by the same scholar.
[17] Heerma van Voss, *Zwischen Grab und Paradies*, Taf. 14.
[18] In this connection he is only once depicted (Taf. 19) as the guide of the triumphant deceased. For the association of justice and a gate in actual juridical practice see G.P.F. van den Boorn, '*Wḏ‘-ryt* and Justice at the Gate', *JNES* 44 (1985), 1–25.
[19] Cf. T.G. Allen, *The Book of the Dead* (Chicago, 1974), 101 (Spell 125 A, b).

whole world; or indeed a vantage-point in the underworld which receives members of several races. One recalls the passage in the Book of Gates which presents Horus and Sakhmet as protectors or saviours of the souls (*bʿw*) of Asiatics, Nubians, and Libyans.[20]

At the same time there can be little doubt that the basic prototype of the tribunal, expansive as it now appears to be, is the *djadjat* or *qenbet* which is firmly localized. Indeed the latter term was used at Deir el-Medîna even of the court through which the god was deemed to pronounce judgement.[21] When transposed to the tribunal of the dead, particularly in the form conveyed by Spell 125 of the Book of the Dead, the ruling personnel are no longer local worthies, but deities with various functions. In the case of Anubis, the exceptional scenario implies, instead of the general moral assessment, an example of the test or ordeal category, although it would be unwise to draw too rigid a distinction.[22]

A further point made by Heerma van Voss, this time in relation to Spell 17 of the Book of the Dead, concerns the participation of the nomes. In the earliest versions of this text (*CT* IV 258 *b*) allusion is made to the activity of Anubis in preparing seats for the spirits who follow *the Lord of the Nomes*; and Heerma van Voss (*De oudste Versie etc.* 36) remarks on the fact that one text (B9C *a*) has *the Lords of the Nomes*, although he queries whether *the Lord* should be read. This at once recalls the fact that in the developed form, textual and pictorial, of the judgement scene, the role of assessors is assigned to forty-two beings, and their number has naturally been linked to the number of the nomes of Egypt. Terms used of them suggest the role of executioners rather than assessors, for they are *Devourers of shades*, *Breakers of bones*, and *Eaters of entrails*.[23] The correspondence of their number to that of the nomes was used in itself as a sufficient indication of their significance. Brugsch and Erman both drew this conclusion, and Breasted[24] ventured into

---

[20] Erik Hornung et al., *Das Buch von den Pforten des Jenseits*, I (Geneva, 1979), 176–81 (Fifth Hour, Scene 30); and II (1980), 134–7 (with Translation and Commentary). On the positive approach to other nations see S. Morenz, *Ägyptische Religion* (Stuttgart, 1960), 54, noting that the context of *BD* 125 refers also to Thoth as an interpreter.

[21] Allam in *BSFE* 68 (1973), 21; cf. id. *Everyday Life in Ancient Egypt* (Prism Arch. Series, 1; Guizeh, Egypt, 1985), 63 describing the *qenbet* as a local council which included the most esteemed inhabitants.

[22] See further M. Heerma van Voss, 'Anubis in *Pyr.* 1713 c', in *L'Égyptologie en 1979*, Vol. II (Paris, 1982), 25 (= Acta of 2nd Congress of Egyptology, Grenoble, 1979); also my own remarks in *Origins of Osiris and his Cult*, 185.

[23] Seeber, *Untersuchungen*, 136.

[24] *The Dawn of Conscience* (New York, 1934), 257.

further detail. Noting that the deceased is said to address these deities by their names and that these names include allusions to places, he propounded the view that the forty-two gods are an 'artificial creation' with a specific purpose:

> The priests doubtless built up this court of forty-two judges in order to control the character of the dead from all quarters of the country. The deceased would find himself confronted by one judge at least who, having come from the deceased's 'home town', was acquainted with his local reputation up and down 'Main Street', and who therefore could not be deceived.

Even if the appealing concept of the last sentence seems fanciful, one might argue that in any case the local court of actual procedures has now become, in the afterworld, a veritable pan-Egyptian judicature whose authority appears accordingly to be more august. A complicating feature is added by Breasted: the deceased is said to address each god in turn with 'a declaration of innocence of some particular sin'. The divine names do not, however, betray any relation to the sins denied, and Breasted remarks that 'the priestly editors had some difficulty in finding enough sins to make up a list of forty-two, and there are several verbatim repetitions, not to mention essential repetitions with slight changes in the wording.'

At first sight the pan-Egyptian theory seems to have received a crushing blow at the hands of Charles Maystre. After examining the names assigned to the Forty-two deities, he finds the topographical connections to be very one-sided. He sees Lower Egypt to be represented by five or six nomes, and the part of Egypt south of Heracleopolis by two or three nomes only; several divinities are found to relate to one nome (three for the nome of Heqa-Adj). His map shows clearly how sparsely Upper Egypt is accounted for.[25] Yet what is strange about Maystre's discussion is that, whereas he boldly rebuts the traditional theory, he does not propound an alternative explanation. A possibility that the presence of seven and repetitions of it reflects the status of seven as a sacred number is regarded by Christine Seeber[26] as the most likely interpretation; but she then proceeds to admit that geographical emphases are plainly present and that some of the deities may well be regarded as ancient local gods. This approach is the more cogent. It is also possible that the original intention was indeed to represent the forty-two nomes, but that the intention was imperfectly executed.

---

[25] Charles Maystre, *Les Déclarations d'innocence* (IFAO, Cairo, 1937), 131, with the whole discussion on pp. 129–33.
[26] Op. cit. 137.

Incidentally, the number of these deities is often less than forty-two in the representations, but the reason for this is evidently spatial.

Other divine roles are assumed by Thoth as the recording scribe, by the sons of Horus, by the Ennead, and by Maat. The last-named has a multiple presence: she is often figured in one of the scales, and is occasionally present as a seated observer or presiding deity. The Two Maats are onlookers as guardians of justice; and the single form of Maat is often seen as a deity who defends and helps the deceased.[27] The Devourer of the Dead is also a divine being, and of the three animals combined in its form—the crocodile, lion, and hippopotamus—the crocodile recalls Thoeris, although the positive aspects of this deity do not accord well with the function of the Devourer.[28]

If there are hints of an all-Egyptian scenario in the connections of the Forty-two assessors, the diversity of the divine participants in general points to the sanction of earth, heaven, and the underworld.

4. The Combination of Test and Ordeal

We saw that a dualism characterizes the Forty-two assessors in that they appear both as examiners sitting in judgement and as intimidating executioners. In the subsidiary episode where Anubis and the demons question the deceased on the name of the door and its parts, the answers depend on the possession of magical knowledge. The location of the episode is noteworthy: it comes at the end of Spell 125 of the Book of the Dead, thus indicating that the Egyptians themselves regarded the episode as being essentially related to the process of posthumous judgement. Such a pointer is not available with the various works concerned with the fate of the deceased in the underworld, save when a judgement scene is expressly included, as in the *Book of Gates*; but their possible relationship is worth considering.

The earliest of these works is the *Book of the Two Ways*, a modern title which rather belies the fact that the work deals with the many ways, often tortuous and fearful, that await the deceased; the text was usually inscribed on the inside base of coffins with a very practical aim—'probably so that the deceased would have this

---

[27] Ibid. 139–47. Thoth, on the other hand, was the impartial Recorder and his role in judgement made him very popular in the Ptolemaic and Roman eras: see Garth Fowden, *The Egyptian Hermes* (Cambridge, 1986), 23.
[28] Ibid. 163–84.

guide at their feet when waking in the underworld'.²⁹ Both maps and text provide help in avoiding the dangers and pitfalls of the grotesque topography thus charted. At the heart of the whole experience is the motif of the Gate, which recurs in the other books of the underworld, especially in the *Book of Gates*. Each gate is defended by a terrifying guardian whose task is to repel all hostile and evil powers and also to threaten danger to uninitiated beings who wish to pass. The movement of the deceased person is conveyed as being parallel to that of the sun-god Rê in his barque, who is likewise threatened by ther hostile powers.³⁰

Horror and intimidation come from the demon-guardians, and the techniques to be used by the deceased include a display of knowledge, especially knowing the names of the guardians and the relevant spells, and also avowals of identity with major gods. Erik Hornung, our foremost authority on the whole range of this literature,³¹ has ably traced the element of horrendous bizzarrerie to the realm of the unconscious, showing how and why the absorption with the underworld reflected a search of man's unconscious processes, not now supressed, but freely and frightfully displayed.³² If we ask what was the moral content, if any, of the judgement theme in this literature, the answer must on the whole be dismissive. It has been said of the *Book of the Two Ways* that 'there are almost no moral criteria connected with reaching the goals . . .'³³ Sporadic moral concern does emerge, it is true, as when the deceased, approaching high walls encircled by flames and snakes, appeals for information on the names of the demons and then implores, *Make a clean way for me, O lord of everlastingness who is in Maat. Broad is the way which does not embrace snakes. May darkness cease and light come to be.*³⁴ Even here the moral element should not be magnified. Maat has it, of course; but *clean* might mean *unencumbered*,

---

²⁹ Leonard H. Lesko, *The Ancient Egyptian Book of Two Ways* (Berkeley, 1972), 4. Cf. my review in *JEA* 61 (1975), 293–4.

³⁰ Cf. H. Kees, *Totenglauben und Jenseitsvorstellungen der alten Ägypter* (2nd Ed., Berlin, 1956), 289–90.

³¹ See Erik Hornung, *Ägyptische Unterweltsbücher* (2nd Ed., Zürich, 1984) and his edition of the *Book of Amduat* in three volumes (Wiesbaden, 1963–67); also his edition, with A. Brodbeck and E. Staehelin, of *Das Buch von den Pforten des Jenseits* (2 Vols., Geneva, 1979 and 1984).

³² Hornung, 'The Discovery of the Unconscious in Ancient Egypt', in *Spring*, An Annual of Archetypal Psychology and Jungian Thought, Vol. for 1986 (Dallas, Texas), 16–28. The types of punishment inflicted on the damned are analysed by him in his *Altägyptische Höllenvorstellungen* (Abh. Leipzig, 59, 3; Berlin, 1968).

³³ Lesko, *The Ancient Egyptian Book of Two Ways*, 7.

³⁴ Lesko, ibid 31 = *CT* VII, 485 *a* ff.

were it not that in the phrase *w3t w'bt* (*CT* VII 485 *a*) the adjective carries the water determinative and has strong associations with both ritual and moral purity. The god asked to secure this boon is *the Lord of Eternity in whom is Maat*[35] (Truth and Justice), thus confirming the moral stress. In a review of a wide sweep of sources which are concerned with the passing of gates, Jan Zandee gives considerable importance to this aspect.[36] He states (p. 114) that 'sometimes it is said that the gate lets only just people through, but keeps sinners at bay', and of the doorkeepers that 'they perform the function of judges, who let the just pass, but keep the sinner at bay or condemn him.' Later he supplies a more precise summary of what is going on:[37]

> The composition of these spells is: invocation of the gate, order to let the dead pass, declaration that he has power over the gate on account of knowing the name, and that he is entitled to pass, because he is pure.

It will be seen that the moral claim is confined to the last clause: *because he is pure*. This doubtless includes ritual purity, just as the phrases *lords of food, lords of offerings,* and *lords of truth* are shown (p. 124) to refer to the justified dead.

In the *Book of Gates* the ethical emphasis is sometimes unequivocal, as in the description of the blessed dead:[38]

> Those who have spoken truth on earth, those who have not approached impurity, they are summoned to this gate, they live on truth, their refreshment is in their lake. Rê says to them, 'Truth belongs to you, through which you live.'
> (*Book of Gates*, Second Hour, Scene 6.)

Maat is the key to the eulogy. On the other hand, the accursed ones who are described soon afterwards are condemned merely for their rebellious attitude to Rê.[39] Theologically one finds already in the *Book of the Two Ways* a commingling of the celestial and underworldly abodes of the dead with the corresponding association of Rê and Osiris in the prospect of the deceased himself, as detailed by Spell 1130:[40]

---

[35] I prefer this rendering with an inverted use of *imy* in *CT* VII, 485 *b*, where B5C reads *imy m3't.f, in whom is his Mâat*.
[36] Jan Zandee, *Death as an Enemy* (Leiden, 1960), 114–25.
[37] Zandee, op. cit. 123.
[38] Hornung et al., *Das Buch von den Pforten des Jenseits*, I, 20–21; and II, 50–51. See also Zandee, 'The Book of Gates' in *Liber Amicorum* (for C.J. Bleeker, Leiden, 1969), 284.
[39] Hornung, op. cit., II, 67; Zandee, op. cit. 285.
[40] Cf. J. Bergman, 'Zum Zwei-Wege-Motiv' in *Svensk Exegetisk Årsbok* 41–42 (1976–7), 52. Cf. Lesko, op. cit. 131–3; Faulkner, *Coffin Texts*, III (1978), 168–9.

> Everyone who knows this spell will be like Rê in the East of Heaven and like Osiris in the underworld. He goes away to the fiery region without being hindered for ever by the fire.
> (*Coffin Texts*, VII 471 c–f.)

It is significant that it is Thoth in this work who is responsible for the union of the Two Ways, and the texts all come from El-Bershe, which has special links with this god.[41]

Knowing the potent and relevant spell; knowing also the names of gates and their guardians: this is the equipment which only priestly lore can supply. If we seek the actual situations demanding similar responses, we think of entry through the gates of towns and temples. It is relevant to recall that no fewer than 35 gates of the Karnak temple are known to us by name.[42]

5. *Magic and Morality*

The powerful influence of the Egyptian imagery is exemplified by the expression *the Gates of Hell* used in Christ's promise to Peter (Matt. 16:18), where the image of the πύλαι ᾅδου, which shall not prevail against the Church, has been unhappily obliterated in *the powers of death* in the translation of the Revised Standard Version.[43] Still closer is the image of the new Jerusalem (Rev. 21:12) which *had a great high wall, with twelve gates, and at the gates twelve angels* ... It must be by way of Jewish apocalypticism[44] that the image has reached the New Testament.

A task not easily essayed is the quantifying of the magical as opposed to the moral element in the posthumous judgement. We have seen that in the *Book of the Two Ways* the magical element is overwhelmingly weightier. The magically potent element is provided in spells replete with secret knowledge, especially concerning the correct names, and they are effectively present in the form of scrolls, inscriptions, and vignettes. In this context the gatekeepers

---

[41] Bergman, ibid.; Lesko, op. cit. 3.
[42] H. Brunner, 'Die Rolle von Tür und Tor im Alten Ägypten', *Symbolon* N.F. 6 (1982), 37–59, this on p. 38.
[43] So also *NEB*, with *the gates of death* as an alternative. For the parallel cf. Brunner, op. cit. 45. Torments and punishments take place not at the gates themselves but at specially prepared *places of destruction*: see Hornung, *Unterweltsbücher*, 42–45.
[44] Cf. the Qumrân Manual of Discipline, 8.7, a *tested bulwark* never to be shaken; T.H. Gaster, *The Scriptures of the Dead Sea Sect* (London, 1957), 65; G. Vermes, *The Dead Sea Scrolls in English* (Penguin, 1962, repr. 1966), 85; S.E. Johnson in *The Scrolls and the New Testament* ed. K. Stendahl (London, 1958), 136, but with no mention of gates.

become judges,⁴⁵ but the expectation of a more widely based tribunal is also pressing, as is made clear in Spell 127 of the *Book of the Dead*:⁴⁶

> O you doorkeepers who guard your portals, who swallow souls and who gulp down the corpses of the dead who pass by you when they are allotted to the House of Destruction, who cause that the soul of every potent, great and holy spirit shall be led aright to the place of the Silent Land, even he who is a soul like Re who is praised and like Osiris who is praised. May you guide N, may you open the portals for him, may the earth open its caverns to him, may you make him triumphant over his enemies.
> (*Book of the Dead*, 127.)

The triumph mentioned is triumph in the tribunal (lit. *make him true of voice*) which is also specifically named in previous lines as *the Great Tribunal*. It follows that the enemies referred to are people who oppose him in the tribunal—*Prozeß-Gegner*, as Brunner rightly calls them. It is well-known that the procedure implies an assessment of a man's conduct in his life on earth; his 'protestations of innocence' are a reply to specific questions and they constitute fixed formulae which vary little from one text to another and therefore show no variation according to the person implicated (apart from distinctions of gender). A suggestion of purely objective appraisal comes from the imagery of sins being weighed against the symbol of Truth. It is true that the 'protestations' seem to put ethical and ritual failures on a par, but that is true of most ancient religions.

The code of conduct assumed as the standard from which aberration is culpable has the impress of a high ideal. Included in the denials are the following:

> I have not blasphemed God. I have not done violence to a poor man. I have not broken the taboo of a God. I have not defamed a servant to his superior. I have not made (anyone) sick. I have not made (anyone) weep. I have not killed. I have not given orders to kill.
> (tr. H. Brunner, 'Egyptian Texts', 65–66.)⁴⁷

It is of some interest that among the sins condemned is male homosexuality.⁴⁸

---

⁴⁵ Cf. Brunner, op. cit. 46, who also goes on to quote from *BD* 127.

⁴⁶ Tr. R.O. Faulkner, *The Ancient Egyptian Book of the Dead* (New York, 1972, rev. ed. London, 1985), 115.

⁴⁷ In *Near Eastern Texts relating to the Old Testament* ed. W. Beyerlin (tr. J. Bowden, London, 1978), translating Naville's text = *BD* 125. Cf. my remarks in 'The Faith of the Pharaonic Era' in *Classical Mediterranean Spirituality* ed. A.H. Armstrong (New York, 1986), 34.

⁴⁸ *I have not had sexual relations with a boy* (Brunner, p. 66, but noting that there is some obscurity). Brunner states that 'homosexuality was strictly taboo'.

The magical potency of the 'Declarations of Innocence' was deemed to come from the fact that a copy of the text, often finely embellished, was placed in the tomb of anyone who could afford it. The same belief went with the early *Book of the Two Ways*, of which Lesko writes:[49]

> If a person could afford to buy the guide, having it was supposed to be enough to guarantee his future life. This could still make some sense if the deceased would have been able to read the book or memorize its contents, but, since the copies were so incomplete and replete with errors, it is questionable whether many of the owners would have or could have read the texts.

This raises the question of the extent of literacy in the population. If three to four million is accepted as the likely estimate of the population for the New Kingdom,[50] the small scribal class with the high officials and priests who would also be literate could scarcely be numbered at more than 300,000. We can be sure, however, that in well-equipped tombs the officiating priests in a funerary rite would be fully able to deal with the task of reciting the textual parts assigned to them. In the case of the deceased King the task was nominally allotted to the living Horus-King, but the permanence of such arrangements was obviously limited. There can be little doubt, at the same time, that a sense of permanence came from a belief that the written sacred word preserves its magical potency. Morenz believed that the permanence came from the deceased's assumed ability to continue with the process of recitation.[51] This explanation does not go far enough. Even without the recitation rites the written texts retained their saving power. It has often been urged that the texts imply ritual procedures additional to recitation. In a widely-ranging study of the afterworld guides of the New Kingdom and their meaning for the deceased King, Winfried Barta has argued against the claimed ritual implications, apart from minor accompaniments like incense-burning and libations to go with the recitations.[52] In this he may be right, as also in regard to the Pyramid Texts, but one cannot believe that with the end of recitations these sacred writings were thought to lose their power.

---

[49] Lesko, *Book of Two Ways*, 7.
[50] Cf. David O'Connor in *Ancient Egypt, A Social History* (Cambridge, 1983), 190. Philippe Derchain in a newspaper article by Horst Zimmermann (undated), discussing his forthcoming study of Egyptian love poetry, gives five per cent as his estimate of the literate class.
[51] Morenz, *Ägyptische Religion*, 241; cf. my *Origins of Osiris and his Cult*, 188.
[52] W. Barta, *Die Bedeutung der Jenseitsbücher für den verstorbenen König* (MÄS 42; Munich, 1985), 151 ff.; cf. my remarks in *CdE* (forthcoming).

The closing speech assigned to the deceased in the *Book of the Dead* (125) is noteworthy for its positive claims relating to conduct:

> See, I have come to you without sin, without guilt, without evil, without there being any evil in me, without there being a witness against me, without one against whom I might have done anything (evil). Rather, I live off Maat and drink of the truth ... I have given bread to the hungry and water to the thirsty, clothes to the naked and a ferry to the one without a boat. I have provided sacrifices for the gods and dead-offerings for the dead. So save me, protect me, do not make any report about me to the great god.
> (tr. H. Brunner, 'Egyptian Texts', 67.)

What strikes one here is that parallels can be cited from biographies more than a thousand years earlier, as in that of Nefer-Seshem-Rê of the Sixth Dynasty:

> I saved the weak from one stronger than he as far as was in my power, I gave bread to the hungry, clothes ⟨to the naked⟩, I brought to land him who had no boat.
> (*Urk.* I, 199.2–3.)[53]

Similar claims are made by Harkhuf, also of the Sixth Dynasty, and it is significant that in his case the claims are associated with the idea of judgement, as when he says, *Never did I speak any evil thing to a powerful one against any man, for I desired that it might be well with me before the Great God.* (*Urk.* I, 123.1–2.)[54]

It seems likely that the problem about the relative importance of magic and morality in the concept of posthumous judgement is best resolved on the basis of the varying standards of the people involved. For the great illiterate majority the main emphasis was probably magical. It was doubtless explained to them by priests and scribes that a judgement followed death, but that the sacred writings deposited in the tomb, together with the proper rites, would ensure the passing of the test. What we cannot measure is the impact of such a belief. A fear of the process of judgement, with its deeply moral implications, must have been present even if an acceptance of the magical guarantee was the prevailing factor. It is quite clear, at the same time, that to a literate and thoughtful minority the significance of the judgement went far beyond the ritual and magical equipment provided. The earliest expression of this conviction is the Instruction of Ptahhotep, a work which may well derive from the Fifth Dynasty. We have seen[55] that it contains

---

[53] Cf. M. Lichtheim, *Lit.* I (1973), 17.
[54] Cf. my *Conflict of Horus and Seth*, 79–80.
[55] See above, p. 190.

the belief that the operation of Maat brings recompense to man in this life; but it also seems to imply that the process extends to the life after death.[56] Two doctrines, it appears, are combined in this text, relating in turn to this world and the next, and the combination is significant, albeit rather rare. We have assembled numerous references to both types of judgement, but a conscious consideration of their relation is not often revealed. When that does happen, as with Ptahhotep, the natural and logical suggestion is that the judgement on earth can be continued in a life to come—at least that the threshold to that life can stage a rigorous ethical assessment which implies the completion of any unfinished business left over from the earthly process.

If a certain vagueness nevertheless attends the expression of the duplicated doctrine,[57] the Instruction for Merikarê, which derives from the Ninth or Tenth Dynasty (*c.* 2100 B.C.), contains a reference which is unambiguous in its description of a Court that is clearly placed after death, for it says of its members that *they view a lifetime in an hour*:[58]

> You know they are not lenient,
> On the day of judging the miserable,
> In the hour of doing their task.
> It is painful when the accuser has knowledge;
> Do not trust in length of years,
> They view a lifetime in an hour!
> When a man remains over after death,
> His deeds are set beside him as treasure,
> And being yonder lasts forever.
> (Merikarê, 52–55; tr. M. Lichtheim, *Lit.* I, 101.)

The continuity of this conviction through a long period of Egyptian spirituality is well attested. It reaches its culmination in the words of Petosiris, who was a priest at Hermopolis in the fourth century B.C.:[59]

> There no distinction is made between the inferior and superior person ... No one is free from the reckoning. Thoth as a baboon holds [the balance], to assess each man according to what he has done on earth.

But he was no isolated figure. Similar sentiments were expressed

---

[56] Morenz (tr. Ann E. Keep, London, 1973), 127, following Gerhard Fecht.
[57] Cf. H. Brunner, 'Die Lehren', in *Hdb. der Orientalistik*, I.1.2. *Literatur* (2nd Ed., Leiden, 1970), 122; Yoyotte, 'Jugement des Morts', 35.
[58] Cf. J.A. Wilson, in *ANET*³ 415 and Ch. Seeber in *LÄ* III (1980), 249–52.
[59] Cf. Morenz (tr. Keep), *Egyptian Religion*, 133; M. Lichtheim, *Lit.* III, 46.

before him by Baki, a high official of the New Kingdom[60] who impresses with his moral intensity; in a stela set up at Abydos by Ramesses IV; and in a Memphite funerary text of Ptahnefer in the Nineteenth Dynasty where the deceased is said to state that *if a man be glorified for his integrity, then shall my soul be the Master of the Balance before the Great God, Lord of the West.*—a bold assumption of the role of Anubis or Thoth.[61]

6. *The Priestly Connection and the Basic Situation*

To explain the institutional mechanics which gave rise to a concept of such impelling force and influence is not a difficult task. The religion of Ancient Egypt consistently inculcated a belief that life persists after death and that this continued life is marked by many of the qualities and activities of the life which preceded it. Among such activities were judicial processes of the types which we discriminate as functions of either civil or criminal law. The fear arose that one was in danger, after death, of having to face charges in a celestial or underworld location and that such charges would relate to conduct in the previous life. Allusions to the fear of litigation do not refer to any exact timing of the process; nor indeed is any suggestion given, at first, that the process is either inevitable or compulsory. What is clear, however, is that the judicial settings of this world are boldly projected to the next; the terminology points incisively to the projection—it talks of a court, a presiding judge, a plaintiff, a defendant, a witness, and arbiters.[62]

A much more difficult task is to explain the emergence of the idea that a compulsory moral test faces every one immediately after death. In its developed form the idea also includes the proviso that immortality itself depends on the successful passing of the test. It is possible, as we have seen, that the doctrine is present in the lore of Ptahhotep in the Fifth Dynasty; it is indubitably present in the Instruction for Merikarê in the Tenth. In the New Kingdom it achieves indelible expression both textually and pictorially. The mechanics of the development remain the same: the transposition of a court scenario. Yet the moral insistence, with its application to persons of every class and sex, has a universal sweep which defies a

---

[60] G. Roeder, *Die ägyptische Religion in Text und Bild*, IV (Zürich, 1961), 243–50.
[61] For such texts, with refs., see Spiegel, *Die Idee vom Totengericht*, 71–77; Yoyotte, in 'Jugement des Morts', 65–69; Brandon, *The Judgment of the Dead*, 41–43.
[62] See especially, R. Grieshammer, *Jenseitsgericht*, 18 ff.

merely institutional explanation. The likely source of this moral compulsion which challenged the very texture of the social inequality so manifest in Egyptian life in other ways was the concept of Maat. Ample witness to the force of the concept is found in the Wisdom Literature; and what is significant is the way in which the concept compelled the broadening of the judicial basis of the judgement of the dead. In mundane practice the type of process envisaged would obviously have been confined in each case to a narrow range of particular charges. Now, in the posthumous judgement, the assessment touches the whole of life with a detailed and searching list of questions. It is a far cry from the triviality of the cases emanating from the Egyptian court-rooms; the broad sweep and the austerity of the probing are impressive qualities which can be connected principally with Maat, although the association of the concept with the deities Rê and Osiris was clearly also a powerful factor.

The personal protestations of innocence in *BD* 125 have been rightly compared with statements addressed to priests in inscriptions engraved on side doors leading into the temples of Graeco-Roman Egypt. H.W. Fairman collected some of these from the temple of Edfu, and a typical example includes a list of prohibitions relating to service in the great temple of Horus:[63]

> Do not initiate wrongfully; do not enter when unclean; do not utter falsehood in his house; do not covet the property <of his temple>; do not tell lies; do not receive bribes; do not discriminate between a poor man and a great; do not add to the weight or the measuring-cord but (rather) reduce them; do not tamper with the corn-measure.
> (*Edfou*, III, 360.12–361.5.)

The text with which Fairman was mainly concerned (*Edfou*, V, 334. 1–6) is inscribed above a figure of Seshat, goddess of writing, on the lintel of a door. Horus is addressed by the goddess and told that she has come to him *that I may set down in writing before thee the doer of good and the doer of evil*, the latter being then described as *he who initiates wrongfully, [he who enters] when unclean; he who speaks falsehood in thy house*, whereas the doer of good is *he who knows right from wrong, he who is pure, he who is upright and walks in (the path of) righteousness*—a contrast which recalls that of the First Psalm. While Fairman properly notes (p. 87) that 'Seshat appears to be acting after the manner of a "recording angel"', he does not comment on resemblances to the Declarations of

---

[63] H.W. Fairman, 'A Scene of the Offering of Truth in the Temple of Edfu', *MDAIK* 16 (1958: FS. H. Junker), 86–92, this on p. 90; cf. Serge Sauneron (tr. A. Morrissett), *The Priests of Ancient Egypt* (New York, 1960), 25.

Innocence. The emphasis is on purity and is found in both the texts quoted above and also in the Declarations; the theme of falsifying weights or measures is found in the first text and in the Declarations. When the priestly King or his deputy addresses the gods, he too affirms that he is pure and free from sin, with a denial of specific charges, such as *I have not stolen things*. It is also of interest that he appeals to *the Council of the Great God in this temple*—a distinct suggestion of affinity with the posthumous Tribunal.[64] On a more mundane level, of course, a large temple had an administrative council with the prince of the nome often at its head.[65]

A priestly connection has been more clearly illumined in a Greek papyrus of the second century A.D. from Oxyrhynchus published by Verne B. Schuman.[66] The verso deals with rules concerning sacred animals and sacrificial victims; the recto gives regulations by which priests were governed. An oath enjoined on a newly installed priest is given: he promises not to eat or drink things that are not lawful, not to *measure a measure on a threshing floor*, not to touch sheep's hair. These statements are in the future tense. But then come statements with past reference:[67]

> I have not cut off the head of a living being.
> I have not killed a man.
> I have not bound a man.
> I have not had sexual union with a boy.
> I have not had sexual union with a wife of another.

It is to Reinhold Merkelbach that we owe the perceptive realization that here we are very close to the Declarations of Innocence.[68]

The text from Oxyrhynchus relates to an Egyptian temple, and Merkelbach remarks on the more stringent definition of the priest's conduct as compared with that expected in Pharaonic times; for instance, priests then were called on to slaughter the accepted sacrificial animals. In addition to the texts assembled by Fairman there are sayings from other Ptolemaic sources which represent avowals of purity to be made by priests on entering the temple and which sometimes contain phrases similar to those found in the Declarations relating to judgement.[69] The natural inference is that

---

[64] See Fairman, op. cit. 91, translating *Edfou*, III, 78, 10–79, 4.
[65] Sauneron, op. cit. 60.
[66] *Harv. Theol. Rev.* 53 (1960), 159–70.
[67] Ibid. 163–6 with notes.
[68] R. Merkelbach, 'Ein Griechisch-Ägyptischer Priestereid und das Totenbuch', in *Religions en Égypte hellénistique et romaine* (Paris, 1969), 69–73; and more fully in *ZPE* 2 (1968), 7–30.
[69] See E. Otto as quoted by Merkelbach in *ZPE* 2 (1968), 29–30.

the similarity of the textual material demanded led to a rather fluid adoption of sayings from one category to another, although the situation might be radically different. A good example is seen in the remarkable parallels found in poems by the Roman elegists Lygdamus and Tibullus: the former, when he feels that death is near, protests to the gods that he has not revealed secrets of the Mysteries, has not poisoned any one or stolen anything from the temples. L. Koenen points to parallels in the Egyptian Declarations and in the biographical inscriptions of the Late Period; but he wisely concludes that the confessions expected in the Isis Mystery-cult are the immediate source.[70]

It is a matter of some surprise, in view of these instances of literary interpenetration, that the suggestion has been made that the priest's prelude to vocation and duty is the basic *Sitz im Leben* of the entire concept of the judgement of the dead as presented in the Book of the Dead.[71] It is the more surprising in view of the fact that the scholar who has propounded it, Reinhard Grieshammer, had made clear in his earlier study, *Das Jenseitsgericht in den Sargtexten* (1970), that the origins of the idea are much wider—the belief that judicial litigation was possible in the life after death. The relevant early material contains no hint of restriction to a priestly class; indeed an impressive feature of the doctrine of a compulsory posthumous judgement, first firmly enunciated in the Instruction for Merikarê, is that it is binding on all. Perhaps the earliest connection of the idea with the image of weighing in the balance occurs in the stela of Antef in the Eleventh Dynasty;[72] and a significant development in this direction is that the deceased's heart takes the place of the opposing litigant.[73] It should be noted that the priestly parallels to the Declarations of Innocence occur only in the Graeco-Roman era, at a time when the scenario of judgement after death was long since firmly established. It is much more likely, therefore, that the borrowing was from the Declara-

---

[70] L. Koenen in *ZPE* 2 (1968), 31–38. For confession in the Isis-Cult cf. my *Apuleius, The Isis-Book* (Leiden, 1975), 53; 252; 271; and M. Heerma van Voss in *Studies in Hellenistic Religions* ed. M.J. Vermaseren (Leiden, 1979), 26.

[71] R. Grieshammer in *ZDMG* Suppl. II (Wiesbaden, 1974), 19–25; cf. F. Junge in *Aspekte der spätägyptischen Religion* ed. W. Westendorf (Wiesbaden, 1979), 110; H. Brunner in *Symbolon* N.F. 6 (1982), 48. In his *Jenseitsgericht in den Sargtexten*, 58 n. 313, Grieshammer already makes a tentative approach to his later theory.

[72] See W. Schenkel's translation in *Memphis Herakleopolis Theben* (Wiesbaden, 1965), 298–9; see also Seeber, *Untersuchungen*, 1 with refs.; and D. Müller on Merikarê in *ZÄS* 94 (1967), 117 ff.

[73] Grieshammer, *Jenseitsgericht*, 52. He also shows that the idea of weighing the heart occurs in several of the *Coffin Texts*.

tions (cf. Kákosy, *Selected Papers*, 228); and that behind them was the sequence of ideas which we have outlined. The early biographies, with their allusions to a day of reckoning before the Great God, certainly played their part. Along the line too comes the association of judgement with doors or gates with its basic tenet that a right of entry must be ritually or morally established. This association, be it noted, never ousts the central motif of a court of judgement. There is a nexus here, of course, with right of entry into a temple or its privileged areas, and it is only the latter category that concerned the priesthood as such. In a recent discussion of purity as a qualification of entry Grieshammer wisely includes several spheres of thought, referring to similar demands made for entry to the grave, the afterworld, and the tribunal of the dead.[74] The priestly element does not seem to dominate in any of these contexts; and the prescriptions of priestly purity in the Graeco-Roman era do not normally include parts of the Declarations of Innocence.[75] Indeed some of the eulogies of the priest's life and function are more positive in their approach to God's blessings, as in the text from Edfu:[76]

> Enter in peace, leave in peace, go in happiness! For life is in His hand, peace is in His grasp, all good things are with Him . . . There is food for the one who remains at His table; there is nourishment for the one who eats of His offerings! There is no misfortune or evil for the one who lives on His benefits; there is no damnation for the one who serves Him; for His care reaches to heaven and his security to the earth.

Here the lofty tone is admittedly marred a little by one crass note of materialistic pleasure.[77]

We are not abundantly informed about the rules of entry. According to Sauneron[78] the priesthood was 'too liberally open and above all subjected to a very anarchistic method of recruiting', while another view[79] sees priestly offices as 'highly coveted positions' with appointment 'no easy matter'. The higher echelons were

---

[74] Grieshammer, 'Reinheit, kultische', *LÄ* V (1984), 212–13.

[75] One might insist too that the example noted by Merkelbach is in a Greek papyrus. But it is quite probably a translation from the Egyptian, as Stephanie West suggested in *ZPE* 2 (1968), 21 n. 10.

[76] Sauneron, *The Priests of Ancient Egypt*, 26, following M. Alliot's translation of *Edfou* V, 343, 13 ff.

[77] In the Late Period emoluments in land and stipend were a still greater inducement: see Alan B. Lloyd in *Ancient Egypt, A Social History* (Cambridge, 1981), 308.

[78] Op. cit. 27.

[79] Lloyd, op. cit. 303.

plainly controlled by royal patronage or the hereditary principle, particularly in the Late Period; in all eras ritual purity was much emphasized. It can be argued, in relation to the judgement of the dead, that the priest and the deceased person have the same status.[80] It is true that this simple equation is not so effective when we consider the matter of origins. The first stages are apparent, as Leclant has reminded us, in the Pyramid Texts, and the broad source thus indicated is royal ritual.[81] But other funerary sources, especially the early private biographies, show that the idea was by no means restricted to the King. One might argue, of course, that the Pharaoh was pre-eminently a priest, and that this is true of the Pyramid Texts. Yet the Pharaoh was much else besides, and the functions of judgement were both vested in him and, in some contexts, applied to him. If the theory of the priestly origin of the Declarations of Innocence were true, one would expect to encounter early traces of it in the material in which the King figures as a defendant. Such statements as

> There is no living one who complains against the King.
> (*Pyr.* 386 a.)

> I have not opposed the King.
> (*Pyr.* 892 a.)[82]

illustrate two facets of the developing idea; and the second one, in the form of a denial, plainly points to the typical form of the later Declarations. Yet it betrays no special link with the priesthood. Even a statement like *this King is far removed from what men abominate, his hands have not touched what the gods abominate* (*Pyr.* 2082 b–c.) is susceptible of a non-priestly interpretation, although it claims purity.

The same is true of most of the Declarations of Innocence. Perhaps Grieshammer is right (p. 23 of his article in *ZDMG* Suppl. II, 1974) in questioning whether they constitute, as is often claimed, 'das ethische Gesamtideal der Ägypter'; he notes that several areas dealt with in the Wisdom Literature are not touched on here, or at least very little. To relate the Declarations, however,

---

[80] F. Junge in *Aspekte der spätägyptischen Religion*, 110, following Grieshammer.

[81] J. Leclant, *Annuaire du Collège, 1982–3* (Résumé des cours et travaux, Paris, 1983), 532.

[82] The first clause points to a non-royal origin. See also H. Junker, *Pyramidenzeit* (Zürich, 1949), 82. In *ZDMG* Suppl. II (1974), 22 Grieshammer refers to an 'Utterance for entry into the temple' of Sethos in Abydos and also to the Berlin Amûn-ritual for earlier examples of priestly dicta which are comparable to the *BD* Declarations.

to one narrow priestly class is not a convincing ploy, especially in view of the claims pointedly made as early as Merikarê, that no one is exempt from the assessment. Merikarê is important in the argument, for the theory does not posit that the developed doctrine applied only to priests, only that the priestly situation gave rise to the claims of purity and integrity. If *BD* 125 talks of *bringing the Horus-Eye*, that is admittedly a priest's task; but a recitation by a lector-priest could include such a rite (or merely an allusion to it). It does not affect the wide application of the content of the Declarations.

7. *Some Changed Emphases and their Influence*

It was to be expected that a concept which held spiritual sway for such a long period would experience several changes in the detailed manner of its presentation. Several of these changes relate to the pictorial records and the following brief survey is indebted for an indication of these to the admirable study by Christine Beinlich-Seeber.[83] Previously an important study of one aspect had been published by László Kákosy.[84]

(1) *The Weighing of the Heart*

In the most prevalent type of representation the symbol of the human heart, as the seat of the intellect and conscience, is shown in one of the scales, while a figure of Maat appears in the other, sometimes in an abbreviated form. In a variant detail which occurs in Ptolemaic and Roman times and also occasionally in earlier examples the figure of a man is depicted instead of the heart.[85] This recalls the Greek vase-paintings which depict the weighing of small figures of armed warriors (probably Achilles and Hector) by the god Hermes before Zeus.[86] Indeed one might consider the possibility of Greek influence on the Egyptian motif; but the earlier examples in Egypt, from the Nineteenth or Twentieth Dynasty, suggest that the Egyptians were developing an innovation which

---

[83] Christine Seeber, *Untersuchungen zur Darstellung des Totengerichts im Alten Ägypten* (Munich, 1976).

[84] L. Kákosy, 'Selige und Verdammte in der spätägyptischen Religion', *ZÄS* 97 (1971), 95 ff. = id. *Selected Papers* (Studia Aegyptiaca, 7; Budapest, 1981), 227–37.

[85] Kákosy, op. cit. (*Selected Papers*), 229–30; Seeber, op. cit. 75. Cf. Emma Brunner-Traut, *Gelebte Mythen* (Darmstadt, 1981), 76, a depiction from Akhmîm (ii A.D.) showing the man in the scale as a skeleton.

[86] See below, 289.

had already appeared among them. In the Roman era occurs another deviation from the norm: instead of the desired equilibrium which is regularly portrayed as the ideal result, now the scale with the dead man is shown in a downward fall.[87]

For the weighing of other parts of the body see below, pp. 230–31; 241.

(2) The Blissful Right and the Baleful Left

In the Egyptian tradition the blessed and vindicated dead are led on the right to a life of happiness, while the damned are led on the left to a fate of torture and destruction.[88] The dual linkage is furthered in Egyptian by the fact that the words for 'Right' and 'Left' can also mean 'West' and 'East', the former being the abode of the blessed dead. It seems to be a distinctive notion since other directional associations appear elsewhere; thus in both Hebrew and Arabic 'Left' can refer to the 'North' and 'Right' to the 'South'.[89] Of course the favourable and unfavourable connotations of 'Right' and 'Left' respectively are well-known[90] over an almost universal span.[91] What tends to confirm the view of Morenz on the way in which Egypt has here influenced Orphic practices and the thought of Plato and Vergil is the use of the image in phases which form a sequel to judgement. The same is true of the role ascribed to the Son of Man:

> Before him will be gathered all the nations, and he will separate them one from another as a shepherd separates the sheep from the goats, and he will place the sheep at his right hand, but the goats at the left.
> (Matt. 25:32–33.)

Jewish apocalyptic doubtless provides the immediate source of this judgement scene;[92] but its original source may well be in Egypt.[93]

---

[87] Kákosy, op. cit. 229; Seeber, op. cit. 77 with n. 280 and Fig. 23.

[88] See below, 296 with n. 65.

[89] J. Chelhod in *Right and Left* ed. Rodney Needham (Chicago, 1973), 247.

[90] Ibid. passim; a work devoted mainly to present-day societies. The only essay dealing with the ancient world is 'Right and Left in Greek Philosophy' (pp. 167–86) by Geoffrey Lloyd, and even this omits the eschatology of the Orphics and Plato. On the Egyptian attitude cf. my remarks on 'The Deserters on the Left of the King', *ASAE* 53 (1955), 144–9.

[91] Geoffrey Lloyd, op. cit. 172, says of the ancient Chinese that 'they held the left to be more honorable than the right.'

[92] J.A.T. Robinson, in *NTS* 2 (1955–56), 228, suggests that the Similitudes of Enoch are a likely source of the image of a Messianic figure on the throne of God's judgement; and he compares allusions in Enoch 45:3; 51:3 and elsewhere.

[93] Cf. Beate George, *Zu den altägyptischen Vorstellungen vom Schatten als Seele* (Bonn, 1970), 31 ff.

(3) *Shaï, Meskhenet, and Renenet*

The deceased is often shown standing and watching the weighing process; his heart is shown in one of the scales; sometimes too his *ba* or his shadow (*šwyt*) are depicted. In addition we occasionally see a divine triad with whom the deceased is intimately connected: the god Shaï, Fate; Meskhenet, goddess of birth; and Renenet, goddess of nourishment. The clearest representation is that in the Papyrus of Ani.[94] Any meaning assigned to the group must refer to the personal history of the deceased person: Meskhenet to his birth, Renenet to his vital growth, and Shaï to his allotted life-span which has now been destined to end.[95] Explication cannot here be based on detailed textual appendages, and the idea that Shaï and Meskhenet imply that the weighing of merits takes account of the joy and pain which have been allotted by destiny is rather speculative.[96] It is generally assumed that the whole approach is to the deceased's past; his life-record is of course basic to the judgement scene. But there are several instances in the Twenty-first Dynasty where the objects connected with birth and with Meskhenet[97] appear above the mummified squatting figure of the deceased; and it has been cogently urged that the portrayed meaning is the hope that the deceased will be reborn to a new life.[98]

One instantly recalls the importance of such a doctrine in the Isis Mystery-Cult, but the time-factor from the Twenty-first Dynasty prevents an easy equation. In the Graeco-Roman era the idea of Fate was of far-reaching import, and the Isis religion, while it claimed power over fate, shows some impress of non-Egyptian ideology.[99] The role of Shaï in the judgement process probably did not impart any sense of tension between an ethical assessment and a fatalistic determinism; man's conduct was not envisaged as predestined,[100] and the presence of Shaï emphasized the distinctive

---

[94] Seeber, op. cit. 83–88 with Fig. 24. She points out that usually Shaï and Renenet appear as a pair without Meskhenet. See also J. Quaegebeur, *Le Dieu égyptien Shaï* (Leuven, 1975), 149.

[95] Cf. J. Broekhuis, *De Godin Renenwettet* (Assen, 1971), 90–95.

[96] Yoyotte in 'Jugement des Morts', 46 and 74 n. 74, where the description of Setne in the Demotic tale is taken as the basis. See M. Lichtheim, *Lit.* III (1980), 140 (Setne II): the tribunal is said to assess the number of good and bad deeds.

[97] Cf. John Baines, *Fecundity Figures* (Warminster, 1985), 64.

[98] Seeber, op. cit. 88 and 102–106.

[99] See J. Bergman, 'I Overcome Fate, Fate Harkens to Me', in *Fatalistic Beliefs* ed. H. Ringgren (Stockholm, 1967), 35–51. In the end he agrees with Morenz's dictum: 'Im Kern blieb Isis Ägypterin.'

[100] His birth and life-span were so regarded, it seems: cf. S. Morenz (with D. Müller), *Untersuchungen zur Rolle des Schicksals in der ägyptischen Religion* (Abh.

individualism of the deceased. In the Homeric psychostasia Zeus weighs the *kêres* of people—their fates.[101] But the parallel is not exact, for Shaï in the Egyptian scene is a subsidiary accompanying figure, though closely connected with the person who is assessed. A sharp contrast emerges in the idea of Agathos Daimon, when equated with Shaï, as a pantheistic god, lord of the earth and the cosmos, creator and nourisher of all.[102]

(4) *A Triad of Assistant Arbiters*

Whereas Rê or Osiris is usually shown as the president of the tribunal, the latter being often accompanied by Isis and Nephthys, there is a considerable range of divinities also involved in the procedure. We have mentioned above the Forty-two Assessors. In the weighing scene a curious variant occurs in the depiction of the balance as shown in the *Book of Gates*: here the balance is seen above the shoulders of a mummiform god who faces the presiding Osiris and is in close proximity to him.[103] This figure may well be regarded as a personification of the balance.[104]

Broadly speaking we may observe that three deities are regularly shown as participating in the procedure which an enthroned Osiris is witnessing. Anubis or Horus is often shown in charge of the balance, while Thoth is regularly the Recorder. The goddess Maat appears also, not as an active participant but as a bystander who lends her spiritual sanction.[105] Further, the hall of judgement is from early times[106] designated as that of the Two Maat-goddesses

---

Leipzig, 52; Berlin, 1960), 23. Later he discusses the equation of Shaï and Agathos Daimon, two snake deities; but the latter did not stand for the Greek idea of destiny; cf. J. Lindsay, *The Origins of Alchemy in Graeco-Roman Egypt* (London, 1970), 311–12 and J. Quaegebeur, op. cit. 170–76.

[101] See below, 289.

[102] Cf. J. Assmann, *Ägypten—Theologie und Frömmigkeit einer frühen Hochkultur* (Stuttgart, 1984), 281, quoting Preisendanz, *Papyri Graecae Magicae*, 12, 242 ff. (= Leiden P.Gr. J 384 (v), found in a tomb in Thebes). The Greek Agathos Daimon was not likely to provide this expansive vision; indeed the Alexandrian form was primarily seen as a patron of the city and of domestic prosperity; cf. P.M. Fraser, *Ptolemaic Alexandria*, I (1972), 209–11. On p. 211 Fraser refers to the equation with Psais, 'bringer of individual good luck'. The Egyptian Shaï was very much more than that.

[103] Hornung et al., *Das Buch von den Pforten*, II (1980), 143–4.

[104] See M. Heerma van Voss in *Travels in the World of the Old Testament* (Amsterdam, 1974), 86. He notes that on two sarcophagi the figure is called *The Master of the Balance* (*iry mh3t*).

[105] For an ably detailed exposé of the role of these gods see Seeber, *Untersuchungen*, 63–175, with due attention also to the gods who follow Osiris, the four sons of Horus, the Ennead, the 42 Assessors, and the Devourer of the Dead.

[106] They appear in the earliest of the *Pyramid Texts* (317 *a–b* W); cf. my *Conflict*

and the two figures sometimes appear in depictions. The figure of Maat also appears in one of the scales, sometimes with simply the feather-symbol.

In the Greek tradition it is Zeus who corresponds to Rê or Osiris; he is the god who presides over the psychostasia, and in the Homeric allusions he holds the scales himself. In Greek art, however, the function of enacting the weighing is sometimes assigned to Hermes, so that a parallel to the Egyptian situation again appears.[107] In his *Gorgias* (523 E) Plato mentions a divine triad of judges assessing the dead in Hades: they are Minos, Rhadamanthys, and Aeacus; and of these Aeacus is to deal with persons from Europe, while the other two deal with those from Asia. Minos, however, is designated afterwards as deciding cases which are found difficult by the other two judges. In Plato's *Apology* (41 A) Socrates contrasts the judges who are trying him in Athens with the true judges of Hades—Minos, Rhadamanthys, Aeacus and Triptolemus, the group now forming a tetrad. A parallel to the Egyptian set-up thus emerges, save that there is no Zeus- or Osiris-figure to preside in Hades. In Pindar (*Isthm.* 8.27–28) Aeacus is one who judges between the gods. But it is Plato who comes closest to the Egyptian paradigm, for the judgement in the *Gorgias* gives details of the two ways which form a sequel to the verdict: one leads to the Isles of the Blest, the other to Tartarus.[108] It is generally agreed that Plato is indebted in such matters to the Orphic tradition; and this is where the discussion by Morenz is especially enlightening, for he has been able to show that several elements of Orphic teaching, particularly the theory of the primal cosmogonic egg, have their origins in Egypt.[109] Accordingly, in discussing the Pla-

---

of Horus and Seth, 55–57. Seeber, op. cit. 63, strangely ignores these early occurrences. Anubis *ỉp ỉbw*, who searches (or, reckons) hearts, appears in *Pyr.* 1287 *a* P, and Beate George, *Zu den altägyptischen Vorstellungen vom Schatten als Seele*, 31, argues that this refers to judgement. Hornung, *Altägyptische Höllenvorstellungen*, 10–11, takes *sỉp* in the more extreme sense of 'condemn' (*verdammen*).

[107] Cf. below p. 290.

[108] Cf. J. Bergman, 'Zum Zwei-Wege-Motiv', 49, where he also compares the vision of Er at the end of Plato's *Republic* (614 C): the righteous ascend to heaven through the opening on the right, whereas the wicked descend to the earth through the opening on the left. On the popular Greek idea of a triad of judges see Nilsson, *Geschichte der Griech. Rel.* I (3rd Ed., 1967), 824, noting that Demosthenes (18.127) mentions Minos, Rhadamanthys, and Aeacus.

[109] See Morenz, 'Ägypten und die altorphische Kosmogonie', in id. *Religion und Geschichte des alten Ägypten* (Weimar, 1975), 452–95 (first publ. in 1950). M.L. West, *Early Greek Philosophy and the Orient* (Oxford, 1971), 30 and 95–96, discusses the Iranian cosmic egg, but seems not to have heard of the Egyptian doctrine; he makes ample amends, however, in his *The Orphic Poems* (Oxford, 1983), 188–9.

tonic passages concerned with judgement of the dead, Morenz rightly treats of the Orphic 'gold leaves' used as passes, and firmly connects them with the Egyptian funerary tradition.[110]

A similar delegation of the actual procedure of judgement appears in the Judaeo-Christian tradition. In the Book of Daniel (7:9–10) *one ancient in years* seems to preside, but no detail is given of the ministrants who proceed with *the opening of the books*; in Enoch 61:8 it is *the Elect One* that is *on the throne of glory*, and a weighing of deeds takes place without a further indication of the performers. When the theme was developed in Christian art, a clear designation of the divine beings appears: Christ the enthroned Saviour presides, and the archangel Michael is in charge of the balance.

An assumption of intellectual contact underlies such claims[111] and when we come to Hellenistic and Roman times it may be taken for granted. Nor is it any one-way traffic. Literature in Egypt now shows the impress of Graeco-Roman traditions. Thus we read in the story of Setne Khamwas and Si-Osire, a work which belongs to the second century A.D., in a description of punishments in the underworld:

> Now let me learn [what is happening] to those people who are plaiting ropes while donkeys chew them up; and those others whose provisions of water and bread are hung above them, and while they scramble to bring them down, others dig pits at their feet to prevent them from getting at them.
>
> (M. Lichtheim, *Lit*. III, 141.)

Here are evident allusions to the fate in Greek tradition of Ocnus and Tantalus, both bearers of a punishment which consists of vain and hopeless endeavour. Ocnus tries in vain to make a rope while an ass tears it up again; Tantalus has delicious fruit dangled above him which ever recedes from his grasp. Another feature of this story may be of Greek origin, for it tells of the visit made to the underworld by Setne, a living person, who has his son, Si-Osire, as guide. Greek traditions concerning Odysseus, Orpheus, and Aeneas told of such visits and of converse with the dead.

---

[110] Ibid. 289 ('Rechts und links im Totengericht').

[111] Cf. Günther Hölbl, *Beziehungen der ägyptischen Kultur zu Altitalien* (2 Vols., EPRO 62; Leiden, 1979). He deals in the main with material prior to 300 B.C. and expressly refrains (I, 6) from discussing relations between Egyptian religion and Orphic-Pythagorean doctrines. He refers, however, to the view of A.A. Barb in *The Legacy of Egypt* (2nd Ed., Oxford, 1971) ed. J.R. Harris, 149–50, accepting the theory of Egyptian influence in this matter; Barb's Fig. 2 (p. 150) shows a tomb amulet from Sardinia where he finds 'a purely Egyptian scene of the Judgement of the Dead'.

A different kind of contact is suggested by another story in the same papyrus. It relates how a rich nobleman who was sumptuously buried faced nothing but misery and torture in the underworld, whereas a poor man whose burial was unadorned and unlamented was exalted after death to a position of great honour. The parable of Dives and Lazarus in Luke 16:19–31 is a close parallel and it was the view of Gressmann that the Egyptian tale supplied the main motifs of the New Testament parable as well as of similar Jewish stories,[112] although the Demotic papyrus may itself be later than Luke's gospel.[113] However that may be, Dr Lichtheim is clearly right when she says that 'elements of Greek origin' have been absorbed into the Demotic text; and she refers to the 'many testimonies to the intermingling of Egyptian and Greek cultures in Greco-Roman Egypt'.[114]

(5) *Heaven, Hell, and a Pointer to Purgatory*

Egyptian ideas of heaven and hell are abundantly attested in both pictures and texts. Although they are properly brought into connection with the scenario of judgement, it is not often that they are expressly linked with it. Pictorially and textually it is the *Devourer of the Dead*, the composite monster depicted in the weighing episode, that is plainly the instrument of inflicting the punishment that awaits the guilty. It is not until the Roman period, however, that the monster is shown in action, as in the representation from Akhmîm to which allusion has already been made. Here we see the monster preparing to devour the deceased's skeleton or shadow after it has been cooked in a cauldron with two handles. What is satisfying about this tomb-painting is that it is placed immediately adjacent to a depiction of the judicial weighing and is therefore explicitly seen as a possible sequel.[115] If the victim's form is that of a shadow it is in line with much earlier depictions; if it is intended to

---

[112] Hugo Gressmann, *Vom reichen Mann und armen Lazarus* (Abh. Berlin, 1918), 59: the Egyptian tale arose in Memphis in the Hellenistic era, but received Greek motifs which were mediated by Orphic circles; it was in Memphis that Jews got to know of the tale and through them it reached Palestine in an Aramaic version which became known already in the pre-Christian era.

[113] F. Ll. Griffith, *Stories of the High Priests of Memphis* (Oxford, 1900), 41, suggests a date in the late first century A.D. for the Demotic text. Hornung, *Altägyptische Höllenvorstellungen* (Berlin, 1968), 10 n. 1, says of 'Setna II' that its date veers between the first century B.C. and the second century A.D.

[114] M. Lichtheim, *Lit.* III (1980), 126.

[115] For a finely coloured reproduction see F.W.F. von Bissing, *ASAE* 50 (1950), Pl.1, facing p. 576, with a description of the whole painting on p. 557.

be a skeleton, that may show Roman influence.[116] The monster's tongue protrudes a little, suggesting eagerness for a good meal.[117] It seems that in the texts it is the shadow of a condemned man that is peculiarly amenable to humiliation and destruction in various ways.[118]

The heavenly alternative is less effusively portrayed in representations, but includes idyllic scenes of bliss by the Nile, and notably a concept of 'Isles of the Righteous'.[119]

Was a third alternative ever presented? The second Setne tale describes the judgement of the dead in a way that makes this idea possible. Its first editor, comparing the doctrine of the *Book of the Dead*, maintained that 'in the present text the division is made on a different principle and into three classes, viz. the actively virtuous, the actively vicious, and those whose good and evil acts balanced each other.'[120] Erik Hornung[121] accepts this statement, but emphasizes that no process of purification is envisaged. He points out too that more subtle distinctions according to individual faults, such as the Coptic apocalypses, especially those of Peter and Paul, show after the second century A.D., have no Egyptian prototype; nor has the possibility of purification. The three categories are thus demarked in the second Setne tale:

> He who would be found to have more misdeeds than good deeds [is handed over] to the Devourer who belongs to the lord of the netherworld. His *ba* is destroyed together with his body, and he is not allowed to breathe ever again.
> He who would be found to have more good deeds than misdeeds is taken in among the gods of the tribunal of the lord of the netherworld, while his *ba* goes to the sky together with the august spirits.
> He who would be found to have good deeds equal to his misdeeds is taken in among the excellent spirits who serve Sokar-Osiris.
> (M. Lichtheim, *Lit*. III, 140.)

If the third category might appear to be well treated, they are not allowed, nevertheless, to ascend to heaven and have to remain in the netherworld as servants of the funerary sovereign. Later in the story we are told that the governing principle is one of reciprocity in relation to life in this world:

---

[116] Thus Erik Hornung, *Höllenvorstellungen*, 26 n. 7. A line-drawing is there given and the painting is dated to the second century A.D. (probably).
[117] Emma Brunner-Traut, *Gelebte Mythen*, 76.
[118] Beate George, *Zu den altägyptischen Vorstellungen vom Schatten als Seele*, 31–63.
[119] Cf. J. Gwyn Griffiths, 'In Search of the Isles of the Blest', *Greece and Rome* 16 (1947), 122–6, and *The Origins of Osiris and his Cult*, 32 ('Island of the Justified').
[120] F. Ll. Griffith, *Stories of the High Priests of Memphis*, 48 n. on line 8.
[121] *Höllenvorstellungen*, 10 n. 1. Cf. Walters, *JEA* 75 (1989), 200 ff.

He who is beneficent on earth, to him one is beneficent in the netherworld. And he who is evil, to him one is evil.

(Ibid. 141.)

There are clear differences between these descriptions and the pictorial and textual evidence of the *Book of the Dead*. One is the open admission that evil deeds have sometimes been committed; another is the exact distinction between two commended classes, the first class being allowed to join the gods in heaven and the second being accepted among the excellent spirits in the netherworld.[122]

A question that immediately arises is whether the intermediate verdict may reflect early Greek tradition about Purgatory, the intermediate state between Heaven and Hell. Just as Setne's allusions to Ocnus and Tantalus plainly have a Greek source, here the apparent deviation from the traditional Egyptian approach may have a similar explanation.[123] According to Plato, *Gorgias* (525 B), in a passage added by Socrates to the myth there presented, sinners who arrive in Hades are regarded by the judges as either incurable or curable; the former suffer terrible punishments to serve as an example, but the treatment of the latter is remedial: through painful experiences souls are prepared for a return to Earth and reincarnation.[124] Vergil presents a similar idea in the Sixth Book of the *Aeneid* (739–51): a favoured few go to the joyous fields of Elysium, while the damned are tortured for ever. Many others endure a long process of expiation so that they may return to Earth; and this they are allowed to do after drinking the waters of Lethe in order to forget their former lives. Penance is exacted for offences committed. Vergil stresses the element of purification in the process: 'from some the pervasive guilt is washed away under a deep whirlpool or it is burned out by fire':

aliis sub gurgite vasto
infectum eluitur scelus, aut exuritur igni.

As we have noted, this is precisely the element that Hornung finds missing in the third category of Setne's account.

Of course there is plenty of fire in the Egyptian sources, but

---

[122] Cf. Seeber, *Untersuchungen*, 81 and 115.

[123] Cf. L. Kákosy, *Selected Papers*, 235–6; J. Bollók, 'Die Tartaros-Szene in der Aeneis', *Ann. Univ. Budapest, Sectio Classica*, 4 (1976), 47–61.

[124] Not mentioned in the *Gorgias*; but cf. *Phaedo* 113 A–114 C and *Republic* 615 A ff.; see E.R. Dodds, *Plato, Gorgias* (Oxford, 1959), 375. The curables are also subdivided into two groups—those guilty of serious crimes and those whose lives have been varied between good and evil.

mostly it is fiercely destructive, including the 'Lake of Fire' and cauldrons of fire. Ideas of Hell in Iranian religion also give prominence to fire; and the Greek tradition depicts the torches of the Erinyes and blazing pitch and metal as instruments of torture, aided too by the concept of a world conflagration. The Egyptian hell-fire is much earlier, however, and it is surprising that Nilsson takes no account of it in reaching with gloomy pride his conclusion that the whole idea of Hell is a Greek invention.[125] In the Books of the Underworld the variety of the means by which defaulters are destroyed seems endless. The Devourer of the Dead, the monster of the judgement, himself annihilates the guilty, but fire, stake and sword through demon agents pursue the same end relentlessly and decapitation ensues, until one is ready to ask how many times is it possible to destroy a human being. The aim is complete destruction and reduction to a state of 'non-being'.[126]

Yet purification is certainly not absent from the Egyptian ideology. Flame Island (*iw nsrsr*) is a place fabled as the home and birth-place of the sun-god. Every dawn recalls the dawn of creation and the victory over darkness and chaos. The justified dead will share in Flame Island the joy of rebirth and the triumph over evil.[127] A phrase like *the house of the living in Flame Island* (*CT* I, 168 *c*) has led to the idea that the sun-god's island is located in this world; and some contexts imply that a living son approaches his dead father about action in Flame Island.[128] But preponderantly it is linked to the afterworld. What concerns our theme is that, whereas purification and rebirth appear to ensue there, these processes apply to beings already justified. It is not a third alternative to life or death, but a privilege extended to those who have triumphed in the judgement. This does not exclude the idea that Flame Island is regarded as a 'Zwischenreich' between this world and the next, as Grieshammer suggests.

In contrast, the second Setne story does delineate a third

---

[125] Nilsson, *Geschichte der Griech. Rel.*, II, 535: 'Leider bleibt es dabei, daß die Hölle eine griechische Erfindung ist.' In I, 328 f., however, he acknowledges that the Isles of the Blest form a concept which has come from Egypt to Greece via Minoan Crete.

[126] Hornung, *Unterweltsbücher*, 42–45; on destruction by fire see id. *Tal der Könige* (Zürich, 1982), 155–64.

[127] See the Ninth Hour of the *Book of Gates*, Hornung et al., *Das Buch von den Pforten*, II, 212–13, where the context tells of nourishment brought to the deceased and his *ba*. Kees, *Totenglauben*, 102, shows it to be sometimes a place of judgement. For Rê as a 'living flame' see Assmann, *Re und Amun* (1983), 148 and 150.

[128] Grieshammer, *Jenseitsgericht*, 101–104. *The house of the living* may, in spite of this, refer to the abode of the dead.

alternative, a true Purgatory. If one faces the possibility of non-Egyptian influence, Iranian ideas need to be considered. The Gāthās refer to a judgement after death when rewards and punishments will be assigned by a triad of judges (Mithra, Sraosh and Rashnu); also to an ordeal of molten metal which will lead to the destruction of the wicked while blessed souls return to a purified and peaceful earth. Only in post-Sasanian times (after A.D. 651) does a doctrine emerge which envisions the purging and eventual salvation of the wicked: see Mary Boyce, *A History of Zoroastrianism*, I (Leiden, 1975), 240–44; and J. Duchesne-Guillemin in *Religions of the Ancient East* (London, 1959), 144, on Heaven, Hell, and 'an intermediate place'.

In its later stages Etruscan eschatology supplements the Greek Hades to include horrendous demons who suggest a sequel of punishing tortures of the wicked: see M. Pallotino, *Etruscan Painting*, I (Geneva, 1952), 91–92 and 125–7; but there is no suggestion of Purgatory as an intermediate phase. We may well conclude that the second Setne story reveals, in this respect, a facet of Greek influence, especially as that influence is attested too in the figures of Ocnus and Tantalus. At least, that is the likely immediate source.

(6) *Transference to the Living*

A feature of Osirian beliefs in the Graeco-Roman era was the application of the god's power to the world of the living. Although he was primarily a funerary god, the Mysteries of both Isis and Osiris celebrated the emergence of a new life in the experience of the initiate, while including, at the same time, a blessed assurance of eternal bliss.[129] In the Roman era, especially, the cult of Osiris became more prominent,[130] while in the Hellenistic period he was to some degree supplanted by Sarapis. In much earlier times at Abydos Osiris was invested with cosmic powers and tended to be regarded accordingly as a universal god, thus equipping him for a status among the living.[131] In the Festival of Khoiak, which was celebrated throughout Egypt in the Graeco-Roman era, attention

---

[129] J. Gwyn Griffiths, 'Osiris', *LÄ* IV (1981), 629; and id. *Apuleius, The Isis-Book*, 51–55.

[130] V. Wessetsky, *Ausgewählte Schriften* (Budapest, 1981), 175–80 (first publ. 1976); M. Malaise, *Les Conditions de pénétration et de diffusion des cultes égyptiens en Italie* (EPRO 22; Leiden, 1972), 208.

[131] H. Kees, *Der Götterglaube im Alten Ägypten* (2nd Ed., Berlin, 1956), 336–7; cf. J. Černý, *Ancient Egyptian Religion* (London, 1952), 137, who dates the process from the New Kingdom.

was given to the Passion of Osiris and his revivification; but the culminating rite was the raising of the *djed*-pillar, and this rite, while also alluding to the new life achieved by the god, implied in a general sense that 'life will go on in the world.'[132]

That even the tribunal of the dead could sometimes be transferred to a temple of the living and be thus made to implicate the living, is a possibility suggested by the reliefs in a temple of Ptolemaic date at Deir el-Medîna. In these reliefs Osiris presides over a judgement scene which mostly follows the standard pattern,[133] save that the deceased is a nameless figure.[134] A statement by Diodorus (1.92.1–5) locates the judgement in a council of forty-two judges (a clear allusion to the posthumous trial) who examine charges and eulogies relating to the deceased's conduct in life; only if the verdict is favourable is the funeral allowed to proceed. Diodorus (1.72.4) makes a similar statement about royal burials, but in this case he places the assessment (*kritêrion*) of the life-record at the entrance to the tomb. His claim that many kings were refused the traditional burial because of an adverse verdict is plainly incredible; and there is no tangible evidence to support his account of the general practice.[135]

There is evidence, on the other hand, that the living King was sometimes subjected to a form of moral examination. A papyrus now in Brooklyn, which probably dates to the fourth century B.C., deals with ceremonies concerning the New Year. After a fervent paean of praise to the Pharaoh's celestial power as an ally of the sun-god Rê comes a disturbing rebuttal of an implied charge:

> He is without sins and his obstacles are dispelled.
>
> (III, 17.)[136]

The source of the first clause is manifestly in the Declarations of Innocence (*BD* 125): *I am without sin and I have committed no evil* (Naville, Tb. 125, Conf. 34). What is suggested is that the Pharaoh,

---

[132] R.T. Rundle Clark, *Myth and Symbol in Ancient Egypt* (London, 1959), 236. Clark treats the *djed* as essentially Osirian; originally, however, it was associated with other gods, such as Ptah, Rê and Khons. The rite concluded the festival; see E. Chassinat, *Le Mystère d'Osiris au mois de Khoiak*, I (Cairo, 1966), 73 with refs.

[133] See below, 'Judgement in the Mystery Religions', 313 ff.; 326 f.

[134] Deemed to represent Imhotep by L. Kákosy: see his *Selected Papers*, 179. If one objects that Imhotep was a divine figure by then, Kákosy would argue (as I have heard him argue in Budapest) that the universal application of the judgement is thereby emphasized: even a divinized being is not exempt.

[135] See Anne Burton, *Diodorus Siculus Book I: A Commentary* (EPRO 29; Leiden, 1972), 268–70.

[136] See Jean-Claude Goyon, *Confirmation du pouvoir royale au nouvel an* (BÉ 52; Cairo, 1972), 62.

in spite of his joy in the renewal of power, has had to account for his conduct in the past year. About a century later a hymn to the goddess Isis in the Temple of Philae (Room 7)[137] and in a similar context—that of the New Year—the King denies possible charges brought against him:[138]

> He has not done anything disgraceful against the god of his town,
> He has not committed any evil;
> Nothing will be counted against him in the Court of the Scribes of the Two Lands.

An actual annual process of scrutiny is strongly suggested; and there is again a parallel (in the first two lines) to the Declarations of Innocence. In a wider sense there are parallels too with ideas connected with New Year Festivals in other cultures. In the Babylonian New Year Festival there was an episode of marked humiliation when the king was struck in the face by the High Priest and made to kneel while uttering several denials of sins:

> I have not sinned, O lord of the lands,
> I have not been negligent regarding the divinity.
> I have not destroyed Babylon . . .

Afterwards the king was allowed to take back the royal insignia, since 'by his penance and confession the king cleansed himself of the taint of past sins.'[139] Rather similar is the tradition in Israel that the Davidic king has to suffer although he is the Messiah of Yahweh:[140]

> Remember, O Lord, the mockery of Thy Servant.
> (Psalms 89:50.)

It is accordingly possible that Egyptian tradition received a new influence at this time on a phase of judgement in this life.

---

[137] Removed between 1972 and 1980 to the adjacent island of Agilkia.

[138] Translation by Louis V. Žabkar in his *Hymns to Isis in Her Temple at Philae* (University Press of New England, 1988), 119. I am most grateful to Professor Žabkar for allowing me to peruse the typescript and plates of his book, which includes a Translation and detailed Commentary, prior to publication; and also for permission to use it here. Cf. his studies in *JEA* 66 (1980), 127–36 and 69 (1983), 115–37; and in *ZÄS* 108 (1981), 141–71. See also 183 above.

[139] H. Frankfort, *Kingship and the Gods*, 320; H. Ringgren, *Religions of the Ancient East*, 106–7.

[140] Aubrey R. Johnson, *Sacral Kingship in Ancient Israel* (Cardiff, 1955), 104 (but in an autumnal festival); id., *The Cultic Prophet and Israel's Psalmody* (Cardiff, 1979), 80.

8. Facets of Impact on Judaeo-Christian Thought

(1) The Second Death

From Coffin Texts as early as the third millennium B.C. we find spells against having *to die for the second time* (*mt m whm*);[141] and it was a belief that persisted long and vigorously in the *Book of the Dead*, as in Spells 175 and 176.[142] In the latter text dying again seems to be a fate enacted in the slaughtering-places of the East where enemies of the gods are slain.[143]

It is remarkable that a similar phrase occurs several times in the Book of Revelation, a work probably written in the reign of Domitian (A.D. 81–96). Here we are told (2:11) that he who is victorious shall not be harmed *by the second death* (ἐκ τοῦ θανάτου τοῦ δευτέρου). It is said (20:6) that he who shares *in the first resurrection* is blessed and that *the second death* will have no power over him; hereby the doctrine is implied that only the martyrs will experience *the first resurrection* and that others will have to wait for the general resurrection of the dead; but 'first' in this phrase does not affect the idea of *the second death*. In 20:14 it is said that *Death and Hades were thrown into the lake of fire. This is the second death, the lake of fire.* The same equation occurs in 21:8, where all manner of evil doers are said to end up in this lake, *which is the second death*. In 20:13 Death and Hades are said to have given up their dead, *and all were judged by what they had done*, so that *the second death* follows an episode of judgement—an idea that exactly corresponds to that portrayed in Egyptian sources.

Commentators, notably R.H. Charles (ICC, 1920), quote from Rabbinic parallels which do not make this idea clear at all. In fact they refer merely to a death that occurs in the next world, as when the Jerusalem Targum on Deut. 33:6 (*Let Reuben live, and not die, nor let his men be few*) says *Let Reuben live in this age, and not die the second death whereof the wicked die in the next world*. T.F. Glasson (Cambridge, 1965, 26) takes the first death to mean 'natural physical death' whereas 'for some its sequel is judgement and retribution.'[144] The Egyptian sources certainly locate the idea as a sequel to judgement that is adverse. Such a penalty is carried out, it seems, by the devouring monster which is often called in the Twenty-first Dynasty

---

[141] Zandee, *Death as an Enemy*, 186–7.
[142] Cf. Morenz (tr. Keep), *Egyptian Religion*, 207 with refs.
[143] Hornung, *Totenbuch*, 518, describes this slaying as 'the second, final death'.
[144] J. Massyngberde Ford (Anchor Bible, New York, 1975), 393, says that the phrase 'seems to differentiate this death from martyrdom, or physical death,' but with no further distinction of detail.

t3 '3t mwt, the *Great One of Death*[145]—a pointer to death as the consequence of failure. It is the second death since in these representations the deceased men and women appear to attend the judgement as living persons.

What is clear in the Egyptian material is that a distinction is made between the nature of the first and second deaths. In the first the end of the physical life is denoted; in the second the end of the spiritual life of the *ba* is meant, together with the end of the personal magical power which was termed *heka*. For those, on the other hand, who were deemed to escape this fate through a favourable judgement the spiritual faculties were renewed and reinforced; and they were given a warrant of survival for ever.[146] *Not to die a second time on the part of the* ba *of a man*, a locution in the *Book of the Dead* (64, Naville, Varianten, Ca, Vol. II, p. 139) suggests that the experience particularly concerns the *ba*,[147] while the first death concerns the body. It is rather striking that some recent commentators on Revelation have seen a similar, though not identical, distinction there. According to Martin Kiddle[148] 'the *second death* was the eternal damnation of the soul on the day of final judgment;' and G.B. Caird[149] draws the contrast more incisively: 'He cannot promise immunity from the death which kills the body, but he can promise immunity from the death which annihilates the soul.' He shows that a similar antithesis occurs in Matthew 10:28: *And do not fear those who kill the body but cannot kill the soul; rather fear him who can destroy both soul and body in hell.* (Cf. Luke 12:4–5.) While it is true that soul and *ba* are not exact counterparts, the latter meaning 'the manifestation of spiritual power' (cf. Žabkar, 'the *alter ego* of the deceased'), the Egyptian distinction is probably behind the idea of the *second death* ultimately.

(2) *The Crown of Righteousness*

Another concept in the New Testament which bears the stamp of

---

[145] Seeber, *Untersuchungen*, 169.

[146] Zandee, *Death as an Enemy*, 186–7.

[147] Morenz (tr. Keep), *Egyptian Religion*, 207. Cf. Emma Brunner-Traut, *Gelebte Mythen*, 71; and esp. Louis V. Žabkar, *A Study of the Ba Concept in Ancient Egyptian Texts* (Chicago, 1968), 142–3.

[148] Moffat N.T. Comm. (London, 1940), 29.

[149] Black's N.T. Commentary, 2nd Ed., London, 1984, 36. G.R. Beasley-Murray, New Century Bible, London, 1974, 83 n. 1, posits another idea as a Jewish belief: 'Resurrection was limited to the holy land'; and this too has a clear parallel in Egyptian thought. Since this section of Rev. (2:11) is addressed, however, to the Church in Smyrna, such a belief would hardly be of comfort to them.

Egyptian origin is that of the 'Crown of Righteousness'. This is portrayed as the reward of success in the judgement:

> Henceforth there is laid up for me the crown of righteousness, which the Lord, the righteous judge, will award to me on that Day ...
> (2 Tim. 4:8.)

> And when the chief Shepherd is manifested, you will obtain the unfading crown of glory.
> (1 Peter 5:4.)

> Be faithful unto death, and I will give you the crown of life.
> (Rev. 2:10.)

In the first quotation the *crown of righteousness* is explicitly the reward conferred by the divine judge, and this crown is exactly equivalent to the 'Crown of Justification (or Victory)' which in the Egyptian tradition is assigned as a *m3ḥ n m3ʿ-ḥrw* to the deceased person who triumphs in the judgement. *Crown of Life* and *Crown of Glory* are obvious variants of the idea.[150] It is also the crown presented to the initiate Lucius in the Isiac rite described in the *Metamorphoses* of Apuleius (11.24).[151]

(3) Weighing and Recording

It has been suggested that the Jewish literature concerned with divine judgement presents two images—'the image of the heavenly account-book and that of the weighing of people's deeds'.[152] It is suggested, at the same time, that the two images are entirely unconnected and do not imply 'an adding up or a weighing of individual deeds, so that God may recompense men in strict proportion to their deeds'. This is scarcely confirmed by the detailed allusions. It is true that in a scene of judgement in Daniel 7:10 it is merely said that *the books were opened*. Elsewhere detail is supplied:

> From now on do know that all your injustices which you have committed unjustly are written down every day until the day of your judgement.
> (1 Enoch 98:8; tr. E. Isaac.)[153]

---

[150] See Ph. Derchain, 'La couronne de la justification', *CdÉ* 30 (1955), 225–87; *BD* 19; Morenz, op. cit. 254; *Wb.* III, 16, 6–7.
[151] Cf. my *Apuleius, The Isis-Book*, 314–15; also 159 and 357.
[152] Stephen H. Travis, *Christ and the Judgement of God* (Basingstoke, 1986), 16.
[153] In *The Old Testament Pseudepigrapha* ed. J.H. Charlesworth, I (London, 1983), 79.

> And I recorded all those who have been condemned by the judge, and all their sentences and all their corresponding deeds.
>
> (2 Enoch 40:13; tr. F. I Andersen, ibid.)

> For behold, the days are coming, and the books will be opened in which are written the sins of all those who have sinned, and moreover, also the treasuries in which are (*sic*) brought together the righteousness of all those who have proven themselves to be righteous.
>
> (2 Baruch 24:1; tr. A.F.J. Klijn, ibid.)

The last piece, which dates from the second century A.D., shows the concern with good as well as evil deeds, and this appears also in 1 Enoch 108:10, whose date is more uncertain (several sections probably derive from the second century B.C.): *And I have recounted in the books all their blessings. He has caused them to be recompensed.*

A *book of the living* is mentioned in Psalms 69:28, where Yahweh is asked to blot out the cultic prophet's enemies *out of the book of the living* (or, *The Book of Life*).[154] A similar salvation-bringing book seems to be intended in Daniel 12:1 with its promise of deliverance for *your people . . ., every one whose name shall be found written in the book*.[155] Several allusions in the New Testament appear to point to such a book, as in the exhortation, *Rejoice that your names are written in heaven* (Luke 10; 20).[156] In Revelation there are similar mentions,[157] but in a portrayal of judgement we are told (20:12) that the dead appeared before the great white throne and that *books were opened*:

> Also another book was opened, which is the book of life. And the dead were judged by what was written in the books, by what they had done.
>
> (Rev. 20:12.)

It seems, accordingly, that the names of the righteous have already been recorded in the Book of Life, whereas the deeds of the sinners are recorded in other books, a process implied in the previous quotations from Jewish literature. The compilation of names in the Book of Life might suggest a list of heavenly citizens on the lines of a worldly civic list;[158] and a confusing result of this idea would be a kind of pre-selection of the righteous, thus removing the validity of

---

[154] Cf. Aubrey R. Johnson, *The Cultic Prophet and Israel's Psalmody*, 392–3; and id., *The Vitality of the Individual* (Cardiff, 1949), 105, noting the ambiguity of the Hebrew.
[155] Cf. Exod. 32:32.
[156] Cf. Phil. 4:3 (*the book of life*); Hebr. 12:23 (*enrolled in heaven*).
[157] Rev. 13:8, *the book of life of the Lamb that was slain*; cf. 20:15 and 21:27.
[158] Cf. Leo Koep in *RAC* II (1954), 725. For two opposing lists he also compares the Babylonian 'Tablet of Grace' and 'Tablet of Sin'.

a verdict based on a scrutiny of the records.[159] Yet such a validity is explicitly retained by the statement (Rev. 20:12) that *the dead were judged by what was written in the books, by what they had done*. It is true that the Book of Jubilees mentions the *book of life* (30:22; cf. 36:10) and *the book of those who will be destroyed* (30:22, where a Latin text has *libro perditionum*), inviting the explanation that 'all names go into one book or the other, according to whether they are basically righteous . . . or wicked.'[160] The heavenly account-book, if this view is correct, is not a book with a 'credit and debit account' which seeks to recompense men in strict proportion to their deeds. If so, why is so much stress laid on the recording of good and bad deeds at the time of their doing? It is admitted[161] that 'particular good or evil deeds are the evidence by which a person is shown to belong to "the righteous" or "the wicked".' That is possible, obviously, only in the final count, and the process of recording rules out any predetermined categories. A mixed category, one has to concede, is not mentioned, but it can be assumed that a greater number of good deeds is regarded as the saving factor.

Essentially this is the approach of the Egyptian material, and the weighing is there intimately linked to the recording. Not only is the final result to be recorded and announced to Osiris, but particular deeds are to be weighed and recorded. The whole weighing process was associated with the Declarations of Innocence, each denial being regarded as contributing no extra adverse weight to the scale in which the heart is placed. A minor difference in the Jewish tradition is that deeds seem to be viewed as being recorded at the time of their enactment; in Egypt the process is retrospective—a record in reply to scrutiny of the past life. It would have been difficult to portray all this in relation to the weighing; yet there are sporadic attempts to do just that. Brief inscriptions reveal the idea that not only the heart, but other parts of the body have also been weighed, with a clear verdict of NOT GUILTY. A good example is found in a Leiden papyrus of the Ptolemaic era (T 16) where Thoth speaks thus of the result achieved by a deceased woman:

> Her heart is guiltless (*wḏ3*) in the balance like that of excellent glorified spirits, her heart, her eyes, her legs, are guiltless in the balance.
> (Seeber, *Untersuchungen*, 79, with further instances on pp. 80 and 111.)

We can only guess how the specific sins named in the Declarations

---

[159] Cf. Brandon, *The Judgment of the Dead*, 104.
[160] Stephen H. Travis, *Christ and the Judgment of God*, 16.
[161] Ibid.

were severally connected with the body's members, and only a small minority of the allusions reveal this idea. Pictorially such allusions have normally no counterpart since it is the heart only that is represented.[162] Difficulties would have arisen, in any case; and as with the significance of the Forty-two Assessors, a degree of failure attended the attempt to present an elaboration of the life-assessment.

The representations show Thoth, the scribe of the gods, either actively recording during the process of weighing or approaching the enthroned Osiris with a scroll which conveys the final result, but not without, presumably, the detailed record. It has been urged that the weighing process should be envisaged as a single act.[163] If a connection is sought, however, between the words spoken by the deceased (particularly in the Declarations) and the weighing process, then a more persuasive interpretation is that each claim relating to conduct is accompanied by an act of weighing, thus ensuring a detailed coverage of the many deeds involved.[164]

In spite of one minor difference concerning the time of the recording, the Judaeo-Christian pattern corresponds closely to that of the Egyptian material, in respect of both weighing and recording. In both areas the two procedures go together. It was in the second century B.C. that Jewish ideas on divine judgement in eschatology developed with some elaboration; and the concern with it is revealed in Daniel and especially in 1 Enoch.[165]

B) Iran, Judaism, and the Christian Consummation

Jewish and Christian apocalyptic relates, in its important manifestations, to the literature of the four centuries between 200 B.C. and A.D. 200, but religious influences on this literature may of course derive from earlier eras. A view often accepted is that the main influence was Iranian, and a discussion of this popular theory is clearly imperative if the counter-claim of Egypt is to be properly assessed. Two cautionary points seem to be in order. First, we are not concerned with the whole range of apocalyptic, nor that of

---

[162] In one instance two eyes are depicted with the heart in one of the scales: see Seeber, *Untersuchungen*, 80.
[163] J.J. Clère in *BIFAO* 30 (1931), 430 ff.
[164] Spiegel, *Die Idee vom Totengericht*, 68; cf. Seeber, op. cit., 81; J. Vandier, *La Religion égyptienne* (2nd Ed., Paris, 1949), 137.
[165] R.H. Charles, *A Critical History of the Doctrine of a Future Life* (2nd Ed., London, 1913), 242–6.

eschatology, but only with that part of eschatology that deals with divine judgement. Secondly, we must be prepared to consider multiple sources of influence. It is *prima facie* unlikely that every influence on religious thought came from a single source.

1. *The Impact of Iranian Eschatology*

The historical possibility of contact with Iranian or Egyptian ideas is a general factor which must be considered. It can be quickly stated without further ado that the Hellenistic and Roman eras facilitated such contact in every way—and contact also, obviously, with ideas prevalent in Greek and Roman culture as well as in other cultures of the Near East, including that of Babylon. Alexandria, the cultural capital of the Greek world in this period, was itself a simmering melting-pot of religious amalgam, and its literary importance for both Jews and Christians is hard to overestimate. The considerable Jewish presence in Alexandria and in other parts of Egypt, especially in Lower Egypt, effected a significant and constant exposure to Egyptian ideas.

Nor is evidence lacking for plentiful contact between the Jews and Iranians. Politically the sway of the Persian Empire, which began in 539 B.C. with the fall of Babylon to Cyrus the Great and eventually extended to the whole of the Near East, meant direct contact, beginning with the proclamation by Cyrus in 538 B.C. to the Jewish exiles in Babylon through which they were urged to return to Jerusalem. It is not surprising that several books of the Old Testament, in particular Ezra and Nehemiah, which were written during the Persian period, provide details of the Persian political and administrative framework. The later books of Esther and Daniel, both of which were probably written in the second century B.C., have their setting in the Persian court.[166] If there is an influence on Jewish eschatological ideas, the question arises as to which period tended to favour such influence most. Protagonists of Iranian penetration in this respect have hitherto advocated the Achaemenid period as the likely influential span.[167] It has been argued,[168] however, that a 'time lag of some 200 years' between the

---

[166] Saul Shaked in *The Cambridge History of Judaism*, I (1984), 313. His whole chapter ('Iranian Influence on Judaism: First Century B.C.E. to Second Century C.E.') is very relevant.

[167] For Persian religion in this age (550–330 B.C.) see Mary Boyce in *Camb. Hist. of Judaism* I, 279–307.

[168] John R. Hinnells, 'Zoroastrian Influence on Judaeo-Christian Tradition', *Journal of the K.R. Cama Oriental Institute* 45 (1976), 1–23.

source and the time of reception tends to vitiate an aspect of this theory and that the age of Parthian rule in Asia (247 B.C.—A.D. 224, covering an area from the Euphrates to the Indus) was the more likely temporal medium of impact. John Hinnells instances contacts between Jews and Parthians: the reception of Parthian ambassadors by Alexander Jannaeus the Jewish king (103–76 B.C.); the Parthian invasion of Jerusalem in 40 B.C., when there were pro-Parthian parties in the city;[169] the Jews who lived in Parthia itself and the Parthian contacts established in other parts of the Jewish Diaspora. The Arsacid Parthians, be it noted, were Iranian in culture and religion.

Through such channels, it is urged, flowed the influence of Zoroastrian ideas, but Hinnells (p. 9) has a salutary comment on the danger of explaining 'influence' as 'the sudden taking over of a new and strange idea'. Rather does it often imply 'a subconscious process involving the development or emphasis of some ideas already held and the neglect of others'; a modification of existing ideas results, but in other cases there is a 'conscious imitation of another's ideas'. While Hinnells is cautious about connecting the Iranian myth about the primordial man Gayomart with the Judaeo-Christian figure of the Messiah as the Son of Man,[170] he posits three areas where he finds the impress of Iranian beliefs:

(1) In Revelation 19:11–16 he regards the depiction of Christ as being coloured by the worship of Mithra (as a challenge to it).
(2) The concept of a devil and his demons.
(3) The concept of a saviour who could 'cast out demons and destroy them as well as introducing the judgement scene and the resurrection'.

Clearly it is the third area that mainly concerns our theme.

A doctrine of resurrection is closely linked to that of judgement, for it is only the premiss of a possible life after death that gives meaning to a posthumous trial. In the Egyptian sources it is the deceased that is justified and becomes *maa-kherw* who achieves new life. The Iranian tradition has a rather similar word—Old Persian *artāvan*, Avestan *ašavan*, 'possessing *Arta, Truth*',[171]—and the *Daiva*-

---

[169] Cf. W.D. Davies in *Peake's Comm. on the Bible* (1962, repr. 1981), 687.

[170] More often it is the Iranian belief in a type of saviour, the Saoshyant, that is adduced; cf. Hinnells, op. cit. p. 4, and Mary Boyce, *Zoroastrianism* (Manchester, 1984), 90.

[171] Chr. Bartholomae, *Altiranisches Wb.* (Berlin, 1904 and 1961), 192; (1) 'Gesetz, Recht, heiliges Recht'; (2) 'was das Gesetz (usw.) verlangt, religiöse Pflicht'.

Inscription of Xerxes (486–465 B.C.) clearly expounds its significance:[172]

> The man who conforms to the law which Ahuramazdāh has commanded, and worships Ahuramazdāh in proper style in accord with *Arta*, becomes happy while living and *artāvan* when dead.

Gershevitch (ibid.) remarks that 'here obviously Arta, viz. Truth, is something to cultivate in life, as well as a reward after death, and the *artāvan* is one who has obtained, or owns, this reward.' It is the righteous, then, who are to be saved after death. 'Righteous' (*tsadiq*) is also the Hebrew term used of those who will survive the judgement.[173]

In the Inscription of Xerxes, in spite of the use of *artāvan*, there is no precise allusion to judgement, nor indeed to resurrection. On the latter question the Iranian contribution is rather unclear. If the Book of Daniel reflects Iranian thought in its promise of resurrection, one might think that an astral element is conspicuous:

> And many of those who sleep in the dust of the earth shall awake, some to everlasting life, and some to shame and everlasting contempt.
> And those who are wise shall shine like the brightness of the firmament; and those who turn many to righteousness, like the stars for ever and ever.
> (Dan. 12:2–3; cf. 1 Enoch 104:2.)

It is a doctrine of selective resurrection and if we ask whether the emphasis on *the brightness of the firmament* and on *the stars for ever and ever* goes beyond mere metaphor and points to anything in Iranian religion, the close association of Mithra with the sun is noteworthy, achieved through his reliance on the agency of fire.[174] In the Roman imperial period Mithras came to be regarded as a solar deity, but that could not affect a text of the second century B.C. The origin of the resurrection theme has been located in Iranian religion or in the dying and rising deities of the Near East.[175] For the idea that the

---

[172] Lines 51 ff., tr. by Ilya Gershevitch, *The Avestan Hymn to Mithra* (Cambridge, 1959), 153. For the text see Roland G. Kent, *Old Persian* (New Haven, 1953), 150–52. Instead of 'in accord with *Arta*' he renders 'and worship Ahuramazda and Arta'.

[173] Cf. Mary Boyce in *Camb. Hist. of Judaism*, I, 294, showing how the inscription also attacks the old worship of the *daivas*, gods of war.

[174] Boyce, *Hist. of Zoroastrianism*, I, 28–29. The worship of Sol Invictus in imperial Rome was a cult of Syrian origin: see Gaston H. Halsberghe, *The Cult of Sol Invictus* (EPRO 23; Leiden, 1972), who notes (p. 173) that Julian saw it 'as an expression of Mithraism'.

[175] Hengel, *Judaism and Hellenism*, I, 196 with notes in II, 574 ff.

dead became stars one can cite Pahlavi books[176] whose compilation is not earlier than c. A.D. 500 although their content may preserve earlier material.[177] In Egypt, however, the idea is much earlier and much more persistent; in fact it is a constant feature of the celestial hereafter as depicted initially in the Pyramid Texts, then in the Book of the Dead and in sources of the Graeco-Roman era.[178] The depiction of the sky-goddess Nut on the inside of coffin lids became an enduring practice and the clear connotation was that the dead person was to be reborn as a star in her womb.[179] At the same time, Egyptian beliefs were multiple and complex, and alongside of stellar immortality they stressed the resurrection of the body; hence the basic import of the rites of mummification and Opening of the Mouth. Here Iran supplies a telling contrast: its earliest tradition seems to exclude a resurrection of the body, and even goes further in its maltreatment of the corpse.[180] Theopompus, however, in the fourth century B.C. said that *according to the Magi men will live again and be immortal*.[181] Yet the Jewish doctrine in its developed form is closer in this matter to Egypt than to Iran. The resurrection of the body is stressed; and Jewish tendance of the dead, although it did not normally include mummification, was far removed from Iranian practice. In the Hellenistic and Roman eras Egypt itself shows clear signs of the influence of Mesopotamian astrology: funerary representations now include, alongside traditional Egyptian motifs, planetary themes and the signs of the zodiac.[182] It is of interest, though, that Kákosy in his presentation of this ideological influx cites only Egyptian sources for the continuing belief that the

---

[176] M.L. West, *Early Greek Philosophy and the Orient* (Oxford, 1971), 188 n. 2, but referring also to Egypt, India, and Greece.

[177] Cf. Mary Boyce, *Zoroastrianism* (1984), 4–5 and 82–83.

[178] Bonnet, *RÄRG* 749. The circumpolar stars are especially the object of equation. Cf. *Pyr.* 374 a, *This King leads the imperishable stars*; *BD* 69, 5–6 (with mention of Orion and Nut); *BD* 177, 3–4 (Naville).

[179] See my *Origins of Osiris and his Cult*, 187; Černý, *Ancient Egyptian Religion*, 82. For stars as the souls of gods see Plutarch, *De Iside et Osiride*, 21, 359 C; *Asclepius*, 37 with the note by W. Scott, *Hermetica*, III, 225 ff., quoting the Egyptian prayer in Porphyry, *De abst.* 4.10.

[180] Boyce, *Hist. of Zoroastrianism*, I, 300–301. On p. 236 she states that Zoroaster's doctrine sees final happiness in the reunion of the soul with the body 'in a physical world restored to a flawless state'. These teachings envisage a resurrected body raised after the Last Judgement; they are teachings 'as they reach us largely through the tradition'. But Hengel, op. cit. II, 130 n. 574, says that 'The Gāthās do not know the resurrection, but only the later Avesta . . .'

[181] Quoted by Diogenes Laertius (iii A.D.): see Carl Clemen, *Fontes Hist. Rel. Persicae* (Bonn, 1920), 75; cf. 95, quoted by Aeneas of Gaza (v A.D.), but with a phrase which recalls New Testament usage (πάντων νεκρῶν ἀνάστασις, cf. 1 Cor. 15:13 and Phil. 3:11).

[182] Kákosy, *Selected Papers* (1981), 195–205 (first publ. 1969).

deceased person becomes a star (his p. 198). There are naturally doubts about the origins of certain ideas. If Jewish and Rabbinic literature knows of Seven Heavens, it might seem likely that Babylonian and Iranian systems, intent as they were on astrology, have supplied this; yet it occurs in the Demotic Magical Papyrus of London and Leiden (iii A.D.), while the Seven Gates of the underworld are known to the Book of the Dead and the Book of Gates.[183] By the time of Cicero[184] astral immortality was a popular feature of Stoicism, and Posidonius, who came from Apamea in Syria, was a formative influence.[185] The precise lines of transmission to Posidonius himself remain untraced.[186]

If we look at details of Iranian teaching on posthumous judgement, we note that the earliest sources for Zoroastrianism, the Gāthās, occasionally give some attention to the necessity of coming after death to the Bridge or Crossing of Chinvat.[187] A portion of the Yasna (Liturgy) voices the anxiety of the believer:

> Whom, Mazda, hast Thou appointed protector for one like me, if the Wicked One shall dare to harm me? Whom but Thy Fire and Thy (Good) Purpose, by whose acts, Lord, Truth is nourished. Proclaim this teaching to my Inner Self! . . . Whosoever, Lord, man or woman, will grant me those things Thou knowest best for life—recompense for truth, power with good purpose—and those whom I shall bring to Your worship, with all these shall I cross over the Chinvat Bridge.
> (From Yasna, 46; tr. Mary Boyce, *Zoroastrianism* (1984), 42.)

It is then stated that those guilty of evil acts will be tormented by *their own soul and Inner Self*, so that they will be *guests for ever in the House of the Lie*. In the phrase činvato . . . pərətūm, the *Separator's Bridge* or *Crossing*, the first word has attracted slight variations of translation. Reichelt (*Avesta Reader*, 230) explains it as the genitive of a participial form činvant-, 'separating';[188] a similar meaning is

---

[183] Kákosy, ibid. 202 with refs. to *BD* 144 and 147; also to Griffith and Thompson on the papyrus, p. 132.

[184] *Tusc. Disp.* 19; *Somnium Scip.* 25–27.

[185] Franz Cumont, *After Life in Roman Paganism* (1922, repr. New York, 1959), 27–28 and Ch. 3 on 'Celestial Immortality', pp. 91–109. He shows that the ascent to heaven was a part of Mithraic doctrine in the first century A.D., but uses the vague phrase 'of Chaldeo-Persian origin' (p. 107); cf. his *L'Égypte des Astrologues* (Brussels, 1937), 202. It was certainly a part of Zoroastrian teaching; see Boyce, *Zoroastrianism*, 38–39 (from the Gāthās) on 'heavenly glory' and Boyce, *Hist. of Zoroastrianism*, I, 236.

[186] Cf. the curiously indecisive attitude of J. Duchesne-Guillemin, *The Western Response to Zoroaster* (1958, repr. Westport, Conn., 1973).

[187] Cf. below, 253; 350–51.

[188] For the text see Hans Reichelt, *Avesta Reader* (1911, repr. Berlin, 1968), 86; also his note on pp. 151–2.

given by Boyce (*Hist.* 240), but she avers that 'there is no evidence as to how Činvatō Pərətu itself acquired its name—whether the Separator was originally water, or a chasm, or some power who waited there for souls to attempt the crossing.'[189] However that may be, the term *Separator* has affiliations with judicial activity; cf. *wpi*, Egn., of separating and therefore judging contestants at law; and the locution *judge or divider* (κριτὴν ἢ μεριστήν) in Luke 12:14, *who made me a judge or divider over you?*

The precise origin of *činvat-* has, nonetheless, been debated. Bartholomae (*Wb.* 596–7) gives 'separating' as its meaning, explaining this as the separation of the good and evil by the Bridge of the Judges; yet adds a designation of it as the Present Active Participle of the verb *kay* which he renders (p. 464) 'retaliate' or 'atone for' with reference again to the action of a judge who punishes. From this verb is also derived *kaēnā-*, 'punishment, retaliation, vengeance' (ibid. 429). That this is the basic meaning of *činvat-* was firmly maintained by H.W. Bailey, as Zaehner pointed out in his *Zurvan* (Oxford, 1955), 203 n. 3; he there cited the view of Nyberg, 'the crossing over (from this world) of him who aims at directing to (the other world)'; but he was clearly attracted more to Bailey's view (which Bartholemae, however, had long since propounded). Whereas Zaehner renders the phrase in *Zurvan*, 203, as 'the bridge of the Separator', in his later work *The Dawn and Twilight of Zoroastrianism* (1961), Pp. 56, 59, and 111, he consistently renders 'Bridge of the Requiter', remarking also (p. 111) that whereas in the later literature Rashnu is the judge and Requiter, in the Gāthās it is Ahura Mazda who has this role. Conceptually both 'Separator' and 'Requiter' suit this context of judgement, but the latter meaning is better supported philologically.

Whether the process at the Bridge included the weighing of deeds according to the Gathic evidence is a matter of some doubt. It has been well expounded that Zoroaster used ancient beliefs, which included judgement at the Bridge, and gave them greater moral significance. The earlier belief, it is urged, assigned merit to merely ritual qualifications, while the undeserving were consigned to fall from the Bridge to an existence as 'hapless disembodied

---

[189] On p. 117, ibid., she refers to 'the place of the dogs' there, and remarks that *pərətu* 'can denote crossings of various kinds, and it is possible that in the remote past this term was used of a ford or ferry-place over underground waters, and that it was with the development of belief in Paradise on high that it became a bridge over an abyss, of which one end rested on the highest peak of earth, the other on the road to heaven.'

shades';[190] but Zoroaster made it a 'strict moral judgement' in which each man's thoughts, words and deeds were carefully weighed in precise scales. One looks in vain, however, for a clear mention of the scales. Zoroaster is said (Boyce, p. 241) to allude to them in Yasna, 48.8; good thoughts, words and acts are admittedly of deep concern to the worshipper here, but no allusion seems to be made to a balance in which they are weighed.[191] This Gāthā begins with a mention of *the time of the rewards*, probably after death, when evil will, it is hoped, be conquered by good; and it ends with an allusion to the future saviours of the lands (*saoshyants*) who will carry on the purpose of Mazda.[192]

So far we have been discussing the Iranian doctrine of the final judgement of the individual. A further feature of that doctrine is that it points also to the end of the world. In Yasna 34 allusion is made to a fire of ordeal and also, less clearly, to the fire of the Last Day which will encompass the ruin of the enemy of Ahura Mazda:

> Then we wish Thy fire, Lord, strong through Truth, very swift, mighty, to be of manifest help to Thy supporter, but of visible harm, O Mazda, with forces in his hands, to Thy enemy.
> (Yasna, 34.4; tr. Boyce, ibid. 38.)

Another Gathic text (Yasna, 51.9) refers to blazing fire and molten metal as ordeals used in judgement which will ensure the salvation of the just and the destruction of the wicked:

> That requital which Thou wilt assign to the two parties, O Mazda, by Thy bright blazing fire and molten metal, is a sign to be given among all living beings, to destroy the wicked man, to save the just.
> (Yasna, 51.9; tr. Boyce, ibid. 43.)

It appears, then, that in this early material the ordeal by fire and molten metal is the important procedure and not any weighing of deeds. A detailed exposition of these ideas occurs in the Greater Bundahishn, a much later work whose composition is dated between the fourth and tenth centuries A.D. Here a general resurrection of the dead is portrayed, but the mode of judgement is again fire and molten metal:

> In fifty-seven years the Soshyant will raise up all the dead. And all mankind will arise, whether just or wicked ... Then the assembly of

---

[190] Boyce, *Hist. of Zoroastrianism*, I, 237.
[191] See Helmut Humbach, *Die Gathas des Zarathustra* (Heidelberg, 1959), I, 138–41, esp. 140; and II, 75–79; cf. the parts rendered by Boyce in *Zoroastrianism*, 39.
[192] Boyce, ibid.; cf. J. Duchesne-Guillemin (tr. M. Henning), *The Hymns of Zarathustra* (1952, repr. Westport, Conn. 1979), 34–39 (Yasna 48).

Isadvaster (eldest son of the prophet) will take place. In that assembly everyone will behold his own good or bad deeds, and the just will stand out among the wicked like white sheep among the black. Fire and the gazad (deity) Airyaman will melt the metals in the hills and mountains, and it will be upon the earth like a river. Then all men will be caused to pass through that molten metal.
(Greater Bundahishn, 34.6 ff; tr. Boyce, ibid. 52.)

This terrifying ordeal, we are told, will not affect the just; for them it will be like walking through warm milk; but the wicked will feel it like *walking in the flesh through molten metal*. In spite of this *all men will become immortal*. Abandoned now is the destruction of the wicked.[193]

A marked change appears in the doctrine of immortality for all, although earlier emphases persist in the ideas about judgement. The question of chronology raises its battered head once more, and there can be little doubt that different phases of Iranian literature reflect some development and change. In his positing of Iranian influence on Judaism during the Parthian period (141 B.C.—A.D. 224) Hinnells pays scant attention to this matter. It is clear, for instance, that in the early centuries of our era Zervanism was flourishing within Zoroastrianism as a doctrine that claimed priority and pre-eminence for the god Zervan ('Time' as the First Cause) as the creator of both Ahura Mazda and Ahriman, rejecting thus the basic dualism of Zoroaster.[194] In Judaism the Old Testament concept of Satan as a being created by Yahweh still prevails to some extent, but an independent Devil with an entourage of demons appears in non-canonical writings, and this may reflect the Zoroastrian position.[195] In fact Zervanism, by making Ahriman a creature of Zervan, is closer to the orthodox Hebrew tradition; and thus a specific influence from the Parthian period tends to be negated.

A more important matter of chronology concerns the Later Avestan writings. It is not surprising that the Gāthās have formed the main source on which theories of Iranian influence on Judaism have depended. At the Uppsala Colloquium on Apocalypticism to which I contributed in 1979 a number of Swedish Iranists vigor-

---

[193] Cf. the Pahlavi texts quoted by Zaehner in his *Dawn and Twilight of Zoroastrianism*, Ch. 15 ('The End'), 302–21. He remarks (p. 302) that in these there is no eternal damnation and that 'no soul is eternally punished for the sins it has committed;' rather is there a 'final Rehabilitation of all existence'.

[194] W.B. Henning, *Zoroaster* (London, 1951), 49. Plutarch, *De Iside et Osiride*, 46, describes offerings to Ahriman which may possibly allude to Zervanism; but see R.C. Zaehner, *Zurvan: A Zoroastrian Dilemma* (Oxford, 1955), 13 f. and my remarks on Plutarch's statement ad loc. pp. 474–5.

[195] J.R. Hinnells in *Journal of the K.R.Cama Or. Inst.* 45 (1976), 12–13.

ously presented the view that the Later Avestan writings incorporate much earlier material and that even the subsequent Pahlavi literature includes such material. Geo Widengren[196] in his long and learned contribution states that Avestan ceased as a living language *c*. 300 B.C. and that the Pahlavi literature uses a medium that is linguistically mixed while its content is a mixture of Zervanism and Zoroastrianism. What must be rejected, he urges, is the frequent claim that the Pahlavi literature is post-Sasanian (i.e. after A.D. 651) with ideas of very late origin; in reality, he maintains, they are of early origin, deriving from the Avesta and revealing an astonishing continuity of thought. In spite of his strong aura of assurance Widengren is not really claiming a blanket guarantee of early origin for all this literature. Thus he concedes the importance of Zervanism, a movement which began to appear in Achaemenid times (550–330 B.C.); but Zervan was probably not an ancient divinity.[197] In the Bundahishn (34), as we have noted, there is some deviation from earlier eschatology, and Widengren (p. 151) is rather cautious in positing the possibility that all this material is Avestan.

Writing on the dating of the Later Avestan apocalyptic, Sven S. Hartman,[198] a pupil of Widengren, refers to the doctrine of the four ages as it appears in three stages of Iranian literature (the Avesta, the Bundahishn, and the Bahman Yasht), in Hesiod (*c*. 700 B.C.), and in Daniel, Chapter 2. The Avesta stratum he dates, at the latest, to about 600 B.C.; Hesiod is therefore earlier, but there is a firm and distinctive link between the Avestan teaching and that of Jewish and Christian apocalyptic: the idea, namely, that the final outcome is brought about by the cyclical incarnation of an *Urmensch*, a prophet and an eschatological saviour—an idea not found in Hesiod.[199] Philological data are also adduced: whereas Gayōmart (the *Urmensch*) does not occur in the early Gathic Avesta, yet the constitutive words *gaya* and *maretan* do; similarly with Ahura Mazda: the separate words occur in the Gāthās, while the combined appellative usage is found only in the Later Avesta. Yet the name A(h)uramazda occurs in Achaemenid inscriptions; and it

---

[196] 'Leitende Ideen und Quellen der iranischen Apokalyptik', in *Apocalypticism in the Mediterranean World and the Near East* ed. David Hellholm (Tübingen, 1983), 77–162.
[197] Boyce, *Hist. of Zoroastrianism*, I, 199 n. 84.
[198] In *Apocalypticism etc.* ed. Hellholm, 61–75.
[199] The 'metallic ages' in Hesiod nevertheless derive, probably, from Iranian or Mesopotamian sources; see my 'Archaeology and Hesiod's Five Ages', in *Journal of the History of Ideas* 17 (1956), 109–119; also ibid. 19 (1958), 91–93 ('Did Hesiod Invent the "Golden Age"?').

252 IRAN, JUDAISM, AND THE CHRISTIAN CONSUMMATION

follows that parts of the Later Avesta must be dated to before the Achaemenid period.

A similar attitude is upheld by Tord Olsson,[200] but he gives more attention to corroborative evidence emanating from sources other than the Iranian texts. Although he was writing in the early second century A.D., Plutarch in a description of Iranian religion quotes statements by Theopompus:

> The earth shall be flat and level and one way of life and one government shall arise of all men, who shall be happy and speak the same language. Theopompus says that, according to the Magians, for three thousand years alternately the one god will dominate the other and be dominated, and that for another three thousand years they will fight and make war, until one smashes up the domain of the other. In the end Hades shall perish and men shall be happy; neither shall they need sustenance nor shall they cast a shadow.
> (Plutarch, *De Iside et Osiride*, 47, 370 B; tr. J. Gwyn Griffiths.)

This rather detailed eschatology was penned by a Greek writer who was born about 378 B.C., and it is remarkable that his picture of the Last Things corresponds in several respects to that found in the *Bundahishn* and the *Dēnkart*, Iranian works of much later origin.[201] It is also noteworthy that such ideas about world-ages were ascribed to the Magi some centuries before the Book of Daniel was written. Further, there are similarities between the apocalyptic vision assigned to the Oracles of Hystaspes by Lactantius and parts of the Bahman Yasht; and the Oracles were disseminated, it is thought, in the first century B.C.[202] It is a little strange, by the way, that Olsson finds space to discuss 'Phenomenological Parallels from Other Cultures' (pp. 28 ff.), among them the religions of the Mayas and the Aztecs, while not even mentioning the ample parallels in Egypt which are so near in time and space.

By and large the chronological thesis advanced by these scholars is undoubtedly acceptable. The Later Avestan, and even the Pahlavi, writings include elements that derive from the early phases of Zoroastrianism. They do not claim, however, that later elements are not eventually subsumed, especially those produced by Zer-

---

[200] 'The Apocalyptic Activity. The Case of Jāmāsp Nāmag', in *Apocalypticism etc.* ed. Hellholm, 21–49.

[201] See my *Plutarch's De Iside et Osiride* (1970), 480–82; cf. Boyce, *Zoroastrianism* (1984), 96–97, where the passage is classified under 'Zurvanism'.

[202] T. Olsson, op. cit. 27, referring especially to the comparisons noted by Widengren, ibid. 121–7. The Bahman Yasht includes the dream of Zoroaster about a tree with four branches which turn out to be metallic and are explained by Ahura Mazda as indicating four future periods. For a translation see E.W. West, *Pahlavi Texts* (SBE 51 Oxford, 1880, repr. Delhi, 1965), 191–235.

vanism. Nor does their work remove all the problems concerning the origin of certain elements. We have noted, for instance, that whereas the Gāthās refer to the judgement made at the Bridge of the Requiter, they do not refer to a weighing of deeds or souls. In the *Bundahishn* 34.6 ff. (quoted above) mention is made of an assembly where *everyone will behold his own good or bad deeds, and the just will stand out among the wicked like white sheep among the black*. There is no suggestion of a balance here; indeed the picture is rather of a shepherd separating white sheep from the black. On the other hand, prominence is given in the Gāthās to a retributive process implemented by fire and molten metal:

> That requital which thou wilt assign to the two parties, O Mazda, by Thy bright blazing fire and molten metal, is a sign to be given among all living beings, to destroy the wicked man, to save the just . . .
> (Yasna, 51.9 (Gathic); tr. Boyce, *Zoroastrianism*, 43.)

It is only in the Pahlavi sources that a weighing at the Chinvat Bridge is clearly described, as in the *Menog i Khrad* ('Spirit of Wisdom'), a work assigned to about 600 A.D., where three deities are located at the Bridge, of whom Rashn is said to conduct the weighing—*the righteous Rashn who lets the scales of the spiritual gods incline to neither side, neither for the saved nor yet for the damned, nor yet for kings and princes: not so much as a hair's breadth does he allow (the scales) to tip, and he is no respecter of persons, for he deals out impartial justice both to kings and princes and to the humblest of men.*[203] Here the sentiment is strongly reminiscent of the words of Petosiris in the Egypt of the fourth century B.C., who likewise emphasizes the universal application of the divine tribunal. But in the *Dadestan i denig* ('Religious Judgements') the Bridge itself is presented as an ordeal or test; it gives a broad crossing to the just, while *for the wicked it becomes a narrow crossing, just like a razor's edge*;[204] perhaps we would say 'just like walking a tightrope'.[205] What emerges clearly is that the Iranian tradition about weighing deeds or souls does not give this idea much prominence at any stage and its earliest sources do not mention it. In Egypt, on the contrary, it is a conspicuous and

---

[203] Tr. R.C. Zaehner, *The Teachings of the Magi* (1956, repr. London, 1975), 134; cf. Boyce, *Zoroastrianism*, 82, with one variant: *In the weighing Rashn the just, who holds the balance for souls* . . .

[204] Boyce, ibid. 83, cf. 85 (ad fin.), from *Arda Viraz Nāmag*, with an allusion also to the weighing of the just and the wicked.

[205] Cf. James H. Moulton, *Early Zoroastrianism* (1913, repr. Amsterdam, 1972), 166, but stressing the ethical note. A beautiful girl was said to await the just at the end of the crossing: 'Zarathustra had no use for Blondins, any more than for houris, in his Paradise.'

central part of the eschatology, and Judaism is much more likely to have borrowed it from Egypt, especially as the details about recording reflect a similar concern in both areas.

Again, the role of fire and molten metal does not find a counterpart in Jewish literature. In Daniel 7:9–10 fire accompanies the Ancient of Days, but with no suggestion of a testing function. Its function admittedly varies somewhat in the Iranian writings. In the passage we quoted from the *Bundahishn* (34) it functions as an ordeal faced by both the saved and the damned with very different results; yet both here and in the *Menog i Khrad* the eschatological sequel is now given a beneficent twist, for all will be saved in the end. In the latter text a kind of Purgatory, however, is envisaged for a certain group of souls, who are taken to a place called *hamēstagān*, 'the place of the mixed'; these souls are deemed to have enacted an equal number of good and evil deeds. A degree of punishment is now inflicted on them, but after this correction they emerge to enjoy immortal bliss. Yet since punishment rather than purification is denoted, the term Purgatory, at least in the Christian sense, is not properly applied to this phase.[206] It remains, however, as a third possible verdict in the process of judgement.

The Judaeo-Christian pattern contains the following strands:

(1) An individual judgement which occurs immediately after death and is described as a weighing of good and bad deeds.
(2) A general judgement which also affects individuals and coincides with the end of time and the end of the world.
(3) A general judgement which concerns the nations of the world.
(4) The emergence of a Saviour is associated with (2) and (3).
(5) The verdict leads to Heaven or Hell.
(6) In either verdict a resurrection of the dead body is declared or implied.

The option of Purgatory is not included here since it was not clearly defined in Jewish or Christian thought until later.[207]

It would be proper now to comment briefly on the various elements listed, with a view to assessing possible influences from Iran or Egypt.

(1) The individual judgement of the dead occurs in both these areas, but the Egyptian tradition is much fuller and more compelling in

---

[206] Zaehner, *The Teachings of the Magi*, 131–2; and id. *Zurvan*, 202; 401; 414; cf. Boyce, *Zoroastrianism*, 86, where *Hammistagan* is translated 'the Place of the Motionless Ones'. Moulton, op. cit. 175, cites the Later Avestan *misra gātu*, 'place of the mixed', following Bartholomae in accepting this meaning.

[207] See Jacques Le Goff, *The Birth of Purgatory* (New York, 1983), where attention is given to pre-Christian antecedents.

its emphasis on weighing and recording; it provides the likely source too of ancillary concepts like the Second Death and the Crown of Righteousness.

(2) A general judgement accompanying the end of the world and time is a doctrine which Egypt could not easily have provided.

When Egyptian texts refer to the end of the world, they do not connect it with the operation of judgement. In *BD* 175 Atum and Osiris conduct a dialogue about it, and Atum declares that after millions of years he will destroy everything that he has created; the earth will return to be engulfed in the primal waters from which it arose; only Atum himself and Osiris will survive this regress to the original chaos.[208] A moral causation of the end is perhaps suggested: the harmony of the beginning has been lost through the strife that implicates Osiris, Horus and Seth.[209] Like the island in the *Shipwrecked Sailor*, Plato's Atlantis is swallowed up by the waves and Plato diagnoses a moral decline as the cause; here he doubtless follows the Greek doctrine of nemesis, although in other ways his account shows traces of Egyptian influence.[210]

Among Demotic texts from Saqqâra occurs a fragmentary piece on an ostracon which records a dream experienced in 155 B.C.[211] I have ventured to call it a 'Little Apocalypse',[212] for it tells of *a great* destruction (*sk '3*) in which *Thoth judges: no province shall remain [among them] in any way (on) earth*.[213] In this panic Hor is ordered to *choose a town (of) Egypt* and it seems that he chooses Pi(?)-Thoth in the northern Delta, where he has been a pastophorus of Isis. It is a charming touch: when the whole of Egypt is doomed, he chooses for survival the little town where he had served the goddess Isis. Fragmentary as it is, this brief text is very unusual in that it combines a final cataclysm with a scene of judgement in which Thoth pronounces his edict.

Various future disasters are outlined in *The Prediction of the Lamb under Bokkhoris, The Oracle of the Potter*, and the Hermetic *Asclepius*, but unlike the apocalyptic literature of Iran, the domin-

---

[208] Cf. E. Hornung (tr. J. Baines), *Conceptions of God in Ancient Egypt* (London, 1983), 163–5. H. Brunner in *LÄ* s.v. 'Weltende' (1986), 1213–4, n. 1, suggests that the mention of Osiris is an interpolation; since there is a dialogue, however, between the two gods, this is unlikely, although it may convey a mere gesture of courtesy on the part of Atum. Other mentions of final cataclysm occur in the text of the Celestial Cow and in the Shipwrecked Sailor. In his fine study, 'Schöpfung und Weltuntergang in der ägyptischen Religion', L. Kákosy, *Selected Papers* (1981), 55–68 (from 1963), shows how the end of the world is often regarded as the reversal of the process of creation. Thus, in the latter process the separation of earth and sky was important; now the sky is pulled down on the earth.

[209] Thus Kákosy, ibid. 56. *What is to be done with the Children of Nut?* are the opening words of the spell.

[210] See my 'Atlantis and Egypt', *Historia* 34 (1985), 3–28.

[211] See John D. Ray, *The Archive of Ḥor* (Texts from Excavations, 2; London, 1976), 167 ff.

[212] See my 'Apocalyptic in the Hellenistic Era', in *Apocalypticism etc.* ed. D. Hellholm, 273–93, this on pp. 284–5.

[213] Tr. John D. Ray. I also thank him for drawing my attention to the text.

ant concern here is the fate of one nation in Egypt.[214] The cosmic scope of Zoroastrianism is missing in Egyptian writings of this genre. Above all, the teaching about the Last Things has no centrality, and it is usually unconnected with the theme of judgement. Iranian influence clearly predominates under this heading.

(3) A general judgement which concerns the nations of the world is a distinctively Jewish concept, and will be discussed in our next section.

(4) The emergence of a Saviour is a theme less decisively settled.

In Jewish and Christian accounts of judgement the Son of Man and Christ assume the leading roles. The possible Egyptian counterpart is clearly Osiris, and here the parallelism extends to the ancillary figures. In the Iranian tradition it is Ahura Mazda that is regarded as the Requiter who controls the Bridge or Crossing, itself a means of judgement rather than the Balance, although molten metal has a judging function too. Neither Bridge nor molten metal figures in the Judaeo-Christian imagery. In the Pahlavi texts the Balance does assume some importance and the god Rashn leads the weighing, assisted by Mithra and Sraosha. The Osirian judgement provides a more convincing prototype.

On the other hand, if we consider the wider function of the Saviour in initiating a general judgement at the end of time, we may well favour Iranian influence, or at least a combination of such a factor with the Messianism of Hebrew thought. It is true that the Iranian figure of Gayōmart, the Primal Man, has been adduced, but these affinities are rather vague.[215] The *Saoshyant* ('one who will bring benefit') is really the key figure. Whereas in the Gāthās his function is to give spiritual guidance on *the straight paths of salvation*, later his task is more expansive, for he will bring about the renewal of the world and the final triumph over evil, not without a bloody struggle.[216] He is born miraculously of a virgin from the seed of Zoroaster, but he is a man, born of human parents, destined to become the cosmic Saviour who also confers individual salvation.[217]

Egyptian religion also knows a Saviour. His name is Osiris, and identification with him empowers every believer to achieve triumph in the judgement and renewed life thereafter. While he has cosmic attributes, particularly his power over fertility, it is the bestowal of personal victory over sin and death that gives him his special appeal. In the Hellenistic and Roman eras the goddess Isis often conveys this appeal more attractively, while assuming

---

[214] See my remarks ibid. 287–91.

[215] Cf. Saul Shaked, *CHJ*, I (1984), 323: 'these (affinities) seem to be imprecise and are somewhat equivocal.' But he thinks that 'the idea of a general resurrection of the whole of mankind, in which all people will be put to judgement in their physical bodies for deeds performed while they were alive, seems to have been moulded by contact with Iran.'

[216] Boyce, *Zoroastrianism*, 39–40 and 90–91.

[217] Boyce, *Hist. of Zoroastrianism*, I, 282; cf. Zaehner, *Teachings of the Magi*, 143, 'a hero, not a god'.

too the role of a universal nature-goddess. But in neither case can we discern a doctrine of cosmic renewal—nothing to remind us of the words of the Apocalypse: *then I saw a new heaven and a new earth* (Rev. 21:1). Iranian literature can provide a parallel:

> Then will the final Resurrection take place in the two worlds; and in accordance with its own desire the material world will become immortal for ever and ever.
> *(Bundahishn, 24.)*[218]

Yet Egyptian apocalyptic can produce a deliverer in its own mould. Usually it is a figure who restores order after a time of chaos, as when the Prophecies of Nefer-ti avow that *a King will come from the South*.[219] But he is not basically a figure of cosmic import; his task is primarily political, although the theology of kingship did link him with the maintenance of order in the universe. Such prophecies are roundly and rightly classified by Assmann[220] as 'politische Prophezeiungen'.

The function of Saviour as Judge in an individual judgement, particularly in a psychostasia, is best derived from Egypt; but a Saviour who inaugurates a renewed world at the end of time is likely to be an Iranian contribution. In this latter context, nevertheless, Messianic ideals in the Jewish outlook may be significant. A composite pattern therefore results.

(5) Heaven and Hell appear in Egypt and Iran. In the Iranian tradition Heaven is more exclusively celestial than in Egypt. Neither Sheol nor Gehenna provided detailed antecedents for the Judaeo-Christian Hell, whose lake of fire and other embellishments point to an Egyptian source.[221]

A third alternative verdict is occasionally referred to in both Egypt and Iran, but neither forms a precise anticipation of the much later Christian doctrine of Purgatory.

(6) Resurrection of the body is a conspicuous part of Egyptian belief. It is not attested in the earliest Iranian stratum, but in the fourth century B.C. there is Greek evidence of a Zoroastrian doctrine of immortality.[222]

---

[218] Zaehner, op. cit. 150. The context does not make quite clear what the 'two worlds' are; the second is probably the celestial and spiritual world. In a work written in the ninth century A.D. much earlier ideas may be preserved; but even Widengren in *Apocalypticism etc.* 81 admits that the Gathic Avesta holds no belief in a resurrection; only a heavenly ascent of the soul is there accepted.

[219] Cf. above p. 176.

[220] In *Apocalypticism etc.* 357 ff. Earlier (p. 345 n. 1) he suggests that the term 'eschatology' should not be applied to Egyptian concepts since they do not concern the end of the world. He admits, however, that they definitely propound an 'individual eschatology' relating to man's fate after death; in view of this the suggestion is rather arbitrary.

[221] This applies especially to mediaeval Christian art: see E. Brunner-Traut, *Gelebte Mythen*, 81 ff.

[222] Cf. Anders Hultgaård in *Apocalypticism etc.* 407. He admits, at the same time (p. 406), that some elements in the Pahlavi texts have much more recent relevance, i.e. from the viewpoint of the time of redaction in the ninth or tenth

The Jewish and Christian debt to Egypt centres on the portrayal of the judgement of the individual after death; it extends also to the belief in the resurrection of the body and in the conception of Hell; possibly also to ideas of Heaven, especially of astral immortality. It is from Iran that the Jews probably derived the belief in a general judgement concomitant with the end of the world and inaugurated by a cosmic Saviour.

These simple-seeming conclusions should not be allowed to obscure the possibilities of interaction between the various ancient cultures in the Hellenistic and Roman eras. We have noted, for instance, that Iran influenced Egypt at this time; similarly an Egyptian impact on Iran, especially in the matter of the psychostasia, should not be excluded. The Persians ruled Egypt from 525 to 404 B.C. and for a second briefer span (343–332 B.C.); and conquerors are notoriously exposed to the culture of the conquered. More significant, probably, was the impact of Babylon on Iran. There were early syncretisms of Babylonian and Iranian gods, such as of Ishtar and Anahiti;[223] and the astronomical learning of the Babylonians must have affected Iranian thought in various ways, as in the curiously elaborate scheme of the millennia in the winding up of history. Akkadian literature does indeed contain prophecies of royal dynasties when justice and well-being will replace chaos and misery.[224] Eschatology, however, is for the most part lacking since life after death was not a tenet of religious belief. It is true that a netherworld which is the realm of the dead is known in this tradition, and the god Utu, judge of gods and men, is said to judge disputes among the dead.[225] But the theme seems not to have received elaboration.

2. *Judaism's Distinctive Contribution*

If ideas and imagery about individual judgement were contributed by Egypt and those about a general judgement at the end of time by Iran, Judaism nevertheless developed its own distinctive approach. It was the figure of the Messiah with a special role in judgement

---

centuries A.D.; thus the hope of redemption from the East, particularly from India, 'may correspond to real attempts to restore the national independence of Iran after its subjugation by the Arabs.'

[223] Mary Boyce, *Hist. of Zoroastrianism*, II (Leiden, 1982), 269.

[224] As in the Uruk prophecy, discussed with others by H. Ringgren in *Apocalypticism etc.*, 379–86, comparing (p. 385) the Egyptian Prophecies of Nefer-ti.

[225] Thorkild Jacobsen, *The Treasures of Darkness* (New Haven, 1976), 134; cf. 122 (the lord Nanna as judge in the netherworld).

that constituted this distinction, and the associated doctrine that a judgement of the nations would be conducted by him.

(1) *The Messianic Figure*

Messianism was a post-exilic development which spread the hope and belief that Yahweh would send his Anointed 'son of David' to deliver the Jewish nation from oppression. Although Deutero-Isaiah (45:1) uses the term once of Cyrus the Great, its background is intensely national. The term was used of priests and kings, particularly of ideal kings; and in the Scrolls two types of Messiah are presented. In the Old Testament, however, the general concept is not specifically linked to the term. The idea of a deliverer from the house of David who will not only save Israel but also judge the nations in righteousness is of early origin. In the eighth century B.C. Amos proclaimed doom oracles against the nations, threatening Yahweh's judgement of them; but he was careful to add Judah to the list.[226] The judgement anticipated by him is probably to be located in the disturbing international events of the eighth century which were dominated by Assyria. He was much concerned with the impending 'Day of Yahweh', but insisted on its moral connotation.

The Davidic leader *from the stock of Jesse* is himself credited with penetrating wisdom as a judge:

> He shall not judge by what his eyes see,
>   or decide by what his ears hear;
> but with righteousness he shall judge the poor,
>   and decide with equity for the meek of the earth;
> and he shall smite the earth with the rod of his mouth,
>   and with the breath of his lips he shall slay the wicked.
> Righteousness shall be the girdle of his waist,
>   and faithfulness the girdle of his loins.
>   (Isa. 11:3–5.)[227]

In spite of the hardness of the divine chastisement, an idyllic period of peace is then portrayed, extending even to the animal world and appearing again, perhaps, in Vergil's serene Fourth Eclogue.

Other facets of the Davidic deliverer eventually emerge—the Son of Man and the Suffering Servant. The latter figure may well have

---

[226] See above, Chapter 1, p. 5.
[227] Some scholars have doubted the ascription of these words to Isaiah (or Proto-Isaiah): see H.H. Rowley, *The Faith of Israel* (London, 1956, repr. 1973), 188. Klaus Koch (tr. M. Kohl), *The Prophets*, I (London, 1982), 136 ff., seems content on the whole to accept them as Isaianic.

been accepted by the community of Qumran as embodied in their Teacher of Righteousness, who seems to have suffered martyrdom. In Daniel 7:13 *one like a Son of Man* approaches the Ancient of Days in the judgement scene; it is he, the Son of Man, who is granted dominion and glory by the judge, so that all nations shall serve him. At the end of the Egyptian text which we know as *The Admonitions of Ipuwer* the author refers to the kingship of the sun-god Rê as a theme contrasting with the sad conditions he has described. Of this ideal king he says, *It is said he is the shepherd of all men; there is no evil in his heart*; and he adds pathetically, *Where is he today? Doth he sleep perchance? Behold his might is not seen.* J.H. Breasted[228] remarks on this 'picture of the ideal sovereign', comparing it with the Davidic hope in Hebrew tradition; he then says that 'this is, of course, Messianism nearly fifteen hundred years before its appearance among the Hebrews.' In this matter, unhappily, the comparison does little to enhance the Egyptian ideal; it is particularly jejune when compared with the rich and varied idealism of the Jewish vision; especially does it lack the hope of deliverance in the future.

There is, at the same time, an element of conquest in the portrayal of the triumphant Messiah. Sometimes it is purely defensive in aim, as when the Psalms of Solomon (i B.C.) see *the son of David* as a judge: *He will judge peoples and nations in the wisdom of his righteousness* (17:29). Before that the Messiah's task will be to rid Israel of foreign rule:

> Undergird him with the strength to destroy the unrighteous rulers,
>   to purge Jerusalem from gentiles
>   who trample her to destruction.
>   (Psalms of Solomon, 17:22.)[229]

The foreign rule is clearly that of the Romans, for these Psalms refer in detail to Pompey. Such oppressors are viewed as being eventually in subjection to the Davidic victor:

> And he will have gentile nations serving him under his
>   yoke,
>   and he will glorify the Lord in (a place) prominent
>   (above) the whole earth.
>   (Ibid. 17:30.)

It seems, then, that whereas the first task of the Messiah is to

---

[228] *The Dawn of Conscience* (New York, 1933), 198–9. Cf. above p. 171.
[229] Tr. R.B. Wright in *The O.T. Pseudepigrapha* ed. J.H. Charlesworth, II (London, 1985), 667. Cf. S.P. Brock's translation in *The Apocryphal Old Testament* ed. H.D.F. Sparkes (Oxford, 1984), 678.

restore Israel to her former glory, he is expected to proceed afterwards to secure for her the leading position among all nations.[230] These manifestations of his power are doubtless regarded as acts of war and probably reflect the influence of the Maccabean campaigns. Indeed Mowinckel[231] avers that 'as a rule, the Messiah is not regarded as judge of the world in a legal and forensic sense'; he also finds a view expressed that the acts of the Messiah will be only a preparation for the great judgement of the Last Days, and that this final judgement sees God himself, *the Ancient of Days*, as the judge of the world. He concedes, however, that 1 Enoch envisages the Messiah as appearing only after the final judgement; and that Rabbi Akiba assigns one of the judgement seats in the seventh chapter of Daniel to 'David', that is, the Messiah.[232] It does seem that in the victorious acts of the Messiah judgement and warlike destruction merge into each other: 'the reckoning with the world power is also regarded as an act of judgement in which the Messiah takes part' (Mowinckel, p. 313). Certainly the Apocalypse of Ezra, as he points out, has annihilation following judgement:

> For first he will set them living before his judgement seat, and when he has reproved them, then he will destroy them.
> (Fourth Book of Ezra, 12:33 (late i A.D.) tr. B.M. Metzger in Charlesworth, op. cit. I, 550.)

The Son of Man was manifestly a Messianic figure; not always a personal Messiah (in Daniel 7 he symbolizes the people of Israel), he is transcendental and eschatological; thus he comes, as in the New Testament, with the clouds of heaven. Book 5 of the Sibylline Oracles (*c.* 80–130 A.D.)[233] portrays him thus:

> For a blessed man came from the expanses of heaven with a scepter in his hands which God gave him.
> (Sibylline Oracles, 5.414–15; tr. J.J. Collins.)

while his achievement is thus summed up:

> He destroyed every city from its foundations with much fire and burned nations of mortals who were formerly evildoers. And the city

---

[230] Sigmund Mowinckel (tr. G.W. Anderson), *He that Cometh* (Oxford, 1956), 311, showing also that this characterized the Messianism of later Judaism. Cf. E. Schürer rev. Vermes, Millar, and Black, *The History of the Jewish People in the Age of Jesus Christ*, II (Edinburgh, 1979), 492 ff.
[231] Mowinckel, op. cit. 312.
[232] Cf. ibid. 352. Mowinckel there asks, 'Why, then, is there more than one throne?' The pluralism was clearly supplied by the Egyptian pattern, but Mowinckel restricts himself to Hebraic antecedents.
[233] See J.J. Collins in Charlesworth, op. cit. I, 390.

which God desired, this he made more brilliant than stars and sun and moon.

(Ibid. 5.418–21; tr. Collins.)

To the Son of Man is ascribed a conspicuous role as 'the Judge of the World'.[234] In this task he is associated with God himself. God's Anointed One *will call all nations, and some of them he will spare, and others he will kill* (2 Baruch 72:2, early ii A.D.; tr. A.F.G. Klijn, ibid.)

(2) The Judgement of the Nations

If the figure of a national Saviour is not entirely distinctive, and certainly not unique, the concept of a judgement of the nations, which characterizes Jewish eschatology, clearly merits these terms. We have seen that the religions of both Egypt and Iran inculcated a posthumous judgement of individuals; Iran also evolved a doctrine of general judgement at the end of time, but this equally meant, it seems, a judgement of individuals. It was Judaism alone that conceived of a judgement of nations.

That nations endure loss or experience gain in the course of history on the basis of a divine assessment of their conduct is a notion we have already examined. Israel herself is often included in this category by her own prophets. When transferred to an eschatological context, the idea of judging nations naturally loses the precision which characterizes the application of the process to past history, unless of course that history is now treated with detailed retrospection. Nor is the elaboration of individual judgement easily possible with its assessment of good and bad deeds. Furthermore, a generalizing factor is present in the simplicity of the basic division between Jews and Gentiles.

It is true that some allusions are concerned with an assessment of people in a wide sense without any national reference. Such is the suggestion of an allusion which employs the imagery of weighing actions:

> And after that, I saw all the secrets in heaven, and how a kingdom breaks up, and how the actions of the people are weighed in the balance.
> And there I saw the dwelling place of the sinners and the company of the holy ones . . .
>
> (1 Enoch 41:1–2; tr. E. Isaac.)

---

[234] Mowinckel, op. cit. 393–9.

Here the apparently political reference of the breaking up of a kingdom is not made precise, and the subsequent division of *the sinners* and the *holy ones* shows that a general ethical dichotomy is intended. But in Isaiah (2:4) it is said that *He shall judge between the nations and shall decide for many peoples*, and here the terms *gôîm* and *'ammîm* are used. Of these it is the latter term *'am* that is generally used of Israel as a people or nation. Whether the full sense of people or nation should be ascribed to the group associated with Moses may be questioned; and Möhlenbrink has argued that this group was an exclusively religious alliance, a kind of 'amphictyony'.[235] The later nomadic and tribal periods of Israelite history do not prevent the recognition that eventually the marks of nationhood are apparent. There is some looseness, of course, in the application of the terms *gôîm* and ἔθνη (Rev. 11:18) to the nations that are judged and condemned. The Romans, for instance, were an imperial power which had absorbed many nations.

In the Dead Sea Scrolls the judgement of Rome is implemented by a militant Messianism, as in the text entitled *Benedictions* or *Blessings* (I QSb V. 20–28), where a Warrior Messiah is prophesied who is destined to dominate the whole world:

> Thou shalt smite the peoples with the power of Thy word; with Thy rod thou shalt lay waste ... the earth. Thou shalt tread down the nations as mud in the streets. For God has raised thee up as the sceptre of rulers.
>
> (Tr. Matthew Black.)[236]

Still more forceful is the expression of these Messianic hopes in the *Scroll of the War* which Yigael Yadin[237] has edited. Here the enemy are often called Kittim, and Yadin concludes (p. 25) that the Romans are mainly referred to. He would date this text to the second half of the first century B.C. Angelic hosts from heaven further the Messianic cause, which aims at the conquest of the whole world; and Matthew Black[238] well describes the *Scroll of the War* as 'a kind of blue-print, in this case for an Apocalyptic or

---

[235] See A. Lods in *Record and Revelation* ed. H. Wheeler Robinson (Oxford, 1938), 204. Here Lods goes on to claim that 'Moses did create a people' in the sense of a group of men descended from a common ancestor and covenanted to 'the national worship of Yahweh'.

[236] *The Scrolls and Christian Origins* (London, 1961), 151. Cf. T.H. Gaster, *Scriptures of the Dead Sea Sect* (London, 1957), 101, who uses optatives for the main verbs, as also does G. Vermes, *The Dead Sea Scrolls in English* (Pelican, 1966), 209.

[237] *The Scroll of the War of the Sons of Light against the Sons of Darkness* (Oxford, 1962).

[238] Op. cit. 153. Cf. Schürer rev. Vermes, Millar and Black, *Hist. of Jewish People etc.* II, 554.

Messianic War which will finally bring to an end the oppressions and sufferings of Israel at the hands of one of the great Empires and place the true Israel, as represented and led by this priestly sect, in the dominant world-rôle now occupied by her enemies, the Kittim'. In his *Histories* (5.13.2) Tacitus refers to a belief derived from ancient priestly writings that the East would at that time (A.D. 70) achieve power and that men from Judaea would conquer the world. While Tacitus says that the prophecy applied really to Vespasian and Titus, it seems possible that Jewish writings of this kind were conveyed to a Roman observer with calculated camouflage of their real target.[239]

Most of the allusions to the judgement of nations are a good deal less specific. In Daniel 7:14 dominion is given to a Messianic figure, as we have seen, and he is to be served by *all peoples, nations and languages*; but all these seem to be regarded as on a par. The Book of Enoch (1 Enoch) is packed with judgement scenes in an apocalyptic setting, and the opening words point to the major segregation of categories:

> The blessing of Enoch: with which he blessed the elect and the righteous who would be present on the day of tribulation at (the time of) the removal of all the ungodly ones.
> (1 Enoch 1:1; tr. E. Isaac, as throughout.)

The righteous and the ungodly: this is the basic division which is constantly in mind; the righteous will be blessed and forgiven by God; the ungodly will be cursed and destroyed. After a section telling of the rough treatment meted out to fallen angels and the human beings corrupted by them, we are surprised to learn (10:21–22) *that all nations shall worship and bless me . . . And the earth shall be cleansed from all pollution, and from all sin, and from all plague, and from all suffering.* This recalls rather the Happy End of the *Bundahishn*. On the other hand, the account of Enoch's journeys through the earth and to Sheol (17–36) may recall aspects of Greek tradition. It has also been argued[240] that the depiction of twelve divisions in Sheol has no counterpart in Iranian eschatology, and that Orphic influence may be at work; however, Egypt provides a

---

[239] See my 'Tacitus, *Hist.* 5.13.2 and the Dead Sea Scrolls', in *Rheinisches Mus. für Phil.* 113 (1970), 363–8, noting that a more general prophecy, such as Daniel 2:44, could have provided the source.

[240] T. Francis Glasson, *Greek Influence in Jewish Eschatology*. With Special Reference to the Apocalypses and Pseudepigrapha. (London, 1961), Chapters 2 and 3 ('Journeys to the Realm of the Dead' and 'Divisions in Sheol'), pp. 8–20. There is an Egyptian parallel too in the Second Setne story, as we have noted above, p. 229ff.

closer parallel in the twelve hours dividing the night of Amduat and also in the visit of Rê to this region.

Enoch's First Similitude (Ch. 38) refers to the fate after judgement of the *kings and rulers*—clearly the leaders of nations hostile to Israel:

> At that moment, kings and rulers shall perish,
> they shall be delivered into the hands of the righteous
>   and holy ones,
> and from henceforth no one shall be able to induce
>   the Lord of the Spirits to show them mercy,
> for their life is annihilated.
>
> (1 Enoch 38:5–6; tr. E. Isaac.)

Prayer is made that the blood of the righteous may be avenged (47:1–4); but in Chapter 50 *the others* (the Gentiles) *shall be saved through his name if they repent*; otherwise *oppression cannot survive his judgement; and the unrepentant in his presence shall perish* (50:4). What seems to be an Iranian touch marks the description of the mountains of metal in Chapter 52; but the sequel is quite different: instead of molten metal as an ordeal we are given the assurance that there will be no need of metals any more; they will be removed. A rarely specific allusion occurs in a section concerned with the last struggle of heathen powers against Israel: *In those days, the angels will assemble and thrust themselves to the east at the Parthians and Medes* (56:5).[241] There will be an immense slaughter, but Sheol shall *swallow up the sinners* (56:8). A vindictive note is struck in Chapter 62, which depicts *the punishment of the kings, the governors, the high officials, and the landlords*; they will plead in vain for mercy from the Son of Man, and they shall be delivered to the punishing angels *in order that vengeance shall be executed on them—oppressors of his children and his elect ones* (62:11). Then follows: *It shall become quite a scene for my righteous and elect ones. They shall rejoice over them.* We are then told that even if they repent, it will be of no avail. One may compare the Testament of Moses, 10:7: *In full view will he come to work vengeance on the nations. Yea, all their idols will he destroy.*[242]

The vindictive intensity is, however, surpassed by the Christian rejoicing over the prophesied fall of Rome:

---

[241] The four world kingdoms in Daniel's dream vision include, of course, the Medes and Persians; see M. Hengel, *Judaism and Hellenism*, I, 182. He compares an unpublished fragment from 4 Q.

[242] Tr. J. Priest in Charlesworth, *The O.T. Pseudepigrapha*, I, 932. For this text (probably of i A.D.) and related literature see also Schürer, rev. Vermes, Millar, and Black, op. cit. II, 526–9.

> The kings of the earth may lament
> 'Alas! Alas! thou great city,
> thou mighty city, Babylon!
> In one hour has thy judgment come.'
>
> (Rev. 18:10.)

But God's people are exhorted to recall that *God has remembered her iniquities* and to pay back to her even beyond the due measure:

> Render to her as she herself has rendered,
> and repay her double for her deeds;
> mix a double draught for her in the cup she mixed.
>
> (Rev. 18:6.)

The prophet Isaiah's vision is very different. He too sees the God of Jacob as a judge of the nations[243] and he sees these nations acknowledging the precedence of Jerusalem, not because they have been conquered by a Messianic leader, but because they recognize *the light of the Lord*:

> Nation shall not lift up sword against nation,
> neither shall they learn war any more.
>
> (Isa. 2:4.)

The prophet's aim is not to establish Israel's claim to world sovereignty, but Yahweh's claim to moral sway: *soli deo gloria*.[244]

All three religious traditions we have been comparing in this area—the Egyptian, Iranian, and Jewish—consistently taught that individuals face judgement after death. It was only in Egypt that this kind of judgement was given exclusive importance. In both the other areas a general judgement coinciding with the end of the world was also inculcated. It was only Judaism, however, that exhibited a fervent belief that a judgement of nations would occur as part of the general winding-up of history. The source of this highly distinctive belief is not far to seek. Whereas Egyptian religion was also intensely national, it was in Israel alone that the essence of religion was seen to lie in the sacred covenant sealed between God and his people. A theology of history was firmly based on this foundation.

3. *The Other Ancient Cultures*

None of the other cultures of the ancient world provides a well-

---

[243] An unusual trial scene in the Egyptian Book of Gates also depicts other nations sharing the divine solicitude. See above p. 208. There is a hint of a pleasing parallel, but no more.

[244] Cf. Paul Volz, *Der eschatologische Glaube im Alten Testament* (Stuttgart, 1935), 15.

defined and distinctive concept of posthumous judgement. In the area of the Near East the Hittites, as we have shown (Chapter 1, Section 3), betray a concern with ideas of divine intervention, but it is usually related to the events of the present life. If appearance before a divine tribunal is more than once suggested, the issue does not relate to the fate of an individual or nation in the afterworld, but rather to the removal of dangers which pertain to war or pestilence. In rather similar fashion Babylonian writings (see Chapter 1, Section 4) treat of the divine ordering of human affairs and sometimes question its moral consistency; yet the basic belief is that religious devotion is properly rewarded in this life without any resort to a continuation of the process in a life to come.

The Etruscans, by way of contrast, displayed a profound interest in man's fate after death. Their eschatology must have included the idea of posthumous judgement, for the depiction of tortures suffered by the souls of the dead clearly implies this. A partial dependence on Greek ideas is apparent, as in the demon Charun and monstrous figures recalling the Erinyes; and the Greeks themselves drew on the ideology of Minoan Crete and of Egypt. The Etruscans may have been influenced by Egypt more directly in some ways: the attempt to give the tomb the shape and function of a house may be one indication; the funerary portrait, which was so important in Egypt, may be another.[245] Such influences do not extend to details of imagery relating to judgement, although the terror-raising figures recall those of the Egyptian Books of the Underworld.

In India's Vedic literature the afterlife is portrayed on the lines of blissful or baneful alternatives which are dependent on the earthly display of good or evil conduct (see Chapter 5, Section 2). One assumes that Yama, the god of the dead, is responsible for the arbitration of rewards and punishments, but the early literature gives scant information about any process of judgement. Eventually a doctrine of rebirth after death appears with the attendant concept of a cycle of existence in which many depressing phases of rebirth are possible. When the principle of *karma* was evolved from this belief, an ethical basis relating to good and bad actions was provided; inherent in the system was suitable compensation. While the system was constantly adducing previous and future lives to explain the operation of a moral law, yet it was focussed on the present life. Judgement is seen to be implemented unceasingly, but its implementation after death is not given special emphasis. Later

---

[245] M. Pallottino (tr. J. Cremona), *The Etruscans* (Harmondsworth, 1955), 168–72.

Vedic literature includes an allusion to the weighing of good and bad deeds in a balance,[246] yet in general this tradition does not present, whether in Hinduism or Buddhism, a judicially equipped posthumous trial.[247]

As for early Chinese thought, we have seen (Chapter 6) that it was often finely attuned to questions affecting the relationship between conduct and well-being or suffering. Such questions are confined, at the same time, to considerations about living here and now. The possibility of life after death is treated with agnosticism, so that eschatology is practically absent, including any thought of a posthumous judgement.

4. *The Christian Consummation*

We have already discussed aspects of the Christian beliefs about posthumous judgement, particularly those that reflect the likelihood of Egyptian and Iranian influence. Now it would be useful, I think, to review early Christian ideology in a more general way. If various sources have contributed to its intellectual make-up, certain distinctive features can yet be recognized. I propose to consider, in order of ascending importance, Revelation, the writings of Paul, and the Synoptic Gospels.

(1) *Revelation*

This work probably dates from the last years of the Emperor Domitian (A.D. 90–96) and it gives much prominence to the theme of a judgement at the end of time. Yet this is not the central theme. It is the myth of the combat, set out in Chapter 12, that provides the conceptual framework underlying the book as a whole.[248] In this myth a struggle for universal kingship is depicted

---

[246] Brandon, *Judgment of the Dead*, 167, but noting that elsewhere 'nothing is said of a *post-mortem* judgment as such.'
[247] Jean Varenne in *Jugement des Morts* (Paris, 1961), 226–7. Brandon, op. cit. 197 and Pl.11 (facing p. 131) treats of a Tibetan Buddhist depiction of the Judgement of the Dead. White and black pebbles are weighed; but the picture is modern and its imagery is very composite in origin. Some elements are much older: see W.Y. Evans-Wentz, *The Tibetan Book of the Dead* (3rd Ed., Oxford, 1957), 37–38, the picture being reproduced in his Plate 5 and discussed on pp. xxx–xxxi. Parallels to Osiris and Thoth are seen in two of the figures, and it is the monkey-headed Shinje, equated with Thoth, who holds the scales. These figures, however, do not seem to be mentioned in the text which deals with judgement (pp. 165–9), and the Tibetan form of Buddhism which produced the text was not established, under Indian influence, until the eighth century A.D.
[248] See Adela Yarbro Collins, *The Combat Myth in the Book of Revelation* (Harvard

between two divine beings, one of whom is a woman clothed with the sun, who is pregnant, and the other a great red dragon who threatens the woman. The dragon is identified (Rev. 12:9) with the Devil and Satan, and a war ensues in heaven, where Michael and his angels oppose the cosmic dragon. While the dragon is defeated in this episode, further monstrous beasts appear and the struggle is renewed until final victory is won against the kings of the whole world assembled at Armageddon. The last phase of this victory of the Lamb and of God introduces us to a woman arrayed in purple and scarlet. She is *Babylon the great, mother of harlots*; she is *drunk with the blood of the saints and the blood of the martyrs of Jesus* (17:5–6). Later it is said (17:18) that this woman is *the great city which has dominion over the kings of the earth*. Clearly the city is Rome, and the blood has been shed through Rome's persecution of Christians. It is at this stage that one type of judgement is announced (17:1): it is equated really with the victory-cry over the fall of Babylon-Rome in Chapter 18 (cf. above p. 266). The Romans are likewise the threatened Kittim in *The War of the Sons of Light*. In the Jewish Apocalypses such as the Psalms of Solomon and the Parables of Enoch it is the Messiah who leads the triumphant onslaught, and yet 'the Messiah is not a warrior, but a supernatural being descended from heaven;' he exacts punishment from the enemies of God's people 'not as a general, but as a judge appointed by God'.[249] Revelation is not here concerned, however, with posthumous judgement; the fall of Rome is to occur in a longed-for future, yes, but within history—like Babylon and Sodom.

The Christology of Revelation is often felt to be at variance with that of the rest of the New Testament. The Christ depicted here is equipped with the Messianic fusion of judge and warrior: *in righteousness he judges and makes war* (19:11). In this role he is the answer to the anguished needs of a Church which is beset by the claims of Emperor-worship and by the blood-bath of imperial persecutions.[250] In Revelation he is often[251] called the Lamb. In 5:9 he is a lamb that was slain and therefore worthy *to take the scroll and to open*

Diss., Missoula, Montana, 1976), 57–85, and esp. 231. She points to mythic parallels in Egyptian, Ugaritic, and Akkadian literature: see her pp. 67 ff.

[249] Schürer, rev. Vermes-Millar-Black, *Hist. of Jewish People*, II, 527.

[250] A developed Emperor-cult and the increase of persecution of Christians in Asia Minor are two reasons why an earlier date than the last years of Domitian is unlikely. Both circumstances are mentioned in Rev.; cf. H. Conzelmann and A. Lindemann, *Arbeitsbuch zum N.T.* (Tübingen, 1976), 319. For another view see Moule, *The Birth of the N.T.* (1981), 174.

[251] According to Donald Guthrie, *The Relevance of John's Apocalypse* (Exeter, 1987), 46, the title is used 29 times.

its seals; this action leads in Chapter 6 to a series of prophecies or oracles. A lamb who prophesies recalls the prediction of the lamb under the Pharaoh Bokkhoris of Saïs at the end of the seventh century B.C.; its oracles were also media of doom applied to cities. (See above p. 255.) But the fact that the Lamb in Revelation was one which was slain is a clear pointer to the Jewish tradition of the paschal lamb and to the significance of the crucifixion. A dual aspect is, however, presented. When the Lamb first appears (5:5–6) he is referred to as the *Lion of the tribe of Judah, the Root of David*, who has conquered. *The wrath of the Lamb* (6:16) is a key phrase,[252] but the warrior Christ gives way to Christ as judge. After his Messianic victory he reigns with the saints for a thousand years; Satan is freed and a final war leads to his defeat once more, he and his allies being either consigned to eternal torment or, as with Gog and Magog, consumed by fire. Then, and only then, comes the general judgement of the dead (20:11 ff.) following their resurrection. Although Christ has previously figured as a judge (19:11 ff.) holding the forensic sword after his sacred marriage to a bride who represents the Church, in the final judgement he that sits on the great white throne is God himself. In spite of this it is Christ who assumes the role of judge in later Christian portrayals of the Last Judgement.

We have already discussed details of the scene in Revelation. Its atmosphere is calmly judicial with its emphasis on assessment in the light of recorded deeds. Previously (19:15) it is said of Christ as warrior-judge that *he will tread the wine press of the fury (thumos) of the wrath of God the Almighty*. In the final judgement scene the picture is rather different. On the whole, none the less, it is not surprising that Revelation's treatment of our theme has evoked adverse reactions. Ideas of judgement in it are often merged with bloodthirsty martial motifs although it gives no detailed accounts of warfare. 'The God of the Apocalypse can hardly be recognized', says Dodd,[253] 'as the Father of our Lord Jesus Christ.' Punishment after the trial is ruthless: those not named in the Book of Life are thrown into the lake of fire (20:15), presumably for the same eternal

---

[252] See H. Kleinknecht et al., *Wrath* (Bible Key Words from Kittel's *TWNT* (London, 1964). Anthony T. Hanson, *The Wrath of the Lamb* (London, 1957) surveys the whole theme in the N.T. He notes (p. 195) the danger of undue anthropomorphism and while seeing the wrath as a process of retribution, prefers to regard all the N.T. references as inherently impersonal.
[253] C.H. Dodd, *The Apostolic Preaching and its Development* (3rd Ed., London, 1963), 49, quoted by Donald Guthrie, op. cit. 38. A. Yarbro Collins in *Apocalypticism* ed. D. Hellholm, 746, gives a wise summation: 'The idea that God executes judgement does not exclude the human feeling of envy or desire for revenge.'

torment as was meted out to the Satanic allies (20:10). But here, of course, the Gospels too provide parallels. The apocalyptic tradition plays a big role in the presentation. Yet a bigger and more urgent role was that of the storm and stress of actual persecution. If Christ as the warrior-judge has a robe dipped or sprinkled in blood (19:13), this is not merely a garish dramatic ploy: it is a true reflex of the suffering and martyrdom of early Christians.[254]

At the same time a fervent and benign universalism is found in Revelation. The new song addressed to the Lamb tells of his redemptive sacrifice for people of all nations:

> for thou wast slain and by thy blood didst ransom men for God from every tribe and tongue and people and nation.
> (Rev. 5:9; cf. the multitude from every nation, 7:9–10.)

The angel with an eternal gospel to proclaim (14:6–7) *to every nation and tribe and tongue and people* tells them, '*Fear God and give him glory, for the hour of his judgement has come.*' This implies a call to repentance since the general assize of all the nations is imminent.

There is a realization withal that an element of eschatology has already been experienced in the life, death, and resurrection of the Saviour, who is accepted as the Lord of both history and cosmic power. There is a conviction that 'the future judge Jesus Christ has already in the past inaugurated eschatological salvation and resurrection'[255] and that a prophetic function of encouragement and exhortation is thus sustained.

(2) *Paul*

The writings of Paul show some affinities to Revelation in their outlook on judgement. Paul is clear and firm on the matter of the final assessment: *For we must all appear before the judgment seat of Christ, so that each one may receive good or evil, according to what he has done in the body* (2 Cor. 5:10). It is true that the *great white throne* in Revelation 20:11 is apparently occupied by God rather than Christ, but the two divine powers are often paired, as in the promise that the martyred saints *shall be priests of God and of Christ* (Rev. 20:6). Paul

---

[254] The Neronic repression counted heavily here; probably also the fall of Jerusalem in the eyes of an author who was a Jewish Christian. See A. Yarbro Collins, 'Persecution and Vengeance in the Book of Revelation' in D. Hellholm (ed.) op. cit. 729–49. She accepts (pp. 730 and 747) the view of D.H. Lawrence (1931) that hatred and envy were powerful factors. On the arguments for an earlier dating of the book see Moule, *The Birth of the N.T.*, 152 ff. Yarbro Collins, 733 and 739 defends A.D. 95 as a likely date.
[255] Elisabeth Schüssler Fiorenza in D. Hellholm (ed.), op. cit. 313.

sees Christ at the end of time delivering *the kingdom to God the Father after destroying every rule and every authority and power* (1 Cor. 15:24); and one may compare the proclamation of the seventh angel in Revelation 11:15: '*The kingdom of the world has become the kingdom of our Lord and of his Christ.* Another parallel can be seen in the Pauline[256] idea that the forces of good and evil are stridently ranged against one another and that Christ and the devil are the protagonists; the forces of evil include *the spiritual hosts of wickedness in the heavenly places* (Eph. 6:12). This is close to the central motif of Revelation, and in particular to its 'war in heaven'.

On the other hand there are certain differences, and they concern the structure of Paul's eschatology. In the third chapter of Philippians (10–11) Paul voices his aspiration for identification with Christ and through that for resurrection: *that I may know him and the power of his resurrection, and may share his sufferings, becoming like him in his death, that if possible I may attain the resurrection from the dead.* There may be a suggestion in *if possible* (εἴ πως) that the achievement of resurrection will depend on success in passing the test of the final judgement; and the following verses indicate his struggle to attain a just reward: *I press on toward the goal for the prize of the upward call of God in Christ Jesus* (14). An important part of his expectation is the Second Coming of Jesus: *but our commonwealth is in heaven, and from it we await a Saviour, the Lord Jesus Christ . . .* (20). A little later he assures the Philippians that *the Lord is at hand* (4:5)—an allusion probably to the Parousia rather than to the Lord's nearness in the general sense of Psalms 145:18.

It is in the second chapter of Romans (1–16) that we find Paul expatiating on the significance of God's verdict on man. After listing the sins which invoke God's wrath, he has observed (1:32) that men persist in their wickedness *though they know God's decree that those who do such things deserve to die*. Inconsistency is condemned in those who judge others while doing the same things themselves: do they suppose that they *will escape the judgement of God?* (2:3). Refusal to repent will be repaid on *the day of wrath*, when the reward for good works will be *eternal life* and the punishment for disobedience and evil will be *wrath and fury, tribulation and distress*:

> But by your hard and impenitent heart you are storing up wrath for yourself on the day of wrath when God's righteous judgment will be revealed. For he will render to every man according to his works; to those who by patience in well-doing seek for glory and honour and immortality, he will give eternal life; but for those who are factious

---

[256] Ephesians was probably the work of one of Paul's followers.

and do not obey the truth, but obey wickedness, there will be wrath and fury. There will be tribulation and distress for every human being who does evil . . .
(Rom. 2:5–9.)

The dependence on deeds is noteworthy.[257] It is thoroughly in accord with traditions we have studied in Jewish, Iranian, and Egyptian sources.

Other allusions maintain this interpretation. The day of reckoning is *that day when, according to my gospel, God judges the secrets of men through Jesus Christ* (Rom. 2:16). The whole world is said to be held *accountable to God* (Rom. 3:19); and *each of us shall give account of himself to God* (Rom. 14:12). When Paul says (1 Cor. 3:13) that *each man's work will become manifest, for the Day will disclose it, because it will be revealed with fire*, it is clear that the Day is that of judgement. The fire, however, since it will test, but not destroy, is not that of Gehenna or of the Egyptian Hell; it must be, in origin, the Iranian fire ordeal. In the same epistle Paul stresses the comparative unimportance of human assessments; only the divine judgement will count:

> It is the Lord who judges me. Therefore do not pronounce judgment before the time, before the Lord comes, who will bring to light the things now hidden in darkness and will disclose the purposes of the heart. Then every man will receive his commendation from God.
> (1 Cor. 4:4–5.)

From the last quotation it is evident that Paul expects the final judgement to follow the Second Advent of Jesus. The view that he posits a Messianic kingdom as the immediate sequel of the Parousia (as in Revelation and 4 Ezra) must be rejected. His eschatology may be described as a sequence in these terms: 'the early expectation of the Parousia when there would be a final judgement, a general resurrection of the righteous (and possibly of all the dead), the transformation of the righteous living, and ensuing upon all this the final consummation, the perfected Kingdom of God when God would be all in all'.[258]

A problem arises over the emphasis on the assessment of deeds which I have noted. It is concisely conveyed in Romans 2:6: *For he*

---

[257] Cf. Morna D. Hooker in *Paul and Paulinism* ed. M.D. Hooker and S.G. Wilson (1982), 49.

[258] W.D. Davies, *Paul and Rabbinic Judaism*, 297. Cf. id., *Jewish and Pauline Studies* (1984), 100 ff., showing that Paul did regard Jesus as the Messiah and believed that 'in Jesus, crucified but raised from the dead, the Messianic Age had begun' (p. 102).

will render to every man according to his works. Yet Brandon[259] is able to say, after discussing the same material, that 'Paul taught that through the death of Christ alone could men and women be saved from eternal damnation and not by their own moral effort.' He is referring, of course, to the well-known doctrine of 'justification by faith' which is often given a central place in Paul's thought.[260] A detailed and thorough analysis has led to the conclusion that 'the notion of judgment according to works is part of a genuinely Christian doctrine of judgment.'[261] A crucial question about 'justification by faith' is whether it has a forensic meaning, and, if so, whether it refers especially to the final court of God's judgement. Paul's best known dicta are in Romans:

> Therefore, since we are justified by faith, we have peace with God through our Lord Jesus Christ.
>
> (Rom. 5:1.)

He uses present tenses, be it noted, and goes on to speak of a state of grace now enjoyed by the believer. A little later he makes a pointed reference to the final judgement:

> Since, therefore, we are now justified by his blood, much more shall we be saved by him from the wrath of God.
>
> (Rom. 5:9.)

Now again stresses a justification already achieved,[262] but the operation of saving grace is envisaged also in the final reckoning. This does not exclude an assessment of conduct after the baptism which has sealed justification in the initial sense of salvation.

Paul offers little detail on the process of judgement or on the rewards or punishments which result. To him eternal life is the reward and it is the free gift of God. A suggestion of differing degrees of reward or punishment might be read into the words *so that each one may receive good or evil, according to what he has done in the body* (2 Cor. 5:10), but such degrees do not seem to be specified. If the wages of sin is death (Rom. 6:23), the idea probably goes beyond the traditional Jewish view that physical death was a

---

[259] *The Judgment of the Dead*, 106.
[260] Cf. W.D. Davies, *Jewish and Pauline Studies*, 185: 'so often given an exaggerated significance'.
[261] Stephen H. Travis, *Christ and the Judgment of God* (1986), 59. The literature is immense; cf. his pp. 204 ff.
[262] Cf. F.V. Filson, *St Paul's Conception of Recompense* (Leipzig, 1931), Chapter 10, and Travis, op. cit. 91. The latter urges cogently that 'justification involves not merely a verdict of acquittal, but a relationship with God in which people experience God's power at work'.

punishment, in origin at any rate, for sin, a view mirrored by Paul in Romans 5:12-14. Paul was thinking, presumably, of death in the absolute and spiritual sense—a concept close to that of the Second Death. It is true that he once (1 Cor. 11:27-34) refers to death and illness as a result of moral failure. Eschatologically, however, death or annihilation, though not eternal torment, is the fate of those who reject God's proffered grace.[263]

(3) The Synoptic Gospels

Unlike Paul's writings, the Synoptic Gospels display a wholehearted belief in the eternal torment of the damned and often ascribe it to Jesus himself. The place of punishment is Gehenna, the part of Sheol to which the wicked were believed to be sent. It is portrayed as *the unquenchable fire* (Mark 9:43) and as a place (48) *where their worm does not die, and the fire is not quenched*. Gehenna was a valley west of Jerusalem which after its desecration by Josiah had been used as a refuse area for the city. (See D.E. Nineham ad loc.) The words about the worm and the fire are taken from Isaiah, where the Lord is speaking:

> 'And they shall go forth and look on the dead bodies of
> the men that have rebelled against me; for their worm
> shall not die, their fire shall not be quenched, and
> they shall be an abhorrence to all flesh.'
>
> (Isa. 66:24.)

In 4 Ezra 7:36 (late i A.D.) we find a less graphic description of this *pit of torment* and *furnace of Gehenna* (tr. B.M. Metzger). Nineham remarks that 'the suggestion is of maggots preying on offal and fires perpetually smouldering for the destruction of refuse;' he goes on, though, to say that 'it is not an original saying expressly designed to convey the Christian view about the fate of the "lost", but a quotation of traditional language ... designed to call up an image of utter horror.' This last phrase agrees with his *caveat*, following Vincent Taylor, that the words should not be dismissed too lightly as simply 'picturesque metaphor'.

Fire figures in other images of Hell. The parable of the tares or weeds ends with an apocalyptic exhibition of punitive power and judgement:

> Just as the weeds are gathered and burned with fire, so will it be at the close of the age. The Son of man will send his angels, and they will

---

[263] Cf. Bornkamm, *Paul*, 124-5; Travis, op. cit. 73-77; E. Earle Ellis, *Paul and his Recent Interpreters* (Grand Rapids, 1961), 33.

gather out of his kingdom all causes of sin and all evildoers, and throw them into the furnace of fire; there men will weep and gnash their teeth. Then the righteous will shine like the sun in the kingdom of their father.

(Matt. 13:40–43.)

Here the clamant contrast between the fate of the righteous and that of the evildoers[264] is heightened by the run-over of the fire symbolism: for the weeds to be burned with fire is the expected thing, but the burning of the evildoers goes further than the merely metaphorical application. There is a literalism in the words *there men will weep and gnash their teeth*—an expression connected with the fate of those in 'outer darkness' in Matthew 8:12; 22:13, and 25:30. Elsewhere (Matt. 25:41) the Son of man seated on his royal throne orders the defaulters on his left hand, who have failed to feed the hungry and so forth, to depart *into the eternal fire prepared for the devil and his angels*; and at the end of this splendidly impressive judgement scene we are told that *they will go away into eternal punishment, but the righteous into eternal life* (Matt. 25:46).

I have given some attention to Gehenna[265] and the eternal fire in order to avoid any glossing over of this element in the teaching of Jesus. The quotation from Isaiah clearly indicates continuing torment and pain.[266] We find the idea in Rabbinic writings, as in Aboth 5.22, where the disciples of Balaam inherit Gehenna and the pit of destruction. So too in the Qumran Scrolls the Levites are instructed in the Community Rule (II, Vermes tr., p. 73) to deliver the wicked up for torture at the hands of those who wreak vengeance and to damn them in *the shadowy place of everlasting fire*. Contemporary and conventional Jewish belief (with the exception of the Sadducees, a priestly aristocracy) is therefore reflected. In spite of the literalism of the 'gnashing of teeth etc.', we may argue that the language is merely symbolic. But symbolic of what? The concept of eternal punishment, if only in a spiritual sense, remains. Of close relevance here is the saying about the death of body and soul:

---

[264] For the mistaken idea that the 'enemy' mentioned earlier in this parable is a cryptic allusion to Paul as a sower of seeds of moral indifference in the Church, see W.D. Davies, *The Sermon on the Mount* (Cambridge, 1966), 93.

[265] Travis, op. cit. 197 n. 6, questions the antiquity of the tradition about the city's refuse being burnt in the Valley of Hinnom (= Gehenna). Early evidence on this point is absent, but Jer. 7:32 ff. refers to it as the Valley of Slaughter, where dead bodies will be food for birds and beasts.

[266] Travis, 137, differs on this: 'It is conventional language, which need not imply everlasting torment. The worm and the fire which abide are symbols of an irreversible fate, but that need not imply that their victims endure conscious pain for ever.'

> And do not fear those who kill the body but cannot kill the soul; rather fear him who can destroy both soul and body in Gehenna.
> (Matt. 10:28.)

> I tell you, my friends, do not fear those who kill the body, and after that have no more that they can do. But I will warn you whom to fear: fear him who, after he has killed, has power to cast into Gehenna; yes, I tell you, fear him!
> (Luke 12:4–5.)

The threat envisaged is that of the persecution facing the disciples, and there is a parallel in 4 Maccabees 13:14–15: *Let us not fear him who thinketh he kills; for a great struggle and peril of the soul awaits in eternal torment those who transgress the ordinance of God.*[267] There has been some debate as to who is deemed to have the power to cast into Gehenna—Satan or the Son of man or God? Satan is often associated with Gehenna, but he is never assigned the supreme sovereignty implied here. The priority of soul over body is indicated by Luke in consonance with Greek ideology; but Matthew favours the Jewish view of the union of soul and body.

We have noted in Chapter 4 that several of the sayings ascribed to Jesus show little regard for the operation of rewards and punishments in the present life, but that the reward in Heaven is emphasized. In the story of Dives and Lazarus (Luke 16:19–31) the two contrasting states in the afterworld are presented. The poor man, Lazarus, enjoys the bliss of being in Heaven after being *carried by the angels to Abraham's bosom*; the rich man goes to Hades, where he is *in torment*. We have seen that this story is of Egyptian origin; its Biblical end, however, is differently slanted with its emphasis on Moses and the prophets. Otherwise there is little depiction of the places of reward and punishment, save that Gehenna is outlined in the manner we have discussed. Only once (Luke 23:43) is Jesus said to refer to Paradise, in his promise to the penitent thief. But he talked a great deal about the Kingdom of God or the Kingdom of Heaven, claiming that it had dawned with his coming. In his deeds and in his parables he made clear its spiritual dimensions. It is a hidden treasure and a pearl of great price, but is readily available to repentant sinners. Several of the parables show a concern with judgement at the end of time. We have referred to this element in the parable of the tares or weeds; it appears also in other parables related to the idea of growing and of the consummation found in harvest. The parable of the ten virgins (Matt. 25:1–13) has a

---

[267] T.W. Manson, *The Sayings of Jesus*, 107.

similar emphasis. The theme of the Great Banquet (Luke 14:12 ff.) also illustrates his doctrine of repayment after death:

> When you give a dinner or a banquet, do not invite your friends or your brothers or your kinsmen or rich neighbours, lest they also invite you in return, and you be repaid. But when you give a feast, invite the poor, the maimed, the lame, the blind, and you will be blessed, because they cannot repay you. You will be repaid at the resurrection of the just.
>
> (Luke 14:12–14.)

That there was a Jewish national dimension to the concept of the end-time judgement held by Jesus is plainly shown by his words to the disciples:

> Truly, I say to you, in the new world (lit. the rebirth), when the Son of man shall sit on his glorious throne, you who have followed me will also sit on twelve thrones, judging the twelve tribes of Israel.
>
> (Matt. 19:28; cf. Luke 22:28–30.)

Whereas the 'great promise' thus made gives prominence to the upheld role and indeed restoration of Israel, with an affirmation of the bond between the twelve disciples and the twelve tribes,[268] there is no suggestion here of the vindication of Israel vis-à-vis the Gentiles. E.P. Sanders[269] compares the words of Paul: *Do you not know that the saints will judge the world?* (1 Cor. 6:2.) A similar idea is found, as we have seen, in Revelation 20:6 (at least in the sense of reigning with Christ). In the two last loci, however, the national note is missing.

To find the most richly distinctive and spiritually arresting expression of Christ's concept of the final judgement we must revert to the description given by Matthew (25:31–46). It begins with the Messianic idea of an assize in which all the nations appear: *When the Son of man comes in his glory, and all the angels with him, then he will sit on his glorious throne. Before him will be gathered all the nations* ... (25:31–32). But after this the whole pan-ethnic concourse is abandoned; and so too, temporarily, is the juridical *mise-en-scène*, for we are told that *he will separate them one from another as a shepherd separates the sheep from the goats, and he will place the sheep at his right hand, but the goats at the left*. An ancient tradition, as we have remarked above, lies behind the left and right demarcation. Then the Son of man, as King and Judge, welcomes those on the right, urging them to inherit the kingdom prepared for them. They are welcomed be-

---

[268] Cf. K. Stendahl, ad loc. in Peake's Comm. (1962).
[269] *Jesus and Judaism* (1985), 115.

cause of their kindly and merciful actions on behalf of the hungry, the thirsty, the strangers, the naked, the sick, and the imprisoned. These actions were done, he says, to the King himself; and when they show surprise, he tells them that *as you did it to one of the least of these my brethren, you did it to me* (25:40). The praise then becomes a rebuke to those who have failed to do these things.

A salutary kind of shock is thus administered. So this is the big concern of the Last Tribunal—the way in which the suffering and the oppressed have been treated. The Son of man in his glory, sitting on his glorious throne, identifies himself with *one of the least of these my brethren* (40) or *one of the least of these* (45). The word *brethren* has given rise to some debate. Brandon[270] speaks of 'good works for the benefit of Christ's disciples'. J.C. Fenton (1963) ad loc. remarks that 'Matthew probably thought of the *brethren* here as the disciples of Jesus; but in the original parable it may have referred to anyone who was in distress.'[271] Certainly the parable of the Good Samaritan (Luke 10:29–37) indicates the belief of Jesus that the duty to take compassion on suffering humanity transcends both religious and ethnic divisions.

---

[270] *The Judgment of the Dead*, 101.
[271] He compares Matt. 10:42: *Whoever gives to one of these little ones even a cup of cold water because he is a disciple* . . ., a version which leaves unclear whether *he* refers to the giver or the receiver. The Greek has εἰς ὄνομα μαθητοῦ, 'for the sake of the name of disciple'. On the further confusion of 'little ones' as 'children' or 'disciples' see Manson, op. cit. 138 f. According to him, pp. 249–52, the idea of an assize of the nations in our passage is not abandoned, since 'the true Israel is covered by the concept "Son of man"' and *all the nations* refers to all the Gentiles. The brethren, he argues, will be disciples of Jesus who suffer in their missionary tasks. For the equation of the Son of man and Israel see also Morna D. Hooker, *The Son of Man in Mark* (London, 1967), 184–5.

CHAPTER TEN

FROM EGYPT TO GREECE VIA CRETE

Egypt offered a cheerful eschatology to those who passed the test after death; a radiant afterlife awaited those who triumphed in the tribunal before Osiris. Early Greek religion, on the other hand, usually presented only the prospect of Hades, where nothing but a gloomy and shadowy existence was possible.

The brighter prospect of Elysium and the Islands of the Blest is, however, presented in a minority of Greek allusions. According to Homer (*Od.* 4.561 ff.) Elysium is on the western border of the earth, near to Ocean. It is only favoured heroes that are allowed to pass without death to this region, where they live a blessed life under the rule of Rhadamanthys. One of these favoured mortals is Menelaus, and he receives the privilege because he is the son-in-law of Zeus; and the Elysian plain, where he is promised an endless future life, is described rather as Olympus is described elsewhere. Proteus is speaking to Menelaus:

> But thou, Menelaus, offspring of Zeus, art not fated to die and meet thy doom in horse-grazing Argos, but the immortal Gods shall conduct thee to the Elysian plain and the end of the world, where dwells fair-haired Rhadamanthys, where life is most pleasant to men. No snow is there, nor mighty storm, nor any rain, but Ocean ever sendeth forth the breeze of the shrill West to blow refreshingly on men; yea, for thou hast Helen as thy wife, and art to them the son of Zeus.
>
> (*Od.* 4.561–9.)

The same idea appears in the account given by Hesiod of the fourth race of men created by Zeus: they met death in various ways, but Zeus gave them endless life in the Islands of the Blest:

> And they with souls unafflicted by grief dwell in the Islands of the Blest by deep eddying Ocean; blessed heroes, for whom the fertile earth brings forth fresh honied fruit thrice a year.
>
> (Hesiod, *Op.* 170–73.)

These happy islands are also portrayed by Pindar in his Second Olympian Ode (lines 76–84). Virtue, he says, brings its reward, and the good are allowed after death to live a life free from toil; but a still greater reward awaits those of proven purity:

> Whosoever have dared in either world to live three times a life pure

from all evil, pass on the road of Zeus by the tower of Cronus, where the breezes of Ocean breathe around the Islands of the Blest, and flowers are radiant with gold, some on the shore from the shining trees, while the water fosters others. With wreaths of these and with crowns they entwine their hands, living the while by the righteous counsels of Rhadamanthys.

(Pindar, *Ol.* 2.76–84.)

It is well known that the Egyptian idea of a blissful afterlife was sometimes portrayed in similar terms, as our discussion above (Chapter 9, Section 5) has shown. 'Islands of the Righteous' are referred to, and a celestial heaven envisages an idealized Nile Valley. As early as the *Pyramid Texts* we find a celebration of its happiness and comfort. The deceased King shall reach the *great island* with its *Field of Offerings* and shall be given *this tree of life on which they live* (Pyr. 1216, PMN). In time the privilege was extended and its popularity increased. A good pictorial record of it appears in a painting on a tomb wall in Deir el-Medîna in Western Thebes (Twentieth Dynasty, *c.* 1880 B.C.), where a man called Sen-Nedjem is shown with his wife in the Fields of Iaru.[1] Branches of the Nile intersect the scene, suggesting islands. There are fruitful trees and scenes which show Sen-Nedjem and his wife ploughing, sowing and reaping. In the top register they greet a barque in which the sun-god and Osiris are figured. It is not surprising that boats are a frequent feature of Egyptian funerary concomitants whether in burial deposits or in depictions of the afterlife.

In his elaborate and enduring study *The Minoan-Mycenaean Religion and its Survival in Greek Religion*,[2] Martin Nilsson gave much attention to his thesis that the Greeks borrowed the idea of Elysium and of the Isles of the Blest from Crete, and that the Minoans in turn derived it from Egypt.[3] Pride of space was given to the Late Minoan sarcophagus from Haghia Triada, and one prominent factor in the depictions thereon is the boat carried by the foremost youth and presented to the dead—an idea that eminently suits the need to provide for the voyage to the afterworld.[4] Other boats

---

[1] E. Otto (tr. K.B. Griffiths), *Egyptian Art: The Cults of Osiris and Amon* (London, 1967), Pl. XV.

[2] 2nd Ed., Lund, 1950. In his Preface (p. viii) Nilsson rightly tends to disavow the term 'Minoan-Mycenaean', recognizing now that there were radical differences between the two traditions, even if the end product was almost a merger. Cf. John Chadwick, *The Mycenaean World* (Cambridge, 1976), 85, and Robin Hägg in *Linear B: A 1984 Survey* (Louvain-la-Neuve, 1985), 203–4.

[3] See esp. his pp. 619–33.

[4] Ibid. 438–9, with Fig. 196. Cf. H.Th. Bossert, *Altkreta* (2nd Ed., Berlin, 1923), Abb. 71–77.

represented on rings and seals point in the same direction, especially as several of them show a cabin and an animal-headed prow in the Egyptian manner.[5] This formal, concrete, and objective resemblance is the easiest type of influence to establish; in itself it does not prove ideological borrowing although here the funerary context strongly supports it. The whole question of the validity of types of influence is thus raised, and in the case of Minoan Crete difficulties arise through the absence of direct literary evidence.

1. *Types of Influence*

A close connection between Crete and Egypt by way of commerce is amply attested by the archaeological record in both areas. In his *Aegyptiaca*[6] J.D.S. Pendlebury listed Egyptian objects found on Greek archaeological sites with the exception of Rhodes, where they were deemed to be too numerous (some 1500 in all).[7] In Crete occurrences relate to the Egyptian Old Kingdom, but are more frequent in the Middle Kingdom and later, with a notable emphasis on the southern area which faced Libya and allowed quick contact within Crete with Knossos and adjacent centres, the route of penetration being from the Messara Plain, Pyrgos on the road north, Knossos and Gournes on the north coast.[8] Phaestos, Haghia Triada, and Haghios Onouphrios are within this particular sphere of influence. Nor should the impact in the opposite direction be ignored. Minoan pottery in Egypt has recently evoked an elaborate study although its sum total is comparatively small.[9] The direct route from Egypt to Crete would have to use the southern or the eastern coast of Crete, and in the latter case Zakro would have provided the receiving point. The direct route, however, involved a distance of about 550 kilometres on the open sea and a voyage both dangerous and difficult, and Jean Vercoutter[10] has cast serious doubts on its likelihood, arguing that the long and round-about route to the east via Rhodes, Anatolia, and Syria probably pro-

---

[5] Ibid. 38–39. See also Arthur Evans, *Palace of Minos* (London, 1921–35), IV, 952, Fig. 920 and A.W. Persson, *The Religion of Greece in Prehistoric Times* (Berkeley, 1942), 84, Rings 25–28, where the Egyptian barque of Rê is compared.

[6] *A Catalogue of Egyptian Objects in the Aegean Area*. Cambridge, 1930.

[7] Much less in number were Egyptian objects found in Corinth, although Humfry Payne, *Necrocorinthia* (Oxford, 1931), p. x, refers to them as 'a very remarkable number of scarabs and other imported Egyptian objects, sixty in all'.

[8] Pendlebury, op. cit. xviii.

[9] B.J. Kemp and S. Merrilees, *Minoan Pottery in Second Millennium Egypt* (Mainz, 1980).

[10] *Essai sur les Relations entre Égyptiens et Préhellènes* (Paris, 1954), 13–18.

vided the contacts. He is doubtful too about the shorter passage from Crete to Cyrenaica with a coastal follow-up to the Nile Delta; but the fact that this coast has not been explored archaeologically is scarcely a valid argument against the feasibility of this route.

The most immediate type of influence results from immigration. Whereas a large influx of population from Anatolia and Syria is often adduced to explain Minoan ethnic origins, a smaller influx from Libya was propounded by Arthur Evans[11] for the Early Minoan Period (c. 3000-2200 B.C.). Among notable archaeological similarities connecting the two areas are the tholoi of the Mesara and the Libyan mapalia, both being in essence circular collective burial-places, and it has been urged[12] that 'a migration from north-western Egypt to Crete at the time of the Early Dynastic period' would suit the chronology of Early Minoan I and also with what is known of 'political events in Egypt at this time'. Some imprecision has clouded this argument. 'North-western Egypt', although much influenced by Libya, is not the same as Libya, and if navigation from Cyrenaica is envisaged, an initial trek across the vast Libyan desert would have been a formidable obstacle.[13] The mention of 'political events in Egypt' is an ingenious suggestion, for King Peryebsen in the Second Dynasty uniquely shows the god Seth above his *serekh*-name.[14] A renewed ascendancy of Upper Egypt might have led to 'a number of refugees fleeing westwards', but Brannigan (p. 199) rightly faces the difficulties of the hypothesis (though not the question of transport) and turns for parallels instead to the Ghassulian Chalcolithic culture of Palestine.

Any large-scale immigration would produce a type of influence other than what we are looking for. Immigrants bring their own culture and techniques with them and cannot therefore be expected to reflect the extent of the impress on the native culture. Thus the long catalogue of imported Egyptian objects which Pendlebury provided is really concerned with the results of trade. When elements of religious practice and belief are borrowed, one does not

---

[11] Cf. J.D.S. Pendlebury, *The Archaeology of Crete* (London, 1939), 279; and his *Handbook to the Palace of Minos*, Knossos (London, 1954), 16: 'Probably there was emigration from Egypt, which was easier than it appears . . . There was certainly very early contact also between Crete and Libya.'

[12] Keith Brannigan, *The Foundations of Palatial Crete. A Survey of Crete in the Early Bronze Age.* (London, 1970), 198.

[13] Vercoutter, op. cit. 32-33, referring to a desert route of about 800 km. But he ignores the possibility of navigation near the coast from the Delta to Cyrenaica.

[14] Cf. my *Conflict of Horus and Seth* (Liverpool, 1960), 124. Sinclair Hood, *The Minoans* (London, 1971), 34, would link the movement of refugees with Narmer-Menes, founder of the First Dynasty, following Arthur Evans.

expect exact replicas of external forms; yet there must be enough basic resemblances to equate facets of Minoan and Egyptian cult. Perhaps artistic borrowings are easiest to trace, and they include the whole function of several technical media, such as the use of faience and, in the Late Minoan era, the treatment of whole walls for fresco painting instead of the small panels previously used.[15] A Nilotic scene shows cats stalking pheasant-like birds;[16] it has been remarked[17] that 'the cats are not Cretan wild cats but domesticated Egyptian ones', but this goes beyond my competence in feline matters whether ancient or modern. A fresco at Knossos shows two blue monkeys and a papyrus plant[18]—probably a straight copy of an Egyptian original.

Far less slavish is the presentation of Egyptian religious motifs. When this occurs in an artistic background that is otherwise distinctively Minoan, we can be sure that a vital impact has been made. The fragmentary black steatite vase from Haghia Triada is a case in point. (Late Minoan II.) Usually called 'The Harvesters' Vase',[19] it figures a procession, more probably, of seed-sowers who are singing boisterously in some kind of revel. Several groups are shown and one is led by a person who is rattling an Egyptian sistrum. Pendlebury[20] describes him as 'a thick-set man in a skull-cap, . . . who looks remarkably like an Egyptian priest.' I would question the last statement, while admitting that Pendlebury, as an archaeologist who excavated in both Crete and Egypt, has a special standing in these matters. It is the 'skull-cap' that is the objection; although priestly dress varied, the head was usually bare and shaven. Still, the Egyptian sacral instrument is there.[21] The work has been brilliantly executed, but interpretation of the presumably agricultural rite defies precision.

---

[15] Pendlebury, *Archaeology of Crete*, 287.

[16] Ibid. Pl. 32, 2; Hood, *The Minoans*, Pl. 57.

[17] R.W. Hutchinson, *Prehistoric Crete* (Harmondsworth, 1962), 277. He cites his Pl. 20, but the ref. is wrong.

[18] Ibid. 275; cf. Hood, op. cit. 90 with Fig. 39.

[19] Evans, *Palace of Minos*, I, 83.

[20] *Archaeology of Crete*, 213 with Pl. 37, 3. For better reproductions see Hall, *The Civilization of Greece in the Bronze Age* (London, 1928), 157; H.Th. Bossert, *Altkreta* (2nd Ed., Berlin, 1923), Abb. 94–97.

[21] In Egypt itself the sistrum is always handled by women, as K. Bosse-Griffiths reminds me; and here the sistrum-player is followed by three girl choristers. Hood, *The Minoans*, 221 n. 38, identifies another figure as the priest: he has long hair and wears a big quilted cloak or cuirass, see Hood's Pl. 38. A 'sowing festival' is recognized. Cf. Reynold Higgins, *The Archaeology of Minoan Crete* (London, 1973), 63. Gerald Cadogan, however, *Palaces of Minoan Crete* (2nd Ed., London, 1980), 45, thinks that the 'rods' carried by the peasants are for 'beating the olives from the trees'; the implements look more like forks.

From the same place and period comes the Haghia Triada sarcophagus, where the funerary purpose is plain and where the Egyptian concept of a blissful afterworld, as we have seen, is pointedly presented. At the same time scarcely any of the borrowed facets are rigid replicas. One instantly recognizes, of course, the Egyptian flavour of the scene in front of the tomb, where the deceased man stands near a tree and faces the figures who are bringing offerings. Nilsson argues for the deification of the dead, and this agrees fully with the Egyptian belief that every dead person became an Osiris, although the funerary cult embodies it only marginally. There is nothing specifically Osirian about the Minoan scene unless the link of tree and tomb be seen as such.[22] It is true that R. Paribeni[23] urged a close point-by-point comparison with Egyptian prototypes; it is not easy to accept in every case, as in the equation of the dead man's figure with a mummified form. He was right, however, as opposed to Nilsson, on the basic matter that the offerings to the dead are not an expression of deification. Yet they agreed, and were supported by Picard and Persson, on the Egyptian eschatological outlook, especially on the significance of the boat.[24]

I have argued that some variation from the Egyptian forms suggests a more vital acceptance of the original impulse. This may admittedly prove, on occasion, to be difficult terrain to defend unless there are some firm elements which point clearly to a borrowing process. In a whole book devoted to the sarcophagus from Haghia Triada Charlotte R. Long[25] has rejected the Egyptian thesis *in toto*, arguing that this person was buried in accordance with Minoan practices which were untainted by Egyptian traditions. To Paribeni's claim that the birds shown on the double axes and above the griffins are the *ba* of the deceased man, she replies (p. 31), perfectly correctly, that the *ba* was represented with a human head during the Eighteenth Dynasty in Egypt; indeed that was so in most other periods too. But the quest for exact correspondence is surely misplaced. The important parallel is the role of the

---

[22] See my *Origins of Osiris and his Cult* (Leiden, 1980), 31 and 91.
[23] *Monumenti Antichi*, 19 (1908), 1 ff.
[24] The shape has proved puzzling. E.A.S. Butterworth, *The Tree at the Navel of the Earth* (Berlin, 1970), 135, finds its crescent shape suggestive of the moon, but suited to the transport of spirits. A happy afterworld is figured on several rings and seals, as on the gold ring from Vafio which shows two dancing persons with an '*ankh*-shaped variety of the double axe'. See Nilsson, *M-M. Rel.*, 275 with Fig. 138.
[25] *The Ayia Triadha Sarcophagus* (Göteborg, 1974). J.T. Hooker tends to support her in his essay 'Minoan Religion in the Late Palace Period', *Minoan Society* (Proc. Cambridge Colloquium, 1981) ed. O. Krzyszkowska and L. Nixon), 137–42.

bird in a funerary context. More convincing is her rejection of Paribeni's proposal that the ceremony of 'Opening the Mouth' is also being suggested; at least there is no concrete detail, such as the presence of an adze, which can be related to the ceremony. Like Martin Nilsson, C.R. Long has zealously compared other evidence from Crete and Mycenae. So did A.W. Persson,[26] but in his case and that of Nilsson there was a readiness to accept the palpable pointers to Egypt.

Such pointers are available in numerous other facets of religion,[27] although it is by no means a wholesale take-over of one religion by another. A blissful afterlife seems to follow the Egyptian pattern, but in that pattern it is contingent on success in the tribunal. If we ask whether the Minoan funerary tradition provides evidence of this idea, we seem at first to face a blank. In the case of Egypt the evidence was most fully presented in a papyrus of the *Book of the Dead*; in addition, representations on coffins and on mummy cartonnage often depicted the weighing of the heart. I shall refer later to a possible Mycenaean expression of this concept. At the moment the occurrence in Cretan religious imagery of the Egyptian cynocephalus ape is worth noting. The adorant posture of the raised arms or forelegs is several times represented.[28] Another specimen on a gold signet-ring from the necropolis of Phaestos may add a more significant feature. Here there is another adorant in the form of a female votary with raised hands, and both are facing a pillar or column in front of which is a seated figure of the Minoan goddess. Above the cynocephalus is a plume-like object in which Arthur Evans saw a further link with an Egyptian original. 'This', he says, 'is the ostrich feather of Maat, the Goddess of Truth and Justice, the weighing of which against the heart of the deceased it was the special function of the Cynocephalus to observe.'[29] The Minoans were not familiar with the Egyptian dog-ape and perhaps they borrowed details which they but faintly understood. Can we really believe that Thoth as an assistant judge of the dead is implied here? A necropolis of course suits the theme, but the plume-like object which is floating in the air above the dog-ape is not easily con-

---

[26] *New Tombs at Dendra near Midea* (Lund, 1942), 176 ff. ('Mycenae and Egypt').

[27] Cf. my unpubl. Liverpool Diss., 'The Influence of Ancient Egypt on Greek and Mycenaean religious cults before the Hellenistic age' (1936), where I was probably too ready to accept the many suggestions of this character made in *The Palace of Minos* by Sir Arthur Evans.

[28] Evans, *Palace of Minos*, II, 763; cf. D.G. Hogarth, 'Zakro Sealings', *JHS* 22 (1902), 78, Fig. 4 et alia.

[29] Evans, *Palace of Minos*, II, 764; cf. Nilsson, *M.M. Rel.*, 257 with Fig. 125; also 346 and 370–71.

nected with the feather of Maat; nor do the Egyptian judgement scenes supply a close parallel, for as a Recorder of the weighing Thoth is normally shown with an ibis-head; he appears often as a baboon seated on the centre of the balance, but Maat is otherwise represented. Occasionally he is shown as a seated baboon who is surveying the process in company with the goddess Maat with her ostrich-feather;[30] the latter attribute would not be out of place with him, for he is shown writing the sign.[31] But the identity of the object on the Phaestos ring is in doubt.

A clearer body of evidence comes from the symbolic scales found in tombs.

2. *Symbolic Scales*

Scales of thin gold plate or of bronze have been discovered in tombs. Although the Mavrospilio cemetery near Knossos[32] provided some of the evidence, the sites concerned were mostly in mainland Greece—Mycenae, Vafio, Dendra, Myrsinochorion, Prosymna, Argos, and Pylos.[33] The Third Shaft Grave at Mycenae produced the gold example, which was also more elaborate in other ways. If the Vafio prince had with him only 'bronze discs of scale pans',[34] that betokens a style at once humbler and sturdier, but a cogent interpretation will have to cover all the examples. Unlike the larger vases and swords found in these tombs, the scales are all smaller in size than any which might figure in actual use. Many give the impression of being tiny models. In this simple sense they are all symbolic scales, although a practical connection is not thereby eliminated, as in the theory of J. Svoronos that the Mycenae gold balances are models of the instruments used to weigh gold as a form of currency.[35]

These examples were discovered by Schliemann himself and they include figures of butterflies embossed on gold discs and attached by means of perforation through the upper ends to small chains. In their wings they have eyes and they are enclosed in the golden scales. The beams of these scales consist of tubes of thin gold plate,

---

[30] Christine Seeber, *Untersuchungen*, Abb. 3.
[31] Ibid. 31, 32. In one instance, Abb. 26, the threatening monster has the feather perched on his head.
[32] Evans, *Palace of Minos*, II, 556; III, 150–54.
[33] Emily Vermeule, *Greece in the Bronze Age* (Chicago, 1964), 298 and 349 n. 7, citing more than twenty examples in all.
[34] Ibid. 298.
[35] A theory cited by Nilsson, *M.-M. Rel.*, 47 with n. 43. There was no need, surely, to have balances of gold in order to weigh gold.

which are attached to the scales by long, thin straps of gold. One pair of scales has a floral decoration, while the other represents butterflies which have large, tapering bodies and wings divided symmetrically.[36] Schliemann[37] did not hesitate to posit a symbolical meaning, stressing that the objects were found in a grave. He makes a vague and brief reference to wall-paintings in Egyptian tombs, 'in which are weighed the good and bad deeds of the deceased' (this is not strictly correct), but prefers to cite in analogy the *psychostasia* as it occurs in Homer (*Il.* 22.209–13; cf. 8.69 ff.), where scales are said to be used by Zeus to weigh the fates of Hector and Achilles. In these scales were placed *the two lots of death, the prostrator*. The result is that *down sank Hector's day of doom, and fell to Hades*. What is most attractive, perhaps, in the analogy is that Homer describes them as *golden scales*, exactly fitting the Mycenaean find.

Sir Arthur Evans supported this interpretation and explained the butterflies as symbols of the soul, comparing their presence, with a chrysalis (twice), on a large gold signet-ring, the so-called 'Ring of Nestor', which was found at Kakovatos. If the authenticity of the latter object is suspect, Arthur Evans properly reminds us that the Greeks sometimes used the word *psychê*, 'soul', to mean 'a butterfly'. Aristotle (*Hist. An.* 551ᵃ14) does this in a passage where he describes the development of the butterfly from caterpillar and chrysalis. Again, works of art which illustrate the legend of Cupid and Psyche show Psyche with the wings of a butterfly, or indeed simply as a butterfly.[38] Some have firmly rejected any symbolical interpretation of the golden scales from Mycenae, arguing that they 'are simply to be looked upon as a gift just as necessary to the housewife in her grave as sword and drinking-cup are to the man in his.'[39] (The grave belongs to three women and two infants.) The trouble here is that the scales are so very small and fragile; they could have been of no earthly use in a domestic sense.[40] Of course the argument could be sustained, as we have already remarked, by seeing them as mere models. Other occurrences in mainland and Cretan tombs concern balances mostly of bronze which are not equipped

---

[36] Ibid. Pl. 47 A; cf. A.J.B. Wace, *Chamber Tombs at Mycenae* (Oxford, 1932), 37 and 173 f. (with the refs. to Tell el-Amarna).

[37] *Mycenae* (London, 1878), 197, Figs. 301–2.

[38] R. Merkelbach, *Roman und Mysterium in der Antike* (Munich, 1962), 27 with Taf. I–III.

[39] C. Schuchardt, *Schliemann's Excavations* (London, 1891), 206.

[40] Cf. Charles Picard, *Les Religions préhelléniques (Crète et Mycènes)* (Paris, 1948), 290, where the connection with the Egyptian *psychostasia* is accepted.

with butterflies, and in their case it is hard to press the idea of a *post-mortem* judgement unless a kind of 'hieroglyphic' sense is automatically attached to them.[41] What favours an affinity with Egypt in such a situation is the time-factor: the Egyptian *psychostasia* was at the height of its influence in the second half of the second millennium B.C., which is the period involved. On the other hand, no identity of symbolism can be maintained in all the details. It is true that a form of the soul or manifestation of it is often represented in Egypt as the *ba*, a human-headed bird, and sometimes a man's *ba* is depicted above the scene of the weighing of the heart; it is shown, for instance, in the Papyrus of Ani above the scale in which the heart appears. The butterfly is the mark of a different tradition, clearly, but what is puzzling at Mycenae is that it appears in both the scales. Perhaps the identity of the scales implies that the soul is shown in two aspects, the good and the bad.

If Homer is half a millennium later, the parallel may be closer with him in that the two scales hold similar, if not identical, figures. They are the figures of warriors engaged in mortal combat. The presiding god is always Zeus, and we are told that he uses his golden scales to compare the impending fates or death-daemons (*kêres*) of the Trojan and Greek armies (*Il.* 8.69 ff.); the result is that *down sank the Greeks' day of doom*, whereas the fate of the Trojans was lifted up towards heaven. This is not, of course, the final verdict, and the passage may well be a weak doublet of the account of the weighing which concerns Hector and Achilles (*Il.* 22.209 ff.) and to which we have already referred. The collective application, to Greeks and Trojans, is a rare concept, and this is one of the obvious differences from the Egyptian tradition. Again, the Homeric weighing has no ethical content at all; it is concerned simply with the fate of the heroes who are fighting one against the other. One is to die; the other will live. It has to do in the first place with this world, not the next. In a sense, of course, the Egyptian idea involves one's fate—the ultimate fate after death. As for the relationship between Zeus and the fate of men, it would probably be wrong to interpret his resort to the scales as implying that he himself is ruled by fate.[42] The balance is rather his instrument of expressing his will. On the other hand, it is hard to believe that the weighing is introduced merely to heighten the dramatic effect. It is much more likely to derive from religious belief and imagery.

---

[41] Picard, ibid. Cf. A.W. Persson, *New Tombs at Dendra near Midea* (Lund, 1942), 73 f.
[42] Cf. B.C. Dietrich, *Death, Fate and the Gods* (London, 1965), 294 ff.

There are formal resemblances that recall the Egyptian tradition. In Homer the scale which proves the heavier bears the unfortunate loser, and this rather strange feature is found too in the Egyptian pattern, as we have seen. When Vergil describes (*Aen.* 12.725) the fates of Aeneas and Turnus being weighed, he is of course following Homer and reproduces the same Egyptian detail, for the scale that sinks denotes death. Homer is followed too by Milton in *Paradise Lost* (4, 996 ff.) when he describes *Th' Eternal* hanging forth *his golden scales*, with the result that Satan's scale *kicked the beam*, indicating that he was *weighed and shown how light, how weak*. It is perhaps typical of Milton that he begins the episode with a Homeric touch, but continues with an impress of the Book of Daniel.

Homer says in one place (*Il.* 16.658) that Hector knew the *scales of Zeus*, that is, he sensed how fate was working, and upon the death of Sarpedon, he therefore fled. Mention is made elsewhere (*Il.* 19.223) of how Zeus, the *disposer of wars, inclines the scales*. Yet this makes a total of only four allusions in Homer to this idea. By way of contrast the relevant representations in Greek art are fairly numerous. They are mostly vase-paintings, and on a jar which is now in Paris[43] the weighing is depicted as being conducted by the god Hermes. In the scales are two small figures of armed warriors, perhaps Achilles and Hector, as Homer has described. On the right is a woman looking on rather excitedly; we cannot be sure who she is, but she must presumably be a goddess. On the left, surveying the ceremony, is the god Zeus, holding his sceptre and thunderbolt. In Homer it is Zeus himself who is said to hold the balance, but here the disposition of the gods distinctly recalls the Egyptian order. Zeus corresponds in function to the presiding judge Osiris, whereas Hermes has the role assigned in Egypt to Anubis or Thoth. The goddess who shows keen interest recalls the role of Maat.

A feature of the Greek vase-paintings is that the most popular subject is the weighing of the figures of Achilles and Memnon, a theme that also points to the direction of Egypt, for Memnon was the King of the Ethiopians. Indeed a later Alexandrian tradition regarded him as an Egyptian. Memnon's mother was said to be Eos, goddess of the dawn, and in some of the scenes which depict the warrior-souls of Achilles and Memnon being weighed, Eos is

---

[43] Brandon, *Judgment of the Dead*, 79, Fig. 5; Ernst Wüst, *Arch. Rel.* 36 (1939), 164, No. 3. In this study ('Die Seelenwägung in Griechenland und Ägypten') Wüst takes the view that while the Greek *psychostasia* in general derives from Egypt, the Mycenaean balances are unconnected with the theme. See also his 'Psychostasie', *PW* 23.2 (1959), 1439–58.

shown in a pleading posture. Perhaps she is the goddess on the jar in Paris. According to a piece of an epic now largely lost, the *Aethiopis*, she is imploring Zeus to confer immortality on her son.[44] This lost epic was probably earlier than Homer, and it seems to have provided the theme of a play by Aeschylus, which is also lost, but which bore the significant title *Psychostasia*. What has not been hitherto noticed[45] is that if Eos is pleading for the grant of immortality to her son, then the theme of the *psychostasia* is much nearer to that of the Egyptian tradition because it is now concerned with life after death. However, the mother of Achilles, Thetis is sometimes depicted as well, and in such a case the mothers must clearly be pleading for the victory which means life in this world.

A Mycenaean amphora which was found in a chamber tomb at Enkomi in Cyprus and is dated to about 1300 B.C. depicts two persons in a horse-drawn chariot. In front of the horse stands another person who is holding a balance in one hand; a fourth person near the horse is equipped as a warrior. The identity and role of the figure who holds the balance are crucial to the interpretation. According to Nilsson[46] 'the only satisfactory interpretation is that Zeus is the person represented, taking the scales of Destiny in order to determine the fate of the combatants.' The difficulty is that Zeus is normally depicted with the thunderbolt; the figure shown here has no distinguishing attribute and he is dressed like the two in the chariot. Is he just a 'steward' of the deceased man's household?[47] Such a view robs the picture of meaning for the afterlife. The balances found in tombs cannot easily be explained in this retrospective fashion; their symbolism points to a weighing of the souls after death.

3. *The Evidence of Linear B*

If the lack of concomitant texts, or even captions, restricts the study of the archaeology of Crete and Mycenae in its religious aspects, the work on the Linear B script by Ventris, Chadwick and others since 1952 has ostensibly opened up another source of information, at least for the period 1450–1200 B.C. It is true that the inventories

---

[44] G. Kinkel, *Epic. Graec. Fr.* (1877), I. 33. According to Plutarch, *De aud. poet.* 2, 17 A, Thetis, the mother of Achilles, and Eos, the mother of Memnon, are both pleading for their sons who are fighting.

[45] Not even by Ernst Wüst, who has ably elucidated the Egyptian affinities of the theme.

[46] *M.-M. Rel.*, 36 with Fig. 1 on p. 35.

[47] Thus Evans, *Palace of Minos*, IV, 659 and Picard, *Les Rel. préhelléniques*, 290.

of objects thus usually presented are not concerned much with religion[48] save when deities are named as the recipients of offerings. These are said to include Zeus, Hera, Poseidon, Athena Potnia, Artemis, and Eileithyia.[49] Poseidon is especially prominent, as opposed to Zeus.[50] A title *wa-na-ka-te, The Queen*, occurs,[51] and Palmer[52] remarks that this designation is 'widespread in the ancient Near East as the cult title of the Mother Goddess'—a rather facile and vague parallel, although he goes on to mention her 'youthful consort' (e.g. Adonis). More distinctive is the use of the term *wanax, King*, in conjunction with *wa-na-so-i, for the Two Queens* (Pylos, Fr. 1227 and 1235), and Palmer (ibid.) ventures to compare the combination with the ivory from Mycenae which Charles Picard[53] interprets as portraying a male infant with two associated goddesses—the two Eleusinian goddesses, Demeter and Persephone, and the child Dionysus or Triptolemus. Nilsson[54] has questioned whether goddesses are shown, while Mylonas[55] has vigorously challenged the interpretation. If we revert to the Linear B text, it is disconcerting to find that John Chadwick, after all (*Documents*, 479), feels that 'it is clearly simpler to regard *wa-na-so-i* as the address, a locative plural indicating the name of the shrine or locality'.[56] In that case there is no reason to connect the text with the ivory triad from Mycenae.

---

[48] John Chadwick, *Documents in Mycenaean Greek* (2nd Ed., Cambridge, 1973; the 1st Ed. was by Ventris and Chadwick, Cambridge, 1956).

[49] Ibid. 125–9. Dionysus occurs, but with no indubitably divine status: pp. 127 and 411. See also Chadwick on 'What do we know about Mycenaean Religion?', *Linear B: a 1984 Survey*, ed. A. Morpurgo Davies and Y. Duhoux (Louvain-la-Neuve, 1985), 191–202, with its appeal for 'greater caution' (p. 201).

[50] Cf. L.R. Palmer, *The Interpretation of Mycenaean Greek Texts* (Oxford 1963), 103; and id. *Mycenaeans and Minoans* (2nd Ed., London, 1965), 130–42.

[51] On tablets from Knossos and Pylos, Chadwick, *Documents*, 589 with refs.

[52] *Interpretation* etc. 249.

[53] *Les Religions préhelléniques*, 83 and 244. For the ivory itself see A.J.B. Wace, *Mycenae* (Princeton, 1949), Pl. 103 with pp. 83 ff. where he takes them as 'mother, daughter, and boy' and as recalling 'at once the Eleusinian trinity'; also G.E. Mylonas, *Mycenae and the Mycenaean Age* (Princeton, 1966), Fig. 129. The boy seems to be carrying the Egyptian forelock which typifies childhood and raises a finger in the manner of Harpocrates. If the prototype is Egyptian, the figures must be Isis, Nephthys and Harpocrates, a common triad. The dress of the two goddesses, however, as Wace shows, is typically Mycenaean. For Egyptian influence on Mycenaean burials in hints of mummification and the use of 'false doors' see Spyridon Marinatos, *Crete and Mycenae* (London, 1960), 82; cf. Frank H. Stubbings, *Prehistoric Greece* (London, 1972), 28 (artistic motifs). More speculative is the theory of Marinatos, ibid., about Mycenaeans who had fought in Egypt and brought gold therefrom.

[54] *M.-M. Rel.*, xxiv and 314 n. 20.

[55] Op. cit. 155–6.

[56] Cf. Monique Gérard-Rousseau, *Les mentions religieuses dans les tablettes Myce-*

I have devoted some attention to this debate in order to show that Linear B texts are not likely to further the present investigation into the eschatology of Minoan and Mycenaean religion and its possible evidence for divine judgement. The evidence is mainly archaeological and the texts do not accompany the objects. There is one shining exception, nonetheless, which enlightens this gloom, although it is not linked to archaeological evidence: tablets at Knossos allude to *Erinys* in a way which Chadwick[57] thinks may support 'the theory that the Mycenaeans too believed in retribution in an afterlife'. The name occurs three times at Knossos, in the forms *e-ri-nu* and *e-ri-nu-we*.[58] In the first instance an offering of oil is involved; otherwise the contexts are not revealing. The first instance belongs to a series in which each tablet begins with the name of the month; perhaps, then, part of a ritual calendar, or simply store-room dockets relating to the distribution of oil, although the recipients dramatically include the Dictaean Zeus, the Daidaleion, all the gods, Erinys, and the priestess of the winds.[59] That Erinys as a goddess of retribution is intended here seems likely.[60] At this point, at the same time, we have to note a contradiction in the authoritative remarks by John Chadwick. He is the soul of caution, apropos of the allusions to Erinys in the Knossos tablets, in stressing, as we have noted, that these mentions 'might be used to support, though they will not prove, the theory that the Mycenaeans too believed in retribution in an afterlife'. It seems to me that he is throwing caution to the winds in using the phrase 'in an afterlife'. There is not the slightest evidence that Erinys here, any more than the other gods mentioned, is being associated with the

---

niennes (Rome, 1968), 240 ('une notation de lieu'); J.T. Hooker, *Linear B: An Introduction* (Bristol, 1980), 154 ('at the (place of the) *wanax*' or 'the locative of a place-name').

[57] *Linear B: A 1984 Survey*, 193 ('What do we know about Mycenaean Religion?')

[58] (1) KN Fp 1.8 = p. 182 in J. Chadwick, J.T. Killen and J.-P. Olivier, *The Knossos Tablets* (4th Ed., Cambridge, 1971) and No. 1 in *Corpus of Mycenaean Inscriptions from Knossos*, Vol. I, ed. J. Chadwick, L. Godart, J.T. Killen, J.-P. Olivier, A. Sacconi and I.A. Sakellarakis (Cambridge, 1986); (2) Fh 390 = p. 173 in *The Knossos Tablets* and No. 390 in the *Corpus*; (3) *e-ri-nu-we* in V 52, *latus inferius*, on p. 316 of *The Knossos Tablets* and No. 52, *lat. inf.*, in the *Corpus*. Chadwick observes in *Documents*, 127, that it was Furumark who proposed *Erinys* as the interpretation of *e-ri-nu*, which is 'apparently dative'.

[59] Palmer, *Interpretation*, 235–7. On p. 237 he surmises that the oil was 'intended for ritual anointing'. Chadwick, *Documents*, 307, notes that in addition to her function as an avenging deity, Erinys appears as an epithet of Demeter in Arcadia (Pausanias, 8.25.6) and in Hesychius as an image of Aphrodite. On Demeter Erinys see above, Chapter 2, Section 2.

[60] Cf. Alfred Heubeck, *Aus der Welt der frühgriechischen Lineartafeln* (Göttingen, 1966), 98. Monique Gérard-Rousseau, *Les mentions religieuses*, 104, remains uncertain.

afterlife; they are all recipients of oil, doubtless for ritual purposes, but there is nothing funerary in the context. As far as the living cult was concerned, the idea of retribution was probably applied to this life, although what precisely the goddess meant to these worshippers is beyond our information. In much later Greek thought the Erinyes were believed to operate in this world and the next.[61]

4. *The Minoan Judges of the Dead*

It is certainly from later Greek thought that we derive part of the evidence about Minoan ideas of the judgement of the dead. Far removed in time from the era of Crete's flowering as a culture, it yet contains ancient traditions which relate to that culture. It also points to the enduring impact of that culture on one stratum of Greek thought.

The most celebrated king of Crete was Minos, whose name perhaps became titular in force, like 'Pharaoh' or 'Caesar'. In the Eleventh Book of the *Odyssey* Odysseus visits Hades and his encounter there with the spirits of the dead conforms with the traditional picture of Hades as a state of gloomy semi-existence. But a further encounter reveals Minos, *the radiant son of Zeus*, seated on his throne and holding a golden sceptre. He is dealing out judgement to the dead. (*Od.* 11.568–71.) The punishment of three particular sinners is then described: Tityus is being gnawed by vultures, Tantalus is tormented by water and fruit which he cannot reach, and Sisyphus is rolling a big stone up a hill only to find that it constantly comes down again. All this is very different from Homer's normal approach to life after death. Nowhere else does he suggest a doctrine of posthumous punishment,[62] although in one passage, as we have noted earlier, he does describe the Elysium which is the reward of a happpy and just *élite*.

Many scholars, including W.B. Stanford (ad loc.) regard the account of the judgement in the *Odyssey* as a later interpolation derived from Orphic sources. What is odd is that a similar suggestion is not usually made about the description of Elysium. Clearly the one passage is the counterpart of the other: the one depicts the punishment of the wicked, the other the reward of the just. Whereas the two passages run counter to the Greek idea of Hades,

---

[61] Cf. above, Chapter 2, Section 2.
[62] In *Il.* 3.279 men who take false oaths are said to be punished in the underworld; and in *Il.* 19.259–60 the punishment is ascribed to the Erinyes; the latter allusion might support Chadwick's remarks on Erinys in the Knossos tablets.

which Homer normally presents, they both have the stamp of a Cretan origin, and beyond that the impress of Egyptian ideas of Heaven and Hell. One development which differs from the Egyptian prototype is that the ideas apply only to a select few, and not to men in general.

It is Plato who eventually gives the most elaborate expression to this concept. At the end of the *Republic* the myth of Er tells how the souls of the dead are subject to a judgement which is based on a scrutiny of their lives. For each misdeed a tenfold penalty is exacted, and a similar scale is applied to rewards. The examination is related to records which the souls carry with them, a detail which recalls the *Book of the Dead* in Egypt. Plato here refers to judges in the plural, but he does not name them. In the *Apology* (41 A) and elsewhere he does name them, and prominent among them are Minos and Rhadamanthys, a clear sign that we are dealing with the same tradition. There are many diverse elements, admittedly, in the Orphic amalgam of ideas to which Plato was attracted, but the concept of judgement was probably of Minoan, and ultimately Egyptian, origin. The same ultimate origin has been claimed for another element of Orphic teaching. According to the Orphic writings the world took its beginning from a huge primeval egg which was fertilized by the wind; and it has been shown that this idea is found in Egypt, although it occurs also in the Iranian tradition.[63] Plato's account of the process of judgement invites comparison with that conveyed by Vergil in the Sixth Book of his *Aeneid*. To some extent Vergil is following Homer, for he describes in some detail the penalties inflicted on prominent wrongdoers. In spite of this detail he makes it quite clear, as Plato does, that the judgement concerns everyone, and this is true of the developed pattern transmitted from Egypt. Vergil tells us that the judge is Rhadamanthys of Knossos, who wields pitiless power:

Gnosius haec Rhadamanthus habet durissima regna
(Vergil, *Aen.* 6.566.)

We are told that he compels everyone to confess the sins which he left unatoned in the world above. In another passage (432) Minos is named as the judicial investigator who calls the dead together and learns of their lives and the accusations brought against them.

Both Vergil and Plato enounce the doctrine of the Two Ways.

---

[63] See S. Morenz, 'Ägypten und die altorphische Kosmogonie' in *Aus Antike und Orient: FS.W. Schubart* (Leipzig, 1950), 64–111; cf. my *Plutarch's De Iside et Osiride*, 478; and Martin L. West, *The Orphic Poems* (Oxford, 1983).

The Sibyl tells Aeneas, when they have reached a certain place in the underworld, that two paths lie ahead:

> It is here that the way splits into two paths; one track, on the right, goes straight to mighty Pluto's battlements and by it we make our journey to Elysium; and the other, to the left, brings evil men to godless Tartarus, and, with never a pause, exacts their punishment.
>
> (*Aen.*, 6.540–43; tr. W.F.J. Knight.)

Similarly in Plato's *Republic* (614 C), when judgement has been given, the just are ordered to take the path to the right, which leads to heaven, while the unjust are bidden to take the path to the left, which leads below. Orphic writings inscribed on pieces of gold leaf which derive from the Greek cities of Southern Italy (probably fourth century B.C. in date) show a similar emphasis: the way to the left in the House of Hades is inauspicious, but the deified dead is exhorted to *proceed on the path to the right to the sacred meadows and groves of Persephone*.[64] Both allusions imply a sequel of judgement, and it has been shown (Chapter 9, 7 (2)) that in Egyptian texts the justified dead are similarly committed to the path on the right, which is equated with the bliss of the West, whereas the damned are sent to the left.[65] Precisely the same allocation is found in the Gospel of Matthew (25:33) and it often figures in depictions of judgement in medieval Christian art.

We have seen that Rhadamanthys is prominent as a judge of the dead. His Cretan qualifications, it should be noted, are impeccable. His name is plainly Cretan in origin, containing as it does the element *-nth-* as in Labyrinthos and Berekynthos; it belonged to the pre-Hellenic people, traces of whom are seen also in the Peloponnesian names Hyakinthos and Korinthos.[66] Homer connects him with Crete by naming him in the list of the consorts of Zeus as a son of Zeus and Europa and brother of Minos (*Il.* 14.321 ff.); and Pausanias (8.53.5) states that the old Spartan poet Cinaethon was succeeded genealogically by Cres, Talus, Hephaestus, Rhadamanthys, and Gortys. If Malten's probable emendation into Phaestos is accepted, this means that Rhadamanthys was locally associated

---

[64] G. Zuntz, *Persephone* (Oxford, 1971), 328 ff. and 358 ff.

[65] Zuntz, op. cit. 376 n. 1, although he recognizes other Egyptian analogies in the inscriptions from Southern Italy, is strangely obtuse to the importance of this point. See also M.L. West, *Early Greek Philosophy and the Orient* (Oxford, 1971), 65 f.

[66] L. Malten, 'Elysion und Rhadamanthys', *Jb. des Deutschen Arch. Inst.* 28 (1913), 37. Cf. Nilsson, *M.-M. Rel.*, 623, who goes on to dwell on the connection with Egypt, an idea rejected by Christian Froidefond, *Le Mirage Égyptien* (Aix-en-Provence, 1971), 40–41; cf. my remarks in *CR* 26 (1976), 56 f.

with the south Cretan town of Phaestos. While he is sometimes connected through Europa, his mother, with Boeotia,[67] his son Erythrus is regarded as the founder of Erythrae, which was in part a Cretan colony.[68] Rhadamanthys, accordingly, was pre-eminently Minoan.

These Cretan judges of the dead do not seem to be associated with the *psychostasia* which appears in the balances found in tombs and in the Greek vase-paintings. Yet the general idea of the judgement of the dead as expressed in Egyptian tradition is probably embodied in them. The Homeric *psychostasia* appears to lack ethical colouring, thus differing basically from the Egyptian concept. Plato's depictions of judgement, on the other hand, have a strong ethical background, and we should remember that he was not unfamiliar with Egyptian religion. If the Cretan Elysium was borrowed from Egypt, it is likely that the moral conditions attached to it were not entirely jettisoned.

---

[67] Apollodorus, 2.70; 3.6.
[68] Pausanias, 7.3.7; cf. Diodorus Sic. 79.1; 84.3.

CHAPTER ELEVEN

POSTHUMOUS JUDGEMENT IN ISRAEL

Any concept of the divine which includes moral sovereignty is likely to lead to the belief that God or a god should be regarded as a judge of man's conduct during life in this world. Thus we read in Genesis 18:25: *Shall not the judge of all the earth do what is just?* and there follows the account of the destruction of Sodom and Gomorrah as an instance of judgement carried out in history. It is a further step to locate such a judgement in the life after death as a prerequisite and prelude to the continuation of a life which is regarded as immortal; at least such a step posits, to begin with, the belief that life after death is at all possible.

A third consideration will concern the particular expression given to the idea of judgement. The natural tendency, one would expect, would be to conceive of it as a court or tribunal or public examination, applying to the next world the practices followed in this one. In several ancient societies the processes of law-courts took the form of a dispute or litigation between contending parties and even in criminal cases the accusation at first lay with a private person. This was true of the early phase of Roman law, for instance; it was only later that the state became responsible for a wide range of criminal charges. In Egypt the idea of the judgement of the individual after death is as early as the Pyramid Texts (2340–2200 B.C.), and some of the first allusions seem to involve opposing parties in the court. (See above, Chapter 9, Section 2.) Eventually the weighing of the heart in the balance becomes the accepted symbol of the process, and an unexpected phenomenon is the remarkable stress on the importance of the individual. The weighing of the heart involves every single dead person, whatever his status. Egyptian society was for the most part highly centralized and yet this judgement highlights the individual. Here is a salutary warning that religion is not a mere reflex of sociology.

The picture of the balance[1] is found several times in the Old

---

[1] Cf. Paul Humbert, *Recherches sur les sources égyptiennes de la littérature sapientiale d'Israel* (Neuchâtel, 1929), 42; W.O.E. Oesterley, *The Wisdom of Egypt and the Old Testament* (London, 1927), 48 f. Other parallels are cited by H. Brunner in Walter Beyerlin (ed.), *Near Eastern Religious Texts relating to the Old Testament* (tr. J. Bowden, London, 1978), 49 ff.

Testament. We find allusions, to start with, that are literal and physical as in the injunction

> You shall have true scales, true weights, true measures...
> (Lev. 19:36.)

As in Amos 8:5 where mention is made of *tilting the scales fraudulently*, the negative idea is found in Proverbs 11:1: *False scales are the Lord's abomination*; cf. 20:23. Again Ezekiel (45:10) in urging the maintenance of law and justice says: *Your scales shall be honest, your bushel and your gallon shall be honest*. According to Proverbs 16:11 *scales and balances are the Lord's concern*. Although such statements are paralleled in the Wisdom of Amenemope, the Hebrew dicta do not here involve the idea of judgement. Some of them indeed, even if they have a touch of symbolism, suggest simply a kind of divine Inspector of Weights and Measures.

Rather different is the metaphorical application of the image in a moral sense, and this may be happening in three passages in Proverbs:

> A man's whole conduct may be pure in his own eyes,
> but the Lord fixes a standard for the spirit of man.
> (Prov. 16:2.)

> A man may think that he is always right,
> but the Lord fixes a standard for the heart.
> (Prov. 21:2.)

> God, who fixes a standard for the heart, will take note,
> God, who watches you—be sure he will know;
> he will requite every man for what he does.
> (Prov. 24:12.)

The expressions about 'fixing a standard' are based on the verb תָכַן, 'regulate, measure, estimate', and several occurrences denote 'measuring out', as, for instance, of silver: see *BDB* (1907), 1067; Koehler (1953), 1028–9; Fohrer (1971), 300. 'Measuring hearts' or 'measuring spirits' might recall the fact that in the Egyptian *psychostasia* it is the heart that is weighed, although the Hebrew words are doubtless used in a less sharply visualized sense.[2] The general idea is that God knows the inner thoughts of man and assesses them.[3] Berend Gemser[4] would deny that the verb תָכַן allows the concept of weighing, since שָׁקַל is normally used

---

[2] Cf. A.D. Power, *Side Lights on the Book of Proverbs* (London, 1950), 29 ff.

[3] Cf. Helmer Ringgren, ad loc. (Göttingen, 1962), 68. Glendon E. Bryce, *The Legacy of Wisdom* (London, 1979), 158, finds the contrast drawn between man's evaluation of his moral standard and the right judgement of God reminiscent of

for this idea; however, in his meanings for the former verb he gives 'regeln, anpassen, einstellen' and adds 'und vielleicht "messen"'. But in 2 Kings 12:11 the Puʻal form is used of 'measuring out' or 'checking' silver; and how can silver be measured out except by weighing it?[5] The writers of the Revised Standard Version clearly took this view; and in the passages quoted above they render *the Lord weighs the spirit* and *the Lord weighs the heart*. Indeed Gressmann[6] was hardly too confident in assigning the three phrases in Proverbs to the impact of the Egyptian *psychostasia*; to him the god who measures hearts or spirits (he ignores the variant) will be originally Thoth, who in the Egyptian representations examines the result of the weighing and records it. A conscious and specific allusion to Thoth may be questioned. But a general factor which favours the recognition of this background is that a part of Proverbs shows the influence of the Egyptian Wisdom of Amenemope.[7]

1. *The Lack of a Posthumous Application*

In spite of the debt thus strongly suggested, it may be doubted whether a stage in a future life is envisaged. The confident statement that God *will requite every man for what he does* (Prov. 24:12) probably implies compensation in the present life. If there is no full-hearted belief in life after death, there is obviously no place for a judgement of the life-record. One could envisage, admittedly, even without a belief in immortality, importance being given to a retrospective record of a man's life. Whereas Hebrew religion from the first shows a lively interest in historical records in a communal and theological sense, the custom of providing a tomb with an inscribed record of a man's life was absent; its presence in Egypt proved to be the origin of autobiography as a literary form. Even so, without a belief in an afterlife, the act of recording lacks the motive which concerns us. Among the factors which contributed to the Egyptian concept of a tribunal after death was a mania for

---

Amenemope, 19, 18–21; for a version of the latter locus see Lichtheim, *Lit.* II, 157–8.

[4] *Sprüche Salomos* (2nd Ed., Tübingen, 1963), 70; cf. W. McKane (London, 1970), 496.

[5] G.R. Driver, *VT* 1 (1951), 243, argues for an original meaning of 'fixed, adjusted'. A connection with weighing is not excluded.

[6] *Israels Spruchweisheit im Zusammenhang der Weltliteratur* (Berlin, 1925), 32.

[7] Ronald Williams in *The Legacy of Egypt* ed. J.R. Harris (2nd Ed., Oxford, 1971), 277 ff. A reversal of roles was favoured by Drioton and others, who saw Israel as the original source. A magisterial reply by R. Williams appeared in *JEA* 47 (1961), 100–106; cf. Derek Kidner, *Proverbs* (Leicester, 1964), 24 and W. McKane (London, 1970), 371.

registering and recording everything, an obsession that seems to have survived into modern times, as anyone who has visited Egypt will have noted. The idea is not completely absent from the Hebrew tradition. In Genesis 15:6 it is said of Abraham's faith in Yahweh that it is *counted to him as righteousness*:

> Abram put his faith in the Lord, and the Lord counted that faith to him as righteousness.
>
> (Gen. 15:6.)

Gerhard von Rad[8] has pointed out that although the second clause looks at first sight like a carefully-thought theological formula, there is a statement in Leviticus 7:18 which suggests rather a priestly dictum related to a ritual act. It is there said that if the flesh of the sacrifice of peace offerings be eaten on the third day, instead of on the first or second, then *it shall not be accepted, neither shall it be counted to him*. It suggests a process of priestly accountancy, with a formal statement accompanying the acceptance of the offering. Von Rad goes on to argue convincingly that in Genesis 15:6, which speaks of faith being 'counted to a person as righteousness', the priestly formula is now applied, perhaps unconsciously, to a spiritual state.

Such a moral or spiritual reckoning, however, applies only to this life, and we look in vain for any clear evidence that early Hebrew religion embraced a belief in immortality. Rowley in his *Faith of Israel* (1956), 155, states rather emphatically that 'there is no evidence that it was ever part of the faith of Israel that a man wholly ceased to be when his body was laid in the grave.' He then stresses the great care taken over the burial of the body and the fact that the dead are represented as being in Sheol; he states too (p. 156) that 'necromancy implies a belief that the dead still exist.' These features remind one of the cheerless prospect offered by early Greek religion; there may be differences between Sheol and Hades, but neither is an attractive goal. Aubrey R. Johnson[9] describes Sheol as 'this foul region of virtual annihilation'.

We have seen that Proverbs is a work deeply infused with Egyptian Wisdom. That is true not only of the part borrowed from Amenemope but of several others, as William McKane shows in a Commentary (1970) which includes a fine *exposé* of 'International Wisdom' (pp. 51–208). He is not entirely consistent, admittedly,

---

[8] 'Die Anrechnung des Glaubens zur Gerechtigkeit', *Gesammelte Studien zum Alten Testament* (Munich, 1958, this essay from 1951), 129–35. Cf. his Comm. on Genesis (1956, tr. J.H. Marks, London, 1961), 179 f.

[9] *The Vitality of the Individual in the Thought of Ancient Israel* (Cardiff, 1949), 93.

in his treatment of the evidence. In 16:2, where he translates *but it is Yahweh who weighs up motives*, he finds (p. 496) 'no echo' of a judgement associated with Thoth, but in 24:12, where he renders

> will not the one who weighs up motives get at the truth? He who watches over you will know about it, and he will repay every man for what he has done.

he sees (p. 402) a possible 'element of truth' in this interpretation. It is not, he thinks, that judgement after death is thought of; rather 'the justice of Yahweh which is envisaged is ultimate rather that immediate' and 'in the long run the truth about a man's worth will emerge.' This is an attractive formulation.

If a vigorous belief in immortality is not presented by early Hebrew religion, it would seem to follow that, when such a belief does emerge, it must be the result of influence from outside: Rowley (op. cit. 160 ff.) points out that in a later phase of Old Testament teaching 'we find the beginnings of the thought of a richer and more worth-while survival in another world, and the growth of a belief in a resurrection to life on earth.' He goes on to say that 'both are sometimes traced to the influence of foreign thought, but it is more probable that neither was of foreign origin', adding that 'both emerged on distinctively Israelite lines.' The last statement, if applied generally, is often true of syncretistic processes, and indeed of borrowings in art and literature. Any virile and vital culture is sure to adapt and modify foreign influences in accord with its national genius. But when Rowley claims that these ideas of immortality were probably not of foreign origin, he appears to be contradicting his own previous portrayal of early Hebrew religion.

It was the religion of Canaan that was most adjacent and therefore the most likely source of outside influence in early periods. Some of the Hebrew psalms, as several scholars[10] have shown, reflect the feelings of the cultus personnel in the temple; and the end of Psalm 73, which dates from the post-exilic period, seems to express a hope for the afterlife:[11]

> thou dost guide me by thy counsel
> and afterwards wilt receive me with glory.
> Whom have I in heaven but thee?
> And having thee, I desire nothing else on earth.
>
> (Ps. 73:24–25.)

---

[10] Cf. G. von Rad, *Gesammelte Studien usw.* 225–47.

[11] The interpretation is denied by H. Gunkel (Göttingen, 1925), ad loc. Mowinckel, *Psalms*, II, 36, thinks that the individual, rather than Israel or the King, is implicated and that it is a song of thanksgiving for Yahweh's 'justifying aid'. J.H. Eaton (London, 1967), 185–6, senses an exegetical dilemma here and in verse 17.

Stripped of magic and mythology as this hope is, it may yet be indebted to the Canaanite religion which included, as Ezekiel (8:14) observed, the worship of Tammuz that had penetrated the temple of Yahweh. Tammuz was identified with both Adonis and Osiris, and each of these gods was regarded as achieving triumph over death.

One well-known locus in the Psalms mentions a judgement:

> So when judgement comes, the wicked shall not stand firm.
> (Ps. 1:5.)

Blackman,[12] following Gressmann,[13] claimed that there was a clear allusion here to posthumous judgement on the Osirian pattern. Oesterley, however, *ad loc.* (London, 1939, 121), avers that 'the thought is not that of the final Judgement;' and that 'the psalmist is dealing with present conditions, not with the world of the future, which belongs to Eschatology.' That seems to be the view of Mowinckel[14] too, who thinks that in this Psalm as in 112, we have the Jewish dogma of retributive justice—'piety will be rewarded and ungodliness punished in this earthly life.' Some difficulty remains with the 'judgement' referred to, if we accept this view. It will not be the process of an ordinary law-court, obviously; perhaps an abstract spiritualized tribunal is meant, or 'God's providential judgement in the course of human history'.[15] B. Gemser in the Rowley Festschrift (Leiden, 1955), 128, refers to the many Psalms which have judicial terminology, but thinks it is metaphorical. According to him, 'to interpret this class of Psalms as representing a real lawsuit and trial before a temple tribunal with decision by ordeal looks like a hermeneutic "transubstantiation," or substantializing of metaphor into reality.' But since the following, and parallel, dictum claims *nor shall sinners stand in the assembly of the righteous*, the idea may well be that God's judgement 'sifts the membership' and that the allusion is to 'ceremonies of admission and purging in the Temple assemblies'.[16]

Judicial terminology is also prominent in the Book of Job, and it is worth examining the kind of significance that is there implied.

---

[12] In D.C. Simpson (ed.), *The Psalmists* (Oxford, 1926), 195.
[13] *Israels Spruchweisheit usw.* 32.
[14] *Psalms*, II, 112. The ref. is to the translation by D.R. Ap-Thomas, *The Psalms in Israel's Worship* (Oxford, 1962). C.A. and E.G. Briggs (ICC, 1906), 6–7, explained it as 'Wicked men will not rise up, that is, in the resurrection which takes place in the Judgment, at the end of the age of the world.' They date the Psalm to the Greek period.
[15] A modern view cited by C.A. and E.G. Briggs ad loc. and rejected by them.
[16] J.H. Eaton, *Psalms* (London, 1967, repr. 1976), 30. Cf. above, 18.

2. The Book of Job

We have seen that an early form of the Egyptian belief was the possibility that one would have to face litigation after death in the manner of a civil dispute or of a law-suit involving an accuser.

Thus an appeal to Thoth reads as follows:[17]

> O Thoth, turn thy face towards me, vindicate me concerning my enemies . . . as thou didst vindicate Osiris against his enemies in the presence of the Great Council which is in Heliopolis, that night of the conflict against the enemies, the day of destroying the enemies of the Lord of the Universe.

A much-discussed passage in the Book of Job may invite comparison:

> But in my heart I know that my vindicator lives and that
> he will rise last to speak in court; and I shall discern
> my witness standing at my side and see my defending
> counsel, even God himself, whom I shall see with my
> own eyes, I myself and no other.
>
> (Job 19:25–27.)

The New English Bible brings out very plainly the judicial background of the passage, although it adds that the clause *I shall discern my witness standing at my side* is a 'probable reading' and that the Hebrew there, as it stands, is 'unintelligible'. It is also true that in verse 25 the term translated 'vindicator' derives from a verb גָּאַל which has a variety of meanings such as 'redeem, act as kinsman, redeem from bondage or exile, be an avenger of blood', but some of these actions involve legal procedures. We are dealing here, of course, with a difficult and corrupt text, and it has invited a vast extent of commentary. The weight of modern exegesis seems to favour the interpretation which points to a legal vindicator,[18] who is pledged by his position to protect the helpless kinsman. In this case the vindicator of Job seems to be God himself, although Samuel Terrien[19] has argued that in the sequel, far from proclaiming the honour and integrity of the hero, God inflicts greater

---

[17] J. Lieblein, *Le Livre égyptien Que Mon Nom Fleurisse* (Leipzig, 1895), No. XLIV. For similar passages see my *Conflict of Horus and Seth*, 75 ff.

[18] Cf. the Commentaries of Bernh. Duhm (Freiburg, 1897), 102; S.R. Driver and G.B. Gray (ICC, 1921), 172; Paul Dhorme (Paris, 1926), 256, also in H. Knight's translation (London, 1967), 282 f.; Paul Szczygiel (Bonn, 1931), 114. A.R. Johnson, 'The Primary Meaning of √גאל', *VTS* 1 (1953), 67–77, assigns the meaning 'protect' to the root, but seeks to connect it with the root √גאל, 'defilement', suggesting that 'cover' is the basic meaning present in both.

[19] *Job* (Neuchâtel, 1963), 151.

indignity on him. The vindicator is therefore, he urges, some one other than God, and he quotes an Ugaritic liturgical formula as a parallel:

> And I know that he lives, the powerful sovereign!
> He exists, the prince, the sovereign of the earth!

Or, as Cyrus H. Gordon[20] translates it:

> And I know that Aliyn Baal is alive,
> That the Prince, Lord of Earth, exists.

It is fairly clear that the Ugaritic text is referring to the achievement by Baal of life after death;[21] and one wonders whether Job is referring to any such idea. What is quite different in the Ugaritic text is the absence of any allusion to a vindicator or indeed to any judicial background. In spite of the resemblance in the opening phraseology, there is scarcely a valid parallel.

If the vindicator to whom Job is referring is not Yahweh, then who is he? Terrien (p. 151) says that Job is now abandoned by men and gods and anchors his hope on 'a divine being, endowed with eternal life', who will act as protector to him after his death. Robert Gordis[22] has attacked this idea of an independent mysterious figure who has the power to summon God and Job to judgement and to vindicate Job. He avers that 'the idea that there could be a being more powerful than God would be more than blasphemy to a Hebrew thinker— it would be the ultimate absurdity.' In his French Commentary, however, Terrien leaves the question fairly open. Indeed he goes on to admit that the Ugaritic parallel which he adduces has not been established and he proceeds to quote from the Egyptian text which is generally referred to as the *Lebensmüde*: *Why surely, he who is yonder will be a living god, punishing a sin of him who commits it . . . Why surely, he who is yonder will be a man of wisdom, not hindered from appealing to Re when he speaks!* (tr. J.A. Wilson, *ANET*³ 1969, 407.) The allusion to Rê probably implies a posthumous court, and Egyptian funerary texts are replete with appeals for vindication in this court. For instance:

---

[20] *The Loves and Wars of Baal and Anat* (Princeton, 1943), 10, lines 8–9; cf. Ch. Virolleaud, *Syria* 12 (1931), 213, lines 8–9 (Text 49, III); H.L. Ginsberg, *ANET*³ (1969), 140. For the verb *ydʻ*, 'know', see Gordon, *Ugaritic Textbook* (Rome, 1965), 409, No. 1080.

[21] Cf. Julian Obermann, *Ugaritic Mythology* (New Haven, 1948), xx; Robert Gordis, *The Book of God and Man* (Chicago, 1965), 60, says that the idea of immortality in the Ugaritic text would have been 'totally meaningless' to the Hebrew poet.

[22] Op. cit. 88.

Hail to you, Council of the gods, in which they judge this Osiris-N today, concerning what he said and did when he was ignorant and young (*var.* and happy) and carefree. Go around N, stand behind him. Osiris-N is vindicated against his enemies before Geb, the leader of the gods.

(De Buck, *Coffin Texts*, I, 24 a ff.)

The clause 'stand behind him' (25 a) recalls the meaning assigned by some scholars to וְאַחֲרוֹן[23] in verse 25 of Job 19. Yet in Egyptian thought the vindicator is not only present in the court; he is its president, and the deceased defendant is identified with him in name and experience.

The first chapter of the Book of Job refers (verse 6) to the members of the court of heaven taking their place in the presence of the Lord, Satan being among them. The Egyptian concept does not include a Satan; in later tradition the god Seth becomes a kind of Satan, but his original membership of the Ennead of Heliopolis does not imply such a rebellious status. On the other hand, the composite monster shown in the vignettes is the divine enemy who is ready to punish. Whether the Book of Job in the closing section of chapter 19 is taken to allude to a divine tribunal in the Egyptian manner depends partly on our estimation of the book's affinities in a general sense. Babylonian literature has been shown to contain compositions with a similar structure and sometimes with similarity of thought-content.[24] The pessimistic mood, at the same time, and the poetic inspiration are paralleled by the Egyptian *Lebensmüde*. Furthermore, Ronald Williams[25] has called attention to a number of clear traces of Egyptian influence, including allusions to the ostrich, crocodile and hippopotamus. Again, Gerhard von Rad[26] has compared the order in which things relating to heaven are listed in Job 38:12 ff. with that given in the Egyptian Onomasticon of Amenemope, which Gardiner edited. On a matter of style he has also compared the long series of rhetorical questions in Job 38

---

[23] Cf. 'Hintermann', cited by Dhorme (1926, 257), though rejected; see also W.B. Stevenson, *Critical Notes on the Hebrew Text of the Poem of Job* (Aberdeen, 1951), 86 f.

[24] See W.G. Lambert, *Babylonian Wisdom Literature* (Oxford, 1960), 21 ff. ('The Poem of the Righteous Sufferer'); also 63 ff. ('The Babylonian Theodicy') and 139 ff. ('The Dialogue of Pessimism'). See above Chapter 1, Section 4, for a fuller discussion.

[25] In *The Legacy of Egypt* (2nd Ed.), 282 ff.

[26] 'Hiob 38 und die altägyptische Weisheit' in his *Gesammelte Studien*, 262–7. A valuable exposition of aspects of Egyptian Wisdom is available in *Studien zu altägyptischen Lebenslehren*, ed. Erik Hornung and Othmar Keel (OBO 28; Freiburg, Schweiz, 1979) and in Miriam Lichtheim, *Late Egyptian Wisdom Literature in the International Context* (OBO 52; Freiburg, 1983).

with that found in P. Anastasi (*temp.* Ramesses II) in the section on Syria.²⁷ The comparison concerns the structure only, for the Egyptian passage conveys matter-of-fact details of geography, whereas the chapter in Job is sublime poetry.

In view of these affinities, may not the author of Job have followed also the Egyptian concept of a divine tribunal? It might seem difficult to locate such a tribunal in the hereafter, for elsewhere the idea of immortality appears to be rejected:

> If a tree is cut down,
> there is hope that it will sprout again, ...
> But a man dies, and he disappears.
>
> (Job 14:7 and 10.)

Yet it is instructive that among the parallels to which Ronald Williams has called attention are Egyptian texts which are funerary in character. He quotes the words of Harkhuf in the Sixth Dynasty:

> I gave bread to the hungry, clothing to the naked: I brought to land him who had no ferry-boat.
>
> (*Urk.* i, 122, 6–8.)

He then compares Job's claim to good deeds:

> Whoever heard of me spoke in my favour,
> and those who saw me bore witness to my merit,
> how I saved the poor man when he called for help
> and the orphan who had no protector ...
> I was eyes to the blind
> and feet to the lame;
> I was a father to the needy,
> and I took up the stranger's cause.
>
> (Job 29:11 ff.)

Perhaps the motives of the two statements are slightly different. Harkhuf's words are inscribed in his tomb and they include also a warning that passers-by should not interfere with it. But his main motive is given in the words *for I desired that it should be well with me in the presence of the Great God*—a clear reference to his hope that his good deeds will stand him in good stead when the day of judgement comes. Job, on the other hand, after replying to his friends, is delivering a monologue in which he justifies his conduct both to himself and to God. It is true that his attitude to God is partly one of rebuke:

---

²⁷ Von Rad, loc. cit. See also Humbert, *Recherches sur les sources égyptiennes etc.*, ch. 3. On p. 89 Humbert cites Job 26:11 (*the pillars of heaven*) as a likely Egyptianism. Certainly the image occurs often in Egyptian; cf. D. Kurth, *Den Himmel stützen* (Brussels, 1975).

> I call for thy help, but thou dost not answer:
> I stand up to plead, but thou sittest aloof.
>
> (Job 30:20.)

But in chapter 31 he is appealing to God as the judge and arbiter:

> What is the lot prescribed by God above,
> the reward from the Almighty on high?
> Is not ruin prescribed for the miscreant
> and calamity for the wrongdoer?
>
> (Job 31:2–3.)

Then comes the great 'Avowal of Integrity' which has been rightly compared with the 'Declarations of Innocence' found in Spell 125 of the *Book of the Dead*.[28] The term 'Negative Confession' was formerly used of the Egyptian material, and the same designation could be applied to the Hebrew statement, for in essence it is a series of denials. Gordis[29] refers to the Hebrew chapter as 'the code of the Jewish gentleman', and it may equally be said that this part of the *Book of the Dead*, whatever its immediate religious incentive, reflects the standard of morality accepted in Egypt as the ideal norm. Both Hebrew and Egyptian statements put the main emphasis on the ethical code, although they contain brief denials relating to ritual demands. Job, for instance, denies that he has worshipped the sun and the moon (31:26–27).

A further parallel is that each statement has a clearly juridical character. Spell 125 of the Book of the Dead[30] refers to *Words spoken when one enters the Hall of the Two Truths*. In the Book of Job the position seems to be a little complicated in this respect. There are several allusions to the law-courts of this world and their code of law. Adultery is described in verse 11 as *an offence before the law*, but the New English Bible regards this and the following verse as a late addition. In verses 21–22 Job says, *If I have raised my hand against the innocent, knowing that men would side with me in court, then may my shoulder-blade be torn from my shoulder* . . ., words that show how close to the writer's mind is the idea of the process of justice. Again, Job says of his denial that he has worshipped the heavenly bodies, *This would have been an offence against the law, for I should have been unfaithful to God on high* (verse 28). According to Deuteronomy 17:2–7 the punishment for this offence was to be stoned to death.

Yet Job is represented as thinking mainly in terms of a divine

---

[28] Cf. Humbert, op. cit. 91 ff. See also above, Chapter 9, Section 2.
[29] *The Book of God and Man*, 99.
[30] See H. Brunner, op. cit. in n. 1 above, 63 ff. for an annotated translation with a citation of parallels.

tribunal. This is true of the opening words of the chapter (31:2–4). It is clear in the denial of the maltreatment of slaves:

> If I have ever rejected the plea of my slave
> or of my slave-girl, when they brought their complaint to me,
> what shall I do if God appears?
> What shall I answer if he intervenes?
>
> (Job 31:13–14.)

According to Hebraic law the rights of slaves were few (Exod. 21:1–11), as Dhorme points out; the process of a higher tribunal is therefore envisaged here.

The end of the chapter is again explicit in its portrayal of such a tribunal:

> Let me but call a witness in my defence!
> Let the Almighty state his case against me!
> If my accuser had written out his indictment,
> I would not keep silence and remain indoors.
> No! I would flaunt it on my shoulder
> and wear it like a crown on my head;
> I would plead the whole record of my life
> and present that in court as my defence.
>
> (Job 31:35–37.)

The New English Bible has here transposed a number of verses from their traditional order. A witness and an accuser are mentioned, and the Almighty is himself involved. If one were in any doubt as to the nature of this trial, there is one line which makes it very clear:

> I would plead the whole record of my life.

This is exactly the underlying purpose of the Egyptian posthumous judgement. One other quotation clinches the parallel unmistakably:

> Let God weigh me in the scales of justice
> and he will know that I am innocent!
>
> (Job 31:6.)

Even the *psychostasia*, then, is a part of the process, and the whole weight of the lengthy series of denials is to ensure, as in the Egyptian trial, a verdict of innocence.[31] Further, Job emphasizes the writing out of the proceedings, at least of the indictment. We see exactly the same emphasis in the Egyptian vignettes, where the god Thoth is producing a written record.[32] Paul Humbert argues

---
[31] Cf. Humbert, op. cit. 93.
[32] Ibid. 95.

that there is a similarity also in the content of the Hebrew and Egyptian Declarations of Innocence. He adduces from the Egyptian texts the attention to the rights of servants and slaves and of the poor; the denial of adultery; the respect to the code of hospitality in relation to the needy and to strangers; and the denial of usurpation of neighbouring land. One difference is that the Egyptian texts lay slightly greater stress on sins of ritual; nor do they mention the widow and the orphan, although they refer to sins against infants, inferiors, and the dead.

Chapter 31 of Job, then, is very close to the Egyptian tradition, and some commentators, notably Dhorme, have recognized this. A passage in Chapter 16 is rather similar:

> For look! my witness is in heaven;
> there is one on high ready to answer for me.
> My appeal will come before God,
> while my eyes turn again and again to him.
> If only there were one to arbitrate between man and God,
> as between a man and his neighbour!
> For there are but few years to come
> before I take the road from which I shall not return.
>
> (Job 16:19–22.)

The judgement desiderated here is in heaven, but it is not placed after death. What is unclear is God's role: at one moment he is the presiding judge (*my appeal will come before God*); at another he is a contestant in court against Job, another person being sought as an arbiter.

Finally, the *dénouement* of the book can be regarded as a kind of verdict. It is true that the Epilogue has been rejected by some scholars; and it does seem an easy way out, rather like the facile use of the *deus ex machina* condemned by Aristotle. *So the Lord restored Job's fortunes and doubled all his possessions* (42:10). There is no express allusion to a court here. The matter of the Prologue is taken up, but with no reference to the *members of the court of heaven* mentioned in 1:6. Yet it is the *Diktat* of the Lord that settles Job's condition in the end, and it is natural to regard it as the divine acquittal. Indeed Rowley[33] argued that the Epilogue is artistically and morally necessary. In a formal sense, then, the whole structure of the book is built around the judgement of a divine tribunal, but its verdict concerns the life and condition of Job in this world. The impact of Egyptian ideas is clear, but they have been modified to fit into a

---

[33] 'The Book of Job and its Meaning', *Bull. Ryl.* 41 (1958), 167–207, this point on pp. 185 f. Cf. James Barr, 'The Book of Job and its Modern Interpreters', ibid. 54 (1971), 28–46.

system which does not include a belief in immortality. The Book of Job is usually dated to the post-exilic period: about 400 B.C. is given by many as a likely date. Samuel Terrien[34] has argued for a pre-exilic origin of the prose narrative and he regards the poet as a man of Judaean birth who lived partly in Asia Minor at the beginning of the exile. Certainly this would have enabled him, perhaps in an international circle of writers, to become familiar with the literatures of various peoples of the Fertile Crescent, including those of the Egyptians and Babylonians.

The theory of Egyptian influence on parts of the book is not, I think, vitiated by the fact that the literature of the Old Testament contains many examples of what Berend Gemser has called, in an impressive study, 'The *Rîb-** or Controversy Pattern in Hebrew Mentality'.[35] He rightly stresses (pp. 134–5) that 'the book not only abounds in judicial phraseology, but formally it cannot be better understood than as the record of the proceedings of a *rîb* between Job and God Almighty in which Job is the plaintiff and prosecutor, the friends of Job are witnesses as well as co-defendants and judges, while God is the accused and defendant, but in the background and finally the ultimate judge of both Job and his friends.' In one respect I should modify this description: chapter 31, which betrays Egyptian influence most clearly, shows Job as the defendant and God as the judge.

Apart from the borrowings we have indicated above, especially in chapter 31, the Book of Job does not follow, for the most part, any outline of Osirian eschatology. It adheres, rather, to the early Hebraic rejection of immortality. The opening setting of a heavenly court may reflect the impact of Egyptian ideas and can be paralleled elsewhere in the Old Testament, as in the Psalms:

> God takes his stand in the court of heaven
>   to deliver judgement among the gods themselves.
> (Ps. 82:1; cf. 89:6–7.)

Such a court, however, is not connected with the afterworld, as it often is in Egypt;[36] and the impress of Egyptian thought, even at its

---

[34] (1963), 21. He dates the poetic parts to about 575 B.C. (pp. 23 f.). Albright in the Rowley FS. (Leiden, 1955), 14, thinks it very likely that the author 'lived in the cosmopolitan atmosphere of the sixth or fifth century B.C.'

[35] In *Wisdom in Israel and in the Ancient Near East* (Rowley FS.; Leiden, 1955), 120–37. For further lit. on this *Gattung* see Terrien, *Job* (1963), 19 n. 2.

[36] Ronald Williams suggests that the Canaanite worship of Baal-Hadad is influential here: see his essay on 'Theodicy in the Ancient Near East' in *Theodicy in the Old Testament* ed. J.L. Crenshaw (London, 1983), 42–56, esp. pp. 54–55. The essay dates from 1953.

clearest, as in the content of the 'Declarations of Innocence' by Job, falls short of a posthumous location.

Let God weigh me in the scales of justice (31:6), as we have seen, is indubitably from the same source, and it would be a mistake to regard this as the borrowing of a mere metaphor. Just as, in mythic and magical thought, 'there is no such thing as a *mere* picture', so too in mythic thinking 'there is much more in metaphor than a bare "substitution".'[37] It is a moot point, admittedly, how far the original mythic impulse retains its potency when it is imported into another culture and language. In the case of Job the retained potency is attested only fitfully, and he conveys the impression that he has transmuted the idea of a tribunal in the afterworld into one of a higher heavenly process which is effective here and now. A distinctive feature of his presentation is its call for the intervention of a third party to mediate between God and man.

As it stands, the book is of composite origin, and the original Book of Job is undoubtedly the Dialogue (chapters 3–31).[38] Here the problems of theodicy and unjust suffering are dealt with in a spirit of fearless honesty; and the happy ending of the Epilogue, although formally a divine verdict in the edited structure of the whole, could not have been written by the same superbly profound writer.[39]

---

[37] Ernst Cassirer (tr. S.K. Langer), *Language and Myth* (New York, 1946), 94.
[38] Ronald Williams, op. cit. 52; W.A. Irwin in *Peake's Comm.* (1962), 391.
[39] W.A. Irwin, ibid. 407: 'The author of the Dialogue was too penetrating and too honest ever to have offended his readers with these superficialities.'

The above chapter, esp. in its second part, embodies some material published by me in *Fontes atque Pontes*, ed. M. Görg (Festgabe für H. Brunner = *Ägypten und Altes Testament* 5, Wiesbaden, 1983), 186–204. This material in turn was partly based on a lecture by me in 1974 to the Society for Old Testament Study with Mr D.R. Ap-Thomas in the chair; a revised form was presented at the Hebrew University, Jerusalem in 1980 with Professor Sarah Groll in the chair. I have profited from comments made on those occasions.

CHAPTER TWELVE

DIVINE JUDGEMENT IN THE MYSTERY RELIGIONS

Although the Mystery Religions usually reveal considerable concern with life after death and with a process of judgement that occurs on the threshold of that life, yet in the experience of the initiate the operation of a type of judgement is seen to characterize phases of the initiation itself. A kind of transposition accordingly emerges. There is some variety of emphasis, naturally, in the various cults, and the idea of posthumous judgement is not abandoned. It is worth examining how far the Mysteries of Isis, of Demeter at Eleusis, of Mithras, and of Dionysus conform to this new pattern of development.

1. *The Isiac Mysteries*

The clearest and most eloquent example of the role of divine judgement in the Mystery Religions appears in the account which Apuleius has given us of the initiation of the central character of his *Metamorphoses*, the Greek Lucius, into the Mysteries of Isis. It is also the loftiest in its devotional intensity and spiritual tenor, but in making this claim we have to admit that the lack of any detailed literary elaboration of what went on in the other Mystery Religions makes a fair comparison impossible. With the others we often have to rely on the evidence of archaeology, of inscriptions, and of literary allusions that are all too brief. Admittedly we must bear in mind in the case of Apuleius the possibility that this accomplished author may have embellished his account with rhetorical flourishes or even with some details drawn from his rich imagination.

Here the question of his own experience of the rites arises. Clearly the account in his Eleventh Book is not all pure autobiography. Several details apply to a man from the neighbourhood of Corinth who is keen, after his initiation in Cenchreae, to visit his home which is not far off, before proceeding to Rome to undergo further initiation ceremonies. We know that Apuleius was an African from Madauros, but that he had travelled in Greece and also lived for some time in Rome. His account of initiation into the rites of both Isis and Osiris bears the stamp of one who actually experienced it. At one point indeed he allows the mask of Lucius the Corinthian to drop from his face and he refers to him (at the end of Ch. 27) as *a man from Madauros* (*Madaurensem*). Perhaps it is a deliberate insertion of the author's signature. In a recent edition and commentary Jean-Claude Fredouille (Paris, 1975, p. 17) emends *Madaurensem*, the reading of the manuscripts (with *Maudarensem* and *Mandaurensem* as variants), to *Corinthiensem*, arguing that this restores consistency to the narrative. It most certainly does, but all too tidily and effectively. In the same way he tries to question the autobiographical element. In his *Apologia* (55, p. 62, 20 ed. Helm) Apuleius says: *I have taken part in a number of initiation ceremonies in Greece* (*sacrorum pleraque initia in Graecia participavi*); in the *Metamorphoses* likewise (3.15) the slave-girl Photis tells Lucius that he has been *initiated into many sacred rites* (*sacris pluribus initiatus*). Here it is natural to see confirmation of the equation Lucius-Apuleius; thus too in the allusions (*Metam.* 11.28 and 32) to the forensic activities pursued by Lucius: they give an autobiographical flavour, as Solmsen remarks in his *Isis among the Greeks and Romans* (Cambridge, Mass., 1979), 146 n. 29. Fredouille[1] justly emphasizes, at the same time, that Apuleius does not reveal, outside the *Metamorphoses*, any particular attraction to the Egyptian religion, although he boasts in the *Apologia*, as we have seen, about the number of initiation ceremonies in which he has taken part in Greece. One reference[2] suggests that he was an Eleusinian initiate.[3] To press these points, however, to produce a suggestion that the Isiac account is not based on personal experience is a procedure that has little to commend it; a simple fact of chronology may explain the discrepancy. We know that the *Apologia* was written in A.D. 158/9. It is very likely that the *Metamorphoses* is more than ten years later, and clearly the religious experience portrayed in it may have come later too. Also misleading, it seems to me, is the argument deployed by Françoise Dunand[4] when she urges, against the theory of an autobiographical element, that Lucius, from the moment when he is admitted to initiation, consecrates himself entirely and definitively to the service of the Egyptian gods; she adds that 'the adhesion to the Isiac religion seems with him to be exclusive of every other form of religious engagement, which is certainly not the case of Apuleius.' It is true that there is a suggestion of this exclusive claim in Chapter 6, where Isis tells Lucius to remember that the remaining course of his life is to be dedicated to her. The

---

[1] Op. cit. 20. He finds only one reference to Osiris (*De deo Soc.* 154) and none to Isis.
[2] *Apol.* 55 (p. 62, 23 Helm).
[3] Cf. my *Apuleius of Madauros, The Isis-Book* (EPRO 39; Leiden, 1975), 4.
[4] In *CdE* 52 (1977), 295.

address of the priest also, in Chapter 15, makes it clear to Lucius that from now on he must serve the goddess. Not even Osiris is mentioned in these important passages relating to the First Initiation. On the other hand an exclusive claim is not made *expressis verbis*. There is no specific ban on the worship of other gods, and nothing like the henotheistic emphasis of *Thou shalt have no other gods before me*. Indeed we are told in Chapter 22 that the High Priest in charge of the rites was called Mithras and that he was linked to Lucius *by a certain divine association of constellations*. Here then acknowledgement is made to both Mithraism and astrology. From other sources, of course, there is plentiful evidence of the tolerance and even active symbiosis practised by the Mystery cults. It was possible for a person to be initiated into several of them.

(1) *Confession*

Let us now turn to the episodes which concern us. They are experiences through which expression is given to confession, judgement, and forgiveness. They do not belong to the initiation itself, but are presented as part of the necessary preliminaries. As soon as Lucius has received the promised boon of transformation back into human shape after his many adventures in the form of an ass, a dialogue ensues between him and the priest who had offered him the crown of roses. It was by eating these, as foretold by Isis herself, that Lucius achieved his return to human form. The priest had also been enlightened by Isis beforehand, and in carrying the crown of roses he is said by Lucius to be bringing with him *my destiny and my very salvation (fata salutemque ipsam meam gerens)*. This priest, by the way, seems to be a different person from the priest Mithras who is put in charge of the initiation; he is called simply a *sacerdos* (Chs. 12 and 13), whereas Mithras is called a *sacerdos praecipuus* (Ch. 22). When Lucius is changed back into a man he is of course naked, and the priest who had carried the roses gives him a linen garment to wear—a dress which anticipates his initiation. Another of the band of devotees gives him his outer cloak. In the meantime Lucius has been anxious to express his gratitude to the goddess for the wondrous miracle she has performed, but it is the priest who speaks although he too is astonished at the form which has now become thoroughly human.[5]

In many ways it is the speech of the priest in Chapter 15 that

---

[5] *Perhumanum in aspectum meum attonitus*. By reading *perhumanum* one supplies a reason for the priest's astonishment; cf. my *Isis-Book*, 183.

constitutes the most important chapter in the whole of Book XI and indeed of the whole work. It provides an analysis of the spiritual state of Lucius, especially of the state resulting from his change into an ass and the events and moral causes which led to that. Although no reference is made to an act of confession by Lucius, one has to assume that this has taken place and that it was a constant procedure in the Isiac Mysteries before a candidate was accepted for initiation. It is true that we are told in Chapter 14 that *the priest had by divine communication, as ever, become acquainted with all my misfortunes from the start.* When we examine, however, the analysis presented by the priest, it becomes clear that he reveals far more than an acquaintance with the outward events which have caused trouble to Lucius. He proceeds to dissect his social and intellectual status and then to lay bare the most profound questions of motivation and conduct. A detailed confession punctuated by question and response would seem to be the indispensable basis for such a spiritual examination and judgement. The likely quality of the confession can be assessed by the description in Chapter 19. Here Lucius tells how he took a lodging within the precinct of the temple although he still had no official standing and had not yet been accepted as a candidate for initiation. But now Isis herself tells him how he has been predestined for initiation into the Mysteries and how the time has arrived. Ardent as is his devotion to the goddess, a sense of uncertainty and withdrawal is nevertheless conveyed at this point:

> Nor did I spend a single night or indulge in any sleep without being blessed by the vision and counsel of the goddess, but in frequent sacred injunctions she opined that now, after being long since destined for the Mysteries, I should at length be initiated. For my part, however, while I ardently desired this end, I was restrained by religious fear. For I had taken care to ascertain how arduous was the service of the faith, how extremely hard were the rules of chastity and abstinence, and how needful it was to fortify cautiously and carefully a life exposed to many blows of chance. Revolving such thoughts repeatedly in my mind, for some reason, in spite of my ardour, I kept delaying the matter.
>
> (Apuleius, *Metam.* 11.19.)

The state of apprehension, uncertainty, and desire to delay is paralleled, as Festugière[6] has pointed out, in documents concerned with the cult of Asclepius. In the two examples cited by him a person who hesitates to carry out a divine command is punished by

---

[6] *Personal Religion among the Greeks* (Berkeley, 1954, repr. 1960), 79, referring to *P. Oxy.* 1381 and Aelius Aristides, 48.71 ff.

the god, with the result that the hesitation is abandoned. No punishment is mentioned here, and it is therefore doubtful whether Apuleius is simply following a literary convention. The description is notable for its subjectivity and is one of the features that attest the authenticity of the narrative; the writer is bringing to it the stamp of genuine personal experience.[7]

(2) *Judgement*

When we turn to the judgement delivered by the priest in Chapter 15, we observe at once that it begins with a note of sympathy and understanding. He points out that Lucius, after his many troubles and storms, has now reached *the haven of Rest and the altar of Mercy* (*ad portum Quietis et aram Misericordiae*). Here, then, is no suggestion of a terrible and final judgement, no hint of a *Dies Irae* which will reduce the judged one to prostration. Yet it is a quite ruthless examination of the spiritual aberrations which have troubled Lucius. His high birth and respected social status are referred to, and also his claim to be a learned man. These qualities are certainly ascribed to Lucius in the narrative. He boasts of Greek ancestors in Attica, in the Corinthian Isthmus, and in Sparta; he tells us that his mother was descended from the famous Plutarch and his nephew Sextus, the philosopher; he has learnt Attic Greek and later has mastered Latin in Rome without the help of a teacher. For a Greek of respected origin to have learned Attic Greek is an odd claim. It has force only when applied to Apuleius himself. He was neither Greek nor Roman, but of African origin. Yet, as he boasts elsewhere, he mastered both the classical languages; in the *Apologia* (4, init.) he takes pleasure in quoting what his accusers had said about his eloquence in both Greek and Latin. On this point what applies to Lucius in the priest's *exposé* applies also to Apuleius and even more so.

In the Third Book (Ch. 15) Photis, the slave-girl with whom he has become infatuated, assures him of her confidence in him not only because of his nobility of birth but also because of his learning (*doctrina*) and his highly gifted talent. Both the *Apologia* and the *Florida* contain boasts about learning; they refer to his linguistic ability and also to his discerning in religious matters. If he has a knowledge of many religious rites, it is because of his *enthusiasm for the truth and sense of duty towards the gods*.[8] Now the priest stresses that

---

[7] Cf. my *Isis-Book*, 272–3.
[8] *Apol.* 55 (p. 62, 26 f.).

all these things, including learning, were of no avail to Lucius. Are we to infer, then, that learning was opposed by exponents of the Isis-cult? This is the view of Wittmann,[9] who maintains that to the Isiacs *doctrina*, which he defines as the embodiment of human spiritual freedom ('der Inbegriff menschlicher Geistesfreiheit'), was rejected as a thoroughly unprofitable *curiositas* which could only lead to evil. One feels here that the definition of *doctrina* is somewhat one-sided, echoing specifically the autonomous claim of the Stoic man of virtue with his emphasis on ἐγκράτεια and αὐτάρκεια.[10] Certainly the Stoics attacked learning in its conventional sense. Seneca[11] in his celebrated discussion of Liberal Studies condemns current education root and branch because its idea of wisdom does not include the basic ideal of moral insight, the pursuit of *sapientia*. The suggestion, however, that believers in Isis were opposed to learning in its higher sense is unfounded. Plutarch in his *De Iside et Osiride* (2, 351 E) devotes some attention to the theme and states that Clea worships the goddess Isis *as one who is exceptionally wise and devoted to wisdom*. In his discussion Plutarch makes it clear that he regards this wisdom as including both the devotion to truth in an intellectual sense and the process of *gnôsis* which leads to knowledge of *the First and the Lord*, a knowledge aided by the self-discipline demanded in the cult.[12] Clearly the priest who is addressing Lucius cannot be interpreted as condemning *doctrina* in all its aspects. His point is that whatever learning Lucius may have possessed, it did not save him from falling into gross sins which brought him dire misfortune.

These are the sins of lust and curiosity, and on them falls the scourge of divine judgement as wielded by the priest. There have been many allusions to both of them in earlier parts of the narrative, and this is one reason why the priest's address is also a conscious effort on the part of Apuleius to bind the whole novel together thematically.[13] Lucius is rebuked by the priest thus:

---

[9] *Das Isisbuch des Apuleius* (Stuttgart, 1938), 80–81.
[10] Cf. Max Pohlenz, *Die Stoa*, I (Göttingen, 1948), 241 (on Hecaton); F.H. Sandbach, *The Stoics* (London, 1975), Index s.v. Self-sufficiency.
[11] *Epist. Mor.* 88.
[12] Cf. my *Plutarch's De Iside et Osiride* (Cardiff, 1970), 256. In 1 Cor. 1:30 it is said of Christ, *for God has made him our wisdom*; see H.D. Betz and E.W. Smith Jr. in *Plutarch's Theological Writings and Early Christian Literature*, ed. H.D. Betz (Leiden, 1975), 41.
[13] See my 'Isis in the *Metamorphoses* of Apuleius' in *Aspects of Apuleius' Golden Ass*, ed. B.L. Hijmans Jr. and R.Th. van der Paardt (Groningen, 1978), 141–66, esp. 141. See also the discussion G.N. Sandy, ibid., 123–40.

... on the slippery path of your hot-headed youth you fell into low pleasures ...
(... lubrico virentis aetatulae ad serviles delapsus voluptates ...)
(Ibid. 11.15.)

The main reference is, of course, to the affair with the slave-girl Photis, and the phrase *ad serviles delapsus voluptates* may well contain an allusion, expressed in the adjective, to the fact that Photis was a slave. But the sense is also more general: such lustful pleasures are low and degrading. In a recent attempt at a re-interpretation Gerald N. Sandy[14] has argued that 'Fotis, far from being a symbol of sexual lust, represents one face of the coin of mysticism, the face that is discredited in Book 11.' 'In other words', he goes on, 'the servitude ... denotes Lucius' obsessive desire to meddle in the malevolent affairs of witchcraft.' It is quite true that Photis is linked to the two themes of lust and magic; but the short answer to Sandy's argument is that the priest, in his address to Lucius, separates the two themes, and that he clearly subsumes magic under the second theme, which he names *curiositas*. A well-known difficulty, when we consider the sin of lust as applied to Lucius, is that the people, after the priest's speech, congratulate Lucius on his new-found happiness and praise the goddess for the wondrous favour she has bestowed on him, adding then that Lucius has deserved such treatment by his upright manner of living:

> Happy is he, by Heaven, and thrice blessed, to have clearly deserved, by the purity of his former life and his pious loyalty, such a wondrous favour from Heaven that he is, as it were, born again and has at once pledged himself to service in the sacred rites.
>
> (Felix hercules et ter beatus, qui vitae scilicet praecedentis innocentia fideque meruerit tam praeclarum patrocinium ut renatus quodam modo statim sacrorum obsequio desponderetur.)
> (Ibid. 11.16.)

Sandy[15] argues that the words *innocentia* and *fides*, used here to characterize Lucius, imply that the sin of sensuality in his record is minimized and that naiveté was responsible for his fall, an idea he finds adumbrated in *lubrico virentis aetatulae ... delapsus*. In the interpretation of the *Isis-Book*, however, one of the instruments which must often be applied is Form Criticism. Several literary

---

[14] 'Serviles Voluptates in Apuleius' Metamorphoses', in *Phoenix* 28 (1974), 234–44. That a fusion of lust and magic is attacked is also the view of Serge Lancel in *Rev. Hist. Rel.* 160 (1961), 32 f. L.A. MacKay in *Arion* 4 (1965), 474–80 argues that the basic sin of Lucius is 'disobedience, self-will'.
[15] Ibid.

forms prominent in the religious tradition are employed, and in the eulogy of Lucius we have, without doubt, a traditional *Macarismos* or Felicitation, so that the special details of the present situation are ignored.[16] A further point about the condemnation of sensuality is that it has a significance, when viewed from a consideration of the novel as a whole, which goes beyond the lustful attachment of Lucius to Photis. There are episodes in the life of Lucius as an ass, especially his willingness to have sexual union with a rich lady in Book 10, which might similarly be objected to. Lucius has become an ass, but retains human sensibilities. Thus he is shocked by the idea that he should have intercourse in public with a convicted murderess. On the whole Lucius-Asinus is more sinned against than sinning. The extension of application to which I referred can be also related to the many tales which are introduced by way of digression and in which sexual immorality is a prominent theme. James Tatum[17], in a discussion of these tales, shows how several of them are relevant to the theme of love, true and false, especially the tales grouped by him under the title 'Tales of Revenge and Adultery' (pp. 514 ff.). He designates these as tales that 'create the need in Lucius for a salvation in Isis by discrediting the kind of indulgence which marked his life as a man' (p. 525). What is condemned both in the life of Lucius and in these tales of immorality points to the radiant contrast provided by the end of the novel. Sensuality is replaced by the higher *Voluptas* which centres on Isis. The process of sublimation is of course in full accord with the Platonism of Apuleius.

Divine judgement as voiced by the priest then castigates *curiositas* as the second evil which has led to the downfall of Lucius. Much has been written about this concept. It will suffice now to stress its importance in the novel as a whole. In particular it is the leading motif of the story of 'Cupid and Psyche', and it appears there under the shadow of the same moral disapproval as it does in Book 11. Here the priest establishes a causal nexus between the sin of *curiositas* and the crowning misfortune that befell Lucius in his transformation into an ass. He tells him: *you have gained a grim reward*

---

[16] See Joseph Berreth, *Studien zum Isisbuch Apuleius' Metamorphosen* (Ellwangen, 1931), 102, who also suggests that the mention of the previous part of his life may refer to the life of Lucius before the narrative of the novel begins. See further my *Isis-Book*, 257. A more general doxology appears in Ch. 13. Cf. the shout of the people at the end of the Ephesiaca of Xenophon of Ephesus: *Isis is a great goddess*, on which see R. Merkelbach, *Roman und Mysterium in der Antike* (Munich, 1962), 111–12; cf. J. Gwyn Griffiths in *Hommages Vermaseren*, I (Leiden, 1978), 423.

[17] *TAPA* 100 (1969), 487–527.

for your ill-starred curiosity. This is patently borne out by the actual narrative: it was the curiosity of Lucius about the magical practices of Pamphile that led to his unfortunate transformation. In the person of the slave-girl Photis this urge to meddle with magic is merged in the motive of love, but it was the sin of *curiositas* that produced the catastrophe. In the context of magic and religion it is a forbidden urge. When Apuleius wants to refer to what we would regard as the highly acceptable virtue of intellectual curiosity, he avoids the word *curiositas* and uses an expression like *studium veri*, 'enthusiasm for the truth'.[18] To him the context of the Mystery Religions was one which especially inhibited the exercise of a prying curiosity; of this he uses the adjective *temerarius*, 'daring' (Ch. 23), but proceeds to provide a more favourable expression— *desiderium religiosum*, 'religious longing'—to which he does make a brief concession in the synopsis then given of the First Initiation.

A theological antithesis between Fortuna and Isis concludes the priest's spiritual diagnosis. Through his sins Lucius has endured the infamy of the asinine transformation and in this form he has afterwards suffered various troubles which have exposed him to the buffetings of Fortuna. Here the priest catalogues briefly the painful experiences which Lucius has faced, noting that eventually they were of no avail to wicked Fortuna. According to the priest Fortuna is blind and wilful, and delights in inflicting tortures. Yet in her unforeseeing evil she led Lucius to his state of religious bliss. Lives redeemed by Isis are no longer under the power of hostile fate; they are protected by a Fortuna who is not blind, but sees; that is, by Isis Tychê. Through the providence of mighty Isis Lucius is victorious over his Fortune. The reference to Isis as *Fortuna videns* implies knowledge of the syncretistic Isis Tychê,[19] an instance where syncretism in a double name indicates the dominance of the first-named deity. In the case of Lucius it is Isis who is deemed to have overruled the evils brought by Fortuna, so that in spite of them all he achieves a state of bliss.

Here and in his subsequent words the priest tends to abandon his role of Pater Confessor and judge. He is now addressing himself not so much to Lucius as to the multitude around. His speech has

---

[18] See my *Isis-Book*, 248–50 and 354, with refs. to various discussions. See further Friedrich Solmsen, *Isis among the Greeks and Romans* (Martin Classical Lectures, 25; Cambridge, Mass. 1979), 100–102.

[19] In origin Tychê, like Moira, is subordinate to Zeus. Cf. Ugo Bianchi, ΔΙΟΣ ΑΙΣΑ: *Destino, uomini e divinità nell'epos, nelle teogonie e nel culto dei greci* (Rome, 1953); Walter Burkert (tr. J. Raffan), *Greek Religion: Archaic and Classical* (Oxford, 1985), 129–30.

become a medium of propaganda for his faith, a veritable missionary effort which exploits the miracle in order to win new believers for Isis.

(3) *Forgiveness*

Rigorous as the priestly judgement is, it nevertheless proffers the hand of pity, mercy and forgiveness. The first hint of this is in the priest's opening sentence: Lucius has reached, after many troubles and storms, *the haven of Rest and the altar of Mercy*. There was an Altar of Mercy according to Pausanias (1.17.1) in the Athenian agora; and in the Roman era there was a similar altar at Epidaurus. The goddess Isis is often depicted as merciful and loving, although she can also be a stern judge and avenger. In this book she is pre-eminently the Savious Goddess who takes mercy on the asinine Lucius.

The second hint comes in the statement that Lucius has now reached a state of religious bliss (*religiosa beatitudo*). Clearly if his sins had merited a grim reward, it is divine forgiveness that has reversed the situation. In accordance with this the priest asks Lucius to show a happier face in keeping with the white cloak he has assumed; he is to follow the procession of the Saviour Goddess with triumphant step. A call to the service of the goddess then ensues. It seems that the formal proclamation of forgiveness comes later. It occurs in the preliminary rites of the initiation. Lucius is led by the priest—now it is Mithras, the High Priest—with an escort of the faithful to the temple baths where he is submitted to the customary ablution (*sueto lavacro*). After this we are told that the priest *prayed for the forgiveness of the gods* (*praefatus deum veniam*) and besprinkling Lucius, cleansed him most purely (Ch. 23). An interval of ten days follows in which the candidate had to abstain from meat and wine. Then, during a nocturnal visit to *the very heart of the holy shrine* comes the ceremony proper of the initiation.

The forgiveness of the gods is therefore imparted in a rite of baptism. It is a little uncertain whether Apuleius intends us to envisage two ceremonies of ablution. The *customary ablution* would seem to indicate the purification of all people entering a temple, whereas the elaborate cleansing that follows appears to be a ceremony specially related to initiation.[20] Certainly the stress on for-

---

[20] Françoise Dunand, *CdE* 52 (1977), 298–9, would deny the application of the term 'baptism' to either of these rites of ablution. She avers that it is the ceremony of initiation that makes of Lucius a *renatus*. One must agree on the latter point; but

giveness is thus related. Ritual purity, as Festugière[21] reminds us, was an age-old pre-requisite in the Eleusinian Mysteries; he finds, however, a deeper meaning in the Apuleian context, where the vocation and grace of the goddess are needed, together with her forgiveness. Later on, in Chapter 25, where Lucius has offered to Isis an exquisite prayer, he is said to beg Mithras, the High Priest, for forgiveness (*veniam postulabam*); but the sense here is more personal on a human level—he had been unable, he says, to recompense Mithras for the great favours he had bestowed on him.

2. *Anticipated Eschatology*

It is fairly clear how the sequence of confession, judgement, and forgiveness fits into the pattern of soteriology in the doctrine of the Isiac Mystery Religion. The candidate who has reached this stage can be prepared to regard his sinful past as a closed chapter and to look forward hopefully, in view of the forgiveness bestowed on him, to a new and brighter chapter which is opened for him through the grace of the goddess and through his vows of consecration to her service. In other words, his old life has come to an end, and he is dead to its folly and sin. Now he begins a new life of purity and service. He is born again, *renatus*—a term used of the new-found humanity of the *Eselmensch*, but also of the new spiritual life to be achieved by Lucius. In the record presented by Apuleius the idea of death and rebirth through initiation comes through very lucidly. The experience of initiation implies a voluntary death and a life obtained by grace. These are expressions used by the High Priest to Lucius in an attempt to explain the significance of the rites that are imminent:

> For the gates of hell and the guarantee of life were alike in the power of the goddess, and the very rite of dedication itself was performed in the manner of a voluntary death and of a life obtained by grace ...
> (Ibid. 11.21.)

Here the reference to *the gates of hell* (*inferum claustra*, lit. *of the underworld*) reminds us that the promises of the cult embraced one's fate in the next world; and the term *salus, salvation*, certainly covers the idea of life saved and protected in this world as well as the next.

---

the forgiveness of the gods is an important preliminary experience, and it is explicitly connected with the second purification.

[21] Op. cit. 79. On confession as a pre-requisite of healing in the Isis cult, though not in the Mysteries, see Burkert, *Ancient Mystery Cults* (Cambridge, Mass. 1987), 16.

The new life, in fact, is viewed as beginning at once, and here is a significant idea shared by the other Mystery Religions and also by Christianity. Within the framework of Egyptian religion we find a parallel concept of judgement which at the same time points a contrast. Very prominent in that religion is the idea of judgement after death, with an approximation also to the ideas of confession and forgiveness. A process of confession lies behind the 'Declarations of Innocence' in Spell 125 of the *Book of the Dead*, even if denials such as *I have done no wrong against men* or *I have done no evil* could be regarded, in the context of a papyrus deposited in a tomb, as ready-made guarantees. In the New Kingdom and later the frequency of the pictorial portrayal of the weighing of the heart may produce a sense of uniformity in spite of the numerous minor variations, and Eberhard Otto[22] once argued that the earlier expressions of the idea in literature, as in the *Instruction for Merikarê*, show a more vibrant vitality in the spiritual sense. He goes on to admit, though, that the line which demarks magic from ethical awareness is often not easy to draw, and that some areas of Egyptian literature, especially after the time of Akhenaten, reveal a consciousness of sin and a profound confessional approach.[23] Just as in the tradition of the judgement of the dead, the individual is starkly alone[24] before the gods, so in these hymns and prayers does he appear in humility as a single person before his divine rulers. A good instance of this in the context of judgement is the tomb of Khaemweset, son of Ramesses III, in Thebes (Theban Tombs, No. 44). In several scenes the King is shown accompanying his young son; but before Osiris and Thoth the son is shown on his own.[25]

(1) *The Change of Perspective*

When we compare the portrayal of divine judgement given by Apuleius with that found in the traditional doctrine, we are struck by the change in perspective. What related in the earlier phase only to eschatology has now been transferred to the life of the believer

---

[22] *Osiris und Amun* (Munich, 1966), 35–36.
[23] See the section 'Personal Prayers and Hymns' in H. Brunner, 'Egyptian Texts' in *Near Eastern Religious Texts relating to the Old Testament* ed. W. Beyerlin, tr. J. Bowden (London, 1978), 30–44; also the parallel section in Jan Assmann, *Ägyptische Hymnen und Gebete* (Zürich, 1975), 349 ff.
[24] He is guided often by a deity, and occasionally accompanied by his wife, but of necessity he is himself alone involved in the assessment.
[25] Observed by the writer, 15.1.1966.

here and now. Although eschatology in the shape of a happy afterlife is still included in the promise of salvation, the immediate emphasis is on the death and new life which are experienced at once in the process of initiation. Confession, judgement, and forgiveness form an important part of the experience and these elements now seem to be transferred from the eschatological context in the judgement of the dead to the present consciousness of the candidate for initiation.

The question naturally arises whether the idea of spiritual regeneration in this life can be traced back to aspects of the Egyptian tradition or whether it derives from the impact of the Greek Mysteries which in the Hellenistic era influenced all the rites, whatever their origin, which are called Mysteries. We know of no Egyptian ceremonies specifically related to the prospect of posthumous judgement in the sense of a preparation for it, although several works are extant which were intended as guides to the gloomy or happy possibilities of the next world. Among these are the *Book of the Two Ways*,[26] the *Book of Amduat*, and the *Book of Traversing Eternity*. However, there were several rites connected with the cult of Osiris which undoubtedly had the effect of linking the worshipper intimately with the god who could promise him triumph in the tribunal to come, and it must be remembered that the believer's identification with Osiris was the key to this triumph. It is significant that Herodotus, when he refers (2.171) to the sufferings of an unnamed god (it is clearly Osiris) being enacted on a sacred lake in Saïs, says that the Egyptians call the rite Mysteries (μυστήρια). Obviously the dramatic aspect of the rite was one element which recalled for him the Greek Mysteries. Sometimes the Egyptians also emphasized the element of secrecy, and in several allusions to Osiris Herodotus upholds his avowal of silence or reticence. On the other hand, the element of personal initiation seems to have been absent in the early Egyptian rites except in the case of priestly functionaries. See also A.B. Lloyd, ad loc. (Leiden, 1988), 209.

The idea of the judgement of the dead persisted strongly in the Late, Ptolemaic, and Roman periods, and is attested mostly on coffins and linen-covers. Dr Christine Seeber in her valuable compilation (*Untersuchungen usw.*) shows that a shortened form or an

---

[26] For the preservation of some ideas of this book in the synopsis given by Apuleius in Ch. 23 of the initiation experience see Jan Bergman, 'Zum Zwei-Wege-Motiv' in *Särtryck Ur: Svensk Exegetisk Årsbok* 41–42 (1976–77), 27–56, esp. 53–54.

isolated scene is often used. An example which probably derives from the Roman era occurs in the Wellcome Museum of the University College, Swansea.[27] It is a painting on linen, and the style is somewhat cruder than that of earlier eras. In the scales are shown, in the traditional manner, the symbol of the heart and a figure of the goddess Maat. The two gods concerned with the weighing are Thoth and Horus. Thoth, of course, is regularly depicted, but usually in the role of Recorder; here he helps with the weighing, as in other examples of this period; and the presence of Horus is also distinctive of the later eras. Another distinctive point is the frontality of the figure of the deceased, and especially the fact that she is shown in Greek or Graeco-Roman dress. She recalls the tradition of Tuna el-Gebel with its fusion of Egyptian and Greek forms; and indeed the object may well derive from this area since Thoth is called, in the hieroglyphic inscription above, *Nb Ḥmnw, Lord of Hermopolis*.

During the Ptolemaic era there appeared one remarkable representation of the judgement scene. Its special significance lies in the fact that it occurs not in a tomb but in a temple. I refer to the relief in the West Theban temple of Deir el-Medîna, which was begun under Ptolemy IV Philopater (221–204 B.C.) and finished under Ptolemy VIII Euergetes II (145–116).[28] Although the temple was dedicated to the three deities Amûn, Hathor Lady of the West, and Maat, the patron goddess of Deir el-Medîna,[29] it is Osiris who dominates this scene, for the judgement takes place before him. Admittedly the goddess Maat is also important here, for she is shown introducing the person who is to be judged, but this time in the double form of the two Maats. Horus (specifically Harsiesis) and Anubis are in charge of the scales, and Thoth stands outside busily recording. We see the traditional forty-two assessors and the devouring monster who is ready to deal with the guilty. Immediately before Osiris is a symbol of embalming and then, standing on a large lotus-bud, the four sons of Horus. Now this is a temple for the use of the living, and even if the traditional scene of the *Totengericht* is fairly faithfully followed, we cannot accept that the purpose here is funerary. It is noteworthy, for instance, that the person who faces the judgement is not named; and this is quite contrary to the custom in the Book of the Dead. Eberhard Otto[30]

---

[27] J. Gwyn Griffiths, 'Eight Funerary Paintings with Judgement Scenes in the Swansea Wellcome Museum', *JEA* 68 (1982), 228–52
[28] See E. Otto, *Osiris und Amun*, 64, No. 8 and Pl.8; cf. above 235.
[29] Christine Seeber, op. cit. 29.
[30] *Osiris und Amun*, 64. It is certainly true that the influence of Osiris in the Late

argues that the temple in general emphasizes the funerary gods and the life after death and points to the final victory of Osiris over Amûn, the lord of Thebes, and this even on his own ground in Thebes. That the relief is not really concerned with the magical protection of the dead is the view of Christine Seeber;[31] she suggests rather a connection with the cult of the Maat, the patron goddess of Deir el-Medîna, for she is also the mistress of the righteousness which holds sway in the court. If we press the point, though, that temple reliefs normally represent rites that went on in the temple, according to the principle of *Raumfunktion*,[32] and in particular in an area of the temple adjacent to the representation (and this relief was in a southern sanctuary of the building), then we must agree with Yoyotte[33] that we have here a ceremony that was practised for the living. He compares the statement in the Rubric at the end of Spell 125 of the *Book of the Dead*, to the effect that he for whom this roll is used shall prosper, together with his children; and that *he shall be a favourite of the King and his courtiers*—a somewhat materialistic approach, but one which indubitably implies success in this world.

What exactly happened in the rite in Deir el-Medîna is a matter of surmise. Yoyotte suggests that the participants may have been people who were getting worried about their prospects in the afterlife in view of their feelings of guilt. One recalls the statement of the High Priest to Lucius (Ch. 21), that the goddess tended to choose for initiation persons who were approaching the end of life.

3. *The Eleusinian Experience*

Although living people participated, doubtless with confession and remission of sins, the emphasis on preparation for life after death would still be retained. A similar emphasis was present in the Eleusinian rites. It has been argued that they were not so patently

---

Era and afterwards becomes much stronger, and that he invades the world of the living. Cf. J. Černý, *Ancient Egyptian Religion* (London, 1952), 137, who points to the use of the name Osiris in proper names (e.g. Petosiris, whose *floruit* was *c*. 420 B.C.), a practice which was earlier eschewed because of the god's association with death. Černý misleads, though, when he goes on to say that 'the cult of the sun-god Rē vanished.' As Rē-Harakhty he is prominent in the Edfu temple.

[31] Op. cit. 29. Kákosy, *Selected Papers* (1981, this paper of 1968), 179, tentatively suggests that the unnamed plaintiff is Imhotep, but his alternative suggestion ('a figure of a priest of the temple') is more cogent. Cf. above, 235.

[32] Cf. Dieter Arnold, *Wandrelief und Raumfunktion in ägyptischen Tempeln des Neuen Reiches* (MÄS 2; Berlin, 1962).

[33] In *Le Jugement des Morts*, 66; cf. Brandon, *The Judgment of the Dead*, 204 n. 96.

concerned with eschatology. Thus A.D. Nock,[34] after describing the Greek rites at Eleusis, refers to the worship of Egyptian and other Oriental gods in the Hellenistic era and states that this worship 'was subjected to Greek influences which humanised its mythology and caused it to be less otherwordly and to stress mystic redemption in this life and not exclusively happiness hereafter.' How far can we accept 'mystic redemption in this life' as a part of the Eleusinian experience?

In the early concepts associated with the Eleusinian rites there is intense concern with death; but also, of course, with the possibility of life after death. The divine retribution proclaimed in the Homeric Hymn to Demeter is to fall on the unjust. Possibly it is envisaged as beginning already in this life, but the stress is on its operation in the afterlife:

> But on the unjust vengeance shall for ever fall.
> Τῶν δ'ἀδικησάντων τίσις ἔσσεται ἤματα πάντα.
> (Hom. Hymn to Demeter, 366.)

The basic theme is thus 'an eschatology of compensation'.[35] Happiness is experienced, for the same hymn says (480 ff.) that *happy* (ὄλβιος) *is he among men on earth, who has seen these things* (i.e. the Mysteries). But it adds that *the uninitiate, who has no share in them, never experiences blessings of this kind once he is dead in the misty darkness below.* Clearly the happiness is envisaged mainly as belonging to the next world; it begins now, but it is firmly linked to the prospect of a blessed afterlife. The same word (ὄλβιος) is used by Pindar[36] of the blessedness of the Eleusinian initiate: he is said to understand the end of mortal life and its God-given beginning. This is from a dirge in memory of an Athenian initiate (perhaps of Hippocrates, brother of the statesman Cleisthenes), so that a funerary emphasis is natural in the context. John Sandys,[37] in his Loeb translation, interprets the words *God-given beginning* (διόσδοτον ἀρχάν) in the sense of 'the beginning (of a new life) given of god'; but *the beginning*, as contrasted with *the end* in death, probably refers to the divine source of life. The position is doubtless rightly summed up by saying that 'the neophyte acquires privileges and is promised happiness in this life and in the life after death',[38] provided that the

---

[34] *Early Gentile Christianity and its Hellenistic Background* (New York, 1964, first publ. 1928), 8.
[35] Ugo Bianchi, *The Greek Mysteries* (Iconography of Religions, 17, 3; Leiden, 1976), 12.
[36] Fr. 137 a, ed. Bruno Snell.
[37] *The Odes of Pindar* (2nd Ed., London, 1919, repr. 1930), 592–5.
[38] Bianchi, op. cit. 2.

present happiness is explained as one which is based on the hope of immortality.

Discussing the passages here quoted, Walter Burkert[39] cites and translates two others:

> Thrice blessed are those mortals who have seen these rites and thus enter into Hades: for them alone there is life, for the others all is misery.
> (Sophocles, Fr. 837, from his *Triptolemos*.)

> (The initiates) have more pleasing hopes for the end of life and for all eternity.
> (Isocrates, 4.28.)

In spite of these clear statements, Burkert feels able to say that 'it is remarkable that the concept of immortality is never mentioned in connection with Eleusis', adding that 'death remains a reality, even if it is not an absolute end, but at the same time a new beginning.' Hopes *for all eternity* are hard to reconcile with this view; admittedly the Sophoclean dictum *for them alone there is life* implies 'life in a worthwhile sense' since the non-initiates too have life after death, albeit a miserable one. If Eleusis did not offer an explicit dogma about immortality (Greek religion is in any case not notable for its dogmas), its votaries may be assumed to have held a belief in a life after death which for them would be blessed.[40]

Some of the iconographical evidence is concerned with divine judgement. A number of painted vases from Apulia in southern Italy depict scenes in Hades: the judges are shown, together with, occasionally, the tortures of the damned.[41] A fragment of an amphora now in Karlsruhe[42] shows three judges: Dikê in the top register, and below Aeacus and Triptolemus. Seated and apparently bound is Perithous, King of the Lapithae. They can all be

---

[39] *Greek Religion: Archaic and Classical*, 289; cf. id. (tr. Peter Bing), *Homo Necans* (Berkeley, 1983), 255. In the latter work, 296, he sees in the rites 'an encounter with death, through which death is overcome', adding that 'in sacrifice, in the act of killing, the will to live rises triumphant over the fallen victim.' This hermeneutic of sacrifice at Eleusis (and elsewhere) is not entirely convincing. It is said to be 'truly frightening' p. 280); but the maiden-sacrifice of Korê uses an animal-substitute (p. 65); and the burning of Demophon is a torch-ritual (p. 281).

[40] Guthrie, *The Greeks and their Gods* (London, 1954), 284 ('immortality for the human soul'); cf. Rohde, *Psyche* (9–10th Ed., Tübingen, 1925), I, 294; Günter Wagner, *Das religionsgeschichtliche Problem von Römer 6, 1–11* (Zürich, 1962), 96. Ramsay MacMullen, *Paganism in the Roman Empire* (New Haven, 1981), 53–59, utterly rejects the view that any of the Mystery cults offered immortality. His discussion is littered with *argumenta ex silentio*; e.g. his paragraph on Plutarch (p. 56).

[41] Bianchi, *The Greek Mysteries*, 11–12.

[42] Ibid. Fig. 72 with Bianchi's note on p. 34.

330   DIVINE JUDGEMENT IN THE MYSTERY RELIGIONS

identified from inscriptions, whole or partial, and it is noteworthy that Dikê is lifting a sword high. Peirithous is shown with a huge serpent, probably as a punishment. In the myth he is said to have tried to carry off Persephonê from Hades to be his wife, and in this Theseus is said to have aided him. In a more aggressive scene on another vase, Peirithous and Theseus have been bound by a winged Fury.[43] Pluto is seated above them and Persephonê stands holding torches in both hands. Again the scene is drawn from mythology: Peirithous and Theseus are being punished for their attempt to take Persephonê away from Hades. The question naturally arises whether the two heroes who are being thus chastised have a more generalized significance. This is probably the case, the myth being interpreted to mean that this is what happens after death to those who act violently and criminally.[44] It is an example of mythology becoming paradigmatic, as happened with the better known sinners Tantalus, Sisyphus, and Ixion.

Admittedly these depictions have no demonstrable connection with initiation into the Mysteries, and the judgement seems to be posthumous in context. Yet there are others which are closely related to initiation. Another Apulian amphora[45] depicts a female initiate seated on a chair. To her right a second female figure is standing, and with her left hand this figure is pushing forward a small winged female attendant who is in the act of placing a garland or crown on the initiate's head. The initiate herself is holding up a large basket on her lap and she is looking to her left, where a young man is presenting her with a bird. If this is a clear instance of an initiate being honoured, there are other non-mythological figures which cannot be interpreted so easily, although Günther Zuntz[46] is prepared to explain such figures as 'initiates of the Eleusinian mysteries'. These vase-paintings, some of which we have already discussed, have been dated to the second half of the fourth century (about 340–310 B.C.),[47] and the view of Zuntz (p. 411) is that 'they represent typical figures of Attic mythology, adding to the traditional denizens and visitors of Hades (such as Tantalos, Sisyphos, and Herakles) the judges of the dead

---

[43] Ibid. Fig. 73 with Bianchi's note on p. 34.
[44] Cf. Bianchi's caption: 'Two damned souls bound by a winged fury'.
[45] Ibid. 34, No. 74 and Fig. 74 ('Symbols probably representing the privileges of an initiate in the world beyond').
[46] *Persephone. Three Essays on Religion and Thought in Magna Graecia.* (Oxford, 1971), 412.
[47] Ibid. 297, given as the view of R. Pagenstecher.

whom we know from Plato, and the Furies in the shape which Aischylos and Euripides had made canonical.'

Whether the rites at Eleusis offered a spiritual rebirth of the individual initiate is a problematic question. Such a phase might be symbolized by the return of Korê from Hades as enacted or by the announcement of the hierophant that Demeter had given birth to a boy: *the Mistress has given birth to a holy boy, Brimo to Brimos*.[48] New life in a general sense is probably meant, without a suggestion of regeneration in the initiate.[49] Furthermore, in the early rites a collective significance was prominent.[50] Bianchi[51] speaks of 'the individual initiation of groups of citizens'; and he adds, 'therefore we have a collective intention, shared by all the citizens.' This contrasts with the Egyptian emphasis on the individual. In fact, the Greeks, unlike the Egyptians, provided one instance where even the psychostasia was used in a collective sense. As we have noted above (Chapter 10, Section 2), in the *Iliad* (8.69 ff.) Zeus is said to weigh in his golden scales the fates or death-daemons of the Trojan and Greek armies. One figure is envisaged in each scale, but it has a collective reference. The Egyptians, on the other hand, adhered resolutely to the individualism inherent in the concept. Doubtless the compulsion of the symbol was operative here: normally one can only weigh one thing at a time and a thing of limited size.

By the Hellenistic era the importance of the individual was much enhanced. It was favoured by the influence of astrology and it is clearly attested in the Mystery cults. It is true that societies of worshippers were very popular in Egypt and the Greek world, and they had the attraction of a kind of club. But the cohesion of these groups was based on the shared experience of individual initiation. Certainly the essence of confession, judgement, and forgiveness in the context of the Mysteries is that the individual takes part on his own. The pattern is not fully discernible in the Eleusinian tradition. Divine judgement is certainly attested, but it seems to concern one's fate after death. There is a kind of preliminary judgement, it is true, since murderers were excluded and elaborate purification rites enacted, these latter amounting only to preparatory ceremonial with never a hint of the confessional approach.[52] The holy

---

[48] Hippolytus, *Ref.* 5.8.40; G. Wagner, op. cit. 91, denies that this can symbolically apply to the initiate.
[49] Burkert, *Homo Necans*, 289-90. Cf. A.D. Nock, *Early Gentile Christianity*, 110.
[50] Cf. Burkert, *Homo Necans*, 146 f. (on Eleusis and Athens).
[51] Bianchi, op. cit. 4.
[52] For the atrophy of the confessional element in Greek and Roman religion see R. Reitzenstein, *Die hellenistischen Mysterienreligionen* (3rd Ed., Leipzig, 1927), 137 ff.

hushed climax seen in the revelation of an ear of corn must be given, in the first place, its simple meaning of the new life and sustenance bestowed by Demeter, the earth-goddess, emphasizing the cult's agrarian core.[53] That it also implies new life after death is likely, especially when we recall the many parallels in the Near East which equate reborn vegetation with immortality, as with Osiris,[54] Tammuz, and Adonis. A third possible implication of new life here and now in the experience of the initiate is hard to establish.

4. *Mithraism: Judgement as Ordeal*

A strong sense of self-examination and spiritual *Angst* appears early in Babylonian literature, as in *I Will Praise the Lord of Wisdom* (see above, Chapter 1, Section 4), and Reitzenstein[55] does not hesitate to compare its ethos with that of the later Mystery cults. An element of confession and moral revision is attested for the cult of the Cabeiri at Samothrace. The Mysteries there have been described as 'involving a preliminary confession of sins';[56] the initiand is asked by a priest to state what is the worst deed he has ever committed during his life. According to Diodorus Siculus[57] the gods (the Cabeiri) *bring unexpected help to those of the initiates who call upon them in the midst of dangers*—a clear indication of their saving power in this life. Diodorus refers then to the moral influence which is immediately operative: *they say that those who have participated in the Mysteries become more devout and upright and in every way better than they were before.* Yet this is a somewhat vague and general statement,[58] unlike the previous one, and probably could be applied to other Mysteries too.

---

[53] Burkert, *Homo Necans*, 290–91, presents an amazing feat: the cutting of the blade of corn, he argues, implies castration and 'a transposition of hunting behavior onto agriculture'. The fantasy must be firmly rejected. Fair play, though, he himself talks of it as a 'seemingly far-fetched fantasy'. He wisely omits it in *Greek Religion*, 289–90.

[54] A.A. Barb in *The Legacy of Egypt* ed. J.R. Harris (2nd Ed., Oxford, 1971), 149 ff. rightly posits Egyptian influence on Greek eschatology and ideas of judgement, but goes on rather uncritically to derive most of the Eleusinian cult from Osirian origins. This was attempted much earlier and more thoroughly, though not successfully, by Paul Foucart in his *Les Mystères d'Éleusis* (Paris, 1914). Cf. my remarks in *CR* 25 (1975), 307–8.

[55] Op. cit. 161 ff., esp. 165; cf. G. Wagner, *Problem*, 175 ff.

[56] A.D. Nock, *Early Gentile Christianity*, 6; Plut. *Mor.* 217 D; 229 D; 236 D; cf. Burkert, *Greek Religion*, 283.

[57] 5.49.5–6 (ed. C.H. Oldfather, Loeb, III, 1939, p. 234).

[58] Cf. Bloch, 'wertlose Redensart', quoted by O. Kern in *PW* s.v. Kabeiros und Kabeiroi (1919), 1433 f.

In the iconography of the initiation rites of the Mithraic Mysteries we find clearer evidence of a phase of judgement and also of punishment. It was said of the Emperor Commodus (A.D. 180–92), who himself became a devotee of both Isis and Mithras, that he stained the Mithraic rites with an act of homicide.[59] This was obviously not a feature of the rites, but the writer adds that in them it was usual to say or represent something that would give a show of terror (*ad speciem terroris*). It is possible that these words may be applied to some of the quite tough and difficult ceremonies which the novice had to enact. Several of the relevant representations recall the role of Mithras as judge, although he is not depicted as such in these scenes. Like Aryaman and Varuna he had a disciplinary judicial function.[60] He figures as one of the three judges of the dead when they arrive at the Bridge of the Separator.[61]

We are now interested, however, in a judgement that may have characterized the initiation. A worshipper of Mithras has stated on a wall of the Santa Prisca Mithraeum in Rome that on the 20th November of the year A.D. 202 he was *natus prima luce, born at the break of dawn*.[62] But the term *renatus, born again*, is also used.[63] From the evidence of iconography we can confidently say that this process was not without birth-pains, reflected in the trials imposed on the initiand. Some of the inscriptions also refer to this. Two lines from Santa Prisca refer to consuming by fire:[64]

> Accipe thuricremos pater accipe sancte Leones.
> Per quos thuradamus per quos consumimur ipsi.

After a detailed discussion Vermaseren[65] translates them thus:

> Accept, O holy Father, accept the incense-burning Lions
> Through whom we offer the incense, through whom we
>   ourselves are purified.

He shows that the Lions, who represent the fourth grade of initiation,

---

[59] *SHA, Commodus*, 9.6 (ed. D. Magie, Loeb, 1922, p. 288): *sacra Mithriaca homicidio vero polluit*. Cf. M.J. Vermaseren in *The Excavations in the Mithraeum of the Church of Santa Prisca in Rome* (Leiden, 1965), 125.
[60] Cf. H.W. Bailey in *Mithraic Studies* ed. J.R. Hinnells, I (Manchester, 1975), 14.
[61] See above, Chapter 1, Section 5 (ad fin.) and Chapter 9, Section 8 (4).
[62] Vermaseren, *CIMRM*, 498; id. *Santa Prisca*, 208; cf. R.E. Witt in *Mithraic Studies*, II (1971), 489.
[63] Vermaseren, *Santa Prisca*, 207 ff. in a couplet which he translates (p. 208), *Sweet are the livers of the birds, but Mithras's care guides him who is piously reborn and created by sweet things*. Cf. Ramsay MacMullen, *Paganism in the Roman Empire*, 54 (predictably dismissive).
[64] Vermaseren, *Santa Prisca*, 224 with Fig. 70 and Pl. 69, 1.
[65] Ibid. 232.

are especially connected with the element of fire. They wear a bright-red dress; and in these rites fire, like incense, has a purifying force. At the same time baptism with water was necessary. The initiate in the previous grade, that of Miles, received on his forehead, in a baptism of fire, a mark which was made by burning the skin.[66]

Apposite in this connection are the wall-paintings found in the Mithraeum in Capua. They were first discovered in 1922 and published two years later by the Italian scholar A. Minto; but it is only fairly recently that they have been published in colour and with an elaborate documentation: I refer to the study by Vermaseren in his *Mithriaca* I (Leiden, 1971), where he has added a detailed commentary on the symbolism, drawing also from texts. In one scene[67] a mystagogue, who is perhaps also a *Pater*, is shown wearing a white tunic with red borders. He is pushing the initiand by the shoulders; and this person is naked and blindfolded. His hands are outstretched and he is proceeding slowly and uncertainly, relying obviously on his guide. There is doubtless a symbolism attaching to the temporary blindness. The novice has not yet seen the secrets of the Mysteries. As for the nakedness, he has not yet put on the new garments pertaining to the new life; perhaps the state of nudity in birth is suggested. In another scene[68] the novice is kneeling on his right knee before the mystagogue; another figure approaches with a red tunic and red helmet; he is holding a flaming torch near the head of the novice, and he is identified by Vermaseren as one of the grade of Miles. A similar scene was represented on a marble base which was perhaps found at Velletri but which has since disappeared; the neophyte again had to face a flaming torch. A third scene[69] again shows the neophyte being treated somewhat aggressively. Behind him stands the mystagogue who is pressing his left foot on one of the calves of the neophyte; the latter is kneeling on both knees and his arms are crossed on his breast; and yet with one he appears to be offering a rhyton to the mystagogue, who is pouring liquid into it from a little cup. Some of these details are not very clear in the photograph; nor is the action of the approaching *Pater* clear.

Serene relief may have followed one of the punishments or

---

[66] Vermaseren, ibid.; also id, *Mithras, the Secret God* (London, 1963), 145, quoting Tertullian, *De praescr.* 40, *(Mithras) signat illic in frontibus milites suos.*
[67] Vermaseren, *Mithriaca*, I (1971), 26–27 with Pl. 21. The whole series is also discussed by him in *Mithras, the Secret God*, 131–3 with Figs. 51–53.
[68] Id. *Mithriaca*, I, 28 ff. with Pl. 22.
[69] Ibid. 45–47 with Pl. 28.

ordeals. Vermaseren[70] quotes the dictum of the fourth-century writer Ambrosiaster about the tying of hands. He says that *some of them have their hands tied together with chicken guts, and they are then thrown over pits filled with water while someone approaches with a sword, cuts through the gut bonds and so calls himself the Liberator.* It is doubtful whether this hint of a 'theology of liberation' in the saving process has deep roots in Mithraism. The Isiac candidate, at the end of Apuleius' Chapter 15, is told to combine the idea with that of a 'voluntary yoke' and here there is a clear parallel to Christian teaching.

The ordeal by water mentioned by Ambrosiaster and also the ordeals by fire prompt a comparison with the rites of initiation by which primitive societies admit persons to a special status, as, for instance, the admission of youths to the rank of adulthood. Trials and ordeals are frequently practised, as Mircea Eliade shows in his *Rites and Symbols of Initiation* (1958, repr. New York, 1965).[71] Eliade is not so convincing, however, when he deals with 'patterns of initiation in higher religions' (his Chapter VI). He can say, for instance (p. 117):

> But even so, it is impossible not to realize all that distinguishes Christianity from the Essenes and in general from all contemporary esoteric cults. Above all, there is the feeling of joy and newness.

To claim this feeling as being distinctively Christian is wide of the mark, for *gaudium*, 'joy', is the dominant note of the experience conveyed by Apuleius.[72] Eliade[73] strangely describes the *taurobolium* as 'the chief rite of the mysteries of Mithra'; it is found with Mithras, but is primarily associated with the cult of Cybele and Attis. The only other Mithraic ceremony he refers to, and it belongs to the category of ordeal, is 'climbing a ladder with seven rungs', where the rungs, as he rightly says, are connected by Celsus with the seven planetary heavens.

Was there a moral element in the Mithraic ordeals? The Suda says, under *Mithras*, that no one could be initiated into his Mysteries if, after having faced a certain number of ordeals, he did not

---

[70] *Mithras, the Secret God*, 133; cf. Nicolaus Turchi, *Fontes Historiae Mysteriorum Aevi Hellenistici* (Rome, 1930), 291.

[71] Cf. several discussions in C.J. Bleeker (ed.), *Initiation* (Leiden, 1965); also Bianchi, *The Greek Mysteries*, 3–4.

[72] See Festugière, *Personal Religion among the Greeks*, 80–84; my *Apuleius, Isis-Book*, 54–55; 345.

[73] *Rites and Symbols of Initiation*, 93–94. For the dictum of Celsus see Origen, *Contra Cels.* 6.22 = N. Turchi, *Fontes*, 284; cf. Vermaseren, *Mithras, the Secret God*, 138.

show himself to be sanctified (ὅσιος). It would be clearly unwise to give a purely physical or externally ritualistic meaning to them. Certainly the religious interpretation of ordeals which prevailed right up to the Middle Ages and afterwards was that they expressed, in the fate of the person tried, the judgement of God.[74]

It seems advisable, in the case of the Mithraic ordeals, to look for possible antecedents in the early Iranian cult, although the precise situation of the probing of a neophyte may not be present. We have seen that trials involving fire are prominent in the process of initiation, and the role of fire in early Mithraism is likewise conspicuous. A graffito from Santa Prisca was read by C.W. Volgraff[75] as *Te cauterio i Saturne i Ata[ri] Opi* (*I brand thee, come Saturn, come Atar, come Ops*), where Atar is a Persian god of fire, although the word also occurs as a common noun for 'fire'. We have seen that branding did occur in Mithraic rites, but the reference just quoted must remain doubtful, as is the reading itself. What is significant is that in early Iranian religion fire was intimately associated with Mithra as the personified power of the covenant. It was customary to swear covenants by Mithra in the presence of fire; and it was through fire, in a judicial ordeal, that the man who was false to his covenant was convicted and consigned to death.[76] Describing various forms of ordeal by fire in the ancient religion, Mary Boyce[77] refers to one inflicted on a warrior prince: he has to ride fast between two huge fires, and his innocence is demonstrated if he remains unscathed, for *when . . . God doth so vouchsafe, the breath of fire is even as the wind*. Here the God referred to is doubtless Mithra the judge.

Another form of the fire-ordeal was the pouring of molten metal on to a naked breast; survival proved innocence—a test which appears in Zoroaster's vision of the Last Judgement. (See above Chapter 9, Section 8 (4) with the quotation from Yasna 51.9.) If we recall the priest who holds a blazing torch before the eyes of the neophyte in the Capuan Mithraeum, the idea of a sacred covenant made in the presence of fire may well be denoted, for the neophyte is in the process of making such a covenant of allegiance to the god.

---

[74] See Hermann Nottarp, *Gottesurteilstudien* (Bamberger Abh, II; Munich, 1956).
[75] See Vermaseren, op. cit. 42 and in more detail in *Santa Prisca*, 147 with Fig. 33, where he also gives R. Egger's very different reading, *M. Aur . . . [? pa]t(er) Cauti dat l(ibenti) a(nimo)*.
[76] See Mary Boyce, *Hist. of Zoroastrianism*, I, 28-29.
[77] Ibid. 35.

In Section 1.3 of the Avestan Hymn to Mithra, which was written in the fifth century B.C., the god Atar (Fire) assists Mithra, and they both favour those who are not false to the contract.[78] On the other hand, the blazing torch might be a medium of testing the neophyte's innocence, in which case the judgement of Mithras on him is expressed through the ordeal.[79] A branding is probably not implied here. Whereas the links between Western Mithraism and the early Iranian tradition are not always easy to indicate, if only because the time-gap is so large, there can be little doubt that the fire-ordeals, which are so closely related to Mithra himself, should be derived from the ancient source.[80]

5. *The Dionysiac Mysteries*

While there are many scattered texts concerned with this theme, it may be worth considering, first of all, a work of art which sheds particular illumination on it.

(1) *From the Villa dei Misteri.*

A doctrine of punishment and reward is vividly presented in an episode of the 'Great Fresco' in the Villa dei Misteri near Pompeii. The series to which the episode belongs is clearly related to the Dionysiac Mysteries, and the work is dated to the era of the Late Republic or the Early Empire. Its Dionysiac character is proved by the scene depicting the marriage of Dionysus and Ariadne (or Persephone or Aphrodite), by the presence of Silenus and Satyrs, and by other obvious elements of Dionysiac symbolism. A female neophyte seems to be present in the scenes, and the first episode, which shows a sacred text being read, points to a ritual aspect,

---

[78] See Ilya Gershevitch, *The Avestan Hymn to Mithra*, 74–75; cf. his remark on p. 30 that 'Indo-Aryan contracts' were concluded in front of a blazing fire under the sanction of Mitra or Mithra.

[79] According to LeRoy A. Campbell, *Mithraic Iconography and Ideology* (EPRO 11; Leiden, 1968), 299, the action was 'symbolic of an engendering of the *pneuma* or *asthma* in the reborn *mystes*'; he compares the 'flame of Fire' on the head of Mithra 'while being engendered in the Petra genetrix'.

[80] On fire in Mithraism see Vermaseren in *Santa Prisca*, 299 f.; id. *Mithriaca*, IV (Leiden, 1978), 33 (the lion as a symbol of fire); LeRoy A. Campbell, op. cit. 147 et al.; Robert Turcan, *Mithras Platonicus* (EPRO 47; Leiden, 1975), 92 ff. on statements by Firmicus Maternus. Ramsay MacMullen, *Paganism in the Roman Empire*, 119, opposes Iranian interpretations: 'Mithraism's ties with the east amount to so little that they can be denied entirely'. The role of fire in the rites, however, is not easy to explain from any Western tradition.

probably that of initiation, although we may well doubt whether the whole process is being depicted.[81]

One of the closing scenes shows a young woman who is kneeling and is partly stripped; she is also being whipped. She is bending on the knees of another seated woman who is apparently keeping her in a position so that the whipping may be properly carried out. Yet the following scene shows a joyful dance under the auspices of the god Dionysus. A scene which may be unconnected with this—it is apart from the series—shows a bride preparing her toilet, and a widely accepted explanation of the whole series is that it portrays and symbolizes Dionysiac rites that precede the wedding of a human bride.[82] If we may ask why on earth a young woman should be scourged on the occasion of her wedding or in a rite immediately preceding her wedding, we are told that in ancient ritual flagellation was believed to confer fertility, as in the Roman Lupercalia. There is clear evidence too that occasionally this happened in Dionysiac rites: see Pausanias, 8.23.1 and Nonnus, *Dionysiaca*, 9.261–4. But I can find no evidence that such a rite ever formed part of a marriage ceremony or of a prelude to it. It might be urged that whipping can provide sexual stimulation, but its use in ancient or modern marriage ties does not seem to be attested. It would certainly not be a very nice thing to inflict on any bride in connection with her wedding.

The marriage theory collapses rather badly when we observe who is responsible for the flagellation. It is a tall female figure with high boots. She is fitted with huge dark wings, and must therefore have divine associations. She is raising her left arm, perhaps as though to deprecate the phallus in the *liknon*-basket which is being exposed by another woman; but others have seen in this gesture an involuntary concomitant of the whipping posture. Certainly there are affiliated representations which show Aidos, Modesty, fleeing at the sight of the phallus; see Bianchi, *The Greek Mysteries*, 14. Günther Zuntz[83] has gone so far as to explain the flagellation as 'a

---

[81] The work has been much discussed. See Nilsson, *The Dionysiac Mysteries of the Hellenistic and Roman Age* (Lund, 1957), 66–76 and 123–32; Reinhard Herbig, *Neue Beobachtungen am Fries der Mysterien-Villa in Pompeji* (Baden-Baden, 1958), with his bibliography; Erika Simon in *JDAI* 76 (1961), 111–72; K. Lehmann in *JRS* 52 (1962), 62–68; G. Zuntz in *Proc. Brit. Acad.* 49 (1963), 176–201; Bianchi, *The Greek Mysteries*, 11–15 and 36–37 with Figs. 90–92.

[82] Thus Margarete Bieber in *JDAI* 43 (1928), 298–330; Jocelyn Toynbee in *JRS* 19 (1929), 67–87; A. Maiuri, *La Villa dei Misteri* (Rome, 1931), 155 ('cerimonia di inizione di giovani spose ai misteri', with a flagellation of the bride to confer fertility); R. Herbig, op. cit. 48; Erika Simon, op. cit. 116.

[83] Op. cit. 194 ff. Cf. E. Pottier, in *Rev. Arch.* 1915, 2, 342.

Roman intrusion' and a reflection of Augustan[84] Puritanism, in this case implying 'a deprecation of extra-marital sexual relations'. However, if anything is clear and indubitable about the Pompeian fresco, it is its thoroughly Dionysiac tone and theme. The right procedure, it seems to me, in seeking to interpret the judgement implemented in these scenes, is to look back to the history and content of the cult. While its early excesses were doubtless modified in a Roman setting, the ecstatic message of Dionysus remained the same: the life-force associated with the god must be accepted in the sense of sexuality and physical fertility, and with this acceptance comes a warrant of continued bliss after death. It is the opponents of the cult and its message that are punished. The classic case is Pentheus, whose main attack on the cult derives from condemnation of its sexual freedom; he says of the cult's female devotees, *they creep away one by one to a solitary place to serve the lust of males* (Euripides, *Bacch.* 222-3); Pentheus is 'the dark puritan whose passion is compounded of horror and unconscious desire'.[85] His savage and cruel death was a result of the triumph of Dionysus, and it is relevant to our theme that it was portrayed in the *Casa dei Vettii* at Pompeii.[86] In this vibrant painting Pentheus is attacked by three Maenads, one of whom holds her thyrsus aloft, ready to strike him; behind are two Lyssai or Furies, also threatening him, each being equipped with a torch and a whip. The raised thyrsus and the whip recall the scourging female in the Great Fresco. Admittedly, the kneeling female is not openly associated with the resistance of a Pentheus; but we must assume that what is being punished is the rejection of sexuality.

Yet the female who carries out the whipping is not a Maenad. She is winged and solemn, a figure from another world. While she is acting on behalf of the Dionysiac code, the initiation must be partly focussed on the afterworld. She may be Dikê, as Nilsson calls her; perhaps an Erinys or Anankê or Adrasteia; but in a context that is so intensely Dionysiac she must be inflicting punishment for resistance to the ecstatic call of the cult. Only after the punishment can the joy of union with the god's followers ensue; and it is a joy

---

[84] Some scholars would admit an Augustan date for the work, but the majority opt for an earlier date. See Zuntz, op. cit. 200 n. 1. It is, in any case, generally accepted that it imitates an earlier original.

[85] E.R. Dodds, *Euripides, Bacchae* (Oxford, 1944), 93.

[86] Herrmann-Bruckmann, *Dkm. der Malerei*, I (Munich, 1904), 54 (Text) with Pl. 42; cf. Karl Schefold, *Pompejanische Malerei* (Basel, 1952), 42 with Pl. 44; for another fragmentary scene in which Pentheus figured at Pompeii see Schefold, *Vergessenes Pompeji* (Bern, 1962), 91.

that implies a blessed immortality. The marriage symbolism, denoted especially in the depiction of Dionysus and Ariadne, will refer to the union of the neophyte's soul with the god.[87] In the final scene there is shown, in the background, a tall female dressed in black who is holding the thyrsus in her hand; in front is a nude female figure raising her arm and clashing cymbals together. She is evidently beginning the Dionysiac dance, and the ecstasy of this rite was probably associated with the promise of a joyous immortality. On the other hand—and this is where I disagree with Nilsson—the happiness thus achieved is not exclusively applied to the afterlife. It is more likely that it was envisioned as beginning at the time of the initiation, that is, here and now.

The episode of judgement is therefore a phase, as here presented, in a Dionysiac initiation, though not of Dionysus himself (as a child) according to the view of G.E. Rizzo,[88] nor yet, in a specific sense, of a bride. What is problematic is how far, at this time, the ideas which Bianchi[89] terms 'mysteriosophic concepts of *kolasis* and liberation of the soul, the divine element', should belong to the interpretation. Thus the phallus as a symbol may be given a universal and cosmic application. I would urge, however, that in a Dionysiac rite the *kolasis* should not be given an anti-Dionysiac meaning.

(2) *Textual Evidence*

That the Dionysiac Mysteries in the Hellenistic age and afterwards included an emphasis on life after death is abundantly clear, and the evidence extends to funerary inscriptions and symbolism.[90] Textual evidence for a belief in divine judgement is not easy to come by. Two statements merit attention:

[1] Plutarch, *Consol. ad uxorem*, 611 D. *You have often heard it said—and most people believe it—that the departed experience no evil or pain whatever. I know that you are prevented from believing this by our ancestral doctrines and by the mystic symbols of the Dionysiac initiations, of which we two have a shared knowledge.*

---

[87] Cf. M. Rostovtzeff, *Mystic Italy* (1927), 42 ff. on 'the sacred marriage of the soul', following the views of V. Macchioro; cf. the latter's *Die Villa der Mysterien in Pompei* (1928).

[88] *Dionysos Mystes* (Naples, 1915), 39 ff. To him the wielder of the whip is Adrasteia, who has come to disturb the mystic rite of unveiling the phallus.

[89] *The Greek Mysteries*, 14.

[90] Nilsson, *The Dionysiac Mysteries etc.*, 116–32 = Ch. 8 ('The Afterlife'); Burkert, *Greek Religion*, 293–5; MacMullen, *Paganism etc.*, 53 (with some scepticism).

The loss of their little daughter Timoxena has led, it seems, in this piece, to a curious kind of consolation. After death all will not be pure and painless: ancestral doctrines (unspecified) and the Dionysiac faith point to some difficult encounters. He goes on to suggest that Timoxena's brief life means that she will have less trouble with the process of entering another body, having been not long accustomed to the previous body. But metempsychosis has nothing to do with Dionysiac beliefs; the allusion to these in a discomforting sense must be to a phase of judgement which is expected after death. In the case of little Timoxena such a thought is hardly fitting or felicitous. Her brief life has left scant room for rigorous examination, particularly as Plutarch has stressed her natural goodness.[91]

[2] Celsus apud Origen, *Contra Celsum*, 4.10. *Hence he compares us* (the Christians) *to those who introduce apparitions and horrors into the Bacchic initiation rites.*

Here the Christian parallel is to be found in the punishments of Hell, and Nilsson finds a prime example in the scourging female of the Great Fresco at Pompeii.[92] Yet there is a vital difference of temporal location. The punishments of Hell come after death, but the Bacchic initiation rites (*teletai*) have to do with a living person.

[3] Texts claiming Penance and Purity.

I come pure from the pure, Queen of those below.

The soul addresses Persephone in a text from Thurii in S. Italy of the fourth century B.C.[93]

I have paid the penalty for deeds that were not just.[94]

The simplest explanation of the second dictum is that the *penalty* refers to the fate of a person struck by lightning, an event explicitly mentioned. Yet other words point to the experience of Dionysiac initiation: *happy and blessed one, god shalt thou be instead of mortal* (A 1, line 8). Apotheosis[95] as a culmination of initiation is found also in the Isiac rites. Rebirth is suggested by *I went down beneath the lap of*

---

[91] Moses Hadas, *Plutarch On Love, the Family, and the Good Life* (New York, 1959), 93, contrasts 'the well-fed infant in *St. Augustine's Confessions* who would not let his mother nurse a starving stranger'.

[92] Other sinister aspects of the rites may be meant, such as the whitening of the initiand's face with gypsum. Cf. M.L. West, *The Orphic Poems*, 155.

[93] Zuntz, *Persephone*, 300 ff., A 1–A 3, line 1; Kern, *Orphicorum Fr.*, 32 d; cf. M.L. West, op. cit. 22–23; Burkert, *Greek Religion*, 295.

[94] Zuntz, A 2–3, line 4.

[95] See my Apuleius, *The Isis-Book*, 316; cf. Vermaseren, *Liber in Deum: l'apoteosi di un iniziato Dionisiaco* (EPRO 53; Leiden, 1976). The initiate at Thurii claims, however, to be of divine origin himself (A 1, line 3).

the Lady, the chthonic queen (A 1, line 7).[96] These are texts, it is true, in which Pythagorean[97] and Orphic ideas also commingle, but it is the context of Dionysiac ritual that provides the setting. Thus the initiate's crown is mentioned in A 1, line 6: *I stepped with swift feet on the longed-for crown.* It follows that the allusions to the purity achieved and to the judgement whose demands are met are also likely to relate to the initiate's experience; and confession, it may be assumed, was a part of the spiritual probing.

It is very likely that the Mystery Religions of the Hellenistic and Roman ages influenced one another both ritually and ideologically, especially as it was always possible for a person to be accepted as a candidate in several cults. It remains true that considerable variety of practice and belief is indicated. The Isiac sequence of confession, judgement, and forgiveness, implying a transposition of the eschatological schema, is not fully apparent in the evidence for the other cults, although a phase of judgement is consistently present.

The Eleusinian rites were clearly concerned to some degree with this element, but it is constantly placed after death. At Samothrace the initiation rites of the Cabeiri provide a hint of the practice of confession, while the rites of Mithras give a distinctive form to the operation of judgement: the neophyte has to face a series of ordeals which are definitely part of the process of acceptance and which in one respect (the role of fire) probably derive from the early Iranian cult. In the Dionysiac Mysteries the neophyte encountered demands of ritual and moral purity; with the promise of happiness after death comes a warrant of present joy and of spiritual rebirth after a phase of chastisement.

Discussing the theme of death and rebirth in these rites, Burkert[98] rightly remarks that 'the evidence is less explicit and more varied than the general hypothesis would postulate.' He is referring to the hypothesis that this theme was the essential basis of the rites. After admitting, however, that the passage in Apuleius is 'most telling', he goes on to say that 'there is no corroborating evidence.' If he means evidence for the initiand having to lie in a coffin and being raised to new life, then he is right. One would hardly expect such evidence. But the paradigm of all this is Osiris, and the evidence is overwhelming: witness the many depictions of

---

[96] Burkert, *Greek Religion*, 295.
[97] On punishment cf. the maxim ascribed to Pythagoras: Having come for punishment one must be punished. See Iamblichus, *V. Pyth.* 85; cf. M.L. West, *The Orphic Poems*, 22.
[98] Walter Burkert, *Ancient Mystery Cults* (1987), 99 ff.

the god being awakened and revived from death by Isis; the importance of the Corn Osiris and the Osiris Bed, where renewed vegetation proclaims rebirth; and the prominence, as in the Isiac depiction from Herculaneum, of Osiris Hydreios, where Nile water gives the same message.[99]

---

[99] See my *Apuleius, The Isis-Book*, 294–308. Very oddly Burkert (p. 166 n. 56) has been looking for a mummified Isis. Referring to baptism (p. 101), he says that 'water receptacles in sanctuaries of Isis, again suggestive of baptism to our eyes, were used to represent the flood of the Nile, as Wild's study has shown.' The reference is to Robert A. Wild, *Water in the Cultic Worship of Isis and Sarapis* (Leiden, 1981). In fact Wild shows (pp. 101 ff.) that the Nile water was identified with Osiris; he also shows that ablutions and sprinklings were a regular feature of the Isiac cult (pp. 129 ff.).

In the above chapter I have used some material which appeared in my contribution to *La Soteriologia dei culti orientali nell' Impero Romano*, ed. U. Bianchi and M.J. Vermaseren (Acta of the Colloquium at Rome, September, 1979; EPRO 92, Leiden, 1982), with appended remarks by G. Casadio, Bruce Lincoln, and R. Turcan. On several points I now offer a revised opinion.

EPILOGUE

We began this study with remarks on von Kleist's novel *Michael Kohlhaas* and the devastating sense of disillusion which there attends an individual's search for justice in one particular experience. Several judicial sittings inevitably adorn that account; and it is not surprising that modern literature offers several other examples of the treatment of similar themes.[1]

Kafka's *Der Prozeß* is one of the most striking modern works in this category. At times its satiric power borders on the grotesquely unreal, as when we are told that *the Defence was not actually countenanced by the Law, but only tolerated* and that *the proceedings were not only kept secret from the general public, but from the accused as well*.[2] Kafka was writing this work in 1914 and 1915, and it is still notoriously difficult to know what the main target of his satire was. The accused's alleged guilt is never explained, nor is the charge described;[3] but early in the novel he is advised by his lawyer that it is often better to be in chains than to be free; in the end he is not merely imprisoned, but brutally executed with a butcher's knife. In spite of multiple corruptions, however, in its administration, the Law is given an exalted, almost numinous, position, and man's inherent guilt is stressed, suggesting his Original Sin. If much is frustrating and incomprehensible, that may mirror man's predicament in the universe.[4] There is more than a hint of eschatology in the treatment, although some aspects, such as the radical lack of fairness in the whole procedure, have been compared with Kafka's Letter to his Father, where the father's dominating will should not, however, be projected too easily on to the novelist's idea of a divine retributive power.

In sharp contrast stands the portrayal of posthumous judgement in the ancient religions. Without exception they view the procedures as patterns of absolute rectitude and fairness; the divine judges are beyond bribery, and the social or sexual status of the

---

[1] For a valuable brief conspectus see Valerie P. Minogue, *Trials of Life*. Inaugural Lecture. Swansea, 1982.

[2] *The Trial*, tr. Willa and Edwin Muir (Penguin, 1984), 128–9.

[3] 'What is the Law, what is the guilt?' According to Erich Heller, *Kafka* (Glasgow, 1974, repr. 1977), 91, the failure to answer these questions is 'the decisive flaw' of *The Trial*.

[4] Cf. Minogue, op. cit. 7: 'Is Kafka suggesting that this is Man's position? Born guilty, and condemned to death by a blind irrational force?'

person assessed is of no consequence. One might complain, admittedly, that only occasionally is a third alternative verdict suggested. As a rule everything is decisively black or white, although this may imply an assessment of actions in which good deeds are more numerous than the bad, or vice-versa. The third alternative covers the cases where the two sides are evenly balanced. Divine intervention in the history of a nation or in the life of the individual does not lend itself so easily to a statement in terms of a judicial verdict. A context of conflict in war sometimes produces a divine decision through the medium of an oracle or dream-vision, but usually without details of a process of assessment. On the moral plane of the individual's life there are plentiful instances of the divine insistence on rewards and punishments. Again these are not normally couched in judicial terms, and if there is an allusion to judgement, it may be eschatological.

In the consideration of the present life the concept of Destiny or Fate plays a varying role in the explanation of man's lot. Some of the Greeks and Romans tended to give it, especially in the Hellenistic era, a role that was dominant, and astrology furthered the emphasis. In Egyptian religion there was a constant affirmation that Destiny was under divine control, and a similar attitude is apparent in Judaism and Zoroastrianism. Shaï, Destiny, as relating to the individual, is expressly subordinated in the Egyptian weighing of the heart to the edict of the divine judges. Very different is the temper of some modern interpretations of human life. One recalls the way in which Thomas Hardy ends his novel *Tess of the D'Urbervilles*, when his heroine, Tess, has been executed for murder:

> 'Justice' was done, and the President of the Immortals, in Aeschylean phrase, had ended his sport with Tess.

In spite of her misdeeds, Tess is 'a pure woman', as the subtitle tells us; she has become the plaything of the malicious forces wielded by Destiny. 'The words are a defiant, despairing cry against the injustice of the universal plan.'[5] Dostoievski, on the other hand, was more interested in the interplay of spiritual forces within the soul of man. In *The Brothers Karamazov* there are tense court scenes concerned with murder; but the confrontation between Christ and the Grand Inquisitor is the most impressive of the ideological clashes.

---

[5] David Cecil, *Hardy the Novelist* (London, 1943, repr. 1969), 101. In his play *Justice* John Galsworthy presents a detailed and forceful case against the oppression of the legal system as it affects the life—and death—of an individual.

A part of Egypt's powerful influence on the concept and imagery of judgement is concerned with the centrality of its symbolism. Weighing the heart is there related to the assessment of actions in the life-record. This does not mean, of course, that other symbols were not in use—in Egypt and elsewhere. In Egypt a concomitant figure of great importance was the goddess Maat. Conceptually and pictorially the adherence to the principle of justice and truth is an essential element; and the feather of Maat is a determining factor in the process. Elsewhere the idea of just compensation for conduct is sometimes expressed through the imagery of bearing fruit, as in Paul's saying:

> Do not be deceived; God is not mocked, for whatever a man sows, that he will also reap.
> (Gal. 6:7.)

The metaphorical use of sowing and harvesting has many ancient parallels, and the compensation referred to may be located in this life or in the judgement after death.[6] Paul may have the Last Judgement in mind especially,[7] but the two meanings may well be combined.

There is also a variety of approach to the mode of interpretation. The posthumous judgement, as portrayed in the *Book of the Dead*, reaches a verdict on the basis of examination, confession, and careful recording. It is all in accordance with Maat. In other contexts, however, the importance of knowledge comes to the fore, as in the *Book of Gates*, where it is vital to know the names of the gatekeepers, who conduct thereby a process of judgement. Such knowledge is, of course, magical, but the importance of knowing in a higher sense is also expressed and it contributes to the experience of confession and repentance as well as to the understanding of punishment.[8] In the Old Testament, too, judgement is sometimes interpreted as going beyond mere compensation, whether by reward or penalty: in purpose it can be disciplinary, purificatory, or revelatory.[9] Nor is it surprising that the New Testament can echo this sense of discipline, using the word *paideia*, as when the writer to the Hebrews delivers the exhortation, '*My son, do not regard lightly the*

---

[6] See Hans Dieter Betz, *Galatians* (Hermeneia; Philadelphia, 1979), 307 ad loc.

[7] Betz, ibid. finds an eschatological reference of the image both in Judaism and in Plutarch. On Paul's belief in an imminent Parousia, followed by a general Resurrection, Judgement, and perfected Kingdom of God, see W.D. Davies, *Paul and Rabbinic Judaism*, 295–8.

[8] Morenz (tr. Keep), *Egyptian Religion*, 122.

[9] Stephen H. Travis, *Christ and the Judgement of God*, 10–11; cf. 17; 24; 27–29 (on Judaism).

discipline of the Lord, nor lose courage when you are punished by him.' (Hebr. 12:5, cf. Prov. 3:11.) By and large, however, the Greeks did not apply the concept of *paideia* to their doctrine of divine retaliation with any thoroughness, although a chorus in Aeschylus (*Ag.* 250 f.) declares that Justice brings wisdom to them that suffer.

Jewish literature also emphasizes precise retribution in the form of the *lex talionis*, and this often means that allusion is made to the records of deeds meticulously preserved and to the weighing of the deeds in a final judgement—the most potent example, as we have urged, of Egyptian influence. Should these allusions be given doctrinal significance? It has been argued[10] that they should not be so treated. Rabbi Judah the Patriarch refers thus to the theme:

> Consider three things and thou wilt not fall into the hands of transgression: know what is above thee—a seeing eye and a hearing ear, and all thy deeds written in a book.
> (Aboth, 2.1, ed. R. Travers Herford, 38–40.)

The mention of the heavenly record book, it is suggested,[11] is merely 'a picturesque device to warn against sin'. One might agree with the suggestion if the mention were something isolated and unparalleled; in fact it is one of a plethora of allusions which constitute a firm doctrine about man's fate after death. Admittedly, it does not amount to 'systematic theology', but this phrase is hardly apposite to the very diverse doctrinal content of Judaism, nor indeed to any other of the ancient religions. Whereas a coming judgement of both nations and individuals[12] is inculcated in Judaism, the verdict based on records of actions seems to apply only to the lives of individuals; in a broad sense, of course, the principle must operate with nations as well.

In the Egyptian prototype the evidence for this belief is found both in detailed textual material and in the massive iconography. It can be argued, it is true, that the pictorial symbolism of the weighing is not essential to the belief. To separate the symbol from what it represents is, however, a hazardous process, especially in the area of the ancient religions. The precision and thoroughness of the assessment are the features displayed by the symbol in this case.[13]

---

[10] E.P. Sanders, *Paul and Palestinian Judaism*, 33–59; cf. Travis, op. cit. 23–24.
[11] Travis, op. cit. 24.
[12] The same is true of the teaching of Jesus, the concern with Israel being clear in Luke 13:1–5 and Matt. 19:28, although E.P. Sanders, *Jesus and Judaism*, 110–119, tries to minimize this element.
[13] Cf. Ugo Bianchi, *The History of Religions* (Leiden, 1975), 133. He refers initially to 'archaic religions', but pursues the theme into the 'classical world'. The

What is very clear in the whole field of divine judgement is the way in which man has attributed to God the human activities through which man seeks to achieve justice. The compensation for good or bad conduct in this life is seen to be implemented in various ways. Rewards and punishments are allocated by the ruling powers of a society, and in the case of punishments are often the result of a court trial. When divine intervention in the lives of individuals is portrayed, the juridical element is not usually prominent, since prosperity is regarded as the reward of virtue and failure as the punishment of sin in a direct correlation. In the lives of nations such a process must evidently be more complex and involves reflection on a long historical span; it is given most attention in the Hebrew and Greek traditions. Both these traditions also reflect the force of the vendetta on a personal and family level. When projected to divine activities, it means that God becomes a vengeful and determined being who pursues even the descendants of the offender. Although its punishments are often condign and irrevocable, posthumous judgement is generally represented in a calmly inquisitorial style. Now the juridical setting is all-important. That is true of the Judaeo-Christian tradition and also of many Greek portrayals, and Egypt provides the prototype. Early Iranian sources give attention rather to the Bridge and to molten metal as the instruments of judgement.

For the most part, the doctrine of punishment is squarely based on the principle of retribution. If it is spelled out most clearly in the Hebrew *lex talionis*, it is stated or implied in all the ancient religions. It appears in the *Iliad* (18.309) in a saying about Ares: *Impartial is Enyalios (Ares), and he kills him who kills.* This would seem to rebut the statement of H.J. Rose[14] that in the Augustan cult of Mars Ultor the Italian Mars 'was capable of embodying the idea of righteous vengeance, while Ares is little more than a divine swashbuckler'. Indeed Simone Weil[15] finds here a principle of 'the justice of retaliation' and an anticipation of the Gospel saying (Matt. 26:52) that all who take the sword will perish by the sword (cf. Rev. 13:10). Yet Ares in Homer does not normally assume the role of just retaliator, and Rose is right in this. In the line quoted from the *Iliad* he is probably treated as a personification of war.[16]

Egyptian 'Declarations of Innocence' amount to a detailed code of conduct which cannot well be correlated to the symbol.

[14] *A Handbook of Greek Mythology* (5th Ed., London, 1953), 157.

[15] *Intimations of Christianity among the Ancient Greeks* (from a work which she entitles *La Source Grecque*), 34.

[16] Cf. Otto Kern, *Die Religion der Griechen*, I (Berlin, 1926), 120.

In the wider spectrum there is some variety of emphasis, it is true, when the divine role is considered. Outside the Vedic tradition the doctrine of *karma* in India is often divorced from belief in a personal God, becoming rather an impersonal law which ensures the punishment of sin either in the present life or in a future reincarnation.[17] The other systems rest the retribution on the sanction of deities who are either wrathful in their pursuit of the sinner or at least inexorable in their implementation of justice. Whether the doctrine of *karma* is fatalistic and deterministic in essence has been the subject of debate. Deterministic it certainly is, but in theory it is the person himself that determines his own fate. From this point of view it is not in the category of divine judgement, but one might compare instances in the Old Testament where man is regarded as bringing judgement upon himself through the effecting of the in-built results of his actions. While the later 'theistic Upanishads' assign the operation of *karma* to divine control,[18] the traditions of both Buddhism and Jainism reject this idea.

A vital element in all forms of the system is the belief in the transmigration of souls. Judgement on the basis of the life-record, according to this belief, cannot be confined to the course of a single life; it must apply to a whole series of lives. Jainist doctrine sees the soul moving, immediately after the death of one body, into a new embryo within a single moment, the identity and nature of the embryo, which may be in animal form, depending on the record of previous lives. Such a prospect is admitted to produce sometimes an attitude of despair. The system claims a possible means of release, however, in the concept of *moksha*, 'liberation'. In the teaching of Mahayana Buddhism this can be achieved only after rigorous self-discipline, but it leads to a blissful *nirvana*. As a means of salvation this teaching has few affinities elsewhere, since *nirvana*, however exalted an ideal, implies the extinction of personality.[19]

A problem with the early Chinese literature is the lack, for the most part, of a clearly defined concept of divinity. Confucius in his *Analects* often talks of Heaven, but refrains from giving it a sense of personal godhead, not even when he says *Heaven is the author of the virtue that is in me*. Yet he wants to show reverence to *the gods and*

---

[17] Cf. Edwyn Bevan, *Symbolism and Belief* (London, 1938), 245.

[18] See 'Karma and God' in T.P. Day, *The Conception of Punishment in Early Indian Literature* (1982), 77 ff.

[19] Cf. A.T. Hanson, *The Wrath of the Lamb*, 221, who contrasts the system with 'faith in Christ as salvation from wrath.' Hans Küng, *On being a Christian* (1978), 94, is more sympathetic, finding that in Mahayana Buddhism *nirvana* 'acquires a positively theological content and is identical with the Absolute and happiness.'

spirits and he laudably puts service *before the reward you get for it*. To him disease and death are decided by Destiny and have no moral causation. Heaven maintains the cosmic order and doubtless a moral order too, although there is no suggestion of heavenly intervention by way of rewards and punishments in this life, not to mention an afterlife.

A different view was taken by Mo Tzu, probably a little later than Confucius. He enunciated a doctrine of the Will of Heaven and of universal love. The former doctrine impelled him to support the idea of divine intervention in human affairs, with the regular rewarding of virtue and punishing of evil, mainly in this world. He cites cases of premature death due to blasphemy and evil-doing. To him Heaven takes on the character of a personal god. That is not true of Lao Tzu and his famous classic *Tao Te Ching*, where the Way, *Tao*, is expounded as something which is in harmony with the divine principle behind the cosmic creation. Failure to live in the spirit of this harmony brings unhappiness, for the Way of Heaven, although viewed as an impersonal power, intervenes in the life of man and *is for ever on the side of the good man*. While conventional morality is sometimes challenged, the ethical emphasis is often impressive, as in the precept *Do good to him who has done you an injury*. A principle several times presented is that good conduct brings happy results in this life.

Another adherent of Taoism, Chuang-tzu, refers to Heaven as *the maker of things* and talks in one place of its action of recompense to man; yet what is being recompensed, it is added, is *not the man but what is from Heaven in the man*. On the whole Chuang-tzu seems not to be much concerned with the details of recompense, although one poem ascribed to him extends felicitation to the believer who *knows the joy from Heaven* since *there is no wrath from Heaven, no blame from man* and also *no retribution from ghosts*. In some historical writing, on the other hand, from the third century B.C. the idea of retribution plays a part in episodes which feature avenging ghosts.

The Iranian contribution has several distinctive features. Ahura Mazda was regarded as the arbiter of rewards and punishments, acting through his chosen spirit of truth, Asha. This applies to the present life, but in several instances the allusions to judgement are equivocal in that they can refer equally, if not exclusively, to judgement after death. Nor is this surprising when we remember that the major impetus of Zoroastrianism was in the direction of eschatology. After death a judgement of the individual was believed to be enacted at the 'Bridge of the Separator', the Bridge itself being a means of test or ordeal; fire and molten metal are other methods of ordeal. It is only in the later Pahlavi sources (from c. A.D. 600) that a weighing in a balance is said to occur at the Bridge. Iran's most distinctive and influential contribution was without doubt the doctrine concerning a Last Judgement coinciding with the end of the world and of time. Its thousand-year sequences and cosmic scope have force and grandeur, and its impact on Judaism and Christianity is very clear, even if the detailed symbolism of the judgement of the individual owes more to Egypt.

Judaism, at the same time, developed its own emphases within this setting. One was the special role of the Messiah, allied to the concept of an impending 'Day of Yahweh' which was prominent already in the eighth century B.C., as in the Book of Amos. The Davidic Messiah was given the role of judge, and the Psalms of Solomon in the first century B.C. see him in this role after his triumphant restoration of freedom to Israel. *One like a Son of Man* in Daniel 7:13 is a Messianic figure, although symbolic of the people of Israel rather than a personal Messiah; there he approaches the *Ancient of Days* in the scene of judgement and is awarded dominion and glory by him. The son of David, according to the Psalms of Solomon, *will judge peoples and nations in the wisdom of his righteousness*; and that is another highly distinctive feature of the tradition of Judaism. The Final Judgement will deal with nations rather than individuals. This feature again arises from Israel's ancient experience, for at the heart of her religion is the sense of dedicated nationhood based on the covenant between God and Israel.

The evidence for Christian ideology is quite varied. Whereas the Gospel of John voices the belief that Jesus in his coming was himself enacting a process of judgement by judging and being judged, the Synoptic Gospels give more attention to a final reckoning at the end of time associated with his Second Coming. They also supply details, though, on his interpretation of events in the present life and within history. The woes pronounced by him on the little towns of Galilee relate to *the day of judgement*, but with a fate worse than that of Sodom—a fate realized in history. Several sayings are concerned with rewards and punishments here and now and they firmly reject any idea that conduct should be based on such considerations. There is always a divine reward, but it is beyond this world, and is freely promised and given. In line with this attitude is the rejection by Jesus of any attempt to see God's judgement being enacted in recent tragic events in Jerusalem. His reported prophecies of the fall of Jerusalem as an act of God's condemnation raise some problems. The precise details of certain sayings suggest later embellishment, but there is an authentic nucleus which is fully in keeping with Israel's prophetic tradition. An element of judgement is present in accounts of the sacraments, especially the eucharist. Jesus provides a touch of eschatology in the words *until that day when I drink it new in the Kingdom of God* (Mark 14:25). It is Paul who stresses this element in the sense of present condemnation, maintaining that unworthy participation has sometimes resulted in death and disease. In his writings the theme of the wrath of God is prominent; and accounts of the cleansing of the Temple by Jesus, although they do not use the term, include sayings which are suffused with righteous indignation.

The idea of judgement after death is dramatically presented in the Book of Revelation, where Jesus appears as the warrior-judge. The Pauline writings are also much concerned with it, but with a great deal more spiritual discernment. In Paul's view *the day of wrath* will offer *eternal life* as the reward for good works, while the disobedient and evil will face as a penalty *wrath and fury, tribulation and distress*. Elsewhere Paul emphasizes his belief in justification by faith and *not by the works of the law*; but *works* here has a specialized sense. Justification refers to the initial saving grace conferred through identity with Christ in his death and resurrection; the grace thus bestowed in salvation will continue in its saving power, but an assessment of the life-record will nevertheless be part of the final reckoning. Kümmel[20] phrases it thus: 'there can be no doubt that Paul anticipates the divine judgement upon men on the basis of their deeds and does not except Christians from this expectation.'

A feature of the sayings of Jesus in the Synoptic Gospels is the full acceptance of the contemporary belief in Gehenna as a place of the eternal torment of the damned. If symbolism is the key to the meaning, annihilation of soul and body remains a possibility, and that is above all to be feared. The reward in Heaven is depicted in the story of Dives and Lazarus, but the Kingdom of Heaven is more often described, mainly in parables. For Jesus the judgement at the end of time will include a Jewish national dimension. When he says that the Son of man will come in his glory, it is possible that he is thinking of the Son of man as a figure representing Israel. Further, *all the nations* will be gathered before him. But this concept is not apparently persisted with. When the King welcomes the blessed of his Father, it is for their acts of kindness and mercy *to one*

---

[20] *Theology of the New Testament*, 229.

of the least of these that he praises them, and in so doing the King identifies himself with the lowly sufferers.

It is the criterion of compassion, then, that counts in the end. The idea is not new, for it appears in Egypt in the third millennium B.C. in funerary sayings assigned to certain dignitaries. Looking ahead to the judgement of the Great God, they claim that they have given food to the hungry and clothes to the naked. (See above p. 216.) The Gospel scene is, of course, far more impressive in its spiritual scope and depth, and it adds the exquisite stress on the humility of the Royal Judge, for the King in his glory is at one with the least of his needy brethren.

Yet it must be admitted that the depiction of the Last Judgement in Christian art is not always calculated to uplift or edify. So often is it devoted to the fire of Hell and the torturing of sinners. The artistic motifs vary, it is true, and in the earliest examples, from the third to the fifth centuries, preference is given to Christ the Judge shown as a shepherd (Matt. 25:32–33).[21] From the eleventh century onwards representations become much more frequent and the archangel Michael often assumes the role of supervisor. Angels blowing trombones are a pleasing feature, but the special attention given to the never-resting Worm and the miseries of Hell is depressing. In his splendid painting on the west wall of the Sistine Chapel Michelangelo shows the nations gathered before Christ the Judge; his Christ is refreshingly naturalistic with no outward symbols of pomp and power, while the Lord's mother, seated on his right, looks perhaps too young for the role. Meditating on this masterpiece, Hans Küng[22] asks, 'just *what* could *still be relevant* today in such a mythologically depicted assembly of all nations for judgment?' Relevant still, he suggests, is the thought that 'I cannot, in the last resort, judge myself, nor can I leave this judgement to any other human tribunal.' More positively, he suggests that 'only in the encounter with the manifest ultimate reality of God will my life acquire its full meaning, will the history of mankind become transparent, will the individual and human society reach their true fulfillment.'

Even this serene and cautious statement seems to overlook one consideration—the fate of the vast number of the damned, many of them, according to some interpreters, predestined to be damned.

---

[21] See Desanka Milošević, *The Last Judgment* (Vaduz, 1964), 10–13; cf. Brandon, *Judgment of the Dead*, 123–35 and the many illustrations in L. Kretzenbacher, *Die Seelenwaage* (1958).

[22] Op. cit. 394.

Hans Küng (p. 395) reminds us that whereas the New Testament accounts of judgement divide mankind into two categories, the saved and the damned, yet there are statements which suggest 'that there will be mercy for all.' He refers to Paul's claim (Rom. 5:18) that *as one man's trespass led to condemnation for all men, so one man's act of righteousness leads to acquittal and life for all men.*[23] Paul's teaching, however, makes the wide offer dependent on repentance and faith; it also calls for a right relationship to God and views damnation as extinction rather than eternal torment. To him it is not retribution, but the rejection of divine grace that brings condemnation.

Greek religion contained a rich ideology relating to the divine control of human life. The early poets and playwrights had strong convictions on this matter, particularly the conviction that the gods were sure to penalize excessive pride in wealth and power. Perhaps it is Aeschylus who conveys this belief most memorably, applying it to both nation and individual. Not always was religion invoked to justify the idea. Thus Heraclitus said that arrogance was more to be extinguished than a conflagration; he also said that a man's character is his daemon, suggesting that his fate is decided by what he is. In the philosopher's thought, in spite of this, God has an important place, and Zeus for many Greeks was the just arbiter who maintained a moral order. By the end of the fifth century traditional religious beliefs were being challenged. Whereas Herodotus devoutly applied to his interpretations of history a scheme of divine rewards and punishments (especially the latter), Thucydides refrained from this, although certain strong moral implications are implied by some of his comments too, as in his condemnation of imperial greed and cruelty. In eschatology, on the other hand, the Greeks were at first rather barren of confident convictions. In time they tended to abandon Hades for the more cheerful Elysium, and with that a pattern of posthumous judgement. These ideas probably came ultimately from Egypt, but Crete seems to have acted as the transmitting agency.

A plain prerequisite of a belief in judgement after death is the conviction that there is an assured immortality. In early Israel this was notably absent, even if Sheol offered some kind of continued existence. No ancient culture surpassed Israel in the attempt to make moral sense of this life, and the 'Deuteronomic History'

---

[23] He also cites 1 Cor. 15:24–28 and 1 Peter 4:6. See too Rom. 11:32: *For God has consigned all men to disobedience, that he may have mercy upon all*; and other texts cited by Travis, *Christ and the Judgment of God*, 65, who rightly observes that Paul also calls for faith in those seeking salvation.

pursues the idea of a covenantal give-and-take in a fairly rigid sense. The writings of the prophets show a keen appreciation of the providential shaping of history. Nor was this concern confined by them to Israel. The prophets Amos and Isaiah achieved a vision of God's universal solicitude; so did the writer of the Book of Jonah, although his narrative lacks historicity. As for judgement after death, Proverbs and the Book of Job show some clear signs of accepting this idea. Indeed the Book of Job stands out for its double achievement in relation to our theme: it provides the most searching analysis of the validity or otherwise of a divine moral order in the present life; at the same time, in certain sections, it looks forward to a complete vindication of God's purpose in a judgement after death.

In the world of the Mystery Religions of Isis, Demeter, Mithras, and Dionysus, an element of judgement is certainly present, albeit with varying prominence. We are told in the Homeric Hymn to Demeter that *on the unjust vengeance shall for ever fall*, and there are vase-paintings connected with Eleusis which depict evil-doers being punished. The account of the Isiac initiation portrayed by Apuleius outlines a sequence which conveys confession, judgement, and forgiveness. Since the experience also includes a spiritual death and rebirth, it seems that an eschatological pattern is now being transferred to a present experience.

The rigid pursuit of justice has some moral force, and the retributive theory of punishment has gained respectable support among philosophers, being upheld by Kant, Hegel, and F.H. Bradley.[24] Indeed retribution is itself a respectable word, but the respect for justice suggested by it may invite the objection that it is 'elegant draping for naked revenge'.[25] Punishment may serve other ends, such as deterring other potential offenders or reforming persons who have already offended. In the context of divine judgement after death it is only in the concept of Purgatory that a reforming motive is possible. An anticipation of this concept appeared in Egypt, but it probably originated among the Greeks.

Perhaps the most affecting, and certainly the most intensely anguished, ancient writings on these and related themes are those which question the validity of the divine order and its claim to hold sway over human life. From time to time even the most committed

---

[24] See Edmund L. Pincoffs, *The Rationale of Legal Punishment* (New York, 1966), 1–16. Essays by them are included in Gertrude Ezorsky, *Philosophical Perspectives on Punishment* (New York, 1972, repr. 1977).

[25] Pincoffs, op. cit. 16.

of pious minds have failed to convince themselves that life makes moral sense. The failure may be a fleeting phase, but its despairing depths have an enduring appeal. When the crucified Christ feared for a moment that God had forsaken him, his words—*Eli, Eli, lama sabachthani?* (Matt. 27:46)—were a quotation from the Psalms (22:1), but they expressed none the less a personal experience. In the Old Testament attempts are sometimes made to face the problems raised by the sufferings of the righteous and the prosperity of the wicked. Intellectually and poetically the theodicy of the Book of Job is the finest example; several Babylonian writings are impressive attempts to deal with the same theme; nor is Egyptian literature without its searing scepticism concerning the traditional faith.

Theologians have naturally continued the debate in the modern world. The Holocaust and other human disasters in the twentieth century have troubled both Jewish and Christian writers who are concerned with the question of God's judgement and control of history. Never has man's evil been so evident as in a century which has witnessed the enormities of Belsen and Buchenwald, Hiroshima and Dresden. If God is omniscient, omnipotent and benevolent, his relation to such events cannot easily be explained. Ernest Becker[26] has urged that 'something entirely different had to be done to explain evil in the world, a theodicy without divine intervention.' In that case it is no longer theodicy, and Becker rightly goes on to use the word 'anthropodicy'. It could apply to man's nuclear death.

It is a feature of several of the ancient religions which have concerned us that the belief in divine judgement was not confined to the interpretation of the present life, although it certainly began thus. A judgement after death provided a final settling of the account. A parallel approach appears in some facets of the modern debate on theodicy. Pointing to Augustinian theodicy as one which emphasized the Fall of man and explained suffering as a divine punishment for sin, John Hick[27] prefers what he calls the Irenaean view (after the second-century theologian Irenaeus of Lyons) which looks to the future: 'it is eschatological, centring on the belief that in the end good will be triumphantly brought out of evil.' The world becomes, in this way, 'a place of soul-making'. Fulfilment rather than judgement is therefore implied in the final phase. It is rather like the initial belief of Ivan Karamazov when he says that he

---

[26] *The Structure of Evil* (New York, 1976), 18, quoted by Kenneth Surin in *Harv. Theol. Rev.* 76 (1983), 228.
[27] *The Centre of Christianity* (London, 1977), 83; and more fully in his *Evil and the God of Love* (Glasgow, 1968).

believes in *the underlying order and meaning of life*; and also *I believe in the eternal harmony into which we are all supposed to merge one day.*[28]

A little later, however, Ivan avers that there are types of suffering which do not fit the serene belief he has outlined. The sufferings of children are dwelt on; he instances the case of a retired army general whose favourite hound was slightly injured by a stone thrown by a boy of eight; the following day, in front of the boy's mother, he fed the boy to his whole pack of hounds. Ivan goes on to tell his brother Alyosha that he cannot accept this world of God's; and that *if all have to suffer so as to buy eternal harmony by their suffering, what have the children to do with it?* He also says[29]

> I must have retribution or I shall destroy myself. And retribution not somewhere in the infinity of space and time, but here on earth, and so that I could see it myself.

The call for retribution is, of course, itself morally objectionable since it implies repeating the crime. Doubtless it is an instinctive call. We are told that the general, in fact, was deprived of the right to administer his estates, but that does not meet Ivan's reaction. According to John Hick,[30] 'if there is any eventual resolution of the interplay between good and evil, any decisive bringing of good out of evil, it must lie beyond this world and beyond the enigma of death.' Ivan's 'moral atheism' is not countered thus, and the principle of a God who suffers with his creatures is ethically preferable.[31] In the cross of Christ, according to Moltmann, God offers a self-revelation and self-justification; for there 'judgement and damnation are taken up by God himself, so that man may live.'[32]

---

[28] Dostoievsky, *The Brothers Karamazov*, tr. D. Magarshak, 275. Cf. the discussion by Kenneth Surin, op. cit. 236 ff.
[29] Ibid. p. 285.
[30] *Evil and the God of Love*, 375; cf. Surin, op. cit. 239.
[31] Surin, ibid. develops this theme in relation to a 'theology of the cross': 'Only a suffering God can help' (p. 241). See also his book, *Theology and the Problem of Evil* (Blackwell, Oxford, 1986), esp. 142–3. Cf. the views of J. Moltmann, D. Soelle, and P.T. Forsyth as expounded by him.
[32] Jürgen Moltmann, *Hope and Planning* (New York, 1971), 43.

BIBLIOGRAPHY: SECTIONAL AND SELECT

Note: A person referred to as an Editor of a volume or series may also be a Contributor to it.

I. General

Armstrong, A.H. (ed.) *Classical Mediterranean Spirituality: Egyptian, Greek, Roman.* Vol. 15 of *World Spirituality*. New York, 1986.
Bertholet, Alfred, rev. Kurt Goldammer. *Wörterbuch der Religionen.* 3rd Ed., Stuttgart, 1976.
Beyerlin, Walter. (ed.; tr. John Bowden) *Near Eastern Religious Texts Relating to the Old Testament.* London, 1978.
Bianchi, Ugo. *The History of Religions.* Leiden, 1975.
Bleeker, C.J. (ed.) *Initiation.* Leiden, 1965.
Brandon, S.G.F. (ed.) *A Dictionary of Comparative Religion.* London, 1970.
——.*The Judgment of the Dead.* London, 1967.
——.(ed.) *The Saviour God.* (for E.O. James). Manchester, 1963.
Brunner-Traut, Emma. (ed.) *Die fünf großen Weltreligionen.* Freiburg, 1974, repr. 1977.
Douglas, Mary. *Purity and Danger.* London, 1966, repr. 1979.
Eliade, Mircea. (ed.) *The Encyclopedia of Religion.* 16 Vols. New York, 1987.
——.*Myth and Reality.* London, 1964.
——.*Rites and Symbols of Initiation.* 1958, repr. New York, 1965.
——.*The Sacred and the Profane.* New York, 1959.
Evans-Pritchard, E.E. *Theories of Primitive Religion.* Oxford, 1965, repr. 1972.
Glasenapp, Helmuth von. *Die nichtchristlichen Religionen.* Frankfurt am Main, 1957.
Goedicke, Hans, and J.J.M. Roberts. (ed.) *Unity and Diversity.* Essays in the History, Literature, and Religion of the Ancient Near East. The Johns Hopkins Near Eastern Studies. Baltimore, 1975.
Goldammer, Kurt. *Die Formenwelt des Religiösen.* Stuttgart, 1960.
——.v. Bertholet, Alfred.
Griffiths, D.R. (in) *Cerddi Cadwgan.* Swansea, 1953.
Hardy, Thomas. *Tess of the D'Urbervilles.* London, 1891, often repr.
Hellholm, David. (ed.) *Apocalypticism in the Mediterranean World and the Near East.* Tübingen, 1983.
Hinnells, John R. (ed.) *Dictionary of Religions.* Harmondsworth, 1984.
——.*A Handbook of Living Religions.* Harmondsworth, 1985.
Kitagawa, J.M. and C.H. Long. (ed.) *Myths and Symbols* (for Mircea Eliade). Chicago, 1969.
Kleist, Heinrich von. (ed. John Gearey) *Michael Kohlhaas.* First publ. 1810; New York, 1967. Cf. tr. by David Luke and Nigel Reeves in *The Marquise of O- and Other Stories,* Harmondsworth, 1978, 114–213.
Kolakowski, Leszek. *Religion.* Fontana Masterguides. Glasgow, 1982.
Kramer, Samuel Noah. (ed.) *Mythologies of the Ancient World.* New York, 1961.
Lanczkowski, Günter. *Begegnung und Wandel der Religionen.* Düsseldorf, 1971.
——.*Geschichte der Religionen.* Frankfurt am Main, 1972, repr. 1975.
Leeuw, G. van der. (tr. J.E. Turner) *Religion in Essence and Manifestation.* London, 1938, 2nd Ed., 1964.
Lévi-Strauss, Claude. (tr. Rodney Needham) *Totemism.* London, 1964.
Ling, Trevor. *A History of Religion East and West.* London, 1968.
Long, C.H. v. Kitagawa, J.M.
Merkelbach, Reinhold. *Roman und Mysterium in der Antike.* Munich, 1962.

Needham, Rodney. *Belief, Language, and Experience*. Oxford, 1972.
——.*Primordial Characters*. Charlottesville, 1978.
——.*Reconnaissances*. Toronto, 1980.
——.(ed.) *Right and Left*. Chicago, 1973.
Nock, Arthur Darby. *Essays on Religion and the Ancient World*. 2 Vols. ed. Zeph Stewart. Oxford, 1972.
Nottarp, Hermann. *Gottesurteilstudien*. Bamberger Abh., 11. Munich, 1956.
Parrinder, Geoffrey. (ed.) *Man and his Gods*. London, 1971.
——.*Worship in the World's Religions*. London, 1961, 2nd Ed., 1974.
Peake, A.S., rev. Matthew Black and H.H. Rowley (ed.) *A Commentary on the Bible*. New Ed. London, 1962, repr. 1981.
Pettazzoni, Raffaele. (tr. E.A. Voretzsch). *Der allwissende Gott*. Frankfurt am Main, 1960.
Pettinato, G. 'Die Bestrafung des Menschengeschlechts durch die Sintflut', *Orientalia* 37 (1968), 165–200.
Pritchard, James B. (ed.) *Ancient Near Eastern Texts Relating to the Old Testament*. 3rd Ed. with Supplement. Princeton, 1969.
Ringgren, Helmer. *Religions of the Ancient Near East*. London, 1973.
——. 'Judgment of the Dead', *Encycl. of Religion*, ed. Eliade, Vol. 8, 205–8. 1987.
Roberts, J.J.M. v. Goedicke, Hans.
Robertson, Roland. *Sociology of Religion*. Selected Readings. Harmondsworth, 1969, repr. 1971.
Röllig, Wolfgang. (ed.) *Altorientalische Literaturen*. Neues Handbuch der Literaturwissenschaft, ed. Klaus von See, Bd. 1. Wiesbaden, 1978.
Schedl, Claus. *Muhammed und Jesus*. Vienna, 1978.
Sebeok, Thomas A. (ed.) *Myth. A Symposium*. 1955, repr. Bloomington, 1965.
Silz, Walter. *Heinrich von Kleist*. Philadelphia, 1961.
Smart, Ninian. *The Philosophy of Religion*. New York, 1970.
——. *The Religious Experience of Mankind*. 1969, repr. Glasgow, 1971.
Stietencron, H. von. (ed.) *Der Name Gottes*. Düsseldorf, 1976.
Thomas, D. Winton. (ed.) *Documents from Old Testament Times*. London, 1958.
Thouless, Robert H. *An Introduction to the Psychology of Religion*.
Turchi, Nicolaus. *Fontes Historiae Mysteriorum Aevi Hellenistici*. Rome, 1930.
Wach, Joachim. (ed. J.M. Kitagawa) *The Comparative Study of Religions*. New York, 1958, repr. 1961.
——. *Sociology of Religion*. Chicago, 1944, repr. 1962.
Weber, Max. (tr. Ephraim Fischoff) *The Sociology of Religion*. German original 1922, 4th Ed., 1956, tr. 1965. repr. London, 1966.
Weil, Simone. (tr. E. Craufurd) *Waiting on God*. London, 1951, repr. 1974.
Whitehead, A.N. *Religion in the Making*. Cambridge, 1927.
Wollaston, Arthur N. *Muhammad: His Life and Doctrines*. London, 1904.
Yoyotte, Jean, et al. *Le Jugement des Morts*. Sources Orientales, 4. Paris, 1961.
Zaehner, R.C. (ed.) *The Concise Encyclopedia of Living Faiths*. 2nd Ed., London, 1971, repr. 1983.

II. *Israel and Judaism*

Ackroyd, Peter. 'The Jewish community in Palestine in the Persian period', *CHJ* I (1984), 130–61.
Albrektson, Bertil. *History and the Gods*. An Essay on the Idea of Historical Events as Divine Manifestations in the Ancient Near East and in Israel. Coniectanea Biblica, Old Testament Series, 1. Lund, 1967.
Amsler, S. 'Le thème du procès chez les prophètes d'Israel', *Revue de Theologie et de Philosophie* 111 (1974), 116–31.
Baker, A.E. *Prophets for a Day of Judgment*. London, 1945.
Barr, James. 'The Book of Job and its Modern Interpreters', *Bull. Ryl.* 54 (1971), 28–46.

——. 'Daniel', *Peake's Comm. on the Bible*, 591–602. 1962, repr. 1981.
——. *Fundamentalism*. 2nd Ed., London, 1981.
——. 'Jewish Apocalyptic in Recent Scholarly Study', *Bull. Ryl.* 58 (1975), 9–35.
Bentzen, Aage. *Daniel*. 2nd Ed., Tübingen, 1952.
——. 'The Ritual Background of Amos 1.2–2.6'. *Oudtestamentische Studiën* 8 (1950), 85–99.
Bickerman, Elias J. 'The Babylonian Captivity', *CHJ* I (1984), 342–57.
Black, Matthew. *The Book of Enoch or 1 Enoch*. A New English Edition with Commentary and Textual Notes. Studia in Veteris Testamenti Pseudepigrapha, 7. Leiden, 1985.
——. 'The Development of Judaism in the Greek and Roman Periods (c. 196 B.C.–A.D. 135)', *Peake's Comm. on the Bible*, New Ed., 1962, repr. 1981, 693–8.
——. *The Scrolls and Christian Origins*. London, 1961.
Blackman, Aylward M. 'The Psalms in the light of Egyptian research', *The Psalmists* ed. D.C. Simpson, 177–97. London, 1926.
Briggs, C.A. and E.G. *The Psalms*. ICC. Edinburgh, 1906.
Bright, John. *Jeremiah*. New York, 1965.
Brock, S.P. 'The Psalms of Solomon', *The Apocryphal Old Testament*, ed. H.F.D. Sparks, Oxford, 1984.
Brown, F., with S.R. Driver and C.A. Brigg. *A Hebrew and English Lexicon of the Old Testament*. (= BDB).
Bryce, Glendon E. *The Legacy of Wisdom*. The Egyptian Contribution to the Wisdom of Israel. London, 1979.
Buber, Martin. 'The Heart Determines: Psalm 73', *Theodicy in the Old Testament*, ed. J.L. Crenshaw, 109–118. London, 1983 (first publ. 1968).
Caquot, André, and Maurice Sznycer. *Ugaritic Religion*. Iconography of Religions, 15.8. Leiden, 1980.
Carmignac, Jean. 'Description du phénomène d'Apocalyptique dans l'Ancien Testament', *Apocalypticism etc.* ed. D. Hellholm, 163–70. Tübingen, 1983.
Cazelles, Henri. 'Le Jugement des Morts en Israël', *Le Jugement des Morts*, Sources Orientales, 4, 105–42. Paris, 1961.
Charles, R.H. *A Critical History of the Doctrine of a Future Life*. 2nd Ed., London, 1913.
Charlesworth, James H. (ed.) *The Old Testament Pseudepigrapha*. 2 Vols. London, 1983; 1985.
——. 'Treatise of Shem (First Century B.C.)', ibid. I, 473–86.
Christiansen, Irmgard. *Die Technik der allegorischen Auslegungswissenschaft bei Philon von Alexandrien*. Tübingen, 1969.
Clements, R.E. *Prophecy and Tradition*. Oxford, 1975.
Collins, John J. *Between Athens and Jerusalem*. Jewish Identity in the Hellenistic Diaspora. New York, 1983.
——. 'The Genre Apocalypse in Hellenistic Judaism', *Apocalypticism etc.* ed. D. Hellholm, 531–48. Tübingen, 1983.
——. 'Sibylline Oracles', *The Old Testament Pseudepigrapha*, ed. J.H. Charlesworth, I, 317–472. London, 1983.
Crenshaw, James L. *Old Testament Wisdom. An Introduction*. London, 1982.
——. 'The Problem of Theodicy in Sirach: On Human Bondage', *Theodicy in the Old Testament*, ed. J.L. Crenshaw, 119–40. London, 1983 (first publ. 1975).
——. 'The Shift from Theodicy to Anthropodicy', ibid. 1–16.
——. (ed.) *Theodicy in the Old Testament*. Issues in Religion and Theology, 4. London, 1983.
Crowfoot, J.W. and Grace. *Early Ivories from Samaria*. London, 1938.
Danby, H. (tr.) *The Mishnah*. Oxford, 1933.
Daube, David. *Ancient Hebrew Fables*. Inaugural Lecture. Oxford, 1973.
Daumas, François. (ed.) *Philo, De vita contemplativa*. Paris, 1963.

Davies, William David. 'The Jewish State in the Hellenistic World', *Peake's Comm. on the Bible*, 686–92. 1962, repr. 1981.
——. 'A Note on Josephus, *Antiquities*, 15:136', *Harv. Theol. Rev.* 47 (1954), 135–40.
——. 'Reflections about the use of the Old Testament in the New in its historical Context', *The Jewish Quarterly Review* 74 (1983), 105–36.
——. *Torah in the Messianic Age and / or the Age to Come*. Soc. of Biblical Lit., Monograph 7. Philadelphia, 1952.
——. and Louis Finkelstein. (ed.) *The Cambridge History of Judaism. (CHJ)* Vol. I. Cambridge, 1984.
Delcor, Mathias. *Le Testament d'Abraham*. Studia in Veteris Testamenti Pseudepigrapha, 2. Leiden, 1973.
Dhorme, E. Paul. *Job*. Paris, 1926. See also English tr., London, 1966.
Driver, S.R. and G.B. Gray. *Job*. ICC. Edinburgh, 1921.
Duhm, Bernhard. *Job*. Freiburg, 1897.
Eichrodt, Walther. (tr. L.L. Welborn) 'Faith in Providence and Theodicy in the Old Testament', *Theodicy in the Old Testament*, ed. J.L. Crenshaw, 17–41. London, 1983 (first publ. 1934).
——. (tr. J.A. Baker) *Theology of the Old Testament*. I. Philadelphia, 1961.
Eissfeldt, Otto. (tr. Peter R. Ackroyd) *The Old Testament. An Introduction*. Oxford, 1965, repr. 1974.
Emerton, J.A. (ed.) *Studies in the Historical Books of the Old Testament*. SVT 30. Leiden, 1979.
Finkelstein, Louis. v. Davies, W.D.
Fohrer, Georg. *Hebräisches und aramäisches Wörterbuch zum Alten Testament*.
Freud, Sigmund. *Der Mann Moses und die monotheistische Religion*. Frankfurt am Main, 1965.
Frey, P. Jean-Baptiste. *Corpus Inscriptionum Iudaicarum*. 2 Vols. Vatican, 1936; 1952.
Fuks, Alexander. v. Tcherikover, Victor A.
Gaster, Theodor H. *Scriptures of the Dead Sea Sect*. London, 1957.
Gemser, Berend. 'The *Rîb-** or Controversy Pattern in Hebrew Mentality', *Wisdom in Israel and in the Ancient Near East* (Rowley FS.), 120–37. Leiden, 1955.
——. *Sprüche Salomos*. 2nd Ed., Tübingen, 1963.
Gese, Hartmut. (tr. L.L. Grabbe). 'The Crisis of Wisdom in Koheleth', *Theodicy in the Old Testament*, ed. J.L. Crenshaw, 141–53. London, 1983 (first publ. 1963).
——. *Lehre und Wirklichkeit in der alten Weisheit*. Tübingen, 1958.
——. 'Wisdom literature in the Persian period', *CHJ* I (1984), 189–218.
Gilbert, M. (ed.). *La Sagesse de l'Ancient Testament*. Leuven, 1979.
Ginsberg, H.L. 'Ugaritic Myths, Epics, and Legends', *ANET*^{3} 129–55.
Giveon, Raphael. *The Impact of Egypt on Canaan*. OBO 20. Freiburg, Schweiz, 1978.
——. 'Remarks on the Transmission of Egyptian Lists of Asiatic Toponyms', *Fragen an die altägyptische Literatur* (Gedenkschr. E. Otto), ed. Jan Assmann et al., 171–83. Wiesbaden, 1977.
Glasson, T. Francis. *Greek Influence in Jewish Eschatology*. With special reference to the Apocalypses and Pseudepigrapha. London, 1961.
Goldin, Judah. *The Living Talmud: The Wisdom of the Fathers*. Mentor Books. New York, 1957.
Goodenough, Erwin R. *Jewish Symbols in the Greco-Roman Period*. 13 Vols. New York, 1953–1958.
Gordis, Robert. *The Book of God and Man*. Chicago, 1975.
Gordon, Cyrus H. *The Loves and Wars of Baal and Anat*. Princeton, 1943.
——. *Ugaritic Textbook*. Analecta Orientalia, 38. Rome, 1965.
Gray, G.B. *A Critical Introduction to the Old Testament*. London, 1913.
——. v. Driver, S.R.
Gray, John. *I and II Kings*. 3rd Ed., London, 1977.

Gressman, Hugo. *Israel's Spruchweisheit im Zusammenhang der Weltliteratur.* Berlin, 1925.
Griffiths, J. Gwyn. 'Egypt and the Rise of the Synagogue', *JTS* n.s. 38 (1987), 1–15.
——. 'The Egyptian Derivation of the Name Moses', *JNES* 12 (1953), 225–31.
——. 'Tacitus, *Hist.* 5.13.12 and the Dead Sea Scrolls', *Rh. Mus.* 113 (1970), 363–8.
——. 'Tacitus and the *Hodayot* in the Dead Sea Scrolls', ibid. 122 (1979), 99–100.
Gunkel, H. *Die Psalmen.* Göttingen, 1925.
Gutmann, Joseph. *The Jewish Sanctuary.* Iconography of Religions, 23.1. Leiden, 1983.
Habel, Norman G. *The Book of Job.* Cambridge Bible Comm. Cambridge, 1975.
Harnisch, Wolfgang. 'Der Prophet als Widerpart und Zeuge der Offenbarung. Erwägungen zur Interdependenz von Form und Sache im IV. Buch Esra', *Apocalypticism etc.* ed. D. Hellholm, 461–93. Tübingen, 1983.
Heilman, Samuel G. *Synagogue Life.* Chicago, 1976.
Hengel, Martin. (tr. John Bowden) *Judaism and Hellenism.* 2 Vols. London, 1974.
——. *Juden, Griechen und Barbaren.* Stuttgart, 1976.
——. 'Messianische Hoffnung und politischer "Radikalismus" in der "jüdisch-hellenistischen Diaspora"', *Apocalypticism etc.* ed. D. Hellholm, 655–86. Tübingen, 1983.
Herford, R. Travers. *Pirke Aboth: The Ethics of the Talmud: Sayings of the Fathers.* Text, Translation, Commentary. New York, 1945, repr. 1975.
Herrmann, Siegfried. (tr. M. Kohl) *Israel in Egypt.* Studies in Biblical Theology, 27. London, 1973.
Humbert, Paul. *Recherches sur les sources égyptiennes de la littérature sapientiale d'Israel.* Neuchâtel, 1929.
James, M.R. *The Testament of Abraham.* Texts and Studies, II. 2. Cambridge, 1892.
Johnson, Aubrey R. *The Cultic Prophet and Israel's Psalmody.* Cardiff, 1979.
——. *The One and the Many in the Israelite Conception of God.* Cardiff, 1942.
——. 'The Primary Meaning of √גאל', *VTS* 1 (1953), 67–77.
——. *Sacral Kingship in Ancient Israel.* Cardiff, 1955.
——. *The Vitality of the Individual in the Thought of Ancient Israel.* Cardiff, 1949.
Johnson, Sherman E. 'The Dead Sea Manual of Discipline and the Jerusalem Church of Acts', *The Scrolls and the New Testament*, ed. K. Stendahl, 129–42. London, 1958.
Jones, Gwilym H. 'Deng Mlynedd o Astudio'r Proffwydi' (Ten years of Studying the Prophets, 1960–70), *Efrydiau Beiblaidd Bangor* (FS. B.J. Roberts), 44–79. Swansea, 1973.
——. *Diwinyddiaeth Yr Hen Destament.* (Theology of the Old Testament) Cardiff, 1979.
——. *I and II Kings.* 2 Vols. New Century Bible. London, 1985.
Juster, Jean. *Les Juifs dans l'Empire Romain.* New York, 1914.
Keel, Othmar. (tr. T.J. Hallett) *The Symbolism of the Biblical World.* London, 1978.
Kissane, Ed. J. *The Book of Isaiah.* Dublin, 1941.
Kitchen, Kenneth A. *Ancient Orient and Old Testament.* London, 1966.
Koch, Klaus, et al. *Amos.* Alter Orient und Altes Testament, 30.2. Neukirchen-Vluyn, 1976.
——. (tr. T.H. Trapp) 'Is There a Doctrine of Retribution in the Old Testament?', *Theodicy in the Old Testament*, ed. J.L. Crenshaw, 57–87. Cf. id., 'Vergeltung und Sühne usw.' (1972).
——. (tr. M. Kohl). *The Prophets.* I. The Assyrian Period. London, 1982.
——. (tr. M. Kohl). *The Rediscovery of Apocalyptic.* London, 1972, repr. 1981.
——. (ed.) *Um das Prinzip der Vergeltung in Religion und Recht des alten Testaments.* Wege der Forschung, 125. Darmstadt, 1972.
——. 'Vergeltung und Sühne im altisraelitischen Strafrecht', ibid. 236–77.
——. 'Vom profetischen zum apokalyptischen Visionsbericht', *Apocalypticism etc.*

ed. D. Hellholm, 413–46. Tübingen, 1983.
Koehler, L., and W. Baumgartner. *Lexicon in Veteris Testamenti Libros*. 2nd Ed., Leiden, 1958.
Koep, Leo. 'Buch. III', *RAC* II (1954), 717–24.
Kraeling, Emil G. *The Brooklyn Museum Aramaic Papyri*. New Haven, 1953.
Krause, Martin. 'Die literarischen Gattungen der Apokalypsen von Nag Hammadi', *Apocalypticism etc.* ed. D. Hellholm, 621–37. Tübingen, 1983.
Krauss, Samuel. *Synagogale Altertümer*. Berlin, 1922.
Lebram, Jürgen C.H. 'The Piety of the Jewish Apocalyptists', *Apocalypticism etc.* ed. D. Hellholm, 171–210. Tübingen, 1983.
Lieberman, Saul. *Hellenism in Jewish Palestine*. New York, 5722–1962.
Lods, Adolphe. 'The Religion of Israel: Origins', *Record and Revelation* ed. H. Wheeler Robinson, 187–215. Oxford, 1938.
Loffreda, Stanislao. *A Visit to Capharnaum*. 7th Ed., Jerusalem, 1980.
Löhr, Max. Untersuchungen zum Buch Amos. Giessen, 1901.
Malamat, Abraham. 'A Political Look at the Kingdom of David and Solomon and its Relations with Egypt', *Studies in the Period of David and Solomon*, ed. T. Ishida, 189–204. Tokyo, 1982.
——. 'The Twilight of Judah: in the Egyptian-Babylonian Maelstrom', VTS 28, 123–43. Leiden, 1975.
Mars, Leonard. 'What was Onan's Crime?', *Comparative Studies in Society and History* 26 (1984), 429–39.
Marsh, John. *Amos and Micah*. London, 1959.
McKane, William. *Prophets and Wise Men*. London, 1965.
——. *Proverbs: A New Approach*. London, 1970, repr. 1980.
Mayes, A.D.H. *Deuteronomy*. New Century Bible, London, 1979.
Mays, James L. *Amos*. London, 1969.
Morgan, Donn F. *Wisdom in the Old Testament Traditions*. Oxford, 1981.
Mowinckel, Sigmund. (tr. G.W. Anderson) *He that Cometh*. Oxford, 1984.
——. (tr. D.R. Ap-Thomas) *The Psalms in Israel's Worship*. 2 Vols. Oxford, 1962.
Musaph-Andriesse, R.C. (tr. John Bowden) *From Torah to Kabbalah*. London, 1981.
Neusner, Jacob. *The Way of Torah: An Introduction to Judaism*. The Religious Life of Man. 3rd Ed., North Scituate, Mass. 1979.
Nickelsburg, George W.E. 'Social Aspects of Palestinian Jewish Apocalypticism', *Apocalypticism etc.* ed. D. Hellholm, 642–54. Tübingen, 1983.
Nikiprowetzky, Valentin. *La Troisième Sibylle*. Paris, 1970.
Nötscher, F. *Jeremia*. Bonn, 1934.
North, C.R. *Isaiah 40–55*. Torch Comm. London, 1952, repr. 1959.
Noth, Martin. (tr.) *The Deuteronomistic History*. 1943, rev. 1957. Sheffield, 1981.
——. *Exodus*. London, 1962.
Obermann, Julian. *Ugaritic Mythology*. New Haven, 1938.
Oesterley, W.O.E. *The Psalms*. London, 1939, repr. 1962.
——. *The Wisdom of Egypt in the Old Testament*. London, 1927.
——. and Theodore H. Robinson. *Hebrew Religion: Its Origin and Development*. London, 1930, repr. 1966.
Paul, Shalom M. 'Amos 1:2–2:3: A concatenous literary pattern', *Journal of Biblical Lit.* 90 (1971), 397–403.
Peake, A.S. 'Job: The Problem of the Book', *Theodicy in the Old Testament* ed. J.L. Crenshaw, 100–108. London, 1983, (first publ. 1905).
——. for Peake's *Commentary on the Bible* see Section I, 'General'.
Phillips, Anthony. *Deuteronomy*. Cambridge, 1983.
Philonenko, Marc. 'L'apocalyptique qoumranienne', *Apocalypticism etc.* ed. D. Hellholm, 211–18. Tübingen, 1983.
Porten, Bezalel. *Archives from Elephantine*. Berkeley, 1968.
——. 'The Jews in Egypt', *CHJ* I (1984), 372–400.
Porteous, Norman W. *Daniel: A Commentary*. London, 1965.
Power, A.D. *Side Lights on the Book of Proverbs*. London, 1950.

Priest, J. 'Testament of Moses', *The Old Testament Pseudepigrapha*, ed. J.H. Charlesworth, I, 919–34. London, 1983.
Rad, Gerhard von. (tr. A.J. Ehlin) 'The Confessions of Jeremiah', *Theodicy in the Old Testament*, ed. J.L. Crenshaw, 88–99. London, 1983 (first publ. 1936).
——. (tr. J.H. Marks) *Genesis*. London, 1956.
——. *Gesammelte Studien zum Alten Testament*. Munich, 1958.
——. (tr. D.M.G. Stalker) *Old Testament Theology*. Edinburgh, 1961.
Rankin, O.S. *Israel's Wisdom Literature*. Edinburgh, 1954.
Reichert, Victor E. *Job*. Soncino Books of the Bible. Hindhead, Surrey, 1946.
Reventlow, H. Graf. *Das Amt des Propheten bei Amos*. Göttingen, 1962.
Ringgren, Helmer. *Israelite Religion*. London, 1969.
——. *Sprüche / Prediger*. Das Alte Testament Deutsch, 16 / 1. Göttingen, 1962.
Roberts, Bleddyn J. *The Old Testament Text and Versions*. Cardiff, 1951.
——. 'Helenistiaeth ac Iddewiaeth' (Hellenism and Judaism), *Cefndir y Testament Newydd*, ed. J. Gwyn Griffiths, 27–39. Llandysul, 1966.
Robinson, Bernard P. 'Which Book of Daniel?', *New Blackfriars* 66 (1985), 424–37.
Robinson, H. Wheeler. (ed.) *Record and Revelation*. Oxford, 1938.
——. *The Religious Ideas of the Old Testament*. London, 1913, repr. 1930.
Robinson, J. *The Second Book of Kings*. Cambridge, 1976.
Robinson, Theodore H. *The Book of Amos*. Tr. into colloquial English. London, 2nd Ed., n.d.
——. *Prophecy and the Prophets in Ancient Israel*. London, 1923; 3rd Ed., 1979.
——. v. Oesterley, W.O.E.
Rose, Martin. *Deuteronomist und Jahwist*. Zürich, 1981.
Rowley, Harold H. 'The Book of Job and its Meaning', *Bull. Ryl.* 41 (1958), 167–207.
——. *The Faith of Israel*. London, 1956, repr. 1973.
——. *Job*. New Century Bible. London, 1970.
——. *The Relevance of Apocalyptic*. London, 1944.
——. (FS.) *Wisdom in Israel and in the Ancient Near East*. Leiden, 1955.
Russell, D.S. *The Jews from Alexander to Herod*. Oxford, 1967.
——. *The Method and Message of Jewish Apocalyptic*. London, 1971.
Sanders, E.P. 'The Genre of Palestinian Jewish Apocalypses', *Apocalypticism etc.* ed. D. Hellholm, 447–59. Tübingen, 1983.
Sanders, Jack T. *Ben Sira and Demotic Wisdom*. Chicago, 1983.
Scholem, Gershom. 'On Sin and Punishment: Some Remarks concerning Biblical and Rabbinical Ethics', *Myths and Symbols* (FS. M. Eliade), ed. J.M. Kitagawa and C.H. Long, 163–77. Chicago, 1969.
——. *Major Trends in Jewish Mysticism*. London, 1955.
Shaked, Saul. 'Iranian Influence on Judaism: First Century B.C.E. to Second Century C.E.', *CHJ* I (1984), 308–25.
Simon, Marcel. 'Sur quelques aspects des Oracles Sibyllins juifs'. *Apocalypticism etc.* ed. D. Hellholm, 219–33. Tübingen, 1983.
——. *Verus Israel*. 2nd Ed., Paris, 1964.
Simpson, D.C. (ed.) *The Psalmists*. Oxford, 1926.
Smallwood, E. Mary. *The Jews under Roman Rule*. Leiden, 1976.
Smith, Morton. 'Jewish religious life in the Persian period', *CHJ* I (1984), 219–78.
——. *Palestinian Parties and Politics that shaped the Old Testament*. London, 1971.
Soggin, J. Alberto. (tr. John Bowden). *Introduction to the Old Testament*. Revised Ed. London, 1980.
——. *Judges. A Commentary*. London, 1981.
Sparks, H.F.D. (ed.) *The Apocryphal Old Testament*. Oxford, 1984.
Stegemann, Hartmut. 'Die Bedeutung der Qumranfunde für die Erforschung der Apokalyptik', *Apocalypticism etc.* ed. D. Hellholm, 495–530. Tübingen, 1983.
Stein, Edmund. *Die allegorische Exegese des Philo aus Alexandria*. Giessen, 1929.
Stendahl, Krister. (ed.) *The Scrolls and the New Testament*. London, 1958.

Stevenson, W.B. *Critical Notes on the Hebrew Text of the Poem of Job*. Aberdeen, 1951.
Sugden, Edward H. *Israel's Debt to Egypt*. London, 1928.
Sukenik, E.L. *Ancient Synagogues in Palestine and Greece*. Schweich Lectures, 1930. London, 1934.
Szczygiel, Paul. *Job*. Bonn, 1931.
Sznycer, Maurice. v. Caquot, André.
Tcherikover, Victor A., with Alexander Fuks et al. *Corpus Papyrorum Judaicarum*. Vols. I–III. (*CPJ*) Cambridge, Mass, 1957–1964.
Terrien, Samuel. *Job*. Neuchâtel, 1963.
Thompson, John Mark. *The Form and Function of Proverbs in Ancient Israel*. The Hague, 1974.
Vermes, Geza. *The Dead Sea Scrolls in English*. Harmondsworth, 1962, repr. 1966.
Volz, Paul. *Der eschatologische Glaube im Alten Testament*. Stuttgart, 1935.
Vriezen, T.C. *Outline of Old Testament Theology*. Oxford, 1960.
Wanke, Gunther. 'Prophecy and Psalms in the Persian period', *CHJ* I (1984), 162–88.
Weber, Max. (tr. H.H. Gerth and D. Martindale) *Ancient Judaism*. Glencoe, Illinois, 1952.
Weinfeld, Moshe. *Deuteronomy and the Deuteronomic School*, Oxford, 1972, repr. 1983.
Williams, Ronald J. 'Egypt and Israel', *The Legacy of Egypt*, ed. J.R. Harris, 257–90. 2nd Ed., Oxford, 1971.
———. 'Theodicy in the Ancient Near East', *Theodicy in the Old Testament*, ed. J.L. Crenshaw, 42–56. London, 1983 (first publ. 1956).
Winston, David. *Philo of Alexandria*. Classics of Western Spirituality. London, 1981.
Wolff, Hans Walter. *Amos*. Neukirchen-Vluyn, 1967.
Wright, R.B. 'Psalms of Solomon', *The Old Testament Pseudepigrapha*, ed. J.H. Charlesworth, II (1985), 639–70.
Yadin, Yigael. *Masada*. London, 1966.
———. *The Scroll of the War of the Sons of Light against the Sons of Darkness*. Oxford, 1962.

III. The Hittites

Bittel, Kurt. *Hattusha*. New York, 1970.
Furlani, Giuseppe. 'The Basic Aspect of Hittite Religion', *Harv. Theol. Rev.* 31 (1938), 251–62.
———. 'Il giudizio del dio nella dottrina religiosa degli Hittiti', *Rev. Hittite et Asianique* III. 18 (1934), 30–44.
———. *La Religione degli Hittiti*. Bologna, 1936.
Goetze, Albrecht. Translations of Hittite texts, *Ancient Near Eastern Texts Relating to the Old Testament* (ANET) ed. James B. Pritchard. 3rd Ed., Princeton, 1969.
Güterbock, Hans G. 'The Composition of Hittite Prayers to the Sun', *JAOS* 78 (1958), 237–45.
———. 'Hethitische Literatur', *Altorientalische Literaturen*, ed. W. Röllig, 211–53. Wiesbaden, 1978.
———. 'Hittite Mythology', *Mythologies of the Ancient World*, ed. S.N. Kramer, 141–79. New York, 1961.
———. 'Hittite Parallels', *JNES* 33 (1974), 323–7.
———. 'Religion und Kultus der Hethiter', *Neuere Hethiterforschung* ed. G. Walser (Historia Einzelschriften, 7), 54–73. Wiesbaden, 1964.
Gurney, O.R. 'Hittite Prayers of Mursili II', *Liverpool Annals* 27 (1940), 3–163.
———. *The Hittites*. 1952, repr. London, 1975.
———. *Some Aspects of Hittite Religion*. Schweich Lectures, 1976. Oxford, 1977.
Hoffner, Harry A., Jr. 'On the use of Hittite -*za* in nominal sentences', *JNES* 28 (1969), 225–30.
———. 'Propaganda and Political Justification in Hittite Historiography', *Unity and*

Diversity, ed. Hans Goedicke and J.J.M. Roberts, 49–62. Baltimore, 1975.
Kitchen, Kenneth A. *Suppiluliuma and the Amarna Pharaohs*. Liverpool Monographs in Archaeology and Oriental Studies. Liverpool, 1962.
Kühne, Cord. (tr. John Bowden) 'Hittite Texts', *Near Eastern Religious Texts Relating to the Old Testament*, ed. Walter Beyerlin, 146–84. London, 1978.
Kümmel, H.M. *Ersatzrituale für den hethitischen König*. Wiesbaden, 1967.
Malamat, Abraham. 'Doctrines of causality in Hittite and Biblical historiography: a parallel', *VT* 5 (1955), 1–12.
Weidner, Ernst F. *Politische Dokumente aus Kleinasien*. Boghazköi Studien, 8. Leipzig, 1923.

IV. *Mesopotamia*

Albright, W.F. 'The Mari Letters', $ANET^3$ 482–3.
Aynard, Jeanne-Marie. 'Le Jugement des Morts chez les Assyro-Babyloniens', *Le Jugement des Morts*, Sources Orientales 4, 83–102. Paris, 1961.
Borger, R. *Die Inschriften Asarhaddons*. Graz, 1956.
Brandon, S.G.F. *Creation Legends in the Ancient Near East*. London, 1963.
Dandamayev, M. 'Babylonia in the Persian age', *CHJ* I (1984), 326–41.
Ebeling, Erich. *Tod und Leben nach den Vorstellungen der Babylonier*. Berlin, 1931.
Frankfort, Henri. *The Birth of Civilization in the Near East*. London, 1954.
——. *Kingship and the Gods*. Chicago, 1948.
Gadd, C.J. *Ideas of Divine Rule in the Ancient East*. Schweich Lectures, 1945. London, 1948.
Heidel, A. *The Gilgamesh Epic and Old Testament Parallels*. 2nd Ed., Chicago, 1949.
Hooke, S.H. *Babylonian and Assyrian Religion*. London, 1953.
——. (ed.) *Myth and Ritual*. Oxford, 1933.
Jacobsen, Thorkild. 'Mesopotamia', *Before Philosophy*, ed. H. and H.A. Frankfort, 137–234. Harmondsworth, 1949.
——. *The Treasures of Darkness*. New Haven, 1976.
Jastrow, Morris, Jr. *Aspects of Religious Belief and Practice in Babylonia and Assyria*. 1911, repr. New York, 1971.
Kramer, Samuel N. *Lamentation over the Destruction of Ur*. Assyriological Studies, 12. Chicago, 1940.
——. 'Sumerian Lamentations', $ANET^3$ 455–63; 611–19.
Lambert, W.G. *Babylonian Wisdom Literature*. Oxford, 1960.
——. 'Destiny and divine intervention in Babylon and Israel', *OTS* 17 (1972), 65–72.
——. '*Dingir.šà.dib.ba* Incantations', *JNES* 33 (1974), 267–322. with Appendix by Hans G. Güterbock, 'Hittite Parallels', 323–27.
——. and A.R. Millard. *Atra-Ḫasīs. the Babylonian Story of the Flood*. Oxford, 1969.
Landsberger, B. *Three Essays on the Sumerians*. Los Angeles, 1974.
Millard, A.R. v. Lambert, W.G.
Pfeiffer, Robert H. 'Akkadian Observations on Life and the World Order', $ANET^3$ 434–40.
Reiner, Erica. 'Die akkadische Literatur', *Altorientalische Literaturen*, ed. W. Röllig, 151–210. Wiesbaden, 1978.
Ringgren, Helmer. 'Akkadian Apocalypses', *Apocalypticism etc.* ed. D. Hellholm, 379–86. Tübingen, 1983.
——. *Religions of the Ancient Near East*. (tr. J. Sturdy) London, 1973.
Saggs, H.W.F. *Assyriology and the Study of the Old Testament*. Inaugural Lecture. Cardiff, 1969.
——. *The Encounter with the Divine in Mesopotamia and Israel*. Jordan Lectures, 1976. London, 1978.
——. *Everyday Life in Babylonia and Assyria*. London, 1965.
——. *The Greatness that was Babylon*. London, 1962.
——. *The Might that was Assyria*. London, 1985.

Schmökel, Hartmut. 'Mesopotamian Texts', *Near Eastern Religious Texts Relating to the Old Testament*, ed. Walter Beyerlin, 68–145. London, 1978.
Schützinger, Heinrich. 'Tod und ewiges Leben im Glauben des Alten Zweistromlandes', *Tod und Jenseits im Glauben der Völker*, ed. H.-J. Klimkeit, 48–61. Wiesbaden, 1978.
Soden, W. von. With E. Ebeling, B. Meissner, E. Weidner, and D.O. Edzard. *Reallexikon der Assyriologie und vorderasiatischen Archäologie*. 7 Vols. Berlin, 1928–1987.
Speiser, E.A. 'The Epic of Gilgamesh', *ANET*³ 72–99.
Wiseman, D.J. 'Historical Records of Assyria and Babylon', *Documents from Old Testament Times*, ed. D. Winton Thomas, 46–83. London, 1958.

V. *Greece*

Abrahams, E.B. *Greek Dress*. London, 1908.
Adkins, Arthur W.H. *From the Many to the One*. London, 1970.
———. *Moral Values and Political Behaviour in Ancient Greece*. London, 1972.
Armstrong, A.H. (ed.) *Cambridge History of Later Greek and Early Medieval Philosophy*. Cambridge, 1967.
———. (ed.) *Classical Mediterranean Spirituality*. Vol. 15 of *World Spirituality*. New York, 1986.
Barrett, W.S. *Euripides, Hippolytus*. Oxford, 1964.
Benardete, Seth. *Herodotean Inquiries*. The Hague, 1969.
Bergman, Jan. 'I Overcome Fate, Fate Harkens to Me', *Fatalistic Beliefs*, ed. H. Ringgren, 35–51. Stockholm, 1967.
———. *Ich bin Isis*. Acta Univ. Upsal., Hist. Religionum, 3; Uppsala, 1968.
———. 'Zum "Mythus von der Nation" in den sog. hellenistischen Mysterienreligionen'. *Temenos* 8 (1972), 7–28.
Betz, Hans Dieter. (ed.) *The Greek Magical Papyri in Translation*. Vol. I Chicago, 1986.
———. with Peter A. Dirkse and Edgar W. Smith, Jr. *Plutarch's Theological Writings and Early Christian Literature*, ed. H.D. Betz. Studia ad Corpus Hellenisticum Novi Testamenti, 3. Leiden, 1975.
Bianchi, Ugo. ΔΙΟΣ ΑΙΣΑ: *Destino, uomini e divinità nell' epos, nelle teogonie e nel culto dei greci*. Rome, 1953.
———. *The Greek Mysteries*. Iconography of Religions, 17.3. Leiden, 1976.
Bischoff, Heinrich. 'Der Warner bei Herodot', *Herodot*, ed. W. Marg, 302–19. Wege der Forschung. Munich, 1962.
Bowra, C.M. *Pindar*. Oxford, 1964.
———. *Tradition and Design in the Iliad*. Oxford, 1930.
Brenk, Frederick E. *In Mist Apparelled*. Mnemosyne Suppl. 48. Leiden, 1977.
Broadhead, H.D. *The Persae of Aeschylus*. Cambridge, 1960.
Brown, Truesdell S. *Timaeus of Tauromenium*. Berkeley, 1958.
Burkert, Walter. *Ancient Mystery Cults*. Cambridge, Mass., 1987.
———. 'Apokalyptik um frühen Griechentum: Impulse and Transformationen', *Apocalypticism etc.* ed. D. Hellholm, 235–54. Tübingen, 1983.
———. (tr. J. Raffan) *Greek Religion: Archaic and Classical*. Oxford, 1985.
———. *Griechische Religion*. Stuttgart, 1977.
———. *Homo Necans*. RVV 33. Berlin, 1972. Also tr. Peter Bing, Berkeley, 1983.
———. *Structure and History in Greek Mythology and Ritual*. Berkeley, 1979, repr. 1982.
Burn, A.R. *Persia and the Greeks*. London, 1962.
Burton, Anne. *Diodorus Siculus, Book I: A Commentary*. EPRO 29. Leiden, 1972.
Burton, R.W.B. *Pindar's Pythian Odes*. Oxford, 1962.
Calhoun, George M. *The Growth of Criminal Law in Ancient Greece*. 1927, repr. Westport, 1973.
Callahan, John F. 'Dialectic, Myth and History in the Philosophy of Plato', *Interpretations of Plato*, ed. Helen F. North, 64–85. Leiden, 1977.

Collard, Christopher. *Euripides*. New Surveys in the Classics, 14. Oxford, 1981.
Croix, G.E.M. de Ste. *The Class Struggle in the Ancient Greek World*. London, 1981.
Denniston, J.D. and D.L. Page. *Aeschylus, Agamemnon*. Oxford, 1957.
Diehl, Ernst. *Anthologia Lyrica Graeca*. 3rd Ed., Leipzig, 1949–1952.
Diels-Kranz: H. Diels and W. Kranz, *Die Fragmente der Vorsokratiker*. 5th Ed., Berlin, 1934.
Dietrich, B.C. *Death, Fate and the Gods*. London, 1965.
——. *A Sense of Guilt*. Inaugural Lecture. Cardiff, 1980.
Dillon, John. *The Middle Platonists*. London, 1977.
Dirkse, Peter A. v. Betz, H.D.
Dodds, E.R. *Euripides, Bacchae*. 2nd Ed., Oxford, 1960.
——. *The Greeks and the Irrational*. Berkeley, 1951, repr. 1963.
——. *Plato, Gorgias*. Oxford, 1959.
Drachmann, A.B. *Atheism in Pagan Antiquity*. London, 1922.
Drexler, Hans. *Herodot-Studien*. Hildesheim, 1972.
Dunand, Françoise. *Le Culte d'Isis dans le bassin oriental de la Méditerranée*. 3 Vols. EPRO 26. Leiden, 1973.
Evans, Sir Arthur. *The Palace of Minos*. I–IV. London, 1921–36, repr. 1964.
Fahr, Wilhelm. *Theous Nomizein*. Spudasmata, 26. Hildesheim, 1969.
Farnell, Lewis R. *Greek Hero Cults*. Oxford, 1921.
Farrington, Benjamin. *The Faith of Epicurus*. London, 1967.
Festugière, André-Jean. *Personal Religion among the Greeks*. Berkeley, 1954, repr. 1960.
Fisher, N.R.E. (ed.) *Social Values in Classical Athens*. The Ancient World: Source Books. London, 1976.
Fontenrose, Joseph. *The Delphic Oracle*. Berkeley, 1978.
Fornara, Charles W. *Herodotus*. An Interpretative Essay. Oxford, 1971.
Fowden, Garth. *The Egyptian Hermes*. Cambridge, 1986.
Fraenkel, Eduard. *Aeschylus, Agamemnon*. 3 Vols. Oxford, 1950, repr. 1962.
Fraser, P.M. *Ptolemaic Alexandria*. 3 Vols. Oxford, 1972.
Freeman, Kathleen. *The Murder of Herodes*. New York, 1963.
Frisk, H. *Griechisches Etymologisches Wörterbuch*. Heidelberg, 1954–70.
Fritz, Kurt von. *Die Griechische Geschichtsschreibung*, I. Berlin, 1967.
Froidefond, Christian. *Le Mirage égyptien dans la littérature grecque*. Aix-en-Provence, 1971.
Garvie, A.F. *Aeschylus, Choephori*. Oxford, 1986.
——. 'The Resentment of the Gods', *Proc. Class. Ass.* 83 (1986), 15–16.
Garzya, Antonio. *Theognis, Elegeia*. Florence, 1958.
Glotz, Gustave. *La Solidarité de la famille dans le droit criminel en Grèce*. Paris, 1904, repr. New York, 1973.
Glover, T.R. *Herodotus*. Berkeley, 1924.
Graf, Fritz. 'Die lokrischen Mädchen', *Studi Storico-Religiosi* 2 (1978), 61–79.
Grant, Frederick C. (ed.) *Hellenistic Religions*. The Age of Syncretism. New York, 1953.
Griffiths, J. Gwyn. 'Atlantis and Egypt', *Historia* 34 (1985), 3–28.
——. 'In Search of the Isles of the Blest', *Greece and Rome* 16 (1947), 122–6.
——. *Plutarch's De Iside et Osiride*. Edited with a Translation and Commentary. Cardiff, 1970.
——. 'Xenophon of Ephesus on Isis and Alexandria', *Hommages à M.J. Vermaseren*, I, 409–37. Leiden, 1978.
Hadas, Moses. *On Love, the Family, and the Good Life*. Selected Essays of Plutarch. New York, 1957.
Heerma van Voss, M. 'The Cista Mystica in the Cult and Mysteries of Isis', *Studies in Hellenistic Religions*, ed. M.J. Vermaseren, 23–26. Leiden, 1979.
Heinen, Heinz. 'Die Tryphè des Ptolemaios VIII. Euergetes II.', *Althistorische Studien* (FS. H. Bengston), Historia Einzelschr. 40, 116–28. Wiesbaden, 1982.
Hengel, Martin. (tr. John Bowden) *Judaism and Hellenism*. 2 Vols. London, 1974.

Henley, Jane. *Greek Myths: A Vase Painter's Notebook.* Bloomington, 1973.
Herbig, Reinhard. *Neue Beobachtungen am Fries der Mysterien-Villa in Pompeji.* Baden-Baden, 1958.
Herrmann, Paul. *Denkmäler der Malerei des Altertums.* I. Munich, 1904.
Herter, Hans. 'Effeminatus', *RAC* 4 (1959), 620–50.
Hirzel, Rudolph. *Plutarch. Das Erbe der Alten,* 4. Leipzig, 1912.
How, W.W. and J. Wells. *A Commentary on Herodotus.* 2 Vols. Oxford, 1912, repr. 1928.
Hudson-Williams, T. *The Elegies of Theognis.* London, 1910.
Ingenkamp, Heinz G. *Plutarchs Schriften über die Heilung der Seele.* Hypomnemata, 34. Göttingen, 1971.
Jacoby, Felix. *Fragmente der griechischen Historiker.* (= *FGrH*). Berlin and Leiden 1923–1958.
Jaeger, Werner. (tr. Gilbert Highet). *Paideia.* I and II. Oxford, 1939.
Kamerbeek, J.C. *The Ajax.* Leiden, 1953.
Kern, Otto. 'Kabeiros und Kabeiroi', *PW* (1919), 1433 f.
———. *Die Religion der Griechen.* I and II. Berlin 1926; 1935.
Kinkel, Gottfried. *Epicorum Graecorum Fragmenta.* Leipzig, 1877.
Kirk, G.S. *The Nature of Greek Myths.* Harmondsworth, 1974.
Klaerr, Robert. v. Vernière, Yvonne.
Kretzenbacher, Leopold. *Die Seelenwaage.* Buchreihe des Landesmuseums für Kärnten, Bd. IV. Klagenfurt, 1958.
Lacy, Phillip H. De, and Benedict Einarson. *Plutarch's Moralia,* Vol. VII. Loeb Classical Library, London, 1959.
Lehmann, K. 'Ignorance and Search in the Villa of the Mysteries', *JRS* 52 (1962), 62–68.
Lesky, Albin. *Greek Tragedy.* 2nd Ed., London, 1967.
———. *Die tragische Dichtung der Hellenen.* 3rd Ed., Göttingen, 1972.
Leutsch, E.L. von, and F.G. Schneidewin. *Corpus Paroemiographorum Graecorum.* 2 Vols, the second by von Leutsch alone. Göttingen 1839, repr. Hildesheim, 1958.
Lindsay, Jack. *The Origins of Alchemy in Graeco-Roman Egypt.* London, 1970.
Lloyd, Alan B. *Herodotus Book II.* 3 Vols. EPRO 43. Leiden, 1975–1987.
Lloyd, Geoffrey. 'Right and Left in Greek Philosophy', *Right and Left,* ed. Rodney Needham, 167–86. Chicago, 1973.
Lloyd-Jones, Hugh. *Agamemnon.* Tr. with Commentary. Prentice-Hall, 1970.
———. *The Justice of Zeus.* Berkeley, 1971.
Lonis, Raoul. *Guerre et religion en Grèce à l'époque classique.* Paris, 1979.
Macan, R.W. *Herodotus IV-VI; and VII-IX.* Text and Commentary. London, 1895; 1908.
Macchioro, Vittorio. *Die Villa der Mysterien in Pompei.* Berlin, 1928.
MacDowell, Douglas M. *The Law in Classical Athens.* London, 1978.
Maiuri, Amedeo. *La Villa dei Misteri.* Rome, 1931.
Marcovich, M. *Heraclitus.* Merida, Venezuela, 1967.
Marg, Walter. (ed.) *Herodot.* Wege der Forschung. Munich, 1962.
Merkelbach, Reinhold. 'Ein ägyptischer Priestereid', *ZPE* 2 (1968), 7–30.
———. 'Ein Griechisch-Ägyptischer Priestereid und das Totenbuch', *Religions en Égypte hellénistique et romaine,* 69–73. Paris, 1969.
———. and M.L. West. *Fragmenta Hesiodea.* 2nd Ed., Oxford, 1983.
Michelini, Ann N. *Tradition and Dramatic Form in the Persians of Aeschylus.* Leiden, 1982.
Momigliano, Arnaldo. *Alien Wisdom.* Cambridge, 1975.
———. *The Development of Greek Biography.* Harvard, 1971.
———. *Essays in Ancient and Modern Historiography.* Oxford, 1977.
———. *Studies in Historiography.* London, 1966.
More, Paul Elmer. *The Religion of Plato.* 2nd Ed., Princeton, 1928.
Murray, Oswyn. *Early Greece.* Glasgow, 1980.

——. 'Hecataeus of Abdera and Pharaonic Kingship', *JEA* 56 (1970), 141–71.
Nilsson, Martin P. *The Dionysiac Mysteries of the Hellenistic and Roman Age.* Lund, 1957.
——. *Geschichte der griechischen Religion.* I (3rd Ed.); II (2nd Ed.) Munich, 1967; 1961. (= *Gr. Rel.*)
——. *Greek Folk Religion.* 1940, repr. New York, 1961.
——. *The Minoan-Mycenaean Religion.* 2nd Ed., Lund, 1950.
Nock, Arthur D. *Early Gentile Christianity and its Hellenistic Background.* 1928, repr. New York, 1964.
——. v. Section I. *General.*
North, Helen F. (ed.) *Interpretations of Plato.* Suppl. *Mnemosyne*, 20. Leiden, 1977.
Norwood, Gilbert. *Pindar.* Berkeley, 1945.
Oakesmith, John. *The Religion of Plutarch.* London, 1902.
Oldfather, C.H. (ed.) *Diodorus Siculus*, Vol. III. Loeb Classical Library. London, 1939.
Parke, H.W. *History of the Delphic Oracle.* Oxford, 1939.
Parker, Robert. *Miasma. Pollution and Purification in early Greek Religion.* Oxford, 1983.
Parlasca, Klaus. *Repertorio d'arte dell' Egitto greco-romano.* B. 1. Palermo, 1969.
Paton, W.R. *Polybius*, Vols. I–VI. Loeb Classsical Library, London, 1922–1927.
Persson, A.W. *New Tombs at Dendra near Midea.* Lund, 1942.
——. *The Religion of Greece in Prehistoric Times.* Berkeley, 1942.
Picard, Charles. *Les Religions préhelléniques (Crète et Mycénes).* Paris, 1948.
Pötscher, Walter. 'Moira, Themis and τιμή im homerischen Denken', *Wiener Studien* 73 (1960), 5–39.
Pohlenz, Max. *Herodot.* Leipzig, 1937, repr. Stuttgart, 1961.
——. *Die Stoa.* 2nd Ed., Göttingen, 1959.
Preisendanz, Karl. *Papyri Graecae Magicae.* 2 Vols. Leipzig, 1928; 1931.
Ranulf, Sven. *The Jealousy of the Gods and Criminal Law at Athens.* I. London, 1933.
Rist, J.M. *Stoic Philosophy.* Cambridge, 1969.
——. (ed.) *The Stoics.* Berkeley, 1978.
Rizzo, G.E. *Dionysos Mystes.* Naples, 1915.
Rohde, Erwin. *Psyche.* 9th and 10th Ed., Tübingen, 1925.
——. (tr. W.B. Hillis). *Psyche.* 8th Ed., London, 1925, repr. 1950.
Rose, H.J. *A Handbook of Greek Mythology.* 6th Ed., London, 1958.
Russell, D.A. *Plutarch.* London, 1972.
Ruyt, Franz de. *Charun, Démon Etrusque de la Mort.* Brussels, 1934.
Sandbach, F.H. *The Stoics.* London, 1975.
Sandys, Sir John. *The Odes of Pindar.* Loeb Classical Library. 2nd Ed., London, 1919, repr. 1930.
Saunders, Trevor J. *Plato, The Laws.* Harmondsworth, 1970, repr. 1972.
Schachter, Albert. *The Cults of Boeotia.* Vols. 1, 2, 4. London, 1981; 1986.
Schliemann, Heinrich. *Mycenae.* London, 1878.
Schneidewin, F.G. v. Leutsch, E.L. von.
Schuchardt, C. *Schliemann's Excavations.* London, 1891.
Schuman, Verne B. 'A Second-Century Treatise on Egyptian Priests and Temples', *Harv. Theol. Rev.* 53 (1960), 155–70.
Simon, Erika. 'Zum Fries der Mysterienvilla bei Pompeji', *JDAI* 76 (1961), 111–72.
Smith, Edgar W., Jr. v. Betz, H.D.
Snell, Bruno. (tr. T.G. Rosenmeyer) *The Discovery of the Mind.* Oxford, 1953.
——. *Die Entdeckung des Geistes.* 3rd Ed., Hamburg, 1955.
——. 'Die Welt der Götter bei Hesiod', *Hesiod.* ed. E. Heitsch. Wege der Forschung, 44. 708–25. Darmstadt, 1966.
Soury, Guy. *La démonologie de Plutarque.* Paris, 1942.
Stallmach, Josef. *Ate. Zur Frage des Selbst- und Weltverständisses des frühgriechischen Menschen.* Beitr. zur klassischen Philologie, 18. Meisen-

heim am Glan, 1968.
Steiner, George. *After Babel.* London, 1975.
Stough, Charlotte. 'Stoic Determinism and Moral Responsibility', *The Stoics* ed. J.M. Rist, 203–31. Berkeley, 1978.
Thomson, George. *Aeschylus and Athens.* London, 1941; 3rd Ed., 1966.
——. *The Oresteia of Aeschylus.* 2nd Ed., Amsterdam, 1966.
Toynbee, Jocelyn. 'The Villa Item and a Bride's Ordeal', *JRS* 19 (1929), 67–87.
Vermaseren, M.J. (ed.) *Studies in Hellenistic Religions.* EPRO 78. Leiden, 1979.
Vernant, Jean-Pierre. (tr. Janet Lloyd) *Myth and Society in Ancient Greece.* London, 1982.
——. *Myth and Thought among the Greeks.* London, 1983.
——. *The Origins of Greek Thought.* London, 1982.
Vernière, Yvonne, and Robert Klaerr. *Plutarque, Oeuvres Morales*, Tome VII. with 'Sur les délais de la justice divine', Edition, Tr., Comm. by Y. Vernière. Collection Budé. Paris, 1974.
——. *Symboles et mythes dans la pensée de Plutarque.* Paris, 1977.
Vlastos, Gregory. 'The Theory of Social Justice in the *Polis* in Plato's *Republic*', *Interpretations of Plato*, ed. Helen F. North, 1–40. Leiden, 1977.
Wace, A.J.B. *Chamber Tombs at Mycenae.* Oxford, 1932.
Walbank, F.W. *A Historical Commentary on Polybius.* I–III. Oxford, 1957; 1967; 1979.
Walcot, Peter. *Envy and the Greeks.* Warminster, 1978.
——. *Greek Drama in its Theatrical and Social Context.* Cardiff, 1976.
——. *Greek Peasants, Ancient and Modern.* Manchester, 1970.
——. 'Hesiod and the Instructions of 'Onchsheshonqy', *JNES* 21 (1962), 215–19.
——. *Hesiod and the Near East.* Cardiff, 1966.
Waters, Kenneth H. *Herodotos on Tyrants and Despots.* Wiesbaden. 1971.
——. *Herodotus the Historian.* London, 1985.
Wells, Joseph, v. How, W.W.
West, Martin L. *Early Greek Philosophy and the Orient.* Oxford, 1971.
——. *Hesiod, Theogony.* Oxford, 1986.
——. *Hesiod, Works and Days.* Oxford, 1978.
——. *The Orphic Poems.* Oxford, 1983.
——. v. Merkelbach, R.
West, Stephanie. 'Lycophron Italicised', *JHS* 104 (1984), 127–51.
Wilamowitz-Moellendorff, U. von. *Griechische Tragoedien übersetzt*, II. 8th Ed., Berlin, 1919.
Wood, Ellen M. and Neal. *Class Ideology and Ancient Political Theory.* Oxford, 1978.
Woodhead, A.G. *The Greeks in the West.* London, 1962.
Wüst, Ernst. 'Psychostasie', *PW* 23.2 (1959), 1439–58.
——. 'Die Seelenwägung in Griechenland und Ägypten', *Arch. Rel.* 36 (1939), 162–71.
Young, Douglas. *Theognis.* Teubner, Leipzig, 1961.
Žabkar, Louis V. 'Herodotus and the Egyptian Idea of Immortality', *JNES* 22 (1963), 57–63.
Zuntz, G. 'On the Dionysiac Fresco in the Villa dei Misteri at Pompeii', *Proc. Brit. Acad.* 49 (1963), 176–201.
——. *Persephone.* Oxford, 1971.

VI. *Rome*

Altheim, Franz. (tr. H. Mattingly) *A History of Roman Religion.* London, 1938.
Bailey, Cyril. *Religion in Virgil.* Oxford, 1935, repr. New York, 1969.
Bailey, D.R. Shackleton. *Profile of Horace.* London, 1982.
Berreth, Joseph. *Studium zum Isisbuch Apuleius' Metamorphosen.* Ellwangen, 1931.
Bollók, J. 'Die Tartaros-Szene in der Aeneis', *Ann. Univ. Budapest, Sectio Classica* 4 (1976), 47–61.
Briscoe, John. *A Commentary on Livy Books XXXI–XXXIII.* Oxford, 1973.

Brunt, P.A. 'Laus imperii', *Imperialism in the Ancient World*, ed. P.D.A. Garnsey and C.R. Whittaker, Cambridge, 1978.
Büchner, Karl. *P. Vergilius Maro. PW* 1961. Sonderdruck.
Costa, C.D.N. (ed.) *Horace*. London, 1973.
Cumont, Franz. 'La fin du monde selon les mages occidentaux', *Rev. Hist. Rel.* 103 (1931), 29–96.
Daube, David. *Roman Law*. Edinburgh, 1969.
Dorey, T.A. (ed.) *Livy*. London, 1971.
Dumézil, Georges. (tr. P. Krapp.) *Archaic Roman Religion*. Chicago, 1970.
DuQuesnay, I.M. Le M., 'Horace and Maecenas', *Poetry and Politics in the Age of Augustus*, ed. T. Woodman and D. West, 19–58. Cambridge, 1984.
Earl. D.C. *The Political Thought of Sallust*. Cambridge, 1961, repr. Amsterdam, 1966.
Eliot, T.S. Preface to Simone Weil, *The Need for Roots*. London, 1952.
Erkell, Harry. 'Caesar und sein Glück', *Caesar*, ed. D. Rasmussen, 48–60. Wege der Forschung, 43. Darmstadt, 1967.
Essen, C.C. van. v. Vermaseren, M.J.
Evans, A.W. Wade. *Welsh Christian Origins*. Oxford, 1934.
Festugière, André-Jean. 'Lucius and Isis', id., *Personal Religion among the Greeks*. Berkeley, 1954, repr. 1960.
Finley, Moses I. *Ancient History: Evidence and Models*. London, 1985.
Fraenkel, Eduard. *Horace*. Oxford, 1957.
Frank, Tenney. *Vergil: A Biography*. Oxford, 1922.
Fredouille, J.C. *Apulée, Metamorphoses, Livre XI*. Coll. Erasme. Paris, 1975.
Gabba, Emilio. 'The Historians and Augustus', *Caesar Augustus; Seven Aspects*, ed. F. Millar and E. Segal, 61–85. Oxford, 1984.
Galinsky, G. Karl. *Aeneas, Sicily, and Rome*. Princeton, 1969.
Garnsey, P.D.A. and C.R. Whittaker, (ed.) *Imperialism in the Ancient World*. Cambridge, 1978.
Grant, Frederick C. *Ancient Roman Religion*. New York, 1957.
Griffiths, J. Gwyn. *Apuleius of Madauros: The Isis-Book (Metamorphoses, Book XI)*. EPRO 39. Leiden, 1975.
——. 'Hadrian's Egyptianizing Animula', *Maia* n.s. 36 (1984), 263–6.
——. 'Isis in the *Metamorphoses* of Apuleius', *Aspects of Apuleius' Golden Ass*, ed. B.L. Hijmans Jr. and R.Th. van der Paardt, 141–66. Groningen, 1978.
Hijmans, B.L., Jr. and R.Th. van der Paardt. (ed.) v. preceding item.
Hölbl, Günther. *Beziehungen der ägyptischen Kultur zu Altitalien*. 2 Vols. EPRO 62. Leiden, 1979.
Hosius, Carl. v. Schanz, Martin.
Hubbard, Margaret. 'The Odes', *Horace*, ed. C.D.N. Costa, 1–28. London, 1973.
——. v. Nisbet, R.G.M.
Huxley, H.H. *Virgil, Georgics I and II*. London, 1963, repr. Bristol, 1979.
Kajanto, Iiro. 'Die Götter und das Fatum bei Livius', *Wege zu Livius*, ed. Erich Burck, 475–85. Wege der Forschung, 132. Darmstadt, 1967.
Klingner, Friedrich. *Virgil: Bucolica, Georgica, Aeneis*. Zürich, 1967.
Koenen, Ludwig. 'Die Unschuldsbeteuerungen des Priestereides und die römische Elegie', *ZPE* 2 (1968), 31–38.
Lancel, Serge. '"Curiositas" et préoccupations spirituelles chez Apulée', *Rev. Hist. Rel.* 160 (1961), 25–46.
Latte, Kurt. *Römische Religionsgeschichte*. Munich, 1960.
Leach, Eleanor W. *Vergil's Eclogues*. Ithaca, 1974.
Liebeschuetz, J.H.W.G. *Continuity and Change in Roman Religion*. Oxford, 1979.
Lipovsky, James. *A Historiographical Study of Livy, Books VI–X*. New York, 1981.
Luce, T.J. *Livy: The Composition of his History*. Princeton, 1977.
MacKay, L.A. 'The Sin of the Golden Ass', *Arion* 4 (1965), 474–80.
Magie, D. (ed.) *Scriptores Historiae Augustae: Commodus*. Loeb Classical Library. London, 1922.

Malaise, Michel. *Les Conditions de pénétrations et de diffusion des cultes égyptiens en Italie.* EPRO 22. Leiden, 1972.
Mason, Sheila M. 'Livy and Montesquieu', *Livy*, ed. T.A. Dorey, 118–58. London, 1971.
Mazzarino, Santo. (tr. G. Holmes) *The End of the Ancient World.* Westport, Conn., 1966.
Millar, Fergus, and E. Segal (ed.) *Caesar Augustus: Seven Aspects.* Oxford 1984.
Momigliano, Arnaldo. (ed.) *The Conflict between Paganism and Christianity in the Fourth Century.* Oxford, 1963.
Netoliczka, von. 'Inaures', *PW* (1914), 1229–41.
Nisbet, R.G.M., and Margaret Hubbard. *A Commentary on Horace, Odes, Book I.* Oxford, 1970, rev. ed. 1980.
Ogilvie, R.M. *A Commentary on Livy, Books 1–5.* Oxford, 1965.
———. *The Romans and their Gods.* London, 1964.
Paardt, R.Th. van der. v. Hijmans, B.L., Jr.
Pallottino, M. (tr. J. Cremona) *The Etruscans.* Harmondsworth, 1955.
Pattie, T.S. v. Williams, R.D.
Rose, H.J. *The Eclogues of Vergil.* Berkeley, 1942.
Rostovtzeff, M. *Mystic Italy.* New York, 1927.
Sandy, Gerald N. 'Book 11: Ballast or Anchor?', *Aspects of Apuleius' Golden Ass*, ed. B.L. Hijmans, Jr. and R.Th. van der Paardt, 123–40. Groningen, 1978.
———. '*Serviles Voluptates* in Apuleius' *Metamorphoses*', *Phoenix* 28 (1974), 234–44.
Schanz, Martin, rev. Carl Hosius, *Geschichte der römischen Litteratur*, I.1[4] Munich, 1935.
Schefold, Karl. *Pompejanische Malerei.* Basel, 1952.
———. *Vergessenes Pompeji.* Bern, 1962.
Segal, E. v. Millar, Fergus.
Solmsen, Friedrich. 'Horace's First Roman Ode', *AJPh* 68 (1947), 337–52.
———. *Isis among the Greek and Romans.* Martin Classical Lectures, 25. Cambridge, Mass. 1979.
Stübler, Gerhard. *Die Religiosität des Livius.* Stuttgart, 1941, repr. Amsterdam.
Syme, Ronald. *The Roman Revolution.* Oxford, 1939, repr. 1967.
Tatum, James H. 'The Tales in Apuleius' *Metamorphoses*', *TAPA* 100 (169), 487–527.
Tschudin, Peter F. *Isis in Rom.* Aarau, 1962.
Vermaseren, M.J. and C.C. van Essen. *The Excavations in the Mithraeum of the Church of Santa Prisca in Rome.* Leiden, 1965.
Vogt, Joseph. (tr. J. Sondheimer) *The Decline of Rome.* London, 1965.
Walsh, P.G. *Livy: His Historical Aims and Methods.* Cambridge, 1961, repr. 1976.
Weil, Simone. (tr. A.F. Wills) *The Need for Roots.* London, 1952.
Weinstock, Stefan. *Divus Julius.* Oxford, 1971.
Whittaker, C.R. v. Garnsey, P.D.A.
Williams, R.D., and T.S. Pattie. *Virgil: His Poetry throughout the Ages.* London, 1982.
Wilson, L.M. *The Clothing of the Ancient Romans.* Baltimore, 1938.
Witt, R.E. *Isis in the Graeco-Roman World.* London, 1971.
Wittmann, Willi. *Das Isisbuch des Apuleius.* Stuttgart, 1938.
Woodman, Tony, and David West. (ed.) *Poetry and Politics in the Age of Augustus.* Cambridge, 1984.

VII. *Christianity*

Bammel, Ernst, and C.F.D. Moule. (ed.) *Jesus and the Politics of His Day.* Cambridge, 1984.
Beasley-Murray, G.R. *Revelation.* New Century Bible, London, 1974.
Bornkamm, Günther. (tr. I. and F. McLuskey) *Jesus of Nazareth.* London, 1960.
———. (tr. D.M.G. Stalker) *Paul.* London, 1971.
Brandon, S.G.F. *The Fall of Jerusalem and the Christian Church.* London, 1951.

——. *Jesus and the Zealots*. Manchester, 1967.
——. '"Jesus and the Zealots": A Correction', *NTS* 17 (1971), 453.
——. *The Trial of Jesus of Nazareth*. London, 1968.
Brandt, S., and G. Laubmann. (ed.) *Lactantius, Divinae Institutiones*. Vienna, 1890.
Bultmann, Rudolf. (tr. G.R. Beasley-Murray) *The Gospel of John*. Oxford, 1971.
——. (tr. R.H. Fuller) *Primitive Christianity in its Contemporary Setting*. London, 1956, repr. Glasgow, 1960.
——. (tr. K. Grobel) *The Theology of the New Testament*. 2 Vols. London, 1952; 1955.
Caird, G.B. *Revelation*. 2nd Ed., London, 1984.
——. *Saint Luke*. Harmondsworth, 1963, repr. 1974.
Collins, Adela Yarbro. *The Combat Myth in the Book of Revelation*. Harvard Diss. Missoula, Montana, 1976.
——. 'Persecution and Vengeance in the Book of Revelation', in *Apocalypticism* ed. D. Hellholm (1983), 729–49.
Court, John M. 'Paul and the Apocalyptic Pattern', in *Paul and Paulinism* ed. M.D. Hooker and S.G. Wilson (London, 1982), 57–66.
Cross, F.L. and E.A. Livingstone. *Oxford Dictionary of the Christian Church*. 2nd Ed., Oxford, 1974.
Daniélou, Jean. (tr. D. Attwater) *Primitive Christian Symbols*. London, 1964.
Davies, William David. *The Gospel and the Land*. Berkeley, 1974.
——. *Jewish and Pauline Studies*. Philadelphia, 1984.
——. 'Paul and the Dead Sea Scrolls: Flesh and Spirit', *The Scrolls and the New Testament*. ed. K. Stendahl (1957, repr. Westport, 1975), 157–82.
——. *Paul and Rabbinic Judaism*. London, 1948; 2nd Ed. 1955, repr. 1962; New Ed., Philadelphia, 1980.
——. *The Sermon on the Mount*. Cambridge, 1966.
——. *The Setting of the Sermon on the Mount*. Cambridge, 1964.
——. (In honor of). R. Hamerton-Kelly and R. Scroggs (ed.), *Jews, Greeks, and Christians: Religious Cultures in Late Antiquity*. Leiden, 1976.
Deichmann, F.W. *Ravenna: Geschichte und Monumente*. Wiesbaden, 1969.
Dodd, C.H. *The Founder of Christianity*. 1970, repr. Glasgow, 1986.
——. *Historical Tradition in the Fourth Gospel*. Cambridge, 1965.
——. *The Interpretation of the Fourth Gospel*. Cambridge, 1953.
——. (Presented to). W.D. Davies and D. Daube (ed.), *The Background of the New Testament and its Eschatology*. Cambridge, 1954, repr. 1964.
Dostoievsky, Fyodor M. (tr. D. Magarshack). *The Brothers Karamazov*. Harmondsworth, 1958, repr. 1986.
Ellis, E. Earle. *Paul and his Recent Interpreters*. Grand Rapids, 1961.
Ezorsky, Gertrude. *Philosophical Perspectives on Punishment*. New York, 1972, repr. 1977.
Filson, F.V. *St Paul's Conception of Recompense*. Leipzig, 1931.
Ford, J. Massyngberde. *Revelations*. Anchor Bible. New York, 1975.
Fortna, R.T. *The Gospel of Signs*. Cambridge, 1970.
Fournée, Jean. *Le Jugement dernier*. Paris, 1964.
Fuller, Reginald H. *The Foundations of New Testament Christology*. 1965, repr. Glasgow, 1969.
Glasson, T.F. *Jesus and the End of the World*. Edinburgh, 1980.
Goff, Jacques Le. (tr. A. Goldhammer) *The Birth of Purgatory*. London, 1984.
Gressmann, Hugo. *Vom reichen Mann und armen Lazarus*. Abh. Berlin, 1918.
Griffiths, D.R. *The New Testament and the Roman State*. Swansea, 1970.
Griffiths, J. Gwyn. 'The Disciple's Cross', *NTS* 16 (1970), 22–25.
——. 'Zealot and Para-Zealot', *NTS* 19 (1973), 483–5.
Grundmann, Walter, v. Leipoldt, Johannes.
Guthrie, Donald. *The Relevance of John's Apocalypse*. The Didsbury Lectures, 1985. Exeter, 1987.
Harvey, A.E. *Jesus and the Constraints of History*. London, 1982.

Heller, Erich. *Kafka*. Glasgow, 1974, repr. 1977.
Hengel, Martin. (tr. J. Bowden) *The Son of God*. London, 1976.
——. (tr. Wm. Klassen) *Was Jesus a Revolutionist?* Philadelphia, 1971, repr. 1975.
——. *Die Zeloten*. Leiden, 1961.
Hick, John. *The Centre of Christianity*. London, 1968, repr. 1977.
——. *Evil and the Gospel of Love*. Glasgow. 1968.
Hinnells, John R. 'Zoroastrian Influence on Judaeo-Christian Tradition', *Journal of the K.R. Cama Oriental Inst.* 45 (1976), 1–23.
Hooker, Morna D. *Jesus and the Servant*. London, 1959.
——. 'Paul and "Covenantal Nomism"', *Paul and Paulinism* ed. M.D. Hooker and S.G. Wilson (London, 1982), 47–56.
——. *The Son of Man in Mark*. London, 1967.
——. and S.G. Wilson (ed.), *Paul and Paulinism* (For C.K. Barrett). London, 1982.
Hoyles, J. Arthur. *Punishment in the Bible*. London, 1986.
Jaeger, Werner. *Early Christianity and Greek Paideia*. 1961, repr. Oxford, 1969.
Jeremias, Joachim. (tr. N. Perrin) *The Eucharistic Words of Jesus*. London, 1964.
——. (tr. F.H. and C.H. Cave) *Jerusalem in the Time of Jesus*. London, 1969.
——. (tr. S.H. Hooke) *The Parables of Jesus*. Rev. Ed., London, 1963.
Johnson, Sherman E. 'The Dead Sea Manual of Discipline and the Jerusalem Church of Acts', *The Scrolls and the New Testament*, ed. K. Stendahl (New York, 1957, repr. Westport, 1975), 129–42.
Kiddle, Martin. *Revelations*. Moffatt N.T. Comm. London, 1940.
Kingdon, H. Paul. 'The Origins of the Zealots', *NTS* 19 (1973), 74–81.
Kittel, Gerhard, and G. Friedrich (ed.). *Theologisches Wörterbuch zum Neuen Testament*. Vols. I–X. (*TWNT*) Berlin, 1933–1976.
——. Bromiley, G.W. (tr. ed.). *Theological Dictionary of the New Testament*. ed. Kittel and Friedrich. Vols. I–X. (*TDNT*) Grand Rapids, 1964–1976.
Kleinknecht, H., Fichtner, J., Stählin, G. et al. (tr.) *Wrath*. Bible Key Words from Kittel's *TWNT*. London, 1964.
Knox, Wilfred L. *St. Paul*. Edinburgh, 1932.
——. *St. Paul and the Church of Jerusalem*. Cambridge, 1925.
——. *Some Hellenistic Elements in Primitive Christianity*. London, 1944.
Kümmel, W.G. (tr. J.E. Steely) *The Theology of the New Testament*. London, 1974.
Küng, Hans. (tr. Ed. Quinn) *On being a Christian*. London, 1978.
Lampe, G.W.H. 'A.D. 70 in Christian reflection', *Jesus and the Politics of His Day* ed. E. Bammel and C.F.D. Moule (Cambridge, 1984), 153–71.
——. 'Church Discipline and the Interpretation of the Epistles to the Corinthians', *Christian History and Interpretation*, Studies presented to John Knox, ed. W.R. Farmer, C.F.D. Moule, and R.R. Niebuhr (Cambridge, 1967), 337–61.
——. 'Luke', *Peake's Comm. on the Bible* (2nd Ed., 1962), 820–43.
——. *The Seal of the Spirit*. 2nd Ed., London, 1967, repr. 1976.
Leipoldt, Johannes, and Walter Grundmann. *Umwelt des Urchristentums*. 3 Vols. 2nd Ed., Berlin, 1967; 1970.
Lohse, Eduard. *Umwelt des Neuen Testaments*. 2nd Ed., Göttingen, 1974.
Mâle, Émile. *L'art religieux de XIIIe siècle en France*. 8th Ed., Paris, 1948.
——. (tr.) *Religious Art from the Twelfth to the Eighteenth Century*. London, 1949.
Manson, T.W. *The Sayings of Jesus*. London, 1949, repr. 1957.
——. *The Servant-Messiah*. Cambridge, 1953, repr. 1966.
McKane, W. *Proverbs: A New Approach*. London, 1970, repr. 1980.
Meer, F. van der, and Christine Mohrmann (tr. ed. M.F. Hedlund and H.H. Rowley) *Atlas of the Early Christian World*. London, 1958.
Milošević, Desanka. (tr. G.H. Genzel and H. Rosenwald) *The Last Judgment*. Pictorial Library of Eastern Church Art, 3. Vaduz, 1964.
Mohrmann, Christine. v. Meer, F. van der.
Moltmann, Jürgen. (tr. M. Kohl) *The Crucified God*. London, 1974.
——. *Hope and Planning*. New York, 1971.

———. (tr. M. Kohl) *The Trinity and the Kingdom of God*. London, 1981.
Morenz, Siegfried. 'Feurige Kohlen auf dem Haupt', *Theol. Literaturzeitung* 78 (1953), 187–92.
———. *Die Geschichte von Joseph dem Zimmermann*. Berlin, 1951.
Moule, C.F.D. *The Birth of the New Testament*. 3rd Ed., London, 1981.
———. *Essays in New Testament Interpretation*, esp. 'Punishment and Retribution: an Attempt to Delimit their Scope in New Testament Thought'. Cambridge, 1982.
———. and Ernst Bammel, ed. *Jesus and the Politics of His Day*. Cambridge, 1984.
———. 'The Judgment Theme in the Sacraments', *The Background of the New Testament and its Eschatology*, ed. W.D. Davies and D. Daube (FS. C.H. Dodd, Cambridge, 1954, repr. 1964), 464–81.
———. *The Origin of Christology*. Cambridge, 1977.
Painter, John. 'Paul and the πνευματικοί at Corinth', *Paul and Paulinism*, ed. M.D. Hooker and S.G. Wilson (London, 1982), 237–50.
Perrin, Norman. *Rediscovering the Teaching of Jesus*. London, 1967.
———. *What is Redaction Criticism?* 1970, repr. London, 1974.
Pincoffs, Edmund L. *The Rationale of Legal Punishment*. New York, 1966.
Prestige, G.L. *Fathers and Heretics*. Bampton Lectures. London, 1940 repr. 1968.
Richardson, Alan, (ed.) *Theological Word Book of the Bible*. London, 1957, repr. 1969.
Robinson, John A.T. 'The Parable of the Sheep and the Goats', *NTS* 2 (1955–56), 225–37.
(ed. J.F. Coakley) *The Priority of John*. London, 1985.
Rogers, R.S. *Datguddiad Ioan* (The Revelation of John). Swansea, 1944.
Ruef, J.S. *Paul's First Letter to Corinth*. Harmondsworth, 1971.
Sanders, E.P. *Jesus and Judaism*. London, 1985.
———. *Paul, the Law, and the Jewish People*. Philadelphia, 1983.
Schnackenburg, Rudolf. (tr.) *The Gospel according to John*. 1970, tr. London, 1980.
Schoeps, H.J. (tr. H. Knight) *Paul: the Theology of the Apostle in the light of Jewish Religious History*. London, 1961.
Schürer, Emil, rev. G. Vermes, F. Millar, and M. Black. *The History of the Jewish People in the Age of Jesus Christ*. (= *Hist. Jewish People*) Edinburgh, I (1973); II (1979); III.1 (1987).
Schüssler Fiorenza, E. 'The Phenomenon of Early Christian Apocalyptic', *Apocalypticism etc.* ed. D. Hellholm (1983), 295–316.
Schweitzer, Albert. *Geschichte der Leben-Jesu-Forschung*, I. 6th Ed., 1950, repr. Munich, 1966.
Scott-Moncrieff, P.D. *Paganism and Christianity in Egypt*. Cambridge, 1913.
Shore, A.F. 'Christian and Coptic Egypt', *The Legacy of Egypt*, ed. J.R. Harris, 390–433. Oxford, 1971.
Smallwood, E. Mary. *The Jews under Roman Rule*. Leiden, 1976.
Stendahl, Krister. 'Matthew', *Peake's Comm. (1962)*, 769–98.
———. (ed.) *The Scrolls and the New Testament*. 1957, repr. Westport, 1975.
Stevenson, J. *A New Eusebius*. London, 1957, repr. 1970.
Strack, H., and Billerbeck, P. *Kommentar zum Neuen Testament aus Talmud und Midrasch*. 4 Vols. Munich, 1922–1928.
Surin, Kenneth. *Theology and the Problem of Evil*. Oxford, 1986.
———. 'Theodicy?', *Harv. Theol. Rev.* 76 (1983), 225–47.
Synofzik, Ernst. *Die Gerichts- und Vergeltungs-aussagen bei Paulus*. Göttingen, 1977.
Travis, Stephen H. *Christ and the Judgment of God*. Foundations for Faith. Basingstoke, 1986.
Vermes, Geza. *Jesus the Jew*. London, 1973, repr. 1976.
———. *Jesus and the World of Judaism*. London, 1983.
Wagner, Günter. (tr. J.P. Smith). *Pauline Baptism and the Pagan Mysteries*. Edinburgh, 1967. Cf. id., *Das religionsgeschichtliche Problem von Römer 6, 1–11*. Zürich, 1962.

Walters, C.C. 'Christian Paintings from Tebtunis', *JEA* 75 (1989), 191–208.
Weil, Simone. *Intimations of Christianity among the Greeks*. London, 1957, repr. 1987.
Wilson, S.G. (ed.) v. Hooker, M.D.

VIII. *India*

Appasamy, A.J. *Temple Bells*. Readings from Hindu Religious Literature. Calcutta, 1930.
Basham, A.L. *The Wonder that was India*. 3rd Rev. Ed., London, 1967, repr. 1988.
Brough, John. *Poems from the Sanskrit*. Harmondsworth 1968, repr. 1977.
Conze, Edward. *Buddhist Scriptures*. Harmondsworth, 1959, repr. 1976.
Cousins, L.S. 'Buddhism', *Handbook of Living Religions*, ed. J.R. Hinnells (Harmondsworth, 1985), 278–343.
Das Gupta, Ramaprasad. *Crime and Punishment in Ancient India*. New Delhi, 1973.
Day, Terence P. *The Conception of Punishment in Early Indian Literature*. Waterloo, Ontario, 1982.
Embree, Ainslie T. *The Hindu Tradition*. Readings in Oriental Thought. New York, 1972.
Evans-Wentz, W.Y. (ed.) *The Tibetan Book of the Dead*. 3rd Ed., Oxford, 1957, repr. 1985.
Folkert, Kendall W. 'Jainism', *Handbook of Living Religions*, ed. J.R. Hinnells, 256–77.
Geldner, K.F. *Der Rig-Veda*. 4 Vols. Cambridge Mass., 1951–1957.
Glasenapp, H. von. *Der Buddhismus—eine atheistische Religion*. Munich, 1966.
Gombrich, Richard. *On Being Sanskritic*. Inaugural Lecture, Oxford, 1978.
———. *Precept and Practice*. Traditional Buddhism in the Rural Highlands of Ceylon. Oxford, 1971.
Gonda, Jan. *Change and Continuity in Indian Religion*. Disputationes Rheno-Trajectinae, 9. The Hague, 1965.
———. *Prajāpati's Rise to Higher Rank*. Orientalia Rheno-Traiectina, 29. London, 1986.
———. *Die Religionen Indiens*. I. Stuttgart, 1960.
———. *Triads in the Veda*. Amsterdam, 1976.
———. *Vedic Literature*. Wiesbaden, 1975.
Jaini, Padmanabh S. 'Jainism', *Man and his Gods*, ed. Geoffrey Parrinder (London, 1971), 198–209.
———. 'Karma and the Problem of Rebirth in Jainism', *Karma and Rebirth in Classical Indian Traditions*, ed. Wendy Doniger O'Flaherty (Berkeley, 1980), 217–38.
Keith, Arthur S. *The Religion and Philosophy of the Veda and Unpanishads*. Harvard, 1925, repr. Westport, 1977.
Ling, Trevor. *The Buddha*. Harmondsworth, 1976.
———. *A History of Religion East and West*. London, 1968.
Macdonell, Arthur A. *A Sanskrit Grammar*. 3rd Ed., 1927, repr. Oxford, 1973.
———. *The Vedic Mythology*. Strassburg, 1897, repr. Delhi, 1971.
———. *A Vedic Reader*. Oxford, 1917, repr. Madras, 1965.
Mackay, E.J.H. *Further Excavations at Mohenjo-daro*. I and II. Delhi, 1938.
Marshall, Sir John. *Mohenjo-daro and the Indus Civilization*. 3 Vols. London, 1931.
Mascaró, Juan. *The Dhammapada*. Harmondsworth, 1973, repr. 1978.
———. *The Upanishads*. Harmondsworth, 1965, repr. 1975.
Masson-Oursel, P., and Louise Morin. 'Mythology of India', *Larousse Encyclopedia of Mythology* (tr.), ed. Felix Guirand (London, 1959), 339–92.
Matilal, B.K. *The Logical Illumination of Indian Mysticism*. Inaugural Lecture, Oxford, 1977.
Moore, Charles A. v. Radhakrishnan, S.
Nakamura, Hajune. *Indian Buddhism*. Tokyo, 1980.
O'Flaherty, Wendy Doniger. *Dreams, Illusion, and Other Realities*. Chicago, 1984.
———. *Hindu Myths*. Harmondsworth, 1975, repr. 1976.
———. (ed.) *Karma and Rebirth in Classical Indian Traditions*. Berkeley, 1980.

———. *The Origins of Evil in Hindu Mythology*. Berkeley, 1976.
———. *The Rig Veda*. Harmondsworth, 1961, repr. 1984.
———. *Sexual Metaphors and Animal Symbols in Indian Mythology*. Oxford, 1980.
Radhakrishnan, S. *The Hindu View of Life*. London, 1927, repr. 1960.
———. *Religion and Culture*. New Delhi, 1968.
———. and Charles A. Moore, *A Source Book in Indian Philosophy*. Princeton, 1957.
Renou, Louis. *Vedic India*. London, 1957, repr. Delhi, 1971.
Ross, Nancy Wilson. *Buddhism*. London, 1981.
Santucci, James A. *An Outline of Vedic Literature*. American Academy of Religion, Aids to the Study of Religion Series, 5. Missoula, Montana, 1976.
Satprakashananda, S. *The Use of Symbols in Religion*. St. Louis, Missouri, 1970.
Schulberg, Lucille. *Indien: Reiche zwischen Indus und Ganges*. Reinbeck, 1971, repr. 1976.
Smart, Ninian. *The Religious Experience of Mankind*. New York, 1969, repr. Glasgow, 1971.
Thieme, Paul. 'Diskussionsnotiz', *Die fünf großen Weltreligionen*, ed. E. Brunner-Traut, 62–65. Freiburg, 1977.
———. *Der Fremdling im Ṛgveda*. Abh. DKM, 23.2. Leipzig, 1938, repr. Nendeln, 1966.
———. *Gedichte aus dem Rig-Veda*, Stuttgart, 1964.
———. *Mitra and Aryaman*. Transactions of the Connecticut Academy, 41. New Haven, 1957.
Ramanujan, A.K. *Speaking of Śiva*. Harmondsworth, 1973, repr. 1979.
Thomas, Edward J. *Vedic Hymns*. Wisdom of the East. London, 1923.
Trautmann, Thomas R. 'Hinduism', *Man and his Gods*, ed. G. Parrinder (1971), 160–97.
Vakil, Kanaiyalal H. *At Ajanta*. Bombay, 1929.
Varenne, Jean. 'Le Jugement des Morts dans l'Inde', *Le Jugement des Morts*, (Paris, 1961), 209–30.
Varma, V.P. 'The Origins and Sociology of the Early Buddhist Philosophy of Moral Determinism', *Philosophy East and West* 13 (1963), 25–47.
Weightman, Simon. 'Hinduism', *Handbook of Living Religions* ed. John R. Hinnells (1985), 191–236.
Zaehner, R.C. *Hindu Scriptures*. London, 1966.
———. *Hinduism*. Oxford, 1962, repr. 1975.
———. *Our Savage God*. London, 1974.
Zimmer, Heinrich. (ed. Joseph Campbell) *Myths and Symbols in Indian Art and Civilization*. Bollingen Series, VI. Pantheon Books. New York, 1946, repr. 1953.

IX. China

Dobson, W.A.C.H. 'China', *Man and his Gods*, ed. G. Parrinder (London, 1971), 263–305.
Eberhard, Wolfram. *Guilt and Sin in Traditional China*. Berkeley, 1967.
Eichhorn, Werner. *Die Alte Chinesische Religion und das Staatskultwesen*. Hdb. der Orientalistik, IV, 4, 1. Leiden, 1976.
———. *Die Religionen Chinas*. Die Religionen der Menschheit, 21. Stuttgart, 1973.
———. 'Taoism', *Concise Encyclopedia of Living Faiths*, ed. R.C. Zaehner (1977), 374–92.
English, Jane. v. Feng, Gia-fu.
Feng, Gia-fu, and Jane English. *Lao Tsu, Tao Te Ching*. London, 1973, repr. 1978.
Giles, Herbert A. *A History of Chinese Literature*. London, 1901.
Goodrich, Anne Swann. *Chinese Hells. The Peking Temple of Eighteen Hells and Chinese Conceptions of Hell*. Monumenta Serica. St. Augustin, 1981.
———. *The Peking Temple of the Eastern Peak*. Monumenta Serica. Nagoya, Japan, 1964.

Graham, A.C. *Chuang-Tsǔ, The Inner Chapters.* London, 1981, repr. 1986.
——. *Poems of the Late Tang.* Harmondsworth, 1965, repr. 1981.
Granet, M. *The Religion of the Chinese People.* Oxford, 1975.
Groot, J.J.M. de. *The Religious System of China.* 6 Vols. 1892, repr. Taipei, 1972.
Hawkes, David. *Chinese: Classical, Modern, and Humane.* Inaugural Lecture, Oxford, 1961.
——. *Ch'u Tzǔ. The Songs of the South.* An Ancient Chinese Anthology. Oxford, 1959.
Khoury, A. Theodor. 'Buddhismus', *Die fünf großen Weltreligionen*, ed. E. Brunner-Traut (Breisgau, 1977), 40–61.
Lau, D.C. *Confucius, The Analects.* Harmondsworth, 1979, repr. 1986.
——. *Lao Tzu, Tao Te Ching.* Harmondsworth, 1963, repr. 1976.
Legge, James. *The Chinese Classics.* Vol. I. The Confucian Analects, The Great Learning, and The Doctrine of the Mean. 2nd Ed., Oxford, 1893.
——. *The Four Books.* Confucian Analects, The Great Learning, The Doctrine of the Mean, and the Works of Mencius. Shanghai, 1923, repr. New York, 1966.
——. Sacred Books of the East, ed. F. Max Müller. Vol. 3: *The Sacred Books of China.* Part I. The Texts of Confucianism. Oxford, 1879.
——. Vol. 16. Part II (of Vol. 3). Oxford, 1882.
——. Vol. 27. Part III. Oxford, 1885.
Ling, Trevor. *The Buddha.* London, 1973, repr. Harmondsworth, 1976.
——. *A History of Religion East and West.* London, 1968.
Liou, Kia-Hway. *L'Oeuvre complète de Tchouang-tseu.* Traduction, Préface et Notes. Paris, 1969.
Maby, Cedric. *Y Cocatŵ Coch.* Blodeugerdd o gerddi byrion o'r Tseinaeg. (*The Red Cockatoo.* An anthology of short poems from the Chinese, rendered into Welsh.) Cardiff, 1987.
McFarlane, Stuart. 'Mo-Tzu', *Dictionary of Religions*, ed. J.R. Hinnells (Harmondsworth, 1984), 217–18.
Rowley, H.H. *Prophecy and Religion in Ancient China and Israel.* Jordan Lectures, 1954. London, 1956.
——. *Submission in Suffering.* Cardiff, 1951.
Saso, Michael R. 'Chinese Religions', *Handbook of Living Religions*, ed. J.R. Hinnells (1985), 344–64.
——. *Taoism and the Rite of Cosmic Renewal.* Washington, 1972.
Smart, Ninian. *The Religious Experience of Mankind.* New York, 1969, repr. Glasgow, 1971.
Thompson, Laurence G. *Chinese Religion.* 3rd Ed., Belmont, California, 1979.
Vandier-Nicolas, Nicole. 'Le Jugements des Morts en Chine', *Le Jugement des Morts* (Paris, 1961), 233–54.
——. *Le Taoïsme.* Paris, 1965.
Waley, Arthur. *The Analects of Confucius.* London, 1938.
——. *Chinese Poems.* London, 1946.
Watson, Burton. *Basic Writings of Mo Tzu, Hsün Tzu, and Han Fei Tzu.* New York, 1967.
——. *Early Chinese Literature.* New York, 1962.
Williams, Cyril G. *Crefyddau'r Dwyrain.* (Religions of the East). Cardiff, 1968.
Zaehner, R.C. *Drugs, Mysticism and Make-Believe.* London, 1972.

X. *Egypt*

Abd-ul Rahman, M.H. v. Reisner, G.A.
Aldred, Cyril. *The Development of Ancient Egyptian Art.* London, 1962.
——. *Jewels of the Pharaohs.* London, 1971.
Allam, Schafik. 'De la Divinité dans le droit Pharaonique', *BSFE* 68 (1973), 17–30.
——. *Everyday Life in Ancient Egypt.* Prism Archaeology Series, 1. Guizeh, Egypt, 1985.

———. *Das Verfahrensrecht in der altägyptischen Arbeitersiedlung von Deir el-Medineh*. Tübingen, 1973.
Allen, T.G. *The Book of the Dead*. Chicago, 1974.
Altenmüller, Brigitte. *Synkretismus in den Sargtexten*. Wiesbaden, 1975.
Altenmüller, Hartwig. *Die Texte zum Begräbnisritual*. Wiesbaden, 1972.
———. 'Zum Abwiegen von Metall im Alten Reich usw.', *Göttinger Miszellen* 89 (1986), 7–14.
———. 'Ist die Waage im Gleichgewicht?', ibid. 97 (1987), 7–14.
Arnold, Dieter. *Wandrelief und Raumfunktion in ägyptischen Tempeln des Neuen Reiches*. MÄS 2. Berlin, 1962.
Assmann, Jan. *Ägypten—Theologie und Frömmigkeit einer frühen Hochkultur*. Stuttgart, 1984.
———. *Ägyptische Hymnen und Gebete*. Bibliothek der Alten Welt. Zürich, 1975.
———. 'Königsdogma und Heilserwartung. Politische und kultische Chaosbeschreibungen in ägyptischen Texten', *Apocalypticism etc.* ed. D. Hellholm, 345–77. Tübingen, 1983.
———. *Re und Amun*. OBO 51. Freiburg, Schweiz, 1983.
———. 'Schrift, Tod und Identität', *Schrift und Gedächtnis*, ed. Assmann and Hardmeier, 64–93. Munich, 1983.
———. 'Weisheit, Loyalismus und Frömmigkeit', *Studien zu altägyptischen Lebenslehren*, ed. Hornung and Keel, 12–72. Freiburg, 1979.
———. *Zeit und Ewigkeit im alten Ägypten*. Abh. Heidelberg, 1975.
Baines, John. *Fecundity Figures*. Warminster, 1985.
Bakir, Abd el-Mohsen. *The Cairo Calendar No. 86637*. Cairo, 1966.
Barb, A.A. 'Mystery, Myth, and Magic', *The Legacy of Egypt*, ed. J.R. Harris, 138–69. Oxford, 1971.
Barguet, Paul. *Le Livre des Morts*. Paris, 1967.
Barta, Winfried. *Die Bedeutung der Jenseitsbücher für den verstorbenen König*. MÄS 42. Munich, 1985.
———. 'Königsbezeichnung', *LÄ* III (1980), 477–81.
———. *Untersuchungen zur Göttlichkeit des regierenden Königs*. MÄS 32.
Beckerath, Jürgen von. *Handbuch der ägyptischen Königsnamen*. MÄS 20. Munich, 1984.
Begelsbacher-Fischer, Barbara L. *Untersuchungen zur Götterwelt des alten Reichs*. OBO 37. Freiburg, Schweiz, 1981.
Bennett, John. 'The Restoration Inscription of Tut'ankhamūn', *JEA* 25 (1939), 8–15.
Bergman, Jan. 'Introductory Remarks on Apocalypticism in Egypt', *Apocalypticism etc.* ed. D. Hellholm, 51–60. Tübingen, 1983.
———. 'Zum Zwei-Wege-Motiv', *Svensk Exegetisk Årsbok* 41–42 (1976–7), 27–56.
Berlev, Oleg. v. Hodjash, Svetlana.
Bianchi, R.S. 'Not the Isis Knot', *Bull. Egyptol. Seminar Brooklyn* 2 (1980), 9–31.
Bierbrier, Morris. *The Tomb-Builders of the Pharaohs*. London, 1982.
Bissing, F.W.F. von. 'Tombeaux d'époque romaine à Akhmîm', *ASAE* 50 (1950), 547–76.
Blackman, A.M. 'Myth and Ritual in Ancient Egypt', *Myth and Ritual*, ed. S.H. Hooke, 15–39. Oxford, 1933.
Bleeker, C.J. *Hathor and Thoth*. Leiden, 1973.
Blumenthal, Elke. 'Die Prophezeiung des Neferti', *ZÄS* 109 (1982), 1–27.
———. *Untersuchungen zum ägyptischen Königtum des mittleren Reiches. I. Die Phraseologie*. Abh. Leipzig, 61. Berlin, 1970.
Bonnet, Hans. *Bilderatlas zur Religionsgeschichte*, ed. D. Hans Haas. 2–4. *Ägyptische Religion*. Leipzig, 1924.
———. *Reallexikon der ägyptischen Religionsgeschichte*. (RÄRG). Berlin, 1952.
Boorn, G.P.F. van den. '*Wḏ ʿ-ryt* and Justice at the Gate', *JNES* 44 (1985), 1–25.
Borghouts, J.F. 'Divine Intervention in Ancient Egypt and its Manifestation (*b3w*)', *Gleanings from Deir el-Medîna*, ed. R.J. Demarée and Jac J. Janssen, 1–70. Leiden, 1982.

——. *The Magical Texts of Papyrus Leiden I 348*. OMRO 51. Leiden, 1971.
Bosse-Griffiths, Kate. 'Baboon and Maid', *Studien zu Sprache und Religion Ägyptens* (FS. W. Westendorf), II, 743–8. Göttingen, 1984.
Bothmer, B.V. *Egyptian Sculpture of the Late Period*. Brooklyn, 1963, repr. 1973.
Breasted, James H. *The Dawn of Conscience*. New York, 1933.
——. *Development of Religion and Thought in Ancient Egypt*. London, 1912.
Broekhuis, J. *De Godin Renenwetet*. Assen, 1971.
Brovarski, Edward. *Canopic Jars*. Mainz / Rhein, 1978.
Brugsch, Heinrich. *Dictionnaire Géographique de l'Ancienne Égypte*. Leipzig, 1879.
Brunner, Hellmut. *Altägyptische Weisheit*. Die Bibliothek der alten Welt. Zürich, 1988.
——. 'Blindheit', *LÄ* I (1975), 828–33.
——. 'Der freie Wille Gottes in der ägyptischen Weisheit', *Les Sagesses du Proche-Orient Ancien*, 103–30. Paris, 1963.
——. *Die Geburt des Gottkönigs*. 2nd Ed., Wiesbaden, 1984.
——. 'Gottesnähe und -ferne', *LÄ* II (1977), 817–19.
——. 'Die Lehren', *Hdb. der Orientalistik: Ägyptologie, Lit.*² 113–39. Leiden, 1970; cf. id. 'Lehren', *LÄ* III (1980), 964–8.
——. 'Petbe', *LÄ* IV (1982), 992–3.
——. 'Die Rolle von Tür und Tor im Alten Ägypten', *Symbolon* N.F. 6 (1982), 37–59.
——. 'Weltende', *LÄ* VI (1986), 1213–4.
Brunner-Traut, Emma. *Altägyptische Märchen*. Düsseldorf, 2nd Ed., 1965.
——. *Gelebte Mythen*. Darmstadt, 1981.
——. *Lebensweisheit der Alten Ägypter*. Freiburg im Breisgau, 1985.
——. 'Der Sehgott und der Hörgott in Literatur und Theologie', *Fragen an die altägyptische Literatur* (Gedenkschr. E. Otto), 125–45. Wiesbaden, 1977.
——. 'Weiterleben des ägyptischen Lebenslehren in den koptischen Apophthegmata am Beispiel des Schweigens', *Studien zu altägyptischen Lebenslehren*, ed. E. Hornung and O. Keel, 174–216. Freiburg, Schweiz, 1979.
Budge, E.A. Wallis. *The Book of the Dead*. BM Handbook. London, 1920, repr. 1933.
——. *The Dwellers on the Nile*. London, 1926.
——. *The Mummy*. 2nd Ed., Cambridge, 1894, repr. 1972.
Caminos, Ricardo A. *The Chronicle of Prince Osorkon*. Analecta Orientalia, 37. Rome, 1958.
——. 'Fragments of the *Book of the Dead* on Linen and Papyrus', *JEA* 56 (1970), 117–31.
——. *Late-Egyptian Miscellanies*. London, 1954.
Castiglione, L. 'Kunst und Gesellschaft im römischen Ägypten', *Acta Antiqua Acad. Hung.* 15 (1967), 107–52.
Černý, Jaroslav. *Ancient Egyptian Religion*. London, 1952.
——. *A Community of Workmen at Thebes in the Ramesside Period*. Cairo, 1973.
——. *The Inscriptions of Sinai*. Vol. II. 2nd Ed., London, 1955.
——. and Sarah I. Groll. *A Late Egyptian Grammar*. Rome, 1978.
Chassinat, Émile. *Le Mystère d'Osiris au mois de Khoiak*. 2 Vols. Cairo, 1966; 1968.
Clark, R.T. Rundle. *Myth and Symbol in Ancient Egypt*. London, 1959.
Clerc, Gisèle. v. Leclant, Jean.
Clère, J.J. 'Un Passage de la Stèle du Général Antef', *BIFAO* 30 (1931), 425–47.
Daumas, François. *Les Mammisis des temples égyptiens*. Paris, 1958.
Derchain, Philippe. 'La couronne de la justification', *Chronique d'Égypte* 30 (1955), 225–87.
Derchain-Urtel, Maria-Theresia. *Thot*. Rites égyptiens, 3. Brussels, 1981.
Desroches-Noblecourt, Christiane. 'Une coutume égyptienne méconnue', *BIFAO* 45 (1947), 185–232.
——. *Tutankhamen*. London, 1963.
Drioton, E. v. Gabra, Sami.

Dunham Dows. *Naga-ed-Dêr Stelae of the First Intermediate Period.* Boston, 1937.
Edel, Elmar. *Untersuchungen zur Phraseologie der ägyptischen Inschriften des alten Reiches.* *MDAIK* 13.1 (1944).
Edgar, C.C. *Graeco-Egyptian Coffins, Masks and Portraits.* Cairo Cat. Gén. 1905.
Edwards, I.E.S. *A Handbook to the Egyptian Mummies.* London, 1938.
——. *Hieratic Papyri in the British Museum, Fourth Series: Oracular Amuletic Decrees of the Late New Kingdom.* 2 Vols. London, 1960.
——. *Treasures of Tutankhamun.* London, 1972.
Erman, Adolf, and Hermann Grapow. *Wörterbuch der ägyptischen Sprache.* 7 Vols. Berlin, 1926–63, repr. 1982.
Fairman, H.W. 'An Introduction to the Study of Ptolemaic Signs and their Values', *BIFAO* 43 (1945), 51–138.
——. 'A Scene of the Offering of Truth in the Temple of Edfu', *MDAIK* 16 (1958, FS. H. Junker), 86–92.
——. *The Triumph of Horus,* London, 1974.
Faulkner, Raymond O. 'The Admonitions of an Egyptian Sage', *The Literature of Ancient Egypt,* ed. W.K. Simpson, 210–29. New Haven, 1973.
——. *The Ancient Egyptian Book of the Dead.* New York, 1972, rev. ed. London, 1985.
——. *The Ancient Egyptian Coffin Texts.* 3 Vols. Warminster, 1973–1978.
——. *The Ancient Egyptian Pyramid Texts.* Oxford, 1969; Warminster, 1985.
——. 'The Bremner-Rhind Papyrus, I', *JEA* 22 (1936), 121–40.
——. *A Concise Dictionary of Middle Egyptian.* Oxford, 1962.
Fecht, Gerhard. *Literarische Zeugnisse zur 'Persönlichen Frömmigkeit' in Ägypten.* Heidelberg, 1965.
Fořtová-Šámalová, P. *Egyptian Ornament.* London, 1963.
Fowden, Garth. *The Egyptian Hermes.* Cambridge, 1986.
Frankfort, Henri. *Kingship and the Gods.* Chicago, 1948.
Gaballa, G.A., and K.A. Kitchen. 'The Festival of Sokar', *Orientalia* 38 (1969), 1–76.
Gabra, Sami. *Chez les derniers adorateurs du Trismégiste.* Cairo, 1971.
——. and E. Drioton. *Peintures à fresques et scènes peintes à Hermoupolis-Ouest (Touna el-Gebel).* Cairo, 1954.
——. *Rapport sur les fouilles d'Hermopolis-Ouest (Touna el-Gebel).* Cairo, 1941.
Gardiner, Alan H. *Ancient Egyptian Onomastica.* 3 Vols. Oxford, 1947, repr. 1968.
——. *Egypt of the Pharaohs.* Oxford, 1961.
——. *Egyptian Grammar.* 3rd Ed., Oxford, 1957.
——. *Late-Egyptian Miscellanies.* Bibliotheca Aegyptiaca, 7. Brussels, 1937.
Gauthier, Henri. *Dictionnaire des Noms Géographiques.* 7 Vols. Cairo, 1925–1931.
George, Beate. *Zu den altägyptischen Vorstellungen vom Schatten als Seele.* Bonn, 1970.
Glanville, S.R.K. *Catalogue of Demotic Papyri in the British Museum.* Vol. II, 1955.
Goedicke, Hans. (ed.) *Perspectives on the Battle of Kadesh.* Baltimore, 1985.
——. *The Protocol of Neferyt.* (The Prophecy of Neferti.) Baltimore, 1977.
——. *Die Stellung des Königs im Alten Reich.* Ägyptologische Abh. 2.
——. 'Unity and Diversity in the Oldest Religion of Ancient Egypt', *Unity and Diversity,* ed. H. Goedicke and J.J.M. Roberts, 201–210. Baltimore, 1975.
Goff, Beatrice L. *Symbols of Ancient Egypt in the Late Period.* Religion and Society, 13. The Hague, 1979.
Goyon, Jean-Claude. *Confirmation du pouvoir royale au nouvel an.* BdE 52. Cairo, 1972.
——. *Rituels funéraires de l'ancienn Égypte.* Paris, 1972.
Grapow, Hermann. v. Erman, Adolf.
Grieshammer, Reinhard. *Das Jenseitsgericht in den Sargtexten.* Wiesbaden, 1970.
——. 'Reinheit, kultische', *LÄ* V (1984), 212–13.
——. 'Zum "Sitz im Leben" des negativen Sündenbekenntnisses', *ZDMG* Suppl. II, 19–25. Wiesbaden, 1974.
Griffith, F. Ll. *Stories of the High Priests of Memphis.* Oxford, 1900.
Griffiths, J. Gwyn. 'Apocalyptic in the Hellenistic Era', *Apocalypticism etc.* ed. D. Hellholm, 273–93. Tübingen, 1983.

——. *The Conflict of Horus and Seth.* Liverpool Monographs in Archaeology and Oriental Studies. Liverpool, 1960.
——. 'The Deserters on the Left of the King', *ASAE* 53 (1955), 144–9.
——. 'The Faith of the Pharaonic Period'; 'The Great Egyptian Cults of Oecumenical Spiritual Significance', *Classical Mediterranean Spirituality*, ed A.H. Armstrong, 3–38; 39–65. *World Spirituality*, Vol. 15. New York, 1986.
——. 'Hellenistic Religions', *The Encyclopedia of Religion*, ed. Mircea Eliade, Vol. VI, 252–66. New York, 1987.
——. 'Motivation in Early Egyptian Syncretism', *Studies in Egyptian Religion* (for Jan Zandee) ed. M. Heerma van Voss et al., 43–55. Leiden, 1982.
——. *The Origins of Osiris and his Cult.* Supplements to Numen, 40. Leiden, 1980.
——. 'Osiris', *LÄ* IV (1981), 623–33.
——. 'Remarks on the Horian Elements in the Royal Titulary', *ASAE* 56 (1959), 63–86.
——. 'Wisdom About Tomorrow', *Harv. Theol. Rev.* 53 (1960), 219–22.
Grimm, Günter. *Kunst der Ptolemäer- und Römerzeit im Ägyptischen Museum, Kairo.* Mainz, 1975.
——. *Die römischen Mumienmasken aus Ägypten.* Wiesbaden, 1974.
Groll, Sarah I., with J. Černý. *A Late Egyptian Grammar.* Rome, 1978.
Grumach (- Shirun), Irene. *Untersuchungen zur Lebenslehre des Amenope.* MÄS 23. Munich, 1972.
——. 'Lehre des Amenemope', *LÄ* III (1980), 971–4.
Harris, J.R. (ed) *The Legacy of Egypt.* 2nd Ed., Oxford, 1971.
Hassan, A. *Stöcke und Stäbe im pharaonischen Ägypten.* MÄS 33. Munich, 1976.
Hayes, William C. *The Scepter of Egypt.* Vol. II. Cambridge, Mass. 1959.
Heerma van Voss, M. *Anoebis en de demonen.* Leiden, 1978.
——. 'Anubis in Pyr. 1713 c', *L'Égyptologie en 1979*, Vol. II, 25. Paris, 1982.
——. 'Een dodendoek als dodenboek', *Phoenix* 20 (1974), 335–8.
——. 'De Gerichtsscene in het egyptische Poortenboek', *Travels in the World of the Old Testament* (for M.A. Beek), 80–90. Amsterdam, 1984.
——. 'Le Livre des Morts au Nouvel Empire au Musée de Leyde', *BSFE* 105 (1986), 10–22.
——. *Een man en zijn boekrol.* (Valedictory Lecture.) Leiden, 1988.
——. *De oudste Versie van Dodenboek 17 a.* Leiden. 1963.
——. *Zwischen Grab und Paradies.* Basel, 1971.
Helck, Wolfgang. *Die Beziehungen Ägyptens zu Vorderasien im 3. und 2. Jahrtausend v. Chr.* 2nd Ed., Wiesbaden, 1971.
——. *Die Prophezeiung des Nfr-tj.* Kleine Ägyptische Texte. Wiesbaden, 1970.
——. *Der Text der 'Lehre Amenemhets I. für seinen Sohn'.* Kleine Ägyptische Texte. Wiesbaden, 1969.
——. (ed.) with E. Otto and W. Westendorf. *Lexikon der Ägyptologie.* I–VI. Wiesbaden, 1971–1986.
Hodjash, Svetlana, and Oleg Berlev. *The Egyptian Reliefs and Stelae in the Pushkin Museum of Fine Arts, Moscow.* Leningrad, 1982.
Hooper, Finlay A. *Funerary Stelae from Kom Abou Billou.* Ann Arbor, 1961.
Hornung, Erik. *Ägyptische Unterweltsbücher.* 2nd Ed., Zürich, 1984.
——. *Altägyptische Höllenvorstellungen.* Abh. Leipzig, 59. 3. Berlin, 1968.
——. *Das Amduat.* 3 Vols. Ägyptologische Abh. 7; 13. Wiesbaden, 1963; 1967.
——. with A. Brodbeck and E. Staehelin. *Das Buch von den Pforten des Jenseits.* 2 Vols. Aegyptiaca Helvetica, 7, 8. Geneva, 1979; 1984.
——. (tr. J. Baines) *Conceptions of God in Ancient Egypt.* London, 1983.
——. 'The Discovery of the Unconscious in Ancient Egypt', *Spring*. Annual of Archetypal Psychology and Jungian Thought. Vol. for 1986, 16–28. Dallas, Texas.
——. 'Die Israelstele des Merenptah', *Fontes atque Pontes* (FS. H. Brunner), ed. M. Görg, 224–33. Wiesbaden, 1983.
——. 'Lehren über Jenseits?', *Studien zu altägyptischen Lebenslehren*, ed. Hornung and

Keel, 218–24. Freiburg, Schweiz, 1979.

——. 'Monotheismus im pharaonischen Ägypten', *Monotheismus im Alten Israel und seiner Umwelt*, ed. Othmar Keel, 84–97. Freiburg, Schweiz, 1980.

——. *Tal der Könige*. Zürich, 1982.

——. *Das Totenbuch der Ägypter*. Bibliothek der Alten Welt. Zürich, 1979.

——. and Othmar Keel. (ed.) *Studien zu altägyptischen Lebenslehren*. OBO 28. Freiburg, Schweiz, 1979.

——. and E. Staehelin. *Skarabäen und andere Siegelamulette*, I. Mainz, 1976.

——. 'Zeitliches Jenseits im Alten Ägypten', *Jahrb. Eranos* 47 (1978), 269–307.

Iversen, Erik. *Egyptian and Hermetic Doctrine*. Copenhagen, 1984.

James, T.G.H. *Hieroglyphic Texts in the British Museum*. Vol. 9. London, 1970.

Jansen-Winkeln, Karl. *Ägyptische Biographien der 22. und. 23. Dynastie*. 2 Vols. Ägypten und Altes Testament, 8. Wiesbaden, 1985.

Janssen, Jac J. *Commodity Prices from the Ramessid Period*. Leiden, 1975.

Johnson, Janet H. 'The Demotic Chronicle as a Historical Source', *Enchoria* 4 (1974), 1–17.

——. 'The Demotic Chronicle as a Statement of a Theory of Kingship', *JSSEA* 13 (1983), 61–72.

——. 'Is the Demotic Chronicle an Anti-Greek Tract?', *Grammata Demotika* (FS. E. Lüddeckens), ed. Heinz-J. Thissen and Karl-Th. Zauzich, 107–24. Würzburg, 1984.

Junge, F. 'Isis und die ägyptischen Mysterien', *Aspekte der spätägyptischen Religion*, ed. W. Westendorf, 93–115. Wiesbaden, 1979.

——. 'Die Welt der Klagen', *Fragen an die altägyptische Literatur* (Gedenkschr. E. Otto), 275–84. Wiesbaden, 1977.

Junker, Hermann, and Erich Winter. *Das Geburtshaus des Tempels der Isis in Philä*. Wien, 1965.

——. *Pyramidenzeit*. Zürich, 1949.

Kákosy, László. 'Probleme der ägyptischen Jenseitsvorstellungen in der Ptolemäer- und Kaiserzeit', *Religions en Égypte hellénistique et romain*, 59–68. Paris, 1969.

——. *Selected Papers*. Studia Aegyptiaca, 7. Budapest, 1981.

——. 'Selige und Verdammte in der spätägyptischen Religion', ibid. 227–37. (first publ. 1971)

Kamal, A. 'Fouilles à Gamhoud', *ASAE* 9 (1908), 8–30.

——. *Stèles ptolémaïques et romaines*. Cairo Cat. Gén. 1904–1905.

Kaplony, Peter. 'Demotische Chronik', *LÄ* I (1975), 1056–60.

Keel, Othmar. v. Hornung, Erik.

Kees, Hermann. *Der Götterglaube im Alten Ägypten*. 2nd Ed., Berlin, 1956.

——. *Totenglauben und Jenseitsvorstellungen der alten Ägypter*. 2nd Ed., Berlin, 1956.

Kemp, Barry J. 'Divine Kingship' (sub-section), *Ancient Egypt, A Social History*, 71–76. Cambridge, 1983.

Kitchen, Kenneth A. *Ramesside Inscriptions*. 6 Vols. Oxford, 1968–1983.

——. v. Gaballa, G.A.

Koefoed-Petersen, O. *Catalogue des sarcophages et cercueils égyptiens*. Copenhagen, 1951.

Leahy, M.A. 'The Name of Osiris Written 𓊩 ', *Studien zur altägyptischen Kultur* 7 (1979), 141–9.

——. 'The Osiris "Bed" Reconsidered', *Orientalia* 46 (1977), 424–34.

Leclant, Jean, with Gisèle Clerc. *Inventaire Bibliographique des Isiaca*, I–III. EPRO 18. Leiden, 1972; 1974; 1985.

——. 'Aegyptiaca et milieux isiaques', *ANRW* II. 17. 3 (Berlin, 1984), 1692–709.

——. with Gisèle Clerc, 'Ammon', *Lexicon Iconographicum Mythologiae Classicae*, I (Zürich, 1981), 666–89.

——. 'Anubis', ibid. I, 862–73.

Lefebvre, Gustave. *Le Tombeau de Petosiris*. 3 Vols. Cairo, 1923–1924.

Lesko, Leonard H. *The Ancient Egyptian Book of Two Ways*. Berkeley, 1972.

Lichtheim, Miriam. *Ancient Egyptian Literature*. 3 Vols. I. The Old and Middle Kingdoms; II. The New Kingdom; III. The Late Period. Berkeley, 1973; 1976; 1980.

——. *Late Egyptian Wisdom Literature in the International Context*. OBO 52. Freiburg, Schweiz, 1983.

——. 'Observations on Papyrus Insinger', *Studien zu altägyptischen Lebenslehren*, ed. Hornung and Keel, 283–305. Freiburg, Schweiz, 1979.

Lieblein, J. *Le Livre égyptien Que Mon Nom Fleurisse*. Leipzig, 1895.

Lloyd, Alan B. 'The King' (sub-section), *Ancient Egypt: A Social History*, 288–99. Cambridge, 1983.

——. 'Nationalistic Propaganda in Ptolemaic Egypt', *Historia* 31 (1982), 33–55.

Maehler, H., and V.M. Stroka. (ed.) *Das ptolemäische Ägypten*. Mainz, 1978.

Maystre, Charles. *Les Déclarations d'innocence*. IFAO. Cairo, 1937.

Meulenaere, H. De. *Scarabaeus Sacer*. Hoechst, Belgium, 1972.

Meyer, Eduard. 'Ägyptische Dokumente aus der Persenzeit', *SPAW* (Berlin, 1915), 287–311.

Möller, Georg. *Die beiden Totenpapyrus Rhind*. Leipzig, 1913.

——. *Hieratische Paläographie*. 3 Vols. Leipzig, 1927–1936.

Moorey, P.R.S. *Ancient Egypt*. Ashmolean Museum, Oxford, 1970.

Morenz, Siegfried. 'Ägypten und die altorphische Kosmogonie', id. *Religion und Geschichte des alten Ägypten*, 452–95 (first publ. 1950). Weimar, 1975.

——. *Ägyptische Religion*. Religionen der Menschheit, 8. Stuttgart, 1960, repr. 1977.

——. 'Anubis mit dem Schlüssel', *Wiss. Z. der Karl-Marx. Univ. Leipzig* 3 (1953–4), 127–31.

——. *Egyptian Religion*. (tr. Ann E. Keep). London, 1973.

——. 'Das Problem des Werden zu Osiris in der griechischen-römischen Zeit Ägyptens', *Religions en Égypte hellénistique et romaine*, 75–91. Paris, 1969.

——. 'Rechts und links im Totengericht', *ZÄS* 82 (1957), 62–71. Also in ——. id. *Religion und Geschichte des alten Ägypten*. Weimar, 1975.

——. with Dieter Müller, *Untersuchungen zur Rolle des Schicksals in der ägyptischen Religion*. Abh. Leipzig, 52. Berlin, 1960.

Moret, Alexandre. 'La Doctrine de Maât', *RdE* 4 (1940), 1–14.

Morschauser, Scott. 'Observations on the Speeches of Ramesses II in the Literary Record of the Battle of Kadesh', *Perspectives on the Battle of Kadesh* ed. H. Goedicke, (1985), 123–206.

Müller, Dieter. *Ägypten und die griechischen Isis-Aretalogien*. Abh. Leipzig, 53.1. Berlin, 1961.

——. 'Grabausstattung und Totengericht in der Lehre für König Merikare', *ZÄS* 91 (FS. R. Anthes, 1967), 117–24.

——. (Mueller, Dieter). 'Three Mummy Labels in the Swansea Wellcome Collection', *JEA* 59 (1973), 175–80.

——. v. Morenz, Siegfried.

Munro, Peter. *Die spätägyptischen Totenstelen*. 2 Vols. Ägyptologische Forschungen, 25. Glückstadt, 1973.

Nakaten, Susanne. 'Petosiris', *LÄ* IV (1982), 995–8.

Naville, Edouard. *Das Aegyptische Todtenbuch der XVIII. bis XX. Dynastie*. 3 Vols. Berlin, 1886, repr. Graz, 1971.

Needler, Winifred. *An Egyptian Funerary Bed of the Roman Period*. Toronto, 1973.

Nims, Charles, 'The Term *HP*, 'Law, Right', in Demotic', *JNES* 7 (1948), 243–60.

Nur El-Din, M.A.A. *The Demotic Ostraca in the National Museum of Antiquities at Leiden*. Leiden, 1974.

O'Connor, David. 'The Egyptian World-View, 1552–664 B.C.' (sub-section), *Ancient Egypt, A Social History*, 188–202. Cambridge, 1983.

Otto, Eberhard. 'Biographien', *Hdb. der Orientalistik*, ed. B. Spuler, I.i.2, *Ägyptologie: Lit.*, 179–88. 2nd Ed., Leiden, 1970.

——. *Die biographischen Inschriften der ägyptischen Spätzeit*. Leiden, 1954.

——. (tr. Kate Bosse-Griffiths). *Egyptian Art: The Cults of Osiris and Amon.* London, 1967.
——. (Gedenkschr. für). *Fragen an die altägyptische Literatur,* ed. Jan Assmann et al. Wiesbaden, 1977.
——. v. Helck, Wolfgang.
Parlasca, Klaus. *Mumienporträts und verwandte Denkmäler.* Wiesbaden, 1966.
Parlebas, Jacques. 'Über das Zeichen ⤫', *SAK* 4 (1976), 273–5.
Petrie, W.M. Flinders. *Egyptian Decorative Art.* London, 1895.
Posener, Georges, 'Ächtungstexte', *LÄ* I (1975), 67 ff.
——. *De la divinité du Pharaon.* Paris, 1960.
——. (ed.) *A Dictionary of Egyptian Civilization.* London, 1962.
——. 'Lehre für Merikare', *LÄ* III (1980), 986–9.
——. 'Lehre, loyalistische', *LÄ* III (1980), 982–4.
——. *Littérature et Politique dans l'Égypte de la XIIe Dynastie.* Paris, 1956.
Quaegebeur, Jan. *Le dieu égyptien Shaï.* Leuven, 1975.
——. 'Ptolémée II en adoration devant Arsinoé II divinisée', *BIFAO* 69 (1971), 191–217.
Quibell, J.E. *The Ramesseum.* London, 1898.
Ranke, Hermann. *Die altägyptischen Personennamen.* (= PN). 2 Vols. Glückstadt, 1935; 1952.
Ray, John D. 'Ancient Egypt', *Divination and Oracles,* ed. M. Loewe and Carmen Blacker, 174–90. London, 1981.
——. *The Archive of Ḥor.* Texts from Excavations, 2. London, 1976.
——. 'Mu3at and the M3'-Ritual', *Abstracts of Papers, International Association of Egyptologists. Fourth Congress, Munich, 1985,* 183–4. ed. Sylvia Schoske.
——. 'Psammuthis and Hakoris', *JEA* 72 (1986), 149–58.
Reisner, G.A., and M.H. Abd-ul-Rahman. *Canopics.* Cairo Cat. Gén. 1967.
Roeder, Günther. *Die ägyptische Religion in Texten und Bildern.* 4 Vols. Bibliothek der Alten Welt. Zürich, 1959–1961.
Rössler-Köhler, Ursula. *Kapitel 17 des ägyptischen Totenbuches.* Wiesbaden, 1979.
Sauneron, Serge. (tr. A. Morrissett). *The Priests of Ancient Egypt.* New York, 1960.
——. *Le Temple d'Esna.* 5 Vols. PIFAO. Cairo, 1959–1969.
——. 'Le Temple d'Esna', *Textes et langages de l'Égypte pharaonique,* 249–57. BdE 64 / 3. IFAO, Cairo, 1974.
Schäfer, Heinrich. (tr. John Baines). *Principles of Egyptian Art.* Oxford, 1974.
Schenkel, Wolfgang. *Memphis, Herakleopolis, Theben.* Wiesbaden, 1965.
Schott Siegfried. *Urkunden Mythologischen Inhalts,* 1–2. Leipzig, 1929–1939.
Seeber, Christine. 'Jenseitsgericht', *LÄ* III (1980), 249–52.
——. *Untersuchungen zur Darstellung des Totengerichts im Alten Ägypten.* MÄS 35. Munich, 1976.
Seters, John Van. 'A Date for the "Admonitions" in the Second Intermediate Period', *JEA* 50 (1964), 13–23.
——. *The Hyksos.* New Haven, 1966.
Sethe, Kurt. *Die Achtung feindlicher Fürsten, Völker und Dinge.* APAW, Berlin, 1926.
——. *Die altaegyptischen Pyramidentexte.* 4 Vols. (= *Pyr.*) Leipzig, 1908–1922.
——. *Übersetzung und Kommentar zu den altägyptischen Pyramidentexten.* 6 Vols. Glückstadt, 1935–1962.
Siegler, K.G. v. Stock, Hanns.
Shore, A.F. *Portrait Painting from Roman Egypt.* 2nd Ed., London, 1972.
Simpson, William Kelly. (ed.) *The Literature of Ancient Egypt.* New Haven, 1972.
Smith, Henry S. 'The Story of 'Onchsheshonqy', *Serapis* 6 (1980, for Charles Nims), 134–56.
Smith, W. Stevenson. *The Art and Architecture of Ancient Egypt.* Harmondsworth, 1958, repr. 1965.
Spalinger, Anthony. 'The Concept of Monarchy during the Saïte epoch—an Essay of Synthesis', *Orientalia* 47 (1978), 12–36.
Spiegel, Joachim. 'Admonitions', *LÄ* I (1975), 65–66.

——. *Die Idee vom Totengericht in der ägyptischen Religion*. Leipziger Ägyptologische Studien, 2. Glückstadt, 1935.
Staehelin, Elisabeth. v. Hornung, Erik.
Stock, Hanns, and Siegler, K.G. *Kalabsha*. Wiesbaden, 1961.
Stroka, V.M. v. Maehler, H.
Thissen, H.-J. *Die Lehre des Anchscheschonqi*. Papyrologische Texte und Abh., 32. Bonn, 1984.
Vandersleyen, C. (ed.) *Das alte Ägypten*. Propyläen Kunstgeschichte, 15. Berlin, 1975.
Vandier, Jacques. *Mo'alla*. Cairo, 1950.
——. *La Religion ëgyptienne*. 2nd Ed., Paris, 1949.
Vilímková, M. *Altägyptische Goldschmiedekunst*. Prague, 1969.
Vittmann, G. *Priester und Beamte im Theben der Spätzeit*. Wien, 1978.
Weigall, Arthur E.P. *Weights and Balances*. Cairo Cat. Gén. 1908.
Wessetzky, Vilmos. *Ausgewählte Schriften*. (1937–1979). Budapest, 1981.
——. 'hpr—$hprr$', *Bull. Soc. d'Égyptologie, Genève*, 4 (Mél. Vycychl, 1980), 97–98.
Westendorf, W. (ed.) *Aspekte der spätägyptischen Religion*. Wiesbaden, 1979.
——. v. Helck, W.
Wiedemann, Alfred. *Das alte Ägypten*. Heidelberg, 1920.
Wilkinson, Alix. *Ancient Egyptian Jewellery*. London, 1971.
Williams, Ronald J. 'The Alleged Semitic Original of Amenemope', *JEA* 47 (1961), 100–106.
——. 'Egypt and Israel', *The Legacy of Egypt*, ed. J.R. Harris, 257–90. Oxford, 1971.
——. 'The Sages of Ancient Egypt in the Light of Recent Scholarship', *JAOS* 101 (1981), 1–19.
Wilson, John A. Translations of Egyptian Texts in *Ancient Near Eastern Texts Relating to the Old Testament* (ANET), ed. James B. Pritchard. 3rd Ed. with Supplement. Princeton, 1969.
Winter, Erich. *Untersuchungen zu den ägyptischen Tempelreliefs der griechisch-römischen Zeit*. Wien, 1968.
——. v. Junker, Hermann.
——. 'Philae', *Textes et langages de l'Égypte pharaonique*, 229–37. Cairo, 1974.
Wolderung, Irmgard. (tr. Ann E. Keep) *Egypt: the Art of the Pharaohs*. Art of the World, 12. London, 1963.
Wolf, Walther. *Individuum und Gemeinschaft in der ägyptischen Kultur*. Glückstadt, 1935.
Yoyotte, Jean. 'Le Jugement des Morts dans l'Égypte ancienne', *Le Jugement des Morts*, Sources Orientales, 4, 17–80. Paris, 1961.
Žabkar, Louis, V. *Hymns to Isis in her Temple at Philae*. Univ. Press of New England, 1988.
——. *A Study of the Ba Concept in Ancient Egyptian Texts*. Chicago, 1968.
Zandee, Jan. 'The Book of Gates', *Liber Amicorum* (for C.J. Bleeker), 282–324. Leiden, 1969.
——. *Death as an Enemy*. Leiden, 1960.
——. 'Gott ist König', *Studies in the History of Religions*, 167–78. Suppl. to *Numen*, 31. Leiden, 1975.
——. 'Sargtexte um über Wasser zu verfügen', *JEOL* 24 (1975–76), 1–47.
——. (for). *Studies in Egyptian Religion*, ed. M. Heerma van Voss et al. Leiden, 1982.

XI. *Iran*

Bartholomae, Chr. *Altiranisches Wörterbuch*. Strassburg, 1904, repr. 1961.
Bailey, H.W. 'The second stratum of the Indo-Iranian gods', *Mithraic Studies*, ed. J.R. Hinnells, I, 1–20. Manchester, 1975.
Boyce, Mary. *A History of Zoroastrianism*, I and II. *Hdb. der Orientalistik*, I. 8.1.2.

Vol. I. The Early Period; Vol. II. Under the Achaemenians. Leiden, 1975; 1982.
———. 'Persian Religion in the Achemenid Age', *CHJ* I (1984), 279–307.
———. *Zoroastrianism. Textual Sources for the Study of Religion.* Manchester, 1984.
———. *Zoroastrians.* London, 1979.
Browne, Edward G. *A Literary History of Persia.* New York, 1902.
Campbell, LeRoy A. *Mithraic Iconography and Ideology.* EPRO 11. Leiden, 1968.
Clemen, Carl. *Fontes Historiae Religionis Persicae.* Bonn, 1920.
Cumont, Franz. *After Life in Roman Paganism.* 1922, repr. New York, 1959.
———. (tr. J.B. Baker) *Astrology and Religion among the Greeks and Romans.* 1912, repr. New York, 1960.
———. *L'Égypte des Astrologues.* Brussels, 1937.
———. (tr. T.J. McCormack) *The Mysteries of Mithra.* 2nd Ed., New York, 1956.
———. *The Oriental Religions in Roman Paganism.* 1911, repr. New York, 1956.
———. and J. Bidez. *Les mages hellénisés.* 2 Vols. Paris, 1938.
Duchesne-Guillemin, J. (tr. M. Henning) *The Hymns of Zarathushtra.* 1952, repr. Westport, Conn., 1979.
———. 'Iranian Religion', *Religions of the Ancient East.* Faith and Fact Books, 141, pp. 117–64. London, 1959.
———. *Symbols and Values in Zoroastrianism.* Religious Perspectives, 15. New York, 1966.
———. *The Western Response to Zoroaster.* 1958, repr. Westport, Conn., 1973.
———. *Zoroastre.* Paris, 1948.
Gershevitch, Ilya. *The Avestan Hymn to Mithra.* Cambridge, 1959.
Goff, Jacques. *The Birth of Purgatory.* New York, 1983.
Griffiths, J. Gwyn. 'Archaeology and Hesiod's Five Ages', *Journal of the History of Ideas* 17 (1956), 109–119; cf. id., ibid. 19 (1958), 91–93 ('Did Hesiod Invent the "Golden Age"?')
———. *Plutarch's De Iside et Osiride.* Cardiff, 1970.
Halsberghe, Gaston H. *The Cult of Sol Invictus.* EPRO 23. Leiden, 1972.
Hartman, Sven S. 'Datierung der jungavestischen Apokalyptik', *Apocalypticism etc.* ed. D. Hellholm, 61–75. Tübingen, 1983.
Henning, W. Bruno. *Zoroaster. Politician or Witch-doctor?* London, 1951.
Hinnells, J.R. (ed.) *Mithraic Studies.* 2 Vols. Manchester, 1975.
———. *Persian Mythology.* London, 1973.
———. 'Zoroastrian Influence on Judaeo-Christian Tradition', *Journal of the K.R. Cama Oriental Inst.* 45 (1976), 1–23.
Hinz, Walther. *Zarathustra.* Stuttgart, 1961.
Hoffmann, Karl, et al. *Iranistik: Linguistik.* Hdb. der Orientalistik, ed. B. Spuler, I.4.1. Leiden, 1958.
Hudson-Williams, T. *A Short Grammar of Old Persian.* Cardiff, 1936, repr. 1963.
Hultgård, Anders. 'Forms and Origins of Iranian Apocalypticism', *Apocalypticism etc.* ed. D. Hellholm, 387–411. Tübingen, 1983.
Humbach, Helmut. *Die Gathas des Zarathustra.* 2 Vols. Heidelberg, 1959.
Insler, S. *The Gāthās of Zarathustra.* Acta Iranica, 8. Leiden, 1975.
Kákosy, László. *Selected Papers.* Budapest, 1981.
Kent, Roland G. *Old Persian.* New Haven, 1953.
Mackenzie, D.N. *A Concise Pahlavi Dictionary.* London, 1971.
Molé, Marijan. *Culte, Mythe, et Cosmologie dans l'Iran Ancien.* Annales du Musée Guimet, BdE 69. Paris, 1963.
———. 'Jugement des Morts dans l'Iran préislamique', *Le Jugement des Morts,* 145–75. Paris, 1961.
Moulton, James H. *Early Zoroastrianism.* 1913, repr. Amsterdam, 1962.
Olsson, Tord. 'The Apocalyptic Activity. The Case of Jāmāsp Nāmag', *Apocalypticism etc.* ed. D. Hellholm, 21–49. Tübingen, 1983.
Pavry, Jal D.C. *The Zoroastrian Doctrine of a Future Life.* New York, 1926, repr. 1965.
Reichelt, Hans. *Avesta Reader.* 1911, repr. Berlin, 1968.

Scott, Walter. *Hermetica*. I–IV. (Vols. III and IV rev. A.S. Ferguson) Oxford, 1924–1936.
Shaked, Saul. 'Iranian Influence on Judaism: First Century B.C.E. to Second Century C.E.', *CHJ* I (1984), 308–25.
Smith, Maria Wilkins. *Studies in the Syntax of the Gathas of Zarathushtra*. 1929, repr. New York, 1966.
Turcan, Robert. *Mithras Platonicus*. EPRO 47. Leiden, 1975.
Vermaseren, Maarten J. *Corpus inscriptionum et monumentorum religionis mithriacae*. (= *CIMRM*). 2 Vols. The Hague, 1956; 1960.
———. *Mithras, the Secret God*. London, 1963.
———. *Mithriaca*, I, II, III, IV. EPRO 16. Leiden, 1971–82.
West, E.W. *Pahlavi Texts*. Sacred Books of the East, 51. Oxford, 1880, repr. Delhi, 1965.
West, Martin L. *Early Greek Philosophy and the Orient*. Oxford, 1971.
Widengren, Geo. 'Leitende Ideen und Quellen der iranischen Apokalyptik', *Apocalypticism etc.* ed. D. Hellholm, 77–162. Tübingen, 1983.
———. *Die Religionen Iran*. Die Religionen der Menscheit, 14. Stuttgart, 1965.
Witt, R.E. 'Some thoughts on Isis in relation to Mithras', *Mithraic Studies*, ed. J.R. Hinnells, II, 479–93. Manchester, 1975.
Zaehner, R.C. *The Dawn and Twilight of Zoroastrianism*. London, 1961.
———. *The Teachings of the Magi*. London, 1956.
———. *Zurvan: A Zoroastrian Dilemma*. Oxford, 1955.

INDEX OF SUBJECTS AND SOURCES

Abraham, Testament of, 201
Account-book, heavenly, 241
Achan, punishment of, 24
Achilles, fate of, weighed by Zeus, 288; by Hermes, 290; with Memnon, 290 f.
Acquittal, divine, for Job, 310 f.
Act of God, 87
Adam's Fall, 13, 93, 356
Admonitions of an Egyptian Sage, (7.1 ff.) 170 f.; 260
Adonis, and Tammuz, 303; and vegetation, 332
Adrasteia, 339, 340
Adultery, and Mosaic law, 130; woman judged by Jesus, 130 f.; Job's denial, 308, 310
Aeacus, judge in Hades, 228, 329
Aeneas, visits underworld, 229; fate is weighed with fate of Turnus, 290
Aeschylus, 47; on individual and nation, 48–53, 354; and Furies, 331
    Ag. (250 f.) 347; (750 ff.) 49, 52; (921) 49; (946–7) 49; (954–5) 48; (1035 ff.) 49; (1431–47) 49; (1501) 57; (1508) 57; (1523) 71
    Eum. (236) 57; (441, 718) 64; (952; 778–92; 930–37; 954–5) 54
    Pers. (362) 51; (429–32) 68; (718 ff.) 68; (809 ff.) 68
    Psychostasia, 291
Aethiopis, Epic. Graec. Fr. (I.33) 291
Agamemnon, 48 ff.; and blood-feud, 49
Agathos Daimon, and Shaï, 227
Agni, fire-god, 132
Agnosticism, Greek, 73
Ahriman (Angra Mainyu), struggle of, with Ahura Mazda, 40 ff.; and dualism, 250
Ahura Mazda, struggle with Ahriman, 40 ff.; as judge, 248; and dualism, 250; as Requiter, 256; as arbiter, 350
Aidos (Modesty), shuns phallus, 338
Akhenaten, Great Aten-Hymn of, 31; flouting of traditional religion by, 169; indebtedness to, 196; and confessional approach, 324
Akiba, Rabbi, 261
Alastor, spirit of vengeance, 57

Amarna experience, spiritual reaction to, 197
'Amasis (King) and the Boatman', 175
Ambrosiaster, in N. Turchi, *Fontes Hist. Mysteriorum* (291, No. 346) 335
Amduat, divisions of, 265; Book of, 325
Amenemope, Instruction of, (19.16–17) 174 f.; 179, 190, 299, 300
Amenemope, Onomasticon of, 306
Amen-Rê, as judge, 190
Amen-Rê, hymn to, 190
    Caminos, *Late-Egyptian Miscellanies* (9–10) 190 f.
Amida Buddhism, 156
Ammenemes I, Instruction of, 165
Amos, prophet of judgement, 4–11, 259, 351; on God's universal solicitude, 355
Amûn, prayers to, 191 f.; temple of, 326
Anahiti, and Ishtar, 258
Anankê, 339
Anastasi, Papyrus, on Syria, 307
Ancestors, cult of, 156 f.
Anger, of gods, 27
Ani, Instruction of, 174, 190
    (8.15–16) 190
Ani, Papyrus of, 207, 289
    Ed. Budge, Vol. II (Pl.30, 18–26) 207
Animal world, 20; litigious strife of, judged by sun-god Istanu in Hittie hymn, 31–32
Annihilation, following Messianic judgement, 261; fate following rejection of God's grace, 275; and Sheol, 301
Anomia (Lawlessness), altar to, 87
Anonymity, in ancient literature, 47
Antef, and weighing the heart, 221
Anticipated eschatology, 323 f.
Ants, Parade of, and Indra, 141 f.
Anubis, and Dokiel, 201; as judge, 205 f.; Lord of the Balance, 207, 227, 290; Magistrate of the Court, 207; in trial scene, 326
Apatê (Deceit), 72
Apocalypses, Coptic (Peter and Paul), 231
Apocalyptic, and Amos, 5; Jewish-

Christian, 111; and *Demotic Chronicle*, 176 ff.; Jewish, 213; Later Avestan, 251 f.
Apollo, unjust treatment of Coronis, 64 f.
Apollodorus (2.70) 297; (3.6) 297
Apotheosis, through initiation (Dionysiac and Isiac), 341
Apuleius, on list of vices, 122; on baptism in Isis Mystery-cult, 124 f.; on Isiac Mysteries, 313 ff., 355; autobiographical element, 314; mastery of Greek and Latin, 317
   Apol. (4) 317; (55) 314, 317
   Metam. (3.15) 314, 317; (10) 320; (11.6) 314; (11.12, 13) 315, 320; (11.14) 316; (11.15) 315, 319, 335; (11.16) 319; (11.19) 316; (11.21) 124, 327; (11.22) 315; (11.23) 321, 322, 325; (11.24) 239; (11.28; 32) 314
Apulia, painted vases from, 329
Archive of Hor (Demotic text), 255
Arda Viraz Nāmag, Pahlavi work, 253
Areopagus, court of, 50, 54, 94
Ares (Enyalios), impartiality of, 348
Ariadne, and Dionysus, 337; and marriage of soul, 339
Aristotle, on *deus ex machina*, 310
   Hist. An. (551^a 14) 288
Armageddon, 269
Arrogance (*hubris*), 49; 50 f.
Art, Christian, and tortures of Hell, 353
Aryaman, as judge, 333
Ascent to heaven, in Mithraism, 247; in Gathic Avesta, 257
Asclepius (Hermetic text), 255
Asebeia (Blasphemy), altar to, 87
Asha, spirit of truth, 41, 350
Assemblies of Temple, purging of, 303
Assessors, 42, in trial, 209 f., 242
Assyrians, justify fall of Babylon, 35–36
Astral element, (Iranian) in resurrection, 245
Astral immortality, and Stoicism, 247
Astrology, and Mystery-cults, 315; and Fate, 345
Astronomy, of Babylonians, 258
Atar, Persian god of fire, 336
Atê, 47; in early Greek poetry, 58–65; deceitful, 71 f.; in Euripides, 76
Atharva-Veda, and abode of nether darkness, 135
Atheism, Greek, 73; and Euripides, 76
Athena, and court of Areopagus, 54

Atlantis, fall of, 77, 255
Atonement for sin, called for in Rome, 106–109
Atum and Osiris, dialogue of, 255
Augustine, *Confessions*, 341; and Fall of man, 356
Autobiography, non-royal, Egypt as home of, 184 ff., 300
Avenger, divine, as griffin, 182
Avenging Ghosts, in Chinese thought, 157–9, 350
Avesta, 251 f.; Avestan Hymn to Mithra (1.3) 337
Avestan, Later, chronology of writings, 250 f.

Ba and funerary birds (Haghia Triada), 285; in trial scene, 226, 289
Baal, achieves life after death in Ugaritic text, 305
Baal-Hadad, Canaanite worship of, 311
Babylon-Rome, fall of, 269
Babylonian Theodicy, 35–40, 267; New Year Festival, 236; Tablet of Grace and Tablet of Sin, 240
Bahman Yasht, 251 f.
Baki, official of N.K., 218
Balance, personified, 227; in Pahlavi texts, 256, 351; in O.T. lit., 298 ff.
Banquet, and repayment after death (Luke 15), 278
Baptism, 124–5; Isiac, and forgiveness, 322
Behaviourism, and Karma, 145
Benefits, bestowed by gods, 187
Berith, 'convenant', 'bond of communion', 21
Bhagavad-Gita (6.28–29) 139; (18.60) 139
Bible: see next Index
Biography, and society, 66–67; non-royal, and divine impact (Egypt), 184–98; ideal, 195
Blindness, and sin, 117 f.; 123, 185, 189; temporary, of Mithraic initiand, 334
Blood-feud, 15, 16; and Agamemnon, 49; and family or clan, 90
Boat, in Egyptian and Minoan eschatology, 285
Body, parts of, weighed, 241; resurrection of, 257 f.
Bokkhoris, and Prediction of the Lamb, 255, 270
Book of Amduat, 265, 325
Book of the Dead (Egyptian), 232, 246,

247, 286, 295, 346
  (17) and Lord of the Nomes, 208
  (64) and Second Death, 238
  (125) and trial, 204, 207, 208, 214 ff., 224, 235, 308, 324, 327
  (127) and trial, 214
  (144; 147) 247
  (175; 176) on Second Death, 237
  (175) with dialogue of Atum and Osiris, 255
Book of the Dead, Tibetan, 268
Book of Gates, cosmopolitanism in, 197, 208; and judgement, 210 ff., 227, 233, 247, 346
  Ed. E. Hornung (2nd Hour, Scene 6) 212; (9th Hour) 233; (Scene 30) 197
Book of the living (or Book of Life), 240, 270
Book of Traversing Eternity, 325
Book of the Two Ways, 210 ff., 215, 325
Book of the Victory over Seth, 8
Books of the Underworld (Egyptian), 233, 267
Born again (*renatus*), 322 f.; or born (*natus*), 333
Bradley, F. H., on punishment, 355
Bremner-Rhind Papyrus (7, 3–4) 189
Brethren, meaning of, 279
Bridge of the Separator, and judgement, 45–46, 247 f., 253, 256, 333, 348, 350
Bridge of the winter, and Zoroaster, 45–46
Brihad Āranyaka (4.4.5) 145
Brimo (Demeter), gives birth to Brimos, 331
Brooklyn Papyrus, ed. Goyon (III, 17) 235
Brotherhood, universal, taught by disciple of Confucius, 147
Buddha, and popular images, 141
Buddhism, and trial after death, 268; and Karma, 349
Bundahishn, 251, 252, 254, 257
Bundahishn, Greater, (34.6 ff.) 249 f.
Butterflies, embossed on gold discs, 287 ff.; as symbols of soul, 288 f.

Cabeiri, Mysteries of, 332
Caesar, Julius, and divination, 97 *Bell. Afr.* (1.3.44) 97
Calendar of Lucky and Unlucky Days, 185; Cairo Calendar No. 86637 (III) 185
Callimachus, *Fr.* (652 Pfeiffer) 55
Canaan, conquest of, sanctioned by Yahweh, 24; religious influence of, 302
Canaanite municipalities, and Israel, 16
Capua, Mithraeum in, 334, 336
Casa dei Vettii, Pompeii, 339
Cassandra, rape of, 91
Castration, as retribution, 69; and corn-cutting, 332
Cats, Cretan and Egyptian, 284
Celestial Cow (Egyptian text), 255
Celsus, v. Origen
Cenchreae, initiation of Lucius at, 313 ff.
Change of perspective (in Egyptian view of judgement), 324–7
Characterization, in Herodotus, 66
Charun, Etruscan demon, 267
Cheops (Khufu), criticised, 167 f.
Children, and sins of fathers, 15, 30
Chinese thought, 146 ff.; lack of eschatology, 268
Chinvat, Bridge of, 247 f., 253 Yasna (46) 247
Christ, see Jesus Christ
Christianity, and Rome, 109; aspects of doctrine, 110–31
Christology of Revelation, 269 f.
Chuang-tzu, 154–6, 350
  Inner Chapters (32) 155;
  The Way of Heaven, 155 f.
Cicero, *De Nat. Deor.* (2.8) 99; *Div.* (1.16) 98; *Pro Balbo* (31) 101; *Somnium Scip.* (25–27) 247; *Tusc. Disp.* (19) 247
City-state, Sumerian, each with own deity, 35
Civic List, and Book of Life, 240
Clan (*genos*), and blood-feud, 90
Class, and ideology, 90 ff.
Clea, and wisdom of Isis, 318
Clementia, false claim to, 100
Code of conduct, and tribunal, 214; 308
Codex Hammurabi, 15
Coffin Texts (Egyptian), and judgement, 221; and Second Death, 237
Coffin Texts (=CT)
  (I, 24 a ff.) 306; (I, 168 c) 233; (IV, 253 e ff.) 206; (IV, 258 b) 208; (IV, 311 c – 314 e) 206; (VI, 272 d ff.) 167; (VII, 471 c-f) 213; (VII, 485 a ff.) 211
Collective identity, 195; and Eleusinian rites, 331
Collective responsibility, 85, 90, 93
Combat, myth of, in Revelation, 268 f.
Commodus, Emperor, devotee of Isis

and Mithras, 333
Community, punished, 91 ff.; judgement within, 122–4
Comparative Religion, and Herodotus, 66
Compassion, as criterion, 279, 353
Compensation, eschatology of, 328
Confession, and baptism, 124; to Varuna, 134; in the Isiac Mysteries, 221, 315–17; in Mysteries of Cabeiri, 332
Confessional approach, atrophy of in Greek and Roman religion, 331
Confucianism, Mohism, and Taoism, 146–59
Confucius and the Intervention of Heaven, 146–8, 349
Confucius, *Analects*, (6.10) 147; (6.22) 147; (7.21) 146; (7.23) 146; (7.35) 148; (11.12) 147; (12.5) 147; (12.21) 147; (17.19) 147
Conscience of sinner, and Erinyes, 55
Continuum of responsibility, 30; in city, family, individual, 79
Controversy pattern, in Hebrew tradition, 311
Corn, symbolism of in Near Eastern cults, 332
Corn Osiris, 343
Coronis, infatuation of, 64 f.
Cosmic dispersal, doctrine of, in Rigveda, 136
Cosmopolitan outlook, and Amarna, 197
Court setting, invoked by prophets, 11; and Yahweh's judgement of nations, 22; court of heaven (Job 1:6), 306, 311
Covenant, with Israel, 4–5; Book of, 16; 'bond of communion', 21; and Deuteronomy, 23 breaking of, 27; forgiveness in, 123
Creator-god, denied by Jainism and Buddhism, 140
Crete, in commerce with Egypt, 282 ff.
Crime, and punishment, 80, 93
Criminals, treatment of in Egypt, 166
Croesus, 69–70
Cross, of Christ's disciple, 115; theology of, 357
Crown of Righteousness, 238–9; of initiate, 342
Crucifixion, in Palestine, 116; and fall of Jerusalem, 119
Cupid and Psyche, 288, 320
Curiosity, judgement of, 318 ff.
Current events, Christian exegesis of, 114–18

Cynocephalous ape, on signet-ring from Phaestos, 286 f.

Dadestan i denig (Religious Judgements), 253
Daiva-Inscription of Xerxes, 245
Damned, fate of, 353 f.
Dance, Dionysiac, symbolism of, 339
Daniel, Book of, 290; and procedure of judgement, 229, 242
Darius, 68
Darkness, outer, and fate of evildoers, 276
David, son of (Messiah), 259; as wise judge, 259
Day of Requital (Qumrân), 123
Day of Yahweh, 6, 121, 259, 351
Dead, becoming stars (Egypt and Iran), 246
Dead Sea Scrolls, strict code of, 122; two types of Messiah in, 259 ff.; *Benedictions* or *Blessings* (1 QSb V.20–28), 263; *Scroll of the War*, 263, 269; and Tacitus, 264; see also Manual of Discipline
Death, and pollution, 56; voluntary, 124, 323; the Second, 237 f.; Great One of Death, 238; death as result of moral failure, 275; nuclear, 356
Death-daemons of armies, weighed, 289
Deborah, Song of, 17
Deceit, imputed to divine will, 70 ff.
Declarations of Innocence, 204, 214 f., 219 f., 241, 324, 348; compared with 'Avowal of Integrity' by Job, 308, 312
Deeds, import of, in judgement, 272 f.
Deification of dead, in Crete and Egypt, 285
Deir el-Medîna, biographical cameos from, 197; Asiatic deities in, 198; civil and criminal procedures in, 205, 208; Ptolemaic temple in, 235 f.; tomb painting at, 281
Deliverance, promise of, in apocalyptic, 176
Deliverance of Mankind, Egyptian myth, 14
Demeter, Homeric Hymn to, 328; gives birth to boy, 331; revelation of ear of corn, 332
Demeter Erinys, 55 f., 293
Democracy of Athens, as cause of victory, 68
Demon-guardians, 211
Demonology, of Plutarch, 82

Demosthenes, (18.127) 228
Demotic Chronicle, 176 ff. (II, 4) 176; (III, 16) 177; (IV, 9–10) 176; (IV, 11–12) 177
Demotic Magical Papyrus of London and Leiden, 247
Dēnkart (Iranian work), 43, 252
Derveni, Orphic text from, 56
Descendant punished, 79, 93
Despair, and Karma, 143
Destiny (Heimarmenê), and Providence (Pronoia), 73; as arbiter of disease and death (Confucius), 147; and prosperity, divine control of, 193, 345
Determinism, of Stoics, 72; in Old Testament and in Karma, 138 f.; as a heresy, 142
Deus ex machina, 74 f.; in Epilogue of Job, 310
Deutero-Isaiah, on judgement of nations, 22
Deuteronomic History, 23–25, 47, 354
Deuteronomy, Law of, 178 f.
Devil, and his demons, and Iranian impact, 244
Devourer of the Dead (Egyptian), 230 f., 233, 237 f.
Dharma, as source of moral law, 137
Dialogue of Pessimism, 39
Dikê, as judge, 329; 339
Diodorus Siculus, on posthumous trial, 235
  (1.72) 235; (1.92) 235; (5.49) 332; (20.65) 86; (20.70) 86; (79.1) 297; (84.3) 297
Dionysiac Mysteries, 337–43
Dionysus, and Euripides, 75; and Ariadne, 337, 339
Discipline (paideia), 346 f.
Disease, and sin, 32, 133; and Destiny, 147; result of moral failure, 275
Disobedience, brings penalty to whole family (Hittite), 32
Dives and Lazarus, 110, 230, 277, 352
Divination and dependence (Roman), 96–98
Divination, scepticism on, 71, 96
Divine roles, diverging (in tribunal after death), 204 ff.
Djed-pillar, and revivification of Osiris, 235
Dogma, doubted (divinity of Pharaoh), 161–3
Dokiel, archangel, as keeper of the balance, 201
Dostoievski, *The Brothers Karamazov*, 345, 356 f.
Doxology, 320
Dragon, red, cosmic, in Revelation, 269
Dream-visions (Mari), 39–40; and Magians, 70–71
Dualism, in Iranian system, 40 ff., 250

Earth, renewal of, 256 f.
Economic conditions, and Zoroastrianism, 44
Ecstasy, Dionysiac, 75
Edfu temple texts, 219 f.
  Chassinat, *Temple d'Edfou*, (III, 78, 10–79, 4) 220; (III, 360, 12–361, 5) 219; (V, 334, 1–6) 219; (V, 343, 13 ff.) 222
Education, zeal for, in Confucius, 146
Egg, primal, in Orphic tradition and Egypt, 228, 295
Egypt: The Gods and the God-King, 160–83
  Judgement after death, in Egypt and Judaeo-Christian thought, 201–42; from Egypt to Greece via Crete, 280–97
Eleusinian Mysteries, and Apuleius, 314; and ritual purity, 323; the Eleusinian experience, 327–32, 355
Elysium, 232, 280 ff., 294, 296, 354
Emperor-cult, 269
End of the world, Iranian doctrine of, 249 ff.; Egyptian, 255; and reversal of creation, 255; in Paul's thought, 273
Enkomi (Cyprus), amphora from, perhaps showing Zeus with scales, 291
Envy of the gods, 49; 52 f.
Eos, mother of Memnon, 290 f.
Epicureanism, and rejection of divine control, 73; and Horace, 108
Epicurus, 78
Equilibrium, as desired result, 225
Er, Myth of, 76, 295
Erinyes, 47; and Orestes, 50; ministers of Dikê, 51; activity in two worlds, 53–57; and Athenian law, 54; and conscience of sinner, 55; in the mind, 73; and death of Caesar, 82; and Greek law, 94; retributive anger of, 128, 267; as avenging ghosts, 158; torches of, 233; and false oaths, 294
Erinys (*e-ri-nu* and *e-ri-nu-we*), in Linear B tablets at Knossos, 293; in scene of punishment, 339
Eschatology, force of, in Iranian religion, 40, 243–58; sequence in Paul's thought, 273; anticipated, 323 f.; and compensation, 328

INDEX OF SUBJECTS AND SOURCES

Essenes, 335
Esther, and Persian court, 243
Eternal life, as reward, 274; eternal torment of the damned, 275, 352; rejected, 354
Ethical emphasis, lack of, 185; varied place of, 297
Etruscans, and divination, 96; and tortures of wicked, 234, 267
Eucharist, and judgement, 125 f.
Eudaemonism, and utilitarianism, 18
Eumenides, and Erinyes, 56
Euripides, 47; and Dionysus, 75; and Furies, 331
  Bacch. (222-3) 330; *Hipp.* (241) 76;
  Orest. (396) 55; *Troad.* (530) 71
Evil, as primary state, 39; relation to good, 144, 152
'Exaltation of Inanna', 17
Examination, spiritual, of Isiac initiand, 316 f.
Execration texts, Egyptian, 6-7
Expiation, Hittite, for defeat, 27
Ezekiel, 6, 15, 30, 31
Ezra, and Persian period, 243

Faith, justification by (Paul), 274
Fatalism, and Croesus, 69-70; and Karma, 142
Fate, and Zoroaster, 41; and Livy, 99; and Shaï in tribunal scene, 226; fates weighed by Zeus, 288; and divine control, 345
Father and Mother, of deities, 31; also Father-Mother, 31
Fathers, sins of, punished in children, 15, 30, 177
Felicitation (*Macarismos*), 320
Female, role of, lauded by Lao Tzu, 153
Feminism, and the *Medea*, 76
Fields of Iaru, 281
Fire of hell, 275 f.
Fire of ordeal, 249; 253 f., 273, 336. Yasna (34; 48; 51) 249, 253 f.
Flagellation, and fertility, 338
Flame Island, and rebirth, 233
Flood, and moral causation, 13-14
Forgiveness, 123; in Baptism of John, 124; Varuna as source of, 133; after confession, 186, 322 f.
Form Criticism, 319 f.
Forty-two Assessors, 209 f.; 242, 326
Fortuna, and Isis, 321
Fortuna populi Romani, 99
Fortune, 81, 87 ff., 97, 99

Four ages, doctrine of, 251 f.
Freeman, Kathleen, and feminism of *Medea*, 76
Furies, v. Erinyes; 339
Fury, winged, 330

Gain (*kerdos*), 61-62
Galileans, killed by Pilate, 114 f.
Gate, religious role of, 213
Gates of Hell, Egyptian background of, 213; 323
Gāthās (Zoroastrian), 41 ff., 247 ff.
Gayomart, Iranian primal man, 244, 251 f., 256
Geb, as judge, 205
Gehenna, 257, 275 ff., 352
General judgement, 110, 256
Gentiles, in worship at Jerusalem, 130
Ghassulian Chalcolithic culture of Palestine, 283
God, personal, 32; likeness to, as highest aim in life, 78; vengeance left to, 170, 174; unknown, 186; wrath of, 127 ff., 270, 274; Kingdom of, 277; unclear role in Job's trial, 310; God who suffers, 357
God-given qualities, ascribed to Pharaoh, 164-7
Godliness, and prosperity, 18 and passim
Gods, anger of, in Hittite myth, 27; found to be evil, 75
Gog and Magog, punishment of, 270
Gold leaves, Orphic, and Egypt, 229; on blessed right path, 296
Golden Ages, return of, 105, 106
Gomorrah, 11 f., 111, 298
Good Action – Blessings Construct, 123
Good and evil, distinction of transcended, 144; questioned, 152
Gospel of John, 177 f., 351
Gospels, Synoptic, 275-9
Great God, and judgement, 204
Greek concept of a moral law, 47-93
Greek Magical Papyri, and Fate, 227
  PGM (12, 242 ff. = Leiden P.Gr. J 384 (v)) 227
Greeks and Persians, encounter of, 66-67
Guardian deities, of cities and individuals, 35
Guilt-Culture, 48

Hades, torment in, 55; judgement in, 294 f. 354; and Sheol, 301; Korê's return from, 331

INDEX OF SUBJECTS AND SOURCES

Haghia Triada, sarcophagus from, 281 ff.; vase from, with agricultural scene, 284
Hakoris, King, judgement of, 176 f.
Hammurabi, Code of, 15
Hannahanna, Hittite mother goddess, 28
Happy End, 74; in *Bundahishn* and 1 Enoch, 264; in Job, 310, 312
Hardy, Thomas, 345
Harkhuf, funerary claim of, 307
  Urk. (I, 123, 1–2) 195, 216
Harsiesis, and trial scene, 326
Hathor, Lady of the West, 326
Heaven, as giver of wealth and honour (Confucius), 147, 349; as the maker of things (Chuang-tzu), 154; Kingdom of, 277, 352
Heaven, Hell, and Rebirth (Vedic), 135–7; and pointer to Purgatory (Egyptian), 230–4
Hector, fate of, weighed by Zeus, 288; by Hermes, 290
Hegel, on punishment, 355
Heliopolis, Great Council of, 304
Hell, of Greek tradition, 54, 233; Chinese, 157 f.; Egyptian, 230 f.; Iranian, 233; Egypt's influence, 257
Heraclitus, and Erinyes, 51; on arrogance and character, 354
Heraclitus (Diels-Kranz, *Vorsokr.*, I, 22, 94) 51
Herakles, 330
Hermeneutic transubstantiation, 303
Hermes, and psychostasia, 228, 290
Hermetic literature, and Egyptian religion, 182
Herodotus, 47; and nemesis, 52; theology and history in, 65–72, 354; and Comparative Religion, 66; on Mysteries in Saïs, 325
  (I.1) 65; (I.13) 69; (I.66; 75) 71; (I.86) 69; (I.87) 70; (I.107 ff.) 66; (I.135 f.) 67; (2.171) 325; (5.44) 86; (5.91) 71; (7.10) 67; (7.12–19) 70 f.; (7.16) 71; (7.49) 68; (7.139) 68; (8.79) 69; (8.106) 69; (8.109) 68; (9.122) 66
Hesiod, 58; and *atê*, 61–62; and Onkhsheshonqy, 180 f.; and Four Ages, 251 f., 280; and Islands of Blest, 280
  Op. (170–73) 280; (213–16) 61; (230–31) 61; (238 ff.) 94
  Theog. (217, 220, 472) 54; (230) 61
Hesitation, of Isiac initiand, 316 f.
Hinduism, and doctrine of rebirths, 137; and trial after death, 268
Hinnom, Valley of (= Gehenna), 276
'Hippies' Charter' (Lao Tzu), 151
Hippolytus, *Ref.* (5.8.40) 331
Historiography, early Chinese, 157 ff.
History, divine control of, 11–25; revelation in, 26; theology and history, in Herodotus, 65–72
Hittite parallels, 25–34; 267
Holocaust, 93, 356
Homer, 47; and *atê*, 58–61; and divine deceit, 71–72
  Iliad. (3.279) 294; (8.69 ff.) 289, 331; (9.108, 119, 505) 59, 60; (9.628–42) 60 f.; (10.391) 71; (14.321 ff.) 296; (16.658) 290; (18.309) 348; (19.86–92) 58, 60 f.; (19.97) 71; (19.223) 290; (19.259–60) 294; (19.270 f.) 60; (22.209–13) 288; cf. (8.69 ff.) 289
  Od. (4.561–9) 280; (11.568–71) 294; (15.329) 62
Homeric Hymn to Demeter (366; 480 ff.) 328; cf. 355
Homicide, 16; Greek law on, 55, 93 f.
Homosexuality, male, condemned, 214
Horace, 95; and Augustan revival of religion, 106 ff.
  Carm. (1.2.29–30) 107; (1.21) 34; (1.34) 108; (3.6.1–5) 107; (4. *Carm.Saec.*) 108
  Epist. (1.4.16) 108; (1.18) 108
Horus, judicial strife of, with Seth, 204; and balance in tribunal, 227, 326; and Pharaoh, 160 f.
Hubris, 50 ff., 77; altar to, 87; and aristocracy, 89
Hystaspes, Oracles of, 252

I will praise the Lord of Wisdom, Babylonian text, 36 ff., 332
Iamblichus, *V. Pyth.* (85) 342
Iaru, Fields of, 281
Ibn Ezra, 21
Imhotep, and Deir el-Medîna, 235
Imitatio Dei, 78
Immigration, into Crete from Anatolia, Syria, and possibly Libya, 283
Immortality, selective (Daniel), 245; universal (Bundahishn, Greater), 250; Eos pleads for, 291; absent in early Hebrew thought, 300 ff.; and Eleusis, 329; and Dionysus, 339
Imperialism, of Athenians, 73
Incarnation, Christian doctrine, 162
Incest, punished by death, 122; penalty set by Paul in Corinth, 128

Indian doctrines, 132–45; legal systems, 145
Individual, judgement of, 257, 298, 331
Indra, warrior-god, 132; stimulated by Soma, 135; and 'The Parade of Ants', 141
Inequalities, explained by Karma, 140
Infatuation, caused by gods, 58 ff.; of Coronis, 64 f.
Influence, types of, 282–7
Initiate, crowned (vase-painting), 330
Initiation, into several cults, 314–15; rites of, 335
Injury, to be recompensed with good (Lao Tzu), 153
Inner suffering, as real penalty, 84
Innocence, primitive, 106
Inscriptions:
    From Teos (*CIG* 3044) 94;
    Ramesside Inscriptions ed. Kitchen (III, 687, No.12) 185;
    Inscrs. of Sinai, ed. Černý (II), 187;
    Of Xerxes (51 ff.) 245
Inscrutability, of divine mind, 38, 70
Insinger Papyrus, 181 f.
Internalization, 55
International wisdom literatures, 181
Ipuwer, 170 f., 260
Iranian eschatology, 243–58
Iranian religion, and concept of justice, 40–46
Irenaeus, on ultimate triumph of good, 356
Isaiah, 6; and Babylon, 111; on God's universal solicitude, 355
Ishtar, and Anahiti, 258
Isis, linked with Logos and Sophia, 182; hymn to, from Philae, 183; pastophorus of, 255; universal nature-goddess, 256 f.; and wisdom, 318; and revival of Osiris, 343
Isis, Mystery-cult of, 124 f., 313–23; and new life after death, 226; and new life here and now, 234; initiate's crown, 239
Isis Tychê, 321
Islâm, and punishment of sin, 13
Isles of the Blest and Tartarus, 228; of the Righteous, 231, 281; in Egypt, Crete, and Greece, 280 ff.
Isocrates (4.28) 329
Israel, 3–25; 298–311; at mercy of imperial powers, 121; and posthumous judgement, 298–311
Israel Stela, 7–8
Italy, ancient, and Egypt, 229
Ixion, 330

Jainism, and Karma, 139, 144, 349
Jeremiah, 6, 31
Jerusalem, judgement on, in her fall, 118–24, 351 f.
Jesus Christ, crucifixion of, 93, 357; and Second Advent, 110; and Galilean towns, 111; rejection of Zealotism, 116; as wisdom, 318; as warrior-judge, 352; as shepherd-judge, 353
Job, Book of, and judgement, 304–312
Job, and suffering of righteous, 18–21, 36 ff., 355
Joel, 6
Jonah, and Nineveh, 25; and God's universal solicitude, 355
Josephus, on outrages under Pilate, 114;
    Ant. (17.10.10) 116;
    Bell.Iud. (2.5.2) 116; (2.9.4) 116; (5.1.3) 114
Joy, of initiation, 335
Judah the Patriarch, Rabbi, 347
Judaism, distinctive contribution of, 258–66; diverse doctrinal content of, 347
Judas the Galilean, and Zealot movement, 115
Judgement, Particular and General, 110; and the Sacraments, 124–6; and wrath, 128; here and now, 143; after death, 201 ff.; present and future, 202 f.
Judges, tribal, 16; of the dead (Egyptian), 204 ff.; (Minoan), 294 ff.
Justice, human and divine 3–4; sacral and civic, 16; in Iranian religion, 40–46; of Zeus, 50; Plato's views, 76 f.
Justification by faith (Paul), 274, 352

Kant, on punishment, 355
Kantuzilis, Hittite prayer of, 198
Karma or Karman, compensation and retribution in, 137–45, 267, 349
Kafka, Franz, *The Trial*, 344
Khaemweset, son of Ramesses III, in judgement scene, 324
Khakheperrê-sonbe, Lamentations of, 172
Khoiak, Osirian festival, 234–5
Kingdom of God or Heaven, 277
Kittim (= Romans), in *Scroll of the War*, 263, 269
Kleist, Heinrich von, 3, 344
Knossos, cemetery near, 287; Linear B tablets from, 293

Knowledge, importance of, 346
Kolasis (punishment), mysteriosophic, 340
Korê, return from Hades, 331
Koros (surfeit), and Hubris, 63
Krishna, and hero Arjuna, 139
Kumarbi, Hittite Epic of, 180

Lactantius, on Oracles of Hystaspes, 252; *De div. inst.* (6.9.4) 101
Ladder, with seven rungs, in Mithraic ordeal, 335
Lake of Fire (Egyptian), 233
Lamb, victory of, 269; wrath of, 270
Lao Tzu, 150 ff., 350
Lao Tzu, *Tao Te Ching* (tr. mainly D.C. Lau), (I.2) 150; (2, init.) 151; (8.21) 152; (9.23) 152; (10.24–26) 152; (19) 151, tr. Waley; (20) 152; (21.48) 152; (30.70) 152; (42.97) 152; (44.100) 153; (46.105) 153; (49.110) 153; (51.114 a) 153; (63.148) 153; (67.164) 153; (67.165) 154; (77.184; 184 a) 150; (79.192) 150; (81.196) 153
Last Judgement, 110 ff., 346; and impact of Iran, 351
Law, Egyptian, and recompense, 166
Law (*hp*, Egyptian), upholding of, as criterion, 177
Lebensmüde, Egyptian M.K. text, (*ANET* 407) 305
Left, baneful in judgement, 225, 296
Legend of the Winged Disk, 8
Leiden Papyrus T 16 (Ptolemaic), 241
Letters to the Dead, 203
  Ed. Gardiner and Sethe (Pl.10, No. 2) 203
Lex talionis, 5, 14–15, 93, 347; cf. *ius talionis*, 145
Liberation (*moksha*), and Hinduism, 139; and Jainism, 144
Liberator (Mithraic), 335
Libya, in link with Crete and Egypt, 282 f.
Life, eternal, as reward, 274
Likeness to God, as highest aim of life, 78
Linear B, evidence of, 291–4
Lions, and Mithraic grade, 333
Literacy in Egypt, 215
Litigation, posthumous, 203 f.
Lives of Plutarch, and retribution, 81
Le Livre égyptien Que Mon Nom Fleurisse (44) 304
Livy, 95; on Rome's success, 98–102 (*Praef.*) 98; (1.28.11) 100; (1.53.4) 100; (4.20.7) 101; (5.28.11) 100
Locrian Maidens, 91 ff.
Logau, Friedrich von, 3, 80
Longevity, as reward of virtue, 163, 177; 187 f.
Longfellow, on mills of God, 3, 80
Lord, as warrior, 22
Louvre Demotic Papyri 2414 and 2377, 181
Loves and Wars of Baal and Anat (10.8–9) 305
Lucretius, *De Rerum Nat.* (6.68 ff.) 73
Ludlul Bêl Nēmeqi (*I will praise the Lord of Wisdom*), Babylonian text, 36 ff., 332
Lupercalia, 338
Lust, judgement of, 318 ff.
Lycophron, 55
  Alex. (153) 55; (1141–73) 92
Lygdamus, Roman elegist, 221
Lyssae or Furies, 339

Maat, and Pharaoh, 163, 173, 178; and confessional literature, 189; in tribunal, 210, 346; moral import of, 211 f.; brings recompense, 217; broad impact of, 219; in weighing, 224, 227, 290, 326; feather of, 286 f.
Maats, Two, 205, 210, 227, 326
Macarismos, 320
Maccabean campaigns, influence of, 261
Maenads, 339
Magians, and dreams, 70
Magic, prophylactic, 8; magic and morality, 213–18
Mahayana Buddhism, and circumvention of Karma, 141, 349
Man who was Tired of Life, 171 f.
Manifestation, of god to individuals, 185
Manu, Laws of, and Indian punitive stress, 145
Manual of Discipline (Qumrân), strict code of, 122; and image of gate, 213; and torture of wicked, 276
Marduk, Lord of Wisdom, 36
Mari, Akkadian documents from, 39 ff.
Mars Ultor, and righteous vengeance, 348
Martyrdom, 237
Matriarchy, 50
Matrilinear society, 50
Meal, communal, shared by gods and men (Vedic), 136
Medes and Persians, 265; Parthians and Medes, 265
Megasthenes, on Northern India, 145

Memnon, King of Ethiopians, in scene of psychostasia, 290
Menelaus, and Elysium, 280
Menog i Khrad (Spirit of Wisdom), 253, 254
Mercy, altar of in Athens and Epidaurus, 322; mercy for all (Paul), 354
Merikarê, Instruction for, 163, 164 f., 169 f., 185, 217, 221, 224, 324 (52–55) 217; (110 f.) 169 f.; (115 ff.) 164
Meskhenet, goddess of birth, 226
Mesopotamia, 17, 35 ff.; kingship in, 162
Messiah, as Son of Man, 244; as Cyrus the Great, 259; two types in Scrolls, 259 ff.; and role of conquest, 260 ff.; as people of Israel, 261; judge, not warrior, 269; or fusion, 269; Paul's view of, 273; and Day of Yahweh, 351
Messianic Figure, 259–62
Messianism, 173; 236, 256 f.; Egyptian parallel to, 260
Metallic Ages, and Hesiod, 251
Metaphor and myth, 312
Metempsychosis, 137 ff., 341
Michael, Archangel, 3; and balance, 229, 353
Michael Kohlhaas, 3, 344
Michelangelo (Sistine Chapel), and nations before Christ the Judge, 353
Miles, Mithraic grade, and baptism of fire, 334
Mills of God, 3, 80
Milton, *Paradise Lost* (4, 996 ff.) 290
Minoan Judges of the Dead, 294–7
Minoan pottery in Egypt, 282
Minos, judge in Hades, 228, 294 ff.
Miracle-stories, about Jesus, 118
Mithra, and depiction of Christ, 244; and the sun, 245; and judgement, 256; and fire ordeals, 336; Avestan Hymn to, 337
Mithraism: Judgement as Ordeal, 332–7
Mithras, seen as solar deity in Roman era, 245; name of Isiac High Priest, 315, 322 f.; judicial function of, 333
Mitra, linked with Varuna (Indian), 133
Mo Tzu, and doctrine of universal love, 148; tract, *The Will of Heaven*, 149; and a personal God, 149, 350
Mo Tzu, *The Will of Heaven* (26) 149
Moderation, and middle class, 89

Mohenjo-daro, and yogic figure, 138
Moirae, 55; Moira and Zeus, 321
Moksha, 'liberation', 139, 144, 349
Mohism, 148 f.
Molten metal, in Iranian doctrine of judgement, 249; 253 f., 348; in Mithraic initiation, 336
Moral freedom, and Zoroaster, 41
Morality, in rebuke of David, 25; decline of, in Rome, 107; conventional, attacked by Lao Tzu, 151; in Karma, 267
Mosaic law, and adultery, 130
Mother-Father, 31
Mycenaean Religion, Ch. 10, 280 ff.; Linear B evidence for, 292 ff.
Mystagogue (Mithraic), 334
Mysteries, of Cabeiri at Samothrace, 332
Mysteries, Eleusinian, 314, 323
Mysteriosophic concepts (*kolasis* and liberation), 340
Mystery-cults, and Paul, 124 f.; divine judgement in, 313–43, 355; tolerance and symbiosis in, 315
Mysticism, and lust, 319
Myth and metaphor, 312; paradigmatic, 330

Nahum, and Nineveh, 25
Nanna, lord, as judge in the netherworld (Babylonian), 258
Narmer-Menes, 283
National Eisteddfod of Wales, 104
National emphasis, by Jesus, 278
Nations, judged, 4–10; 22; 262–6; Persians and Aeschylus, 50 f.; in Jewish doctrine, 256; assize of, 278 f., 351
Natural goodness, 83; and true morality (Lao Tzu), 151
Nature, Return to, urged by Chuang-tzu, 154
Necromancy, and belief in survival, 301
Neferabw, and hymn to Ptah, 189
  T.G.H. James, *Hieroglyphic Texts in the B.M.* 9 (1970), (36–37 and Pl.31) 189
Nefer-Seshem-Rê, biography of, 216
  Urk (I, 199, 2–3) 216
Nefer-ti, Prophecy of, 172 f., 176, 257, 258
Negative Confessions, 204
Negligence, divine, 34
Nehemiah, and Persian period, 243

Nemesis, as goddess, 51 f.
Nemesis, retribution, 51 f.; and Atlantis, 77, 255
Neronic repression, 271
New earth, 257
New heaven, 257
New life, and Meskhenet, 226
New Year ceremonies, 183; and trial of King, 235 f.
Nile, idyllic scenes of, 231; celestial, 281
Nile water, and Osiris, 343
Nirvana, in Buddhism, 139, 144, 349
Nobel Prize for Literature, 104
Nomes, 42, and assessors, 208
Non-action, urged by Lao Tzu, 153; and by later Taoists, 155
Nonnus, *Dionysiaca* (9.261–4) 338
N*tr*. 'god' (Egyptian), 162 f., 164
Nuclear death, 356
Nudity, of Mithraic initiand, 334

Oaths, false, punished, 294
Ocnus, 229, 234
Odysseus, visits underworld, 229
Onkhsheshonqy, Instructions of, 179 ff. (IV, 19–20) 180 (V, 2–7) 180 (XII, 16) 180
Opening of the Mouth, 246, 286
Oracle of the Potter, 255
Oracles against nations, 4–10; and Herodotus, 69; in *The Demotic Chronicle*, 176 ff.
Ordeal, and test, combined, 210–13; 332 ff.; by water, 335; and judgement of God, 336
Origen, *Contra Cels.* (4.10) 341; (6.22) 335
Original Sin, 39; and Augustine, 341; and Kafka, *The Trial*, 344
Orpheus, visits underworld, 229
Orphic tradition, and Egypt, 228 f.; gold leaf writings on blessed right path, 296
Orthodoxy, in the *Bacchae*, 75
Osiris, president of tribunal, 227, 268; and the living, 234 ff.; and festival of Khoiak showing his Passion, 234 f.; and Deir el-Medîna, 235; and recording process, 241; dialogue with Atum, 255; as saviour and judge, 256 f.; gives victory over sin and death, 256 f.; in barque with Rê, 281; linked with tree and tomb, 285; and Tammuz, 303; vindicated, 304; identification with, 325; invades world of living, 327

Osiris Bed, 343
Osiris Hydreios, 343
Osiris, and vegetation, 332; as paradigm of new life, 342 f.
Ovid, *Metam.* (7.20) 139
Oxyrhynchus, Papyrus from, with rules for priests, 220
= P.Wash.U.Inv. (138: Recto), 220

Paederasty, and the Greeks, 67
Pahlavi literature, claimed to embody ideas from the Avesta, 251
Paideia, in N.T., 346 f.
Paintings, funerary, with judgement scene of Roman era, 326
Pamphile, and magical acts, 321
Pan-Egyptian judicature, 209
Parables of Jesus, and recompense, 113; and Israel's fate, 117; and theme of rejection, 119; and judgement, 277 f.; Good Samaritan, 279
Paradigmatic mythology, 330
Paradise, mentioned once by Jesus, 277
Parousia, 110, 129, 272, 273, 346
Parthian impact on Jews, 244
Parthians and Medes, attacked by angels, 265
Pastophorus of Isis, 255
Pastor, divine, and Zoroaster, 44
Pastoral discipline, 129
Pater, highest Mithraic grade, 334
Pater Confessor and judge, Isiac priest as, 321
Patronage, of Maecenas and Augustus, 102
Paul, and Second Advent, 110 f.; and justification by grace, 113; on rewards and punishments, 122; and mystery-cults, 124 f.; and admission of failure, 139; on judgement, 271–5, 352
Pausanias, (7.3.7) 297; (8.23.1) 338; (8.34.2) 56; (8.53.5) 296; (11.17.1) 322
Peace, and claim of Rome, 105
Peasant audience, 181
Penance and purity, 341
Penitence, Egyptian ritual of, 127; in Hittite prayers, 198
Pentheus, punishment of, 339
Perithous, punishment of, 329 f.
Persephonê in Hades, 330; addressed by initiate, 341
Persians and Greeks, encounter of, 66–67
Personal god (Sumerian, Akkadian,

Hittite), 32; 35
Personal piety, 190
Peryebsen, King, and Seth, 283
Pessimistic mood, of Hebrew, Egyptian, and Babylonian texts, 306
Petbe, and retaliation, 182
Petosiris, inscriptions of, 188; and God's benefactions, 196; and tribunal, 217, 253
    G. Lefebvre, *Tombeau de Petosiris* (II, 30, 31, 38) 188
Petubastis, King, obeisance to, 196
Phaestos, signet-ring from. 286-7
Phallus, in Dionysiac *liknon*-basket, 338
Pharaoh, theological status of, 160 f.; human qualities of, 162 ff.; Cheops criticised, 167 f.; dignity ridiculed, 175; status demeaned, 183; living Pharaoh examined, 235
Pherecydes of Syros, and transmigration, 144
Philae, hymn to Isis from, 183, 236
Philanthropia, benevolence, in Plutarch, 83
Philo, *De vita contemplativa*, 182
Philoctetes, and *deus ex machina*, 74 f.
Photis (in Apuleius), linked with lust and magic, 319
Pindar, and Nemesis, 52; on sequence of guilt and punishment, 63–65
    Fr. (5.9–10) 63; (137 a) 328
    Isthm. (1.41 ff.) 90; (8.27–28) 228
    Ol. (1.54 ff., 56–57) 63; (2.76–84) 280 f.; (13.10) 63
    Pyth. (2.25 ff.) 63, 64; (3.13) 64; (4.291) 64; (10.44) 52
'Place of the mixed', and Purgatory, 254
Plague Prayer (Hittite) of King Mursili II, 26, 34
Plato, 72 ff.; on justice, 76 f.; on providence, 77; on Isles of the Blest and Tartarus, 228; and Purgatory, 232; on judgement, 295 ff.
    Apol. (41 A) 228, 295
    Gorg. (523 E) 228; (525 B) 232
    Laws (694 C) 67; (716 B) 78; (716 C) 94; (903 B) 77
    Phaedo (113 A–114 C) 232
    Phaedrus (248 A) 78
    Prot. (325 D) 174
    Resp. (614 C) 228, 296; (615 A ff.) 232
Plutarch, 72 ff.; on delays of divine vengeance, 77 ff.; retribution theme in *Lives*, 81; and image of bearing fruit, 346
    De aud. poet. (17 A) 291
    Consol. ad uxorem (611 D) 340
    De Is. et Os. (351 E) 318; (369 A) 79; (369 E) 40; (370 B) 252
    De sera (549 D–E) 80; (550 D) 78; (551 D) 82; (553 F–555 F) 84; (555 C) 81; (555 E–F) 82; (556 A–D) 84; (556 E) 85, 92; (557 E–F) 80; (558 F–559 F) 85 (560 F–561 A) 82, 85
Poem of the Righteous Sufferer, 36
Political prophecies, 257
Pollution, and death, 56
Polybius, 86 ff.
    (1.84) 87; (11.24) 87; (18.54) 87; (36.17) 88
Pompeii, 337 ff.
Popular religion, and punishments, 83
Porphyry, *De Abst.* (4.10), 246
Portrait statue, in tombs, 195, 267
Posidonius, and astral immortality, 247
Posthumous litigation, 203 f.
Prediction of the Lamb under Bokkoris, 255
Priest, and divine blessings, 222
Priestly connection, and judgement after death in Egypt, 218–24
Primal Man, blessed sacrifice of (Vedic), 135
Primogeniture, injustice of, 38
Prophecy of peaceful ruler (Vergil's Fourth Eclogue), 106
Prosperity, causes envy of gods, 49
Protestations of Innocence, 204, 214 f.
Proverbs, and posthumous judgement, 299 ff., 355
Providence (Pronoia), and Destiny (Heimarmenê), 73; seen as unjust, 75; and Plato, 77
Psychê, 'soul' and 'butterfly', 288
Psyche in legend of Cupid and Psyche, 288, 320
Psychology, moral, 82
Psychostasia, Greek, 224; and fates of people, 227; enacted by Zeus or Hermes, 228; in vase-paintings, 290 f.; in Israel and Egypt, 299, 309
Ptah-hotep, wisdom of, 190, 216 f. (115 f.) 190
Ptahnefer, Memphite text of, 218
Punishment, divine, deflected elsewhere in Hittite ritual, 33–34
Punishment, eternal, rejected in Pahlavi texts, 250; and by Paul, 354
Punishments and rewards, and Ahura Mazda, 41 ff.
Purgatory, 110; in Jainism, 140; Chin-

ese, 157 ff.; Greek, 232; Iranian, 234, 254; Egyptian, 257; and Greek, 355
Puritanism, Augustan, 339
Purity, moral and ritual, 212, 223, 323
Purusha, Primal Man, sacrificed (Vedic), 135
Pyramid Texts, 298
  Pyr. (157 c) 206; (316 d) 205; (317 a–b) 205, 227; (323 e) 205; (386 a) 203, 223; (892 a) 203, 223; (1216) 281; (1287 a) 205, 228; (1713 c) 206, 208; (2082 b–c) 223
Pythagoras, and transmigration, 144

Qadesh Inscriptions of Ramesses II, 166 f.
Quietism, naturalistic, and Lao Tzu, 150, 153
Qumrân, sect at, 122 f.; claimed highest sanction, 128 f.; and tested bulwark, 213; martyred Teacher of Righteousness, 260

Radhakrishnan, Sir S., on Karma, 143
Rashnu or Rashn, as judge and Requiter, 248; 253, 256
Rationalism, and Ionian writers, 65
Rê, and Pharaoh, 160 f.; president of tribunal, 227; as ideal king, 260; and Amduat, 265; with Osiris in barque, 281
Rebirth, and baptism, 124; in Indian thought, 136 ff., 267; and Eleusis, 331; in Mystery cults, 342
Reciprocity, hope of, through offerings, 136
Recompense, divine, and Egyptian law, 166
Regeneration, spiritual, and Eleusis, 331
Registering, mania for, 300 f.
Reincarnation, 137 ff., 143 f., 232
Religion, as social cement, 99
Religious revival, under Augustus, 101 f.
Renenet, goddess of nourishment, 226
Repayment after death, 278
Repentance (*metanoia*), 82; national, call to, 117; and baptism, 124; in Taoist communities, 156 f.; condition of grace, 354
Reproduction, physical, ascribed to entry of spirit, 138
Requital, Day of, (Qumrân), 123
Resurrection, first, 237; astral element in, 245; of the body, 246; not in

Gathic Avesta, 257; Pauline link with judgement, 272
Retaliation, no central place in Israel's sacral law, 15
Retribution, divine, confined to this life (Babylon), 35; in Avestan, 44; and castration, 69; and judgement, 348; retributive theory of punishment, 355; morally objectionable, 357
Retribution, moral, and Karma, 137 ff.; no retribution from ghosts, but joy from Heaven (Chuang-tzu), 155–6
Retrospective scrutiny, 241
Revelation, Book of, and myth of combat, 268 f.; and judgement, 352
Revelation, and judgement in history, 26
Reward, and sacrifice (Vedic), 135
Rewards, rejected (Confucius), 147
Rewards and punishments, and Ahura Mazda, 41–42; in Christian doctrine, 112–14; eternal life as reward, 274; human and divine, 348
Rhadamanthys, judge in Hades, 228; in Elysium, 280; of Cretan origin, 295 f.; and Phaestos, 296 f.
Rib-Pattern (Controversy), and Hebrew tradition, 311
Right, blissful in judgement, 225, 296
Righteous, survive judgement, 245
Righteousness, Crown of, 238–9
Rigveda (ed., tr. K.F. Geldner), 132 ff. (4.28.1) 135; (7.61.5) 133; (7.86.5) 132; (7.86.6–8) 133 f.; (7.87.7) 133; (7.89.5) 133 f.; (7.104) 135; (10.14) 135; (10.36) 136; (10.90.3–4) 135; (10.119.2–9) 142
Rome, and blood of martyrs, 269; Decline and Fall of, 109; imperial role sanctioned by gods, 98 ff., 95–109
Royal biographies (Egypt), 165

Sacraments, and judgement, 124–6, 352
Sacrifices, condemned by Jesus, 130; linked with reward (Vedic), 135
Sadducees, and rejection of punishment after death, 276
Sallier Papyrus IV (BM 10184), 185
Salvation (*salus*), 323
Salvation-history, 12–13
Samaritan, Parable of, 279
Samothrace, Mysteries at, 332
Samsāra, cycle of existence with sequence of rebirths, 137 ff.; 143 f.
Saoshyant, Iranian Saviour, 244, 249; brings triumph of good and cosmic

renewal, 256
Sarapis, and Osiris, 234
Sardinia, and Egyptian scene of judgement, 229
Satan, becomes an independent devil through Iranian influence, 250; final fate of, 270; and casting into Gehenna, 277; member of court of heaven, 306
Satapatha Brahmana, priestly Vedic commentary, 136 f.
Saviour, and judgement, 256 f.; Saviour Goddess (Isis), 322
Scales, symbolic, from Crete and Mycenae, 287–91
Scapegoat, Hebrew and Hittite, 34
Scepticism, of divine order, 36 f.; on divination, 71
Scriptores Hist. Aug., Commodus (9.6) 333
Scrolls, in tombs, with Jewish debt to Egyptian practice, 182
Second Advent and Judgement, 110–112, 272, 273, 351
Second Death, 237 f., 275
Sed Festival, and renewal, 165
Sehetep-ibrê Stela, Loyalist Instruction from, 172
Self, correction of, 83; self-judgement and Eucharist, 126
Self-operating system, and Karma, 145
Self-sufficiency, Stoic, 318
Seneca, *Epist. Mor.* (88) 318
Sen-Nedjem, happy afterlife of, 281
Servant of Yahweh, and judgement of nations, 22
Service, extolled without thought of reward (Confucius), 148
Seshat, goddess of writing, 219
Seth, judicial strife of, with Horus, 204; and King Peryebsen, 283
Setne Khamwas, story of, 229, 231 f., 234, 264
Seven Gates of the underworld, 247
Seven Heavens, 247
Sexual jealousy, 48–49; sexuality of Dionysiac cult, 339
Shaî, Fate, 226, 345
Shamash, sun-god and judge, 32
Shame-Culture, 48
Sheol, 257, 354; Enoch's visits to, 264; 12 divisions of, 264 f.; and Gehenna, 275 f.; and Hades, 301
Shinje, monkey-headed Tibetan god, 268
Shipwrecked Sailor (Egyptian story), 255
Sibyl, on the two ways, 296

Sibylline Oracles, and Jewish-Alexandrian influences, 106; 261
Sicily, history of, 85 f.
Silent Man, in Egyptian tradition, 181
Siloam, tower of, and death of 18, 114 f.
Silver, weighing of, 300
Sin, and disease, 32; Sin-Disaster Construct, 123; agitated sense of, in Vedic hymn, 134
Sin and punishment, in Jewish mysticism, 13
Sin and suffering, in confessional literature (Egypt), 189–95; victory over, 256 f., 356
Sins of ritual, 310
Sinuhe, God-given success of, 186 f.; (B 206, 210) 186
Si-Osire, story of, 229
Sistrum, on vase from Crete, 284
Sisyphus, punishment of, 294, 330
Social order, inversion of, 170
Societies, of worshippers, 331
Sociology of religion, 89 ff.
Socrates, and Purgatory, 232
Sodom, 11 f., 111, 298, 351
Sol Invictus, and Mithraism, 245
Solon, fatalism of, 62–63
  Eleg. (1.9–15) 62; (1.63–66) 63
Soma, and Indian sacrificial rites, 132; gives victory to Indra, 135
Son of Man, as Judge and Saviour, 130 f., 225, 256 f., 259 ff., 277
Songs of the South (Chinese), 158–9.
Sophocles, 47; theology and psychology of, 73;
  Ajax (132, 1061) 74
  Ant. (603) 73
  Fr. (837) 329
  Phil. (452) 75
  Trach. (850–51) 71
Soul, therapy for, 83; priority over body, or union with it, 277
Sowing and reaping, 346
Spirituality, in Plutarch's *De Sera*, 82
Sraosha, and judgement, 256
Stars, and the dead, 246
Stoics, determinism of, 72; and Nature, 150; on learning and self-sufficiency, 318
Sublimation, 320
Suetonius, *Iul.* (59) 97;
Suffering Servant, 259 ff.
Sun-god, as judge in several religions, 33
Swansea, Wellcome Museum at, linen paintings, 326
Symbolic scales, from Crete and Myce-

nae, 287–91
Synagogue, origin of, in Egypt, 182 f.
Syncretism, of Babylonian and Iranian gods, 258
Synoptic Gospels, 275–9

Tablet of Grace and Tablet of Sin, 240
Tacitus, and Dead Sea Scrolls, 264
    Ann. (2.21 ff.) 105
    Hist. (5.13.2) 264
Tajoeheriet, Papyrus of, 207 f.
Tammuz, and temple of Yahweh, 303
Tantalus, 229, 234, 294, 330
Tao Te Ching (Classic of the Way and of Power), 149 ff., 350
Taoism, 149–54
Targum, Jerusalem, on Deut. (33:6), 237
Tartarus, and Isles of the Blest, 228; and Elysium, 296
Taurobolium, with Cybele and Attis; also Mithras, 335
Tefnut legend, with griffin as divine avenger, 182
Telipinu, in Hittite myth, 27
Temple of Jerusalem, desecrated by Titus, 120; cleansing of by Jesus, 129 f.
Temple tribunal, and Psalms, 303
Temples, restoration of in Rome, 108
Tertullian, 110
    De praescr. (40) 334
Test and ordeal, combined, 210–13
Theodicy, 19, 20; Babylonian, 35–40; and Plato, 77; and Plutarch, 85
Theogamy, Egyptian royal, 161 f.
Theognis, on gods as arbiters, 62
    Eleg. (1.133–6; 833–6) 62
Theology and history, in Herodotus, 65–72; of Plato, 77; theology of the cross, 357
Theopompus, on Iranian immortality, 246; on final restoration of bliss, 252
Therapeutae, Jewish religious community near Alexandria, 182
Therapy, mental, 82
Theseus, punishment of, 330
Thetis, mother of Achilles, and *psychostasia*, 291
Thoth, as assessor, 176, 268, 290, 300, 302, 304, 309; and Petosiris, 188; hymn to, 191; as divine scribe, 192 f., 210, 227, 241, 255; linked with dog-ape on signet-ring from Phaestos, 286–7; helps with weighing, 326; Lord of Hermopolis, 326
Thucydides, absent gods of, 73; but moral implications, 354
Tibetan Buddhist depiction of judgement, 268
Tibullus, Roman elegist, 221
Timaeus, of Tauromenium (Sicily), 85 f.
Timoxena, and judgement after death, 341
Titans, pardoned by Zeus, 64
Tityus, punishment of, 294
Tomorrow, wisdom about, 181
Torah, 123; and *Demotic Chronicle*, 178 f.
Torment, eternal, of the damned, 275 f.
Totemism, 17; and war, 95
Transference of merits (Buddhist and Chinese), 156–7; of tribunal, to the living (Egypt), 234–6
Transmigration, and the Satapatha Brahmana, 136; and Karma, 140; 349
Treaties, Near Eastern, with more curses than blessings, 23
Tree of life, 281
Triad of assistent arbiters, 227–30
Triads, Egyptian and Eleusinian, 292
Trial, posthumous, 235; see also Tribunal, and Part II, passim.
Tribunal of the gate, 207; localized, 208; Great Tribunal, 214; universal sweep of, 218 f.
Triptolemus, as judge in Hades, 329
The Triumph of Horus, 8
Truphê, softness, and fall of cities, 86
Tuna el-Gebel, and fusion of Egyptian with Greek forms, 326
Turnus, fate of, weighed, 290
Tutankhamûn, 168 f.
    Stela at Karnak (*Urk.* iv, 2025–32) 168 f., 171
Twelve divisions of Sheol and Amduat, 264 f.
Twelve tribes of Israel, and twelve thrones, for twelve disciples, 278
Two Ladies (Wadjet and Nekhbet), and Pharaoh, 161
Two Truths, 308
Two Ways, doctrine of, 295 f.
Tychê (Fortune), causing retribution, 81, 87 ff.; and Isis, 321
Tychê-Nemesis, 182

Ugaritic text on Baal's life after death, 305
Ullikummi, Song of, 180
Unconscious, and types of punishment, 211
Universalism, in Revelation, 271
Unknown god, 186

Upanishad, Chāndogya, (5.10.7) and rebirth, 137 f.
Upanishads, and theism, 141, 145, 349
Urkunden des aegyptischen Altertums = Urk. (i, 122, 6–8) 195, 307; (i, 122, 13) 195; (i, 123, 1–2) 216; (i, 199, 2–3) 216
Utilitarianism, and eudaemonism, 18
Utu, Babylonian judge among the dead, 258

Varuna, in the Rigveda, 132–5; moral control of, 132 f.; source of forgiveness, 133; as judge, 333
Vase-paintings, Greek, and psychostasia, 290 f., cf. 355
Vedic literature, 132 ff.
Vendetta, family, 53, 348; right of, 90
Vengeance, and justice, 3; and blood-feud, 15, 53; on tribe of Benjamin, 24; on Nineveh, 25; and Erinyes, 56; and Alastor, 57; Plutarch on delays of, 77 ff.; human and divine, 126–31,170, 174; in Revelation, 270 f.
Vergil, 95; commissioned but inspired, 102–106; and purification of dead, 232; Fourth Eclogue, 259
  Aen. (6.432) 295; (6.540–43) 296; (6.566) 295; (6.739–51) 232; (6.752–3) 105; (6.792–4) 105; (6.835) 106; (12.725) 290
  Ecl. (1.6) 103; (4.13) 106
  Georg. (2.198) 103; (3.16) 102; (3.41) 102
Vermaseren, CIMRM (498) 333; Santa Prisca, inscrs. from, 333; 336
Vices to be eschewed, at Qumrân and Jerusalem Church, 122
Victory, given by gods, 26
Videvdat (Late Avestan text), 41
Villa dei Misteri, 337–40
Vindicator, (God), 304
Virgin, Saoshyant born of, 256
Virgins, Parable of ten, 277 f.
Vision, prophetic, 9
Vivekānanda, condemns Christian concern with sin, 134 f.
Voluntary death, 124, 323; yoke (Isiac), 335
Voluptas, higher, 320

Wales, inherited Romanitas of, 109
War, and Yahweh's judgements, 17; in Hittite religion, 33, 267; and Greek thought, 53; and totemism, 95; Civil War as fratricide, 106; war in heaven, 272; personification of, 348
Water, ordeal by, 335
Way of Heaven, and Lao Tzu, 150, 350
Way of Yahweh, 178
Weighing the heart, 185, 202 f., 221, 224 f., 239–42, 346
Weighing and recording, 239–42
Weni, autobiography of (Egypt), 184
Westcar Papyrus, 167
Wickedness, and misfortune, 18
Winged Disk, Legend of, 8
Wisdom literature, 182, 189 f., 301
Wisdom of Solomon, 182
Witchery (baskania), link with hubris and nemesis, 51
Woes, over cities, 4 ff., 35; on towns of Galilee, 111, 351
Word, written, magical potency of, 215
Wrath of God, 127 ff.; of the Lamb, 270; in judgement, 274, 349

Xenophanes, Fr. (7a) 144
Xenophon of Ephesus, Ephesiaca (end) 320
Xerxes, character of, 68
  Inscr. of (51 ff.) 245

Yahweh, anger of, 27; Day of, 6, 121
Yahweh, as Judge of all the earth, 17; Servant of, 22; as lightning-producer, 25; wrathful, 128; way of, 178; his anointed son of David (Messiah), 259; justice of, 302
'Yahweh War', 24
Yama, god of dead (Vedic), 135, 267
Yoga, and self-integration, 139
Yogi figure from Mohenjo-daro, 138
Yogic practices, and Karma, 138
Yoke, voluntary (Isiac), 335

Zadokite Document, 123
Zealot movement, 115
Zervan, Time as the First Cause, 250; probably not an ancient divinity, 251
Zervanism, rejection of dualism, 250
Zeus, justice of, 50; 59–60, 354; pardons Titans, 64; punishes Atlantis, 77; presides over psychostasia, 228, 288, 290 f.; controls Moira, 321; weighs fates of armies, 331
Zoroaster, and struggle of right and false, 40 ff. as ideal pastor, 44; and trial by weighing, 249; his dream of tree with four metallic branches, 252; fathers Saoshyant in virgin, 256; vision of Last Judgement, 336
Zoroastrianism, economic background of, 44; cosmic scope of, 256

INDEX OF
BIBLICAL AND RELATED REFERENCES

OLD TESTAMENT

Genesis
2:17   13
3:19   13
9:9   22
15:6   301
15:9–18   27
17   22
18:25   17, 298

Exodus
18:13ff.   16
20:5   30, 118
21:1–22:19   16
21:24   14f.
24   22
24:8   21
32:32   240
34:7   30

Leviticus
7:18   301
16:22   34
19:18   127
19:36   299

Numbers
14:18   30

Deuteronomy
7:7–10   23
9:5   23
17:2–7   308
26:5–9   12
28   23
29:25f.   27
32:35,36   127
33:6   237

Joshua
1:12   24
7:20   24

Judges
1   24
5:11   17

11:27   17
19–21   24

1 Samuel
17:47   24
18:3   21
18:17   24

2 Samuel
5:3   21
12:7–12   25
21:1–3   26

2 Kings
10:31   179
12:11   300
14:25–28   6
20:20   116

2 Chronicles
12:1,5   179

Job
1:1,3,21,22   20
1:6   306, 310
1:17   21
2:10   20
4:7–8   19
14:7,10   307
16:19–22   310
19:25–27   304
26:11   307
29:11ff.   307
30:20   308
30:29   21
31:2–4,6,11,13–14,26–27,28   308f., 312
31:35–37   309
38:4   19
38:12ff.   306
38:39,41   20
40:4   19
40:8   19
42:6   20
42:10   310

INDEX OF BIBLICAL AND RELATED REFERENCES

Psalms
1   202, 219
1:3–4   18
1:5   202, 303
2:11–12   128
22:1   356
37:36   18
49   18
69:9   129
69:28   240
73   18
73:24–25   302
82:1   311
89:6–7   311
89:50   236
99:80   127
104:8   128
112   303
130:3–4   123
145:18   272

Proverbs
3:11   347
11:1   299
16:2   299, 302
16:11   299
21:2   299
22:17–23:11   179
24:12   299, 300, 302
25:21–22   127

Isaiah
1:2   11, 128
2:4   263
5:1–7   114
10:5   6
11:3–5   259
13:17   111
13:19   111
19:1–25   6
34:8   127
42:1ff.   21, 22
43:9–10,14   22
45:1   259
56:7   130
66:24   275

Jeremiah
7:11   130
7:32ff.   276
31:30   31
46–51   6

Lamentations
5:7   30

Ezekiel
8:14   303
18:2,30   15, 30
25–32   6
45:10   299

Daniel
2   251
2:44   264
7   261
7:9–10   229, 242
7:10   239, 254
7:13   260, 351
7:14   264
11:31   120
12:1   240
12:2–3   245

Hosea
2:22ff.   21
6:6   130

Joel
3:4–8   6

Amos
1:2–2:3   9
1:3   5
2:2   9
2:6ff.   5
3:1   9, 10
3:2   10
3:6   4
3:9   11
3:13   10
4:1   11
4:11   12
4:13   10
5:1   11
5:2   9
5:7,10,24   4
5:8f.   10
5:9   10
5:18ff.   6
7   9
7:1ff.   9
8:2   10
8:5   299
9:5f.   10
9:7   5
9:14   5

Micah
3:12   121

Malachi
2:14   21

NEW TESTAMENT

Matthew
3:15   125
5:11   112
5:23   130
5:39ff.   127
5:44–45   127
6:2   112
6:4   112
6:18   112
6:34   181
8:12   276
8:32   34
9:13   130
10:28   238, 277
11:24   111
11:38   115
12:7   130
13:40–43   275f.
16:18   213
16:24   115
19:28   278, 347
20:15   113
21:12–16   129
21:33ff.   119
22:7   119
22:13   276
23:29–39   118f., 121
24:2   119
24:15f.   120
24:30   111
25:1–13   277f.
25:21,23   113
25:30   276
25:31–46   278f.
25:32–33   225, 353
25:33   296
25:41   276
25:46   276
26:52   348
27:46   356

Mark
2:3–12   118
7:20–23   122
8:34   115
9:43,48   275
10:21   115
11:15–18   129f.
13:14   120
13:30   110
14:25   352

Luke
9:23   115

10:13–15   111
10:20   240
10:29–37   279
11:49   120
12:4–5   238, 277
12:14   248
13:1–5   114, 117, 347
13:34f.   119
14:12–14   113, 278
14:27   115
16:19–31   110, 230, 277
17:10   113
19:45–48   129
22:28–30   278
23:28–31   119
23:43   277

John
2:13–17   129
5:24   125
8:2–11   130
8:15   131
9:1–3   117f.; 122
9:1–12   116
9:2   29
9:39   123
12:48   123

Acts
5   122
5:37   115

Romans
1:32   272
2:1–16   272f.
2:5   128
2:6   273f.
3:19   273
5:1,9   274
5:12–14   275
5:18   354
6:3–4   124f.
6:23   274f.
7:15   139
8:1   126
11:32   354
12:17,19–21   127
14:12   273
14:22   126

1 Corinthians
1:30   318
3:13   273
4:4–5   273

INDEX OF BIBLICAL AND RELATED REFERENCES

5:1–5   122, 129
5:2–4   128
5:32   128
6:2   278
11:24   126
11:26   126
11:27–34   125f., 275
15:13   246
15:24   272
15:24–28   354

2 Corinthians
5:10   271, 274

Galatians
5:13–21   122
6:7   346

Ephesians
6:12   272

Philippians
3:10–11   14, 20, 272
3:11   246
4:3   240
4:5   272

1 Thessalonians
4:15   111

2 Thessalonians
1:6–8   127
3:10   129

2 Timothy
4:8   239

Hebrews
10:30–31   127
12:5   347
12:23   240

1 Peter
4:6   354
5:4   239

Revelation
2:10   239
2:11   237, 238
5:5–6   270
5:9   269f., 271
6   270
6:16   270
7:9–10   271
11:15   272
11:18   263
12:9   269
13:8   240
13:10   348
14:6–7   271
17:1;5–6;18   269
19:11   269
19:11–16   244
19:13   271
19:15   270
20:6   237, 271, 278
20:10   271
20:11ff.   270, 271
20:12   240f.
20:13,14   237
20:15   240, 270
20:1   257
21:8   237
21:12   213
21:27   240

APOCRYPHA AND PSEUDEPIGRAPHA
(order of alphabet)

2 Baruch
24:1   240

Ben Sira
182

1 Enoch
261
1:1   264
10:21–22   264
17–36   264
38:5–6   265
41:1–2   262

45:3   225
47:1–4   265
50:4   265
51:3   225
52   265
56:5   265
56:8   265
61:8   229
62:11   265
98:8   239
104:2   245
108:10   240

2 Enoch
40:13   240

4 Ezra
7:36   275
12:33   261

Jubilees
30:22   241
36:10   241

Maccabees
13:14–15   277

Psalms of Solomon
17:22,29,30   260, cf. 269, 351

Qoheleth
182

Sibylline Oracles
5:414–15   261
5:418–21   261f.

Testament of Abraham
201

Testament of Moses
10:7   265

Wisdom of Solomon
182
8:19–20   118

RABBINIC WORKS

Aboth
2:1   347
5:22   276

Akiba, Rabbi
261

Qumrân Manual of Discipline
6:25   122
8:7   213

DATE DUE

MY 19 '92			
DE 26 '95			
AP 23 '02			

```
BL                    35042
475.6
.G75      Griffiths, John Gwyn
1990           The divine verdict.
```

HIEBERT LIBRARY
Fresno Pacific College - M.B. Seminary
Fresno, CA 93702